EDITION

5th

Developing Critical Reading Skills

DEANNE MILAN SPEARS
City College of San Francisco

Boston Burr Ridge, IL Dubuque, IA Madison, WI New York San Francisco St. Louis
Bangkok Bogotá Caracas Lisbon London Madrid
Mexico City Milan New Delhi Seoul Singapore Sydney Taipei Toronto

McGraw-Hill College

A Division of The ***McGraw-Hill*** *Companies*

DEVELOPING CRITICAL READING SKILLS

This book is printed on acid-free paper.

 1 2 3 4 5 6 7 8 9 0 DOX/DOC 9 3 2 1 0 9 8

ISBN 0–07–041960–4

Editorial director: *Phillip A. Butcher*
Sponsoring editor: *Sarah Moyers*
Editorial assistant: *Rebecca Andersons*
Marketing manager: *Lesley Denton*
Project manager: *Christine A. Vaughan*
Senior production supervisor: *Melonie Salvati*
Designer: *Gino Cieslik*
Compositor: *Shepherd Incorporated*

Typeface: *10/12 Stone Serif*

Printer: *R. R. Donnelley & Sons Company*

Cover photo: *Telegraph Colour Library/FPG International LLC.*

Library of Congress Cataloging-in-Publication Data

Milan Spears, Deanne.
Developing critical reading skills / Deanne Milan Spears. — 5th ed.
p. cm.
Rev. ed. of: Developing reading skills. 4th ed. c1995.
Includes index.
ISBN 0-07-041960-4
1. Reading (Higher education) 2. Reading comprehension.
I. Milan Spears, Deanne. Developing reading skills. II. Title.
LB2395.3.M55 1995b
428.4'071'1—dc21 97-43872
CIP

http://www.mhhe.com

Developing Critical Reading Skills

About the Author

After receiving a B.A. and an M.A. in Comparative Literature from the University of Southern California, Deanne Milan Spears worked for a management consultant firm as a junior editor. A few months of delivering mail, typing, and correcting the consultants' grammar convinced her that a business career was not for her. She found a long-term substitute teaching job at Los Angeles Valley College, then taught at Rio Hondo Community College, and in 1968 joined the English Department at City College of San Francisco. She has done post-graduate work at San Francisco State University, studying logic, anthropology, and literature. At City College of San Francisco she teaches reading, composition, and computer courses. In addition to this text, she is the author of an intermediate reading book, *Improving Reading Skills* (3rd ed.), also published by McGraw-Hill. She recently married a fellow English teacher, David Spears.

For David

The man who has not the habit of reading is imprisoned in his immediate world, in respect to time and place. His life falls into a set routine; he is limited in contact and conversation with a few friends and acquaintances, and he sees only what happens in his immediate neighborhood. From this prison there is no escape.

—Lin Yu-T'ang, "The Art of Reading"

To read, when one does so of one's own free will, is to make a volitional statement, to cast a vote; it is to posit an elsewhere and to set off toward it. And like any traveling, reading is at once a movement and a comment of sorts about the place one has left. To open a book voluntarily is at some level to remark the insufficiency either of one's life or of one's orientation to it. The distinction must be recognized, for when we read we not only transplant ourselves to the place of the text, but we modify our natural angle of regard upon all things; we reposition the self in order to *see* differently.

—Sven Birkerts, *The Gutenberg Elegies: The Fate of Reading in an Electronic Age*

Good prose is like a window pane. The reader notices, not the writing, but the world.

—George Orwell

All other creatures look down toward the earth, but man was given a face so that he might turn his eyes toward the stars and his gaze upon the sky.

—Ovid, *Metamorphoses*

So many books . . . so little time.

—Seen on a bookstore canvas bookbag

Contents

PART III

READING CRITICALLY 247

■ PART IV

READING ESSAYS AND ARTICLES 363

Preface

The fifth edition of *Developing Critical Reading Skills* has evolved in ways both conspicuous and subtle that I never foresaw when the first edition was published in 1983. Our personal lives change, our reading lives and tastes change, perhaps our students' interests and abilities change; but what stays the same is the joy of discovering a new writer, one whose articles, stories, or books we savor and whose work we recommend to our friends, colleagues, and students. It is this feeling—inspiration, perhaps, for lack of a better word—that I always hope to impart to my students in my teaching and in this book.

Why change the title? Several reasons occurred to me and to my editors at McGraw-Hill. The World Wide Web has permeated our culture with dizzying speed, altering the way many of us retrieve information. Further, handwringers concerned about the future of the book point to video games and the web's format of hypertext links as undermining our ability to do sustained, thoughtful reading. (An excellent book on technology's purported role in the demise of reading is Sven Birkerts' eloquent and impassioned *The Gutenberg Elegies: The Fate of Reading in an Electronic Age.*) Fortunately, though, there is contrary evidence for Birkerts and other doomsayers who warn that the death of the book is nigh. Consider these observations: even the most isolated rural dweller can purchase books via Amazon.com or other online booksellers and can order books via home computer from the local library system; Oprah Winfrey's Book Club was an instant success; and my students seem genuinely excited when they encounter a writer they have never read before who shows them a new way of looking at their lives and at the world.

An underlying assumption of the text is that good reading and clear thinking go hand in hand. The title change thus addresses the legitimate concern of teachers and employers about the difficulty students and employees—at all levels—have reading perceptively and thinking critically. This concern has been reflected in the mandatory inclusion of critical thinking and reading skills in the states' curricula from elementary school through college. Perhaps this book can do a small part to help students, and indeed all of us, be better thinkers and more productive citizens. This edition, like its four predecessors, deliberately omits a discussion of speed techniques. Finally, developing analytical skills requires concentration and an intense engagement with the text. Adding "critical" to the title reflected a tilt in this direction, as a glance at the extensively revised Part III will reveal.

My hope in preparing the fifth edition, as it was in previous editions, is to provide college students with engaging, well-written prose. Learning to read well, especially to read well critically, is more enjoyable—and maybe more successful in the long run— with stimulating material. I always tell my students at the beginning of the term that I want them to learn something about the world as they read this book. The book succeeds if students become more self-assured as they move through the course and if they recognize that reading well—with confidence, fluency, and enjoyment—is an important part of both their emotional and academic life. This means going beyond what one is merely required to do. It means discovering, questioning, refuting in some cases. Sometimes, for example, when we read good fiction or travel literature, it means transporting ourselves, as Birkerts has written, to an "elsewhere."

Despite the new title, the basic organization remains unchanged, and this may account for the text's success: Students first practice intensive, analytical reading with high-quality short passages, followed by practice applying these skills to longer and increasingly more challenging essays and articles. As before, the readings explore many subjects and writing styles: anthropology, sports, human behavior, politics, social policy, education, ethics, autobiography, personal reminiscence, the minority experience, humor, satire, and so forth.

BASIC COMPREHENSION AND CRITICAL READING SKILLS

Within the text's framework, the book's five sections and accompanying exercises are directed at these specific skills:

- Improving vocabulary, with particular emphasis on using context clues.
- Identifying the main idea in a paragraph and the thesis of an essay.
- Determining the author's purpose and predominant mode of discourse.
- Making accurate inferences.
- Discerning methods of paragraph development, organizational patterns, and logical connections between ideas.
- Understanding and analyzing connotative and figurative language.
- Determining the author's tone, including the ability to recognize the many shades and subtleties of irony.

- Finding unstated assumptions, identifying arguments, weighing evidence, distinguishing between inductive and deductive reasoning.
- Recognizing false appeals, claims, and common logical fallacies.
- Reading and enjoying short fiction.

In preparing the fifth edition, I have relied extensively on the reviewers' suggestions, implementing them almost without exception. I hope that the many new features will make it attractive and pedagogically useful. Here, briefly, is a summary of those changes:

CHANGES IN THE TEXT AS A WHOLE

- Short "open-ended" questions are interspersed throughout the text and in the exercise sections, requiring students to respond in writing. Such questions force them to read with greater attention and strengthen their writing skills at the same time.

PARTS I AND II

- For greater ease of learning, new terms are boldfaced; key information and lists are set off in boxes.
- Chapter 1 contains an extended discussion of implied main ideas along with exercises where students must write main-idea sentences.
- Inference is now taken up in Chapter 2, accommodating the suggestions of nearly every reviewer who wanted this crucial skill to be treated earlier and more prominently. In addition, Chapter 2 includes these changes: (1) more discussion of the inference-making process, especially at the beginning level; (2) an explanation of how to use evidence in a passage to arrive at inferences; and (3) the choice of only PA (probably accurate) and PI (probably inaccurate) for the multiple-choice inference items. Finally, some exercises ask students to locate and cite the evidence that leads to the inference.
- Chapter 3 contains two additional methods of paragraph development—facts and statistics and explanation.
- Chapter 6 clarifies the reasons that writers employ figurative language and includes a discussion of other figures of speech besides metaphors and similes along with hyperbole and understatement.
- The discussion of tone in Chapter 7 has been divided into two parts. The first takes up the simpler, more accessible kinds of tone (informative, critical, and so forth), followed by a separate exercise section. After that, there is a more extensive discussion of irony and its many shades, followed by another exercise.

PART III

- An expanded critical reading skill section marks the most prominent change in this edition. To make room for additional pages, again at the behest of several reviewers, I dropped the study skills section, saving space for more in-depth treatment of this crucial area. Because Part III had become too unwieldy, it is now divided into two chapters.
- Chapter 8 introduces the basic elements of critical reading, including a discussion of world view, the information revolution (the Internet and World Wide Web), argument, evidence, unstated assumptions, and balance.
- Chapter 9 takes up problems associated with critical reading, specifically with evaluating arguments: inductive and deductive reasoning, appeals used in arguments and in advertising, logical fallacies (now more accessibly divided into two sections), and other manipulative techniques such as slanting, distortion, demonizing, and scapegoating.
- In both chapters each section is followed by a short exercise, allowing students to practice the individual skill before proceeding to the next. Examples in both chapters have been chosen from a wide variety of newspapers and magazines, and they concern contemporary political, social, educational, and ethical problems and assorted events, some humorous, most of some consequence. Last, both chapters end with three newspaper editorials on timely issues for analysis and evaluation.

PART IV

- As with earlier editions, the longer essays at the end of each chapter in Parts I and II and in Part IV aim to give students a diverse assortment of engaging, readable nonfiction. Of the practice essays following Chapters 1–7, four are new. Of the fifteen essays in Part IV, twelve are new. As in the earlier chapters, many of the exercises contain open-ended questions.

PART V

- Three of the short stories in Part V are new. (Over the past few months, as I came across these stories one by one, I simply could not decide which ones to eliminate, and so these three found their way into this edition.) Only Katherine Mansfield's little gem, "Miss Brill," has been retained. All three new stories make for wonderful reading and represent very different writing themes, conflicts, and styles: Tim O'Brien in "On the Rainy River" blends fiction and autobiography in his recounting of the anguishing moral and emotional dilemma he experienced upon receiving his orders to go to Vietnam in 1968. Stephen King's "The Man in the Black Suit" shows us evil incarnate through the eyes of a nine-year-old boy. Last, "Hired Girl" by Canadian writer Alice Munro takes up a young Ontario girl's first encounter with wealth.

ANCILLARY MATERIALS

- The instructor's manual for the fifth edition, in addition to the usual apparatus, includes a large variety of supplementary material: briefly, three additional exercises for each chapter in Parts I and II, a few short paragraphs to analyze, four classic essays and their accompanying exercises from earlier editions, and a packet of readings on affirmative action. For further information, instructors should consult the manual's introduction. As before, a test booklet is available for instructors who adopt the text.

I am grateful for the generous help I received from many sources—from my colleagues at City College of San Francisco who have used the text: Michael Hulbert, Linda Legaspi, Catherine Phillips, Robert Stamps (emeritus), Joan Wilson, and Rosalie Wolf. I also want to thank Marcia Schneider, Chief of Branches/Community Relations for the San Francisco Public Library, for her counsel; Jill Ramsay for ensuring the book's accuracy on Canadian matters; Donald Cunningham, emeritus at City College, Eleanor Brown of the English Department, two old friends Geri McCauley, of Friday Harbor, Washington, and Jennifer Ruddy, of Rockport, Maine, for recommending good new writers for me to read.

Special thanks to my editors at McGraw-Hill, Sarah Moyers, Rebecca Andersons, and Christine Vaughan, for their encouragement, fast responses to frequent e-mail questions, and general handholding. And heartfelt thanks, too, to my husband, David, first, for his good humor and, second, for reading and making suggestions on a few sections of the manuscript. I wish his unerringly concise writing style would rub off on me. And finally, the book's many reviewers also deserve special mention for their careful reading and judicious recommendations: Brenda Armbrecht, DeKalb College; Ruth Becker, Pensacola Junior College; Paula Brooks-Jawitz, Manatee Community College; Joyce Elifritt, Santa Fe Community College; Kathleen Engstrom, Fullerton College; Janice Hill-Matula, Moraine Valley Community College; Corin Kagan,

Normandale Community College; Jean Kaufmann, Belleville Area College; and Robert Mann, Des Moines Area Community College.

Students and instructors who have comments, suggestions, or questions are invited to contact me via e-mail. The address is *dspears@sirius.com*. I can also be reached through the McGraw-Hill Higher Education website at http:\\www.mhhe.com. I will do my best to answer within a day or two of receiving messages.

Deanne Milan Spears
City College of San Francisco
San Francisco, California

To the Student

Three or four years ago I was shopping with the man who is now my husband and his 12-year-old daughter in downtown San Francisco. An older man, a street musician whom my husband was acquainted with from his own musician days, was playing the tenor saxophone on a street corner. His name is Clifford, and he had attracted a crowd with his wonderful performance. After he finished, my husband introduced him to me and his daughter. Clifford asked Sarah if she played an instrument, and when she replied that she was taking trumpet lessons and played in her junior high school band, he said, "That's fine, little lady. Learn your instrument well and you can play anything."

Somehow these simple and wise words struck me as fitting not only for an aspiring trumpet player but also for a reader. When you learn to read well, you can read anything you want—not just the daily newspapers and mass circulation magazines, but more difficult reading like philosophy, anthropology, film criticism, particle physics, military history—whatever interests you. You would not be limited in any way. Assuming you had the vocabulary—or at least a good dictionary at your side—you could pick up a book or article, concentrate on it, and make sense of the writer's words.

Reading is an almost magical process that involves more than merely decoding print. It requires internal translation. In other words, you internalize the writer's words, so that you understand not only their surface meaning but also what the words suggest beyond that. Rather than reading passively, sitting back and letting the writer do all the work, you will learn to interact with the text. When you read, you enter into a peculiar relationship with the writer, a two-way process of communication. Although the writer is physically absent, the words on the page are nonetheless there to be analyzed, interpreted, questioned, perhaps even challenged. In this way, the active reader engages in a kind of silent dialogue with the writer.

Reading instruction in American schools often ends at elementary school, and students sometimes have difficulty as they progress through school. The reading material gets harder and harder, yet they still must tackle their assignments armed with only their elementary school reading skills. The result, too often, is frustration and loss of confidence. And the assigned reading in your college courses will be even more demanding than they were in high school—both in content and in the amount of reading assigned. *Developing Critical Reading Skills* is designed to accomplish several tasks: to teach you the skills that will enable you to read with greater comprehension and retention, to help you undertake reading assignments with confidence, and to show you how to become an active, fluent reader.

This is the fifth edition of *Developing Critical Reading Skills*. With each edition and with each group of students who use the text, I have learned a great deal. You will be the recipient of their many excellent suggestions, which, along with various reviewers' and colleagues' remarks, I have incorporated. You should take some time to look through the table of contents to become familiar with the book's layout and scope. You will begin with basic comprehension skills and end with critical reading skills.

As you glance through Parts I and II, you will see that the seven chapters treat the paragraph extensively including explanations, illustrative passages, and exercises. At first it may seem odd, or possibly artificial, to devote so much time to single paragraphs which, after all, are seldom read in isolation. Yet my students have found that concentrating on short passages promotes careful reading. The paragraph is the basic unit of writing (it is often referred to as the main building block of the essay). Studying paragraph structure closely and examining short passages for placement of main idea, methods of development, patterns of organization, inferences, language (especially connotation and figurative language), and tone will teach you how to analyze on a small scale. Certainly it is less intimidating to practice with a hundred-word paragraph than with a five-page essay. Once you become proficient with paragraphs, you can apply the same analytical skills to longer works.

More specifically, you will learn to identify the main idea and, more important, to put it into your own words; to see relationships between ideas; to determine the writer's tone and purpose; to make accurate inferences; to recognize arguments; to weigh evidence; to detect bias, unstated assumptions, false appeals, logical fallacies, distortions, lack of balance, and the like. In particular, Chapters 8 and 9 in Part III have been extensively revised, expanded, and reorganized for this edition. In addition, more than sixty percent of the readings throughout the text are new. Because the bulk of the reading you must do in college is expository—that is, prose writing that explains, shows, and informs—the readings in this book mostly reflect this kind of writing, although editorials, advertising material, and short fiction are included, as well. The text will provide you with a variety of engaging readings and many exercises, giving you intensive practice in comprehension and analysis.

Entirely too much emphasis has been placed on increasing reading speed, on skimming and scanning, on zooming through material simply to get the "drift" of what the writer is saying. These techniques are occasionally necessary for certain reading tasks—for example, for the baseball fan who wants to find out which team won, for the student looking through the print or electronic card catalog for likely research sources, or for the reader of "Dear Abby" in the daily newspaper. But they are inappropriate for the major part of the reading you will have to do in college. For this reason, *Developing Critical Reading Skills* does not include a discussion of speed techniques.

One final comment: during the course, as you sharpen your skills, your work should have two results. The first will be an improvement in your own writing. Good reading skills and good writing skills are most certainly interrelated. When you understand how professional writers organize, develop, and support their ideas, you will become more aware of how to deal with your own writing assignments. But more important, you will learn to be a better thinker as well. All of these skills will serve you well for the rest of your life.

If you have comments, suggestions, or questions, you are invited to contact me via e-mail. The address is *dspears@sirius.com.* I can also be reached through the McGraw-Hill Higher Education website at http:\\www.mhhe.com. I will do my best to respond within a day or two.

Deanne Milan Spears

Introduction: The Reading Process

CHARACTERISTICS OF A GOOD READER

Becoming a good reader, rather than merely a competent one, is crucial if you are to do well in your college courses. In my teaching experience, it has become clear that some students lack confidence because they do not know what to look for when they read, nor are they sure what their instructors expect of them when they prepare reading assignments. *Developing Critical Reading Skills* will help you with both of these. You will learn how to look critically and analytically at short passages, essays, and articles and how to discern the parts, the substance, their strengths and weaknesses. As you work through the readings and exercises in this text, you will find your confidence, your ability to comprehend difficult prose, and most important, your enjoyment in the experience of reading gradually improving. To accomplish these admittedly ambitious goals, we need to define the characteristics of a good reader.

A good reader, it seems to me, reads carefully and thoughtfully. This requires keeping one's attention on the material, keeping "on track" through the author's discussion, and reading *actively*. (This process is quite different from watching television, where the images wash over us as we sit passively. It is no wonder that the pejorative phrase "couch potatoes" applies only to TV watchers and never to readers!) If the introduction to an essay "invites" us into the author's world, we are engaged with the text and fully participate in this world.

The reading process itself begins with decoding words. That is, the reader recognizes and pronounces the words and looks up any unfamiliar words rather than taking a chance and guessing at their meaning, especially those that are essential to understanding the writer's main points. Ignoring new words and their connotations, hoping that they don't really matter, may seriously impair your comprehension. (The connotative and denotative value of words is discussed in Part II, Chapter 6.)

Although the meanings of individual words are important, the real meaning of a text lies in the relationship the words have with each other. A good reader looks for these relationships and asks questions throughout the reading process. The two most important questions are, what is the principal idea of what the author is saying and what is the author saying about that main point?

Particularly with difficult prose, paraphrasing some of the writer's ideas, meaning putting the author's words into your own words, may make it easier to see the relationship between the words and sentences. The reader then can evaluate the main ideas and the supporting evidence by asking these questions: Does the information seem reasonable? Has the writer offered sufficient support? Is any pertinent information missing? Is the author biased? Does he or she seem to have an "agenda"? Is there an underlying but unstated motive? What beliefs or assumptions underlie the author's statements? What other information does the reader need to make an intelligent appraisal, to accept or reject the key ideas? How does the writer's thinking accord with the reader's own experience, values, observations, or thoughts—what is often called one's world view? (The answers to these last questions will be taken up in detail in Part III, Critical Reading.)

To restate: a good reader is active. He or she thinks and questions all the way through the text. If you find that you have trouble maintaining focus or that your concentration is often diverted by extraneous matters, read with a pencil in your hand. Writing brief textual and marginal notations—noting questions to raise in class, underlining important points, identifying words to look up—is an excellent way to sharpen your comprehension and concentration and to maintain your focus.

To illustrate this process, let us practice with a short passage from an article that is frequently reprinted in college English anthologies—"Helping and Hating the Homeless" by Peter Marin, contributing editor at *Harper's,* where it first appeared. The entire essay appears in Part IV of this text. First, note the title. What point of view about the homeless does it suggest?

To set this excerpt in the context of the whole essay, Marin begins by explaining that the city council in Santa Barbara, California, the town where he lives, decided to do away with "sleeping ordinances," which Marin describes as "a set of foolish laws making it illegal for the homeless to sleep at night in public places." But the council had not anticipated the public outcry against the council's vote. Hundreds of angry residents turned up at the next council meeting in protest. As Marin says, "One by one they filed to the microphone to curse the council and castigate the homeless." The author, present at this meeting, says that he was astonished at "the power and depth of the emotion revealed: the mindlessness of the fear, the vengefulness of the fury."

Here we begin the excerpt:

> [1]What follows here is an attempt to explain at least some of that anger and fear, to clear up some of the confusion, to chip away at the indifference. It is not meant to be definitive; how could it be? The point is to try to illuminate some of the darker corners of homelessness, those we ordinarily ignore, and those in which the keys to much that is now going on may be hidden.
>
> [2]The trouble begins with the word "homeless." It has become such an abstraction, and is applied to so many different kinds of people, with so many different histories and problems, that it is almost meaningless.
>
> [3]Homelessness, in itself, is nothing more than a condition visited upon men and women (and, increasingly, children) as the final stage of a variety of problems about which the word "homelessness" tells us almost nothing. Or, to put it another way, it is a catch basin into which pour all of the people disenfranchised or marginalized or scared off by processes beyond their control, those which lie close to the heart of American life. Here are the groups packed into the single category of "the homeless":
>
> [4]
> - Veterans, mainly from the war in Vietnam. In many American cities, vets make up close to 50 percent of all homeless males.
> - The mentally ill. In some parts of the country, roughly a quarter of the homeless would, a couple of decades ago, have been institutionalized.
> - The physically disabled or chronically ill, who do not receive any benefits or whose benefits do not enable them to afford permanent shelter.
> - The elderly on fixed incomes whose funds are no longer sufficient for their needs.
> - Men, women, and whole families pauperized by the loss of a job.
> - Single parents, usually women, without the resources or skills to establish new lives.
> - Runaway children, many of whom have been abused.
> - Alcoholics and those in trouble with drugs (whose troubles often begin with one of the other conditions listed here).
> - Immigrants, both legal and illegal, who often are not counted among the homeless because they constitute a "problem" in their own right.
> - Traditional tramps, hobos, and transients, who have taken to the road or the streets for a variety of reasons and who prefer to be there.
>
> Peter Marin, "Helping and Hating the Homeless," *Harper's*

Now that you have read through the passage once, read it again to see if any unfamiliar words impede your understanding. Five words might cause some difficulty:

illuminate [paragraph 1]
abstraction [paragraph 2]
disenfranchised [paragraph 3]
marginalized [paragraph 3]
pauperized [paragraph 4]

Study these dictionary definitions for each word; the check mark shows the meaning best suited for the **context,** or the way the word is used.

illuminate:
(a) to provide or brighten with light
(b) to decorate or hang with lights
✓ (c) to make understandable; clarify
(d) to endow with fame or splendor; celebrate

(Notice that this word is used metaphorically, since Marin refers to the issue of homelessness as residing in a "dark corner" which needs to be brought to light.)

abstraction:
(a) the act or process of abstracting (removing from)
✓ (b) an abstract concept or term (not concrete)
(c) preoccupation, absent-mindedness

Marin means that the word "homeless" has become an abstraction because we see the homeless as merely an "idea" rather than as real human beings in difficult situations.

disenfranchised (sometimes written *disfranchise*):
✓ (a) to deprive a person of a right of citizenship, as of the right to vote
(b) to deprive (a corporation) of a privilege or franchise

marginalized: ✓ (a) to place in a position of marginal importance, influence, or power (literally, existing in the "margins" of society)

pauperize: ✓ (a) to make a pauper of; to impoverish

If other words in the passage are unfamiliar, look them up now.

Once we know what all the words mean, we can turn to the main idea. Marin's point is this: The term "homeless" has become a meaningless abstraction. The term is a catch-all word that ignores the reality of who the homeless really are. The homeless consist of many categories of people who, for whatever reason, are no longer part of regular American life.

Now let us examine the relationship between the paragraphs. Paragraph 1 states Marin's purpose in writing: to explain why citizens are so angry and fearful about the homeless. In attempting to "illuminate some of the darker corners of homelessness," he will write about some troubling aspects of homelessness that Americans have ignored or denied.

Paragraph 2 extends this discussion and leads to the main point, stated earlier. Look again at the second sentence in paragraph 3, which, because it is more difficult, we can paraphrase like this:

> The term "homeless" is a catch-all term into which we lump all of the people who live on the fringes of society, who have lost their rights to participate in American society, or who have lost control of the ordinary cultural processes that most Americans take for granted.

Paragraph 4 extends this idea and offers support : Marin classifies the homeless into ten distinct types. This classification system, then, reinforces his main point—that the homeless do not constitute a monolithic group. They are as diverse as the reasons that made them homeless in the first place.

The pattern in this excerpt can be diagrammed or mapped out like this:

- Statement of purpose.
- Main idea.
- The author's definition of homelessness.
- Supporting ideas—classifying the homeless into 10 groups.

From this short excerpt, it is apparent that Marin is attempting to give a new interpretation to this difficult and seemingly unsolvable problem. While some critics—undoubtedly reinforcing many Americans' ideas about the problem—lay the blame on the homeless themselves, Marin offers a much more sympathetic view. One can discern this in this phrase from paragraph 3: "Homelessness, in itself, is nothing more than a *condition visited upon* men and women. . . ." In other words, he suggests that the blame lies outside the homeless themselves, that it is a condition *imposed* on them by forces beyond their control. Later in the essay, Marin amplifies this observation, saying: "Homelessness is the *sum total* of our dreams, policies, intentions, errors, omissions, cruelties, kindnesses, all of it recorded, in flesh, in the life of the streets."

This discussion illustrates the analytic method of reading undertaken in this text. As you work through it, you will be asked to read passages, longer ones than this, using these techniques. With practice, the process will become more automatic.

IMPROVING YOUR VOCABULARY

A good vocabulary is probably the single most important prerequisite for good reading. Every other skill—comprehension, retention, making inferences, drawing appropriate conclusions, evaluating—depends on whether you know what the words on the page mean in relation to each other and according to the context. After all, if you aren't sure what the words on the page mean, you cannot fully understand the writer. Sometimes it is possible to "wing it," getting the general drift even if some words and ideas remain unclear. Most often, however, and especially with the analytical reading you will be asked to do in this course, your understanding of a passage may hinge solely on the meaning of a single word, a situation in which guessing is hazardous.

The task of improving your vocabulary is inescapable, and it is a lifelong task as well. At first, learning dozens of new words may seem daunting, maybe even overwhelming, but it *is* possible and definitely satisfying. Everyone has to start somewhere, and everyone's vocabulary can be improved. The number of words in the English language is sufficiently vast to make even the best reader reach for the dictionary occasionally. (The 1996 edition of the *Random House Webster's College Dictionary* lists 180,000 entries or words; the third edition of *The American Heritage Dictionary,* also published in 1996, contains 350,000 entries, 16,000 of them new.)

To put these numbers into perspective and to see the dimensions of acquiring an adult-level vocabulary, consider the findings of Richard C. Anderson and William E. Nagy, authorities in reading and educational theory. They estimate that there are approximately 88,000 words in what they call "school English" (compiled from one thousand items of reading materials from elementary through high school).[1] When they added proper nouns, compound words, multiple meanings of homonyms (words that sound alike but that have different spellings and meanings), and idioms, they estimated that "there may be 180,000 distinct vocabulary items in school English and that an average high school senior may know eight thousand of them."[2]

[1]Richard C. Anderson and William E. Nagy, "The Vocabulary Conundrum," *American Educator* (Winter, 1992), 16.
[2]Anderson and Nagy, 19.

Obviously, a college student is expected to know even more than this figure, since the level of difficulty of college reading assignments is greater than that of high school assignments. Consider these numbers by linguist Robert Claiborne:

> The English Language has far more words than any other tongue on earth. Our most comprehensive lexicon, the *Oxford English Dictionary,* lists no fewer than 600,000 words used in English writing since the twelfth century, of which perhaps 450,000 are still in current use. French speakers must make do with less than a third of that number, and Russians with only a quarter.
>
> Robert Claiborne, *The Roots of English*

These figures confirm the obvious—English is a marvelously complex and linguistically rich language. The sheer number of words in the language partly explains why acquiring a good vocabulary takes so long.

Learning New Words

An exhaustive treatment of vocabulary acquisition is not within the scope of this book, and any number of excellent vocabulary guides are available. The very best way to learn new words is to read a lot; most of the words you recognize in your reading you know because of prior exposure. Memorizing lists of words in isolation is tempting but inefficient. You won't remember many of them, nor will you understand their nuances, their subtleties in meaning, or their meanings in various contexts. New words are best learned—and retained—when you encounter them in your reading.

Aside from that warning, however, here are some suggestions to get you started on an active program to learn new words. First, invest in two dictionaries: an abridged (or shortened) paperback edition for class, and an unabridged (complete) edition to use at home. There are several excellent dictionaries of both varieties on the market. Ask your instructor to recommend one, or choose one from this list:

The American Heritage Dictionary (also available in a college edition)
The Random House Webster's College Dictionary
Webster's New World Dictionary
Merriam Webster's Dictionary
The Shorter Oxford English Dictionary (2 volumes)

Because the language is constantly changing, be sure that your dictionary is a current edition. Trying to save money by using a parent's hand-me-down dictionary from high school is a foolish economy. For example, my faithful first edition of *The American Heritage Dictionary,* published in 1969, does not include the informal meaning of the word *clout,* "having influence or power" (as in "political clout"), although it is listed in later editions. Check to see if your dictionary contains these words or phrases:

brewsky	cybersex	trophy wife	ecotourism	digerati
no-brainer	VFR	wellness	input	soccer mom
multiplex	killer app	yada yada yada	ethnic cleansing	granny-dumping

Second, develop an interest in language. When you look words up in an unabridged dictionary, look at their etymology, or history, because so many English words have unusual origins. The etymology of a word is always printed in brackets [ ] following the definitions. It explains and traces the derivation of the word and gives the original meaning in the language or languages the word is derived from.

For instance, one dictionary traces the history of the word *villain* like this: [Middle English *vilein,* feudal serf, person of coarse feelings, from Old French, from Vulgar Latin *villanus,* feudal serf, from Latin *villa,* country house]. You can easily see how far this word, now denoting a bad guy, has veered from its earlier meanings.

Here is another example. The word *curfew* comes from medieval French. Because most houses were made of wood and had thatched roofs, the danger of fire was always great, particularly at night. Every evening residents had to put out their candles when a bell was rung, signalling the order "Cover fire." The French word *couvre-feu,* brought to England by the Norman French conquerors, later evolved into today's word *curfew.*

Also, try to think of words that share similar meanings and origins as belonging to groups of families. The Latin root *specere,* for example, meaning "to look," gives us the English words *spectacle, spectacular, introspective* ("to look into"), *inspect, speculate, spectrum, spectrograph,* and so on.

The word *matriarchy,* referring to a society where the dominant authority is held by women, derives from these parts: *mater* (Latin for "mother") and the Greek suffix *-archy,* meaning "rule" or "government." The root *mater* also appears in the related words *maternal; maternity; matricide* (killing one's mother); *matrilineal* (tracing one's descent through the maternal line); and *alma mater* (the school one graduated from, from Latin, "cherishing or fostering mother"). The same Greek suffix *-archy* can also be found in *monarchy* (rule by one); *oligarchy* (rule by a small group); and *anarchy* (absence of rule, from the Greek prefix *a-* or *an-* meaning "without"). And this useful prefix can be seen in the

English words *amoral; apolitical; apathy* (literally "without feeling"); and *atheist.*

Last, devise a system for learning important new words. You might try writing new words in a special notebook or on index cards. Adding both the original context and a brief definition and reviewing the list occasionally will ensure your mastery.

Using the Dictionary

The dictionary can provide the curious reader with a wealth of information beyond listing spellings and definitions. We can only scratch the surface in this introduction, but it would be good idea to look through your dictionary's introductory pages and to become acquainted with its myriad features. Unabridged dictionaries may include essays on the history of the English language, on etymology (word origins), on usage notes, and on grammar among other topics. More central for your purposes are the reasons that the dictionary should quickly become the most opened book on your desk. We typically turn to a dictionary for (1) correct spelling; (2) correct pronunciation; and (3) the appropriate definition for a word in the particular passage we are reading. Our concern here is with the third use, the **order of definitions.**

Be sure that you know what method your dictionary uses to arrange definitions. The first definition may not always fit a particular context, and some dictionaries organize their definitions historically rather than by frequency of meaning. You can find this information in the front pages before the first entry. *Random House Webster's College Dictionary* provides this description:

> By reading the various definitions within an entry, you can see how writers and speakers are currently using the word and how it was used in the past. You can discover whether the word has one primary meaning or a variety of meanings—and whether its meanings and uses have a common core or have diversified over the years. You will even find some words with meanings that appear to conflict with one another.

The American Heritage Dictionary under "Order of Senses" in the front matter contains this information:

> Entries containing more than one sense are arranged for the convenience of contemporary dictionary users with the central and often the most commonly sought meanings first. Senses and subsenses are grouped to show their relationships with each other.

In sharp contrast, *Webster's New World Dictionary* cites this information on arranging words:

> The senses have in general been arranged in historical order, from the etymology (usually the sense or senses of a word before modern English times or in the language or languages from which it came) through the original modern English senses (now often archaic or obsolete) to the most recent sense. Thus the most common present-day meaning of a word may appear near the end of the entry.

A knowledge of grammar also helps when you look up unfamiliar words, since many words in English fall into more than one grammatical category (part of speech). The dictionary labels parts of speech by means of abbreviations (*n.* = noun; *v.* = verb; *adj.* = adjective; *adv.* = adverb, and so on.) The word *derelict* is one example of a word that crosses over grammatical lines:

> **der e lict** (dĕr′ ə lĭkt′) *adj.* 1. Deserted by an owner or keeper; abandoned. 2. Run-down; dilapidated. 3. Neglectful of duty or obligation; remiss. See Synonyms at **negligent.—derelict** *n.* 1. Abandoned property, especially a ship abandoned at sea. 2. A homeless or jobless person; a vagrant. 3. Law. Land left dry by a permanent recession of the water line.

In these sentences, *derelict* has three different meanings. Write the number of the definition and the correct part of speech in the space provided.

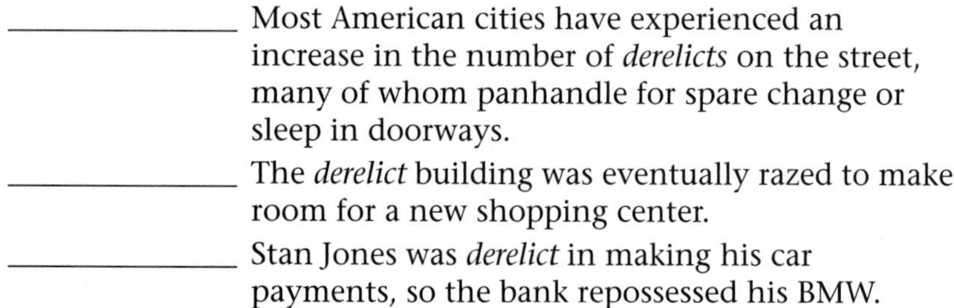

________________ Most American cities have experienced an increase in the number of *derelicts* on the street, many of whom panhandle for spare change or sleep in doorways.

________________ The *derelict* building was eventually razed to make room for a new shopping center.

________________ Stan Jones was *derelict* in making his car payments, so the bank repossessed his BMW.

Before turning to the next section, let us consider the perils that can result from failing to check the meaning of words in the dictionary. In early 1997, Reebok, the athletic shoe manufacturing company, had to decide what to do with 53,000 pairs of a new line of women's running shoes called "Incubus." Although the shoes had been on the market for a year with no customer complaints, ABC learned about the name of the new line and put the story on the evening news. Reebok suffered a corporate red face. It seems that no one at the company had bothered to check in the dictionary to see that an incubus is a male demon who comes to a woman and makes love to her while she sleeps.

Using Context Clues

Although a good dictionary is indispensable, it is unrealistic to think that you must look up every unfamiliar word you come across. Besides looking at the roots, prefixes, and suffixes of words, as we saw earlier, another way to discern the meanings of a new word is to look carefully at the **context,** in other words, the way a word is used in a particular instance. Relying on context clues is not a substitute for looking up exact meanings in the dictionary, nor will every sentence with unfamiliar words necessarily provide you with a clue. But if a clue is present, it is a useful shortcut toward more efficient reading, especially when the word is not absolutely crucial to your understanding the text.

There are four kinds of context clues: (1) synonyms; (2) antonyms; (3) examples and illustrations; and (4) opinion and tone.

1. Synonyms

A synonym is the most frequently used context clue. The writer may provide a word similar in meaning to the unfamiliar one. Although it may not have the exact meaning, it may be close enough to give you an approximate definition. For example:

> The politician was clearly in the wrong occupation. When called upon to give a campaign speech, he was so *reticent* that his long silences made everyone uncomfortable.

The phrase, "long silences," is the context clue, and from that you could probably figure out that *reticent* means "unwilling to speak."

Consider this example:

> When Sarah Smith discovered that her husband had cheated on her, she filed for divorce, citing *infidelity* as the reason.

Does *infidelity* mean (a) lack of respect; (b) addiction; (c) mental instability; or (d) unfaithfulness?

2. Antonyms

Where a sentence suggests a contrast or a contradiction, the context clue may be in the form of an *antonym,* a word that means the opposite of the word in question. If you know the antonym, then you may be able to figure out the new word. For example:

> Although Professor Rivera wants his writing students to develop a concise writing style, Melvin's papers are always returned with lower grades than he would like because his style is too *verbose.*

Since it is obviously being contrasted with *concise,* a word with which you are probably familiar, *verbose* means the opposite, "overly wordy."

Here is another example:

> A well-known writer was most upset when he learned that his publisher planned to release his new novel, which contained profanity and steamy sex scenes, in an *expurgated* version. Instead, he canceled the contract and found a company that would publish the book without removing any of the objectionable parts.

Does *expurgated* mean (a) thoroughly revised; (b) having offensive matter taken out; (c) simplified, made easier to understand; (d) improved?

3. Examples and Illustrations

The meaning of an unfamiliar word may be suggested by proximate examples and illustrations. In this case, no one word or phrase implies the definition, but taken together, the examples help us infer the meaning. For example:

> The *squalid* conditions of many American inner cities—with their burned-out buildings, high crime rates, crumbling schools, and high unemployment—pose a problem for parents trying to raise their children in such grim circumstances.

From the examples printed between the dash marks, you can probably determine that *squalid* means "wretched and neglected."

Now try this one:

> Professor Frederick applies *stringent* rules for his students' papers: margins have to be exactly 1¼ inches on all sides (he even measures them), and after the third sentence fragment or spelling error he assigns a failing grade.

Does *stringent* mean (a) unnecessary; (b) useful; (c) severe; (d) peculiar?

4. Opinion and Tone

This last kind of context clue is less direct and consequently more difficult to rely on. The writer's tone—that is, his or her attitude toward the subject or the opinions the writer expresses—may give you a clue for an unfamiliar word. Study this example:

> Some critics of mass media blame daytime television talk shows for their *insidious* influence on the viewing public, because these programs parade their guests' bizarre and deviant behaviors and create an unhealthy appetite for ever more grotesque revelations.

The obvious critical nature of this sentence suggests that *insidious* is something bad, and indeed it is, since it means "progressing or spreading in a harmful way."

Consider one last example:

> Charley is an *avid* reader whose daily reading habits are admirable. No matter how hectic his schedule or how much studying he has, he manages to find a quiet hour to read just for pleasure from his extensive book collection.

According to the context, does *avid* mean (a) careful; (b) merely competent; (c) enthusiastic; (d) easily distracted?

Whether we turn to the dictionary or rely, when appropriate, on context clues, there is still the matter of choosing the correct definition for the context. And, in fact, students often complain that the hardest part of using a dictionary is determining which of several definitions fit a context. Experience and a careful attention to context will help a great deal in this regard. To practice, always follow these two steps: First consider the context and then study the dictionary meanings carefully. Practice with this example.

> At about the age of eight months or so, a baby learns to *manipulate* her thumb and index fingers to form a pincer, enabling her to pick up small bits of finger food and to feed herself.

The *Random House Webster's College Dictionary* lists these four meanings for the verb manipulate. Which one fits the context here? (1) To manage or influence skillfully and often unfairly; (2) to handle or use, especially with skill; (3) to adapt or change (accounts, figures, etc.) to suit one's purpose or advantage; (4) to examine or treat by skillful use of the hands, as in palpation, reduction or dislocations, or changing the position of a fetus.

Even seemingly easy words can cause difficulty, as these next examples will illustrate. Consider these two sentences from Rosalie Pedalino Porter's book, *Forked Tongue: The Politics of Bilingual Education:*

> My family was poor, so the first necessity was for us to gain the economic means to survive. We children did not *enjoy* the middle-class luxury of a choice of schooling or careers.

What does *enjoy* mean in this context? *The American Heritage Dictionary* lists two meanings. Which is more appropriate for the context? (1) To receive pleasure or satisfaction from; (2) to have the use or benefit of. Obviously the second one is the better choice: Since her family was poor, they could not "enjoy" in the sense we typically use the word what they did not have.

Try this excerpt and, this time, choose the meanings from the definitions provided. Written in a single draft, it is a poignant letter Abraham Lincoln wrote to a woman, the mother of five sons, all of whom died in the Civil War:

> [1]I have been shown in the files of the War Department a statement of the Adjutant General of Massachusetts that you are the mother of five sons who have died gloriously on the field of battle.
>
> [2]I feel how weak and fruitless must be any word of mine which should attempt to beguile you from the grief of a loss so overwhelming. But I cannot refrain from tendering you the consolation that may be found in the thanks of the republic they died to save.
>
> [3]I pray that our Heavenly Father may assuage the anguish of your bereavement, and leave you only the cherished memory of the beloved and lost, and the solemn pride that must be yours to have laid so costly a sacrifice upon the altar of freedom.
>
> Yours very sincerely and respectfully. A. Lincoln

Choose the definition that best fits Lincoln's meaning:

fruitless [para.2]:	(a) bearing no fruit; barren
	(b) unproductive; without results or success
beguile [para. 2]:	(a) to deceive by guile; delude
	(b) to take away from by guile; cheat
	(c) to distract the attention of; divert
	(d) to pass time pleasantly
tendering [para. 2]:	(a) to present formally for acceptance, as in tendering one's resignation
	(b) to offer
	(c) to offer money in payment of an obligation

The appropriate definition of *assuage* in paragraph 3 is easy to determine. The *Random House Webster's Collegiate Dictionary* offers these choices, along with helpful examples, as you see here:

assuage [para. 3]:	(a) to make milder or less severe; relieve; ease: *to assuage one's grief*

(b) to appease; satisfy; allay: *to assuage one's hunger*

(c) to soothe, calm, or mollify: *to assuage one's fears*

Of these four words, which one means something different from the way it is ordinarily used today? (In fact, *The American Heritage Dictionary,* illustrating this definition, quotes this sentence from Lincoln's letter.) ______________________

EXERCISES

Exercise 1

Now try your hand at determining the meaning of words using context clues. Read each passage carefully and, for the first five short excerpts, choose the definition that best fits the way the italicized word is used. It would also be helpful to underline the word or phrase that provides the context clue.

1. Zebra mussels can wreak extraordinary damage in a brief period because they can attach to virtually any surface and are extraordinarily *prolific.* Each female mussel produces up to 1 million eggs per year and reproduces throughout the year. (Alex Barnum)

   (a) highly efficient; (b) highly fruitful; (c) highly energetic; (d) highly damaging.

2. Tide pools contain mysterious worlds within their depths, where all the beauty of the sea is subtly suggested and portrayed in miniature. Some of these pools occupy deep *crevices* or fissures. (Rachel Carson)

   (a) deep, wide holes; (b) earthquake faults; (c) unexplored places; (d) narrow cracks.

3. The hot dry sand in India. . . . A corrosive wind drives rivulets of sand across the land; *torpid* animals stand at the edge of dried-up water holes. The earth is cracked and in the rivers the sluggish, falling waters have exposed the sludge of the mud flats. (Peggy and Pierre Streit)

   (a) physically inactive; (b) domestic; (c) skittish, excitable; (d) malnourished, excessively thin.

4. No aspect of the civil rights movement has generated so much controversy and so little agreement as affirmative action. The idea is a simple one: To help *redress* the long history of racial and gender discrimination in this country, racial minorities and women should be given preference over white males in education, jobs training, hiring and promotion. (Daniel McLoughlin)

   (a) understand; (b) address, consider the problem of; (c) set right, remedy; (d) aggravate, make worse.

Exercise 2

For these excerpts, write your definition for the italicized word(s) in the first space and the dictionary definition in the second.

1. Our sense of smell can be extraordinarily precise, yet it's almost impossible to describe how something smells to someone who hasn't smelled it. The smell of the glossy pages of a new book, for example, or the first solvent-damp sheets from a mimeograph machine, or a dead body, or the subtle differences in odors given off by flowers. . . . Smell is the mute sense, the one without words. Lacking a vocabulary, we are left tongue-tied, groping for words in a sea of *inarticulate* pleasure and exaltation. (Diane Ackerman)

   inarticulate ________________________ ________________________

2. Few people can remember now what the standard of living was half a century ago. . . . Years ago, only a couple of movie theaters and one drugstore had air conditioning to cope with the summer heat. You couldn't buy a pizza or a taco, but as a faded sign on the side of a building . . . reminds us, Coca-Cola was "sold everywhere, 5¢." And only a few lucky people could get television broadcasts beginning in 1948 by WBT in far away Charlotte, N.C. Today, of course, television sets are *ubiquitous.* (John M. Berry)

   ubiquitous ________________________ ________________________

3. To know what to do about vocabulary, you need some basic information about the size of the task students face. If the average high school senior knows 8,000 words, as some people have claimed, then all you have to do is teach 20 words a week for 12 years, and you can cover all of them. But if the average high school senior knows 40,000 words, as other people maintain, you would have to teach 20 words a day to cover them, a much more *formidable* task. Clearly, if high school seniors know anywhere close to 40,000 words, you can be sure that they didn't learn very many of them in vocabulary lessons or by looking them up in the dictionary. (Richard C. Anderson and William E. Nagy)

   formidable ________________________ ________________________

4. Animals' presumed lack of feeling has provided a major excuse for treating them badly. This has been so extreme that animals were long regarded as unable to feel pain, physical or emotional. But when an animal is hurt in a way that would hurt a person, it generally reacts much as a person would. It cries out, it gets away, then examines or favors the affected part, and withdraws and rests. Veterinarians do not doubt that wounded animals feel pain, and use analgesics and anesthetics in their practice. The only *criterion* that an animal fails to meet for feeling physical pain as humans understand it is the ability to express it in words. (Jeffrey Masson and Susan McCarthy)

   criterion ________________________ ________________________

5. In the San Fernando Elementary School, the teaching of non-English-speaking children in their native language enjoys a virtually *religious* status: it is seen as a kind of *panacea* for the generally poor performance of Hispanic children in public schools. But at the Glenwood Elementary School in the San Fernando Valley, a neighborhood of neatly kept stucco homes festooned with bougainvillea, bilingual education is *anathema.* (Richard Bernstein)

   religious ______________________ ______________________

   panacea ______________________ ______________________

   anathema ______________________ ______________________

6. He [P. T. Barnum] put them all on parade for the amusement of the masses: giants and midgets and ladies with beards, Siamese twins, horn-playing seals, rhinos, albinos, girls with no arms but dexterous feet, Zulus, zebras, frog-gulping geeks, Jumbo the elephant, fake missing links. Phineas Taylor Barnum was the greatest showman of the 19th century, a shameless self-promoter who never let the truth get in the way of a good story. He dazzled and delighted an entertainment-hungry public with an endless array of oddities and attractions. . . . P. T. Barnum was the father of the modern entertainment industry. His influence can be seen in the *relentless* hype of movies and sporting events, "once in a lifetime" performances "not to be missed." Admired for his unflagging energy and *ingenuity,* trashed for his *brazen* opportunism and 'vulgarity,' as *The Nation* once put it, Barnum blazed the trail for such skilled self-promoters as Madonna and Michael Jackson. (Jesse Hamlin)

   relentless ______________________ ______________________

   ingenuity ______________________ ______________________

   brazen ______________________ ______________________

PART

I

Reading and Analyzing Paragraphs

1

The Fundamentals of Reading Paragraphs

THE STRUCTURE OF THE PARAGRAPH

The paragraph is the fundamental unit of written thought. Simply put, a paragraph is a group of related sentences that develops and supports one idea, whether stated or implied. A paragraph may be any length as long as it keeps to that one idea. The main idea—a general statement telling the reader what the paragraph is about—may be explicitly present in a sentence that *often* appears at or near the beginning of the paragraph. As you will see later in the chapter, however, many essay writers do not adhere to this pattern. The main idea may be buried in the middle of the paragraph, it may be at the end, or to complicate matters, it may be implied.

Many English textbooks use the term **topic sentence** to refer to the main idea of a paragraph, and in the early grades we are taught this convenient rule. However, the term is misleading: it suggests that a paragraph should contain a sentence that states the main point. As we shall see frequently in this text, this rule is often violated. For this reason, I prefer to use the term **main idea.**

A main idea sentence, if there is one, consists of two parts: the **topic** and the **controlling idea.** The topic is what the paragraph is about—the general subject (though not necessarily the grammatical subject). The controlling idea—often a descriptive word or phrase—limits, qualifies, or narrows the topic to make a broad subject manageable. Another way of looking at the main idea is to ask yourself two questions: What is the topic? What does the author want the reader to understand about the topic? The answers to these two questions will usually give you the topic and controlling idea. Diagrammed, then, a typical main idea sentence might look like this:

Main Idea = Topic + Controlling Idea

Consider this sentence:

> Corporate downsizing in the 1980s and 1990s resulted in severe job displacement for many employees.

In this main-idea sentence, the topic is the phrase "Corporate downsizing in the 1980s and 1990s," and the controlling idea or limiting phrase is " resulted in severe job displacement for many employees." If the writer shifted direction and changed the controlling idea, the focus of the paragraph would change completely:

> Corporate downsizing in the 1980s and 1990s, which eliminated millions of ordinary wage-earners' jobs, occurred at the same time that many corporate executives received enormous salary increases.

And here is a third example, showing yet another possible way that a writer might change the controlling idea and develop the topic differently:

> Corporate downsizing in the 1980s and 1990s often caused severe emotional stress, even for those workers whose jobs were intact.

Thus, the controlling idea serves as a sort of umbrella for the remainder of the paragraph, since every subsequent sentence—assuming the paragraph is well constructed, that is—must adhere to that limiting word or phrase. When you analyze a main idea, label the parts separately, by underlining the topic once and the controlling idea twice. Irrelevant information need not be labeled, as is shown here:

> Although some diehard writers like Danielle Steel still use a typewriter to write,the widespread availability of inexpensive

personal computers has revolutionized and simplified the writing process.

You do not need to include the first clause ("although . . . to write") because the author is not interested in the *disadvantages* of writing on a typewriter. The author mentions this fact only to concede a truth and to avoid generalizing. The topic is "the widespread availability of inexpensive personal computers," and the controlling idea narrows that topic to include only positive *results* of the computer revolution—"has revolutionized and simplified the writing process."

Although this pattern—**topic + controlling idea**—is the typical one, any of the elements may be reversed. Whether the topic precedes the controlling idea or follows it, the meaning is the same.

> The writing process has been revolutionized and simplified because of the widespread availability of inexpensive personal computers, although some diehard writers like Danielle Steel still use a typewriter to write.

Which version, the first or the second, better emphasizes the controlling idea?

Here is a short exercise in labeling main ideas. For each, underline the topic once and the controlling idea twice.

1. The bathroom is the most dangerous room in the house.
2. The most dangerous room in the house is the bathroom.
3. Crows and ravens are the most intelligent of all birds.
4. The most intelligent of all birds are crows and ravens.
5. The southern portion of New Mexico is more desolate and flatter than the northern part.
6. The cow is considered a sacred animal in India for many reasons.
7. Giving children ridiculous names like Petunia or Tiddler can mar their lives in ways that the parents may not anticipate.
8. Tourists who visit New York City's Empire State Building can be classified into three types.
9. Psychologists agree that children who watch too much television may have difficulty distinguishing between fantasy and reality.
10. Two recent experiences illustrate the inefficiency of government bureaucracies.

11. The most useful book a college student can own is an unabridged dictionary.
12. Los Angeles is a city of great contrasts: a burgeoning downtown skyline and blighted ghetto neighborhoods, opulent wealth and abject poverty.
13. Part of the appeal of popular music, from the emergence of rock 'n roll in the early 1950s to the gangsta rap of the 90s, is its ability to irritate adults.
14. The most bizarre form of status seeking studied by anthropologists is the *potlatch,* the ritual feast practiced by many Northwest Native Americans.
15. Success can be measured by the number of imitations a new idea gives rise to, as evidenced by the many television spinoffs of programs that appeal to twenty-somethings like *Friends, Party of Five,* and *Mad About You.*

Now that you have had some practice separating the components of main-idea sentences, let us move to the paragraph as a whole. Read this paragraph once, first, labeling each sentence either with a G (for general statements) or S (for supporting statements.)

> ______ (1) Language originates in magic. ______ (2) The first "words" of a baby are not words at all, but magic incantations, sounds uttered for pleasure and enjoyed indiscriminately to bring about a desired event. ______ (3) Sometime in the last quarter of the first year the baby makes the sounds "mama" or "dada." ______ (4) The baby is surprised and pleased at the excitement he creates in his parents and can easily be induced to repeat this performance dozens of times a day. ______ (5) Unfortunately, he doesn't know who or what "mama" is. ______ (6) He will look right into your eyes and say "mama" and you melt at the lovely sound, and he will look right into his father's eyes and say "mama" and his father, embarrassed, corrects him. ______ (7) He will pursue the dog's tail chanting "mama," and he will reach for a cookie yelling "mama" and he will lie in his crib murmuring "mamamamamamamama"—and he hasn't a thought in his head for M-O-T-H-E-R and the millions of things she gave him. ______ (8) He doesn't connect the word and the person at this point.
>
> Selma H. Fraiberg, *The Magic Years*

Let's see how you did. You should have marked sentences 1, 2, and 8 as general statements and the remaining sentences as supporting ones. Now, read the paragraph again, this time locating the sentence that states the main idea. In that sentence, underline the topic once and the controlling idea twice. Remember that to determine the main idea, ask yourself these questions: What is the topic? What does the writer want me to understand about that topic? If you look carefully at the first two sentences, you will see that sentence 1 expresses a very general idea: "Language originates in magic" would be far too broad and general to be supported in a single paragraph. Sentence 2, the main idea, narrows the focus to the true topic that Fraiberg will support in the rest of the paragraph. You should have underlined once (the topic) "the first 'words' of a baby," and underlined twice (the controlling idea) "not words at all, but magic incantations, sounds uttered for pleasure and enjoyed indiscriminately to bring about a desired event."

We might diagram the paragraph like this:

Sentence 1:	**Introduction (very general idea).**
Sentence 2:	**Main idea (still a general idea, but more specific than sentence 1).**
Sentences 3–7:	**Specific supporting details (developing sentence 2).**
Sentence 8:	**Conclusion (derived from the supporting statements).**

As you can see from this diagram, the sentences in the paragraph operate on two different levels, some general, some specific. The ability to distinguish between the two is necessary in reading so you can see the *texture* (for want of a better word) good writers try hard to achieve. The most important part of the paragraph, clearly then, is the main idea, and specific supporting details are there to support and reinforce the general idea.

However, as a college reader, you must learn to cope with diverse writing styles and techniques and rewrite some of the "rules" you may have been taught in the past. Adult prose is not so neatly formulaic as students would like it to be, and the careful reader has to be alert and ready for any variation. A glance at the paragraphs in the essays in Part IV or at the essays in any freshman English anthology will confirm that the old safe rules are often violated.

THE PLACEMENT OF THE MAIN IDEA

Let us examine a few paragraphs to see the location of the main idea and to determine the direction of ideas. Consult a dictionary if you are unsure of any vocabulary.

> The first Star Wars movie is like a two-hour-long image of raw speed. If you saw it when you were young, this tends to be what you remember—the feeling of going really fast. Lucas is a genius of speed. His first ambition was to be a race-car driver, and it was only after he was nearly killed in a terrible accident, when he was eighteen—he lived because his seat belt unaccountably broke and he was hurled free of the car—that his interest shifted to film. (His first moving pictures were of race cars.) Perhaps the most memorable single image in "Star Wars" is the shot of the millennium Falcon going into hyperspace for the first time, when the stars blur past the cockpit. Like all the effects in the movie, this works not because it is a cool effect (it's actually pretty low tech—merely "motion blur" photography) but because it's a powerful graphic distillation of the feeling the whole movie gives you: an image of pure kinetic energy which has become a permanent part of the world's visual imagination. (The other day, I was out running, and as a couple of rollerbladers went whizzing by I heard a jogger in front of me say to his friend, "It's like that scene in 'Star Wars' when they go into hyperspace.") Insofar as a media-induced state of speed has become a condition of modern life, Lucas was anticipating the Zeitgeist in "Star Wars."
>
> John Seabrook, "Why Is the Force Still With Us?"
> *The New Yorker*

The topic of this paragraph is the film *Star Wars.* Locate and write the phrase that expresses the controlling idea. ______________

____

Now, read the paragraph again, this time circling all of the words and phrases in the paragraph that reinforce the controlling idea, "raw speed."

You should have circled "going really fast," "a genius of speed," "the stars blur past the cockpit," "motion blur," "pure kinetic energy," and "media-induced state of speed." Even the reference to Lucas's earlier fascination with race cars and the reference to the rollerbladers "whizzing by" contribute to this effect. Notice that Seabrook does not repeat the word *speed* over and over. Instead, he uses a variety of synonymous words and phrases. Everything works together to create a network of interlocking thoughts and makes clear the direction of the writer's ideas. In short, every supporting detail reinforces the controlling idea. Reading in this way keeps you on track, makes it easier to follow the chain of ideas, and promotes better concentration.

Another useful comprehension skill is to put a writer's main idea into your own words (in other words, to paraphrase it). Many exercises in the text will ask you to do this. Here is a suggested paraphrase of this paragraph's main idea:

> *Star Wars* effectively conveys a feeling of raw speed and kinetic energy.

However, not all paragraphs are organized so simply, with the main idea stated at the beginning. In the next paragraph, which sentence represents the main idea? After you identify it, restate the main idea in your own words.

> **1**Biology is destiny—or at least more and more people seem ready to believe that it is. **2**Perhaps this is because recent scientific advances—gene splicing, in vitro fertilization, DNA identification of criminals, mapping the human genome—have been repeatedly echoed and amplified by popular culture. **3**From science fact to science fiction (and back again), the gene has become a pervasive cultural symbol. **4**It crops up not just in staid scientific journals and PBS documentaries, but also with increasing regularity in political discourse, popular entertainment, and advertising.
>
> Jeff Reid, "The DNA-ing of America," *Utne Reader*

Main idea sentence ______________________________

Main idea restated ______________________________

And in this one? Again, restate the main idea in your own words after you make your choice.

> [1]The Bear Paw Mountains, a low-slung range south of Chinook, Montana, get their name from an Indian tale of a hunter who ventures into a land of giant bears in order to feed his starving family. [2]When he kills a deer, an angry bear grabs him. [3]In a flash, the Creator severs the bear's paw. [4]Another version tells of an Indian girl who comes to bathe in a virginal lake. [5]A bear bewitched by her beauty reaches out, and the Creator saves her in the same way. [6]The naming of these mountains, like all Indian naming, is poetically exact. [7]From the High Plains, they appear magically inviting, and also remarkably like the just severed paw of a giant bear, its knuckles rippling across the horizon.
>
> Mark Stevens, "Chief Joseph's Revenge," *The New Yorker*

Main idea sentence ______________________________

Main idea restated ______________________________

In this next paragraph about the Beatles, Adam Gopnik uses the first three sentences to state the main idea.

> They [the Beatles] became so famous as to be practically incorporeal. But it was because they were that good. They were literally inimitable. If in those years you played rhythm guitar in a pickup rock band (a rhythm guitarist was someone without rhythm but in possession of a guitar), you knew that to become Led Zeppelin you needed one guy who could actually play the guitar, one guy who could sort of play it, and one guy who could shout hoarsely, all of which was easy. To become the Stones, you needed one guy who could actually play the guitar and one guy who could sort of sing while looking cool, which was hard but conceivable. But to become the Beatles you needed three guys who could actually sing and one guy who could actually play the guitar, and everybody had to look cool. That was why those of us who loved "Penny Lane" ended up playing "Whole Lotta Love" instead, over and over and over.
>
> Adam Gopnik, "Carry That Weight," *The New Yorker*

Using key words, write a main-idea sentence for this paragraph. (Hint: the key word *inimitable* can be broken down into prefix, root, and suffix—*in* ("not") + *imitate* + *able* ("able to"); hence, "not able to be imitated.")

____

____

Another pattern that you will encounter occasionally is sometimes called the "straw man" pattern, in which the writer sets up an idea or popular assumption to be argued against and knocked down, as Tom Regan does in this short passage. After you read it, write a sentence stating the main idea in your own words.

> [1]Someone might think that though what one person thinks or feels about moral issues does not settle matters, what all or most people think or feel does. A single individual is only one voice; what most or all people think or feel is a great deal more. There is strength in numbers. Thus, the correct method for answering questions about right and wrong is to find out what most or all people think or feel; opinion polls should be conducted, statistics compiled. That will reveal the truth.
>
> [2]This approach to moral questions is deficient. All that opinion polls can reveal is what all or most people think or feel about some moral question—for example, "Is capital punishment morally right or wrong?" What such polls cannot determine is whether what all or most people think about such an issue is true or that what all or most people feel is appropriate. There may be strength in numbers, but not truth, at least not necessarily. This does not mean that "what we all think (or feel)" is irrelevant to answering moral questions. Later on, in fact . . . . , we will see how, given that certain conditions have been met, "what we all think" might provide us with a place from which to begin our search for what is right and wrong, and why. Nevertheless, *merely* to establish that all (or most) people think that, say, capital punishment is morally justified is not to establish that it *is* morally justified. In times past, most (possibly even all) people thought the world is flat. And possibly most (or all) people felt pleased or relieved to think of the world as having this shape. But what they thought and felt did not make it true that the world is flat. The question of its shape had to be answered without relying on what most people think or feel. There is no reason to believe moral questions differ in this respect. Questions of right and wrong cannot be answered just by counting heads.
>
> Tom Regan, *Matters of Life and Death*

Main idea ____

IMPLIED MAIN IDEAS

Sometimes a writer leaves the main idea unstated; this is called an **implied main idea.** In paragraphs like this, one needs to locate the key words—those stating the topic and the controlling idea—write them down, and then construct a sentence of one's own. Read this short paragraph and underline the words and phrases that suggest the main idea.

> There are some 16,000 species of lichens in the world. All are slow-growing, but those that encrust the rocks of mountain peaks are particularly so. At high altitudes, there may be only a single day in a whole year when growth is possible and a lichen may take as long as 60 years to cover just one square centimeter. Lichens as big as plates, which are very common, are therefore likely to be hundreds if not thousands of years old.
>
> David Attenborough, *The Living Planet*

You should have underlined *lichens* (the topic) and for the controlling idea—*slow-growing* and *mountainous areas*. Using these key words, one can devise something like this for a main-idea sentence:

> All lichens, especially those growing in mountainous areas, grow slowly.

Read this next paragraph, whose main idea is implied. First, locate the key words by yourself.

> Sagebrush covers 58,000 square miles of Wyoming. The biggest city has a population of fifty thousand, and there are only five settlements that could be called cities in the whole state. The rest are towns, scattered across the expanse with as much as sixty miles between them, their populations two thousand, fifty, or ten. They are fugitive-looking, perched on a barren, windblown bench, or tagged onto a river or a railroad, or laid out straight in a farming valley with implement stores and a block-long Mormon church. In the eastern part of the state, which slides down into the Great Plains, the new mining settlements are boomtowns, trailer cities, metal knots on flat land.
>
> Gretel Ehrlich, *The Solace of Open Spaces*

Now decide which of these statements best represents Ehrlich's implied main idea.

1. Wyoming towns are forlorn-looking.
2. Wyoming's sparse population lives in towns scattered across the state.
3. The eastern part of Wyoming is densely populated in contrast to the rest of the state.
4. There is more sagebrush in Wyoming than there are people.

LEVELS OF SUPPORT

Now we can turn our attention to the paragraph's supporting sentences. Distinguishing between **major supporting statements** and **minor supporting statements** is an important skill. Briefly, **major** statements directly relate to, and develop, the main idea, while **minor** ones further explain or illustrate or otherwise develop the major ones. Analysis of levels of support trains you to think logically because you must weigh the relative importance of ideas in relation to the main idea. Diagramed, using an ideally constructed paragraph, the supporting sentences might look like this:

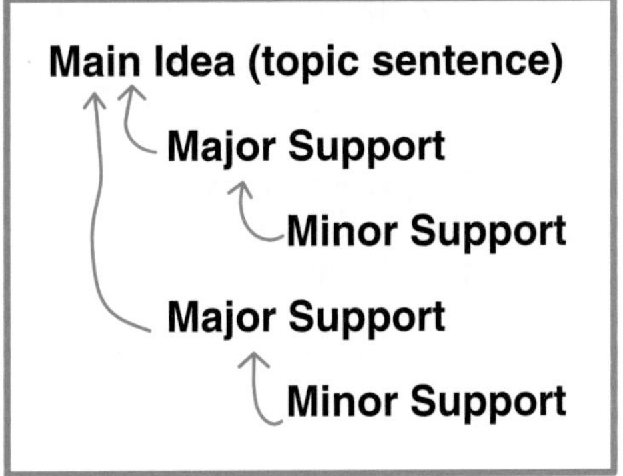

The following paragraph illustrates this alternating pattern of major and minor supporting details. (Notice that the first two sentences are introductory descriptive details; they are minor details of a sort, though not exactly supporting ones.)

> [1]The entire body of a tarantula, especially its legs, is thickly clothed with hair. [2]Some of it is short and woolly, some long and stiff. [3]Touching this body hair produces one of two distinct reactions. [4]When the spider is hungry, it responds with an immediate and swift attack. [5]At the touch of a cricket's antennae the tarantula seizes the insect so swiftly that a motion picture taken at the rate of 64 frames per second shows only the result and not the process of capture. [6]But when the spider is not hungry, the stimulation of its hairs merely causes it to shake the touched limb. [7]An insect can walk under its hairy belly unharmed.
>
> Alexander Petrunkevitch, "The Spider and the Wasp," *Scientific American*

Introductory descriptive details:
The entire body of a tarantula, especially its legs, is thickly clothed with hair. Some of it is short and wooly, some long and stiff. [sents. 1 and 2]

Main idea:
Touching this body hair produces one of two distinct reactions. [sent. 3]

Major support:
When the spider is hungry, it responds with an immediate and swift attack. [sent. 4]

Minor support:
At the touch of a cricket's antennae the tarantula seizes the insect so swiftly that a motion picture taken at the rate of 64 frames per second shows only the result and not the process of capture. [sent. 5]

Major support:
But when the spider is not hungry, the stimulation of its hairs merely causes it to shake the touched limb. [sent. 6]

Minor support:
An insect can walk under its hairy belly unharmed. [sent. 7]

Notice that, if the major supporting sentences were left undeveloped, we would not know how "fast" the spider's rate of capture is when hungry, nor would we see the spider's indifference when not hungry. In addition to promoting better comprehension, being aware of the difference between major and minor details can help your writing, as well, especially if your writing instructors have commented that your writing is too general or too vague or not sufficiently developed. Awareness of these levels also shows you that ideas have relative significance and that ideas are not equally important.

Unhappily, not every paragraph is as balanced as this one is, nor does every paragraph follow this alternating pattern. Try your hand at distinguishing between the two kinds of support in this paragraph. In the space before each sentence, indicate whether the sentence represents the main idea (MAIN), major support (MA), or minor support (MI):

______ (1) People feel safer behind some kind of physical barrier. ______ (2) If a social situation is in any way threatening, then there is an immediate urge to set up such a barricade. ______ (3) For a tiny child faced with a stranger, the problem is usually solved by hiding behind its mother's body and peeping out at the intruder to see what he or she will do next. ______

> (4) If the mother's body is not available, then a chair or some other piece of solid furniture will do. ______ (5) If the stranger insists on coming closer, then the peeping face must be hidden too. ______ (6) If the insensitive intruder continues to approach despite these obvious signals of fear, then there is nothing for it but to scream or flee.
>
> Desmond Morris,
> *Manwatching: A Field Guide to Human Behaviour*

You should have marked the sentences as follows: Sentence 1 (MAIN), sentence 2 (MA), and sentences 3–6 (MI). Notice how Morris helps you keep on track by narrowing the topic in sentence 2 and by restating the key word: "barrier" in sentence 1 is restated as "barricade" in sentence 2. The remainder of the paragraph consists of minor supporting statements all dealing with the way a small child erects a barrier when confronted with a stranger.

Here is a short passage from a popular anthropology book to give you practice with what you have learned so far. Read the passage and circle the key words and phrases. Then indicate the main idea, major support, and minor support in the spaces before each sentence. (Note that in this case there are two paragraphs and therefore two main ideas.) Finally, write a sentence representing the main idea of the *entire passage.*

> ______ (1) Early in the present century, anthropologists were surprised to discover that certain primitive tribes engaged in conspicuous consumption and conspicuous waste to a degree unmatched by even the most wasteful of modern consumer societies. ______ (2) Ambitious, status-hungry men were found competing with each other for approval by giving huge feasts. ______ (3) The rival feast givers judged each other by the amount of food they provided, and a feast was a success only if the guests could eat until they were stupefied, stagger off into the bush, stick their fingers down their throats, vomit, and come back for more.
>
> ______ (4) The most bizarre instance of status seeking was discovered among the American Indians who formerly inhabited the coastal regions of Southern Alaska, British Columbia, and Washington. ______ (5) Here the status seekers practiced what seems like a maniacal form of conspicuous consumption and conspicuous waste known as *potlatch.* ______ (6) The object of potlatch was to give away or destroy more wealth than one's rival. ______ (7) If the potlatch giver was a powerful chief, he might attempt to shame his rivals and gain everlasting admiration from his followers by destroying food, clothing, and money. ______ (8) Sometimes he might even seek prestige by burning down his own house.
>
> Marvin Harris, *Cows, Pigs, Wars, and Witches*

Main idea of the passage ______________________________

____

____

MODES OF DISCOURSE: THE AUTHOR'S PURPOSE

The last topic we will take up in this chapter is **mode of discourse,** or to use an easier term, the writer's **purpose.** If you can ascertain the purpose, later you will be able to accomplish other, more difficult skills (such as detecting bias, understanding the reason one method of development was chosen over another, understanding word choice and connotation, and so on).

The traditional term, modes of discourse, actually refers to the kind of writing a piece of nonfiction prose represents. There are four modes or types: (1) **narration;** (2) **description;** (3) **exposition;** (4) and **persuasion.** But in simpler terms, you can think of mode of discourse as synonymous with the author's purpose.

Narration

The first and most easily recognized mode of discourse is **narration,** meaning simply to tell a story. A writer uses the narrative mode because his or her purpose is to relate events, either real or imagined, in chronological order, usually to provide evidence for some larger truth, as Lewis Thomas does in this passage:

> [1]We may be about to rediscover that dying is not such a bad thing to do after all. Sir William Osler took this view: he disapproved of people who spoke of the agony of death, maintaining there was no such thing.
>
> [2]In a nineteenth-century memoir on an expedition in Africa, there is a story by David Livingston about his own experience of near-death. He was caught by a lion, crushed across the chest in the animal's great jaws, and saved in the instant by a lucky shot from a friend. Later, he remembered the episode in clear detail. He was so amazed by the extraordinary sense of peace, calm, and total painlessness associated with being killed that he constructed a theory that all creatures are provided with a protective physiologic mechanism, switched on at the verge of death, carrying them through in a haze of tranquillity.
>
> Lewis Thomas, "The Long Habit," *Lives of a Cell*

Description

The mode of discourse called **description** shows what someone or something looks like or what something feels like. The author's purpose is to show a visual picture of a *particular* scene, not a generalized one based on a composite of many such scenes. Description almost always relies on sensory details, that is, words that appeal to the reader's senses. Description also can be recognized by its use of figures of speech (imaginative comparisons like metaphors and similes). And although descriptive writing by itself usually does not have a sentence stating the main idea, there usually is a **dominant impression,** revealed little by little as the details accumulate. Study the sensory details in this paragraph from a mystery novel by the great Peruvian writer, Mario Vargas Llosa:

> Amotape is thirty miles south of Talara, surrounded by sun-parched rocks and scorching sand dunes. There are dry bushes, carob thickets, and here and there a eucalyptus tree—pale green patches that brighten the otherwise monotonous gray of the arid landscape. The trees bend over, stretch out and twist around to absorb whatever moisture might be in the air; in the distance they look like dancing witches. In their benevolent shade, herds of squalid goats are always nibbling the crunchy pods that fall off their branches; there are also some sleepy mules and a shepherd, usually a small boy or girl, sunburnt, with bright eyes.
>
> Mario Vargas Llosa, *Who Killed Palomino Molero?*

The dominant impression is of a dry and nearly uniformly gray landscape where the sun glares fiercely and shade is welcome but rare.

In this next paragraph, Gerald Durrell describes a mountain in Africa by using sensory details appealing to the reader's sense of sight.

> N'da Ali[1] was the largest mountain in the vicinity. It crouched at our backs, glowering over the landscape, the village, and our little hill. From almost every vantage point you were aware of the mountain's mist-entangled, cloud-veiled shape brooding over everything, its heights guarded by sheer cliffs of gnarled granite so steep that no plant life could get a foothold. Every day I had looked longingly at the summit, and every day I had watched N'da Ali in its many moods. In the early morning it was a great mist-whitened monster; at noon it was all green and golden glitter of forest, its cliffs flushing pink in the sun; at night it was purple and shapeless,

[1]A mountain in Cameroon, a country in West Africa.

> fading to black as the sun sank. Sometimes it would go into hiding, drawing the white clouds around itself and brooding in their depths for two or three days at a time. Every day I gazed at those great cliffs that guarded the way to the thick forest on its ridged back, and each day I grew more determined that I would go up there and see what it had to offer me.
>
> Gerald Durrell, *The Overloaded Ark*

In your own words, state the dominant impression Durrell's description suggests in this paragraph. ____________________________________

____

In both fiction (imaginative writing, such as short stories and novels) and nonfiction, narration and description frequently overlap. The narrative elements advance the action of the story, and the descriptive elements provide visual or sensory images. The integration of narration and description is illustrated in this excerpt from the novel *On Heroes and Tombs* by the Argentine writer Ernesto Sábato. Notice, too, that this passage shows that descriptive writing can be used to show what something *feels* like. Here the narrator is describing the uncomfortable sensation of waking up in a strange place; embedded in his description is a small but pertinent narrative about an experience by the French writer Antoine de Saint-Exupéry (author of *The Little Prince*).

> I slept very fitfully that night. When I woke up at dawn, I found myself almost in a state of terror; I did not remember immediately what had happened the preceding day and before I was fully awake I looked about in vast surprise at the puzzling reality that surrounded me. For we do not wake up all at once, but rather it is a gradual, complex process whereby little by little we recognize the world that we belong to, as though we were a traveler returning from a very long journey through dim and distant continents, in the course of which, after centuries of obscure existence, we have lost all memory of our previous existence, remembering of it only incoherent fragments. And after a span of time impossible to measure, the light of day begins to feebly illuminate the exits leading out of those labyrinths so full of anguish, whereupon we anxiously break into a run and head toward the everyday world. And we arrive at the edge of sleep like exhausted shipwreck victims who finally reach the shore after a long battle with the storm. And there, still partially unconscious, but feeling our fear gradually draining away, we begin to recognize with gratitude some of the attributes of the everyday world, the tranquil and comfortable universe of civilization. Antoine de Saint-Exupéry tells how after an anxious battle with the elements, lost somewhere out over the Atlantic, when he and his mechanic had lost almost all hope of ever reaching land, they finally spied a faint little light

on the African coast, and touched down safely on their very last gallon of fuel; and how the cup of café au lait that they then drank in a little shack was the humble but transcendental symbol of contact with the whole of life, the trivial but miraculous reunion with existence itself. In the same way, when we return from that universe of sleep, an ordinary night table, a pair of worn shoes, a familiar lamp, are deeply moving lights shining on the coast that we are eager to reach: safety. That is why we are overcome with apprehensions when one of the fragments of reality that we begin to be able to make out is not the one that we were expecting: that little night table we know so well, our pair of worn shoes, the familiar lamp. Which is what usually happens to us when we wake up all of a sudden in a strange place, in a bare, cold, anonymous hotel room, or in the bedroom to which chance circumstances have unexpectedly taken us the night before.

Ernesto Sábato, *On Heroes and Tombs*

Exposition

Exposition, or expository writing, is the most common kind of writing you will encounter in your college reading. It is essentially factual writing with a straightforward purpose: to inform, to explain, to make clear, to discuss, or to set forth. Expository writing is usually *objective,* meaning that in such writing the author attempts not to be influenced by opinions or emotions. In this first example, Genelle Morain explains the significance of eyes to babies in two cultures, Japan and America. (In the last sentence "Argyle" refers to a book by Michael Argyle called *Bodily Communication.*)

Whether the eyes are "the windows of the soul" is debatable; that they are intensely important in interpersonal communication is a fact. During the first two months of a baby's life, the stimulus that produces a smile is a pair of eyes. The eyes need not be real: a mask with two dots will produce a smile. Significantly, a real human face with eyes covered will not motivate a smile, nor will the sight of only one eye when the face is presented in profile. This attraction to eyes as opposed to the nose or mouth continues as the baby matures. In one study, when American four-year-olds were asked to draw people, 75 percent of them drew people with mouths, but 99 percent of them drew people with eyes. In Japan, however, where babies are carried on their mother's back, infants do not acquire as much attachment to eyes as they do in other cultures. As a result, Japanese adults make little use of the face either to encode or decode meaning. In fact, Argyle reveals that the "proper place to focus one's gaze during a conversation in Japan is on the neck of one's conversation partner."

Genelle G. Moraine,
"Kinesics and Cross-Cultural Understanding,"
Language in Education: Theory and Practice

This next example of exposition relates the origins of Johnny Appleseed.

[1]The strangest of all the early American heroes was John Chapman (1774–1845), better known as Johnny Appleseed. If anyone ever exemplified the eccentric trait of obsessive single-mindedness, it was he: he devoted his whole life to the apple, traveling across the country planting countless thousands or millions of apple trees over an area of land estimated to exceed 100,000 square miles. One pioneer who encountered him as he was walking through the Pennsylvania countryside, broadcasting appleseed, described him as "wiry, with long, dark hair and a scanty beard that was never shaved, and keen black eyes that sparkled with a peculiar brightness." He dressed in old coffee sacks with holes cut out for his arms and legs, and went barefoot except in the extreme cold.

[2]Born near Springfield, Massachusetts, Johnny Appleseed was revered by all who met him, particularly the Indians, who believed that he was guided by holy spirits. The one thing that could ruffle his placid demeanor was to hear any slanderous reference made to the apple in the Garden of Eden. "That's wrong!" he would cry. "Look in the Good Book and you'll see that it says that they ate of 'the fruit of the tree.' Now that could be anything—a peach, a plum, a persimmon, a lemon—anything, in short, except an apple. Be sure the Lord wouldn't keep anyone from eating an apple. How many times is the apple mentioned in a favorable way in the Good Book? Eleven times, that's how many!"

David Weeks and Jamie James,
Eccentrics: A Study of Sanity and Strangeness

Not all expository writing, however, is as objective as this. Barbara Grizzuti Harrison, who has spent a good deal of time living in and writing about Italy, uses the expository mode to reveal some information about the origins of pasta. Although Harrison's point of view is undoubtedly more personal than those of the authors in the two earlier examples, the mode is still expository. (Bensonhurst, mentioned in the last sentence, is a lower-to-middle class neighborhood in Brooklyn, New York.) After you read it, underline any words and phrases that contribute to this more personal and casual tone.

[1]The story that pasta was brought to Italy by Marco Polo from China is so romantic and charming that it is almost churlish to refute it. Its charm derives partly from its being one of those Facts we learn in the nursery—proof that Daddy is full of delicious surprises—and so adhere to forever. But food historians tell us that fifty years before Marco Polo left Venice, Indians and Arabs were already eating noodles; they suggest that pasta reached the trading cities of Venice, Florence, and Genoa in the Middle

Ages, by way of Arab lands. Food historian Reay Tannahill says that at a 1972 trade fair in Peking, the Italians tried—one hopes by way of a joke—to sell the Chinese a spaghetti-making machine in which "you put flour, water, and tomato sauce in at one end of the machine and five minutes later hot spaghetti, already prepared and with cheese sauce on top, comes out at the other end." There could not possibly have been a domestic market for this contraption. (If it wasn't a joke, it was proof of the cynicism we are also told—and I am not yet prepared to say—also underlies Italian exuberance.)

[2]Tannahill says that the most common name for pasta in the Middle Ages appears to have been *maccheroni,* which ought to silence food snobs, and which is the generic name by which all forms of pasta, flat and tubular, were called by earlier generations of Italian immigrants. *Pasta* was not a word we ever heard in Italian Bensonhurst; my brother calls it a designer name for "macaronies," and he has a point.

Barbara Grizzuti Harrison, *Italian Days*

Persuasion

This last kind of writing is sometimes called **argumentation,** though technically there is a difference. *Argumentation* traditionally refers to the setting up of logically valid arguments that can be used in defense of a specific point. In contrast, **persuasion** is an attempt to change another person's feelings or opinions by any effective means. A writer persuades when he or she wants to *convince* the reader that a particular idea or opinion is worth holding, to win the reader over to a certain viewpoint, or to get the reader to change his or her mind. By its very nature, persuasive writing deals with controversial issues and relies more on opinion than on fact, since by definition, it represents the writer's subjective point of view. The term *subjective* means the ideas exist in the mind—influenced as it is by emotion and experience and opinion—rather than in external objective reality.

One caution: persuasive writing generally takes up issues about which there is a difference of opinion or a controversy. In the passage above, Harrison writes of the origin of pasta, and it is hard to imagine anyone getting into a heated discussion about whether Marco Polo brought pasta from China to Italy! Her purpose is still to inform, albeit in a light-hearted and rather amusing way.

As you read this first example of persuasive writing, underline the words or phrases that indicate the writer's subjective point of view.

[1]In an era when citizens are upset about needless government agencies, the Central Intelligence Agency may stand out as the ultimate example of a bureaucracy whose lifespan has been pointlessly prolonged. Long after its original mission ceased to matter, a combination of iniquity and inertia has kept the CIA intact.

> [2]Unlike other controversial government agencies that merely squander taxpayer's money, the Central Intelligence Agency is a sinister enterprise with a long criminal record. Its sole rationale—engaging in shadowy combat with its equally nefarious communist counterparts—crumbled at about the same time the Berlin Wall did. Without a Cold War to wage, the CIA has become a dinosaur desperate to avoid extinction.
>
> Kevin J. Kelley, "R.I.P. for the CIA?", *Utne Reader*

What is the author's main objection to the CIA? ______________________

____

In this next paragraph, excerpted from a generally critical essay on professional sports and the astronomical amounts of money involved in their promotion, the writer uses persuasion to underscore the importance of professional sports in American life today. (Note that this subjective point of view could be easily challenged by anyone who thinks that professional sports manifests the worst qualities of American culture, thus, the role of controversy in persuasive writing.)

> Professional sport, it seems fair to say, is a primary expression of the American character at the end of the twentieth century. Like money, it is something we love, a first waking thought and a chronic passion, as well as a vast sector of the economy, a wellspring for contemporary myth and totem, and a media phenomenon of the highest order. Our sports can fend off the brute facts of existence, temporarily arrest the sadness of life, briefly shroud the inevitability of death, and provide the happy illusion of meaning through long, enchanted afternoons. The elation of games can hold us spellbound until finally we are forced to accept their endings, and then we are spent and returned to life, rendered hollow or exuberantly fulfilled, but always afterward cognizant of the real world, with its bits of peanut shell under our shoes and the dark hint of rain to the west. In short, nothing about our national life is quite so national as sport is. Sport is a language we all speak. Sport is a mirror. Sport is life. Through sport we might know ourselves.
>
> David Guterson, "Moneyball!", *Harper's*

A final example of persuasion illustrates a sort of recommendation; in this case, the writer suggests what a person or institution "should" do. One might call this a problem-solution kind of persuasion. Lawrence Otis Graham, an African-American attorney and writer, presents a carefully thought out criticism of the American university and its failure to act as a "moral compass" for students, particularly in the area of race relations.

[1]The best American universities have always been laboratories for the social and political changes that sweep the country from time to time. Ideally, a college campus provides a haven where students, with newfound freedom from the intellectual and social boundaries drawn by their parents and childhood communities, can safely confront different types of people and radical ideas. The best universities provide an environment conducive to such challenges. And yet they stand *in loco parentis* with the authority and responsibility to provide parental direction for the student body. An eighteen-year-old freshman, whether arriving on campus from Topeka, Beverly Hills, or Newark, needs the university and its administration to act as both provocateur and moral compass.

[2]Race is a subject that desperately needs the informed and authoritative voice of the college community. Most black and white students leave their homogeneous communities and arrive on campus curious, intimidated, or even repulsed by students of the other race—and this is true at more places than just Princeton. Filled with doubt or, even worse, derogatory stereotypes regarding the other, they are at a loss about how to treat or identify with those different from them. Without guidance or a higher moral vision from university leaders, the course of least resistance for a student is to re-create that homogeneous community on campus. Unless a university instills a vision of diversity as somehow better, more desirable than homogeneity, a campus naturally begins to mimic the outside world, with its sturdy, racially defined barriers. With well-organized racist militants and demagogues flooding college campuses from groups like the Aryan Nation and the Nation of Islam, it is not surprising that black and white college students have become more racially polarized than ever.

[3]What force other than activism on the part of university administrations can stem such a tide? Certainly, individual students will find their own way toward greater tolerance. But the vast majority will need to be led. College administrators have the ability and obligation to act as moral compasses for their students. To lead by example. For, if they do not, they create a leadership vacuum that can be easily filled by the voices of separatism and racism. Universities should establish moral policies and be willing to back up those policies with moral courage—a courage that acknowledges the existence of a racial problem, but then challenges bigotry and encourages dialogue and interaction between the races.

Lawrence Otis Graham, *Member of the Club*

Mixed Modes of Discourse

Except for the excerpt by Sábato in this section, each passage you have read represents one dominant mode. But prose writers often combine other modes as well besides narration and description. Which *two* modes of discourse are represented in this passage? Defend your choices by pointing to specific words and phrases.

[1]One of the objections to euthanasia often brought forth is the optimistic credo of the imminent cure. What if you let people kill themselves in the early stages of AIDS when a cure might in fact be around the corner? There is a general assumption, born in this century, that disease is curable, and that those diseases which cannot be cured are treatable, and that treating diseases is as logical as eating when you are hungry. It was striking to hear over and over again, in the ACT UP demonstrations of the late nineteen-eighties, declarations that if only the White House would release the funds AIDS could be conquered. This creed is foolish and naïve: until the discoveries of the microbe hunters, everyone accepted the idea that lots of diseases were incurable—that people got them and died, and all you could do was watch and be sad. The arguments against euthanasia are inextricably bound up with our sense that if only you treat disease appropriately it will go away, or at least be mitigated. Euthanasia acknowledges not only the physical weakness of the individual but also the weakness of humanity in the face of disease, and that second admission is anathema to most of us. The doctors who resist euthanasia are in many instances people who entered medicine to conquer their own fear of disease or death: to them anything short of the most aggressive intervention seems like a betrayal.

[2]There is no question that if euthanasia is legalized it will be abused. Some people will kill themselves because of family pressure to do so. Some will kill themselves in depression. Some will kill themselves too soon, and lose precious time on earth. The question is whether these abuses represent a greater crime against life than does keeping alive people who want to die. Is denying people the chance to express love through their own deaths better than denying people the chance to express hatred through the same medium?

Andrew Solomon, "A Death of One's Own,"
The New Yorker

EXERCISES

The three short excerpts and practice essay that comprise the exercises will test your understanding and mastery of main idea, levels of support, modes of discourse, and vocabulary in context. For words that are not part of your active reading vocabulary, first try to determine the meaning from context. Often you will be able to choose the appropriate definition in this way. However, if you are unsure, turn to the dictionary rather than taking a blind stab. It is not cheating to look up words you don't know, even while you are working through exercises. You should follow this procedure for all the multiple-choice vocabulary exercises in this book.

Selection 1

[1]Among the remarkable social developments of the past thirty years is the rapid expansion of the African-American middle class. [2]After the breakthroughs of the civil-rights movement, in the mid-sixties, that class made greater social and economic strides than any black group in the United States ever had before. [3]Yet there has been an equally significant development in the opposite direction—the steady decline in the position of the black poor, who constitute roughly a third of the African-American community. [4]When a leading black scholar like Harvard's Orlando Patterson considers this somewhat divided experience, he cannot help being struck by an odd unison of the best and the worst of times. [5]"Put in the starkest terms, the bottom third of the African-American population—some 10 million persons—live in dire poverty, while the bottom 10 percent or so—the so-called underclass—exist in an advanced stage of social, economic, and moral disintegration," Patterson, a sociologist, wrote in *The New Republic* not long ago. [6]"Thirty-one percent of all black families . . . live in poverty."

[7]That poverty, along with the simultaneous spectacle of middle-class progress and plenty, has become one of the major social and economic contradictions in black America, and has sparked a growing concern. [8]It has also sparked a new kind of pessimism: curiously, the dramatic rise of the black middle class during the past thirty years—with its unprecedented access to major colleges and universities, corporations, high-powered law firms, and elective and appointive office at various levels of government—has led to increasing disenchantment with American possibilities.

Jervis Anderson, "Black and Blue," *The New Yorker*

A. *Vocabulary*

For each italicized word from the selection, choose the best definition according to the context in which it appears.

1. *strides* [sentence 2]: (a) long walking steps; (b) steps forward in progress; (c) innovations, new inventions; (d) short distances.
2. *starkest* [5]: (a) most blunt; (b) most detailed; (c) most understandable; (d) most unfortunate.
3. *dire* [5]: (a) moderate; (b) describing fluctuating levels; (c) having serious consequences; (d) desperate, terrible.
4. *unprecedented* [8]: (a) limited; (b) unnoticed; (c) hard fought; (d) having no previous example.
5. *disenchantment* [8]: The state of (a) being freed from illusion; (b) being politically emancipated or liberated; (c) having one's rights taken away; (d) being unconcerned or apathetic.

B. *Content and Structure*

Complete the following questions.

1. Which of the following sentences best expresses the main idea of the passage? (a) sentence 1; (b) sentence 5; (c) sentence 7; (d) sentence 8.
2. The mode of discourse in the passage is (a) narration; (b) description; (c) exposition; (d) persuasion.
   Defend your choice of mode of discourse. ______________________________
   ____
3. Explain the function of sentences 1–6. (a) To provide background explaining a serious situation; (b) to present the author's personal point of view; (c) to cite historical reasons for a problem; (d) to present a warning for the future.
4. The author's primary concern is (a) the lack of government help for poor African Americans; (b) the growing economic and social divisions between the black poor and the black middle class; (c) the lack of opportunity in education and employment for poor African Americans; (d) the failure of the civil rights movement of the 1960s to solve America's racial divisions.
5. With respect to sentences 1, 2, and 3, mark these supporting sentences as MA (major) or MI (minor):______ sentence 4______ sentence 5______ sentence 6.
6. Look again at this phrase from the end of sentence 4: "an odd unison of the best and the worst of times." Then look at the idea expressed in sentence 7. What is the connection between these two ideas?
   ____

Selection 2

[1]It will not do to blame television for the state of our literacy. [2]Television watching does reduce reading and often encroaches on homework. [3]Much of it is admittedly the intellectual equivalent of junk food. [4]But in some respects, such as its use of standard written English, television watching is acculturative. [5]Moreover, as Herbert Walberg points out, the schools themselves must be held partly responsible for excessive television watching, because they have not firmly insisted that students complete significant amounts of homework, an obvious way to increase time spent on reading and writing. [6]Nor should our schools be excused by an appeal to the effects of the decline of the family or the vicious circle of poverty, important as these factors are. [7]Schools have, or should have, children for six or seven hours a day, five days a week, nine months a year, for thirteen years or more. [8]To assert that they are powerless to make a significant impact on what their students learn would be to make a

claim about American education that few parents, teachers, or students would find it easy to accept.

E. D. Hirsch, Jr., *Cultural Literacy: What Every American Needs to Know*

A. *Vocabulary*

For each italicized word from the selection, choose the best definition according to the context in which it appears.

1. *encroaches on* [sentence 2]: (a) substitutes for; (b) makes irrelevant; (c) makes gradual inroads on; (d) is more important than.
2. *acculturative* [4]: Describing the process of (a) acquiring new ideas; (b) accumulating material goods; (c) restructuring and reshaping the culture; (d) learning about and adopting cultural traits.
3. *assert* [8]: (a) complain about; (b) maintain, postulate; (c) accuse; (d) debate both sides of an issue.

B. *Content and Structure*

Complete the following questions.

1. In your own words, write a main-idea sentence for this paragraph.

   ____

   ____

   ____

2. What is the state of our literacy, according to what the author suggests? ____

   ____

   What word or phrase helped you arrive at your answer? ______________
3. The mode of discourse is (a) narration; (b) description; (c) exposition; (d) persuasion.
4. In relation to the main idea, why does the author include sentence 4?

   ____
5. Who receives the largest measure of criticism in this paragraph for the state of our literacy? (a) The medium of television itself for the poor quality of its programming; (b) the children, who watch television instead of doing their homework or reading; (c) the parents, who do

not supervise or limit their children's television viewing; (d) the schools, which do not demand enough work from children.

6. Which of the following most accurately restates the idea expressed in sentence 6? The decline of the family and poverty are (a) important factors that often account for children's poor performance in school; (b) factors not to be dismissed, but the schools should not use them as an excuse to require little work from their students; (c) factors that make it impossible for many teachers to teach effectively; (d) factors that force teachers to adopt new teaching techniques if children are to learn.

Selection 3

[1]Bats are extremely tidy, comb themselves thoroughly, and do not gather a mess of nesting materials for their homes as birds do. Their guano smells like stale Wheat Thins, and sometimes insects invade the guano so that it appears to be bubbling, but bats themselves live high above in penthouse roosts, where they keep their bodies well groomed. [3]Since they don't build nests, they find shelter in whatever roof eave, cave, open brickwork, hollow tree, or other reasonably clean, secluded place presents itself. [4]Seldom a belfry, despite the myth. [5]Belfries are more often occupied by birds. [6]Perhaps it was the bats darting around the church belfries at twilight, in their normal pursuit of insects, that made people think bats roosted there. [7]Or perhaps it was the image of the devil, traditionally drawn with bat wings, and sermons that warned of his being always in the vicinity. [8]For an orthodoxy to prevail, you need to believe in a heresy waiting at your front door, and the macabre fluttering of bats on devil's wings at sunset in the local churchyard made a persuasive reminder that evil and irrationality are not something you need to keep a day free for. [9]People also think that bats have a special penchant for bedrooms and, if they leave their bedroom windows open when they sleep, as most people do, a wayward bat might indeed be tempted to stray in, but bats much prefer the gables of a house or a chimney or even a place under a porch. [10]Bats roost near wherever there is a good supply of insects to feed on, and that most often is in forests, gardens, parks, along rivers, in churchyards (again, the bats-in-the-belfry idea), or around city streetlamps. [11]Drawn to the free lunch at searchlights, they often frequent airports, along with starlings, finches, and many other winged things; since they don't hear too well in the low registers, they might not be bothered much by the engine noise.

Diane Ackerman, "In Praise of Bats,"
The Moon by Whale Light

A. *Vocabulary*

For each italicized word from the selection, choose the best definition according to the context in which it appears.

1. *orthodoxy* [8]: (a) an approved form of any doctrine or belief; (b) a deviation from an established doctrine or belief; (c) a judicial court specializing only in religious doctrines; (d) a branch of theology concerned with the nature of evil.
2. *heresy* [8]: (a) an example of sinfulness; (b) public condemnation of wrongdoing; (c) any belief at variance with established beliefs; (d) a small splinter religious group or cult.
3. *macabre* [8]: (a) persistent; (b) sickening; (c) gruesome; (d) rapid.
4. *penchant for* [9]: (a) definite liking of; (b) fear of; (c) talent for; (d) connection with.
5. *wayward* [9]: (a) rabid, diseased; (b) lost, confused; (c) hungry; (d) turning irregularly, straying.

B. Content and Structure

Complete the following questions.

1. Write a main-idea sentence for this paragraph.

   ____

   ____

2. A good title for this paragraph would be (a) "Bats in the Belfry"; (b) "Some Habits of Bats"; (c) "Where Bats Live"; (d) "Bats: Myth and Reality."
3. The mode of discourse in this paragraph is (a) narration; (b) description; (c) exposition; (d) persuasion.
4. The author strongly suggests throughout the paragraph that bats (a) are not very interesting mammals to observe or study; (b) are strongly linked with religion, especially with Christianity; (c) are often falsely perceived and have been given a "bad rap"; (d) have pretty much the same characteristics as other mammals.
5. Why does the author include sentences 6–8? (a) To offer two explanations for the idea that bats live in belfries; (b) to show why bats do indeed inhabit belfries; (c) to explain why people are afraid of bats; (d) to show that the bat and the devil are indeed similar both in form and in behavior.
6. Sentence 8 is quite difficult. Consider it carefully and write a paraphrase of it. (Hint: "a day free" for "evil and irrationality" most likely refers to Sunday, the Christian sabbath.)

   ____

   ____

   ____

7. We can conclude that the author finds bats (a) unpleasant and dirty; (b) interesting but misunderstood; (c) scary; (d) remarkably adaptable to every possible environment.

PRACTICE ESSAY

Among the Thugs

Bill Buford

In Great Britain the word football *refers to the game Americans and Canadians call* soccer. *European soccer matches are notoriously rowdy, and British football fans have perhaps the worst reputations of all Europeans in this regard. Many British football club members follow their local teams as they compete all over Europe, drinking, picking fights, and engaging in violence and lawlessness. Bill Buford's book,* Among the Thugs, *takes a look at this phenomenon. Buford writes from a personal point of view: Although he is an American, at the time he resided in England, where he spent several months traveling around with two or three football clubs, observing their fans' behavior and the crowd mentality that marks it. He notes that these fans tend to be working-class people who view these activities as weekend entertainment.*

Until recently, Buford was the editor of Granta, *a well-respected British magazine that publishes high-quality fiction and nonfiction. In 1996 he returned to the United States where he is currently fiction editor at* The New Yorker *magazine.*

1 It is not uncommon, in any sport, to see spectators behaving in a way that would be uncharacteristic of them in any other context: embracing, shouting, swearing, kissing, dancing in jubilation. It is the thrill of the sport, and expressing the thrill is as important as witnessing it. But there is no sport in which the act of being a spectator is as *constantly* physical as watching a game of English football on the terraces. The physicalness is insistent; any observer not familiar with the game would say that it is outright brutal. In fact, those who do not find it brutal are those so familiar with the traditions of attending an English football match, so certain in the knowledge of what is expected of them, that they are incapable of seeing how deviant their behavior is—even in the most ordinary things. The first time I attended White Hart Lane on my own, everyone made for the exit within seconds of the match ending: I looked at the thing and couldn't imagine an exit more dangerous—an impossibly narrow passageway with very steep stairs on the other side. There was no waiting; there was also no choice, and this

peculiar mad rush of people actually lifted me up off my feet and carried me forward. I had no control over where I was going. *Stampede* was the word that came to mind. I was forced up against the barrier, danger looming on the other side, was crushed against it, wriggled sideways to keep from bruising my ribs, and then, just as suddenly, was popped out, stumbling, as the others around me stumbled, to keep from falling down the remaining stairs. I looked up behind me: everyone was grimacing and swearing; someone, having been elbowed in the face, was threatening to throw a punch. What was this all about? This was not an important moment in the game: it was the act of leaving it. This, I thought, is the way animals behave, but the thought was not a metaphoric one. This was genuinely the way animals behave—herd animals. Sheep behave this way—cattle, horses.

2 At the heart of any discussion about crowds is the moment when many, many different people cease being many, many different people and become only one thing—a crowd. There is the phrase, becoming "one with the crowd." In part, it is a matter of language: when the actions of diverse individuals are similar and coherent enough that you must describe them as the actions of one body, with a singular subject and a singular verb. They are . . . It is . . . The many people are . . . The crowd is . . . The English football game expects the spectator to become *one* with the crowd; in a good football game, a game with "atmosphere," the spectator assumes it: it is one of the things he has paid for. But, even here, it is more than an ordinary crowd experience.

3 It is an experience of constant physical contact and one that the terraces are designed to concentrate. The terraces look like animal pens and, like animal pens, provide only the most elementary accommodation: a gate that is locked shut after the spectators are admitted; a fence to keep them from leaving the area or spilling on to the pitch; a place for essential refreshment—to deal with elementary thirst and hunger; a place to pee and shit. I recall attending the Den at Millwall, the single toilet facility overflowing, and my feet slapping around in the urine that came pouring down the concrete steps of the terrace, the crush so great that I had to clinch my toes to keep my shoes from being pulled off, horrified by the prospect of my woollen socks soaking up this cascading pungent liquid still warm and steaming in the cold air. The conditions are appalling but essential: it is understood that anything more civilized would diffuse the experience. It seems fitting that, in some grounds, once all the supporters have left in their herdlike stampede, the terraces are cleaned by being hosed down: again, not just the images but the essential details are those of an animal pen. That is what the terraces offer, not just the crowd experience but the herd experience, with more intensity than any other sport, with more intensity than any other moment in a person's life—week after week.

4 Here, in Cambridge, on a Tuesday night, me a stranger among strangers: the physicalness was constant; it was inescapable—unless you literally escaped by leaving. You could feel, and you had no choice but to feel, every important moment of play—through the crowd. A shot on goal was a felt experience. With each effort, the crowd audibly drew in its breath, and then, after another athletic save, exhaled with equal exaggeration. And each time the people around me expanded, their rib cages noticeably inflating, and we were pressed more closely together. They had tensed up—their arm muscles flexed slightly and their bodies stiffened, or they might stretch their necks forward, trying to determine in the strange, shadowless electronic night-light if this shot was the shot that would result in a goal. You could feel the anticipation of the crowd on all sides of your body as a series of sensations.

5 Physical contact to this extent is unusual in any culture. In England, where touch is not a social custom and where even a handshake can be regarded as intrusive, contact of this kind is exceptional—unless you become a member of the crowd.

6 When I arrived at this match, coming straight from a day of working in an office, my head busy with office thoughts and concerns that were distinctly my own, I was not, and could not imagine becoming, "one" with any crowd. It was windy and cold and that biting easterly weather was felt by *me* personally—in *my* bones. I was, in what I was sensing and thinking, completely intact as an individual. And it was *me,* an individual, who was then crushed on all sides by strangers, noticing their features, their peculiarities, their smells—*except* that, once the match began, something changed.

7 As the match progressed, I found that I was developing a craving for a goal. As its promises and failures continued to be expressed through the bodies of the people pressed against me, I had a feeling akin to an appetite, increasingly more intense, of anticipation, waiting for, hoping for, wanting one of those shots to get past the Millwall goalkeeper. The business of watching the match had started to exclude other thoughts. It was involving so many aspects of my person—what I saw, smelled, said, sang, moaned, what I was feeling up and down my body—that I was becoming a different person from the one who had entered the ground: I was ceasing to be me. There wasn't one moment when I stopped noticing myself; there was only a realization that for a period of time I hadn't been. The match had succeeded in dominating my senses and had raised me, who had never given a serious thought to the fate of Cambridge United, to a state of very heightened feeling.

8 And then the game—having succeeded in apprehending me so—played with me as it played with everyone else. It teased and manipulated and encouraged and frustrated. It had engendered this heightened feeling and, equally, the expectation that it would be satisfied: that there would be gratification—or not. That the team would score—or be

scored against. That there would be victory—or defeat. Climax—or disappointment. Release. But what happens when all that energy, concentrated so deep into the heart of the heart of the crowd, is not let go?

9 At ninety minutes, there was the whistle. There was no score. There would be extra time.

A. *Comprehension*

Choose the answer that best completes each statement. Do not refer to the selection while doing this exercise.

1. Buford was alarmed when he attended the White Hart Lane match because (a) so many uniformed policemen prevented the fans from exiting; (b) the sponsors had run out of tickets for the number of fans present; (c) the home team had threatened revenge against the opposing team for beating them; (d) the exit was too narrow for the number of fans trying to use it to leave.
2. Buford compares the crowd of spectators of football matches to (a) a band of uncivilized men; (b) robbers and thieves; (c) herd animals; (d) political protesters and rioters.
3. Buford emphasizes that when a spectator attends a football match he or she experiences (a) constant and intense physical contact with the crowd; (b) the joys and sorrows of the home team's performance; (c) the thrill of impending or potential violence and danger; (d) the pleasures of watching expert players performing at their best.
4. Once the match began, Buford writes that (a) he gradually became bored with the game's progress; (b) he felt like an outside observer with no connection to the crowd; (c) he felt himself gradually changing, until the game completely dominated his existence; (d) the game's complex rules confused him.
5. With respect to his own reactions to the game and to what he experienced, Buford strongly suggests that he was (a) indifferent; (b) surprised; (c) bewildered; (d) dishonest.

B. *Structure*

Complete the following questions.

1. Which mode of discourse predominates in this essay? (a) narration; (b) description; (c) exposition; (d) persuasion.
2. Explain the reasons for your answer to the question above. ___________

____

3. Read paragraph 1 again. Write the sentence that expresses the main idea in the space. ____
____
____

4. What seems to be Buford's central concern in paragraph 2? __________
____

5. Read paragraph 3 again. Then explain in your own words the meaning of this sentence: "The conditions are appalling but essential: it is understood that anything more civilized would diffuse the experience." ____
____
____

6. The conclusion of the essay is meant to leave the reader with a feeling of (a) confusion; (b) anxiety; (c) suspense; (d) disappointment.

C. *Vocabulary*

For each italicized word from the selection, choose the best definition according to the context in which it appears.

1. dancing in *jubilation* [paragraph 1]: (a) anticipation; (b) joy; (c) religious fervor; (d) a competitive spirit.
2. how *deviant* their behavior is [1]: (a) insulting; (b) threatening; (c) departing from the accepted; (d) unpredictable.
3. *grimacing* and swearing [1]: (a) making an ugly, contorted face; (b) pushing and shoving; (c) engaging in fistfights; (d) yelling obscenities.
4. a *metaphoric* one [1]: (a) clever; (b) unacceptable; (c) describing an imaginative comparison; (d) accurate.
5. *coherent* enough [2]: (a) consistent, sticking together; (b) composed of differing elements; (c) chaotic, lacking order; (d) single-minded, obsessed.
6. *pungent* liquid [3]: Describing a smell that is (a) sweet; (b) sharp, offensive; (c) delicate; (d) hard to define.
7. *diffuse* the experience [3]: (a) scatter; (b) pour out; (c) soften, lessen; (d) change too radically.
8. *audibly* drew its breath [4]: (a) angrily; (b) loudly enough to be heard; (c) collectively, as a group; (d) excitedly.

9. in *apprehending* me so [8]: Here, a metaphorical use, meaning (a) taking fully into custody or authority; (b) understanding the true significance of; (c) perceiving with all the senses; (d) failing to involve or make an impact on.
10. it had *engendered* this feeling [8]: (a) displayed; (b) competed with; (c) enriched, added to; (d) brought about.

D. *Questions for Analysis and Discussion*

1. On balance, would you characterize Buford's description of English football matches as favorable or unfavorable? Explain, citing references to the essay.
2. As Buford has described it, how does a crowd behave? What are its essential features?

2

Making Accurate Inferences

INFERENCES DEFINED

When we make an **inference**—whether in the real world or in our reading—we draw a conclusion from our observations or from facts that are presented to us. Or, as William Lutz defines the term in the Practice Essay at the end of this chapter, "An inference is statement about the unknown based on the known."

Further, we must distinguish between **facts** and **inferences.** A fact is a verifiable piece of information; that is, it can be duplicated, measured, confirmed in other sources, demonstrated, or proved. An inference is different because, as the two definitions in the preceding paragraph suggest, it is *derived* from facts.

For example, in the process of planning a wedding reception, we might measure the reception hall adjoining the church where the ceremony will be held. Our measurements are facts: the hall is 60 feet long and 40 feet wide. Let's say that we are inviting only 25 people; from these two sets of facts, we might draw these inferences:

- The reception hall is too large for that small a crowd.
- People will feel lost in a large space.
- We should find a smaller location.

Inferences and facts, then, are different. Inferences proceed from facts.

Two final definitions: We also need to distinguish between two often confused verbs—"imply" and "infer." To **imply** means to hint at or suggest an idea indirectly, and to **infer** means to draw a conclusion from what the writer's words suggest. A writer or speaker *implies;* a reader or listener *infers*. As we read, we infer by drawing reasonable or probable conclusions from the author's words. In other words, when you make inferences, you "read between the lines." In this chapter, you will examine several passages of varying levels of difficulty followed by inference questions to show how the process works.

PROBLEMS WITH INFERENCES

A personal anecdote will illustrate how the inference process works in everyday life and why making accurate inferences can be troublesome. Recently my husband and I were walking in a residential area near a public beach in the early warm summer evening. The beach had been crowded that day, but at 7 P.M. the street was deserted. Then we saw two dogs—one an adult, the other a puppy—tied by choke chains to a lamppost. The dogs were shaking and appeared afraid and hungry. Even more telling, they wore no collars or ID tags. Simultaneously we reached the same conclusion: these dogs had been abandoned.

We based this inference on our experiences in the world; all the facts pointed to the dogs' abandonment—the lateness of the hour, the deserted street, the lack of tags and of an owner in the vicinity. As it turned out, our inference was dead wrong. As we were debating what to do, a young man rode up on a bicycle. He explained that his girlfriend's bicycle had had a flat tire, and he thought it would be less trouble to ride the mile to town and leave the dogs tied up while it was fixed. (One might also infer something about the intelligence of dog owners who believe they can keep their dogs safe while riding bicycles.)

This illustration suggests something about the nature of inferences: they have a high degree of *probability* rather than of absolute certainty. Our inference was *probably* accurate because we based it on our prior experiences and on our ability to reason from our observations and those experiences. However, because we didn't have all the facts, our inference about this *particular* situation was inaccurate.

To give you another example of what can go wrong with the inference process in the real world, suppose you are driving down the freeway, and you observe a car swerving in and out of lanes, moving erratically, and narrowly missing other cars. Based on your knowledge of the world, you might infer that the driver is probably drunk. But there may be other explanations. Perhaps the driver has suffered a heart attack or a stroke. Perhaps the steering mechanism failed. Or you could engage in more absurd flights of fancy and infer that the driver is a kid who has stolen a car with no idea how to drive it, or that the driver is a stunt car driver who is practicing maneuvers on the freeway. Both of these seem unlikely, since even the most intrepid yet inexperienced car thief would probably not venture out onto a freeway, and stunt car drivers wouldn't use a busy freeway for practice where lives would be endangered. As you can see, the more we get carried away with our assumptions and make inferences from facts we do not have, the less probable it is that these inferences are correct. Thus, our attempts to draw a conclusion as to the reasons for the erratic driving are only speculative.

In addition to inferring inaccurately by straying from the facts, we can also err by assuming that our own cultural practices are universal. For example, in North America a ring on the fourth finger of a person's left hand usually suggests that the wearer is married. However, in many European countries, a married man wears a band on his *right* hand. (And, of course, many married men wear no ring.) So an American might wrongly infer that a European with no ring on his left hand is unmarried, merely because of an incorrect assumption based on our own cultural traditions.

These examples show the importance of thinking and reading carefully, of not leaping to conclusions, and of getting as many facts as possible before making an inference or drawing a conclusion. In reading, the process is the same. We should not "read into" the author's words *beyond what they suggest or imply.* Further, bringing in our own experiences may actually lead us astray from the author's real intentions and may result in misreading, misinterpretation, or confusion.

EXPLAINING SAMPLE INFERENCES

In this chapter you will encounter two kinds of inferences: those that are **probably accurate** and those that are **probably inaccurate.** You should label an inference *probably accurate* if it follows from the facts presented or from the author's own words and observations. You should label an inference *probably inaccurate* if it misstates or misrepresents the author's words, or if it cannot be made because of insufficient evidence, in other words, if you can't tell one way or the other. Of necessity, your inferences should be "safe" ones, meaning that you should stay within the narrow confines of the text. Making inferences, as we have seen, from your past experiences or from strongly held attitudes, values, or cultural practices may result in misreading meanings. The best way to become adept and comfortable with making inferences is to study the examples and the explanations that follow them at the beginning of the chapter.

The first example is from Tobias Wolff's engaging autobiography, *This Boy's Life*. In it Wolff describes the grades he received while attending the public high school in Concrete, a town in eastern Washington state.

> I brought home good grades at first. They were a fraud—I copied other kids' homework on the bus down from Chinook and studied for tests in the hallways as I walked from class to class. After the first marking period I didn't bother to do that much. I stopped studying altogether. Then I was given C's instead of A's, yet no one at home ever knew that my grades had fallen. The report cards were made out, incredibly enough, in pencil, and I owned some pencils myself.
>
> Tobias Wolff, *This Boy's Life*

Decide whether these inferences are probably accurate (PA) or probably inaccurate (PI). Then study the explanations that follow.

1. ______ Students at the high school in Concrete didn't have to study much to get A's.
2. ______ The narrator continued to receive good grades only because he erased the teacher's marks and changed them to higher ones.
3. ______ The teachers were naive to record students' grades in pencil.

Each of these inferences is accurate. If Wolff received A's for studying while walking to class, we can infer that the grading standards must have been pretty lax. We can infer that the second statement is *probably accurate* because, as Wolff so nicely puts it, "I owned some pencils myself." And the third inference is also *probably accurate* because of the adverb Wolff uses to characterize the teachers' use of pencils—"incredibly enough."

This next passage is from a newspaper article published in *The Washington Post* a year before the 1998 Winter Olympics were held in Nagano. Its subject is the tough gun laws and changing attitudes toward guns in Japan.

> **1**TOKYO—Seventeen people were killed by gunfire last year in Japan, about the same number as on a slow afternoon in the United States. In the country of some of the world's toughest gun laws, handguns are illegal, police inspect homes to make sure hunting riffles are under lock and key, and possessing a single bullet can result in a $10,000 fine and five years in prison. The laws are so strict that Japan's national team in the biathlon, an Olympic sport combining cross-country skiing and shooting, has been practicing in Russia because the laws make it so hard to find a place to

practice here. Japanese authorities fret that the athletes might accidentally pick off a bird or a skier if they practiced on the course near Nagano where next year's Winter Olympics will be held.

[2]As strict as the laws are, the public is clamoring for the government to make them even tougher. Although this is still one of the least violent societies in the world, and the vast majority of violence is committed by *yakuza* gangsters against one another, many Japanese people feel the "American disease" of guns is spreading here.

[3]Chinese and Russian mobsters have recently stepped up their smuggling of guns into the country. The street price for many black-market handguns has dropped from about $3,000 a couple of years ago to $500 now. Prices are so low that guns have spread for the first time from organized mobsters into the hands of extortionists, political extremists, petty criminals, and even law-abiding people who have taken a fancy to guns.

[4]Perhaps even more upsetting to Japan's collective psyche is that young people are showing more interest in guns. A recent police survey showed that one in three Japanese men in their twenties would like to own a gun, or at least fire one. In the markets in Tokyo's Ueno district, young people are snapping up $100 black plastic toy guns that look and feel remarkably like the real thing—and thousands more are selling around the country.

[5]"It's become a fad, a cool thing, to like guns," says Michiko Nagashima, 49, a security company employee. "This is a bad import from the West."

Mary Jordan, "Fascinated by Guns," *The Washington Post*

As you work through these inferences, be sure to refer to the paragraph number in brackets for help. Answer PA or PI as before.

1. _____ Compared to the United States, Japan's murder rate is very low. [paragraph 1]
2. _____ Japanese police strictly enforce the prohibition against gun ownership. [1]
3. _____ Japanese gun laws are the strictest in the world. [1]
4. _____ *Yakuza* gangsters are the Japanese version of the American Mafia. [2]
5. _____ Despite strict laws against gun ownership, recently there has been an increase in illegal gun ownership in Japan. [3]
6. _____ Until a couple of years ago, the high price kept guns from being affordable for ordinary citizens. [3]
7. _____ Japanese young people have gotten the impression that guns are cool from American television programs. [4 and 5]
8. _____ Mary Jordan, the author, believes that the United States should emulate Japan and adopt similar anti-gun laws.

Here are the answers. (1) PA; (2) PA; (3) PI; (4) PI; (5) PA; (6) PA; (7) PI; (8) PI. If you answered more than one or two of these inferences incorrectly, study the explanations for the answers carefully.

Question 1 can be inferred by the facts suggested in the first sentence. Question 2 can be inferred by the facts of police inspections, the high fine for possessing a bullet, and the mandatory prison sentence. Question 3 represents a misreading of the sentence beginning "The laws are so strict." They are strict, but Jordan does not suggest that they are the "strictest" in the world. Question 4 is also inaccurate. Since Jordan says nothing about the *yakuza* and any similarity with the Mafia, we cannot assume a connection, nor are all gangsters members of crime syndicates.

Question 5 is obviously accurate because of the information in paragraph 3 about increased smuggling and the spread of handguns into the larger population. Question 6 is a reasonable conclusion from the information given in the remainder of paragraph 3. Question 7 is a tempting but inaccurate inference. The author nowhere implies the specific source of this "bad import from the West." Television is a *possible* culprit (what might be some others?); but we cannot say for sure, therefore making this inference inaccurate. For one thing, we would need to know the extent to which American television programs, especially those depicting guns and violence, are broadcast in Japan. The last inference, similarly, cannot be made because nowhere does the author intrude her opinion, nor does she suggest what "should" be done. In fact, the author suggests, if anything, that Japan's famed strict gun laws no longer work as well as they once did.

Next, read these two well-known fables, one relatively simple, the other more difficult.

> A dispute once arose between the Wind and the Sun as to which was the stronger of the two. They agreed, therefore, to try their strength upon a traveler to see which should be able to take his cloak off first. The Wind began and blew with all his might and main, a cold and fierce blast; but the stronger he blew the closer the traveler wrapped his cloak about him and the tighter he grasped it with his hands. Then broke out the Sun and with his welcome beams he dispersed the vapor and the cold. The traveler felt the genial warmth and as the Sun shone brighter and brighter, he sat down, overcome with the heat, and cast his cloak on the ground. Thus the Sun was declared the conqueror.
>
> "The Wind and the Sun," from *Aesop's Fables*

Which of these moral truths can you accurately infer from this fable?

1. The mighty rule the world.
2. The meek shall inherit the earth.

3. Force is more effective than persuasion.
4. Persuasion is more effective than force.
5. Competition breeds jealousy.

Did you mark answer choice four? The gentle warmth of the Sun's rays—in other words, persuasion—was more effective than the harsh force of the Wind's blowing.

The second fable is slightly more difficult:

> Death speaks:
>
> [1]There was a merchant in Bagdad who sent his servant to market to buy provisions and in a little while the servant came back, white and trembling, and said, Master, just now when I was in the market-place I was jostled by a woman in the crowd and when I turned I saw it was Death that jostled me. [2]She looked at me and made a threatening gesture; now, lend me your horse and I will ride away from this city and avoid my fate. [3]I will go to Samarra and there Death will not find me. [4]The merchant lent him his horse, and the servant mounted it, and he dug his spurs in its flanks and as fast as the horse could gallop he went. [5]Then the merchant went down to the market-place and he saw me standing in the crowd and he came to me and said, Why did you make a threatening gesture to my servant when you saw him this morning? [6]That was not a threatening gesture, I said, it was only a start of surprise. [7]I was astonished to see him in Bagdad, for I had an appointment with him tonight in Samarra.
>
> W. Somerset Maugham, "Death Speaks," *Sheppey*

Based on the evidence in the fable, label these inferences PA or PI.

1. _____ The servant misinterpreted Death's gesture in the market-place.
2. _____ The merchant thought his servant was foolish to go to Samarra.
3. _____ The time and place of our death are predetermined.
4. _____ The servant thought he could outwit Death.
5. _____ Ironically, in trying to escape death, the servant sealed his own fate.

Here are the answers: (1) PA; (2) PI; (3) PA; (4) PA; (5) PA.

The first inference is clearly *accurate* based on the information in sentences 6 and 7, though arriving at this deduction means that we must accept Death's explanation for her gesture and reject the servant's. The second inference should be marked *probably inaccurate;* sentence 4 implies that the merchant willingly lent his horse, thereby suggesting that he agreed with his servant's decision to flee Death's threatening gesture. Further evidence is that later the merchant scolded Death for frightening his servant. Also, a good master would not want his servant to die. Thus this inference statement misinterprets the events of the story.

The third inference is *probably accurate* because Death says that she already knew in advance that the servant would be in Samarra, strongly suggesting that the servant's death was predetermined, meaning planned in advance. And we can conclude that the last two inferences are *probably accurate* by the irony of the situation: in attempting to outwit Death and escape his fate, the servant, instead, must succumb to it. We and Death know what the servant does not. (This fable nicely illustrates the concept of dramatic irony.)

As should be plain by now, these inference questions make you think! While some of these inferences may seem trivial or even "picky," they do force you to look carefully at a passage and to take care in interpreting and drawing conclusions from the evidence. Practicing with inferences will help you both to become an active, questioning reader and a better thinker. And as you become more comfortable with the process, you will find that you do this automatically as you read, assessing the author's evidence and seeing implications beyond the literal words.

Many students find the inference questions in the text quite challenging. As you work through them, be sure you look back at the text to find the phrase or sentence that pertains to each question. Remember that in making inferences, there is some degree of "gray"—that is, you may not be wholly certain that the inference is verifiably true, only that it is, based on the author's words *probably* accurate or *probably* inaccurate. If you disagree with an answer, first look back at the passage to see if you can determine by yourself where you went wrong , and, if you are still unsure, ask your instructor for help.

USING EVIDENCE TO MAKE INFERENCES

As you can see from the foregoing examples, making correct inferences requires you to consider the evidence carefully. Here are two excerpts for you to practice with. In each case you will be asked to locate the evidence that leads to an inference. The first excerpt is a fable that begins Donald Hall's short story "Argument and Persuasion." Read it carefully and then answer the inference question that follows.

> [1]A husband and wife named Raoul and Marie lived in a house beside a river next to a forest. One afternoon Raoul told Marie that he had to travel to

> Paris overnight on business. As soon as he left, Marie paid the Ferryman one franc to row her across the river to the house of her lover Pierre. Marie and Pierre made love all night. Just before dawn, Marie dressed to go home, to be sure that she arrived before Raoul returned. When she reached the Ferryman, she discovered that she had neglected to bring a second franc for her return journey. She asked the Ferryman to trust her; she would pay him back. He refused: A rule is a rule, he said.
>
> [2]If she walked north by the river she could cross it on a bridge, but between the bridge and her house a Murderer lived in the forest and killed anybody who entered. So Marie returned to Pierre's house to wake him and borrow a franc. She found the door locked; she banged on it; she shouted as loud as she could; she threw pebbles against Pierre's bedroom windows. Pierre awoke hearing her but he was tired and did not want to get out of bed. "Women!" he thought. "Once you give in, they take advantage of you. . . ." Pierre went back to sleep.
>
> [3]Marie returned to the Ferryman: She would give him *ten* francs by mid-morning. He refused to break the rules of his job; they told him cash only; he did what they told him. . . . Marie returned to Pierre, with the same lack of result, as the sun started to rise.
>
> [4]Desperate, she ran north along the riverbank, crossed the bridge, and entered the Murderer's forest.
>
> Donald Hall, "Argument and Persuasion,"
> *The Ideal Bakery*

What specific evidence in the story suggests that Marie died? __________

____

Which character is morally directly responsible for Marie's death?

____

The second passage is reprinted from an article called "The End of the Book?" by D. T. Max. Again, read it carefully and then identify the evidence necessary to make the inference which follows.

> Paper has limitations, but the computer may have more. As a physical object, it is hardly comforting. "Who'd want to go to bed with a Powerbook?" John Baker, a vice-president at Broderbund, asks. And even if the laptop goes on shrinking, its screen, whose components represent nearly all the machine's cost, remains at best a chore to read. At the Xerox Palo Alto Research Center (where the receptionist's cubicle still houses an IBM Selectric typewriter) is a display room with half a dozen prototype six-million-pixel

AMLCD screens. The quiet hum of the room, the bright white lighting, the clean, flat antiseptic surfaces, give the impression of an aspirin commercial. "It was clear to us that no reader was going to read a book off any of the current screens for more than ten minutes," says Malcolm Thompson, the chief technologist. "We hoped to change that." A large annotated poster on the wall illustrates point for point the screen's superiority to paper, as in an old-fashioned magazine ad. This flat panel display is indeed better than commercial screens, but it is neither as flexible nor as mobile as a book, and it still depends on fickle battery power. A twentysomething software marketer who began as an editorial assistant in book publishing points out, "A book requires one good eye, one good light source, and one good finger."

D. T. Max, "The End of the Book?" *The Atlantic Monthly*

What inference can you make about the answer to the question posed in the article title, "The End of the Book?" ______________________

Look through the paragraph and identify the evidence that leads to this inference. ______________________

____

____

FURTHER PRACTICE MAKING INFERENCES

In this section are several short passages arranged in order of progressive difficulty, each of which is followed by some inference questions. Follow the same procedure as before. Be prepared to defend your answer choices.

Hypnosis is classed as a psychological rather than a physiological method because it is essentially a form of highly focused mental concentration in which one person allows another to structure the object of the concentration and simultaneously suspends critical judgment and peripheral awareness. When this method is used in a cultic environment, it becomes a form of psychological manipulation and coercion because the cult leader implants suggestions aimed at his own agenda while the person is in a vulnerable state.

Margaret Thaler Singer with Janja Lalich,
Cults in Our Midst

1. _____ Some cult members accept a cult leader's ideas because they have been hypnotized.
2. _____ Hypnosis is always performed as a psychological method to manipulate and coerce.
3. _____ Some individuals never become members of cults because their strong wills makes them resistant to hypnosis.

In this excerpt from an article titled "The Science of Shopping," Malcolm Gladwell explains the rationale behind the way retail merchandise is displayed at stores like the Gap.

> The next thing retailers want to do is to encourage the shopper to walk deep into the store. The trick there is to put "destination items"—basic, staples, things that people know you have and buy a lot of—at the rear of the store. Gap stores, invariably, will have denim, which is a classic destination item for them, on the back wall. Many clothing stores also situate the cash/wrap and the fitting rooms in the rear of the store, to compel shoppers to walk back into Zone 3 or 4. In the store's prime real estate—which . . . is to the right of the front entrance and five to fifteen paces in—you always put your hottest and newest merchandise, because that's where the maximum number of people will see it. Right now, in virtually every Gap in the country, the front of the store is devoted to the Gap fall look—casual combinations in black and gray, plaid shirts and jackets, sweaters, black wool and brushed-twill pants. At the Gap at Fifth Avenue and Seventeenth Street, for example, there is a fall ensemble of plaid jacket, plaid shirt, and black pants in the first prime spot, followed, three paces later, by an ensemble of gray sweater, plaid shirt, T-shirt, and black pants, followed, three paces after that, by an ensemble of plaid jacket, gray sweater, white T-shirt, and black pants. In all, three variations on the same theme, each placed so that the eye bounces naturally from the first to the second to the third, and then, inexorably, to a table deep inside Zone 1 where merchandise is arrayed and folded for petting. Every week or ten days, the combinations will change, the "look" highlighted at the front will be different, and the entryway will be transformed.
>
> Malcolm Gladwell, "The Science of Shopping," *The New Yorker*

1. _____ Retail stores like the Gap display their merchandise randomly, with no apparent purpose.
2. _____ Destination items like denim are put on the back wall so that people must walk through the whole store and see more expensive merchandise on the way.

3. _____ The casual and seasonal clothes one sees in Zones 3 or 4 are more expensive than destination items like denim or sweat shirts.
4. _____ Stores like the Gap hope to entice customers to make impulse purchases.

MAKING OPEN-ENDED INFERENCES

Another kind of inference exercise you will practice making in this text is "open-ended." Rather than labeling choices, you are asked to draw your own inferences after examining a passage. Here are four practice exercises, again arranged in order of difficulty. In the first John Hildebrand describes a horse named Blue.

> Not much bigger than a pony, Blue stood 14-hands high and weighed 950 pounds. His mother was a bucking horse bought from a rodeo, mean and ornery as they come, her history written in overlapping brands that covered her flanks.
>
> John Hildebrand, *Mapping the Farm*

Consider the last sentence again. Why did this horse have so many brands? (Making the correct inference here depends on your knowing the meaning of the word "brand" as it pertains to livestock. If you are unsure, check the dictionary.)

We have all heard that no two snowflakes are identical. Consider what Cullen Murphy says in this paragraph about where this idea originated.

> For all the scientific awareness of the symmetrical character of snow crystals, the ubiquity of their popular image—the one we see in children's paper cutouts and on bags of ice and signs for motels that have air-conditioning—is a relatively recent phenomenon. What snowflakes actually looked like was not widely known until the middle of the nineteenth century, when the book *Cloud Crystals,* with sketches by "A Lady," was published in the United States. The lady had caught snowflakes on a black surface and then observed them with a magnifying glass. In 1885 Wilson Alwyn ("Snowflake") Bentley, of Jericho, Vermont, began taking photographs of snowflakes through a microscope. Thousands of Bentley's photomicrographs were eventually collected in his book *Snow Crystals* (1931).

> The fact that not one of the snowflakes photographed by Bentley was identical to another is probably the basis for the idea that no two snowflakes are ever exactly the same—an idea that is in fact unverifiable.
>
> Cullen Murphy, "In Praise of Snow," *The Atlantic Monthly*

The author ends by saying ". . . the idea that no two snowflakes are ever exactly the same" is "in fact unverifiable." Why is this statement likely to be true? What evidence in the paragraph suggests it? ________

____

____

In *Over the Hills,* David Lamb describes a cross-country bicycle trip he made from Virginia to California. In this excerpt he contrasts the typical overweight American's concern with dieting and his own nutritional intake while on the road.

> Between 1980 and 1991—when the diet business was in full bloom—the average adult American put on eight pounds. That, says the National Center for Health Statistics, is the equivalent of an extra one million tons of fat on the waistline of a nation where one in three persons is certifiably overweight. Ironically, the more we spend trying to get thin—$15 billion a year on diet soft drinks alone, another $4 billion on stuff like Lean Cuisine and pseudo-food appetite suppressants—the plumper we become. Something is clearly out of whack. These contradictions were of no concern to me, however, because I had learned the secret of gluttony without guilt. Day after day I started the morning with French toast or pancakes, enjoyed apple pie with double scoops of ice cream during pre-noon coffee breaks, drank milk shakes, Hawaiian Punch and chocolate milk by the bucketful, snacked on three or four candy bars in the afternoon and often had room for a hot dog or two before I started thinking about dinner. Unlike the rest of America, the more I ate, the less I weighed. I could eat two pieces of coconut custard pie at 11 A.M. and within an hour on the road burn off the 450 calories and then some. By the time I reached western Arkansas, the love handles on my waist had disappeared and I had to tighten my belt an extra notch to keep my pants up.
>
> David Lamb, *Over the Hills*

Based on Lamb's experiences and aside from overeating, why are so many Americans overweight? ____________________

The last practice passage is by Diane Ackerman. The topic is separation experiments performed on monkeys.

[1]At the University of Colorado School of Medicine, researchers conducted a separation experiment with monkeys, in which they removed the mother.

[2]The infant showed signs of helplessness, confusion, and depression, and only the return of its mother and continuous holding for a few days would help it return to normal. [3]During separation, changes occurred in the heart rate, body temperature, brain-wave patterns, sleep patterns, and immune system function. [4]Electronic monitoring of deprived infants showed that touch deprivation caused physical and psychological disturbances. [5]But when the mother was put back, only the psychological disturbances seemed to disappear; true, the infant's behavior reverted to normal, but the physical distresses—susceptibility to disease, and so on—persisted. [6]Among this experiment's implications is that damage is not reversible, and that the lack of maternal contact may lead to possible long-term damage.

[7]Another separation study with monkeys took place at the University of Wisconsin, where researchers separated an infant from its mother by a glass screen. [8]They could still see, hear, and smell each other, only touch was missing, but that created a void so serious that the baby cried steadily and paced frantically. [9]In another group, the dividing screen had holes, so the mother and baby could touch through it, which was apparently sufficient because the infants didn't develop serious behavior problems. [10]Those infants who suffered short-term deprivation became adolescents who clung to one another obsessively instead of developing into independent, confident individuals. [11]When they suffered long-term deprivation, they avoided one another and became aggressive when they did come in contact, violent loners who didn't form good relationships.

Diane Ackerman, *A Natural History of the Senses*

For the first three questions, in the first space, write a sentence stating the inference you can accurately make from the passage. In the second space, cite the evidence—the words, phrases, or sentences—that helped you arrive at your answer.

1. According to the passage as a whole, what can you infer about the effects of touch deprivation in baby monkeys?

   Inference ____________________

   Evidence ____________________

2. What can you infer about the implications of touch deprivation in human infants?

   Inference ____________________

   Evidence ____________________

3. Which of the five senses does the passage suggest is the most important for normal development of infant monkeys?

   Inference ______________________________

   Evidence ______________________________

4. Finally, what can you infer about Ackerman's attitude toward experiments like these conducted on infant monkeys by medical researchers at the Universities of Colorado and Wisconsin? (a) Ackerman suggests that these experiments are needlessly cruel; (b) Ackerman suggests that these experiments yield valuable information about monkeys and, by extension, about humans; (c) Ackerman suggests that such animal experiments should be banned; (d) Ackerman suggests that animal experiments like the ones described here are a necessary evil; (e) Ackerman's discussion does not suggest her attitude one way or the other.

EXERCISES

Selection 1

The author, who lived in Belgium before World War II, had a childhood fascination with the Lowara band of Gypsies who camped every year near his village and who earned their livelihood by horsetrading. At the age of twelve, in the 1930s, he asked his parents if he could leave home and live with the Gypsies, for at least part of each year, and incredibly, they agreed. This is the opening paragraph of his book recounting his experiences.

> [1]As I approached the Gypsy camp for the first time, yellow, wild-looking, stiff-haired dogs howled and barked. [2]Fifteen covered wagons were spread out in a wide half circle, partly hiding the Gypsies from the road. [3]Around the campfires sat women draped in deep-colored dresses, their big, expressive eyes and strong, white teeth standing out against their beautiful dark matte skin. [4]The many gold pieces they wore as earrings, necklaces and bracelets sharpened their color even more. [5]Their shiny blue-black hair was long and braided, the skirts of their dresses were ankle-length, very full and worn in many layers, and their bodices loose and low-cut. [6]My first impression of them was one of health and vitality. [7]Hordes of small barefoot children ran all over the campsite, a few dressed in rags but most nearly naked, rollicking like young animals. [8]At the far end of the encampment a number of horses, tethered to long chains, were grazing; and of course there were the ever-present half-wild growling dogs. [9]Several men lay in the shade of an oak tree. [10]Thin corkscrews of bluish smoke rose skyward and the pungent, penetrating smell of burning wood permeated the air. [11]Even from a distance the loud, clear voices of these Gypsies resounded with an intensity I was not accustomed to. [12]Mingling with them, farther away, were the dull thuds of an ax, the snorting and neighing of

horses, the occasional snapping of a whip and the high-pitched wail of an infant, contrasting with the whisper of the immediate surroundings of the camp itself.

Jan Yoors, *The Gypsies*

A. *Vocabulary*

For each italicized word from the selection, choose the best definition according to the context in which it appears.

1. *bodices* [5]: (a) full skirts; (b) long sleeves; (c) top portions of dresses; (d) shawls.
2. *vitality* [6]: (a) laziness; (b) enthusiasm; (c) curiosity; (d) energy.
3. *rollicking* [7]: (a) rolling; (b) prancing; (c) behaving; (d) romping.
4. *tethered* [8]: (a) restricted; (b) bound up; (c) draped in; (d) decorated.
5. *pungent* [10]: (a) sweetish; (b) biting; (c) sickening; (d) familiar.
6. *permeated* [10]: (a) perfumed; (b) polluted; (c) wafted through; (d) spread throughout.

B. *Content and Structure*

Complete the following questions.

1. The mode of discourse in this paragraph is (a) narration; (b) description; (c) exposition; (d) persuasion.
2. Find the two nouns that Yoors uses to state his dominant impression of these Gypsies. ____________________ and ____________________
3. Yoors uses many words that appeal to our senses. Which sense is *not* emphasized? Words pertaining to (a) sight; (b) smell; (c) sound; (d) touch; (e) color.
4. We can interpret that Yoors found these Gypsies (a) weird; (b) fascinating; (c) alien; (d) lazy.
5. A good title for this paragraph would be (a) "A Study of Gypsy Life"; (b) "The Survival of the Gypsies"; (c) "I Decide to Become a Gypsy"; (d) "First Impressions of a Gypsy Camp."

C. *Inferences*

On the basis of the evidence in the paragraph, mark these statements as follows: PA for inferences that are probably accurate and PI for inferences that are probably inaccurate.

1. ______ The Gypsy camp the author came across was in America.
2. ______ The author had expected the Gypsy camp to be different.

3. ______ Gypsies are persecuted in many European countries.
4. ______ Gypsy culture, at least the culture represented by this group, is essentially nomadic.
5. ______ In Gypsy culture, the women do all the work, while the men lie around, enjoying themselves.
6. ______ Despite the children's ragged appearance, they appeared to be happy.

Selection 2

[1]The first time I ever saw a bear in the wild, I was on my way back from fishing in a beaver meadow on state land next to the Flathead National Forest, about ten miles from the town of Bigfork, Montana. [2]I was coming around a bend on an overgrown logging road when I saw up ahead a large black animal see me and duck into some thimbleberry bushes. [3]I knew it was a bear. [4]I didn't move and he didn't move for maybe three minutes. [5]There was no likely tree nearby for me to climb. [6]Then the bear hopped out of the bushes, took a look at me over his shoulder, and galloped like crazy down the trail. [7]As he ran, his hind feet seemed to reach higher than his head. [8]He splashed water up and made the rocks clack as he crossed a little creek, and then he went into the brush on the other side with a racket that sounded like a car crashing through there. [9]For some reason, I picked up a rock. [10]I felt the weight of the rock in my hand, I smelled the breath from a wild rosebush, I saw the sun on the tops of the mountains, I felt the clothes on my back. [11]I felt like a man—skinny, bipedal, weak, slow, and basically kind of a silly idea. [12]I felt as if I had eyes all over my head. [13]I proceeded, a procession of feelings, down the trail where the bear had run. [14]I saw the dark blots on the trail where he had splashed water from the creek. [15]I kept saying, "A bear! I saw a bear!" [16]I found myself looking over my shoulder for the instant-replay screen. [17]I could not believe that this had happened and then gone by in a second, like trillions of completely unremarkable events. [18]I quickly passed the spot where the bear had disappeared, and then I became happier and happier. [19]I had just moved to Montana at the time, and did not know anyone there. [20]I walked home through the charged twilight and went through the screen door and picked up the telephone and began to call my friends before I even took off my waders.

Ian Frazier, "Bear News,"
Nobody Better, Better Than Nobody

A. *Vocabulary*

For each italicized word from the selection, choose the best definition according to the context in which it appears.

1. *likely* [sentence 5]: (a) sufficiently tall; (b) nearby; (c) suitable; (d) possible.

2. *bipedal* [11]: two (a) hands; (b) feet; (c) arms; (d) eyes.
3. *procession* [13]: (a) a continuous course; (b) a mixture; (c) a list; (d) a parade.
4. *charged* [20]: (a) tense, filled with dread; (b) filled with a sense of wonder and awe; (c) illuminated by electric lights; (d) intensified, saturated.

B. *Content and Structure*

Complete the following questions.

1. The mode of discourse in this paragraph is primarily (a) narration; (b) description; (c) exposition; (d) persuasion. Explain why you chose your answer.

   ____

2. When the bear first spotted the author, it reacted with (a) excitement; (b) curiosity; (c) fear; (d) indifference.
3. Read sentence 8 again. When the author writes that the bear "went into the brush on the other side with a racket that sounded like a car crashing through there," what is he trying to suggest? ______________

   ____

4. Sentences 10 and 11 suggest that this encounter made the author feel—at least in relation to the bear—(a) strong and powerful; (b) vulnerable and open to attack; (c) courageous and daring; (d) small and insignificant.

C. *Inferences*

On the basis of the evidence in the paragraph, mark these statements as follows: PA for inferences that are probably accurate and PI for inferences that are probably inaccurate.

1. ______ Since this incident, the author has probably observed other bears in the wild.
2. ______ The bear was frightened because her cubs were nearby.
3. ______ This bear was more frightened of the author than the author was of the bear.
4. ______ This particular bear was a grizzly.
5. ______ Bears are common in this part of Montana.

Selection 3

[1]In Japan, specially licensed chefs prepare the rarest sashimi delicacy: the white flesh of the puffer fish, served raw and arranged in elaborate floral patterns on a platter. [2]Diners pay large sums of money for the carefully prepared dish, which has a light, faintly sweet taste, like raw pompano. [3]It had better be carefully prepared, because, unlike pompano, puffer fish is ferociously poisonous. [4]You wouldn't think a puffer fish would need such chemical armor, since its main form of defense is to swallow great gulps of water and become so bloated it is too large for most predators to swallow. [5]And yet its skin, ovaries, liver, and intestines contain tetrodotoxin, one of the most poisonous chemicals in the world, hundreds of times more lethal than strychnine or cyanide. [6]A shred small enough to fit under one's fingernail could kill an entire family. [7]Unless the poison is completely removed by a deft, experienced chef, the diner will die midmeal. [8]That's the appeal of the dish; eating the possibility of death, a fright your lips spell out as you dine. [9]Yet preparing it is a traditional art form in Japan, with widespread aficionados. [10]The most highly respected *fugu* chefs are the ones who manage to leave in the barest touch of the poison, just enough for the diner's lips to tingle from his brush with mortality but not enough to actually kill him. [11]Of course, a certain number of diners do die every year from eating *fugu,* but that doesn't stop intrepid *fugu*-fanciers. [12]The ultimate *fugu* connoisseur orders *chiri,* puffer flesh lightly cooked in a broth made of the poisonous livers and intestines. [13]It's not that diners don't understand the bizarre danger of puffer-fish toxin. [14]Ancient Egyptian, Chinese, Japanese, and other cultures all describe *fugu* poisoning in excruciating detail: It first produces dizziness, numbness of the mouth and lips, breathing trouble, cramps, blue lips, a desperate itchiness as of insects crawling all over one's body, vomiting, dilated pupils, and then a zombielike sleep, really a kind of neurological paralysis during which the victims are often aware of what's going on around them, and from which they die. [15]But sometimes they wake. [16]If a Japanese man or woman dies of *fugu* poison, the family waits a few days before burying them, just in case they wake up. [17]Every now and then someone poisoned by *fugu* is nearly buried alive, coming to at the last moment to describe in horrifying detail their own funeral and burial, during which, although they desperately tried to cry out or signal that they were still alive, they simply couldn't move.

Diane Ackerman, *A Natural History of the Senses*

A. *Vocabulary*

For each italicized word from the selection, choose the best definition according to the context in which it appears.

1. *bloated* [sentence 4]: (a) poisonous; (b) swollen; (c) unappealing; (d) intimidating.
2. *lethal* [5]: (a) powerful; (b) bitter-tasting; (c) causing death; (d) dangerous.

3. *deft* [7]: (a) skillful; (b) efficient; (c) clever; (d) well-trained.
4. *aficionados* [9]: (a) customers; (b) trendsetters; (c) gourmets; (d) enthusiastic followers.
5. *intrepid* [11]: (a) serious; (b) courageous; (c) foolish; (d) stubborn.
6. *ultimate* [12]: representing (a) the farthest extreme; (b) the first in a sequence; (c) the largest; (d) the most flavorful.
7. *connoisseur* [12]: (a) a newcomer, novice; (b) a daredevil; (c) a person who does not consider the consequences of his or her actions; (d) a person who has knowledge about food or other esthetic matters.
8. *excruciating* [14]: (a) intensely painful and exact; (b) overly simplified; (c) boring, monotonous; (d) nauseating, sickening.

B. *Content and Structure*

Complete the following questions.

1. Ackerman's purpose in writing the paragraph as a whole is (a) to persuade and encourage the reader to sample puffer fish; (b) to warn the reader about the dangers of eating puffer fish; (c) to explain the preparation and appeal of puffer fish; (d) to describe the appearance of the puffer fish.
2. The mode of discourse in this passage is (a) narration; (b) description; (c) exposition; (d) persuasion.
3. The main idea of the paragraph is best stated in (a) sentence 2; (b) sentence 5; (c) sentence 8; (d) sentence 13.
4. Suppose Ackerman decided to break up this passage, which, after all, is quite long, into three separate paragraphs. Where would she make the divisions?

   Section 1: Sentences ______ to ______

   Section 2: Sentences ______ to ______

   Section 3: Sentences ______ to ______
5. In sentence 4 Ackerman compares the puffer fish's poison to armor. Explain what she means. ______________________________
6. What inference can we make from sentence 11 about why a certain number of diners die each year from eating *fugu?* ______________
7. Which of the following best describes the author's attitude toward puffer fish connoisseurs? (a) She thinks they are weird; (b) She thinks they are foolish; (c) She thinks they are admirable; (d) Her attitude is not evident from the passage.
8. Which of the following can we *reasonably* conclude are characteristics of puffer fish connoisseurs, according to the author's discussion? Mark

any that apply. They are (a) thrill-seeking; (b) cowardly; (c) trusting; (d) daring; (e) idiotic; (f) unafraid of death.

C. *Inferences*

On the basis of the evidence in the paragraph, mark these statements as follows: PA for inferences that are probably accurate and PI for inferences that are probably inaccurate.

1. ______ *Fugu* is another word for puffer fish.
2. ______ The puffer fish is poisonous only when it is served raw as sashimi.
3. ______ The danger in eating puffer fish results from the possibility that the chef may leave too much of the poison in the diner's portion.
4. ______ Connoisseurs who order *chiri* are referred to as "ultimate connoisseurs" because they are getting a double dose of poison.
5. ______ The author has sampled puffer fish.

PRACTICE ESSAY

Abstracting Our Way into Doublespeak

William Lutz

William Lutz, a professor of English at Rutgers University in Camden, New Jersey, for several years has been a zealous crusader warning the public about the dangers of doublespeak, both as head of the Committee on Public Doublespeak for the National Council of Teachers of English and as editor of The Quarterly Review of Doublespeak. *Doublespeak is defined in the dictionary as "deliberately ambiguous or evasive language" and elsewhere defined by Lutz as "language that makes the bad seem good, the negative appear positive, the unpleasant appear attractive or at least tolerable." Each year he presents the annual Doublespeak Award to such people and organizations as Ronald Reagan, Oliver North, the CIA, NASA, the Defense Department, and Exxon Corporation.*

This excerpt is from his latest book, The New Doublespeak. *In it, he examines the origins of doublespeak and the importance of separating facts from inferences. You will have an opportunity to study in more detail doublespeak and its pernicious influence in Chapter 6 of this text.*

1 Heraclitus of Ephesus, writing around 500 B.C., gave us what philosophers call the doctrine of perpetual change. Everything is in a constant state of flux, said Heraclitus, like a flowing river. We cannot step into the "same" river twice because the water we step into the second time is not the same water we stepped into the first time. So it is with the world.

2 The world isn't the stable place we think it is. Like Heraclitus's river, everything is in a constant state of flux, of change. We give stability to this constantly changing world through our ability to re-create it by focusing on similarities and ignoring differences. This process is called abstracting. When we abstract, we select the information we will pay attention to while ignoring the rest, focusing on a limited amount of information that we then arrange into recognizable patterns. Abstracting is a continuous process that allows us to give stability to a very unstable world.

3 All our senses are constantly selecting, organizing, and generalizing the information they receive. When we abstract, we create a kind of summary of what the world is like. We may not be able to step into the same river twice, but by abstracting we act as if we can.

4 **a**Watching television is a simple example of how we constantly abstract without being aware of the process. **b**We see a "picture" on the television screen when there isn't any picture there at all. **c**A television picture is composed of hundreds of thousands of tiny dots. **d**As some dots are lit and some aren't, our brains collect the sensations and organize them into patterns that we see as moving pictures. **e**Those tiny dots on the screen are lit about thirty times per second while our brains organize the dots they see into patterns about ten times per second. **f**Yet even after we understand this process, most of us think the picture is on that screen and not in our heads.

5 Consider this example of the abstraction process involved in seeing a chair. As any physicist will tell you, a chair isn't a "thing" at all; it's an event. A chair is composed of billions of atomic and subatomic particles in constant motion, and even those particles aren't solid matter but are made up of bundles of energy. We can't see these particles, but it's important to remind ourselves that our chair is made up of all these moving particles because then we will remember that the world is not the way we see it. What we see when we look at our chair, and at the rest of world, is a summary, an abstraction, of all the motion of all those particles.

6 Even then we don't see the chair because no one has ever seen a chair in its entirety, all at once. You can see parts of the chair, but not the whole chair—top, bottom, sides—all at once. But we can see enough of the chair that we can construct the entire chair and act as if we know the whole chair. But sometimes our construction can lead us

astray, as when we don't see the crack in the leg and find ourselves on the floor when our chair collapses. Still, our assumptions about our chair will serve us well enough most of the time so that we never question the abstracting process. Indeed, we continue our abstracting when we use language to name the events that make up our world.

Words and Things

7 Naming things—using language—is a very high level abstraction, and when we name something we "freeze" it by placing it in a category and making a "thing" out of it. But now we encounter a curious but most important aspect of this abstracting process. When through the process of abstraction we label an event a "chair," we have created a word for something that does not exist in the world. The word "chair" is an abstraction, a generalization and summary of all those things in the world that look and work in a similar way. The word "furniture" is a still higher abstraction that includes our chair and all those other things that don't look anything like a chair but share some similar features and functions. And we could abstract even further and include our chair in "home decoration" and "personal assets."

8 Here's another example, starting with a specific object and moving through increasingly higher levels of abstraction. Notice how each new level of abstraction ignores more and more differences while focusing on fewer and fewer similarities:

> 1996 red Toyota Camry → Toyota → new car → automobile → motor vehicle → vehicle → private transportation → transportation

9 By the time we get to "transportation" we've moved quite a distance from our 1996 red Toyota Camry. The higher the level of abstraction, the more detail we leave out, the more we ignore differences, and the more we concentrate on similarities, no matter how few or how tenuous those similarities might be. When I talk about transportation, I am including only those aspects of the 1996 Toyota that place it in a category that includes bicycles, airplanes, and trucks.

10 Let's look at a cat named Phil.

> Phil → Maine Coon → male cat → cat → mammal → vertebrate → animal → living thing → thing

11 Phil is a breed of cat known as a Maine Coon. He is also a male cat, and he is a mammal and a vertebrate. But by the time we get to "thing," we're a long way from the collection of atomic and subatomic particles that make up Phil.

12 There is usually less ambiguity at the lower levels of abstraction. If I refer to my 1996 red Toyota Camry, you have a better idea of what I'm talking about than if I refer to my "vehicle" or "private transportation." The words we use reveal the level of abstraction at which we are operating. The word "thing" excludes a lot of detail and can be used to refer to both my Camry and my house, and a whole lot of other objects in the universe. It is a word at the highest levels of abstraction.

13 The less abstract our language, the more concrete and specific we are because we are using language that includes a lot of detail and refers to a very low level of abstraction. I can say, "I like to play sports," or I can say, "I like to play baseball and basketball." Language that is more concrete and specific creates pictures in the mind of the listener, pictures that should come as close as possible to the pictures in your mind.

14 Highly abstract language is a common form of doublespeak, especially among politicians. "Revenue enhancement" is a good example of using a very abstract term to hide what is meant. The government has many forms of revenue besides taxes. And the government can increase its revenues in many ways, with a tax increase being just one of those ways. Indeed, even the term "tax increase" is fairly abstract. Which tax will be increased, and by how much? Are we talking about increasing the tax on corporations by 1 percent, or are we talking about increasing the income tax for anyone making $25,000 a year or less? Those are two very different tax increases, and we might want to talk about them.

15 However, some people would say that they don't care; any tax increase is bad. Of course, we might want to ask them what they mean by "bad," and "bad" for whom? It's bad for the economy, they reply. To which we might say, what do you mean by the "economy"? That's a very abstract term, probably as abstract as calling my 1996 Toyota Camry "transportation" and my cat Phil a "thing." Maybe we would like them to be a little less abstract and a little more specific.

16 Using a high level of abstraction we can call the new dump a "resource development park" and sewage sludge "biosolids" or "organic biomass." Such terms do not call to mind any specific picture because they are so far removed from the concrete reality they are supposed to symbolize. In fact, the terms do exactly what their creators want them to do: They create no picture at all in our minds since we're not sure what they mean. When confronted with such abstractions we have to ask those who use them to give us some specific examples, to move down from their high levels of abstraction to specific examples that clearly illustrate what they are referring to. By using the doublespeak of abstraction, some officials were able to get approval to build a new dump in a residential neighborhood, while other officials won approval for a new sewage plant.

Reports, Inferences, and Judgments

17 At the lowest levels of abstraction we can use language that reports. Reports are based on what we have directly seen, heard, felt, or experienced. Reports are pretty straightforward: "It is raining." "I have a temperature of 101." "I paid $4.99 for that book." We can verify reports and confirm that they are accurate. We can look out the window and see the rain. We can use a thermometer to check a person's temperature. And we can see the sales receipt to verify the price paid for a book. Report language is concrete and specific.

18 In our everyday lives we accept reports of reports all the time. Did General Motors really make a profit last quarter? The newspapers said so, and even though we can't verify that report, we accept it. Without giving it much thought, we accept reports of reports all the time. We follow road maps and our doctor's advice. We read books on science, mathematics, and history, and assume that the authors are giving us reliable information.

Inferences

19 Much as we might like all language to be in the form of reports, we wouldn't get much done if it were. Instead, we use inferences to conduct our daily affairs. An inference is a statement about the unknown based on the known. It is a guess, sometimes an educated guess, and sometimes a wild leap of logic.

20 An inference starts with what is known or observed. You notice the newspapers piling up on your neighbors' porch. Then you notice the mail overflowing the mailbox. Since their car is gone and you haven't seen anyone around the house for a few days, you infer that they have gone on vacation. Your inference is based on your observations, observations that we could call reports because they are all verifiable. However, the statement that the Bergers have gone on vacation is an inference, a conclusion drawn from your observations.

21 It is possible, of course, that you are wrong in your inference. There are other possible inferences that you could draw. Perhaps the entire family has been murdered and the killer fled in their car. Or perhaps Mrs. Berger took the children to her mother's in Florida for a visit while Mr. Berger is out of town on business. Or perhaps the Bergers haven't gone anywhere while their car is being repaired and they have forgotten to collect their mail and newspapers.

22 We make hundreds of inferences every day, and for the most part our inferences work. Since it is a weekday, we infer that stores will be open for business. We go to the bus stop because we infer that the bus will stop there again today to pick up passengers. We can test these inferences because either the stores are open or they aren't, and the bus will stop or it won't.

23 We also make other inferences that aren't so easily or quickly verifiable. We infer a person's economic and social status from the quality of her clothes, jewelry, and car. We infer the geopolitical strategy of Iran from its actions; we infer a person's feelings about us from his words and the way he treats us; we infer the existence of certain creatures based on fossils we collect; we infer the nature of Egyptian civilization from the ruins, written records, and artifacts we examine. Without inferences, we couldn't function in our everyday lives, and without inferences our knowledge of the world would be greatly reduced. However, we have to be aware of our inferences because we can easily draw false inferences without knowing it.

24 A segment on the television evening news shows us a home for unmarried, pregnant teenage girls. The reporter mentions that the home is overcrowded, that there are more pregnant teenagers than there is room at the home. This report is followed by an interview with a politician who says that we have to do something about teenagers having babies, which has become a crisis that demands action. Moreover, our politician adds somberly, teenagers having babies is more evidence of our moral decline. The next day, we mention in conversation that there's a serious problem with all those teenagers having babies.

25 From the television report we have drawn the inference that there are a large number of teenage girls having babies, a number that is growing. We might even infer that there is an "epidemic" of teenage pregnancies. But our inference would be wrong. Teenage pregnancies are not increasing. In fact, the birth rate among teenage girls is lower today than it was forty years ago. In 1955, approximately 90 out of every 1,000 women between the ages of fifteen and nineteen gave birth, while in 1993 the birth rate for that age group was down to 59 out of 1,000. And most of those babies are born to mothers who are eighteen or nineteen years old. So perhaps our inference that there is an epidemic of teenagers having babies is false. And if that inference is false, what about the inference that we are in a moral decline, assuming that we can all agree what we mean by such an abstract term? Drawing false inferences is sometimes called leaping to conclusions.

Judgments

26 Often we move from inferences to a higher level of abstraction known as judgments. Instead of saying, "It is raining," "I have a temperature of 101," and "I paid $4.99 for that book," we might say, "The weather is terrible," "I look terrible," and "I paid too much for that book." These last three statements are judgments. A judgment is an expression of our approval or disapproval of what we are describing. In other words, judgments are nothing more than our personal opinions. We get into trouble when we confuse judgments with reports.

27 Consider these sentences:

1. The man lying in the street is unconscious.
2. The man lying in the street is drunk.
3. The man lying in the street is a bum.

28 The first sentence is a report, a description of fact. The second sentence is an inference, and the third sentence is a judgment. The first sentence is verifiable, while the second sentence is an interpretation of an observation, a statement about the unknown based on the known. We don't know that the man is drunk. We only see him, his physical condition, and his appearance. Based on those observations we may infer that he is drunk. That the man is a bum is a judgment, our evaluation of the man based on our inferences.

29 We often confuse reports and judgments. How often do we accept as a report statements such as: "Hemingway is a great writer." "The Toyota Camry is the best car you can buy," "Allen is stupid," "Socialized medicine is terrible," "Socialism and freedom are incompatible," "Conservatives are fascists," and "America is the greatest country in the world." Yet each of these statements is a judgment, an expression of the speaker's evaluation of the person or thing being discussed. These statements say nothing about the people and things being discussed but do reveal something of the speaker's values. Even if others agree with our judgments we do not have a report, just a similarity of values. Unfortunately, we too often treat judgments as if they were reports.

30 Here's a little story illustrating how we can use the abstraction process to make inferences and judgments that do not coincide with a description of the facts.

A Tale of Faulty Inferences

31 The train rushes across the Hungarian countryside. In a compartment sit a mother and her attractive daughter, a Nazi officer, and a Hungarian official. When the train passes through a tunnel, the compartment is engulfed in darkness. Suddenly there is the sound of a loud kiss followed by a shattering slap. When the train emerges from the tunnel, no one says a word, but the Nazi officer's face bears the unmistakable signs of having been slapped. The mother looks at her daughter and thinks, "What a good daughter I have. She certainly showed that Nazi he can't fool with her." The daughter looks at her mother and thinks, "Mother sure is brave to take on a Nazi officer over one stolen kiss." The Nazi officer stares at the Hungarian official and thinks, "That Hungarian is clever. He steals a kiss and gets me slapped, and there's nothing I can do about it." The Hungarian official stares blankly as he thinks, "Not bad. I kiss my hand and get away with slapping a Nazi."

32 The facts of the story are simple: In the darkness there was a noise that sounded like a kiss, followed by a noise that sounded like a slap.

33 Based on these facts, each person in the compartment drew a different inference and arrived at a different judgment. The mother inferred that the Nazi had kissed her daughter and that her daughter had slapped the Nazi. The daughter inferred that the Nazi had kissed her mother and that her mother had retaliated with a slap. The Nazi inferred that the Hungarian had kissed the girl, prompting her to slap him in error.

34 Each of these people then made a judgment based on the inference. The mother thinks her daughter is "good" because she slapped the Nazi. The daughter thinks her mother is "brave" because she slapped the Nazi. The Nazi thinks the Hungarian is "clever" because he kissed the girl but got the Nazi slapped. The Hungarian, of course, knows what happened. While all the other people think they know the "facts" of the incident, they know only what they have inferred and the judgments they have made.

35 Abstracting is a fundamental and necessary process for dealing with the world. With it we can construct a coherent world with which we can interact. But we must remember that we are constantly engaged in a highly selective process, that we are choosing to ignore large chunks of our world. While abstraction can help us in dealing with our environment, it can also get us into trouble if we forget that we are abstracting and start to treat our inferences and judgments as if they are descriptive statements of the world.

A. *Comprehension*

Choose the answer that best completes each statement. Do not refer to the selection while doing this exercise.

1. According to Lutz, we give stability to the constantly changing world around us by abstracting, which he defines as (a) learning written and spoken language; (b) focusing on similarities and ignoring differences; (c) learning to distinguish the abstract from the concrete; (d) paying attention only to the important things that happen around us.
2. When we look at a chair, we are not really seeing a chair because (a) we can't see every part of the chair, composed of constantly moving particles, at the same time; (b) the word *chair* is an abstract concept that doesn't mean the same thing to everyone; (c) we don't observe things around us, even chairs, very well; (d) the word *chair* only stands for the object, and doesn't represent the thing itself.
3. As we move up the ladder of abstraction, for example, from "1996 red Toyota Camry" to "transportation," we are really (a) showing that we

do not think very clearly; (b) ignoring more differences and focusing on fewer similarities; (c) moving from the general and to the specific; (d) demonstrating that these two terms are more similar than dissimilar.

4. Lutz characterizes doublespeak, especially as used by politicians, as (a) highly abstract and therefore unclear; (b) clear and concise; (c) unclear to everyone except the politicians who use it; (d) the result of lazy thinking and a careless inattentiveness to the meanings of words.
5. When town officials call a new dump a "resource development park," the latter term (a) sounds clearer than what it actually refers to; (b) is too wordy; (c) is far removed from the actual thing it is supposed to symbolize; (d) is too specific on the ladder of abstraction.
6. An inference is a guess based on things we observe, and a judgment is (a) simply a synonym for *inference;* (b) similar to a report but with added subjective observations; (c) another example of abstraction; (d) an evaluation, representing a personal opinion, based on our observation.

B. *Structure*

Complete the following questions.

1. What is the meaning of the sentence "We cannot step into the same river twice"? (See paragraph 1.) ____________________

   ____
2. The mode of discourse in the essay is (a) narration; (b) description; (c) exposition; (d) persuasion.
3. Look again at the sentences in paragraph 4, which are identified by small letters. Label each as MAIN (main idea); MA (major); or MI (minor).

   sentence a _____ sentence b _____ sentence c _____

   sentence d _____ sentence e _____ sentence f _____
4. The purpose of paragraphs 5 and 6 is, specifically, (a) to show that not all things that we call chairs are really chairs; (b) to demonstrate the way we commonly go through the abstracting process to make sense of the world; (c) to show the dangers of abstracting; (d) to show the relationship between abstracting and making incorrect inferences.
5. Look again at paragraphs 24 and 25. How has the viewer made the inference that "there's a serious problem with all those teenagers having babies"?

   ____

Why is that inference, according to Lutz, wrong? ______________

____

6. Consider these three sentences in relation to the discussion in paragraphs 26–28. Then label each according to whether it is a report, an inference, or a judgment.

   a. ______________ Henry must not have studied for his physics test.

   b. ______________ Henry received a D on his physics test.

   c. ______________ Henry is a poor student.

7. The "Tale of Faulty Inferences" in paragraphs 31–35 illustrates (a) how our cultural background can interfere with our good judgment; (b) how people make judgments based on incomplete facts; (c) the importance of never making inferences or judgments; (d) how easy it is to blame the wrong person for a wrongdoing.

8. Which character in the story was the only one who knew the facts?

   ____

C. *Inferences*

Complete the following questions.

1. What is the relationship between abstracting and doublespeak?

   ____

2. Which would be more likely to result in doublespeak—general, more abstract words and phrases at the upper levels of abstraction or specific, more concrete words and phrases at the lower level of abstraction? ______________

3. Why does Lutz object to the term "revenue enhancement"? (See paragraph 14.) ______________

4. Look again at paragraph 16. What does Lutz suggest is the reason government officials use the doublespeak of abstraction? ______________

   ____

D. *Vocabulary*

For each italicized word from the selection, choose the best definition according to the context in which it appears.

1. a constant state of *flux* [paragraph 1]: (a) chaos, confusion; (b) change, movement; (c) serenity, peace; (d) discomfort, uneasiness.

2. no matter how *tenuous* [9]: (a) commonplace; (b) confusing; (c) having a strong connection; (d) lacking a sound basis.
3. usually less *ambiguity* [12]: (a) clarity, understanding; (b) difference of opinion; (c) uncertainly regarding interpretation; (d) dislocation.
4. the more *concrete* and specific [13]: (a) real, perceptible; (b) general, vague; (c) comprehensible; (d) limited in scope.
5. *engulfed* in darkness [31]: (a) made invisible; (b) hindered by; (c) interrupted by; (d) swallowed up.
6. construct a *coherent* world [35]: (a) pleasurable, enjoyable; (b) logically connected, consistent; (c) crucial, significant; (d) economically productive, viable.

E. *Questions for Analysis and Discussion*

1. For a class project, look through the daily newspaper and write down as many examples of doublespeak as you can find over a period of a few weeks. At the end of the designated time period, one student can be chosen to collect the examples, and type and distribute copies to the class for evaluation. How many of the examples of doublespeak result from very high levels of abstraction, as Lutz explains it?
2. Here are the terms in a "ladder of abstraction" from a critical thinking textbook by Marlys Mayfield, *Thinking for Yourself*,[1] but the terms are out of order. Rearrange them by putting the most abstract term at the top and the most specific term at the bottom.
   - Citrus
   - Possession
   - Valencia orange
   - Solid substances
   - Food
   - The orange in my hand
   - Nourishment, fare, provisions
   - Atoms, molecules, elements at the process level in ever-changing characteristics invisible to the naked eye
   - Orange
   - Produce

[1]Fourth edition, Wadsworth Publishing Company, 1997, 55.

3

Five Methods of Paragraph Development

Now that you have studied some of the fundamentals—the main idea, levels of support, modes of discourse, and making inferences—we can begin to analyze paragraph development and organization in more detail. In this chapter you will be introduced to five methods of development, the kinds of evidence used to develop or support the main idea. They are (1) facts and statistics; (2) examples and illustration; (3) process; (4) comparison and contrast; and (5) explanation. (The remaining four methods are more difficult and will be taken up in Chapter 4.) In addition, and as you will see later, a writer can combine two or more methods, but for now, we will examine them in isolation so they are easier to recognize.

As you study these following methods, you will see that the majority are expository; in fact, some composition textbooks refer to these as **expository** methods of development.

FACTS AND STATISTICS

A **fact** is information presented as objectively real. A fact is verifiable, meaning that one can prove its truth by scientific measurement, by personal observation, by duplication, and so on.[1] **Statistics** are, simply put, data in the form of numbers. This is the simplest method of development—though ironically, it is the one most capable of leading readers astray or of presenting false information. One can find statistics to fit any theory, and statistics often contradict each other, depending on their source and their purpose in being compiled.

In this first example, Adam Walinsky writes about guns and gun ownership. After you read the paragraph, answer the question that follows.

> [1]It is a commonplace that many crimes are committed with guns, particularly handguns. In 1993, 69.6 percent of all homicides were committed by gun, four fifths of these by handgun. Guns were also used in 42.4 percent of all robberies and 25.1 percent of aggravated assaults. The total of such gun felonies reported to the police was about 571,000.
>
> [2]As long as surveys have asked the question, about half of all American households have answered that they own at least one gun. Patterns of ownership, however, have changed. In the 1960s weapons used primarily for sport—rifles and shotguns—made up 80 percent of the approximately 80 million guns in private hands. About 12 percent of the population reported owning one or more handguns. By 1976, with the great postwar crime wave under way, more than 21 percent of the population reported owning handguns—an increase of 75 percent. The largest increases were among nonwhites (by 99 percent), college graduates (by 147 percent), and Jews (by 679 percent, to a total of 14.8 percent reporting handgun ownership, which left them well behind Protestants but ahead of Catholics). By 1978 the estimate of total number of guns owned had increased to roughly 120 million.
>
> [3]In every year since, at least four million new guns have been manufactured or imported. In 1993 there were 5.1 million guns manufactured and another 2.9 million imported. Of the eight million new guns in 1993, half—3.9 million—were handguns. The current estimate is that more than 200 million guns are in private hands.
>
> Adam Walinsky, "The Crisis of Public Order,"
> *The Atlantic Monthly*

[1]Compare the definition of *fact* to *factoid,* a word often seen in the media. A *factoid,* according to the *American Heritage Dictionary,* is "unverified or inaccurate information that is presented to the press as factual, often as part of a publicity effort, and that is then accepted as true because of constant repetition."

What *two* specific areas about the topic of guns do Walinsky's facts and statistics support? ________________________________ and ________________________________

In this next passage also published in *The Atlantic Monthly,* Eric Schlosser writes about marijuana laws, his main idea again supported by facts and statistics.

> [1]State marijuana laws were also toughened during the 1980s and now vary enormously. Some states classify marijuana with drugs like mescaline and heroin, while others give it a separate legal category. In New York state possessing slightly less than an ounce of marijuana brings a $100 fine, rarely collected. In Nevada possessing any amount of marijuana is a felony. In Montana selling a pound of marijuana, first offense, could lead to a life sentence, whereas in New Mexico selling 10,000 pounds of marijuana, first offense, could be punished with a prison term of no more than three years. In some states it is against the law to be in a room where marijuana is being smoked, even if you don't smoke any. In some states you may be subject to criminal charges if someone else uses, distributes, or cultivates marijuana on your property. In Idaho selling water pipes could lead to a prison sentence of nine years. In Kentucky products made of hemp fibers, such as paper and clothing, not only are illegal but carry the same penalties associated with an equivalent weight of marijuana. In Arizona, where marijuana use is forbidden, the crime can be established by the failure of a urine test: a person could theoretically be prosecuted in Phoenix for a joint smoked in Philadelphia more than a week before.
>
> [2]Crossing an invisible state line with marijuana in your car can result in vastly different punishments. If you are caught with three ounces of marijuana in Union City, Ohio, you will probably be fined $100. But if you are caught in the town of the same name literally across the road in Indiana, you could face nine months to two years in prison, a fine of up to $10,000, a felony record, suspension of your driver's license, forfeiture of your car, and charges of marijuana possession, of possession with intent to distribute, and of "maintaining a common nuisance" (for the criminal use of an automobile). That one arrest in Indiana might cost you the $10,000 fine and at least $5,000 in legal fees, plus the value of your forfeited car. Wide discrepancies in punishment occur not just between states but also from county to county within a given state. In La Salle County, Illinois, a first-time offender arrested with 300 pounds of marijuana might be sentenced to four months in boot camp. Sixty-five miles to the south, in McLean County, the same person convicted of the same crime would more likely receive a prison sentence of four to eight years.
>
> Eric Schlosser, "Reefer Madness," *The Atlantic Monthly*

What phrase states the controlling idea? ______________________________

Locate the sentence that restates the main idea and serves as a transition (or bridge) between ideas within the paragraph.

____

EXAMPLES AND ILLUSTRATION

The common methods of example and illustration are also relatively easy to identify. An **example** is a specific idea representative of a group as a whole. Concerning the general subject of exotic flavors of ice cream, one could cite several specific instances: mango-mango, coconut-pomegranate, tangerine-mocha, to name just three. Netscape Navigator and Microsoft Explorer are two examples of World Wide Web browsers. A writer, in the same way, may support a general statement, either by citing a series of specific examples, or instances, of the main idea. Or the writer may use a single longer **illustration.** The methods function in the same way: both point to typical and concrete instances of a more general idea. The only difference between them is that examples are short and are usually found in clusters, whereas an illustration supports a general idea in more detail. Without examples, we would be obliged to supply our own, which, of course, would come from a different set of experiences.

In this first sample, Marjorie Garber develops the main idea with two short examples. Which sentence states the main idea?

> [1]At a time when "universal" ideas and feelings are often compromised or undercut by group identities, the dog tale still has the power to move us. [2]Paradoxically, the dog has become the repository of those model human properties which we have cynically ceased to find among human beings. [3]On the evening news and in the morning paper, dog stories supply what used to be called "human interest." [4]There was the story of Lyric, for instance—the 911 dog, who dialled emergency services to save her mistress, and wound up the toast of Disneyland. [5]Or the saga of Sheba, the mother dog in Florida who rescued her puppies after they were buried alive by a cruel human owner. [6]His crime and her heroic single-motherhood were reliable feature stories, edging out mass killings in Bosnia and political infighting at home. [7]Here, after all, were the family values we'd been looking for as a society—right under our noses.
>
> [8]Indeed, at a time of increasing human ambivalence about human heroes and the human capacity for "unconditional love," dog heroes—and dog stories—are with us today more than ever. [9]Near the entrance to Central Park at Fifth Avenue and Sixty-seventh Street stands the statue of Balto, the

heroic sled dog who led a team bringing medicine to diphtheria-stricken Nome, Alaska, in the winter of 1925. [10]Balto's story recently became an animated feature film, joining such other big-screen fictional heroes as Lassie, Rin Tin Tin, Benji, and Fluke.

Marjorie Garber, "Dog Days," *The New Yorker*

Main idea: sentence ______________________________

In this next paragraph, Jeffrey Masson and Susan McCarthy use a single dramatic illustration in support of the main idea, which occurs in the first sentence.

> Tenderness may also cross the species barrier, with some animals showing distinct pleasure in caretaking. When a young sparrow crash-landed in the chimpanzee cage at the Basel Zoo, one of the apes instantly snatched it in her hand. Expecting to see the bird gobbled up, the keeper was astonished to see the chimpanzee cradle the terrified fledgling tenderly in a cupped palm, gazing at it with what seemed like delight. The other chimpanzees gathered and the bird was delicately passed from hand to hand. The last to receive the bird took it to the bars and handed it to the astounded keeper.

Jeffrey Masson and Susan McCarthy,
When Elephants Weep

PROCESS

Process is the next method of development. There are two kinds of process writing, both of which use a step-by-step or chronological pattern. In the first, called the **directive** kind, the author explains the steps that one must *follow* to perform a task, such as how to study for final exams, how to develop a photograph, how to lose 10 pounds, and so on. Process writing is found most often in laboratory or technical manuals and in how-to and self-help books. The following paragraph from a newspaper article on eating Chinese food explains step by step how one goes about learning to use chopsticks.

> Learning to use chopsticks takes only a practice session or two, and using them does enhance the enjoyment of Chinese food: Form a loose fist with your thumb facing up. Slip the lower chopstick into the crux of your hand and over the tip of your middle finger, with the narrow end of the chopstick jutting about 5 inches beyond the tip of your finger. Grip the upper chopstick something like a pencil between the thumb and forefinger. The

tips of the chopsticks should be even. To pick up food, move the top chopstick up and down with your index finger. The lower chopstick, held in place with your thumb, should remain stationary.

Bruce Cost, "Mom Might Faint, But It's OK to Slurp in Chinese Eateries," *San Francisco Chronicle*

Informative process writing, the second kind of process, describes a phenomenon—how something works, how something developed, or how it came into existence. The author uses chronological order, just as in the directive kind, but the underlying purpose is different because either the writer does not expect us to duplicate the process or because it would be impossible to do so. An especially good example of an informative process occurs in this next paragraph, in which the author describes the "Substitution Trunk" a trick performed by the famous magician and master of illusion, Harry Houdini. As they say, don't try this at home.

The very first trick ever performed by Houdini on the professional stage was a simple but effective illusion known generally as the "Substitution Trunk," though he preferred to call it "Metamorphosis." Houdini and his partner would bring a large trunk onto the stage. It was opened and a sack or bag produced from inside it. Houdini, bound and handcuffed, would get into the sack, which was then sealed or tied around the neck. The trunk was closed over the bag and its occupant. It was locked, strapped and chained. Then a screen was drawn around it. The partner (after they married, this was always Mrs. Houdini) stepped behind the screen which, next moment, was thrown aside—by Houdini himself. The partner had meanwhile disappeared. A committee of the audience was called onstage to verify that the ties, straps, etc., around the trunk had not been tampered with. These were then laboriously loosened; the trunk was opened; and there, inside the securely fastened bag, was—Mrs. Houdini!

Ruth Brandon, *The Life and Many Deaths of Harry Houdini*

COMPARISON AND CONTRAST

The **comparison** and **contrast** methods are used to explain similarities and differences between two subjects. The less common of the two, **comparison,** involves a discussion of *similarities* between two seemingly unlike or unrelated things. For example, a writer might explain what the unrelated situations of interviewing for a new job and meeting a new girlfriend's or boyfriend's parents have in common.

Contrast properly refers to a discussion of the *differences* between two related or like things—for example, Clinton's two presidential terms, "Star Wars" and its first sequel, "The Empire Strikes Back"; or the Honda Accord and the Honda Civic automobiles. You may find comparison and contrast used together or singly, depending on the subject and the author's purpose.

The following paragraph uses primarily *comparison*. Peter Steinhart opens with a questionable assertion: that we are more similar to wolves than to any other animal. He then continues to show that, although we are structurally closer to chimpanzees and gorillas, in behavior we are closer to wolves.

> We are drawn to wolves because no other animal is so like us. Of all the rest of creation, wolves reflect our own images back to us most dramatically, most realistically, and most intensely. We recognize chimpanzees and gorillas, which are more like us in body structure and which show capacities for language and tool-making, as our closest evolutionary relatives. But long ago we diverged from chimpanzees and gorillas, and we have been shaped by different habits. As a result, though we are in many ways like chimpanzees, we are in some ways more like wolves. Like wolves, we evolved as hunters; we have long legs and considerable powers of endurance, adaptations to the chase rather than to hiding; we have minds that are capable of fine calculation, not just of spatial relationships, but of strategy and coordination. Like wolves, we band together to kill larger prey, and that has given us a different social system and a different personality from the chimpanzee; we have long childhoods, strong social bonds, complex social roles, and status differences; we tend to claim and defend territories; we have complex forms of communication; we are individuals; we have strong emotions. Humans and wolves are so much alike that they take an unusual interest in one another. Wild wolves have often followed humans with what the humans felt was friendly curiosity, perhaps even a desire for company. And humans have, for thousands of years, adopted wolves and felt with them a mutual sense of companionship.
>
> Peter Steinhart, *The Company of Wolves*

Steinhart's writing is easy to follow because he repeats the key phrase "like wolves" twice at the beginning of sentences. What other words and phrases also contribute to the paragraph's coherence?

Bill McKibben in this next example uses only contrast to show the differences between television news and a newspaper. The only similarity, according to this writer, between a newspaper and television news is that both occur daily; therefore, he focuses on the differences in these two mediums.

> Perhaps the greatest distortion of TV news comes from the very fact of its seeming comprehensiveness. Each day, it fills its allotted hours no matter what, and each day it fills them with a crackling urgency. A newspaper comes out every day, too, but a newspaper has various ways of letting you know whether or not an event is important. The single most useful thing about the *Times* is that the width and type size of the lead headline each morning let you know how it compares, in the view of the paper's editors, with all the other lead stories since the *Times* began. It has a way of saying to its readers, "Nothing earthshaking happened today; it's O.K. to read the reviews or the sports." TV has almost no flexibility of this sort.
>
> Bill McKibben, "Reflections: Television," *The New Yorker*

Of the two methods, contrast is the more common because readers usually need differences pointed out to them rather than obvious similarities. Such is the case in this last passage, in which Jorge Castañeda discusses the class structure in Mexico for an American audience.

> There is, of course, a middle class in Mexico, but it constitutes a minority of the population: somewhere between a quarter and a third. The majority—poor, urban, brown, and often without access to the main attributes of modern life in the United States and other industrialized countries (public education, decent health care and housing, formal employment, social security, the right to vote and serve in government, jury duty, and so forth)—mingles with itself. It lives, works, sleeps, and worships apart from a small group of the very wealthy and a larger but still restricted middle class. The United States is the proverbial mass society (though less so than formerly), in which a white, middle-class, suburban majority coexists with various minorities that are undeniably though unevenly segregated and discriminated against. Mexico is a society terribly riven by class, race, gender, age, region, and future, in which a middle- and upper-class minority segregates and discriminates against the vast majority of the population. It is one of the most unequal societies around, though not one of the poorest. Nonetheless, it is poor: in 1992 nearly 65 percent of wage earners received up to but not more than twice the minimum wage—at the time, around $100 a month. According to a more recent estimate, 55.8 percent of all Mexican households have a yearly purchasing power of less than about $5,000.
>
> Jorge G. Castañeda, "Ferocious Differences," *The Atlantic Monthly*

In your own words, explain Castañeda's two points of contrast:

____ and

____

Besides contrast, what other method of development is evident in the last two sentences? ____

____

EXPLANATION

The last expository method of development taken up in this chapter, **explanation,** might at first glance appear to overlap with or be very similar to process or example and illustration. But if you consider the etymology of the verb *explain,* the distinction will be apparent. From Latin, the verb *explain* means "to make clear" [ex + plānus, "clear"]. A writer using explanation as a method, then, tries to make a complex subject clear and comprehensible. Process also differs from explanation because it uses chronological order, while passages using explanation do not. In the following paragraph, the unnamed author explains the unusual ability of a species of flatfish, *Bothus ocellatus,* to camouflage itself.

> *Bothus ocellatus,* a species of warm-water flatfish, is remarkably adept at camouflaging itself. Researchers at the University of California at San Diego have found that it can change big spots on its skin into small spots or squares, or even eliminate them altogether, if that's what it takes to blend in with its surroundings and avoid predators. Neurologist Vilayanur Ramachandran and his colleagues placed a flatfish in a tank with a variety of patterns on the bottom, including large polka dots, yellow beach sand, and coarse gravel. . . . In each case, within eight seconds or less, the fish rapidly adapted its markings to closely match the pattern on the bottom. The fish accomplish their trick by using different combinations of clusters of pigmented bodies in their skin. "By varying the dispersal of pigment, they use this palette to produce many kinds of patterns," Ramachandran says. Exactly how the fish recognize and re-create the background patterns is a mystery. Ramachandran suspects that there are specialized cells in their brains that can recognize particular patterns and then tell the skin what pigment bodies to expand or contract. "There is probably a hot line from the vision center of the brain to the skin,"

says Ramachandran, "to make these different textures in the skin to match the background."

"Just Trying to Fit In," *Discover*

In this paragraph, the author very briefly describes the process—how the fish adapted its markings to match the pattern—in a single sentence. The remainder of the paragraph explains some theories as to how this camouflage trick is accomplished. The distinction is a fine but perhaps useful one.

David Lamb, the writer of the next sample, bicycled across the United States. Here he explains the origin of the custom in North America of driving on the right-hand side of the road.

Before leaving home, I spent some time researching the evolution of our road system and was surprised to learn that were it not for the Conestoga wagon, we might still be following the British pattern of driving on the left-hand side of the road, as we did in the first few decades of nationhood. Drivers of the Conestoga—or prairie schooner, as it was known during the settlement of the West—were stationed on the left of the wagon, walking, riding the lazy-board or astride the near wheelhorse. To have a clear view over six horses and a wagon that spanned sixty feet, they found it necessary to keep their vehicles to the right. Soon other carriages and cargo haulers were following in the deep ruts cut by the wagons, and in 1813 New Jersey became the first state to order wagons to stay to the right.

David Lamb, *Over the Hills*

COMBINATION OF METHODS

Finally, you should recognize that, like many of life's challenges, the task of reading is a complex undertaking. Not all paragraphs can be as neatly categorized as those you have examined here. Although some writers use an easily recognizable method of development, many do not. In particular, within an essay or article, a writer may use several different methods from paragraph to paragraph or within the same passage. The following paragraph is a good example of a piece of writing that employs a combination of the methods you have studied thus far. David Remnick's subject is Michael Jordan, unquestionably the best basketball player of all time. The passage was written just after Michael Jordan "unretired," returning to play for the Chicago Bulls, in this case against the Knicks in the spring of 1995. As you read it, see if you can identify where these two expository methods occur.

Out on the court, a few players were getting limber, taking desultory jump shots, walking through moves they would later attempt at frenetic speed. Unguarded, unhindered by an opponent whacking him in the ribs or waving a hand in his eyes, even a backup player like the Chicago forward Corie Blount hit seventy or eighty percent of his shots. It means nothing. In baseball, players are competing mainly against the difficulty of the sport itself, the almost laughable improbability of hitting a speeding baseball with a flame-tempered twig. Baseball is such a hard game that small children modify it (they hit off a tee) and the middle-aged *enlarge* it (calling it softball). In basketball, the fundamentals—shooting, passing, rebounding—are relatively easy to manage, at least in the solitude of an empty schoolyard; the difficulty comes in competing against the athleticism, the obstructions and wiles, of an aggressive opponent. Anyone can hit a fifteen-foot shot, sneakers to the floor; only a professional can manage it with a leaping lump of muscle in his face. That's why Jordan is so much better than anyone else who has ever played the game. He plays as if in solitude. High in the air, his legs splayed, his tongue flopping out of his mouth, he seems weirdly relaxed, calm, as if there were no one special around and plenty of time to think through his next move, floating all the while. Faced with double coverage, as he almost always is, Jordan finds a way to wedge between defenders, elevate as if on an invisible forklift, his legs dangling, and then drop the ball through the hoop. The ease of his game makes the rest of the players, all of them stars in college, look rough, somehow—clumsy, a step slow. "Scoring is scoring," Jordan says serenely in "Rare Air," his autobiography. "If I want to average 32 points a game, I can do that easily. It's just eight, eight, eight, eight. No problem. I can do that anytime. That's not being cocky. That's confidence."

David Remnick, "Back in Play," *The New Yorker*

What are the two expository methods in this paragraph?

____________________ and ____________________

With a pencil return to the paragraph and mark the sentences that reflect these methods.

EXERCISES

Selection 1

In each issue of *The Atlantic Monthly,* the magazine's editorial staff publishes a monthly almanac, often reprinting short excerpts from issues 10, 15, or more years ago. This paragraph was originally published in the September 1969 issue.

25 Years Ago

[1]"Our society views dying as being in questionable taste despite the fact that ten out of ten still do it. [2]Perhaps it is part of our emphasis on eternal youthfulness as opposed to maturity. [3]The life-span expands, and we have chosen to put the stretch on the early part. [4]We apparently like to think of ourselves as being young or youngish right up to the moment when we proceed with bouncy step to retirement communities, there to live on forever in spry clusters of ranch-style death houses. . . . [5]The price we pay for this pastel-washed denial of the only inevitable experience of life may be higher than we know. [6]Our abnegation, as a people, of death may be the chief reason we seem to get so little genuine joy out of everyday life. [7]For when life stretches out indefinitely, world without end, there is no yardstick for momentary pleasures, and passing pains are blown up out of all proportion."

Howard Luck Gossage, *The Atlantic Monthly*

A. *Vocabulary*

For each italicized word from the selection, choose the best definition according to the context in which it appears.

1. *bouncy* [sentence 4]: (a) firm, confident; (b) lively, energetic; (c) springy, resilient; (d) halting, slow.
2. *spry* [4]: (a) attractive; (b) active; (c) well-maintained; (d) well-furnished.
3. *inevitable* [5]: (a) unexplainable; (b) impossible to predict; (c) impossible to avoid; (d) occurring without warning.
4. *abnegation* [6]: (a) fear; (b) conflict; (c) avoidance; (d) denial.

B. *Content and Structure*

Complete the following questions.

1. The mode of discourse in the paragraph is (a) narration; (b) description; (c) exposition; (d) persuasion.
2. The method of development is (a) comparison; (b) illustration; (c) process; (d) explanation; (e) contrast.
3. The main idea is implied in this paragraph. In your own words write a main-idea sentence for this paragraph. ______________________

____

____

4. A good title for this paragraph would be (a) "American Views on Death"; (b) "How to Stay Young Forever"; (c) "The Price of Denying Death"; (d) "Why Americans Fear Death."
5. Read sentence 1 again. Which best describes the author's attitude implied in this sentence? (a) informative; (b) concerned; (c) humorous; (d) arrogant.
6. Read sentence 3 again and then write a paraphrase of it. ____________

____

____

7. Gossage sees a connection between (a) our attitudes about aging and good health; (b) our denial of death and diminished enjoyment of our everyday life; (c) retirement communities and the negative effects of aging; (d) older Americans' emphasis on eternal youthfulness, good health, and improved longevity.
8. In the last sentence, the phrase "passing pains" refers to (a) minor aches and pains; (b) serious misfortunes; (c) temporary disappointments and setbacks; (d) serious, life-threatening illnesses.

C. *Inferences*

On the basis of the evidence in *sentence 4,* mark these statements as follows: PA for inferences that are probably accurate and PI for inferences that are probably inaccurate.

1. ______ Old people are happier in retirement communities than they are living among a more diverse population.
2. ______ It is a disgrace that Americans put their old people out of the way in retirement communities.
3. ______ It is ludicrous for old people to pretend that they are young by trying to duplicate youthful activities in retirement communities.
4. ______ Retirement communities offer a wide variety of activities so that people can enjoy their remaining years.

Selection 2

Just before the passage reprinted below, the author, Daniel Duane, mentions that on this particular day a group of surfers spotted a great white shark less than a mile north of where he had been surfing alone that morning near Santa Cruz, California.

1So many disturbing traits, once you look into them—with a somewhat morbid curiosity, I'd begun prowling around the University Science Library,[1] an airy

[1]The library Duane refers to is at the University of California at Santa Cruz.

new building with gestures toward native construction materials, a self-conscious sensitivity to the surrounding redwoods, and the rational and antiseptic calm of too many quantitative minds padding silently down well-carpeted corridors. [2]A few tidbits: sharks are the world's only known *intrauterine cannibals;* as eggs hatch within a uterus, the unborn young fight and devour each other until one well-adapted predator emerges. [3](If the womb is a battleground, what then the sea?) [4]Also, without the gas-filled bladders that float other fish, sharks, if they stop swimming, sink. [5]This explains their tendency to lurk along the bottom like twenty-one-foot, 4,600-pound benthic land mines with hundred-year life spans. [6]Hard skin bristling with tiny teeth sheathes their flexible cartilage skeletons—no bone at all. [7]Conical snouts, black eyes without visible pupils, black-tipped pectoral fins. [8]Tearing out and constantly being replaced, their serrated fangs have as many as twenty-eight stacked spares (a bite meter embedded in a slab of meat once measured a dusky shark's bite at eighteen tons per square inch). [9]And all of the following have been found in shark bellies: a goat, a tomcat, three birds, a raincoat, overcoats, a car license plate, grass, tin cans, a cow's head, shoes, leggings, buttons, belts, hens, roosters, a nearly whole reindeer, even a headless human in a full suit of armor. [10]Swimming with their mouths open, great whites are indiscriminate recyclers of the organic—my sensitive disposition, loving family and affection for life, my decent pickup, room full of books, preoccupation with chocolate in the afternoons, and tendency to take things too personally: all immaterial to my status as protein.

[11]Leftovers from premammalian times, survivors of the dinosaur extinction, sharks evolved completely and always in the sea, never in fresh water. [12]First appearing 350 million years ago, they've descended from sixty-foot, fifty-ton prehistoric monsters, truly overdetermined predators—in one photo a group of scientists stands comfortably inside a pair of fossilized jaws. [13]Great whites are capable of between forty and seventy knots—calculated from photographic blur—and one writer describes a diver in the Mediterranean being hit so hard he exploded. [14]Another mentions a white shark leaping clear out of the water to pull a seal off a rock, and writes that "in most attacks, witnesses see neither seal nor shark, only a sudden explosion blasting spray fifteen feet high, then a slick of blood on the surface." [15]One never sees the white before it strikes, no speeding fin: it surges up in ambush, jaw distended, and tears out fifty-pound chunks of flesh. [16]Death coming truly like a stroke of lightning; in that vast, three-dimensional world of the sea, the surfer's world is quite two-dimensional, all surface and shore, with neither depth nor open sea. [17]Aiding the shark's stealth are jelly-filled subcutaneous canals on its head and sides that are lined with neuromasts called ampullae of Lorenzini, a kind of prey radar detecting faint electrical fields. [18](As a surfer waits for a wave, his very life force pulses like a homing beacon.) [19]And their powerful eyes—with optic nerves thick as ropes—see detail quite poorly, are adapted only to separating prey from background. [20]Among the world's most efficient predators, great whites have a kill

rate better than ninety percent, while the hawks just inland strike all day without luck.

Daniel Duane, *Caught Inside: A Surfer's Year on the California Coast*

A. *Vocabulary*

For each italicized word from the selection, choose the best definition according to the context in which it appears.

1. *morbid* [sentence 1]: (a) healthy; (b) gruesome; (c) unsatisfied; (d) diseased.
2. *lurk* [5]: (a) drift aimlessly; (b) spend time; (c) lie in wait; (d) swim swiftly.
3. *serrated* [8]: (a) notched, like the edge of a saw; (b) smooth, worn down from use; (c) sharp, like the blade of a knife; (d) superfluous, unnecessary.
4. *indiscriminate* [10]: (a) all-purpose; (b) highly selective, picky; (c) highly efficient; (d) not selective.
5. *immaterial* [10]: (a) unimportant; (b) incomprehensible; (c) unconcerned with; (d) unaccustomed to.
6. *distended* [15]: (a) ripped in two; (b) expanded by stretching; (c) open as far as it can go; (d) firmly in place.
7. *stealth* [17]: (a) predatory behavior; (b) prodigious appetite; (c) sensing mechanism; (d) covert movement.
8. *homing* [18]: (a) guiding to a target; (b) returning home; (c) alternating back and forth; (d) shining brightly.

B. *Content and Structure*

Complete the following questions.

1. What *two* modes of discourse are evident in this passage? (a) narration; (b) description; (c) exposition; (d) persuasion.
2. This passage is unusual because you have to infer that the topic is "sharks," since the word doesn't occur until sentence 2. The controlling idea is also in an unusual place. Look at the beginning of the paragraph, find a phrase that represents the controlling idea, and write it in the space.

   ____
3. Consider again the phrase you wrote for the question above. Which of the following methods of development in the remainder of the

paragraph is most evident as support for that phrase? (a) process; (b) comparison; (c) contrast; (d) example; (e) illustration; (f) explanation.

4. Look again at sentence 5, in which Duane imaginatively compares the shark to "a benthic land mine." (*Benthic* is an adjective referring to *benthos,* or organisms that live on ocean or lake bottoms.) What does Duane intend to suggest in this comparison?

   ____

5. From the information given in sentences 9 and 10, we can conclude that sharks (a) can and will eat anything, whether it is food or not; (b) prefer humans to any other food; (c) are basically carnivorous; (d) are able to digest inorganic objects.
6. Consider again the list of contents (sentence 9) found in shark's stomachs. What fact, mentioned later in the passage, explains why the list includes so many inedible items?

   ____

7. In sentence 13, Duane writes, "Great whites are capable of between forty and seventy knots—calculated from photographic blur." What do the words "photographic blur" imply about a shark's swimming speed?

   ____

8. What method of paragraph development is evident in sentences 16 and 20? (a) example; (b) illustration; (c) process; (d) comparison; (e) contrast; (f) explanation.
9. Irony is the discrepancy between what one might expect and what actually occurs. With this definition in mind, what is the irony suggested in sentence 19?

   ____

10. Judging from what Duane writes about the shark, what conclusion can you draw about its predatory behavior? (a) It is a remarkably slow and inefficient killer; (b) it is a remarkably fast and efficient killer; (c) its behavior is unpredictable and therefore erratic; (d) its behavior depends on the conditions of the sea and the available food supply.

Selection 3

This passage concerns His Holiness Shoko Asahara, guru and leader of Aum Supreme Truth, a Japanese religious cult. Asahara masterminded a nerve-gas attack in a crowded Tokyo subway in 1995, in which 12 people were killed and around 5,500 others were injured sufficiently to require hospitalization. Several victims remain in a coma. Charles Manson, mentioned in sentence 3, and his followers murdered actress Sharon Tate (wife of film director Roman Polanski) and other people in Los Angeles in 1969. Jim Jones, mentioned in sentence 7, was the leader of the People's Temple. He and several hundred of his followers committed mass suicide in 1978 in Guyana. David Koresh, mentioned in the same sentence, was leader of the Branch Davidians, a sect whose Waco, Texas, headquarters were burned in 1993—after a 51-day standoff during an FBI raid.

> [1]Many Japanese continue to wonder what mysterious force enabled a man as seemingly unremarkable as Asahara to get as far as he did in building his monstrous empire. [2]On March 20th, the first anniversary of the subway gassing, the mass-circulation newspaper *Mainichi* demanded, "Why were young men and women—many of them [our] intellectual élites—attracted to Aum, and why did they allow themselves to be brainwashed by a bizarre doomsday doctrine that induced them to commit all sorts of atrocities?" [3]Several commentators have named Charles Manson as one of Asahara's murderous predecessors. [4]There are, indeed, parallels. [5]Manson passed most of his youth in children's homes and prisons, and grew to despise his own country; to many young people disillusioned with the middle-class America of the Vietnam era, he seemed to have reached, many years before they did, their own insights. [6]"My thoughts light fires in your cities," Manson spat at his fellow-Americans—a line that could come from an Asahara sermon.
>
> [7]But Asahara differs from Manson, and from other cult leaders like Jim Jones and David Koresh, in his ability to enlist some of the better minds of the younger generation. [8]In this respect, he shares some similarities with our century's most brutal visionary—another unimpressive man, poorly educated, who preached a ragbag of secondhand ideas and harbored a paranoid suspicion of spies and traitors. [9]Hitler once said about his rise to absolute power, "I am totally convinced that this struggle does not differ one hair's breadth from the battle which I once fought out within myself." [10]He was referring not to the battle against the Allies but to one against the Germany and Austria of smug middle-class respectability, which had rejected his paintings and his warped vision, and had never promoted him above lance corporal. [11]Fortunately, Asahara possessed none of Hitler's ability to mobilize a mass audience. [12]But his fiery certainty of hatred, wrapped in the unlikely robes of Buddha and Jesus, made powerful sense to a confused younger generation, many of them frustrated by the laborious old Japan of geriatric professors who block promotion in the universities; by business cartels that allow little room for new competitors; and by old-fashioned fathers who see no further than the archaic Confucian code of work, deference, and waiting your turn. [13]Of course, most clever young Japanese do not see destruction as the logical outlet for frustration, but some—those who could open the laboratories of modern science to the guru—did. [14]Without these willing, dazzled helpers, the unschooled herbalist's techno-terrorism would have been impossible.

Murray Sayle, "Nerve Gas and the Four Noble Truths,"
The New Yorker

A. *Vocabulary*

For each italicized word from the selection, choose the best definition according to the context in which it appears.

1. *doomsday* [sentence 2]: Referring to (a) political terrorism; (b) Judgment Day; (c) a religious controversy; (d) a terrorist plot.
2. *atrocities* [2]: (a) petty crimes; (b) burglaries; (c) unsolvable crimes; (d) cruel, violent acts.
3. *predecessors* [3]: Those who (a) are condemned to death; (b) imitate others' behavior; (c) come before; (d) deserve to be harshly punished.
4. *disillusioned* [5]: (a) deprived of idealism; (b) deprived of legal rights; (c) deprived of material goods; (d) preoccupied with material possessions.
5. *visionary* [8]: One who (a) is given to highly speculative, impractical schemes; (b) has the ability to predict the future; (c) suffers from delusions and nightmares; (d) seeks to rid society of corruption.
6. *smug* [10]: (a) ordinary; (b) prejudiced; (c) admirable; (d) self-satisfied.
7. *warped* [10]: (a) disturbing; (b) unpopular; (c) twisted; (d) ludicrous.
8. *deference* [12]: (a) courteous yielding to others' wishes; (b) striving for success; (c) cut-throat competition; (d) acceptance of one's station in life.

B. *Content and Structure*

Complete the following questions.

1. Write a main-idea sentence for this passage in your own words.

   ____

   ____

2. The mode of discourse in the passage is (a) narration; (b) description; (c) exposition; (d) persuasion.
3. Which *three* methods of development are evident? (a) example; (b) comparison; (c) contrast; (d) facts and statistics; (e) explanation; (f) process.
4. Sayle's purpose is, specifically, (a) to trace significant events in Asahara's life; (b) to offer some possible answers to the question posed by the newspaper *Mainichi;* (c) to explain Asahara's beliefs; (d) to show why Asahara admired Charles Manson, Jim Jones, and David Koresh.
5. According to the author, how does Asahara differ from other cult leaders?

   ____

6. Unlike Asahara, Adolf Hitler was (a) better able to appeal to a mass audience; (b) better educated; (c) more paranoid and suspicious of traitors and spies; (d) justified in his hostility against middle-class respectability.

C. *Inferences*

Complete the following questions.

1. At the end of the passage the author implies that Asahara (a) was remarkably clever and sophisticated in his understanding of explosives; (b) had studied explosives; (c) sought revenge against the upper class for its power and wealth; (d) could not have pulled off the explosion without his followers' technical expertise and their connections.
2. As it is characterized in this passage, Japanese society is (a) traditional and inflexible; (b) rapidly changing; (c) materialistic and preoccupied with making money; (d) hostile to outsiders.

PRACTICE ESSAY

Book of Dreams: The Sears Roebuck Catalog

Rose Del Castillo Guilbault

In 1993 Sears Roebuck & Company announced that it would stop publishing its mail-order catalog, a venerable institution begun in 1886. For generations Americans had shopped at home with the catalog; it was especially important to farm families who made infrequent trips to town. (In the Depression, hard-pressed farm families "recycled" their old Sears and Montgomery Ward catalogs and used them as toilet paper in their outhouses.) But as Rose Guilbault points out in this article from the San Francisco Chronicle, *the Sears catalog represented something abstract and metaphorical to her immigrant family—the possibility of becoming a full-fledged part of the American dream.*

Guilbault was born in Mexico and later immigrated with her family to the US, where they settled in the Salinas Valley, an agricultural area in central California. She formerly wrote a column for the Sunday San Francisco Chronicle *called "Hispanic, USA" and is now director of public affairs and editorials for the ABC affiliate in San Francisco, KGO-TV.*

1 The news that Sears is closing 113 stores and folding its 97-year-old catalog sent me scurrying through the basement in search of one of my

favorite possessions, a 1941 Sears Roebuck & Company catalog. I was relieved to find it, still inside a metal filing cabinet, underneath a jumble of old Chronicles and a 1939 *Liberty* magazine.

2 I've always had an affinity for the 1940s. I love the Big Band music, the movies and the fashions. As a child I sat mesmerized, listening to my mother's stories about dances under the stars where local groups played and my young mother and her sisters flirted the night away.

3 But that's not the only reason I've held onto this ragged catalog through college, marriage, children and numerous moves. It symbolizes the America my parents and I believed in when we arrived in this country from Mexico. An America where everything you could possibly want was in an emporium inside a book. A book that came to your home from which you could leisurely, conveniently choose items that would be delivered to your doorstep. The concept was amazing to us. This wasn't about accumulating goods but about obtaining a piece of the American pie.

4 Many of today's immigrants are easily caught in this country's web of materialism, easy credit and easy debt. But in the early '60s, the values in rural areas were different. These "wish books" were a metaphor for America's bounty and what could be had with hard work.

5 Every new catalog was savored. We all had our own dream sections. Papa, eyes sparkling, would ease himself into his chair after dinner and briskly examine the tools, hunting rifles and cameras. Then he'd pass the catalog to Mama, who—for what seemed to me to be hours—studied the pretty dresses, household appliances, dishes and plants.

6 By the time the catalog made its way into my hands, my palms itched with anxiety. At Easter time, I would lose myself in pages of frilly, pastel dresses with matching hats and purses. In the Christmas season, which brought my favorite edition of the year, I would sit for hours, staring glassy-eyed at the pages of toys, dolls and games.

7 But nothing frivolous was ever ordered. We lived on a farm in the Salinas Valley, miles and miles from a big city and miles from the nearest small town. To get there, you'd turn off the main paved road onto a bumpy dirt trail that led to two farmhouses—one big one where the boss and his family lived, and a small, four-room cottage where we lived. The inside was sparsely furnished, mostly with hand-me-down furniture from the boss, except for the spindly TV and a cheap, forest-green nylon sofa set my father bought my mother as a wedding gift.

8 Extravagances were unaffordable. Only the most practical and necessary items would be given consideration—my mother's first washing machine, a school coat for me, and thick, dark denim overalls to keep Papa warm in the frostiest of dawns.

9 The Sears catalog had other uses. I'd cut out the models and use them as paper dolls. My mother would match English words with pictures, *"Y estas ollas? Seran* "pots" *en ingles?"* And in my most desperate

hours of boredom, when only sports programs dominated afternoon television, rain fell outdoors, and absolutely nothing interested me indoors, I'd pick up the thick catalog, sit in the bedroom with the faded cabbage-rose print linoleum and spin fantasies about living the good life I imagined the Americans in the catalogs lived.

10 In the front of my 1941 Sears catalog are two stories about typical Sears customers. One profiles the Browns of Washington state, who arrived there as homesteaders, lived in a tent with their children, until their farm produced enough for them to build a two-room shack, and eventually build a comfortable white clapboard farmhouse on their land. Photos show Mr. and Mrs. Brown with their new cream separator, daughter Evelyn with her new Elgin bicycle, and the whole family listening to their silver-tone radio-phonograph—all from Sears, of course.

11 The second article describes the Yeamens of Glendale, in Los Angeles County. Mr. Yeamen works at Lockheed Aviation, a mile and a half commute from their "modern, five-room bungalow . . . with a barbecue grill in the back yard and a view of the mountains from every window." Photographs show the various family members with their Sears products: Dad relaxing on a glider swing in the back yard, Mom putting avocado sandwiches in lunch boxes and the kids romping in their stylish clothes.

12 The Browns and Yeamens, the catalog summarizes, are what all of us want to be—good, solid, dependable Americans.

13 As corny and blatantly commercial as these stories are, I like reading them. It reminds me of the America of my youth, or perhaps of my imagination. Even though my family of Mexican immigrants probably didn't have a whole lot in common with the Browns and the Yeamens, we all shopped from that Sears Catalog—a book that made us believe everything was reachable, and ours to have.

14 My family prospered too. Not in great leaps and bounds like the Browns of Washington state, but little by little. Our progress was marked by the occasional splurge from the Sears catalog.

15 When I got to the point where I had to own my own clarinet or drop out of the school band—there was a limit to how long we could borrow from the music department—my family had to make a choice. I was not a great musician; we all knew that. But the band was a wholesome activity that integrated me into school life, into America. One evening after dinner, my parents called me into the living room. I searched their faces for a clue, but they remained mysteriously impassive until my father brought out a wrinkled brown package from behind his back.

16 My heart began pounding when I saw the Sears return address. Out came a compact gray and white case, and inside it, lying on an elegant bed of royal blue rayon velvet, were the pieces of a brand-new ebony clarinet. Never in my stolen afternoons with the Sears catalog had I imagined possessing something so fine!

17 Somehow I can't envision today's kids reminiscing about a Lands' End or Victoria's Secret catalog. Times have changed, and so have demographics. People in rural America no longer need a catalog. They now have Kmarts or Wal-Marts in their own mini-malls.

18 Newspaper articles reporting on the Sears closures have described the catalog as "the best record of American material culture." But to many of us, this catalog wasn't about materialism at all. It was about making dreams come true.

A. *Comprehension*

Choose the answer that best completes each statement. Do not refer to the selection while doing this exercise.

1. The main idea of the article is that, for Guilbault, the Sears Roebuck catalog represented (a) a vision of America that she and her family could never obtain; (b) the possibility of obtaining a piece of the American pie; (c) a way of life that typified the simpler, less stressful era of the 1940s; (d) a convenient way to shop at home to buy both the necessities and expensive luxuries.
2. For the author and her family, the most important American virtue was (a) a competitive spirit; (b) generosity; (c) hard work; (d) the desire for an education.
3. Guilbault's mother looked at the catalog not only to enjoy the pictures of clothing and household items, but also to (a) think of gifts for the family; (b) practice her English; (c) get ideas for making homemade clothing; (d) dream of the good life in America.
4. The catalog's description of the model families—the Browns and the Yeamens—suggested to her that (a) her family was just like them; (b) America was not really the land of opportunity; (c) it was important to buy one's belongings from Sears; (d) everything in America was reachable for her family.
5. Guilbault remembers one especially memorable acquisition, a clarinet. Aside from marking her family's economic prosperity, this purchase was also significant because (a) she could become a great musician; (b) she would improve her status in the class; (c) she would be integrated into American life; (d) she could play music for her family.

B. *Structure*

Complete the following questions.

1. Which *two* modes of discourse are evident in the article? (a) narration; (b) description; (c) exposition; (d) persuasion.

2. This article has a clear beginning, middle, and end. What paragraphs comprise the introduction? ¶ ______ to ¶ ______. What paragraphs comprise the body? ¶ ______ to ¶ ______. And what paragraphs comprise the conclusion? ¶ ______ to ¶ ______.
3. Which of the following adjectives best represents the author's point of view? (a) nostalgic; (b) objective; (c) envious; (d) philosophical; (e) self-pitying.
4. What method of development is used in paragraph 4? (a) example; (b) steps in a process; (c) contrast; (d) definition.
5. What primary method of development is used in paragraphs 5–9? (a) example; (b) comparison; (c) contrast; (d) definition.
6. What is the relationship between paragraph 14 and paragraphs 15 and 16? (a) All represent steps in a process; (b) paragraph 14 includes a term to be defined, and the other two define it; (c) paragraphs 15 and 16 offer a contrast to paragraph 14; (d) paragraph 14 makes a general statement, and paragraphs 15 and 16 serve as a supporting illustration.

C. *Vocabulary*

For each italicized word from the selection, choose the best definition according to the context in which it appears.

1. an *affinity* for the 1940s [paragraph 2]: (a) natural attraction; (b) obsession; (c) slight interest in; (d) reaction.
2. I sat *mesmerized* [2]: (a) silent; (b) amazed; (c) enthralled; (d) withdrawn.
3. an *emporium* inside a book [3]: (a) playground; (b) educational center; (c) imaginary toyland; (d) large retail store.
4. a metaphor for America's *bounty* [4]: (a) high reputation; (b) amalgamation of goods and services; (c) generosity, liberality in giving; (d) treasure chest.
5. every new catalog was *savored* [5]: (a) fought over; (b) relished, enjoyed; (c) perused from cover to cover; (d) worn ragged from use.
6. nothing *frivolous* was ever ordered [7]: (a) insignificant, trivial; (b) attractive, beautiful; (c) expensive; (d) of good quality.
7. the inside was *sparsely* furnished [7]: (a) lavishly, expensively; (b) skimpily, meagerly; (c) poorly, cheaply; (d) cozily, comfortably.
8. as corny and *blatantly* commercial [13]: (a) offensively; (b) typically; (c) ridiculously; (d) obviously.
9. they remained mysteriously *impassive* [15]: (a) silent, withdrawn; (b) showing no emotion; (c) excited, jubilant; (d) embarrassed.

10. times have changed, and so have *demographics* [17]: the study of (a) social values; (b) populations and their characteristics; (c) ethnic groups; (d) social classes.

D. *Questions for Analysis and Discussion*

1. In paragraph 4, Guilbault implicitly criticizes today's culture for its emphasis on materialism, yet it is clear that the Sears catalog, too, promoted materialism. Guilbault suggests a difference, however. What is it?
2. In paragraph 17, Guilbault writes, "Somehow I can't envision today's kids reminiscing about a Lands' End or Victoria's Secret catalog." What does she mean? Do you agree with her?

4

Four More Methods of Paragraph Development

In this chapter we will be concerned with the four remaining methods of paragraph development: (1) cause and effect; (2) analysis and classification; (3) definition; and (4) analogy. These methods are somewhat more complicated than those you studied in Chapter 3.

CAUSE AND EFFECT

The **cause-and-effect method** of development is perhaps easier to identify if you think of the words *reasons* and *results*. A writer may provide *reasons* (*causes*) to explain events, problems, or issues, and the *consequences* (*effects*). Like comparison and contrast, which can be used singly or in combination, with the cause-and-effect method a writer may discuss only causes or only effects, or both, and they can be presented in any order.

The cause-effect pattern always involves the question *why,* whether stated or implied. If you read a paragraph that begins "There are many reasons that college students are borrowing more money now to pay for college than in previous years," it is obvious that the writer will examine the *causes* of increased borrowing. But even if this sentence began with the word "college," you could still predict that the writer would examine the reasons. (Incidentally, anticipating what method of development is likely to follow the main idea of a paragraph is an excellent way to improve your comprehension.)

In the same way, if a paragraph opens with this sentence—"Increased government loan programs for college students are creating an enormous financial burden for graduates"— you can predict that the writer will examine the economic *effects* of borrowing, which is the *cause,* even though words like "effect," "consequence," or "result" are not present.

Cause and effect also refers to a logical relationship between ideas. For example, consider this statement by Peter Steinhart from his book *The Company of Wolves,* in which he implies a cause-effect pattern.

> Cheetahs in Africa suffered a major population decline as human settlement expanded in the nineteenth and twentieth centuries.

Which part of the sentence suggests the cause and which part suggests the effect?

Let us examine a paragraph with an easily-identifiable cause-and-effect relationship. You may remember the exercise in Chapter 3 that alluded to the cult leader, Jim Jones. This passage is from an article published in November 1993 on the 15th anniversary of the Jonestown massacre in Guyana. In it, Lawrence Wright seeks to explain the *reasons* so many urban blacks followed Jones to Jonestown, a remote enclave in the Guyana jungle. In the second paragraph Wright discusses one effect of the temple members' new life after they arrived—their isolation both from their relatives and from reality.

> [1]About seventy percent of those who pulled up stakes and followed Jones were black. Among the many riddles posed by Jonestown, one of the most mystifying was why so many urban blacks would follow a white messiah into the jungle. For some of the elderly members, the dream of living in a black country was ancient and dear: they had embraced Marcus Garvey's Back to Africa movement in the twenties. Close to half the congregation had already made one major migration in their lives, having been born in the South. But, more than anything else, it was the legend of Jim Jones and the Peoples Temple that swayed them. The foundation of his ministry was a promise of racial equality. His followers had grown up in a racist society and suffered economic injustice, and, whether they came from a tenant farm in Mississippi or a cotton mill in Georgia, they had not found redemption in California. Jones made them believe that they could create it themselves—that they could make their own Paradise.
>
> [2]They arrived at a place so remote and undeveloped as to be practically unreachable. Many of their frantic relatives did not even know what continent they were on. Those who tried to get in touch with loved ones who had vanished were discouraged from doing so, but even if they succeeded in being patched through to the radio transmitter in Jonestown they were

> likely to be greeted with a declaration rather than a conversation. The voices that came out of the jungle were shrill and full of recrimination. Leave us alone, the thin, ghostly voices were saying, although even over the wash of static one could sometimes hear Jones, somewhere nearby, telling them what to say.
>
> Lawrence Wright, "Orphans of Jonestown," *The New Yorker*

In this next example, Sissela Bok examines the subject of lying (the *cause*) and its *effects* on those who have been lied to. Notice that the cause-effect relationship here is implied:

> Those who learn that they have been lied to in an important matter—say, the identity of their parents, the affection of their spouse, or the integrity of their government—are resentful, disappointed, and suspicious. They feel wronged; they are wary of new overtures. And they look back on their past beliefs and actions in the new light of the discovered lies. They see that they were manipulated, that the deceit made them unable to make choices for themselves according to the most adequate information available, unable to act as they would have wanted to act had they known all along.
>
> Sissela Bok, *Lying: Moral Choices in Public and Private Life*

Read this short paragraph and then identify the cause-effect relationship in your own words.

> As intelligence becomes more important, youth becomes more protracted. Nature decrees dependency and helplessness as a way of keeping an individual out of trouble until it has sufficient knowledge and experience. To equip an infant with adult bulk and power is to make a destructive monster, a creature that poses danger to its kind and lacks the experience needed to live long enough to pass on its genes. Large carnivores require long schooling. Bear cubs may stay with their mothers two years. Wolves may stay with their parents all their lives.
>
> Peter Steinhart, *The Company of Wolves*

Cause ____

Effect ____

Finally, you should note that the cause-and-effect method often forms a sort of chain, as you see in this paragraph on the disappearance of the Asian elephant population by Sallie Tisdale. The declining population is the *effect.* Read the paragraph and then list the chain of causes and effects pertaining to this decline.

> There are between twenty-five thousand and forty thousand Asian elephants left in the world. Their gradual elimination in the wild is the result of a number of changes, most of them recent and a few subtle. The invention of the chain saw, for instance, made forest-clearing much easier and quicker work. But basically there is just not enough room in Southeast Asia for both elephants and people. The elephant's jungle habitat is being replaced by cropland, and many of the crops are delectable to the now homeless elephant. The elephant raids the millet and sugarcane, and is killed for his efforts, and kills in turn; in India, nearly a hundred and fifty people are killed by elephants every year. Wild elephants are found from India to Indonesia; most inhabit shrinking parks and preserves, in shrinking populations, separated from each other by human settlements as uncrossable as an ocean. Bulls, being more aggressive, are killed far more often than cows. Not only does this deplete the gene pool but the cows' opportunities to breed grow fewer, and as the birth rate falls their mean age increases. Because elephants will feed on the youngest, tenderest trees available, finding them the most appetizing, herds quickly denude small parks beyond the point of natural recovery. Several countries, notably Thailand and India, are attempting to conserve these insular environments and to confront the problems of the diminished gene pool and male-to-female ratio, but quite a few people in elephant biology wonder whether the wild elephant is past saving. There are estimated to be a million elephants left in Africa; however, their numbers are also dropping. Certainly its future, one way or another, resides in zoos.
>
> Sallie Tisdale, "The Only Harmless Great Thing," *The New Yorker*

Effect: The gradual elimination of the Asian elephant population.

Locate and identify the three causes of the population decline.

Cause 1: ______________________________

Cause 2: ______________________________

Cause 3: ______________________________

Now locate and identify the two effects that lead from these causes.

Effect 1: ______________________________

Effect 2: ______________________________

CLASSIFICATION AND ANALYSIS

Classification and analysis are traditionally considered together. Although they are actually separate methods, their underlying purpose is the same. Both involve the author's taking apart a larger subject and examining its separate parts to see how each relates to the whole. With the **classification** method, a writer puts several things (or ideas) into classes or categories, following a consistent system. **Analysis** is different, involving a *single* entity, the parts of which are examined one at a time. Let us look at classification first.

In the real world, we classify all the time. For example, if you decide to reorganize your CD collection, you would first have to determine a *system* for grouping them, and of course the system would have to make sense. Depending on the extent and nature of your collection, you could organize them by type of music (all the hard rock CD's in one group, all the jazz in another, all the blues in a third, and so on). Or if your music collection was international, you could classify them by country. If your collection consisted solely of rock music, you could classify your CD's by artist or group, by subgenres of rock, or perhaps even by decade. The classification system must remain consistent to avoid confusion.

If you read a paragraph that begins, "At the tourist trap where I work during the summers, I have observed three different kinds of customers," or "There are five subspecies of fish called darters," you can expect the writer to use the classification method to follow.

But with analysis, a writer examines the parts of *one* thing. He or she might use analysis to evaluate a current movie by discussing, one at a time, its various features—the credibility and originality of the plot, the acting, the special effects, the cinematography, and so on. Analysis allows a writer to examine the parts in terms of how they relate to the whole—in this case, identifying a worthwhile movie to see.

You can keep these two methods straight if you keep in mind that analysis takes apart a *single* subject, while classification takes several items and groups them into categories. Let us now look at some examples of paragraphs using these methods.

Although the topic of this classification paragraph is a bit grisly, it illustrates the method clearly. In a chapter describing the horrors inflicted on residents of the Central African Republic by its former leader Bokassa, Alex Shoumatoff classifies cannibalism into four types. (In sentence 3 the writer alludes to the Uruguayan soccer team whose plane crashed in the Andes. Their experiences have been recorded in a fine book by Piers Paul Read, *Alive!,* which was also made into a 1993 film of the same name.) After you read it, identify the *system* Shoumatoff uses to classify types of cannibalism.

> There are many kinds of cannibalism. Revenge cannibalism—the gloating, triumphant ingestion of a slain enemy's heart, liver, or other vital parts—is common at the warring-chiefdom stage of social evolution. Emergency cannibalism was resorted to by the Uruguayan soccer team whose plane crashed in the Andes. Ritual endocannibalism is practiced by certain tribes like the Yanonamo of northern Amazonia, whose women drink the pulverized ashes of slain kin mixed with banana gruel before their men go off on a raiding party. In the Kindu region of Zaire there are to this day leopard men who wear leopard skins, smear their bodies with leopard grease (which protects them even from lions), chip their teeth to points, and attack and eat people. Among their victims were some Italian soldiers who were part of the U.N. peace-keeping force during the turbulence after independence in 1960. The rarest kind of cannibals are gustatory cannibals—people who are actually partial to the taste of human flesh.
>
> Alex Shoumatoff, "The Emperor Who Ate His People," *African Madness*

First, list the four types: ______________________________

____

____

____

Basis for the classification ______________________________

In the next passage, Timothy Ferris classifies nebulae, masses of interstellar dust or gas. As you read the paragraph, locate the three types and then determine the basis for his classification system.

> Bright *nebulae* (from the Latin for "fuzzy") are diffuse patches of glowing material found scattered here and there among the stars. Most can be seen only with a telescope. Although they resemble one another superficially, the bright nebulae actually comprise three very different classes of objects. Some, misnamed "planetary" because they are spherical in shape and bear a passing resemblance to planets, are shells of gas thrown off by old, unstable stars; a typical planetary nebula is about one light-year in diameter and has one-fifth the mass of the sun. Others, the reflection and emission nebulae, are clouds of gas and dust illuminated by nearby stars; in many cases, the stars doing the illuminating have themselves recently condensed from the surrounding cloud. These nebulae measure hundreds of light-years in diameter and can harbor the mass of a million or more suns. They represent the bright, congealed parts of the still more extensive dark nebulae

that wend their way throughout much of the disk of the Milky Way galaxy—though this was not recognized at first, since the dark nebulae are too inconspicuous to call attention to themselves. Finally there are the elliptical and spiral nebulae. These are galaxies in their own right, millions of light-years away. A major galaxy can measure over one hundred light-years in diameter and contain hundreds of billions of stars.

Timothy Ferris, *Coming of Age in the Milky Way*

List the three types of nebulae ______________________________,

______________________________, and ______________________________

Basis for the classification ______________________________

As stated before, analysis examines a *single* idea by looking at its separate parts. In this example, Diane Ackerman analyzes the physical structure of an alligator by examining each anatomical feature to show how each helps the whole animal to function efficiently.

Sitting on an alligator is an ideal way to learn about its anatomy. Some people think that "alligators wear a built-in ugly job," as one writer puts it. If so, they haven't looked at one very closely. Alligators have beautiful undulating skin, which feels dense, spongy, and solid, like the best eraser. And they're full of anatomical surprises. Their nostrils are surrounded by strong muscles. Leaning forward, I touched the nostrils with the tips of my fingers, and in response, they squeezed closed and then opened again. An alligator is efficient underwater, aerodynamic and sleek. Not only does it retract its eyes, it can close its nostrils, tuck in the two spongy musk glands under its neck, close its movable ear lids, and seal off its throat with a wide drape of flesh. The throat drape is especially important, so that it doesn't drown when it drags its prey underwater. Though it has a four-chambered heart, it can reroute the blood and stop circulation to the lungs while it's submerged. An alligator should have an excellent sense of smell, because it can close off the glottis and throat, isolate the nostrils, and direct a small sniff of air straight into the olfactory chamber, right next to the brain's olfactory lobe. That a creature so beautiful, wild, and mysterious could be turned into a handbag or pair of shoes gave me a slow chill.

Diane Ackerman, *The Moon by Whale Light*

List the alligator's parts as Ackerman presents them. ______________________________

____

DEFINITION

Unlike the other methods described, **definition** is often used in conjunction with other methods of development. As a method it is nearly self-explanatory, but writers' purposes in using the definition method may differ, as we shall see in this section. Definition is useful when a writer wants to clarify a term because it may be open to varying interpretations (or worse, to misinterpretation) or because he or she is using a word in a subjective or personal way. Definition is especially useful for abstract terms like *machismo, feminism, honor, racism,* or *tolerance.* Even when we think we know what a word means, not every one may share that definition. (One year I received a Christmas card that showed a little girl sitting on Santa Claus's lap. The little girl is saying to Santa: "Define 'good'").

First, let us look at the way definitions are constructed. In traditional rhetoric, a **formal definition** follows this classic model:

Term to be defined = Class + Distinguishing characteristics

For example, using the formal definition model, we can define the word *sofa* like this:

Term: sofa
Class: a piece of furniture
Distinguishing characteristics: with an upholstered seat and back, intended to seat two or more people

Here is another:

Term: schizophrenia
Class: a psychotic mental disorder
Distinguishing characteristics: marked by someone's withdrawal from reality, bizarre behavior, and sometimes delusional behavior

Let us apply this method to a more difficult, more complex word, *racism.*

Term: racism
Class: a belief or doctrine
Distinguishing characteristics: belief that one's abilities and character are determined by race and that one race is superior to another's

Do you accept this definition? Here is a different version:

Term: racism
Class: a belief or doctrine
Distinguishing characteristics: involving the mistreatment and oppression of a member of one race by another

As you can see, it is the distinguishing characteristics part of definitions that poses the problem. Definitions are important in argument, as you will see later in Part III (Critical Reading), because your acceptance of an argument may hinge on your acceptance of an underlying definition. For instance, in challenges to "English-only" rules in the workplace, some employees, forbidden by management to speak their native language on the job, have filed suit to make such rules illegal, often citing racism as a factor. Do either of the definitions here fit this situation? If not, can you write a definition of *racism* that would?

Let us now examine some paragraphs using definition as the method of development. Notice that nearly every example also uses a secondary method as well, and in fact, definition is commonly used in conjunction with one or more other expository methods, chiefly example, comparison-contrast, and analysis.

In this example, a physician, Larry Dossey, defines the word *healing* as he intends to use it in the remainder of the article.

> [1]Though healing is a universal phenomenon that has been recognized by every culture in history, the term has many meanings. By "healing" I mean the *distant,* positive influence of one individual (the healer) on another (the healee) in the absence of any obvious intervening physical influence. It goes by many names: nonlocal, mental, spiritual, psychic, and prayer-based healing. Healing has been linked to spectacular events, such as cancers vanishing without treatment, that cannot be explained by medical science.
>
> [2]These radical healings cause immense intellectual indigestion. "This is the sort of thing I wouldn't believe, even if it really happened," trumpeted one skeptical scientist in an oft-quoted remark.
>
> Larry Dossey, "Healing Happens," *Utne Reader*

What does the author mean by the word "healing"? ________________

____

A writer may use definition to *contrast* similar-sounding or easily confused words, as Jeffrey Masson and Susan McCarthy do in this next example.

Evidence of emotion in captive animals and pets is often discounted as irrelevant. Captive animals, the argument goes, are in unnatural situations, and what domesticated animals do is irrelevant to what animals are *really* like, as if they are not really animals. While genuinely domesticated animals *are* different from wild animals, *domestic* and *tame* do not mean the same thing. Domestic animals are animals that have been bred to live with humans—they have been changed genetically. Dogs, cats, and cows are domestic animals. Captive animals like elephants are not, since through the generations that people have trained elephants, they have almost invariably caught and tamed wild elephants, rather than *bred* elephants. Since the nature of elephants remains unchanged, observations on tame or captive elephants are in fact highly relevant to free-living elephants.

Jeffrey Masson and Susan McCarthy,
When Elephants Weep

Besides definition and contrast, what other method of development is evident here? ______________________________________

What, to you, does the term "sexual harassment" mean? In the 1980s and 1990s this term took on ever greater significance because of numerous highly-publicized lawsuits. Many were serious; others seemed to many observers frivolous (for example, according to *The Washington Post,* a female employee sued her boss—and won several thousand dollars!—because he had given her a scarf for Christmas). One problem with sexual harassment and proving it is that the term may mean quite different things to men and women. A lengthy article in *The Washington Post* in 1997 examined the problem and offered this definition for companies and employers struggling to make sense of the phrase.

[1]What is sexual harassment and how should well-managed companies counsel people who may be engaged in such destructive behavior? Should a company transfer an alleged harasser to another office after receiving a complaint? Should it warn the offender and hope for the best? Offer counseling? Fire the employee?

[2]Companies are learning of the potential pitfalls to each of these approaches, and potentially large liabilities for firms that mismanage the problem.

[3]Susan Webb, president of a Seattle-based consulting group that specializes in dealing with sexual harassment problems, says there are three separate categories of harassers.

[4]Some people are simply unaware of the impact of what they say and do, and when they find out they have been offensive, they are apologetic and

embarrassed. These people, Webb says, are "very trainable." With good instruction about the law and workplace etiquette, their problems can be quickly managed.

[5]A second category is what Webb called "insensitive" workers—people who really don't care if they bother or upset others. Webb says these employees need to be told firmly what the limits are; they need to understand that they will be disciplined or fired if they don't stop doing what is offending other workers. Counseling and training can help in these cases.

[6]Fred Berlin, founder of the Johns Hopkins University Sexual Disorder Clinic in Baltimore, says the first step is making harassers admit and confront what they have done, and how it affects someone else. They need to realize their careers and reputations are at stake and that they risk "public scandal" if a lawsuit should result.

[7]"The bottom line is once a [person] is identified, the company cannot allow itself to be in a position where this continues to happen," Berlin says.

[8]In Webb's third and final category are "hard-core" harassers who have serious psychological problems and cannot easily learn appropriate workplace behavior. "They are such a danger to the company, they're gone," Webb says. "They are scary people. They're nuts—similar to rapists."

Kirsten Downey Grimsley,
"Defining the Problem Is a Start,"
The Washington Post

What other method of development is evident in the discussion?

____

Finally, a writer may define a word according to its **etymology,** or origin (the way the word came into the English language). In this paragraph Charles Earle Funk explains the etymology of the common English verb *fascinate.*

fascinate

From earliest times, and even today among superstitious people, it has been believed that certain persons, if so inclined, have the power to injure or even kill other persons or animals or to destroy crops or commit other injury by no more than a malignant glance. Such a person is held to possess the "evil eye." In ancient Greece, the power of the evil eye was called *baskania,* in Rome *fascinatio.* Because no one knew who that he might meet had the power and the wish to do him injury, it was an almost universal custom, in olden times, to wear an amulet of some kind which was believed to protect the wearer. Even the cattle were sometimes so adorned. Children were thought to be especially susceptible to the power of the evil eye, and no Roman mother, in classical days, would permit a child of hers to leave the house without first suspending from its neck, under the robe, a certain amulet called *fascinum.* Actually, therefore, our word *fascinate,* when first brought into English use, meant to cast the evil eye upon one, to put one under the spell of witchcraft. We use the word rarely now in such a literal sense, but employ it rather to mean to hold one's attention irresistibly or to occupy one's thoughts exclusively by pleasing qualities.

Charles Earle Funk, *Thereby Hangs a Tale*

ANALOGY

The last of the eight methods of development, **analogy,** is perhaps the most difficult method for readers to perceive. An analogy is an *extended metaphor,* in which the writer discusses the literal subject in terms of something else. By imaginatively yoking two unlike things, the writer emphasizes shared characteristics and provides a fresher insight than would a literal discussion. A writer, for instance, might explain the functioning of a human heart in terms of the way a pump works—in other words, compare it to a more familiar object. The way the human eye works could imaginatively be compared to the way a camera works.

An analogy always begins with a metaphor, but rather than being expressed in (typically) a single phrase or sentence, an analogy is a *sustained* metaphor. This means that the comparison is usually extended through at least a few sentences, a paragraph, or—less commonly—even throughout an essay.

Consider this first paragraph developed by analogy. It represents the opening sentences of a news article on the terrible fires that destroyed 25 percent of Yellowstone National Park during the summer of 1988.

> Visiting this fire-scarred but still magnificent park is like watching one of those Hollywood melodramas in which the gorgeous heroine suffers some horrible accident and wakes up in the next scene with her face covered in white bandages. The audience can only wait in suspense to know whether she will still be beautiful when the gauze is removed.

T. R. Reid, "New Yellowstone to Rise from Ashes,"
The Washington Post

The park—the literal subject, mentioned only once—is imaginatively compared to a once-beautiful heroine who has suffered a terrible accident. The "audience," to extend the analogy further, refers literally to people who are interested in the park's future and the likelihood of its recovery. Notice that Reid mentions the burned parkland only once; then he introduces the analogy with the crucial word "like." In other words, the analogy allows the main idea—that visitors to Yellowstone wonder what the long-term effects of the fire will be—to be stated with more drama and suspense, because from movies and television we all have seen a bandaged heroine lying in a hospital bed, waiting anxiously as the doctor enters, scissors in hand. Good analogies like this one are remarkably effective and powerful: they are more than a mere attention-getting device, however, because they provide a new way of looking at things.

Let us examine another example. To set the analogy in context, Richard Harwood, writing in *The Washington Post,* is criticizing the state of journalism today. He begins by using a slim analogy of his own: "It is difficult to tell from the work of analysts whether journalism as we know it in the United States is in a period of terminal decline or is merely going through one of its cyclical periods of malaise and loss of verve." (Harwood imaginatively compares American journalism to a patient suffering either from a terminal disease at the very worst or perhaps just from loss of vitality.) Harwood then continues by quoting Michael Crichton, author of *Jurassic Park* and other best-selling novels and creator of the television program *ER,* as follows:

> The American media produce a product of very poor quality. Its information is not reliable; it has too much chrome and glitz; its doors rattle; it breaks down almost immediately and it's sold without warranty. It's flash but it's basically junk. So people have begun to stop buying it.
>
> (Quoted in Richard Harwood, "Extinct Stained Wretches," *The Washington Post)*

What is being compared to what in this analogy? What is Crichton saying about the American public? Explain the significance of this comparison in your own words.

This next example by African-American writer Eddy L. Harris is from a book he wrote about a trip to Africa where he visited Abidjan, the capital of Ivory Coast (now Côte d'Ivoire).

> [1]A hot wind blows slowly across the land and moisture hangs heavy in the air. The desert has come at last to an end, the sand giving way first to hard red laterite, then to rocky soil and scrub bushes, and finally now to the dark loamy soil of the rain forest.

> [2]Here where forest and sea come together teeters Abidjan, a modern city on the edge of a shelf of antiques, a city where cardboard shacks lie in the shadow of skyscrapers, glass and steel, 50 stories tall. In Abidjan the two worlds are poised side by side, like crippled legs of uneven lengths belonging to a lame man. When he walks there is pain and discomfort. He manages to hobble, but not without a great deal of effort.
>
> Eddy L. Harris, *Native Stranger*

What picture does Harris convey about the city of Abidjan? ____________

____

In this final example, we see a different use of analogy: to offer instruction. In his study of alien abductions, Keith Thompson argues that alternative realities and universes may exist and that, in fact, "we might not be alone." He warns that we should not laugh at or dismiss stories of abductions by aliens as preposterous. To support his theory, he cites the ancient Chinese aphorism, "The fish is the last one to know that it lives in water." He continues, using a narrative as his analogy:

> [1]The fish takes for granted that the medium it knows is the True Element—indeed, the *only* element. Why should it imagine otherwise? But then, one day, a particular fish swims into a remote part of the lake and sees a strange object above. The fish has no name for what it sees from below, but we who are above would call the object a "bobber." Amazed, the fish returns to its school and tells what it has seen. The story is impressive, but the other fish are not so interested. After all, there is always fresh kelp to find, not to mention larger, hungry fish to avoid. News of such strange objects can only be a dangerous distraction to the overall affairs of the school.
>
> [2]Over time, however, others see the bobber, and a robust set of legends grows. Then, on a particular day, a fish happens to swim too close to the object and gets "hooked." Suddenly this fish finds itself pulled *up* and *out,* into a vast and altogether amazing realm of *above* and *beyond.* Those who have snagged the fish and reeled it in, after analyzing the creature according to particular criteria, decide the fish is not a "keeper" and toss it back into the ocean. Bewildered, the fish makes it way back with an even more incredible tale to tell about another world—a very different kind of world—populated by the most marvelous of beings.
>
> [3]Depending on how this news is revealed and received, the fish is deified, eaten, or simply isolated from the rest of the school, where it is left to muse aloud, "Water! We live and swim in *water!* I have just now seen that which is *not* water: I have glimpsed 'dry land,' and 'open sky.' Does anyone hear me? Does anyone *care?*"
>
> Keith Thompson, *Angels and Aliens: UFOs and the Mythic Imagination*

Analogies can also be misused. (See the discussion *False Analogy* in the section on logical fallacies in Part III, Reading Critically.)

COMBINATION OF METHODS

As discussed at the end of Chapter 3, a writer may use a mix of expository methods of development. In this paragraph, Michael Krieger explains the daily lives of Kwaio women. The Kwaio are a mountain people who live on Malaita Island in the Solomon Islands of Oceania. Their lives are brutally hard; their villages are almost completely untouched by outside civilization. As you read the paragraph, locate the main idea and the controlling idea. Then identify the various expository methods of development.

> The existence of Kwaio women, never secure, was also one of continual drudgery. Even today, although a woman no longer has to fear for her life, she has little to smile about. She may walk only on certain trails and in specified areas of the village. She may not enter the men's house or even mingle with the men except under certain prescribed conditions. She must continually tend the gardens, which supply almost all the Kwaio's food, and daily she must carry on her back the heavy bamboo water containers, the yams, and all the firewood, often over miles of steep and narrow mountain trails. Because there is so little flat or terraced ground on which to plant a garden, and because the ravines down which the streams tumble are devastated by flash floods in the wet season, the village may be located an hour's strenuous hike away from the nearest stream or vegetable garden. Consequently, Kwaio women climb three or four hours a day, and their arms and legs are like bands of steel. Owing to their low status—just above the village pigs—and to generations of subservience, the women, for the most part, are like shy, overgrown children. Most have babies clinging to them. Besides rearing the children and all their other jobs, the women are also responsible for caring for the Kwaios' most prized possessions, their pigs. The pigs are either sold or sacrificed and eaten in male-only ceremonies, and so the women generally don't get to eat their charges. In spite of the sexual inequities to which the women are subjected, they seem to harbor no rancor or resentment.
>
> Michael Krieger, *Conversations with the Cannibals*

Main idea ____________________ Controlling idea ____________________

Expository methods of development (Hint: look for three.) ____________

____

EXERCISES

Selection 1

[1]Those of us who have to spend a great deal of time in crowded conditions become gradually better able to adjust, but no one can ever become completely immune to invasions of Personal Space. [2]This is because they remain forever associated with either powerful hostile or equally powerful loving feelings. [3]All through our childhood we will have been held to be loved and held to be hurt, and anyone who invades our Personal Space when we are adults is, in effect, threatening to extend his behaviour into one of these two highly charged areas of human interaction. [4]Even if his motives are clearly neither hostile nor sexual, we still find it hard to suppress our reactions to his close approach. [5]Unfortunately, different countries have different ideas about exactly how close is close. [6]It is easy enough to test your own "space reaction": when you are talking to someone in the street or in any open space, reach out with your arm and see where the nearest point on his body comes. [7]If you hail from western Europe, you will find that he is at roughly fingertip distance from you. [8]In other words, as you reach out, your fingertips will just about make contact with his shoulder. [9]If you come from eastern Europe you will find you are standing at "wrist distance." [10]If you come from the Mediterranean region you will find that you are much closer to your companion, a little more than "elbow distance."

[11]Trouble begins when a member of one of these cultures meets and talks to one from another. [12]Say a British diplomat meets an Italian or an Arab diplomat at an embassy function. [13]They start talking in a friendly way, but soon the fingertips man begins to feel uneasy. [14]Without knowing quite why, he starts to back away gently from his companion. [15]The companion edges forward again. [16]Each tries in this way to set up a Personal Space relationship that suits his own background. [17]But it is impossible to do. [18]Every time the Mediterranean diplomat advances to a distance that feels comfortable for him, the British diplomat feels threatened. [19]Every time the Briton moves back, the other feels rejected. [20]Attempts to adjust this situation often lead to a talking pair shifting slowly across a room, and many an embassy reception is dotted with western-European fingertip-distance men pinned against the walls by eager elbow-distance men. [21]Until such differences are fully understood, and allowances made, these minor differences in "body territories" will continue to act as an alienation factor which may interfere in a subtle way with diplomatic harmony and other forms of international transaction.

Desmond Morris, *Manwatching: A Field Guide to Human Behaviour*

A. *Vocabulary*

For each italicized word from the above selection, choose the best definition according to the context in which it appears.

1. *immune to* [sentence 1]: (a) indifferent to; (b) endangered by; (c) unconcerned about; (d) unaffected by.
2. *charged* [3]: (a) intensified; (b) challenged; (c) excitable; (d) loaded.
3. *suppress* [4]: (a) alter; (b) give into; (c) reduce; (d) hold back.
4. *alienation* [21]: Describing a state of (a) unawareness; (b) being disturbed; (c) isolation; (d) irritation.

B. *Content and Structure*

Complete the following questions.

1. The mode of discourse in this passage is (a) narration; (b) description; (c) exposition; (d) persuasion.
2. This passage represents a combination of various methods of development. Write the method represented in each group of sentences.

   sentences 1–4: ____________________

   sentences 2–4: ____________________

   sentences 6–10: ____________________

   sentences 11–20: ____________________
3. Look again at sentences 2 and 3. What is the relationship between them? (a) Both show steps in a process; (b) sentence 3 shows contrast from sentence 2; (c) sentence 2 introduces an important term and sentence 3 defines it; (d) sentence 2 represents a cause, and sentence 3 shows the effect; (e) sentence 2 presents a general idea, and sentence 3 explains it in more detail.
4. The main idea of the passage is that (a) all diplomats should be trained in other cultures' definitions of Personal Space; (b) the concept of Personal Space is not very well understood; (c) diplomats are especially sensitive to intrusions in their Personal Space; (d) our concept of Personal Space is so linked to powerful feelings that we find it difficult to be immune when it is invaded.
5. Look again at sentences 13–19. From Morris's description of this hypothetical conversation between diplomats, we can conclude that (a) the Briton and the Mediterranean feel equally offended ; (b) the Briton is more offended than the Mediterranean; (c) the Mediterranean is more offended than the Briton; (d) both diplomats are deliberately violating each other's Personal Space to establish dominance.
6. The tone—that is, the emotional feeling the author intends to convey—in sentence 20 is (a) sneering, ridiculing; (b) objective, impartial; (c) mildly humorous; (d) highly negative, critical.

Selection 2

[1]One cannot easily realize what a tremendous thing it is to know every trivial detail of twelve hundred miles of river and know it with absolute exactness. [2]If you will take the longest street in New York, and travel up and down it, conning* its features patiently until you know every house and window and door and lamp-post and big and little sign by heart, and know them so accurately that you can instantly name the one you are abreast of when you are set down at random in that street in the middle of an inky black night, you will then have a tolerable notion of the amount and the exactness of a pilot's knowledge who carries the Mississippi River in his head. [3]And then if you will go on until you know every street crossing, the character, size, and position of the crossing-stones, and the varying depth of mud in each of those numberless places, you will have some idea of what the pilot must know in order to keep a Mississippi steamer out of trouble. [4]Next, if you will take half of the signs in that long street, and *change their places* once a month, and still manage to know their new positions accurately on dark nights, and keep up with these repeated changes without making any mistakes, you will understand what is required of a pilot's peerless memory by the fickle Mississippi.

Mark Twain, *Life on the Mississippi*

A. *Vocabulary*

For each italicized word from the selection, choose the best definition according to the context in which it appears.

1. *trivial* [sentence 1]: (a) silly; (b) ordinary; (c) of little significance; (d) unobserved.
2. *abreast of* [2]: (a) in the vicinity of; (b) near; (c) alongside; (d) behind.
3. *tolerable* [2]: (a) fair, adequate; (b) able to be endured; (c) permissible; (d) exact, accurate.
4. *peerless* [4]: (a) reliable; (b) well-trained; (c) hazy; (d) unmatched.
5. *fickle* [4]: (a) hard to get along with; (b) changeable; (c) undependable; (d) complicated.

B. *Content and Structure*

1. The method of development in this paragraph is clearly analogy. Explain first what Twain is comparing to what.

   ______________________________ is compared

   to ______________________________

*Studying, examining carefully so as to memorize.

2. Now explain in your own words what, in literal terms, the analogy means—that is, what is required of a Mississippi river pilot.

____

____

____

3. Twain probably uses this particular analogy because (a) we can understand the difficulty of learning all of a street's characteristics; (b) the familiar can be explained better in terms of the unfamiliar; (c) a river and a street have nearly identical characteristics; (d) everybody should know the characteristics of a single street as well as Twain suggests.
4. It is apparent from sentence 2 that learning to be a Mississippi riverboat pilot (a) takes an enormous amount of patience; (b) can be quickly accomplished; (c) requires a person who can follow orders; (d) requires a person who can make quick life-and-death decisions.
5. Of the tasks described in sentences 2, 3, or 4, which—in literal terms for the riverboat captain—would probably be the most difficult to accomplish? _______________
   What clue does Twain provide to help you arrive at this answer?

____

6. We usually reserve the word *fickle* to describe human behavior. From what Twain suggests in sentence 4, what are some factors that would cause a river to be described as fickle? _______________

____

Selection 3

[1]Girls' sexual conduct, unlike that of boys, is governed less by hormones than by social controls. [2]But in a cultural climate of sexual freedom, girls have lost much of their authority in boy-girl relationships. [3]Until quite recently girls organized, managed, and regulated the social pursuits of their peer groups, with the strong support of adults. [4]In romantic relationships girls exercised their power by withholding sex, keeping boys in the role of craven sexual petitioners. [5]At the same time, they moved their boyfriends in the direction of commitment and monogamy. [6]"Going steady," the ultimate romantic achievement for teenage girls, offered a pseudomarriage that might include parceling out some of the sexual favors of marriage. [7]Of course, this system was seriously flawed. [8]In the intimacy of a steady relationship, girls could lose control, "give in," and go all the way. [9]Then they had to deal with the dire consequences of their sexual transgression—a guilty conscience, a ruined reputation, and sometimes an unwanted pregnancy.

[10]The sexual revolution overturned this system of social controls by giving women technological control over their fertility. [11]Its emblematic moment came when college health services began providing birth-control pills to eighteen- and nineteen-year-old women. [12]Liberated from many of the penalties of premarital sex and the burdens of a sexual double standard, women were able to behave like men in their sexual pursuits. [13] Yet although a single standard for men and women promised greater honesty and equity in relationships, it tilted away from women's goals of intimacy and commitment in the direction of what one sociologist has aptly called sexual "freedom with a male bias": no holds barred and no strings attached. [14](A nosy mother, I once asked my college-age daughter if there were any differences in the way young men and women conducted their sex lives on campus. [15]"Only that girls wait for a phone call the next day," she said.)

Barbara Dafoe Whitehead, "The Failure of Sex Education," *The Atlantic Monthly*

A. *Vocabulary*

For each italicized word from the selection, choose the best definition according to the context in which it appears.

1. *pursuits* [sentences 3 and 12]: (a) things strived for, interests engaged in; (b) activities, things done to keep busy; (c) actions forbidden by custom or law; (d) rules of behavior, matters of etiquette.
2. *craven* [4]: (a) boastful, bragging; (b) timid, cowardly; (c) overpowering, dominating; (d) obsessed, driven.
3. *petitioners* [4]: (a) those who humbly beg, supplicants; (b) predators of the weak; (c) those who seek social dominance; (d) those who deviate from accepted behavior.
4. *monogamy* [5]: Here, the practice of (a) having two husbands at a time; (b) having multiple sexual partners; (c) having one sexual partner at a time; (d) staying with the same partner for life.
5. *pseudo-* [6]: Prefix meaning (a) half; (b) similar to; (c) unnamed; (d) pretended.
6. *dire* [9]: Indicating (a) easily solved; (b) trouble, disaster; (c) life-threatening; (d) annoying.
7. *transgression* [9]: (a) punishment; (b) enjoyment; (c) relationship; (d) violation.
8. *emblematic* [11]: (a) symbolic; (b) ultimate; (c) most obvious; (d) first.
9. *equity* [13]: (a) emotional stake; (b) burden; (c) equality; (d) inequality.
10. *no holds barred* [13]: (a) no reasons for an explanation; (b) without limits or restraints; (c) establishing limits on behavior; (d) not looking into the future.

B. *Content and Structure*

Complete the following questions.

1. The mode of discourse that predominates in the passage is (a) narration; (b) description; (c) exposition; (d) persuasion.
2. Which methods of development are represented in the passage? (a) cause-effect; (b) contrast; (c) explanation; (d) analogy; (e) classification.
3. In your own words, write a main-idea sentence for the passage.

   ____

____

4. The author's purpose, specifically, is (a) to explain some positive effects of the availability of birth control pills and the sexual revolution; (b) to explain some negative effects of the availability of birth control pills and the sexual revolution; (c) to trace the history of the sexual revolution; (d) to criticize parents, teachers, and college health services for being too tolerant of premarital sexual relationships.
5. Look again at sentences 1 and 2 and 13. What logical relationship is implied *between* sentences 1 and 2 and also *within* sentences 1 and 13? (a) cause and effect; (b) steps in a process; (c) general term and an example; (d) comparison; (e) contrast.
6. Label sentences 2–6 according to whether they represent major support (MA) or minor support (MI).

   _____ sentence 2 _____ sentence 3 _____ sentence 4

   _____ sentence 5 _____ sentence 6
7. Look again at sentence 10. What logical relationship is implied in its parts? (a) cause and effect; (b) steps in a process; (c) general term and an example; (d) comparison; (e) contrast.
8. In terms of the main idea of the passage, in your own words, explain why the author includes sentences 7–9. ______________________

____

   ____

9. On balance, how does the writer characterize the impact of the sexual revolution? Specifically, how has it affected men and women? _______

____

____

10. Sentences 14 and 15, called parenthetical because they appear between parentheses, imply that (a) the daughter thought her mother

was indeed being nosy; (b) there is only a slight difference in the way women and men react after a first sexual encounter; (c) the sexual revolution is still ongoing; (d) a woman is traumatized if the man she has first slept with the night before doesn't call.

PRACTICE ESSAY

How to Talk about the World

Peter Farb

Until his untimely death in 1980 at the age of 49, Peter Farb was a naturalist, an anthropologist, and a writer who popularized the natural sciences. His specialty was Indian languages—in the United States as well as in Mexico, Central America, and Brazil. He is the author of Man's Rise to Civilization as Shown by the Indians of North America and Face of North America, *of* Consuming Passions: The Anthropology of Eating *with George Armelagos and of* Word Play, *a highly readable introduction to the field of linguistics, from which this excerpt comes.*

1 If human beings paid attention to all the sights, sounds, and smells that besiege them, their ability to codify and recall information would be swamped. Instead, they simplify the information by grouping it into broad verbal categories. For example, human eyes have the extraordinary power to discriminate some ten million colors, but the English language reduces these to no more than four thousand color words, of which only eleven basic terms are commonly used. That is why a driver stops at all traffic lights whose color he categorizes as *red,* even though the lights vary slightly from one to another in their hues of redness. Categorization allows people to respond to their environment in a way that has great survival value. If they hear a high-pitched sound, they do not enumerate the long list of possible causes of such sounds: a human cry of fear, a scream for help, a policeman's whistle, and so on. Instead they become alert because they have categorized high-pitched sounds as indicators of possible danger.

2 Words, therefore, are more than simply labels for specific objects; they are also parts of sets of related principles. to a very young child, the word *chair* may at first refer only to his highchair. Soon afterward, he learns that the four-legged object on which his parents sit at mealtimes is also called a *chair.* So is the thing with only three legs, referred to by his parents as a *broken chair,* and so is the upholstered piece of furniture in the living room. These objects form a category, *chair,* which is set apart from all other categories by a unique combination of features. A *chair*

must possess a seat, legs, and back; it may also, but not necessarily, have arms; it must accommodate only one person. An object that possesses these features with but a single exception—it accommodates three people—does not belong to the category *chair* but rather to the category *couch,* and that category in turn is described by a set of unique features.

3 Furthermore, Americans think of *chairs* and *couches* as being related to each other because they both belong to a category known in English as *household furniture.* But such a relationship between the category *chair* and the category *couch* is entirely arbitrary on the part of English and some other speech communities. Nothing in the external world decrees that a language must place these two categories together. In some African speech communities, for example, the category *chair* would most likely be thought of in relation to the category *spear,* since both are emblems of a ruler's authority.

4 The analysis of words by their categories for the purpose of determining what they mean to speakers of a particular language—that is, what the native speaker, and not some visiting linguist, feels are the distinguishing features or components of that word—is known as "componential analysis" or "formal semantic analysis." The aim, in brief, is to determine the components or features that native speakers use to distinguish similar terms from one another so that more exact meanings can be achieved.

5 Anyone who visits an exotic culture quickly learns that the people are linguistically deaf to categories he considers obvious, yet they are extraordinarily perceptive in talking about things he has no easy way to describe. An English-speaking anthropologist studying the Koyas of India, for example, soon discovers that their language does not distinguish between dew, fog, and snow. When questioned about these natural phenomena, the Koyas can find a way to describe them, but normally their language attaches no significance to making such distinctions and provides no highly codable words for the purpose. On the other hand, a Koya has the linguistic resources to speak easily about seven different kinds of bamboo—resources that the visiting anthropologist utterly lacks in his own language. More important than the significance, or the lack of it, that a language places on objects and ideas is the way that language categorizes the information it does find significant. A *pig,* for example, can be categorized in several ways: a mammal with cloven hoofs and bristly hairs and adapted for digging with its snout; a mold in which metal is cast; a British sixpence coin. The Koyas categorize the pig in none of these ways; they simply place it in the category of animals that are edible. Their neighbors, Muslims, think of it in a different way by placing it in the category of defiled animals.

6 Everyone, whether he realizes it or not, classifies the items he finds in his environment. Most speakers of English recognize a category that they call *livestock,* which is made up of other categories known as *cattle,*

horses, sheep, and *swine* of different ages and sexes. An English speaker who is knowledgeable about farm life categorizes a barnyardful of these animals in a way that establishes relationships based on distinguishing features. For example, he feels that a *cow* and a *mare,* even though they belong to different species, are somehow in a relationship to each other. And of course they are, because they both belong to the category of Female Animal under the general category of Livestock. The speaker of English unconsciously groups certain animals into various subcategories that exclude other animals:

Livestock

	CATTLE	HORSES	SHEEP	SWINE
Female	cow	mare	ewe	sow
Intact Male	bull	stallion	ram	boar
Castrated Male	steer	gelding	wether	barrow
Immature	heifer	colt/filly	lamb	shoat/gilt
Newborn	calf	foal	yeanling	piglet

A table such as this shows that speakers of English are intuitively aware of certain contrasts. They regard a bull and a steer as different—which they are, because one belongs to a category of Intact Males and the other to a category of Castrated Males. In addition to discriminations made on the basis of livestock's sex, speakers of English also contrast mature and immature animals. A *foal* is a newborn horse and a *stallion* is a mature male horse.

7 The conceptual labels by which English-speaking peoples talk about barnyard animals can now be understood. The animal is defined by the point at which two distinctive features intersect: sex (male, female, or castrated) and maturity (mature, immature, or newborn). A *stallion* belongs to a category of horse that is both intact male and mature; a *filly* belongs to a category of horse that is both female and immature. Nothing in external reality dictates that barnyard animals should be talked about in this way; it is strictly a convention of English and some other languages.

8 In contrast, imagine that an Amazonian Indian is brought to the United States so that linguists can intensively study his language. When the Indian returns to his native forests, his friends and relatives listen in disbelief as he tells about all the fantastic things he saw. He summarizes his impressions of America in terms of the familiar categories his language has accustomed him to. He relates that at first he was bewildered by the strange animals he saw on an American farm because each animal

not only looked different but also seemed to represent a unique concept to the natives of the North American tribe. But after considerable observation of the curious folkways of these peculiar people, at last he understood American barnyard animals. He figured out that some animals are good for work and that some are good for food. Using these two components—rather than the Americans' features of sex and maturity—his classification of livestock is considerably different. He categorized *stallion, mare,* and *gelding* as belonging to both the Inedible and Work (riding) categories. The *bull* also belonged to the Inedible category but it was used for a different kind of Work as a draught animal. He further placed a large number of animals—*cow, ewe, lamb, sow,* and so on—in the category of Edible but Useless for Work. Since his method of categorizing the barnyard failed to take into account the breeding process, which depends upon the categories of sex and maturity, he no doubt found it inexplicable that some animals—*ram, colt, boar,* and so on—were raised even though they could not be eaten or used for work.

9 To an American, the Amazonian Indian's classification of barnyard animals appears quite foolish, yet it is no more foolish than the American's system of classification by the features of sex and maturity. Speakers of each language have the right to recognize whatever features they care to. And they have a similar right to then organize these features according to the rules of their own speech communities. No one system is better than another in making sense out of the world in terms that can be talked about; the systems are simply different. A speaker of English who defines a *stallion* as a mature, male horse is no wiser than the Amazonian who claims it is inedible and used for riding. Both the speaker of English and the speaker of the Amazonian language have brought order out of the multitudes of things in the environment—and, in the process, both have shown something about how their languages and their minds work.

A. *Comprehension*

Choose the answer that best completes each statement. Do not refer to the selection while doing this exercise.

1. The main idea of the entire passage is that (a) the English system of classifying items in the environment is more logical than and therefore superior to systems used by other linguistic groups; (b) language is an arbitrary collection of words; (c) each culture has its own logical system for classifying items found in that particular environment; (d) the process of naming things shows the intricate working of the human mind.
2. The author stresses that human beings in any culture find it necessary to (a) learn a foreign language; (b) study linguistics; (c) categorize information into broad categories; (d) understand the origin of their vocabulary.

3. According to Farb, the English speaker places *chair* and *couch* together in the category of *household furniture,* whereas, because both words represent a ruler's authority, some speakers of African languages would classify *chair* with the word (a) *king;* (b) *spear;* (c) *throne;* (d) *cattle.*
4. Farb emphasizes throughout the excerpt that every culture's labeling of things in the environment (a) is simply different from every other culture's, and one is not necessarily better or worse than another; (b) is irrational and usually makes little sense; (c) is difficult to learn and explain to outsiders; (d) is based solely on tradition and custom.
5. The hypothetical Amazonian Indian would be puzzled by the American system of naming barnyard animals because, according to *his* system, animals are classified according to whether they are good for (a) breeding or eating; (b) work or food; (c) domestication or nondomestication; (d) recreation or work.

B. *Structure*

Complete the following questions.

1. The mode of discourse in the essay is (a) narration; (b) description; (c) exposition; (d) persuasion.
2. Consider again the first two sentences in paragraph 1. What is the relationship between them? (a) steps in a process; (b) term and its definition; (c) general statement and a specific example; (d) contrasting ideas.
3. Indicate *three* methods of development evident in paragraphs 2 and 3. (a) example; (b) definition; (c) analogy; (d) comparison; (e) classification; (f) contrast; (g) cause-and-effect.
4. Look again at paragraphs 6–9, which suggest a contrast. What two things is Farb contrasting? ______________________ and ______________________
5. In your own words explain the point Farb is trying to make at the end of paragraph 8. Specifically, an Amazonian Indian would not understand why Americans raise animals like rams, colts, and boars, which can neither be eaten or used for work. Why, then, do Americans raise them? ______________________
6. The author, as you remember, was an anthropologist and linguist. Explain how his tone—the way he expresses his ideas—reflects these academic fields.______________________

C. *Inferences*

On the basis of the evidence in the paragraph, mark these statements as follows: PA for inferences that are probably accurate and PI for inferences that are probably inaccurate.

1. ______ Our survival in the world around us depends extensively on our ability to categorize from a mass of sensory impressions.
2. ______ The ability to generalize and to categorize is important in the child's acquisition of language.
3. ______ *Spear* and *chair* are unrelated concepts to English speakers.
4. ______ Dew, fog, and snow are common natural phenomena in India where the Koyas live.
5. _____ A culture's way of classifying items in the environment is arbitrary and is often not readily apparent.

D. *Vocabulary*

For each italicized word from the selection, choose the best definition according to the context in which it appears.

1. to *discriminate* some ten million colors [paragraph 1]: (a) perceive; (b) take in through the senses; (c) tell the difference between; (d) name, codify.
2. a relationship is entirely *arbitrary* [3]: (a) relatively unimportant; (b) logical, precise; (c) not well understood; (d) not based on rational principles or rules.
3. nothing in the external world *decrees* [3]: (a) orders authoritatively; (b) determines precisely; (c) makes effective use of; (d) implies; suggests.
4. both are *emblems* of authority [3]: (a) examples; (b) symbols; (c) tangible objects; (d) mottoes.
5. anyone who visits an *exotic* culture [5]: (a) foreign, unfamiliar; (b) lush, tropical; (c) economically undeveloped; (d) popular with tourists.
6. the category of *defiled* animals [5]: (a) inedible; (b) unclean; (c) lined up in rows; (d) vicious.
7. speakers of English are *intuitively aware* [6]: (a) able to describe a thing's characteristics; (b) skilled at contrasting one thing with another; (c) having knowledge of something without having to use reason; (d) adept at making intelligent decisions.
8. two distinctive features *intersect* [7]: (a) split up, divide; (b) overlap, come together at a point; (c) become identical; (d) contradict, contrast.

9. as a *draught animal* [8] (note: "draught" is the British spelling of "draft"): (a) an animal that is difficult to domesticate; (b) an animal that serves primarily as a pet; (c) an animal suited for pulling heavy loads; (d) a cloven-hoofed animal.
10. he no doubt found it *inexplicable* [8]: (a) impossible to understand; (b) unclassifiable; (c) unrecognizable; (d) difficult to explain.

E. *Questions for Analysis and Discussion*

1. Look around your room and choose a common household object, for example, a lamp, a chest of drawers, a nightstand, or a book. Subject it to the same method to define it, according to its essential characteristics, as Farb does in paragraphs 2 and 3. Then find its distinguishing characteristics. For instance, how does a nightstand differ from a coffee table? How does a book differ from a magazine or a newspaper, two items belonging in the same category?
2. If possible, discuss Farb's ideas with one of your classmates who is from a different culture and speaks another language in addition to English. For example, compare the names of colors and shades; or categorize groups of objects, such as foods eaten at various times of the day or ways of naming relatives. (The English system of naming relatives is quite limited in comparison to those used in other cultures, particularly for relatives like aunts and uncles, sisters- and brothers-in-law, and cousins.)

PART

II

Discovering Meaning through Organization, Language, and Tone

5

Patterns of Paragraph Organization

The three chapters in Part II will introduce you to more sophisticated reading skills. Now that you are probably comfortable with the fundamentals of paragraph structure—placement of main idea, making inferences, modes of discourse, and methods of development, you can now refine your skills by paying more careful attention to the relationship between words, between sentences, and between paragraphs.

In this chapter you will be introduced to some techniques that writers use to ensure unity and coherence, you will learn basic patterns of organization, and by studying transitions, you will learn the various kinds of logical connections between ideas. The chapter concludes with a brief overview of punctuation.

UNITY AND COHERENCE IN PARAGRAPHS

As you learned in Chapter 1, a paragraph is a series of sentences that develops a single idea. Whether a writer uses a single method of development or a mix of them, he or she is careful to help you follow the main idea by ensuring that the paragraph has *unity,* or singleness of purpose. Every sentence in the paragraph—whether short or long—should relate to the main idea, more specifically to the controlling idea. In good writing no irrelevant or extraneous sentences should lead you astray. (In the same way, as you will see later in Part IV, every paragraph in an essay relates to and develops the main idea or thesis statement.)

A good writer's attention to unity means that if you concentrate you should not have too much difficulty following the direction of the ideas, even if the paragraph is long. Let us look at one rather long paragraph to see how its writer maintains unity.

This excerpt by historian Page Smith concerns the Bhagwan Shree Rajneesh, who during the 1970s moved his commune (called a puram) to rural eastern Oregon where he attracted a large number of followers and lived a lavish life. Stories began to circulate about the Bhagwan's physical cruelty to his devotees as well as allegations of free and open sex, as Smith describes here. (The Bhagwan was eventually indicted for tax evasion and was deported to India, his native country, where he later died.) As you read this passage, first find the main idea, paying particular attention to the adjective that serves as the controlling idea. This adjective is later repeated. Notice, too, that every example in support of the main idea *directly* bears out this controlling idea.

> Of all modern cults, that of the Bhagwan Shree Rajneesh in Oregon may well be the most bizarre. After presiding over a puram or Buddhist religious commune in Poona, India, the Bhagwan transferred his operation to a ranch in Oregon. There, as a brochure informed the curious, the Bhagwan (God) and his disciples would "live together in a non-possessive way, neither possessing things nor possessing persons; people living together, creating together, celebrating together and still allowing each one his own space; people creating a certain climate of meditativeness, of love, of living in that climate." Hard to argue with any of that. It was, indeed, the classic utopian dream; it was the aim of the earliest Christian communities and the hope of succeeding generations. Uncounted numbers of men and women have gathered together to live by similar principles throughout history. What was truly bizarre about the Bhagwan's commune was the strain that it might be thought to have imposed on the credulity of the highly—one is tempted to say, extravagantly—educated men and women who flocked to it. What the skeptic saw was a dissipated, self-indulgent Indian guru who encouraged every wild excess from physical violence of the most brutal and degrading kind to ingeniously aberrant sex; who was arbitrary and tyrannical almost beyond belief; who collected jeweled watches and Rolls-Royces on a hitherto unimagined scale. All this was acquiesced in, supported, and praised by his infatuated followers, the great majority of them people with college degrees and many with advanced degrees. Ph.D.'s were a dime a dozen in the puram, and the largest professional group represented were psychologists. Many of the Rajneeshees had given all their worldly goods to the Bhagwan. When the journalist Frances Fitzgerald visited the puram, she was astonished at the professional backgrounds of the Rajneeshees. The commune's city planner, Swami Deva Wadud, had been a professional city planner in San Mateo, California, and boasted an M.A. from the Harvard Graduate School of Design. His assistant was an Australian with a Ph.D. in linguistic philosophy. Another disciple had a degree from Harvard in "visual and

environmental studies." The "president" of the commune had been a systems analyst for IBM and Univac and studied computer sciences at the University of London. The list seemed endless. The chief publicist had a Ph.D. from Yale.[1]

Page Smith, *Killing the Spirit: Higher Education in America*

Notice that in constructing the paragraph, Smith begins with the main idea, followed by a brief explanation of Bhagwan's similarity to earlier cults in American history. Then he repeats the key phrase, "truly bizarre," which in turn is supported by appropriate examples. Even though the paragraph appears dense and forbidding, Smith's careful adherence to paragraph unity makes it relatively easy to read.

Besides unity, well-constructed paragraphs also have *coherence* (literally, the quality of "sticking together"). You may recall from Chapter 1 that good writing was described as a network of interlocking thoughts. Ideally, a writer makes sure that each sentence leads smoothly, logically, even gracefully, to the next, in other words, coherently. At first glance, studying the ways writers achieve coherence may seem more appropriate for a composition course than for a reading course. However, studying these methods will also help you better understand what you read, and equally important, will help you see the logical *connections* between ideas. (And, of course, it may also help your writing.) Sometimes an accurate understanding of a passage may depend on a seemingly unimportant little word like *but* or *for* or *as*.

In this passage about Antarctica, Ann Jones maintains paragraph unity and coherence by repeating key words and by using pronouns, printed with italics for easy identification. (You may recall from your study of grammar that a pronoun is a part of speech that refers to a noun—called its *referent* or *antecedent*.) For each pronoun in the passage, circle its referent or antecedent. Identifying these repetitions and pronouns will keep you focused, alert, and on track as you read.

1Don't expect a postcard from Antarctica. *No* post office. *No* stamps. And *nothing* to write home about. *No* grass. *No* trees. *No* polar bears. *No* land animals at all. *No* indigenous people. *No* art. *No* culture. Unless you count a rock concert held last year at the U.S. research station at McMurdo Sound. They called it *Icestock*.

2That's what Antarctica is, mainly: *ice*. Thirty million billion tons of *it*. So much *ice*, *so* thick, *so* heavy that *it* deforms the planet, denting *it* a little on the south side. The continental landmass is as big as the United States and Mexico put together, and except for the very edges and a few valleys swept

[1]Frances FitzGerald's book, *City on a Hill*, contains an excellent and informative chapter, "Rahneeshpuram," on the appeal of this strange cult. The author has incorrectly spelled FitzGerald's name.

> dry by winds, *it's* covered entirely by *ice,* much of *it* two miles thick. Mountain ranges twice as high as the Alps lie buried in *ice.* Great glaciers descend to the sea and ride upon *it* as *ice* tongues or *ice* shelves. The largest of these, the Ross Ice Shelf, is the size of France and, in some places, as tall as a ten-story building where *it* meets the sea. In winter, when the surrounding ocean freezes, the amount of *ice* is doubled. This is a continent of superlatives: the coldest, driest, highest, windiest, iciest, and most lifeless place on earth. The temperature descends to near 128 degrees Fahrenheit below zero. Theoretically, that's cold enough to shatter human teeth. So *no* polar bears. *No* postcards.
>
> Ann Jones, "Where Penguins Dare," *Lear's*

Now that you have read the paragraph, what is another way—besides repetitions and pronouns—that Jones maintains thematic unity?

____

TRANSITIONS

Writers also establish coherence between ideas by using signposts or markers, called *transitions,* to indicate either a logical relationship or a shift in direction. Transitions can be either single words or phrases, or occasionally a whole paragraph. A transitional word or phrase may appear at the beginning of sentences, but this is not a hard and fast rule. To show you how crucial transitions are, read this paragraph by George Orwell printed without the transitions:

> After getting into the water the toad concentrates on building up his strength by eating small insects. He has swollen to his normal size again. He goes through a phase of intense sexiness. All he knows, at least if he is a male toad, is that he wants to get his arms round something. If you offer him a stick, or even your finger, he will cling to it with surprising strength and take a long time to discover that it is not a female toad. One comes upon shapeless masses of ten or twenty toads rolling over and over in the water, one clinging to another without distinction of sex. They sort themselves out into couples, with the male duly sitting on the female's back. You can distinguish males from females. The male is smaller, darker, and sits on top, with his arms tightly clasped round the female's neck. The spawn is laid in long strings which wind themselves in and out of the reeds and soon become invisible. The water is alive with masses of tiny tadpoles which rapidly grow larger, sprout hind legs, then forelegs, then shed their tails. The new generation of toads, smaller than one's thumbnail but perfect in every particular, crawl out of the water to begin the game anew.

Obviously something is wrong here. Reading this paragraph is like reading a novel with every 10th page missing, or like trying to put a bicycle together when the manufacturer has left out some of the necessary screws. It just does not hold together, and the sentences sound monotonous and choppy. Here is the actual version, this time printed with the transitions restored and italicized, making it much less tedious to read.

> *For a few days* after getting into the water the toad concentrates on building up his strength by eating small insects. *Presently* he has swollen to his normal size again, *and then* he goes through a phase of intense sexiness. All he knows, at least if he is a male toad, is that he wants to get his arms round something, *and* if you offer him a stick, or even your finger, he will cling to it with surprising strength and take a long time to discover that it is not a female toad. *Frequently* one comes upon shapeless masses of ten or twenty toads rolling over and over in the water, one clinging to another without distinction of sex. *By degrees, however,* they sort themselves out into couples, with the male duly sitting on the female's back. You can *now* distinguish males from females, *because* the male is smaller, darker and sits on top, with his arms tightly clasped round the female's neck. *After a day or two* the spawn is laid in long strings which wind themselves in and out of the reeds and soon become invisible. A *few more weeks, and* the water is alive with masses of tiny tadpoles which rapidly grow larger, sprout hind legs, then forelegs, then shed their tails; *and finally, about the middle of the summer,* the new generation of toads, smaller than one's thumbnail but perfect in every particular, crawl out of the water to begin the game anew.
>
> George Orwell, "Some Thoughts on the Common Toad,"
> *The Orwell Reader*

Here is a list of transitions classified by function, meaning the logical relationship they bring to the sentence in which they occur.

1. **Transitions signaling an additional statement** (usually of equal importance): *and, in addition (to), additionally, as well as, besides, furthermore, moreover.*

   Example: The house was badly neglected: the windows were broken, *and* the paint was blistered. *Moreover,* what had once been a well-tended lawn was now only an overgrown weed patch.

2. **Transitions signaling a contrast:** *but, yet, however, nevertheless, nonetheless, while, whereas, on the other hand, in contrast (to), contrary to.*

Example: Newfoundlands and St. Bernards are known for their placid and friendly natures; *in contrast,* terriers are often high-strung and highly excitable.

3. **Transitions signaling an example or illustration:** *for example, as an example, to illustrate, as an illustration, for instance, namely, specifically, a case in point, that is to say.*

   Example: Many residents of urban neighborhoods believe that an influx of national franchise stores can ruin local businesses, destroy a neighborhood's unique quality, resulting in a homogenized, bland environment. *For instance,* neighbors on Larchmont Boulevard, a two-block street in Los Angeles lined with trees and small independent businesses, unsuccessfully fought intrusion by Payless Drugs, Noahs Bagels, and Starbucks in an attempt to preserve its local character.

4. **Transitions signaling steps in a process or chronological order:** *first, second, third, next, the next step, further, then, before, after that, finally, last, in July, last week, in a few days, in 1998, and the like.*

   Example: To use the spelling-checker on your computer, *first* pull down under the "Edit" menu to "Check Document Spelling." The computer will *then* scan through the document to identify any misspelled or questionable words. *After* each word is flagged, select the correct spellings. *Finally,* be sure to save the changes in your file.

5. **Transitions signaling a conclusion:** *therefore, thus, then, to conclude, in conclusion, in summary, to summarize, consequently, hence.*

   Example: Charley spent two hours a day working in the reading laboratory, and he looked up every unfamiliar word he encountered. *As a result,* there was a dramatic improvement in his reading comprehension by the end of the semester.

6. **Transitions signaling emphasis:** *indeed, in fact, certainly, without a doubt, undoubtedly, admittedly, unquestionably, truly.*

   Example: The level of violence directed at abortion clinics and the physicians who perform abortions has seriously escalated in recent years. *In fact,* since 1993 two workers, one in Florida and the other in Massachusetts, have been killed as they entered their clinics.

7. **Transitions signaling a concession or an admission of truth:** *although, even though, in spite of, despite, after all.*

   Although The American Heritage Dictionary is bulky and weighs six pounds, I prefer to carry it to class rather than a lightweight but abridged paperback version. (Note that in this sentence, the first clause *concedes* a truth. Another way to think of a concession is to substitute "regardless of the fact that.")

8. **Transitions signaling spatial order:** *above, below, to the right, to the left, nearby, from afar, beyond, further on, up the road, on top, below, underneath, and so on.*

   Example: "Where the mountains meet the sea" is the official motto of Camden, Maine, a New England village known for its splendid harbor. No wonder. *Behind the harbor, not far from* where the schooners, sailboats, and cabin cruisers are anchored, Ragged Mountain rises precipitously. *Near the peak of the mountain* one can find Maiden Cliffs, where, according to legend, an Indian maiden leaped to her death because of an unhappy love affair.

As stated early, whole sentences can also serve as a transition. In this example, notice that the first three sentences move from the subject of power takeovers in chimpanzee society, which clearly has just been discussed, to the subject of male behavior during these power plays. de Waal signals the shift to the subject of this particular paragraph by using another transition, *however,* in the fourth sentence. Again, being alert to these obvious techniques to keep the discussion coherent is an excellent way to improve your reading comprehension and to improve your reasoning ability.

> There is more to chimpanzee society than power takeovers. The picture I have drawn in this book so far is completely one-sided, in the sense that it only deals with the hard, opportunistic aspect of colony life. It is the impressive charging displays and noisy conflicts between the males which demand immediate attention. However, while the social hierarchy is stable, it is possible to look at a whole host of other, no less fascinating elements of chimpanzee life, such as the formation of social ties, the different ways in which females bring up their children, reassuring and reconciliatory behaviour, sexual intercourse, and adolescence. Each element represents another angle from which the life of the group as a whole can be studied. From some of these viewpoints the three principal males appear to be little more than extras. And it is difficult to say whether any one angle is more correct or more typical or more important than another.
>
> Franz de Waal, *Chimpanzee Politics: Power and Sex among Apes*

To give you practice in locating and interpreting transitions, read the following paragraph about long-term effects of medical advances. Notice that the first sentence itself provides a transition from the preceding paragraph. What can you infer was the particular subject under discussion *before* this paragraph? As you read it, underline the transitions and determine how each functions.

> There is another possibility, however: that advances in medicine will lead people to live longer but without commensurate improvements in health. In other words, science may succeed in pushing the average life expectancy from seventy-five years to ninety-five, but the diseases that used to leave us sick and disabled at eighty-two or eighty-three may still hit at eighty-two or eighty-three—the result being that we would live in a nursing home for the last years of our lives instead of the last two years. Epidemiologists call this possibility the "expansion of morbidity," and it has commanded more and more attention in recent years. Today, many kinds of medical improvements that we have devised are, after all, no longer aimed at saving people from dying at twenty-five or thirty of tuberculosis or smallpox, and so enabling them to enjoy another forty or fifty years of healthy life. Those diseases have been cured. Most attempts to improve longevity today focus on the diseases that primarily afflict the old—cancer, heart disease, stroke, arthritis—which means it is now much more likely that saving people from one disease may only result in their getting sicker and sicker with another.
>
> Malcolm Gladwell, "The New Age of Man," *The New Yorker*

PATTERNS OF ORGANIZATION

Now we can turn our attention to patterns of organization within paragraphs. This term refers to the various ways that ideas in a paragraph can be arranged. As you have seen, although the paragraph is remarkably flexible, we can nevertheless isolate five typical patterns: (1) chronological; (2) spatial; (3) deductive; (4) a variation of deductive; and (5) inductive The first and second patterns are found most often in narrative and descriptive writing; the others tend to occur more in expository or persuasive writing.

Chronological Order

Chronological (or time) order, the easiest pattern to recognize, refers to the order in which events happen. It is used to tell a story, to relate an incident, to recount a historical event, or to describe the steps in a process. In this first example, the anonymous writer describes how Danish zoologists discovered a heretofore unknown animal that lives on the mouths of Norwegian lobsters. (This discovery captured the world's imagination, and the media widely publicized the "lobster lips" organism, *S. pandora*.)

> Biologists divvy up all animals into 40 or so phyla, depending on the classification scheme. Humans, fish, and other vertebrates, for example, are in the phylum Chordata. Late last year, Peter Funch and Reinhardt Kristensen, zoologists at the University of Copenhagen, announced that they'd found an animal strange enough to merit its own phylum, which they have named Cycliophora. Barely visible to the naked eye, *Symbion pandora*—the species name—seems to live exclusively on the mouthparts of a Norwegian lobster, which it clings to with an adhesive disk. Using funnel-like round mouths (*Cycliophora* is Greek for "Carrying a small wheel"), the tiny symbionts eat crumbs from the lobster's meals and reproduce asexually until the lobster molts, which obliterates their home. Then each *S. pandora* gives birth to either a dwarf male or a female. The male . . . lands on another asexual *S. pandora* and waits for it to produce a female. After being fertilized by the dwarf, the female bears a motile larva and immediately expires; the male, which has no digestive system, dies a little later. The larva either finds a new host or lands on the same lobster's new lips, starting a new round of feeding and asexual breeding. "It would be hard to get an answer from a zoologist if you asked what group *S. pandora* belongs to," says Funch. "It's quite impossible to place it in one of the existing ones."
>
> "Life on Lobster Lips," *Discover*

The next passage nicely illustrates two of the most common ways chronological order can be used. In this passage by Murray Sayle, published on the occasion of the 50th anniversary of the Americans' use of the atom bomb on Hiroshima and Nagasaki, the first paragraph uses chronological order to narrate an event (what was going on in Hiroshima on that day and what occurred during the actual bombing). The second paragraph uses chronological order to show the steps resulting from the bomb's detonation. As you read, locate and underline the steps or stages. Also notice the ways Sayle maintains chronological order.

> **1**Monday, August 6, 1945, began like any other wartime day in Japan. By 8 A.M. most Hiroshima office workers were at their desks, children were at school, soldiers were doing physical exercises, high-school students and civilian work gangs were busy pulling down wooden houses to clear more firebreaks. During the night, there had been two air-raid alerts—and then all-clears. At 7:09 A.M., there was another alert, as a B-29 on a last weather check approached the city, and, at 7:31 A.M., another all-clear as it turned away. Minutes after eight, watchers in the city saw two B-29s approaching from the northeast: these were an observation plane and the Enola Gay.

(Colonel Paul Tibbets, the pilot, had only the day before named the bomber after his mother.) The Enola Gay, in the lead, held its course straight and level for ten miles; at eight-fifteen, it let fall its single bomb. Immediately, the other B-29 banked hard to the left, the Enola Gay to the right; both quit the scene. Released at thirty one thousand six hundred feet, or nearly six miles, the bomb fell for forty-three seconds and was triggered (by a barometric switch) by heavily symbolic chance nineteen hundred feet directly above a small hospital that was two hundred and sixty yards from the aiming point, the T-shaped Aoio Bridge.

2Atomic bombs achieve their effects by means different from those of conventional high explosives. The Hiroshima bomb's stated equivalent of eleven thousand five hundred to thirteen thousand five hundred tons of TNT is thus somewhat misleading. When the man-made nuclear chain reaction took place over Hiroshima, the bomb itself was instantly vaporized, at a temperature of several million degrees centigrade, creating a fireball and radiating immense amounts of heat. Heated air then expanded in a shock wave. The blast effect is rapidly attenuated by distance, however, so that in Hiroshima the overpressure at ground level was less than that of a near miss by a conventional one-ton bomb. This explains why the A-Bomb Dome, almost directly under the point of detonation, still stands, and why most of the reinforced-concrete buildings near the hypocenter, having been designed to resist earthquakes, survived the bombing, only to be gutted by the subsequent fire.

Murray Sayle, "Letter from Hiroshima: Did the Bomb End the War?" *The New Yorker*

Spatial Order

The term *spatial* comes from the word *space*. Spatial order refers to the arrangement of things in an environment. Most often used in descriptive writing, spatial order helps a writer organize descriptive details so they are coherent and so we can visualize the scene. Without spatial order, the details would produce a jumble of unrelated impressions.

Some typical ways writers arrange details spatially are from left to right or right to left, near to far or far to near, top to bottom or the reverse. Again, the transitions showing movement from one part of a scene to another allow us to visualize the whole. The next passage by Sallie Tisdale describes a cabin her family owned in southern Oregon in the Klamath National Forest. Here, Tisdale uses prepositional phrases to move our eye from one part of the cabin to another. As you read, underline these phrases so that you become aware of their function.

The cabin was a small, boxy two-story building with a deck, which we called the porch, perched on stilts outside the front door—a room-size platform with a rail on three sides and a dusty porch swing in constant shade. On the first floor was a long, narrow kitchen, which was lined—floor, walls, and ceiling—with a wood so old that it was black from years of lamp-oil and wood smoke. Across from it was a square open stairway, which led to a single room twice as large as the kitchen and extending up the stretch of a hill. To the right at the top of the stairs was the bathroom; the floor of the shower was always gritty with sand, and the shower head yielded no more than a drizzle of cold water. Over the kitchen, facing the river, was a sleeping porch—a narrow screened room with several iron beds, each one piled with musty, lumpy mattresses two or three deep. I slept on them in perfect peace. Oilcloth curtains hung in the kitchen windows but were never closed, even in the blackest night. By the front door was a wooden counter with a chipped white sink, and on the counter there always stood a silvery pail with a ladle. When we arrived, I would grab the pail and run out the back door and down three steps to a spring that trickled from beneath the house. The ground there was boggy, and the plants were wet with dew condensing in the shadows, and I held in my fist the knowledge that we were here for a long time, an infinite time. I would hold the pail under the trickle and wait happily while it filled, inhaling the exuberant scent of the woods, my bare feet cold in the spreading edge of the clear water.

Sallie Tisdale, "The Pacific Northwest," *The New Yorker*

In the last example, Kenneth Boulding uses spatial order in an unusual way: to locate himself first in his narrow environment and then, more philosophically, in the whole galaxy. By repeating the key preposition *beyond,* we easily follow his mind's journey. (A knowledge of basic geography also helps.)

As I sit at my desk, I know where I am. I see before me a window; beyond that some trees; beyond that the red roofs of the campus of Stanford University; beyond them the trees and the roof tops which mark the town of Palo Alto; beyond them the bare golden hills of the Hamilton Range. I know, however, more than I see. Behind me, although I am not looking in that direction, I know there is a window, and beyond that the little campus of the Center for the Advanced Study in the Behavioral Sciences; beyond that the Coast Range; beyond that the Pacific Ocean. Looking ahead of me again, I know that beyond the mountains that close my present horizon, there is a broad valley; beyond that a still higher range of mountains; beyond that other mountains, range upon range, until we come to the Rockies; beyond that the Great Plains and the Mississippi; beyond that the Alleghenies; beyond that the eastern seaboard; beyond that the Atlantic Ocean, beyond that is Europe; beyond that is Asia. I know, furthermore, that if I go far enough I will come back to where I am now. In other words, I have a picture of the earth as round. I visualize it as a globe. I am a little hazy on some of the details. I am not quite sure, for instance, whether Tanganyika is north or south of Nyasaland. I probably could not draw a very good map of Indonesia, but I have a fair idea where everything is located on the face of this globe. Looking further, I visualize the globe as a small speck circling around a bright star which is the sun, in the company of many other similar specks, the planets. Looking still further, I see our star the sun as a member of millions upon millions of others in the Galaxy. Looking still further, I visualize the Galaxy as one of millions upon millions of others in the universe.

Kenneth Boulding, *The Image*

Deductive Order

Deductive order is the most common pattern in the English paragraph. You saw deductive order in the section on placement of main ideas in Chapter 1. Deductive order is sometimes called *general-to-specific order,* because deductively organized paragraphs begin with a general statement (the main idea), which is then supported by a series of specific statements. The deductive pattern, then, is determined by the location of the main idea. You can better visualize deductive order if you imagine an inverted triangle with the base at the top:

Main Idea

Supporting Statements

General ▼ Specific

Typically, expository paragraphs use deductive order, as Lewis Thomas does in this first example. Notice that the main idea in sentence 1 is supported with a single effective illustration.

> Animals seem to have an instinct for performing death alone, hidden. Even the largest, most conspicuous ones find ways to conceal themselves in time. If an elephant missteps and dies in an open place, the herd will not leave him there; the others will pick him up and carry the body from place to place, finally putting it down in some inexplicably suitable location. When elephants encounter the skeleton of an elephant out in the open, they methodically take up each of the bones and distribute them, in a ponderous ceremony, over neighboring acres.

Lewis Thomas, *Lives of a Cell*

In the next example, following the main idea, stated in the first sentence, Alexander Stille uses specific examples and contrast as methods of development. These examples and points of contrast are organized deductively. Identify and underline the two major contradictions the author focuses on.

> Atlanta is a city of contradictions. It is home to the largest concentration of black universities in the United States, has a rich and educated black middle class, and has been run by black mayors for the last twenty-four years; it is referred to as Black Mecca. But the Confederate battle flag still flies over the Georgia statehouse. Between 1915 and 1945, the city was the official headquarters of the Ku Klux Klan, and yet in the fifties and sixties it became the cradle of the civil-rights movement. Atlanta seems obsessed with its history: the heroes of the old Confederacy—Jefferson Davis, Robert E. Lee, and Stonewall Jackson—stand watch over the city from their perch on the side of Stone Mountain, Atlanta's version of Mt. Rushmore. When people in Atlanta speak about "the war," they are talking not about Vietnam or any of the wars of the last hundred years but about "the war of Northern aggression." Yet Atlanta is also an upstart city: it is much younger than Richmond, Charleston, or Savannah, and has a brash, openly commercial nature. While Savannah basks in its former glory, having chosen historic preservation over economic growth, Atlanta has become the boomtown of the fastest-growing region of the United States, going from one million to three and a half million people in about thirty years. Unfortunately, in its drive to become a major capital, it has lost much of its regional character, and looks remarkably like every other new American city: it could be Phoenix, Houston, Denver, or Seattle.
>
> Alexander Stille, "Who Burned Atlanta"? *The New Yorker*

A Variation of Deductive Order

Some writers vary deductive order, especially in long and complex passages. In this kind of order, the main idea at the beginning is followed by supporting sentences; but the writer then *restates* the main idea at the end of the pattern, thereby underscoring its importance. You can visualize this pattern if you imagine, not a triangle, but a tri-level square:

Main Idea	General ▼
Supporting Statements	Specific
Restated Main Idea	▲ General

Bill McKibben here uses variation of deductive order to explain what he calls "the end of nature." After you read it, locate the main idea and the sentence that restates it.

> [1]An idea, a relationship, can go extinct, just like an animal or a plant. The idea in this case is "nature," the separate and wild province, the world apart from man to which he adapted, under whose rules he was born and died. In the past, we spoiled and polluted parts of that nature, inflicted environmental "damage." But that was like stabbing a man with toothpicks: though it hurt, annoyed, degraded, it did not touch vital organs, block the path of the lymph or blood. We never thought that we had wrecked nature. Deep down, we never really thought we could: it was too big and too old; its forces—the wind, the rain, the sun—were too strong, too elemental.
>
> [2]But, quite by accident, it turned out that the carbon dioxide and other gases we were producing in our pursuit of a better life—in pursuit of warm houses and eternal economic growth and of agriculture so productive it would free most of us from farming—*could* alter the power of the sun, could increase its heat. And that increase *could* change the patterns of moisture and dryness, breed storms in new places, breed deserts. Those things may or may not have yet begun to happen, but it is too late to altogether prevent them from happening. We have produced the carbon dioxide—we are ending nature.
>
> Bill McKibben, *The End of Nature*

Inductive Order

Inductive order, the opposite of deductive order, is sometimes called *specific-to-general* order. This pattern actually derives from a kind of thinking called induction, which you learn more about in Part III, Critical Reading. For now, it is enough to know that inductive order involves a series of specific statements leading to a generalization (the main idea) that the reader can validly infer from those statements.

A diagram of an inductively arranged paragraph looks like this:

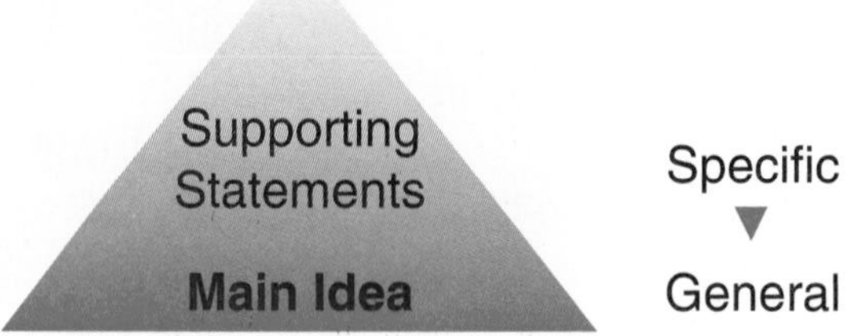

In this first paragraph, the author, a linguist, provides background information in sentences 1 and 2. (These sentences are not the main idea.) Following that, she uses two expository modes—example and contrast—which in turn lead up to the main idea expressed in the last sentence.

> Members of the same culture share a common body idiom—that is, they tend to read a given nonverbal signal in the same way. If two people read a signal in a different way, it is partial evidence that they belong to different cultures. In Colombia, an American Peace Corps worker relaxes with his feet up on the furniture; his shocked Colombian hostess perceives the gesture as disgusting. Back in the United States, a university president poses for a photograph with his feet up on the desk; newspaper readers react with affection for "good old President Jones." While Americans use the feet-on-furniture gesture to signal "I'm relaxed and at home here," or "See how casual and folksy I am," neither message is received by a Colombian, who reads the signal as "boor!" An understanding of the role gestures play within a culture is critical to sensitive communication.

Genelle G. Morain, "Kinesis and Cross-Cultural Understanding," *Language in Education: Theory and Practice*

In the preceding paragraph the writer uses inductive order to arrange the ideas using exposition as a mode of discourse. But inductive order can also be used, less commonly, in descriptive writing, as you can see in this passage by George Orwell, from his classic semi-autobiographical book, *Down and Out in Paris and London*. Which sentence states the main idea?

> It was a very narrow street—a ravine of tall, leprous houses, lurching toward one another in queer attitudes, as though they had all been frozen in the act of collapse. All the houses were hotels and packed to the tiles with lodgers, mostly Poles, Arabs, and Italians. At the foot of the hotels were tiny *bistros,* where you could be drunk for the equivalent of a shilling. On Saturday nights about a third of the male population of the quarter was drunk. There was fighting over women, and the Arab navvies who lived in the cheapest hotels used to conduct mysterious feuds, and fight them out with chairs and occasionally revolvers. At night the policemen would only come through the street two together. It was a fairly rackety place. And yet amid the noise and dirt lived the usual respectable French shopkeepers, bakers and laundresses and the like, keeping themselves to themselves and quietly piling up small fortunes. It was quite a representative Paris slum.

George Orwell, *Down and Out in Paris and London*

PUNCTUATION AND MEANING

An extensive discussion of grammar and punctuation is outside the scope of this text. However, as a closing note to this chapter, it may be worthwhile to review some marks of punctuation, especially the more sophisticated ones like parentheses, dashes, semicolons, and colons. Punctuation marks go beyond the usual definitions of enclosing and separating. Good writers choose punctuation marks carefully—to enclose and separate, to be sure—but also to emphasize, slow us down, speed us up, or clarify. Like well-chosen transitions, punctuation marks help us follow the writers' ideas. The writers' words are meant to be heard in our heads, and punctuation allows us to recreate them as the authors intended us to.

Punctuation often conveys meaning. Even apostrophes, which we don't hear when we speak, can affect meaning. Consider, for instance, these two nearly identical sentences:

- The butler stood at the door and called the guests names as they entered the mansion.
- The butler stood at the door and called the guests' names as they entered the mansion.

In which sentence is the butler insulting the guests?

Commas

Let us begin with the *comma*. There are many and various rules for the use of commas; you can consult any good grammar handbook for a list. A comma, no matter how it is used, always indicates that we should pause, however briefly. Commas determine and affect the rhythm of the prose. To demonstrate this, read aloud this short passage by Gretel Ehrlich. Notice as you read how these little markers enhance the rhythm and flow of her description. Ehrlich here explains and describes winter in Wyoming:

> [1]The name Wyoming comes from an Indian word meaning "at the great plains," but the plains are really valleys, great arid valleys, 1600 square miles, with the horizon bending up on all sides into mountain ranges. This gives the vastness a sheltering look.
>
> [2]Winter lasts six months here. Prevailing winds spill snowdrifts to the east, and new storms from the northwest replenish them. This white bulk is sometimes dizzying, even nauseating, to look at. At twenty, thirty, and forty degrees below zero, not only does your car not work but neither do your mind and body. The landscape hardens into a dungeon of space. During the

> winter, while I was riding to find a new calf, my legs froze to the saddle, and in the silence that such cold creates I felt like the first person on earth, or the last.
>
> Gretel Ehrlich, *The Solace of Open Spaces*

Note: Although the comma following "earth" in the last sentence is grammatically unnecessary, its presence definitely contributes to the effect. What is its purpose?

Semicolons

The *semicolon* is useful for connecting two independent clauses when they have a clear and logical relationship with each other. Stronger than a comma but not quite as strong as a period, the semicolon shows that the writer wants you to consider the clauses together, as a unit, usually because there is some logical connection between them, for example, cause-effect or contrast or a general statement-supporting example. Often a transition indicating the logical relationship is placed between the two clauses, as in this first example:

- But however immature they are, these lovers are not dull characters; on the contrary, they are hauntingly and embarrassingly real. (Arthur Mizener, *The Far Side of Paradise*)
- Steeped in new moods and ideas, I bought a ream of paper and tried to write; but nothing would come, or what did come was flat beyond telling. (Richard Wright, *Black Boy*)
- The man who has not the habit of reading is imprisoned in his immediate world, in respect to time and space. His life falls into a set routine; he is limited to contact and conversation with a few friends and acquaintances, and he sees only what happens in his immediate neighborhood. From this prison there is no escape. (Lin Yu-T'ang, "The Art of Reading," *The Importance of Understanding*)
- The current debate over affirmative action is simply an indication of how far we are from the kind of radical social changes King [Dr. Martin Luther King, Jr.] envisioned. Affirmative action programs were not the culmination of the black freedom struggles of the 1960s; they were instead an outgrowth of conservative ascendancy and the decline of those struggles. (Clayborne Carson, "The Founding Fallacy") Note: The brackets [ ] used in this example indicate that I, the editor, inserted the words to clarify whom "King" refers to in the first sentence. In other words, brackets indicate parenthetical information or explanation by the editor *within* quoted material.

Colons

Besides introducing lists, the *colon* has a special function within independent clauses. A writer may use a colon to separate a clause when it introduces something to be explained in the next phrase or clause, as in these examples.

- Indeed, the life of a sharecropper's wife, which often demanded twelve-hour days in the fields, normally allowed little time for food preparation at all. Typically, she would rise at 4 A.M. in a one- or two-room cabin to prepare breakfast: thinly sliced fat salt pork fried over an open fire and corn bread spread with fat and molasses. (Harvey Levenstein, *Revolution at the Table: The Transformation of the American Diet*)
- Because of Columbus's exaggerated report and promises, his second expedition was given seventeen ships and more than twelve hundred men. The aim was clear: slaves and gold. (Howard Zinn, *A People's History of the United States*)
- The Motion Picture Association of America has proposed a variation on its age-based movie ratings for the V-chip, while others argue for categories that break down shows by content. The end result, though, is the same: the V-chip will give interested parents a chance to exercise some degree of control over the electronic stranger in their living room. (Malcolm Gladwell, "Chip Thrills," *The New Yorker*)

Parentheses

Parentheses enclose additional or "extra" information within a sentence. The related term *parenthetical* simply refers to explanatory or qualifying information enclosed in parentheses. (Note: a parenthetical expression may also be enclosed in commas to suggest that the material is additional material of a straightforward nature or in dashes to suggest that the material is more important and is meant to be emphasized. The dash indicates, then, a stronger pause. You can remember the differences with this little formula: parentheses whisper, commas state, and dashes shout.) Parentheses, on the other hand, suggest that the material enclosed could be dropped without any significant loss of meaning. Study these examples:

- Franz Kafka (1883–1924), the famous Czech writer, is best known for his novels *The Trial* and *The Castle.*
- Packs of wild dogs and wolves, in which both males and females join in the hunt, have only a weak hierarchy, functioning only within each of the sexes (though the pack is usually led by an *alpha* male). (Richard E. Leakey and Roger Lewin, *Origins*)
- A further reason for football's intensity is that the game is played like a war. The idea is to win by going through, around, or over the opposing team, and the battle lines, quite literally, are drawn on every play. Violence is somewhere at the heart of the game, and the combat quality

is reflected in football's army language ("blitz," "trap," "zone," "bomb," "trenches," etc.). (Murray Ross, "Football Red and Baseball Green")

Dashes

The *dash* is a dramatic mark of punctuation. One of its functions is to introduce an afterthought or a punchline at the end of a joke, as you can see in this example:

- People who live in Maine say that they have two seasons—winter and July.

As noted earlier, the dash may enclose parenthetical elements, especially for emphasis, or it can signal an abrupt interruption. Study these remaining examples. Then mentally substitute parentheses for the dashes to see the difference.

- The town part of Sun Valley—it's really just a little shopping center—is built to look like a Bavarian village. I found it oddly charming. (Bill Bryson, *The Lost Continent*)
- Indeed, we live in a world that appears paradoxically to be moving in two conflicting directions. On the one hand, the ideal of racial equality—that individuals "should not be judged by the color of their skin but by the content of their character"—is accepted more than ever before, and anti-discrimination laws exist in most advanced nations. (Clayborne Carson, "The Founding Fallacy," *San Francisco Examiner Magazine*)
- For all the scientific awareness of the symmetrical character of snow crystals, the ubiquity of their popular image—the one we see in children's paper cutouts and on bags of ice and signs for motels that have air-conditioning—is a relatively recent phenomenon. (Cullen Murphy, "In Praise of Snow," *The Atlantic Monthly*)
- Terror, compassion, bravery—accounts like this, systematically developed—could provide evidence for a world of deep emotional experience on the part of animals, but there appears little place for them in scientific literature. (Jeffrey Masson and Susan McCarthy, *When Elephants Weep*)
- The most significant turnaround in [Grand Central Station's] eighty-three-year history is now under way as the result of a momentous, if already ancient, lawsuit. The terminal, which opened in 1913, did not become a permanent part of New York City until 1978, when the Supreme Court ruled that it was a good idea for the city to proclaim this best of buildings, which its then landlord hoped to gut for a high-rise, to be a landmark that—boom, bust, moth, or rust—must not disappear. (Tony Hiss, "Heaven's Gate," *The New Yorker*)

Ellipses

An ellipsis is composed of three dots (. . .). It indicates an omission of material in quotations. A writer quoting someone may intentionally omit a word, phrase, or sentence if it is unnecessary to the idea he or she is discussing. (If the omission occurs at the end of a sentence, as it does in the following example, the ellipsis consists of four dots, the last one being the period.) Notice also Rodriguez's use of dashes to indicate rhetorical questions his observations give rise to in his mind.

- Without question, it would have pleased me to have heard my teachers address me in Spanish when I entered the classroom. . . . But I would have delayed—postponed for how long?—having to learn the language of public society. I would have evaded—and for how long?—learning the great lesson of school: that I had a public identity. (Richard Rodriguez, *Hunger of Memory*)

Quotation Marks

Quotation marks generally indicate quoted material. Double marks (" ") are the standard form. Single quotation marks (' ') indicate quoted material *within* another quotation. Quotation marks can also be used to set off words or phrases used as illustrations. For example, in explaining doublespeak and levels of abstraction, William Lutz uses quotation marks to set off his examples. (In the same sentence, some writers would italicize these examples.)

- Using a high level of abstraction we can call the new dump a "resource development park" and sewage sludge "biosolids" or "organic biomass."

But quotation marks have another use, one not so readily apparent. A writer may use quotation marks to convey irony, to cast doubt on the authenticity of the material quoted. The author is saying, in effect, "I don't accept the meaning of this use of the word." Study these two examples:

- Cuba Shows "Evidence" That Planes Violated Airspace (Newspaper headline for a story by Juanita Darling, *Los Angeles Times*)
- The history of the word "creole" itself dates back to the slave trade. After slaves had been gathered from many parts of Africa, they were imprisoned in West African camps, euphemistically called "factories," for "processing" before being shipped out to "markets." (Peter Farb)

Of the four pairs of quotation marks used here, only one pair does not indicate irony. Which one?

EXERCISES

Selection 1

[1]The value of past experience is neatly demonstrated in an anecdote reported by Colin Turnbull, an American anthropologist who has studied the pygmies of the Congo region. [2]The BaMbuti (the general name given to all pygmies in the Forest of Ituri) spend their entire lives so deeply surrounded by vegetation that the greatest distance they are likely to have experienced is no more than the few tens of yards between them and the other side of a river or a clearing. [3]For the rest of the time their visual world is pressed in closely around them. [4]It is against this background they interpret the size and distance of objects they see. [5]One day Turnbull took Kenge, one of the BaMbuti, with him on a long drive out of the forest and up a mountain overlooking Lake Albert. [6]There Kenge, who found it almost impossible to believe in a world without trees, made a classic perceptual blunder. [7]Pointing to a herd of buffalo grazing several miles away, he asked, "What insects are those?" [8]It took Turnbull a while to realize what Kenge was talking about. [9]Because at that distance buffalo looked so small Kenge supposed they *were* small, in fact no bigger than insects. [10]To a far greater extent than we realize, like Kenge, we "see" what through experience we have come to expect to see.

Richard E. Leakey and Roger Lewin, *Origins*

A. *Vocabulary*

For each italicized word from the selection, choose the best definition according to the context in which it appears.

1. *neatly* [sentence 1]: (a) aptly, appropriately; (b) strangely, inexplicably; (c) effectively, skillfully; (d) humorously, facetiously.
2. *anthropologist* [1]: One who studies (a) human cultures and beliefs; (b) social problems; (c) the history of human language; (d) ancient buildings and human artifacts.
3. *blunder* [6]: (a) gross mistake; (b) observation; (c) error in judgment; (d) witty expression.

B. *Content and Structure*

Complete the following questions.

1. Which of these statements best represents the main idea of the paragraph? (a) We see what we want to see; (b) Our perceptions of the world around us are shaped by what we have seen in the past;

(c) We are often blind to things that are obvious to everyone else; (d) The BaMbuti rarely leave their forest environment.

2. Which *two* modes of discourse are represented in this paragraph?

   ______________________ and ______________________

3. The *two* methods of paragraph development in the paragraph are (a) facts and statistics; (b) explanation; (c) illustration; (d) analogy; (e) classification; (f) process.
4. The pattern of paragraph organization in the paragraph as a whole is (a) chronological; (b) spatial; (c) deductive; (d) variation of deductive; (e) inductive.
5. Write down the phrase(s) that helped you arrive at your answer for

   question 4 above. ______________________

6. The transitional phrase "one day" in sentence 5 indicates (a) chronological order; (b) spatial order; (c) deductive order; (d) inductive order.
7. What is the purpose of the parenthetical remark in sentence 2? ______

   ____

   ____

8. Explain Kenge's "blunder" in your own words. ______________________

   ____

9. Which sentences *best* explain why Kenge made his blunder?

   sentences __________ and __________

10. Which one of these inferences is *probably accurate?* (a) Kenge realized his mistake instantly; (b) Kenge had never been out of the forest and on a mountain before; (c) The buffalo were not where they were supposed to be; (d) Turnbull thought Kenge's blunder was stupid.

Selection 2

[1]Coffee has never been just a drink, but has always been loaded with social and political consequence as well. [2]The desire for it helped spur French, British, and Dutch colonial expansion. [3]Its infusion into 18th-century life helped create a nightlife culture and provided a social context in which political dissidents gathered to discuss the issues of the day. [4]Historians have ascribed to it at least partial responsibility for the Enlightenment—a period that valued alert and rational thought. [5]"The powers of a man's mind are directly proportional to the quantity of coffee he drank" wrote the 18th-century Scottish philosopher Sir James MacKintosh in one of the many pamphlets that circulated through London's coffeehouses in a raging war of arguments for and against the new drink. [6]It was celebrated as a substance that would lengthen the workday and provide stimulation to those engaged in the new sedentary occupations that accompanied the Industrial Revolution, according to Wolfgang Schivelbusch, a German

social scientist and author of *Tastes of Paradise: A Social History of Spices, Stimulants and Intoxicants.* [7]"Not to drink coffee," writes Schivelbusch, "[was] almost as great a sin for the puritanical bourgeoisie as wasting time itself."

[8]Most importantly, it was egalitarian in its easy accessibility to all social classes. [9]In Britain, 17th-century coffeehouses were the first gathering places where ability to pay the bill was far more important than social class in gaining access; tradesmen joined with gentry in consuming the new brew.

[10]That tradition continued in the United States: American colonists heaved tea over the side of a British schooner in Boston Harbor, and coffee became a symbol of defiance against the British. [11]George Washington signed the British terms of surrender to American rebels in a still-operating coffeehouse/tavern in New York. [12]Everywhere they opened, coffeehouses became the centers of political intrigue and philosophical discussion, fostering the concepts of individual liberty and freedom of opinion in the budding republic. [13]Some analysts even claim that coffee has been key to the development of the urban work ethic. [14]"Coffee," says Irene Fizer, a scholar who teaches a course called "Caffeine Culture" at New York's New School, "has been keyed to the construction of a rigidified work life. [15]The urban workaday economy would be unthinkable without coffee."

Mark Schapiro, "Muddy Waters," *Utne Reader*

A. *Vocabulary*

For each italicized word from the selection, choose the best definition according to the context in which it appears.

1. *infusion* [sentence 3]: (a) absorption; (b) introduction; (c) development; (d) purpose.
2. *dissidents* [3]: (a) radicals; (b) those who are discontented; (c) those who disagree with the current political situation; (d) those who make important political decisions.
3. *ascribed* [4]: (a) attributed; (b) devoted; (c) blamed; (d) determined.
4. *sedentary* [6]: (a) highly skilled; (b) requiring a university education; (c) describing assembly work; (d) requiring much sitting.
5. *bourgeoisie* [7]: (a) the proletariat or working class; (b) the middle class; (c) the ruling nobility; (d) members of religious organizations.
6. *egalitarian* [8]: A belief in (a) distinctions made in class, ethnic group, and occupation; (b) political and social equality for all; (c) political conservatism and a reduced role for central governments; (d) universal education.
7. *gentry* [9]: (a) members of the upper or ruling class; (b) manual laborers; (c) members of the middle class; (d) shopkeepers and clerks.
8. *intrigue* [12]: (a) activism; (b) secret plots or schemes; (c) apathy or indifference; (d) corruption or bribery.

B. *Content and Structure*

Complete the following questions.

1. Which sentence expresses the main idea of paragraph 1?

   sentence ______

   Which part of the sentence expresses the topic? ______

   Which part expresses the controlling idea? ______
2. Which sentence expresses the main idea of paragraph 2?

   sentence ______

   The topic is the same in this paragraph as it is for question 1 above, but what is the controlling idea? ______

   ______
3. What is the main pattern of organization for each of the three paragraphs in the passage? (a) chronological; (b) spatial; (c) deductive; (d) variation of deductive; (e) inductive.
4. The mode of discourse in the passage is (a) narration; (b) description; (c) exposition; (d) persuasion.
5. Which *two* methods of development are evident in the paragraph?

   ______ and ______
6. The author evidently sees a strong connection between the increasing popularity of coffee and (a) the beginning of unions to protect laborers; (b) the Industrial Revolution; (c) a rigid workday; (d) the increasing importance of democracy, individual liberties, and social equality.
7. Look again at sentence 5. The author writes that pamphlets circulated in London coffeehouses offering "a raging war of arguments for and against the new drink." From the evidence, on which side of this argument—for or against coffee—does the writer appear to stand?

   ______
8. The transitional phrase "most importantly" in sentence 8 indicates that what follows is (a) an example; (b) a contrast; (c) an idea to emphasize; (d) a conclusion; (e) a cause-effect pattern.
9. Look again at sentence 9. Then explain the logical relationship between the two parts (separated by the semicolon).

   ______

   ______
10. In the last sentence the author quotes Irene Fizer, who writes that the urban workaday economy would be unthinkable without coffee. What

seems to be the author's personal opinion about this statement? (a) His opinion is favorable; (b) his opinion is unfavorable; (c) his opinion is not evident. Explain your thinking.

Selection 3

Note: The reference in sentences 9 and 11 is to William M. C. Lam, an architect in Cambridge, Massachusetts, who, as the author tells us, designed the lighting for that city's Hyatt Regency Hotel.

1What kinds of things enable us to meet our biological needs for visual information? **2**Many of them are conveyed by daylight. **3**Outdoors, the position of the sun in the sky helps us orient ourselves to the time of day, and works to set a series of internal clocks. **4**That is not the simple act it seems, because information about the sun's position comes to us in several ways. **5**If we're standing out in the sun, the sense of touch is involved: we react to the strength of sunlight falling on our skin. **6**But even when the sun isn't directly on us we're still dealing with complex information, because when we look at where the sun is in the sky we're also looking at the brilliance of the light coming from it, which varies during the day. **7**And we're looking at the color of the sunlight; it's bluer in the middle of the day and more orange-red in the morning and evening. **8**How much of this information can we do without before we no longer have access to our daytime sense of orientation? **9**Some two-foot-by-four-foot openings designed by Lam give us a first answer to this question. **10**The openings are high up in the walls that separate bedrooms from dressing rooms at the Hyatt Regency Hotel in Cambridge. **11**(Lam designed the hotel's lighting.) **12**The openings convey natural light to the windowless dressing rooms. **13**You can't actually look through the openings—they're too high up—but they do bring in to an inner room the color and some of the brilliance of the daylight outside. **14**The result, as I found out staying at the Hyatt Regency, is that a perfectly ordinary little nook becomes a friendly place that has, if only faintly, the relaxed and spacious feeling of a room in a resort.

15So we don't always need to feel the sun or to look at it in order to stay oriented, which means we can, if we have to, get by, at least for a while, on about half the information that natural environments provide about orientation. **16**It does seem that the experiences of a place may have a certain amount of give to them, but we're also learning that there are real limits to the amount of experiential diminution we can tolerate. **17**If the Cambridge Hyatt Regency decided to install heavily tinted glass in its bedroom windows, for example, that would distort both the brilliance and the color of the light coming in and might do real damage to the experience available there. **18**The design principle here is that any change made to our surroundings has the potential to affect the way we experience a place, and that the cumulative effect of a number of changes may be at some point to alter the experience entirely.

Tony Hiss, "Experiencing Places," *The New Yorker*

A. *Vocabulary*

For each italicized word from the selection, choose the best definition according to the context in which it appears.

1. *conveyed* [sentence 2; also *convey* in 12]: (a) made known, communicated; (b) perceived by the senses; (c) carried or transported as a load; (d) represented, symbolized.
2. *orient* [3; also *oriented* in 15]: (a) face the east; (b) discover, identify; (c) position or locate; (d) give order to.
3. *nook* [14]: (a) little room or corner; (b) storage closet; (c) hotel lobby; (d) hotel accommodations.
4. *give* [16]: (a) leeway, flexibility; (b) gift, donation; (c) necessary rules and standards; (d) essential requirements.
5. *diminution* [16]: (a) overload, excessive burden; (b) diminishing, decrease; (c) disruption, chaos; (d) experimentation.
6. *cumulative* [18]: (a) acquired by successive additions; (b) overtaking by progressive steps; (c) formed from raw material; (d) intangible, difficult to perceive.

B. *Content and Structure*

Complete the following questions.

1. The mode of discourse in this passage is primarily (a) narration; (b) description; (c) exposition; (d) persuasion.
2. Read the first paragraph (sentences 1–14) again. In your own words, write a sentence that expresses the main idea. ______________________

   ____
3. In sentence 1 Hiss refers to our "biological need for visual information." Here and in the rest of the paragraph he is specifically concerned with our need for (a) warmth and security; (b) adequate sunlight; (c) an internal clock; (d) colors and lights that enhance our enjoyment of life.
4. The pattern of organization in paragraph 1 is (a) deductive; (b) variation of deductive; (c) chronological; (d) inductive; (e) spatial.
5. Which *two* methods of paragraph development are most evident in paragraph 1 (sentences 1–14)? (a) facts and statistics; (b) steps in a process; (c) definition; (d) comparison; (e) explanation; (f) example.
6. Sentence 14 serves both as a conclusion to this paragraph and also as (a) another step in a process; (b) a definition; (c) an effect of a cause; (d) an example; (e) an analogy.

7. In relation to the passage as a whole, sentence 15 serves (a) to state the main idea; (b) to provide a transition or link between paragraphs 1 and 2; (c) to recommend hotel designs; (d) to present the author's opinion on the subject.
8. The pattern of organization in the second paragraph is (a) chronological; (b) spatial; (c) deductive; (d) inductive; (e) variation of deductive.
9. A good title for this passage would be (a) "Sunlight"; (b) "Principles of Hotel Design"; (c) "Experiential Diminution"; (d) "Access to Sunlight and Our Experience of Place"; (e) "Orientation to the Sun."
10. Consider again these two parts of sentence 17: "If the Cambridge Hyatt Regency decided to install heavily tinted glass in its bedroom windows, for example" and "that would distort both the brilliance and the color of the light coming in and might do real damage to the experience available there." What is the logical relationship between these two parts? (a) hypothetical cause and effect; (b) general idea and a supporting example; (c) contrast; (d) steps in a process; (e) the author's opinion and evidence to support it.

C. *Inferences*

On the basis of the evidence in the paragraph, mark these statements as follows: PA for inferences that are probably accurate and PI for inferences that are probably inaccurate.

1. ______ The Cambridge Hyatt Regency Hotel rooms look friendly because the architect was cleverly able to duplicate natural sunlight using artificial lighting.
2. ______ Being deprived of sunlight may have adverse effects.
3. ______ Natural light and artificial light are equally beneficial.
4. ______ Designers of prisons should ensure adequate natural lighting.

PRACTICE ESSAY

Anosmia

Diane Ackerman

The author of five books of poetry and recipient of numerous literary prizes, Diane Ackerman is a poet and writer of nonfiction. She has taught at many universities, among them Washington University, New York University,

Columbia, and Cornell, where she received an M.FA. and Ph.D. Ackerman, a resident of upstate New York, is currently a staff writer at The New Yorker. *Described by the* Boston Globe *as a "narrative journey, one that touches upon biology and anthropology, art and human consciousness,"* A Natural History of the Senses, *from which this essay comes, is an engaging look at the wonders to be found in our five senses.*

1 One rainy night in 1976, a thirty-three-year-old mathematician went out for an after-dinner stroll. Everyone considered him not just a gourmet but a wunderkind,[1] because he had the ability to taste a dish and tell you all its ingredients with shocking precision. One writer described it as a kind of "perfect pitch." As he stepped into the street, a slow-moving van ran into him and he hit his head on the pavement when he fell. The day after he got out of the hospital, he discovered to his horror that his sense of smell was gone.

2 Because his taste buds still worked, he could detect foods that were salty, bitter, sour, and sweet, but he had lost all of the heady succulence of life. Seven years later, still unable to smell and deeply depressed, he sued the driver of the van and won. It was understood, first, that his life had become irreparably impoverished and, second, that without a sense of smell his life was endangered. In those seven years, he had failed to detect the smell of smoke when his apartment building was on fire; he had been poisoned by food whose putrefaction he couldn't smell; he could not smell gas leaks. Worst of all, perhaps, he had lost the ability of scents and odors to provide him with heart-stopping memories and associations. "I feel empty, in a sort of limbo," he told a reporter. There was not even a commonly known name for his nightmare. Those without hearing are labeled "deaf," those without sight "blind," but what is the word for someone without smell? What could be more distressing than to be sorely afflicted by an absence without a name? "Anosmia" is what scientists call it, a simple Latin/Greek combination: "without" + "smell." But no casual term—like "smumb," for instance—exists to give one a sense of community or near-normalcy.

3 The "My Turn" column in *Newsweek* of March 21, 1988, by Judith R. Birnberg, contains a deeply moving lament about her sudden loss of smell. All she can distinguish is the texture and temperature of food. "I am handicapped: one of 2 million Americans who suffer from anosmia, an inability to smell or taste (the two senses are physiologically related). . . . We so take for granted the rich aroma of coffee and the sweet flavor of oranges that when we lose these senses, it is almost as if we have forgotten how to breathe." Just before Ms. Birnberg's sense of

[1]Pronounced vŏon′ dər kint′, *wunderkind* is the German word for a wonder child or child prodigy.

smell disappeared, she had spent a year sneezing. The cause? Some unknown allergy. "The anosmia began without warning. . . . During the past three years there have been brief periods—minutes, even hours—when I suddenly became aware of odors and knew that this meant that I could also taste. What to eat first? A bite of banana once made me cry. On a few occasions a remission came at dinner time, and my husband and I would dash to our favorite restaurant. On two or three occasions I savored every miraculous mouthful through an entire meal. But most times my taste would be gone by the time we parked the car." Although there are centers for treating smell and taste dysfunction (of which Monell[2] is probably the best known), little can be done about anosmia. "I have had a CAT scan, blood tests, sinus cultures, allergy tests, allergy shots, long-term zinc therapy, weekly sinus irrigations, a biopsy, cortisone injections into my nose and four different types of sinus surgery. My case has been presented to hospital medical committees. . . . I have been through the medical mill. The consensus: anosmia caused by allergy and infection. There can be other causes. Some people are born this way. Or the olfactory nerve is severed as a result of concussion. Anosmia can also be the result of aging, a brain tumor or exposure to toxic chemicals. Whatever the cause, we are all at risk in detecting fires, gas leaks and spoiled food." Finally, she took a risky step and allowed a doctor to give her prednisone, an anti-inflammatory steroid, in an effort to shrink the swelling near olfactory nerves. "By the second day, I had a brief sense of smell when I inhaled deeply. . . . The fourth day I ate a salad at lunch, and I suddenly realized that I could taste everything. It was like the moment in 'The Wizard of Oz' when the world is transformed from black and white to Technicolor. I savored the salad: one garbanzo bean, a shred of cabbage, a sunflower seed. On the fifth day I sobbed—less from the experience of smelling and tasting than from believing the craziness was over."

4 At breakfast the next day, she caught her husband's scent and "fell on him in tears of joy and started sniffing him, unable to stop. His was a comfortable familiar essence that had been lost for so long and was now rediscovered. I had always thought I would sacrifice smell to taste if I had to choose between the two, but I suddenly realized how much I had missed. We take it for granted and are unaware that *everything* smells: people, the air, my house, my skin. . . . Now I inhaled all odors, good and bad, as if drunk." Sadly, her pleasures lasted only a few months. When she began reducing the dosage of prednisone, as she had to for safety's sake (prednisone causes bloating and can suppress the immune system, among other unpleasant side effects), her ability to

[2]The Monell Chemical Senses Center in Philadelphia is a research institute where researchers study, as Ackerman says, "the chemistry, psychology, healing properties, and odd characteristics of smell."

smell waned once more. Two new operations followed. She's decided to go back on prednisone, and yearns for some magical day when her smell returns as mysteriously as it vanished.

5 Not everyone without a sense of smell suffers so acutely. Nor are all smell dysfunctions a matter of loss; the handicap can take strange forms. At Monell, scientists have treated numerous people who suffer from "persistent odors," who keep smelling a foul smell wherever they go. Some walk around with a constant bitter taste in their mouths. Some have a deformed or distorted sense of smell. Hand them a rose, and they smell garbage. Hand them a steak and they smell sulfur. Our sense of smell weakens as we get older, and it's at its peak in middle age. Alzheimer's patients often lose their sense of smell along with their memory (the two are tightly coupled); one day Scratch-and-Sniff tests may help in diagnosis of the disease.

6 Research done by Robert Henkin, from the Center for Sensory Disorders at Georgetown University, suggests that about a quarter of the people with smell disorders find that their sex drive disappears. What part does smell play in lovemaking? For women, especially, a large part. I am certain that, blindfolded, I could recognize by smell any man I've ever known intimately. I once started to date a man who was smart, sophisticated, and attractive, but when I kissed him I was put off by a faint, cornlike smell that came from his cheek. Not cologne or soap: It was just his subtle, natural scent, and I was shocked to discover that it disturbed me viscerally. Although men seldom report such detailed responses to their partner's natural smell, women so often do that it's become a romantic cliché: When her lover is away, or her husband dies, an anguished woman goes to his closet and takes out a bathrobe or shirt, presses it to her face, and is overwhelmed by tenderness for him. Few men report similar habits, but it's not surprising that women should be more keenly attuned to smells. Females score higher than males in sensitivity to odors, regardless of age group. For a time scientists thought estrogen might be involved, since there was anecdotal evidence that pregnant women had a keener sense of smell, but as it turned out prepubescent girls were better sniffers than boys their age, and pregnant women were no more adept at smelling than other women. Women in general just have a stronger sense of smell. Perhaps it's a vestigial bonus from the dawn of our evolution, when we needed it in courtship, mating, or mothering; or it may be that women have traditionally spent more time around foods and children, ever on the sniff for anything out of order. Because females have often been responsible for initiating mating, smell has been their weapon, lure, and clue.

A. *Comprehension*

Choose the answer that best completes each statement. Do not refer to the selection while doing this exercise.

1. The mathematician who lost his sense of smell after being hit by a van had a special ability, namely identifying by smell (a) human scents; (b) brands of food; (c) wines according to the soil the grapes were grown in; (d) the ingredients in a dish.
2. According to Ackerman, the most serious effect of this man's loss of his sense of smell was his inability (a) to connect smells with memories and associations; (b) to smell spoiled food; (c) to smell smoke or gas leaks; (d) to taste food.
3. The sense of smell is physiologically most closely related to our (a) sense of touch; (b) sense of hearing; (c) sense of sight; (d) sense of taste; (e) memory.
4. For Judith Birnberg, the most precious scent to her when she temporarily regained her sense of smell was that of (a) her own skin; (b) her husband; (c) a green salad; (d) her house.
5. According to scientific research, (a) women and men are equally sensitive to smells; (b) men are more sensitive to smells than women are; (c) women are more sensitive to smells than men are; (d) children are more sensitive to smells than adults are.

B. *Inferences*

On the basis of the evidence in the paragraph, mark these statements as follows: PA for inferences that are probably accurate and PI for inferences that are probably inaccurate. You may refer to the selection to answer the questions in this section, and all in the remaining sections.

1. ______ The ability to identify precisely the ingredients in a dish is a rare talent.
2. ______ "Smumb" is probably a word the author made up combining "smell" and perhaps "numb."
3. ______ A keen sense of smell is essential for one to lead a normal, relatively happy life.
4. ______ Estrogen apparently plays an important role in a woman's ability to smell.
5. ______ Scientists do not know the exact causes of anosmia.

C. *Structure*

1. The main idea is that (a) anosmia is a physical disorder characterized by loss of the ability to smell; (b) victims of anosmia experience serious emotional trauma as a result of losing their sense of smell; (c) research must be done to find a cure for victims of anosmia; (d) anosmia is only one of many smell dysfunctions.
2. The mode of discourse in this essay is (a) narration; (b) description; (c) exposition; (d) persuasion.
3. The transitional phrase "worst of all" in paragraph 2 indicates (a) an example; (b) a conclusion; (c) a concession; (d) emphasis.
4. The pattern of organization in paragraph 3 and 4 is (a) chronological; (b) spatial; (c) deductive; (d) inductive.
5. Look again at paragraph 3 and find a phrase that represents a controlling idea for the details in both paragraphs 3 and 4.

   ____

6. Also in paragraph 3 locate all of the transitional phrases that indicate chronological order. ______________________________

   ____

7. State the cause-effect relationship Ackerman makes in the first four sentences of paragraph 6. ______________________________

   ____

8. Look again at this sentence from paragraph 6: ". . . it's not surprising that women should be more keenly attuned to smells." The method of development in this sentence and the remaining sentences in the paragraph is (a) classification; (b) example; (c) cause-effect; (d) analogy; (e) steps in a process; (f) definition.

D. *Vocabulary*

For each italicized word from the selection, choose the best definition according to the context in which it appears.

1. the heady *succulence* of life [paragraph 2]: The quality of being (a) absorbing, interesting; (b) juicy, tender; (c) spirited, animated; (d) indulgent, enjoyable.
2. his life had become *irreparably* impoverished [2]: (a) definitely; (b) unable to be explained; (c) unable to be repaired; (d) permanently.
3. food whose *putrefaction* he couldn't smell [2]: (a) chemical additives; (b) pesticides and herbicides; (c) spicy aroma; (d) rottenness.

4. a deeply moving *lament* [3]: A piece of writing expressing (a) grief, remorse; (b) envy, jealousy; (c) anger, bitterness; (d) sarcasm, cynicism.
5. a *remission* came at dinner time [3]: (a) a serious worsening of symptoms; (b) a lessening of symptoms; (c) an unexplainable and complete cure; (d) a return of one's memory.
6. smell and taste *dysfunction* [3 and 5]: The prefix *dys-* means (a) well; (b) faulty; (c) typical; (d) two.
7. the *olfactory* nerve [3]: Contributing to the sense of (a) taste; (b) smell; (c) hearing; (d) touch; (e) sight.
8. her ability to smell *waned* [4]: (a) gradually improved; (b) gradually decreased; (c) became tolerable; (d) stayed the same.
9. it disturbed me *viscerally* [6]: (a) illogically, irrationally; (b) profoundly, deeply; (c) intensely, emotionally; (d) slightly, moderately.
10. more keenly *attuned* to smells [6]: (a) accustomed to as with a special perception; (b) involved with for research; (c) being in harmony with; (d) intrigued or fascinated by.
11. *anecdotal* evidence [6]: Pertaining to (a) factual information; (b) short accounts; (c) rumors, unfounded stories; (d) scientific.
12. Perhaps it's a *vestigial* bonus [6]: Pertaining to a thing that (a) is extra or unnecessary; (b) is not clearly understood; (c) is innate, inborn; (d) is a visible trace of something that no longer exists.

E. *Questions for Analysis and Discussion*

1. Consider again the last part of paragraph 6 where Ackerman discusses some possible theories about women's superior ability to smell. How plausible do you find these theories? Can you think of any others that might account for this phenomenon, assuming, of course, that it is true?
2. Of your five senses, which do you think would be the most difficult to be deprived of? Why?

6

Language

In this chapter, we will be concerned with language in prose writing—with words and the effect the writer intends them to have on you. Specifically, we will examine the denotation and connotation of words; the misuse and abuse of words; several kinds of figurative language, in particular metaphors and similes; and allusions.

DENOTATION AND CONNOTATION

Good writers choose their words carefully to suggest certain ideas, feelings, or attitudes. Much of the pleasure in reading is the ability to savor the emotional associations of the words we read. An understanding of these associations will greatly improve your literal understanding and enhance your enjoyment of reading.

Word choice, or **diction,** involves both denotation and connotation. Some words are meant to arouse positive feelings, some are meant to be neutral or literal, while others are meant to convey a negative impression. **Denotation** refers to a word's explicit, or literal, meaning. Sometimes denotation is called the dictionary definition of a word. Denotatively, the word *lemon,* for example, refers to a sour, yellow-skinned, citrus fruit. In the sentence, "Our lemon tree produced a good crop this year," the speaker or writer is using *lemon* denotatively, and no judgment is implied. However, in the sentence, "Gary's new car turned out to be a lemon. Every conceivable mechanical thing has gone wrong with it since he bought it," *lemon* has a decidedly unfavorable meaning. The dictionary bears this out, giving us an informal meaning of *lemon,* something that proves to be "unsatisfactory or defective."

In this context, the connotation of *lemon* is negative. **Connotation** refers to the cluster of suggestions, emotional responses, or implications—whether positive or negative—that a word carries with it. In other words, the connotation extends the meaning beyond its literal or explicit meaning (its denotation).

Richard Altick, author of *Preface to Critical Reading,* has written: "Nothing is more essential to intelligent, profitable reading than sensitivity to connotation." However, no one can teach you this sensitivity. It comes from a wide exposure to reading and a willingness to consult the dictionary definitions and the accompanying usage notes for help. This sensitivity may take years to develop.

To begin, consider the verb *walk.* It is purely neutral, denoting a forward movement by taking steps. But what of these related verbs: *stride, saunter, stroll, meander, glide, mince, lumber, plod, trudge, stagger, lurch, stomp,* and *march?* Notice what they suggest.

Stride: Walking purposely or resolutely.

Saunter, stroll: Walking in a leisurely, unhurried way.

Meander: Walking in no particular direction; wandering here and there with no fixed destination.

Glide: Walking in an elegant, graceful manner.

Mince: Walking in little steps with exaggerated affectation or primness.

Lumber: Walking heavily and clumsily; often reserved for describing the movement of large, bulky animals like bears.

Plod, trudge: Walking in a heavy or laborious way; *trudge* can also suggest discouragement or defeat.

Stagger, lurch: Walking in an unsteady manner, whether because of illness, drunkenness, or some other affliction; *stagger* is stronger than *lurch.*

Stomp: Walking with purposeful steps, typically in anger.

March: Used in a military sense, this word refers to a formal way of walking in a regiment. Used in an ordinary or civilian sense, it suggests walking purposefully or steadily.

Now consider these pairs of words. In each case, mark the item in the pair that carries a positive connotation with a plus sign; mark the item with the negative connotation with a minus sign. Consult a dictionary if necessary.

secret	underhanded
plump	obese
macho	manly/masculine
binge	spree
pro-life	anti-abortion
nude	naked
childlike	childish
smut	erotica
exotic dancer	stripper
devious	evasive
motionless	passive
energetic	frenetic
frantic	concerned
swamp	wetland
loiter	wait
learned (adj.)	pedantic
assertive	aggressive
hawk (verb)	sell

In addition to the positive or negative "charge" that words can convey, some words in English are restrictive in that they are generally reserved for a particular group. For example, the word *spry* usually applies to old people or animals, particularly dogs. The *American Heritage Dictionary* usage notes (if you have this dictionary, the usage notes follow the definition of "nimble") state that *spry* suggests "unexpected speed and energy of motion," traits that would be more characteristic of an old person or an old dog than, say, a six-year-old child.

The adjective *debonair,* meaning handsome, suave, urbane, usually applies to men. Unfortunately, neither of my two dictionaries suggests this connotation, but from the many contexts where I have encountered this word, that is the mental image I have in my head when a man is described as debonair; a woman may be handsome, attractive, elegant, and so on, but not debonair. Normally, however, your dictionary's usage notes are invaluable for helping you see connotative values. Consider the word *demure.* What connotation does the word have for you? Does it seem to apply to one gender only, and if so, which? Does it suggest any age restriction? Can a middle-aged man be described as demure?

Connotation can be used effectively to change our perceptions of things. The word *cigarette,* for example, is denotative, unambiguously referring to the object without any emotional association one way or another. In recent congressional hearings investigating the tobacco industry, however, the Food and Drug Administration argued that industry executives had proof as far back as the 1960s that cigarettes were addictive. These critics began calling cigarettes *drug-delivery systems,* an effective use of connotation that puts a wholly different slant on the product.

Finally, for some humorous examples of connotation, here is a list titled "Vocabulary Update" by T. O. Sylvester.[1]

1. *Fairy tale:* a lie often involving giants and other imaginary characters.
2. *Fable:* a lie with a moral lesson.
3. *Parable:* a lie with a religious lesson.
4. *Myth:* a lie based on history or tradition.
5. *Politics:* mastery of 1 through 4 above.

To see how connotation works in prose passages, consider these two excerpts on the same topic, one by the American novelist John Steinbeck, the other by Ray Allen Billington, an American historian. Both are concerned with the westward migration following the 1849 Gold Rush, but you will immediately see that the authors' word choices are radically different, reflecting their radically different points of view.

> The railroads brought new hordes of land-crazy people, and the new Americans moved like locusts across the continent until the western sea put a boundary to their movements. Coal and copper and gold drew them on; they savaged the land, gold-dredged the rivers to skeletons of pebbles and debris. An aroused and fearful government made laws for the distribution of public lands—a quarter section, one hundred and sixty acres, per person—and a claim had to be proved and improved; but there were ways of getting around this, and legally. My own grandfather proved out a quarter section for himself, one for his wife, one for each of his children, and, I suspect, acreage for children he hoped and expected to have. Marginal lands, of course, suitable only for grazing, went in larger pieces. One of the largest landholding families in California took its richest holdings by a trick: By law a man could take up all the swamp or water-covered land he wanted. The founder of this great holding mounted a scow on wheels and drove his horses over thousands of acres of the best bottom land, then reported that he had explored it in a boat, which was true, and confirmed his title. I need not mention his name: his descendants will remember.
>
> John Steinbeck, *America and Americans*

[1]*San Francisco Chronicle Sunday Book Review,* June 26, 1996.

> [1]Opportunity was the magnet that drew men westward during those three centuries, for nature's untapped riches promised pioneers the fortunes that fate had denied them in older societies. There, where a king's ransom in furs could be had for the taking, where lush grasslands beckoned the herdsman, where fortunes in gold and silver lay scarcely hidden, where virgin soils awaited only the magic touch of man to yield their wealth, men and women could begin life anew with only their brains and brawn and courage to sustain them. There they could realize the social equality that was the goal of every democratically inclined American. These were the lures that drew the frontiersmen ever westward toward the Pacific.
>
> [2]They moved in an orderly procession. The fur trappers came first, roaming far in advance of the settled areas as they gathered the bales of shiny beaver peltry that would gladden the hearts of Europe's elite. Then came the miners, who also left civilization far behind as they prospected mountain streams and desert wastes in their endless quest for gold or silver. Behind them were the cattlemen, seeking the grassy pastures where their herds could graze without the confinement of fences. Cowboys were a familiar sight on the frontiers of Virginia or Kentucky or Illinois long before they won their places in the sun and cinema on the High Plains of the Far West. These shock troops of civilization made little impression on the wilderness; instead they adapted themselves so completely to the forest environment that they altered the face of the country but slightly.
>
> Ray Allen Billington, "The Frontier Disappears,"
> *The American Story*

Even though each author has a different perspective on the westward migration—Billington takes the broader view, while Steinbeck establishes the background to lead into his grandfather's clever way of evading the homestead law—the difference in connotative words is striking. Billington clearly admires the westward march. To see this for yourself, underline the words in his passage that convey a positive impression. Even his characterization of cowboys as the "shock troops of civilization," which initially sounds negative, turns out to be positive, since he says that their effect on the environment was minimal. Compare this laudatory view with Steinbeck's, whose first two sentences in particular sound extremely negative and harsh.

This next passage is by James W. Loewen, professor of sociology at the University of Vermont. Under the auspices of the Smithsonian Institution, Loewen published a highly readable study of American history textbooks and the false information and narrow perspectives that they reflect. Here he examines the connotations of the word "civilized," particularly as it commonly is used to describe European civilizations.

> For a long time Native Americans have been rebuking textbook authors for reserving the adjective *civilized* for European cultures. In 1927 an organization of Native leaders called the Grand Council Fire of American Indians criticized textbooks as "unjust to the life of our people." They went on to ask, "What is civilization? Its marks are a noble religion and philosophy, original arts, stirring music, rich story and legend. We had these. Then we were not savages, but a civilized race." Even an appreciative treatment of Native cultures reinforces ethnocentrism so long as it does not challenge the primitive-to-civilized continuum. This continuum inevitably conflates the meaning of *civilized* in everyday conversation—"refined or enlightened"—with "having a complex division of labor," the only definition that anthropologists defend. When we consider the continuum carefully, it immediately becomes problematic. Was the Third Reich civilized, for instance? Most anthropologists would answer yes. In what ways do we prefer the civilized Third Reich to the more primitive Arawak nation that Columbus encountered? If we refuse to label the Third Reich civilized, are we not using the term to imply a certain comity? If so, we must consider the Arawaks civilized, and we must also consider Columbus and his Spaniards primitive if not savage. Ironically, societies characterized by a complex division of labor are often marked by inequality and capable of supporting large specialized armies. Precisely these "civilized" societies are likely to resort to savage violence in their attempts to conquer "primitive" societies.
>
> James W. Loewen, *Lies My Teacher Told Me: Everything Your American History Textbook Got Wrong*

In your own words, explain why the Grand Council Fire of American Indians criticized the word "civilized" as it is commonly used in textbooks.

____

____

To what extent does connotative language shape our perceptions? In 1997 Congress wrestled with a bill to outlaw a special kind of abortion called by medical personnel "intact dilation and extraction," while opponents used the phrase "partial birth abortion." Both refer to late-term abortions performed after the 20th week of pregnancy; they are rare and performed only under conditions when the mother's life is threatened. (It is important to note that a fetus is considered viable, that is, able to live outside the uterus, between the 23rd and 26th weeks of pregnancy.) The fetus's viability is probably the reason that some opponents call this type of abortion "infanticide," which clearly carries a more negative connotative effect.

In literature (fiction, as opposed to nonfiction prose), writers may use descriptive details that evoke a particular emotional response to their characters. These details help you both to visualize the character and to assess his or her behavior, motivation, and actions. In this paragraph from *David Copperfield,* Charles Dickens introduces the reader to a character named Miss Murdstone. As you read it, identify and underline the descriptive words associated with metal.

> It was Miss Murdstone who was arrived, and a gloomy-looking lady she was: dark, like her brother, whom she greatly resembled in face and voice, and with very heavy eyebrows, nearly meeting over her large nose, as if, being disabled by the wrongs of her sex from wearing whiskers, she had carried them to that account. She brought with her two uncompromising hard black boxes, with her initials on the lids in hard brass nails. When she paid the coachman she took her money out of a hard steel purse, and she kept the purse in a very jail of a bag which hung upon her arm by a heavy chain, and shut up like a bite. I had never, at that time, seen such a metallic lady altogether as Miss Murdstone was.
>
> Charles Dickens, *David Copperfield.*

Consider the words and phrases you underlined and write a sentence explaining what these connotative words and phrases suggest about Miss Murdstone's character.

____

____

LANGUAGE MISUSED AND ABUSED

From one edition of this book to the next, deceptive and manipulative uses of the language seem to abound, and discouragingly, they become even more entrenched in the language. And so for this edition, I have alphabetized this section for easier reference. For purposes of this discussion, the word *writer* includes not only writers of nonfiction articles and editorials but also politicians, the new breed of political advisors euphemistically called "spin doctors," advertising copywriters, and so forth. Most writers are ethical and honest; they play by the rules of good journalism, strive for integrity in their reporting, and resist the temptation to deal with a subject unfairly or to inject bias into their work. But not all writers are so honest, and advertising and politicking in particular have become so cutthroat that sneaky and deceptive uses of the language are commonly condoned or ignored, almost like elevator music. It's there, but we no longer hear how awful it is.

An unscrupulous writer may use language to exploit the reader, to incite or inflame passions, or to soften the impact of ideas that might otherwise be more realistically or harshly interpreted. As a critical reader, you should be particularly alert to language that attempts to influence you in this way, not through careful, reasoned thought, but through appeals to your emotions or through the clever misuse of words. In this section, we will look briefly at several examples in the general category of misused language: buzzwords and babble, clichés, doublespeak, euphemisms, jargon, politically correct (PC) language, and sneer words.

Do not worry if some of these terms appear to overlap because, in fact, they occasionally do. The point is to develop a sensitivity and appreciation of careful language and to see through linguistic sleaze and sludge when you encounter it. What follow are many examples of language abuses so that you can learn to identify them readily.

Buzzwords, Sound Bites, and Babble

Norman Solomon's book *The Power of Babble,* is a humorous and irreverent compendium subtitled "The Politician's Dictionary of Buzzwords and Double-Talk for Every Occasion." In his preface Solomon writes:

> 1Ambiguity that sounds forthright is a politician's best rhetorical friend. Strive to present your expedient choices as acts of courage; when you stoke the lowest common prejudices, do so with visionary hot air. Keep flattering voters. Don't let on that you're unlikely to lose an election by underestimating their discernment.
>
> 2Your ultimate weaponry comes down to words. Select only the loaded ones. Take aim with steady determination. Make every verbal bullet count. Learn to fire with a single fluid motion of your tongue, which should always be polished and well oiled.

Solomon goes on to define **buzzwords** as words that "commonly precede, and preempt, thought." The term **sound bites** refers to brief snippets that will sound good when broadcast on the evening news, resulting in reducing responses to serious political and social problems to the fewest words possible. **Babble** is just that—nonsense. Here are a few excerpts from Solomon's book, followed by an example and his comments on what each really means. You will undoubtedly recognize many of these common political words and phrases.

aberration
No cause for concern.
Usage: Insistence that the event or pattern is a fluke.
The impropriety committed by my aide was an unfortunate *aberration.*
Antonym: *case-in-point*

afraid to walk the streets
Terrified of violent crime.
USAGE: Conveying that you understand deep worries about criminal elements, this phrase can lay rhetorical groundwork for chipping away at interpretations of the Bill of Rights that you don't like.

feeding frenzy
USAGE: When disclosures threaten your power, declare that they are part of a "feeding frenzy." Evokes imagery of aggressive journalists and opposition politicians as wacko piranha tearing innocent human flesh from bone.

fiscally irresponsible
USAGE: For a budget you don't support.

fiscally responsible
USAGE: For a budget you do support.

good-faith effort
USAGE: When it's under your aegis, every effort is "good-faith," no matter now unsuccessful (or disingenuous). When made by a properly demonized foreigner, no effort can be.

I do not mean to imply
People didn't hear what they may have thought they just heard.
USAGE: A good verbal stratagem for when you've just implied something but don't want to get zinged for it.

"*I do not mean to imply* that protection of the environment is not important. It is very important. However . . ." (Senator Wendell H. Ford, September 8, 1989)

These examples should give you a pretty good idea of the emptiness of these phrases, not to mention the cynical attitude toward the public that they display. (See **cynicism** in the next chapter.)

Clichés

Clichés—fossilized, stale, overused expressions—tell the careful reader that a lazy writer is at work. Good writers avoid clichés because such expressions are tired, having lost their effectiveness long ago. Some clichés do not even make any sense. For example, "Her complexion is like peaches and cream." (Why would anyone want orange and white skin?) Some clichés probably made sense at one time, but now, at the end of the twentieth century, many sound ridiculous. Yet we still hear them, for example, "having an ax to grind," "grist for the mill," or "to fight tooth and nail."

For fun, you might begin your own list of clichés to add to this one:

pretty as a picture	an agonizing defeat
dead as a doornail	chip off the old block
strong as an ox	like water off a duck's back
no skin off my teeth	by the skin of one's teeth
a labor of love	leave no stone unturned
work like a dog	proud as a peacock
pleased as punch	slower than molasses in January
a bolt from the blue	rich as Croesus
as healthy as a horse	out of harm's way
raise a red flag	dig one's own grave
get down to brass tacks	take the bull by the horns

It doesn't take long for expressions to become clichés. A case in point was the omnipresent phrase "information superhighway" (a widely quoted term referring to the Internet and the World Wide Web), which within a couple of years became overworked and wearisome as one writer after another described the Internet's on and off ramps, obstacles, potholes, speed limits (referring to censorship), crashes (meaning system breakdowns), and so forth.

Doublespeak

The word **doublespeak** was coined from the two words "doublethink" and "newspeak," words that George Orwell used in his novel *1984* to describe a future in which the government twists words to manipulate its citizens' thoughts. William D. Lutz, a member of Rutgers University's English department, for many years edited the *Quarterly Review of Doublespeak,* a periodical dedicated to publishing especially egregious examples of doublespeak. (Lutz is also the author of the Practice Essay at the end of Chapter 2.) Lutz has compared doublespeak to "an infection that sickens the language through the pollution of words carefully chosen." In the introduction to his newest book, *The New Doublespeak,* Lutz writes:

> Doublespeak is language that pretends to communicate but really doesn't. It is language that makes the bad seem good, the negative appear positive, the unpleasant appear attractive or at least tolerable. Doublespeak is language that avoids or shifts responsibility, language that is at variance with

its real or purported meaning. It is language that conceals or prevents thought; rather than extending thought, doublespeak limits it.

William Lutz, *The New Doublespeak*

Each year the review gives awards for conspicuous examples of language that is "grossly deceptive, evasive, euphemistic, confusing or self-contradictory" with the potential for "pernicious social or political consequences." Here is a brief list of some current examples of doublespeak, some of which Lutz cites in his book:

Doublespeak Terms Common during Corporate Downsizing in the 1990s:

Uninstalled
A refocusing of the company's skill set
Repositioning
Reducing duplication or *focused reduction*
Reshaping
Involuntary methodologies that result in *involuntary severance*

Doublespeak in Politics

Receipts proposals and *user fees* (President Bush's terms for proposed new taxes in 1991, after he had pledged "read my lips, no new taxes")
Reality augmentation (lying)
Contained depression (a recession)
Wood interdental stimulator (Pentagon doublespeak for a toothpick)
Acquiescent nonvolunteers (phrase used by British and Hong Kong officials for Vietnamese refugees forcibly returned to Vietnam)

Doublespeak in the Military

Predawn vertical insertion (a White House term, used during the Bush Administration, to refer to the invasion of Grenada by parachutists)
Ethnic cleansing (genocide as practiced in the former Yugoslavia)
Civilian irregular defense soldiers (mercenaries paid for by the U.S. government during the Vietnam "conflict")
Ambient noncombatant personnel (refugees fleeing the war)
Suppression of assets (bombing of both people and military targets during Operation Desert Storm)
Airborne sanitation (jamming enemy radio receivers)
Sanitizing an area (bombing)

Miscellaneous Examples of Doublespeak:

User friendly, space effective, flexible desk side sortation unit (a wastebasket)

Intuitively counterproductive (stupid)

Monitored retrievable storage site (a nuclear fuel dump)

Uncontrolled contact with the ground (a safety expert's term for an airplane crash)

Runway incursions (the FAA's term for planes and airport vehicles that stray off course and cause a hazard or a collision)

Water landing (United Airlines term for an airplane crash in the ocean)

Grain-consuming animal units (an agricultural spokesman's term for pigs and cows)

Vertical-transportation corps member (an elevator operator)

Therapeutic misadventure or *diagnostic malpractice of a high magnitude* (the medical profession's terms for medical incompetence that results in a patient's death)

Euphemisms

A **euphemism** is an inoffensive word or phrase substituted for one that might be construed as offensive. Writers use euphemisms to make less harsh our perception of unpleasant events, to change our beliefs, even to cover up wrongdoing. (As you can see from this definition, some euphemisms can also be classified as doublespeak.) Because euphemisms are so pervasive in our culture, you should learn to spot them readily and to recognize the intent behind them.

During World War II, Japanese-Americans living on the West Coast were forced to move to what the government called "relocation centers." However, Nazi Germans and the Soviets imprisoned Jews and other undesirables in "concentration camps," a term of disparagement used by the Allies. "Relocation centers" sounds less sinister than "concentration camps."

During the Vietnam era, euphemisms were widely used in government and military reports about the American presence in Southeast Asia. The 1970 American invasion of Cambodia was described in more positive terms as an "incursion." Herbicides (used to kill the foliage so North Vietnamese troop movements would be more visible from the air) were called "defoliants."

Another example of an attempt to use euphemisms to alter perceptions occurred in the trial of O. J. Simpson, the famous football player and actor, who was accused of killing his former wife, Nicole Brown Simpson and her friend, Ronald Goldman. Simpson's attorneys hoped to deflect the obvious damage references to his alleged wife-battering would have on the jury. They therefore tried to argue that the term "domestic discord" should replace the obviously more damaging "domestic violence" or "spousal abuse" and that the terms "battered wife" and "stalker" should be disallowed. Although Judge Lance Ito refused to "alter reality by altering language, some members of the media complied."[2]

Some euphemisms are more amusing than troubling. For example, at a trendy restaurant, toast is called "grilled peasant bread." A *Jeopardy!* contestant whose occupation is being a bookie called himself a "turf information specialist." The American Hair Loss Council prefers that toupés be called "hair systems." A marriage counselor calls herself a "gender reconciliation specialist."

One last example: A brochure for a memorial park[3] (itself a euphemism for cemetery) advertises its services with advertising copy:

> . . . it must be wise to protect yourself and your family AGAINST THE ONE EVENT THAT MOST CERTAINLY WILL HAPPEN. AND WHAT is the event? It is the same day—it is never a question of IF, only a question of WHEN . . . you will have a break in your family circle and as a result have to make hurried decisions for final arrangements, and we sincerely hope that the need is a remote one.

Aside from the obvious and absurd contradiction, wherein the advertising copywriter of this brochure describes death as both inevitable and remote, the concept of death is nearly absent, described euphemistically as "a break in your family circle."

There is no doubt that euphemisms can color our perception of reality. To illustrate, consider these alternative examples to so-called buzzwords that tour guides at Sea World in Orlando, Florida, must learn. They are reprinted from the park's training manual, excerpts of which appeared in the November 24, 1991, issue of *Florida,* the Sunday magazine of the *Orlando Sentinel* and subsequently were reprinted in *Harper's*.

> Certain words and phrases have negative connotations. At Sea World, we call these "buzzwords." Avoid buzzwords and use more positive words—you'll give guests a better overall impression.

Buzzword	***Alternative***
sick	ill
hurt	injured
captured	acquired

[2]Andrea Dworkin, "In Nicole Brown Simpson's Words," *Los Angeles Times,* January 29, 1995.
[3]Skylawn Memorial Park, San Mateo, California.

Buzzword	***Alternative***
cage	enclosure
tank	aquarium
captivity	controlled environment
wild	natural environment
tricks	behavior
sex	courtship behavior
Other Words to Avoid	
dead, die	If people ask you about a particular animal that you know has passed away, please say "I don't know."
kill	This word sounds very negative. Say "eat" or "prey upon."
play, talk, enjoy	Anthropomorphic; they give human traits to animals.
evolve	Because evolution is a controversial theory, use the word "adapt."

"Chickens of the Sea," *Harper's*

What is the effect of these alternative words and phrases?

Jargon

Jargon refers to the specialized language used by members of a particular trade, group, or profession. Jargon—like doublespeak and euphemisms—can be used to deceive, to make the writer or speaker sound more intelligent or learned than if he or she used ordinary discourse. In and of itself, jargon is not necessarily harmful, at least not in the same way as the other kinds of slanted language we have examined are. Most specialists in a field have their own special terminology that outsiders might not understand.

For example, while most of us associate the word *holiday* with a day at the beach or simply a day when we can sleep late, to a house painter, a holiday means a spot on the wall that his brush missed. Comic book artists use the term *ashcan* to refer to a few sample pages of the first version of a comic book—sort of like a partial prototype. Unsolicited manuscripts to publishing houses and proposals to corporations are referred to as having come in "over the transom."

These are inoffensive uses of jargon that the reader might be able to figure out from the context, but if not, the intention is not to hoodwink. At its best, jargon is useful, providing a verbal shorthand between people who are fluent in the terminology and the subject. At its worst, however, jargon is pretentious, obscure, and often incomprehensible. At the First International Conference of Love and Attraction, delegates came up with the following definition: "The cognitive-affective state characterized by intrusive and obsessive fantasizing concerning reciprocity of amorant feeling by the object of amorance." Translation: love.[4] Jargon is particularly rampant in academic circles, where college instructors, probably because of the "publish-or-perish" atmosphere, are compelled to make their mark in the academic world by delivering high-flown papers at meetings and writing articles and books in their fields.

Politically Correct Language

During the 1980s, the concept of "political correctness" (PC) emerged. Briefly, this doctrine holds that our everyday language is filled with expressions and words that offend or alienate certain groups or call into question their differences. Thus a whole new vocabulary of **politically correct language** has been adopted. Although many of these terms are considered jokes, others have been adopted by oversensitive people who dare not risk offending anyone or do not want to themselves be offended. In the summer of 1997, the National Federation of the Blind demanded that Walt Disney Company stop production on a film starring Leslie Nielsen scheduled to be released at Christmas. The film revives Mr. Magoo, the cartoon character from the 1950s and 1960s whose bad eyesight caused him to stumble around and bump into objects. Disney, bowing to the federation's pressure, went to great lengths to show that the new Mr. Magoo would be a "Forrest-Gump"-like character who has the "greater intuitive ability to see what's going on." Disney also announced that the new Mr. Magoo would not be blind, rather "visually limited."

R. Randy Lee, a lawyer and president of Leewood Real Estate Group on Staten Island, New York, discusses how politically correct language has affected housing advertisements. For example, let's say that a seller wants to advertise a house with "a beautiful ocean view, a spacious master bedroom, walk-in closets, and maid's quarters, and a downstairs family room." The house is located in a private community with shopping and a beach within walking distance.

If a builder or a seller describes the house like this, he or she might be liable for lawsuits because the description discriminates agaist potential buyers in six different ways. Here are the groups that might be offended by the above description: blind people (the house has an ocean view); women ("master bedroom" sounds sexist); the disabled (the

[4] *The 365 Stupidest Things Ever Said Calendar,* February 14, 1997.

house is within "walking" distance to desirable places); singles (the house has a "family room"); and minorities (the word *private* is sometimes used as a code word to keep minorities out of white communities)[5].

The article includes a list of "forbidden words" adopted by the Pennsylvania Association of Realtors, the Pennsylvania Newspaper Association, and the Pennsylvania Human Relations Commission. Here is a sampling of words that can no longer be used:

bachelor pad	landmark
senior citizen	executive buyer
newlyweds	traditional
young family	established

James Finn Garner's *Politically Correct Bedtime Stories* is a satirical collection of rewritten fairy stories. According to the dust jacket, many of these stories that were handed down from one generation to the next were "sexist, discriminatory, unfair, culturally biased, and in general, demeaning to witches, animals, goblins, and fairies everywhere. . . . We'd like to think that future generations of fairy-tale fans will see this as a worthy attempt to develop meaningful literature that is totally free from bias and purged from the influences of a flawed cultural past." Here is Garner's version of "The Three Little Pigs."

> **1**Once there were three little pigs who lived together in mutual respect and in harmony with their environment. Using materials that were indigenous to the area, they each built a beautiful house. One pig built a house of straw, one a house of sticks, and one a house of dung, clay, and creeper vines shaped into bricks and baked in a small kiln. When they were finished, the pigs were satisfied with their work and settled back to live in peace and self-determination.
>
> **2**But their idyll was soon shattered. One day, along came a big, bad wolf with expansionist ideas. He saw the pigs and grew very hungry, in both a physical and an ideological sense. When the pigs saw the wolf, they ran into the house of straw. The wolf ran up to the house and banged on the door, shouting, "Little pigs, little pigs, let me in!"
>
> **3**The pigs shouted back, "Your gunboat tactics hold no fear for pigs defending their homes and culture."

[5]R. Randy Lee, "Housing for the Non-Discriminating Buyer," The Wall Streeet Journal, November 3, 1994.

4But the wolf wasn't to be denied what he thought was his manifest destiny. So he huffed and puffed and blew down the house of straw. The frightened pigs ran to the house of sticks, with the wolf in hot pursuit. Where the house of straw had stood, other wolves bought up the land and started a banana plantation.

5At the house of sticks, the wolf again banged on the door and shouted, "Little pigs, little pigs, let me in!"

6The pigs shouted back, "Go to hell, you carnivorous, imperialistic oppressor!"

7At this, the wolf chuckled condescendingly. He thought to himself: "They are so childlike in their ways. It will be a shame to see them go, but progress cannot be stopped."

8So the wolf huffed and puffed and blew down the house of sticks. The pigs ran to the house of bricks, with the wolf close at their heels. Where the house of sticks had stood, other wolves built a time-share condo resort complex for vacationing wolves, with each unit a fiberglass reconstruction of the house of sticks, as well as native curio shops, snorkeling, and dolphin shows.

9At the house of bricks, the wolf again banged on the door and shouted, "Little pigs, little pigs, let me in!"

10This time in response, the pigs sang songs of solidarity and wrote letters of protest to the United Nations.

11By now the wolf was getting angry at the pigs' refusal to see the situation from the carnivore's point of view. So he huffed and puffed, and huffed and puffed, then grabbed his chest and fell over dead from a massive heart attack brought on from eating too many fatty foods.

12The three little pigs rejoiced that justice had triumphed and did a little dance around the corpse of the wolf. Their next step was to liberate their homeland. They gathered together a band of other pigs who had been forced off their lands. This new brigade of *porcinistas* attacked the resort complex with machine guns and rocket launchers and slaughtered the cruel wolf oppressors, sending a clear signal to the rest of the hemisphere not to meddle in their internal affairs. Then the pigs set up a model socialist democracy with free education, universal health care, and affordable housing for everyone.

[13]*Please note: The wolf in this story was a metaphorical construct. No actual wolves were harmed in the writing of the story.*

James Finn Garner, "The Three Little Pigs," *Politically Correct Bedtime Stories*

Sneer Words

As we saw in the section on euphemisms, a writer can shape our perception of events, making things seem less bad than they actually are. Similarly, a writer can intensify an already bad situation by using **sneer words,** words with strong negative connotations suggesting derision and scorn. When a foreign political leader is out of favor with the American government, he may be described by administration sources as a "strongman." This is the way Slobodan Milosevic, president of Yugoslavia has routinely been characterized in the American media. Oddly, Saddam Hussein of Iraq is generally accorded more respect, being called "president" or "leader," even though his stronghold on Iraq is every bit as ruthless as Milosevic's has been. This sneer word suggests something far more negative than would the more neutral terms "leader" or "president."

Those who view environmentalists as sentimental idealists often call them "tree-huggers," while for their part environmentalists retaliate, using the sneering phrase "toad-stabbers" to describe farmers and corporate executives who are opposed to environmental concerns. During the 1996 presidential campaign, Robert Dole, the Republican nominee, well understood the power of symbols. To remind voters that Albert Gore is a "tree-hugger" interested in environmental issues, Dole's campaign manager hired volunteers to dress up as trees (they were called "Gore trees") to appear at Republican rallies.[6] Here are some other common sneer words:

> *Lackey:* Not only means "servant" but also a fawning, servile follower who does anything the master dictates.

[6]Michael Kelly, "Running Ohio," *The New Yorker,* October 21 and 28, 1996.

Hack: Refers to someone who produces mediocre work and whose motive is to make money.

Do-gooder: This noun denotes someone who naively or unrealistically tries to make the world a better place.

Zealot (as in religious zealot, pro-life zealot): Suggests a fanatic, someone who will stop at nothing to promote his or her ideas.

Self-styled, self-proclaimed, purported (e.g., self-styled leader, self-proclaimed expert, purported authority): Like "so-called," these sneer word labels suggest that their status or reputation is not deserved and has only been conferred by the people themselves.

FIGURATIVE LANGUAGE

Finally, we come to the most difficult, yet the most inventive and interesting use of language: **A figure of speech** or **figurative language** refers to the use of language not in its literal sense, but in a metaphorical or imaginative way. Although you may associate figures of speech primarily with poetry, many prose writers also employ them as well for a variety of reasons: (1) to give immediacy or drama to their writing; (2) to show a striking visual image in the mind's eye; (3) to clarify a philosophical idea; or (4) to show an entirely new way of looking at an otherwise commonplace idea.

Metaphors and Similes

The two most common figures of speech are **metaphors** and **similes.** Both are characterized by imaginative comparisons between two essentially unlike things. The last point is important. The sentence "My house looks like your house" is not figurative; since houses are in the same class, there is no imaginative comparison. A good definition of metaphor can be found in the charming and poignant film, *Il Postino (The Postman).* The main character, a semiliterate postman, wants to write a love poem to Beatrice, the object of his affections. He asks the great Chilean poet, Pablo Neruda, how to go about writing such a thing, and Neruda tells him that a good love poem must have lots of metaphors. Neruda defines a metaphor like this: It is "a way of describing something by comparing it to something else."

A **metaphor** refers to a *direct* comparison, in which a particular quality or characteristic of one thing (the figurative) is transferred to another (the literal). Literally, such transfer of meaning does not make sense, but the reader knows to interpret it as an imaginative comparison. For example, consider this sentence:

> The farmer's leathery, lined face revealed years of toil in the sun.

The writer is directly comparing the farmer's skin to leather (in other words, transferring directly the characteristics of leather to skin), suggesting that the man's skin is browned, thick, and tough.

A **simile,** in contrast, is an imaginative comparison stated indirectly, usually with the words "like," " as," "as though," "as if," or occasionally "seem." If the writer instead used a simile and changed the metaphor "leathery," it would be stated like this:

> The farmer's lined face looked like leather, revealing years of toil in the sun.

It is probably fair to say that metaphors are stronger than similes, if only because the two things—literal and metaphorical—are joined without the reader's being *told* that they are similar as they are with similes. Let us examine a few figures of speech in detail before you analyze some on your own. We will begin with similes. In the first, from the novel *The Kitchen God's Wife* by Amy Tan, the narrator of the novel is describing her mother's house:

> The front of her place is Day-Glo pink, the unfortunate result of her being talked into a special deal by a longtime customer, a painting contractor. And because the outside is bumpy stucco, the whole effect looks like Pepto-Bismol poured over cottage cheese.

To analyze any figure of speech, you first must know what is being compared to what. In this case, the garish pink color of the narrator's house is being compared to the color of Pepto-Bismol, and the bumpy surface texture of the exterior stucco is compared to the texture of cottage cheese. This amusing simile presents a striking visual image.

Jeff Phillips, the author of the next example, frequently visits the Hawaiian Islands. In an article describing the four best beaches in Hawaii, he writes about an incident that occurred during an early morning swim at Kamaole Beach Park in Maui:

> That particular March dawn was calm, and as I churned along watching fish cruise the sandy bottom through my mask, I suddenly heard the faint strains of what sounded like a wildly wavering French horn. Somewhere out in the deep blue, a lone humpback whale was pouring his song into the deep.
>
> Jeff Phillips, "Hawaii's Best Beaches," *Sunset Magazine*

Phillips compares the sounds a humpback whale makes to those of a French horn. But why a French horn? Why not any brass instrument?

Phillips' choice is not accidental, since he is comparing sounds that are apt to be unfamiliar to something familiar. A French horn has a deep mellow tone—not as deep as a tuba's, but not as high-pitched as a trumpet's; the simile allows us to hear the whale's song in our heads. The modifying phrase, "wildly wavering," completes the description: The whale's song is composed in deep notes that go up and down erratically.

Now let us examine two metaphors. The first is from Gabriel García Marquez's novel *Love in the Time of Cholera:*

> The death of his mother left Florentino Ariza condemned once again to his maniacal pursuits: the office, his meetings in strict rotation with his regular mistresses, the domino games at the Commercial Club, the same books of love, the Sunday visits to the cemetery. It was the rust of routine, which he had despised and feared so much, but which had protected him from an awareness of age.

We see first the catalog of Ariza's humdrum weekly activities; then García Marquez ingeniously connects his routine to "rust." The pairing is brilliant. Rust or corrosion usually results from disuse or neglect, but in this case it results in Ariza's "rusting away," doing the same thing week after week. (A similar meaning occurs in the figurative phrase "Rust Belt," often used to describe some areas of northern states like Michigan, Ohio, and Pennsylvania, whose cities are burdened with aging factories and plants that would cost too much to modernize. When they close down for good, the result of industrial obsolescence, the community experiences severe economic hardship, or a kind of social corrosion.)

Here is another metaphor by travel writer and novelist, Pico Iyer. In it, he uses metaphors to explain in a fresh and inventive way what punctuation marks signal to the reader.

> Punctuation marks are the road signs placed along the highway of our communication—to control speed, provide directions and prevent head-on collisions. A period has the unblinking finality of a red light; the comma is a flashing yellow light that asks us only to slow down; and the semicolon is a stop sign that tell us to ease gradually to a halt, before gradually starting up again.
>
> Pico Iyer, "In Praise of the Humble Comma," *Time*

This passage begins with a general metaphor, in which punctuation marks are compared to the more familiar road signs. Iyer then extends the metaphor by classifying three common (and often confused) marks of punctuation. The overall effect is both whimsical and instructive.

Not all figures of speech are used for visual images or for clarification. Some writers simply like to play with language, relishing the chance to show off or to dazzle the reader with ingenious comparisons. One writer who often indulges in bizarre and daring figures of speech is T. Coraghessan Boyle. His story "Beat," included in a collection titled *Without a Hero,* tells of a teenager who embarks on a fictional journey to meet Jack Kerouac, writer of the 1960s cult novel, *On the Road.* The narrator runs away from his home in California and travels to New York, locates Kerouac's house, and finally musters enough courage to knock on the front door. Here is his description of the woman who answers, supposedly Kerouac's mother:

> My first surprise was in store. It wasn't Jack who answered the door but a big blocky old lady with a face like the bottom of a hiking boot. She was wearing a dress the size of something you'd drape over a car to keep the dust off it. . . . She gave me the kind of look that could peel the tread off a recapped tire.

Taken together, what impression of Kerouac's fictional mother do these figures of speech suggest?

The similarity between figurative language and analogies has probably occurred to you. As you may recall from Chapter 4, an analogy begins with a metaphor or simile, an imaginative comparison, but the analogy is *extended,* usually taking up a few sentences. The following excerpt from Jerry Seinfeld's book *SeinLanguage* illustrates how a figure of speech, in this case a simile, becomes a full-fledged analogy.

> Let's face it, the human body is like a condominium apartment. The thing that keeps you from really enjoying it is the maintenance. There's a tremendous amount of daily, weekly, monthly, and yearly work that has to be done. From showering to open heart surgery, we're always doing something to ourselves. If your body was a used car, you wouldn't buy it. You'd go, "Nah, I've heard about these human being bodies. This is one of those Earth models, right? Yeah, a cousin of mine had one. Too much work to keep them going. The new ones are nice looking, though."
>
> Jerry Seinfeld, *SeinLanguage*

Other Kinds of Figurative Language

Metaphors and similes are the most common figures of speech; however, it is worth noting three other kinds of figurative language. One is **metonymy,** a figure of speech in which a term closely associated with the metaphor substitutes for the thing itself. In 1996 anti-smoking advocates failed to convince a judge to allow them to file a huge class action lawsuit on behalf of millions of smokers against the nation's tobacco companies. The newspaper headline for this article was "Tobacco Industry Dodges Another Bullet." (*San Francisco Chronicle,* May 24, 1996) This is metonymy because the word "bullet" substitutes or stands for firing squad.

Next is **oxymoron,** a figure of speech in which the writer deliberately joins two contradictory terms, from the Greek: *oxus* ("sharp") + *moros* ("foolish"). Here is Helen Keller's description of her life before Anne Sullivan Macy came to teach her. Locate the two oxymorons and write them in the spaces.

> Have you ever been at sea in a dense fog, when it seemed as if a tangible white darkness shut you in, and the great ship, tense and anxious, groped her way toward the shore with plummet and sounding-line, and you waited with beating heart for something to happen? I was like that ship before my education began, only I was without compass or sounding-line, and had no way of knowing how near the harbour was. "Light! give me light!" was the wordless cry of my soul. . . .
>
> Helen Keller, *The Story of My Life*

__________________________ __________________________

Last is **personification,** in which inanimate or nonhuman objects—for example, objects, animals, plants, or concepts—are given human attributes, feelings, or ideas. Here are two:

- Just then they heard a faraway rumble: Thunder dragging its furniture. (Joao Guimaraes Rosa, "The Aldacious Navigator," *The Third Bank of the River*)
- Galaxies are gregarious: They tend to huddle together in clusters and superclusters. Our own Milky Way, for instance, has two dozen or so neighbors in a region of space just three million light-years across. ("Filling the Void," *Discover*)

ALLUSION

A writer uses allusions because past associations suggest a new interpretation of things in the present. As Richard D. Altick writes in *Preface to Critical Reading,* "Understanding allusions . . . is simply one way of bringing the memorable ideas of the past to illuminate what we think and say today." An **allusion** is a pointed and meaningful reference to something outside the text. The reference may be from any outside source, but these are the most common:

- The Bible or other religious texts.
- History.
- Literature.
- Greek, Roman, or other mythology.
- Music.

Indeed, although allusions can come from any discipline, they generally come from works or events that educated readers are familiar with.

The reader who misses the associations that an allusion provides misses out not only on the literal content but on the connotative effect as well. The ability to recognize allusions immediately—without turning to reference books, like the dictionary—takes years to develop. It is possible through wide reading and exposure to our cultural tradition. (In the meantime, however, ask your instructor to explain allusions that you do not recognize in your reading or use reference books to help you. Lower-division college students can hardly be expected to be as well grounded in cultural information as older adults are.)

Here is an example of an allusion, whose meaning can be found in any good unabridged dictionary. Here, Joseph Epstein, former editor of *The American Scholar* who writes under the pseudonym "Aristides," humorously explains the trepidation he feels when his students evaluate his teaching performance. (The entire essay from which this paragraph is taken is reprinted at the end of Part IV.)

> Socrates may have had to take the hemlock, but at least he was spared the indignity of that relatively recent addition to the teaching transaction known as "teacher evaluation." On these evaluations, generally made during the last minutes of the final session of the college term, students, in effect, grade their teachers. Hemlock may on occasion seem preferable, for turnabout here can sometimes be cruel play, especially when students, under the veil of anonymity, take the opportunity of evaluation to comment upon their teacher's dress, or idiosyncrasies, or moral character. For the most part I have not fared too badly on these evaluations, though my clothes have been the subject of faint comedy, my habit of jiggling the change in my pockets and my wretched handwriting have been noted, and in one instance I have been accused of showing favoritism (a charge I choose to interpret as my preference, in the classroom, for calling upon the relatively intelligent over the completely obtuse). None of these student

comments, as you can plainly see, affects me in the least; such personal criticisms roll right off me, like buckshot off a duck's heart.

"Aristides" (Joseph Epstein), "Student Evaluations," *The American Scholar*

The allusion in the first sentence is to Socrates, the Athenian teacher and philosopher, who was forced to drink hemlock (a poison) for having corrupted Athenian youth with his teachings. Though Socrates' death was tragic, Aristides' allusion is meant to be playful. It provides an amusing backdrop to his remarks, as does his play on the cliché ("like water rolling off a duck's back") at the end of the paragraph. Can you explain what his last sentence means?

EXERCISES: PART 1—IDENTIFYING AND ANALYZING FIGURES OF SPEECH

Here are several short passages containing figurative language for you to analyze. Using a separate sheet of paper, decide first what kind of figure of speech the excerpt represents. If it is a metaphor or a simile, identify what is being compared to what. Finally, explain briefly the meaning of the figure of speech. (Note: Some of the examples may contain more than one figure of speech, and you may find an allusion or two.)

1. It was a late hour on a cold wind-bitten autumn day when I climbed a great hill spined like a dinosaur's back. (Loren Eiseley, "The Judgment of the Birds," *The Immense Journey*)
2. The band, the spectators, and the dancers were making the Roseland Ballroom feel like a rocking ship. (Malcolm X, *The Autobiography of Malcolm X*)
3. This description is of a river in India:

   The river itself made no sound, though it moved powerfully, eddying like a swarm of greasy snakes in the ravine. (Paul Theroux, *To the Ends of the Earth*)
4. The author is describing the Pacific Ocean at Santa Monica Beach:

   I went into the water. It was like stepping into the small tentacle tips of a monstrous octopus—even in four inches of water you could feel the urgent pull of the water racing out or the force of it boiling back in. (Peter Theroux, *Translating LA*)

5. . . . we watched some of the little brown forest skunks hunting among the roots of the trees around us. These little lizards always looked neat and shining, as though they had been cast in chocolate and had just that second stepped out of the mould, gleaming and immaculate. (Gerald Durrell, *A Zoo in My Luggage*)
6. Newspaper headline: "All-Natural Smokes for Health Nuts" (*The Wall Street Journal,* April 14, 1997.)
7. The author served in the Marine Corps in Vietnam.

   It was noon, without a breath of wind, and the sky seemed like a blazing aluminum lid clamped over the world. (Philip Caputo, *A Rumor of War)*
8. The persistent cloud cover, the almost constant patter of rain, are narcotic. They seem to seal Seattle inside a damp, cozy cocoon, muffling reality and beckoning residents to snuggle up with a good book and a cup of coffee or a glass of wine. (Mary Bruno, "Seattle Under Siege," *Lear's*)
9. Second terms far too often have been marred by scandals, and few reelected presidents have more buzzards circling than Bill Clinton. (David S. Broder, *The Washington Post*)
10. We have waited for more than 340 years for our constitutional and God-given rights. The nations of Asia and Africa are moving with jetlike speed toward gaining political independence, but we still creep at horse-and-buggy pace toward gaining a cup of coffee at a lunch counter. (Martin Luther King, Jr., "Letter from Birmingham Jail")
11. The author is describing central Beirut, scene of some of the heaviest fighting in Lebanon between the Christians and the Muslims from 1975–1980. Central Beirut has still not been rebuilt.

    . . . I was fascinated by the hole in the middle of Beirut. The pulsing central district, once filled with sculpted Ottoman facades and palm-fringed squares, has become an Everest of rubble. This was a no-man's-land and scene of some of the heaviest fighting. Bullet holes mark each surface like acne. (Geoffrey Barraclough, *The London Observer*)
12. The narrator is describing an early-morning reaction to her lover, whom she has decided to dump.

    And then, abruptly, she woke up beside him in her own bed one early spring morning and knew she loathed him and couldn't wait to get him out of the house. She felt guilty, but guilty in the way one feels guilty when about to discommode some clinging slug that has managed to attach itself to one's arm or leg. (Gail Godwin, "Amanuensis," *Mr. Bedford and the Muses*)

13. Parker's wife was sitting on the front porch floor, snapping beans. Parker was sitting on the step, some distance away, watching her sullenly. She was plain, plain. The skin on her face was thin and drawn as tight as the skin on an onion and her eyes were grey and sharp like the points of two toothpicks. (Flannery O'Connor, "Parker's Back")
14. Digna was the first in her house to get up and the last to go to bed. With the rooster's first crow she was already in the kitchen placing twigs on the still-warm coals from the night before. From the moment she began to boil the water for breakfast, she never sat down but was always busy with the children, the washing, the meals, the garden, the animals. Her days were all the same, like a rosary of identical beads shaping her existence. She did not know what rest was, and the only time she found relief was when she had a new baby. Her life was a chain of routines that varied only with the seasons. For her, there was nothing but work and weariness. (Isabel Allende, *Of Love and Shadows*)
15. . . . so few lies are solitary ones. It is easy, a wit observed, to tell a lie, but hard to tell only one. The first lie "must be thatched with another or it will rain through." More and more lies may come to be needed; the liar always has more mending to do. And the strains on him become greater each time—many have noted that it takes an excellent memory to keep one's untruths in good repair and disentangled. The sheer energy the liar has to devote to shoring them up is energy the honest man can dispose of freely. (Sissela Bok, *Lying: Moral Choice in Public and Private Life*)
16. Book title: *Freezer Burn.*
17. A Luddite World Wide Web site.
18. A long-limbed languorous type of showgirl blond lay at her ease in one of the chairs, with her feet raised on a padded rest and a tall misted glass at her elbow, near a silver ice bucket and a Scotch bottle. She looked at us lazily as we came over the grass. From thirty feet away she looked like a lot of class. From ten feet away, she looked like something made up to be seen from thirty feet away. Her mouth was too wide, her eyes were too blue, her makeup was too vivid, the thin arch of her eyebrows was almost fantastic in its curve and spread, and the mascara was so thick on her eyelashes that they looked like miniature iron railings.

    She wore white duck slacks, blue and white open-toed sandals over bare feet and crimson lake toenails, a white silk blouse and a necklace of green stones that were not square cut emeralds. Her hair was as artificial as a night club lobby. (Raymond Chandler, *The High Window*)
19. Some words keep their heads down, fingers in ears, waiting behind the tree for their impact, hoping always for the worst. RUMOR is an example. (Lewis Thomas, *Et Cetera, Et Cetera: Notes of a Word-Watcher*)
20. Editorial title: "The Toxic Saddam Hussein." (*The Washington Post,* November 24, 1997)

EXERCISES: PART 2

Selection 1

[1]The Mission was a small oasis in the heart of an expanse of voluptuous vegetation writhing and twisting from the banks of the river to the feet of the monumental geologic towers that rose toward the firmament like one of God's mistakes. [2]There time is bent and distances deceive the human eye, persuading the traveler to wander in circles. [3]The humid, heavy air smells of flowers, herbs, man's sweat, and animal breath. [4]The heat is oppressive, unalleviated by any breeze; the stones steam and blood boils in the veins. [5]At dusk the sky is filled with phosphorescent mosquitoes whose bites produce endless nightmares, and the still night air carries the distinct cries of birds, the chattering of monkeys, and the distant roar of the waterfalls born high in the mountains to crash far below like the thunder of warfare. [6]The modest mud-and-wattle Mission building, with its tower of woven stakes and a bell to toll for Mass, balanced, like all the huts, on piles driven into the mud of a river of opalescent waters whose banks evaporated in the reverberating light. [7]The dwellings seemed to drift amid silent canoes, garbage, carcasses of dogs and rats, and inexplicable white blossoms.

Isabel Allende, *Eva Luna*

A. *Vocabulary*

For each italicized word from the selection, choose the best definition according to the context in which it appears.

1. *voluptuous* [sentence 1]: (a) decaying, rotting; (b) carefully tended; (c) straggly, sparse; (d) sensually pleasing.
2. *writhing* [1]: (a) twisting, contorting; (b) growing; (c) dying; (d) producing flowers.
3. *monumental* [1]: (a) aesthetically pleasing; (b) traditional; (c) exceptionally large; (d) of no particular artistic merit.
4. *unalleviated* [4]: (a) made more bearable; (b) unexplainable; (c) disturbed; (d) unaffected by.
5. *opalescent* [6]: (a) clear, transparent; (b) having a milky iridescence; (c) jewel-like, sparkling; (d) rushing, torrential.
6. *reverberating* [6]: (a) shadowy; (b) receding, fading; (c) intensifying; (d) reflecting over and over.

B. *Content and Structure*

Complete the following questions.

1. The mode of discourse in the paragraph is (a) narration; (b) description; (c) exposition; (d) persuasion.

2. In your own words, state the dominant impression Allende gives the reader about the Mission and its immediate environment. ___________

____

3. In sentence 2, when Allende writes "distances deceive the human eye, persuading the traveler to wander in circles," she implies that (a) there are no distance markers for travelers to get their bearings; (b) the area is often visited by tourists; (c) the vegetation is so lush that one can easily lose one's way; (d) there are no paths through the vegetation for one to walk on.

C. *Language Analysis*

Complete the following questions.

1. In sentence 1 Allende describes the Mission as being "a small oasis." Is she using this term literally or figuratively? ___________________
2. The simile in sentence 1, in which Allende compares the geologic towers near the Mission to "one of God's mistakes," suggests that these towers (a) are taller than one would expect; (b) are misshapen; (c) are smaller than one would expect; (d) are crumbling and decaying.
3. The beginning of sentence 4 says, "The heat is oppressive, unalleviated by any breeze." This statement is (a) purely denotative; (b) connotative with positive overtones; (c) connotative with negative overtones; (d) an example of a cliché.
4. In sentence 4, Allende writes "the stones steam and blood boils in the veins." One of these details is literal, and one is figurative. Which is which?

   stones steam ___________ blood boils in the veins ___________

   Which idea in the paragraph are these details meant to reinforce?

   ____
5. On balance, do the details and figures of speech in this passage suggest a positive or a negative impression?___________________

   Explain. ____

Selection 2

[1]The ridge lunged upward like a dragon's spine bristling with fir and birch, and clouds were low and flying out from the mountains. [2]Snow from a late-winter storm balanced on boughs and logs. [3]When a riffle of wind stirred the branches, the snow drifted down in crystal veils that added a ghostlike radiance to the forest. [4]Bamboo grew in the understory, the crowded ranks of stems claiming the hillside so completely that the light beneath the bamboo's canopy

was a translucent undersea green. [5]The sunless scent of moss and moldering wood choked the gloom. [6]The bamboo was rigid with frost, and a dense silence hung over the ridge; there was no movement and seemingly no life.

[7]In the stillness, leaves suddenly rustled and a stem cracked like breaking glass. [8]Shrouded in bamboo was a giant panda, a female, slumped softly in the snow, her back propped against a shrub. [9]Leaning to one side, she reached out and hooked a bamboo stem with the ivory claws of a forepaw, bent in the stem, and with a fluid movement bit it off near the base. [10]Stem firmly grasped, she sniffed it to verify that it was indeed palatable, and then ate it end-first like a stalk of celery. [11]While her powerful molars sectioned and crushed the stem, she glanced around for another, her movements placid and skillful, a perfect ecological integration between panda and bamboo. [12]She ate within a circle of three feet, moved a few steps and ate some more, consuming only coarse stems and discarding the leafy tops; she then sat hunched, forepaws in her lap, drowsy and content. [13]Within a circle of three thousand feet was her universe, all that she needed: bamboo, a mate, a snug tree-den in which to bear young.

George B. Schaller, *The Last Panda*

A. *Vocabulary*

1. *translucent* [sentence 4]: (a) transparent; (b) permitting light to pass through; (c) deep, dark; (d) bright, garish.
2. *moldering* [5]: (a) burning; (b) snow-covered; (c) dense; (d) decaying, crumbling.
3. *palatable* [10]: (a) acceptable to one's taste; (b) of the correct species; (c) ripe, mature; (d) of the proper texture.
4. *placid* [11]: (a) efficient; (b) lazy; (c) purposeful; (d) peaceful.

B. *Content and Structure*

Answer the following questions.

1. The mode of discourse in the passage is (a) narration; (b) description; (c) exposition; (d) persuasion.
2. State the subject of the *first* paragraph. ______________________
   In your own words, explain the dominant impression conveyed in this paragraph.
   ____
3. State the subject of the *second* paragraph. ______________________
   In your own words, explain the dominant impression conveyed in this paragraph. ______________________________________

____

4. The pattern of organization in the *second* paragraph is (a) spatial; (b) inductive; (c) deductive; (d) variation of deductive.
5. The author makes the point in sentence 11 that the panda (a) is near extinction; (b) finds all her needs in the immediate environment; (c) eats bamboo only when there is no other food available; (d) is a solitary and shy animal.

C. *Language Analysis*

Complete the following questions.

1. Find two figures of speech in the first paragraph and state what is compared to what.

   ________________________ is compared to ________________________

   ________________________ is compared to ________________________
2. Are these figures of speech meant to convey visual images or to clarify philosophic concepts? ________________________
3. Look again at sentence 7, which contains a description and a simile intended to appeal to our sense of (a) touch; (b) taste; (c) hearing; (d) sight; (e) smell.
4. In the second paragraph the words "fluid," "powerful," "placid," "skillful," "drowsy," and "content" are (a) purely denotative; (b) connotative with positive overtones; (c) connotative with negative overtones; (d) examples of scientific jargon.

Selection 3

[1]The noses of a great many Canadians resemble Porky Pig's. This comes from spending so much time pressing them against the longest undefended one-way mirror in the world. The Canadians looking through this mirror behave the way people on the hidden side of such mirrors usually do: They observe, analyze, ponder, snoop and wonder what all the activity on the other side means in decipherable human terms.

[2]The Americans, bless their innocent little hearts, are rarely aware that they are even being watched, much less by the Canadians. They just go on doing body language, playing in the sandbox of the world, bashing one another on the head and planning how to blow things up, same as always. If they think about Canada at all, it's only when things get a bit snowy, or the water goes off, or the Canadians start fussing over some piddly detail, such as fish. Then they regard them as unpatriotic; for Americans don't really see Canadians as foreigners, not like the Mexicans, unless they do something weird like speak French or beat the New York Yankees at baseball. Really, think the Americans, the Canadians are just like us, or would be if they could.

3Or we could switch metaphors and call the border the longest undefended backyard fence in the world. The Canadians are the folks in the neat little bungalow with the tidy little garden and the duck pond. The Americans are the other folks, the ones in the sprawly mansion with the bad-taste statues on the lawn. There's a perpetual party, or something, going on there—loud music, raucous laughter, smoke billowing from the barbecue. Beer bottles and Coke cans land among the peonies. The Canadians have their own beer bottles and barbecue smoke, but they tend to overlook it. Your own mess is always more forgivable than the mess someone else makes on your patio.

4The Canadians can't exactly call the police—they suspect that the Americans are the police—and part of their distress, which seems permanent, comes from their uncertainty as to whether or not they've been invited. Sometimes they do drop by next door, and find it exciting but scary. Sometimes the Americans drop by their house and find it clean. This worries the Canadians. They worry a lot. Maybe that Americans want to buy up their duck pond, with all the money they seem to have, and turn it into a cesspool or a waterskiing emporium.

Margaret Atwood, "The View from the Backyard,"
The Nation

A. *Vocabulary*

For each italicized word from the selection, choose the best definition according to the context in which it appears.

1. *ponder* [paragraph 1]: (a) argue about; (b) criticize; (c) make estimates about; (d) consider carefully.
2. *snoop* [1]: (a) interrogate, question; (b) pry into others' affairs; (c) establish official surveillance posts; (d) admire unquestioningly.
3. *decipherable* [1]: Able to be (a) seen clearly; (b) interpreted accurately; (c) controlled; (d) judged fairly.
4. *piddly* [2—also piddling]: (a) necessary; (b) insignificant; (c) irrelevant; (d) incomprehensible.
5. *sprawly* [3—slang for *sprawling*]: (a) tasteful; (b) elegant; (c) spread out; (d) garish.
6. *raucous* [3]: (a) tinkling, musical; (b) bitter, scornful; (c) good-natured; (d) loud, harsh.
7. *distress* [4]: (a) anxiety; (b) unhappiness; (c) lack of concern; (d) lack of certainty.
8. *emporium* [4]: (a) educational exhibit; (b) business enterprise; (c) school; (d) vacation spot.

B. *Content and Structure*

Complete the following questions.

1. The mode of discourse in the passage is (a) narration; (b) description; (c) exposition; (d) persuasion.
2. In your own words, write a sentence stating Atwood's main idea.

____

____

3. When Atwood writes at the beginning of paragraph 2 in referring to Americans, "bless their innocent little hearts," she is being (a) honest; (b) scornful; (c) sarcastic; (d) hostile; (e) laudatory.
4. From what Atwood implies in paragraph 2, explain what Americans think about Canadians. _______________

____

5. From the information in paragraph 4, why specifically do Canadians "worry a lot" about their southern neighbors?

____

6. What are the broader implications of Atwood's passage? What is the central inference you can make about the relationship between Canada and the United States? _______________

____

C. *Language Analysis*

Answer the following questions.

1. Paragraph 1 contains two metaphors. Why do Canadians' noses resemble Porky Pig's? _______________
   What does Atwood mean when she refers to the border between Canada and the United States as a "one-way mirror"? What does this say about Canadians? about Americans? _______________

____

____

2. Atwood says in paragraph 2 that Americans go on "playing in the sandbox of the world, bashing one another on the head and planning how to blow things up, same as always." What, literally, does the sandbox metaphor refer to? _______________

Explain what the metaphor means. ______________________

____

From this metaphor, how would you describe Canadians' attitude toward Americans? ______________________

3. In paragraph 3 Atwood switches metaphors, comparing the border between Canada and the United States to "the longest undefended backyard fence in the world." In your own words, explain Atwood's thinking about how these neighboring nations get along. Specifically, try to determine what she means when she refers to the Canadians' "neat little bungalow," the Americans' "sprawly mansion," and the "perpetual party" with the "raucous laughter" and beer bottles and Coke cans thrown in the peonies. ______________________

____

4. In paragraph 4, what is the literal meaning of this excerpt? "Sometimes they do drop by next door, and find it exciting but scary. Sometimes the Americans drop by their house and find it clean."

____

____

5. The last sentence employs *hyperbole,* deliberate exaggeration for effect. Underneath the humor, what does this sentence say about Canadians' real concerns about their southern neighbors?

____

____

PRACTICE ESSAY

On Leavened Bread

Salman Rushdie

Salman Rushdie is a contemporary writer who was born in India. He is best known for his controversial novel, The Satanic Verses, *a book whose 1988 publication was bitterly attacked by Muslims because he committed blasphemy (a character was modeled on the Prophet Mohammed). Iran's Ayatollah Khomeini issued a death threat against Rushdie, which has forced him to live in virtual hiding for many years. He now divides his time between England and America and still lives a circumspect life out of the public eye. This personal essay first appeared in* The New Yorker. *(The leavened bread mentioned in the title refers to bread that is made to rise by adding a leavening agent like yeast, in contrast to Indian breads which are flat.)*

1 There was leavened bread in Bombay, but it was sorry fare: dry, crumbling, tasteless—unleavened bread's paler, unluckier relative. It wasn't "real." Real bread was the chapati, or phulka, served piping hot; the tandoori nan, and its sweeter Frontier variant, the Peshawari nan; and, for luxury, the feshmi roti, the shirmal, the paratha.[1] Compared with these aristocrats, the leavened white loaves of my childhood seemed to merit the description that Shaw's immortal dustman, Alfred Doolittle, dreamed up for people like himself: they were, in truth, "the undeserving poor."[2]

2 My first inkling that there might be more to leavened bread than I knew came while I was visiting Karachi, Pakistan, where I learned that a hidden order of nuns, in a place known as the Monastery of the Angels, baked a mean loaf. To buy it, you had to get up at dawn—that is, a servant had to get up at dawn—and stand in line outside a small hatch in the monastery's wall. The nuns' baking facilities were limited, the daily run was small, and this secret bakery's reputation was high. Only the early bird caught the loaf. The hatch would open, and a nun would hand the bread out to the waiting populace. Loaves were strictly rationed. No bulk buying was permitted. And the price, of course, was high. (All this I knew only by hearsay, for I never got up at such an unearthly hour to see for myself.)

3 The nuns' bread—white, crusty, full of flavor—was a small revelation, but it was also, on account of its unusual provenance, eccentric. It came from beyond the frontiers of the everyday, a mystery trailing an anecdote behind it. It was almost—well, fictional. (Later, it became fictional, when I put the monastery in my novel "Midnight's Children.") Now, in the matter of bread such extraordinariness is not good. You want bread to be a part of daily life. You want it to be ordinary. You want it to be there. You don't want to get up in the middle of the night and wait by a hatch in a wall. So, while the Angels' bread was tasty, it felt like an aberration, a break in the natural order. It didn't really change my mind.

4 Then, aged thirteen and a half, I flew to England. And, suddenly, there it was, in every shopwindow. The White Crusty, the Sliced and the Unsliced. The Small Tin, the Large Tin, the Bloomer. The abandoned, plentiful promiscuity of it. The soft, pillowy mattressiness of it.

[1]The breads listed here are varieties of traditional Indian flat breads which are unleavened, meaning that because they contain no yeast, they do not rise.

[2]Rushdie is referring to the play *Pygmalion* by George Bernard Shaw, which was later made into the Broadway musical and film, *My Fair Lady.* It concerns Eliza Doolittle, a flower stall clerk, and Henry Higgins's attempts to rid her of her Cockney accent. Alfred Doolittle, mentioned here, is Eliza's father. A dustman in England is a garbage collector.

The well-sprung bounciness of it between your teeth. Hard crust and soft center: the sensuality of that perfect textural contrast. I was done for. In the whorehouses of the bakeries, I was serially, gluttonously, irredeemably unfaithful to all those chapatis next door, waiting for me back home. East was East, but yeast was West.

5 This, remember was long before British bread counters were enlivened by the European invasion, long before ciabatta and brioche; this was 1961. But the love affair that began then has never lost its intensity; the new exotic breads have served only to renew the excitement.

6 I should add that there was a second discovery, almost as thrilling; that is, water. The water back home was dangerous and had to be thoroughly boiled. To be able to drink water from the tap was a privilege indeed. I have never forgotten that when I first arrived in these immeasurably wealthy and powerful lands I found the first proofs of my good fortune in loaf and glass. Since that time, a regime of bread and water has never sounded like a hardship to me.

A. *Comprehension*

Choose the answer that best completes each statement. Do not refer to the selection while doing this exercise.

1. The leavened bread that Rushdie remembers from his childhood in Bombay was (a) of excellent quality; (b) of very poor quality; (c) made only by aristocrats; (d) made by nuns.
2. Rushdie found the bread baked at the Monastery of the Angels in Karachi "eccentric" because of its (a) unusual origin; (b) resemblance to the traditional Indian breads of his youth; (c) strange color and flavor; (d) weird shape and texture.
3. According to the author, bread should be (a) made only at home; (b) served with every meal; (c) ordinary and easily available; (d) difficult to come by and therefore more desirable.
4. The author characterizes the white leavened bread he encountered in England as almost (a) miraculous; (b) seductive; (c) mysterious; (d) addictive.
5. The safe water in England was, to Rushdie, another indication of England's (a) immense influence in the colonial world; (b) immeasurable wealth and power; (c) concern with the environment; (d) advanced technology.

B. *Structure*

Answer the following questions.

1. Which *two* modes of discourse are represented in this essay?

   ______________________ and ______________________

2. The author's purpose is, specifically, (a) to explain the differences between Indian unleavened bread and Western leavened bread; (b) to classify types of bread; (c) to explore his various pleasurable sensory discoveries of different kinds of bread; (d) to convince us that leavened breads are superior to unleavened varieties.
3. In paragraph 1, why does author include Alfred Doolittle's quotation, "the undeserving poor," referring to poor people? What does Rushdie use the phrase to refer to? ______________________
4. Rushdie strongly implies in paragraph 2 that (a) the Monastery of the Angels' bread was a very well kept secret; (b) Rushdie's family was sufficiently rich that they could afford to send a servant to buy the monastery's bread rather than to go themselves; (c) the monastery's white bread was superior to the bread which he discovered later in England; (d) the nuns were probably English.
5. Look again at paragraph 6. The transitional phrase, "that is," in the first sentence means (a) so to speak; (b) in contrast; (c) in other words; (d) in conclusion.

C. *Language Analysis*

1. In paragraph 1 Rushdie uses two metaphors to contrast the white unleavened bread of Bombay and the "real" Indian breads like chapati, nan, and paratha. White leavened breads are imaginatively compared to ______________________, while traditional Indian breads are imaginatively compared to ______________________.
2. In paragraph 1, Rushdie describes leavened bread from his childhood as "dry, crumbling, tasteless," and the monastery bread he ate in Karachi as "white, crusty, full of flavor." These phrases are (a) denotative; (b) connotative; (c) ironic; (d) examples of bakers' jargon; (e) euphemisms.
3. In your own words, explain the metaphors in this sentence from paragraph 3: "It came from beyond the frontiers of the everyday, a mystery trailing an anecdote behind it." ______________________

____
4. At the beginning of paragraph 4, why does Rushdie capitalize the varieties of white bread? ______________________
5. At the heart of the essay, in paragraph 4, what does Rushdie imaginatively compare the English variety of white bread to? ______________________

____

____

Locate and identify the details in the paragraph that bear out this comparison.____________________

6. Rushdie apparently enjoys playing with language. Look through the essay and find two sayings that he has rewritten as clever and humorous puns. ____________________

____

7. Toward the end of paragraph 6, Rushdie writes, "I found the first proofs of my good fortune in loaf and glass." "Loaf and glass" are examples of (a) similes; (b) metaphors; (c) metonymy; (d) oxymorons; (e) personification.
8. The emotional expression that this essay conveys is (a) playful, amusing; (b) nostalgic, melancholy; (c) earnest, serious; (d) philosophic, questioning.

D. *Vocabulary*

For each italicized word from the selection, choose the best definition according to the context in which it appears.

1. it was *sorry fare* [paragraph 1]: (a) dry and unpleasant to taste; (b) shaped like a disk; (c) light and airy; (d) poor food.
2. nuns . . . baked a *mean* loaf [2]: Here, slang for (a) world-famous; (b) nasty; (c) excellent; (d) undiscovered.
3. its unusual *provenance* [3]: (a) composition; (b) reputation; (c) appearance; (d) place of origin.
4. it felt like an *aberration* [3]: (a) deviation from the normal; (b) something unexpected and surprising; (c) something associated with guilty pleasure; (d) a betrayal.
5. the abandoned, plentiful *promiscuity* [4]: Here, used ironically and humorously to mean (a) indiscriminately present everywhere; (b) infidelity; (c) low cost; (d) lack of moral standards.
6. *irredeemably* unfaithful [4]: Describing one who is (a) lacking in self-restraint; (b) overcome by remorse; (c) capable of improvement; (d) impossible to reform.

E. *Questions for Analysis and Discussion*

1. Examine a food that, as bread does for Salman Rushdie, reveals something more profound about the culture that produces it.
2. Explore the concept of food as a trigger for memory. What foods serve this function for you?

7

Tone

In this last chapter of Part II we examine how a writer's words—whether denotative or connotative—contribute to the tone of a piece of writing. In addition, this chapter will introduce you to the subtleties of some of the more sophisticated kinds of tone: irony, wit, sarcasm, satire, and cynicism. The chapter ends with a brief discussion of special effects and allusions.

AN EXPLANATION OF TONE

Some of the exercises in the preceding chapters have asked you to identify the tone of a passage, so the term should not be completely unfamiliar. **Tone** refers to the feeling, mood, or emotional quality of a piece of writing. In technical and scientific prose, the author's tone is usually objective and impartial, as befits the purpose—to convey information. It is not used to convince us to accept a controversial opinion, to arouse our emotions, to describe a scene, and so forth. The content is factual, and the tone corresponds to it. Newspaper articles (but not editorials) are usually written in an objective manner, since their purpose is to convey the news—factual information— rather than to provide a subjective viewpoint.

But in all other kinds of writing, whether fiction or nonfiction, the writer's tone can reflect any emotional feeling or mood, as you can see from the adjectives in the following box. Be aware that these are only some examples. Like the emotions of the complex beings we humans are, tone runs the gamut. (If you are unsure of the meanings of some of these descriptive words, check an unabridged dictionary. Sometimes readers have difficulty articulating the tone of a passage because they lack the vocabulary to express the emotion it embodies.) For convenience and ease of learning, I have grouped them into broad categories.

Informative, impartial, objective, unemotional
Admiring, laudatory
Modest, unassuming, humble
Earnest, sincere
Solemn, dignified
Serious, grave
Frank, honest, straightforward, candid
Pensive, thoughtful
Philosophical, reflective
Concerned, worried
Critical, fault-finding, disparaging
Confused, befuddled
Naive, impressionable
Callous, hard-hearted, world-weary
Disheartened, dejected
Lamenting, mourning, sorrowful
Whining, aggrieved, complaining
Witty, humorous, ironic
Ironic, sarcastic
Cynical, skeptical, pessimistic
Nasty, mean-spirited, abusive
Sarcastic, scornful, biting, caustic
Bitter, angry, resentful, hostile

In conversation, a speaker's tone is readily apparent because the listener can also use gestures, tone of voice, vocal pitch (the rise and fall of the voice), and facial expression, in addition to the actual words spoken. We do not even need to see the person's face or gestures because tone of voice can reveal much of the speaker's attitude.

But in print we have only the black print on the white page, and so we must infer tone from the writer's choice of words and their connotative values, from the details the writer has chosen to include, occasionally from the sentence structure, as you will see later, and from the writer's purpose. The reader's task is to recreate the "sounds" of the sentences as the writer intended you to hear them. Because complete objectivity, even in expository prose, is nearly impossible for a writer to achieve (assuming it were desirable), the careful reader must be alert to the subtle nuances that contribute to a reading's emotional mood or feeling.

Recreating the feelings the printed words are meant to arouse—as indeed with any other reading skill—requires studying several examples. The remainder of this chapter gives you numerous short passages to practice with. In the initial passages, the tone is distinctive and clearly evident. As you read each one, first identify the main idea, the mode of discourse, and the purpose—a good review of the early chapters in this book. Then locate and underline words with particular connotative value. See if you can figure out how all of these elements show the writer's tone.

In the first example, Harvard biologist Edwin O. Wilson discusses the contributions of indigenous people to the world's crops.

> From the mostly unwritten archives of native peoples has come a wealth of information about wild and semicultivated crops. It is a remarkable fact that with a single exception, the macadamia nut of Australia, every one of the fruits and nuts used in western countries was grown first by indigenous peoples. The Incas were arguably the all-time champions in creating a reservoir of diverse crops. Without the benefit of wheels, money, iron, or written script, these Andean people evolved a sophisticated agriculture based on almost as many plant species as used by all the farmers of Europe and Asia combined. Their abounding crops, tilled on the cool upland slopes and plateaus, proved especially suited for temperate climates. From the Incas have come lima beans, peppers, potatoes, and tomatoes. But many other species and strains, including a hundred varieties of potatoes, are still confined to the Andes. The Spanish conquerors learned to use a few of the potatoes, but they missed many other representatives of a vast array of cultivated tuberous vegetables, including some that are more productive and savory than the favored crops. The names are likely to be unfamiliar: achira, ahipa, arracacha, maca, mashua, mauka, oca, ulloco, and yacon. One, maca, is on the verge of extinction, limited to 10 hectares in the highest plateau region of Peru and Bolivia. Its swollen roots, resembling brown radishes and rich in sugar and starch, have a sweet, tangy flavor and are considered a delicacy by the handful of people still privileged to consume them.
>
> Edwin O. Wilson, *The Diversity of Life*

The purpose is clearly expository, but the tone is more admiring and laudatory than strictly objective. Did you underline these phrases with a positive connotation?— "a wealth of information," "a remarkable fact," "the all-time champions," "a sophisticated agriculture," and "their abounding crops." Besides word choice, the impressive list of foods he provides further reveals admiration, especially since these foods were grown "without the benefit of wheels, money, iron, or written script," all inventions that seem like essential prerequisites for agriculture.

The second passage is an example of a eulogy, a short writing published after a person's death. It was written a few days after the death of Jerry Garcia, leader of the Grateful Dead, in August 1995. As you did earlier, locate and underline any words and phrases that help contribute to the tone of the piece.

> As word of the death of Jerry Garcia spread last Wednesday, via news reports and phone calls and E-mail, the scale of the reaction and the depth of the response quickly surpassed what anyone might have expected. It was suddenly obvious that Garcia had become, against all odds, an American icon: by Thursday morning, the avuncular old reprobate had smuggled his way onto the front pages of newspapers around the world. That his battered, ruined body had finally given out was somehow less surprising than the abrupt recognition of how much he had meant to so many. He was eulogized as a rock star and as a guitar god, of course; he was praised as a businessman who marketed his mystique both shrewdly and generously; and, in the obituaries that recounted the intermittent struggles with addiction that preceded his demise, at the age of fifty-three, in a Marin County drug-rehabilitation center, he was inevitably, and with some justice, pronounced a casualty of drug abuse. But Jerry Garcia was a more graceful and complicated figure than those categories can encompass: he transcended show business, and it's impossible, even now, to think of him as a victim or a sad case. The choices he made in life, whatever their ultimate cost to him, command respect. He was a lyrical hipster, an outlaw with a sense of humor, a fount of profound pleasure for tens of millions of people.
>
> Hal Espen, "American Beauty," *The New Yorker*

Jerry Garcia's many contributions to music receive the emphasis, not his personal failings. He is described with fondness and reverence. The tone is respectful, admiring, and affectionate.

In contrast, study these opening paragraphs from a newspaper story written by sportswriter Bruce Jenkins, whose subject is the 1994 strike by baseball players against team owners, which resulted in the World Series being canceled for the first time in baseball history.

> **1**The game of baseball is too strong to die. It will survive on the fields of American youth and in the dreams of anyone who fancies hitting that ball over the fence. But the "national pastime" was put to rest yesterday, extinguished by a group of men who didn't seem to notice.

> [2]Our romance with the game had already been in peril, soured by greed and arrogance and a labor crisis too senseless to understand. But now there is no World Series, and the breakup will be easy. Even for those willing to maintain a friendship, things will never be quite the same.
>
> [3]Major league baseball is a blackened wasteland now, still simmering from the fires that killed it. The ballparks are empty, the fans don't care, and the executors of this disaster are left to ponder what they've done. Incredibly, they have no idea. They've been too busy hating each other. Save the game? Never came into play. Stubbornness, name-calling and pure hatred felt so much better.
>
> Bruce Jenkins, "Dark Day—Our Pastime in Ruins," *San Francisco Chronicle*

In the space provided, write the connotative words and phrases that indicate Jenkins's tone. ______________________________

The author's tone in this excerpt is more difficult to analyze than those we have seen in earlier passages. He is angry, sad, and accusatory—a mix of complex emotions as befits a complex situation. Using a metaphor—the public's love affair with baseball—Jenkins plainly states that the owners' and players' greed and arrogance ruined the romance. (Indeed, baseball attendance figures three years later as I am writing this still have not reached their pre-1994 strike levels.)

Notice that in this excerpt, the opening paragraphs of a newspaper article, the writer achieves a breezy, informal tone. After you read it, underline the phrases and sentences that contribute to this tone.

> [1]Evil lurks in many insidious forms. I am staring at one form right now, this TV-like machine with the soothing blue screen perched atop a box that looks like a mutant VCR.
>
> [2]Don't get me wrong. The computer is a boon to anyone's job, with its promise of efficiency, speed, and skills never before imagined and I'll slug anyone who tries to take it away from me.
>
> [3]But the computer also promised to relieve me of all my paper. It hasn't. Instead, I now have both paper files and digital files. The computer has presented me with gigabytes of new material to organize: interview notes, story drafts, half-cocked ideas, project lists, research downloaded from online services, and contact lists.
>
> [4]Then there's the time element. I spend hours every month backing up files to protect myself from accidental deletions, lethal viruses, hard-disk crashes, or faulty floppies. Hey, I never had to clone my filing cabinet.
>
> Hal Lancaster, "Chaos in a Box: Messy Computer Files Can Strain Your Job," *The Wall Street Journal*

In this opening paragraph of J. D. Salinger's classic novel, *Catcher in the Rye,* the narrator, Holden Caufield, age 13, introduces himself:

> If you really want to hear about it, the first thing you'll probably want to know is where I was born, and what my lousy childhood was like, and all that David Copperfield kind of crap, but I don't feel like going into it, if you want to know the truth.
>
> J. D. Salinger, *Catcher in the Rye*

What is Caufield's tone? He is casual and direct, but he also sounds alienated and disillusioned beyond his years.

EXERCISES: PART 1—DETERMINING TONE

Here are some passages for you to practice with. Read each carefully, paying attention to word choice (denotation and connotation) and to the quality and "sound" of the prose, underlining words and phrases that strike you as being particularly connotative. In addition, you might want to read each passage aloud. Consider the list of possible tones at the beginning of the chapter and write your answer in the space after each passage.

Selection 1

The reference in the first sentence is to a facsimile of Menlo Park's complaint form that victims of sexual harassment are required to fill out. The complaint form was printed along with the article in the original source.

> [1]This is the complaint form used by the city of Menlo Park, California, for allegations of discrimination or harassment in the workplace. On March 1, 1993, Donna Vincent, a twenty-nine-year-old computer operator, charged that an exhibition in Menlo Park's City Hall of woodcuts by Brazilian artist Zoravia Bettiol constituted sexual harassment because it disrupted her work environment. "The new art display in city hall has several (3 or more) drawings of women who are nude from the waist up and one that is a full nude," she wrote. "I have to walk through the hallways each day as part of my work and would prefer not to have to see this type of 'Art.' " One day after the complaint was filed, city officials removed two woodcuts: portraits of Aphrodite . . . and "Luxuria." The issue raised by Vincent's complaint is being faced by universities and municipalities across the country: Can a work of art be sexually harassing? In more than a dozen recent cases, allegations of sexual harassment have been used to force the removal of artwork from classrooms, municipal buildings, and public art galleries.
>
> [2]How can one be a "victim" of art? In 1558, when Pope Paul IV viewed the male genitalia painted by Michelangelo on the ceiling of the Sistine Chapel, he

insisted that they be brushed over with flowing draperies (only recently removed after more than 400 years). When Donna Vincent, a Seventh-Day Adventist, first objected to the naked female torsos, the Menlo Park Arts Commission ordered that the offending parts be covered. Canary yellow Post-It notes fluttered from Aphrodite's breasts overnight before the woodcuts were removed from the exhibit altogether. The artist, who was an outspoken proponent of artistic freedom under Brazil's former military government, brought a legal complaint against the city for violating her First Amendment rights. The case is pending.

Mark Schapiro, "The Fine Art of Sexual Harassment," *Harper's Magazine*

Tone ______________________________

Selection 2

[1]Lost in the cities of America, the immigrant Jews succumbed to waves of nostalgia for the old world. "I am overcome with longing," wrote an early immigrant, "not only for my Jewish world, which I have lost, but also for Russia." Both the handful of intellectuals and the unlettered masses were now inclined to re-create the life of the old country in their imaginations, so that with time, distance and suffering, the past they had fled took on an attractive glow, coming to seem a way of rightness and order. Not that they forgot the pogroms, not that they forgot the poverty, but that they remembered with growing fondness the inner decorums of *shtetl* life. Desperation induced homesickness, and homesickness coursed through their days like a ribbon of sadness. In Russia "there is more poetry, more music, more feeling, even if our people do suffer appalling persecution. . . . One enjoys life in Russia better than here. . . .

[2]There is too much materialism here, too much hurry and too much prose—and yes, too much machinery." Even in the work of so sophisticated a Yiddish poet as Moshe Leib Halpern, who began to write after the turn of the century, dissatisfaction with the new world becomes so obsessive that he "forgets that his place of birth was very far indeed from being a paradise." "On strange earth I wander as a stranger," wrote Halpern about America, "while strangeness stares at me from every eye."

Irving Howe, *World of Our Fathers*

Tone ______________________________

Selection 3

Back in the days when everyone was old and stupid or young and foolish and me and Sugar were the only ones just right, this lady moved on our block with nappy hair and proper speech and no makeup. And quite naturally we laughed at her, laughed the way we did at the junk man who went about his business like he was some big-time president and his sorry-ass horse his secretary. And we kinda hated her too, hated the way we did the winos who cluttered up our parks and pissed on our handball walls and stank up our hallways and stairs so you couldn't halfway play hide-and-seek without a goddamn gas mask. Miss Moore was her name. The only woman on the block with no first name. And she was black as hell, cept for her feet, which were fish-white and spooky. And she was always planning these boring-ass things for us to do, us being my cousin, mostly, who lived on the block cause we all moved North the same time and to the same apartment then spread out gradual to breathe. And our parents would yank our heads into some kinda shape and crisp up our clothes so we'd be presentable for travel with Miss Moore, who always looked like she was going to church, though she never did. Which is just one of the things the grown-ups talked about when they talked behind her back like a dog. But when she came calling with some sachet she'd sewed up or some gingerbread she'd made or some book, why then they'd all be too embarrassed to turn her down and we'd get handed over all spruced up. She'd been to college and said it was only right that she should take responsibility for the young ones' education, and she not even related by marriage or blood. So they'd go for it. Specially Aunt Gretchen. She was the main gofer in the family. You got some ole dumb shit foolishness you want somebody to go for, you send for Aunt Gretchen. She been screwed into the go-along for so long, it's a blood-deep natural thing with her. Which is how she got saddled with me and Sugar and Junior in the first place while our mothers were in a la-de-da apartment up the block having a good ole time.

Toni Cade Bambara, "The Lesson," *Gorilla, My Love*

Tone ____

Selection 4

[1]While coaches fine-tune their playbooks and college football fans await the excitement of crisp autumn Saturdays, men you've never heard of are making secret plans to funnel cash or gifts (or grades or drugs or women) to the college athletes (or their friends and families) most likely to play in the National Football League or the National Basketball Association next year.

[2]Despite their best efforts, the details of some of these schemes will become public. By the end of the season we'll have another scandal or two or 10 in college sports. Columnists will decry the opportunism of the "student athletes" who make such rotten role models for kids. Fans will shake their heads and wonder what happened to "love of the game."

[3]Last season's college basketball player of the year, Marcus Camby of the University of Massachusetts, admitted taking cash and gifts worth several thousand dollars from the guys who wanted to be his agent and rake off a percentage when he landed his NBA contract. Georgetown's Allen Iverson signaled his intentions and hopes of going pro by tooling around in a $100,000 Mercedes "borrowed" from a local car dealer.

4 But since the future of college sports is predictable, there's no point in moralizing or whining or holding onto a willful innocence. "Say it ain't so," after all, was a little boy's plea to the adult world of professional sports corruption back in 1920. It's well past time to grow up and abolish the hypocrisy of college sports.

Warren Goldstein, "Time Out for a Change In College Athletics," *The Washington Post*

Tone ______________________________

Selection 5

1 Four score and seven years ago our fathers brought forth on this continent, a new nation, conceived in Liberty, and dedicated to the proposition that all men are created equal.

2 Now we are engaged in a great civil war, testing whether that nation, or any nation so conceived and so dedicated, can long endure. We are met on a great battle-field of that war. We have come to dedicate a portion of that field, as a final resting place for those who here gave their lives that that nation might live. It is altogether fitting and proper that we should do this.

3 But, in a larger sense, we can not dedicate—we can not consecrate—we can not hallow—this ground. The brave men, living and dead, who struggled here, have consecrated it, far above our poor power to add or detract. The world will little note, nor long remember what we say here, but it can never forget what they did here. It is for us the living, rather, to be dedicated here to the unfinished work which they who fought here have thus far so nobly advanced. It is rather for us to be here dedicated to the great task remaining before us—that from these honored dead we take increased devotion to that cause for which they gave the last full measure of devotion——that we here highly resolve that these dead shall not have died in vain—that this nation, under God, shall have a new birth of freedom—and that government of the people, by the people, for the people, shall not perish from the earth.

Abraham Lincoln, "The Gettysburg Address"

Tone ______________________________

Selection 6

Glenn Close wrote the following excerpt on the occasion of her last performance playing Norma Desmond in the long-running play, "Sunset Boulevard." At the beginning, she recounts the story of Mary Ure, a beautiful and accomplished English actress, who had suffered a series of personal setbacks in her career and was having difficulty remembering her lines. One day, before the matineé performance, the producer finally decided to replace Miss Ure with her understudy, Glenn Close, who hurried to her dressing room before the play began. These are the last five paragraphs:

> [1]Down I went. They put me in her costume, suffused with her distinctive, evocative perfume. They put her wig, still damp from her performance, on my head, and I was taken up to her dressing room—the star dressing room, on stage level. On the empty walls were the hooks from which she had just taken down all the pictures of her children. I was overwhelmed by the sudden realization that my chance of a lifetime was her terrible tragedy. An uncanny calm came over me. The cast was called back early from dinner. We had an hour to walk through the show.
>
> [2]Half an hour before curtain, in the strange, haunted dressing room, I tried to prepare myself. People kept running in and out. Last-minute flowers from the cast, the producers, and Hal. Heads popping in with "Break a leg!" and "Knock 'em dead!"
>
> [3]A few minutes before curtain, a note was brought to me. I opened it and read, "Dear Glenn, It is a tradition in the English theatre for one leading lady to welcome the next leading lady into her dressing room. I learned this when I was very young and making my début at the Haymarket. I was surprised to find a letter for me from Dame Peggy Ashcroft, who had just closed after a long run. I salute you and welcome you. Be brave and strong. Mary Ure."
>
> [4]Life went on. I did the show and was adequate. I had a lot to learn, but I did learn with every performance, graciously supported by my fellow-actors. When the run was over, I was sent back up to my garret of a dressing room and resumed my life as an understudy.
>
> [5]The following spring, Mary Ure died. At the time, I thought that hers had been a curious choice of words: "Be brave and strong." How could that apply to me, so full of hope and possibility? Now, twenty-one years later, I think I understand. On July 2nd, I will welcome Betty Buckley into Dressing Room No. 1. I will leave a note on the table. I will make my exit.
>
> Glenn Close, "Leaving the Role," *The New Yorker*

Tone ______________________________

THE IRONIC STANCE

In the end of the list you studied at the beginning of the chapter, you may recall these examples of tone:

Witty, humorous, ironic
Ironic, sarcastic
Cynical, skeptical, pessimistic

The tones involving irony are harder to detect and cause more difficulty than those you have studied so far. **Irony** results when a writer deliberately says the opposite of what he or she really means, whether for humorous intent, to poke fun at human foibles, or, more seriously, to criticize, to encourage reform, to cast doubt on someone's motives, or to make a comment about the human condition. The writer assumes that the reader will see through the pretense and recognize that the words express something different from their literal meaning.

The *American Heritage Dictionary* lists many definitions for irony; for our purposes, here are the most relevant:

1. a. The use of words to express something different from and often opposite to their literal meaning.
   b. An expression or utterance marked by a deliberate contrast between apparent and intended meanings.
   c. A literary style employing such contrasts for humorous or rhetorical effect.
2. a. Incongruity between what might be expected and what actually occurs.

Recognizing irony is tricky because it is a general term with many shades of meaning, as these definitions suggest—from simple amusement and a keen appreciation of life's absurdities to scathing sarcasm. Richard Altick, in his fine book, *Preface to Critical Reading,* defines irony like this:

> The essence of irony is the implied contrast between what is and what, in a more nearly perfect world, might be; and the effect of irony, similarly, lies in the striking disparity between the writer's apparent attitude—that is, his seeming seriousness, or his pretended lack of seriousness—and what he really means. When an author adopts an ironical manner, he is commenting upon the shortcomings of life, the weaknesses of mankind, or, sometimes, the frailties of individual beings. The ironist often is said to be a disappointed idealist, who laughs only to keep from crying or committing suicide. His disillusionment may be only temporary and may spring from a trivial cause; it may, on the other hand, be almost cosmic in its scope and represent a sweeping rejection of the whole of life and all of mankind. Thus

> irony has a wide variety of tones and shadings, running the gamut from unmitigated, pathological bitterness to mere gay amusement.
>
> Richard Altick, *Preface to Critical Reading*

Consider these real-life examples of irony. In the 1940s and 1950s North America experienced a terrible epidemic of polio. According to Geoffrey C. Ward in an article called "War on Polio,"[1] this epidemic was, ironically, a byproduct of new standards of middle-class cleanliness. In earlier decades babies and small children had routinely come in contact with the polio virus and developed a lifelong immunity to it. But with new standards of hygiene and the increasing use of household disinfectants like Lysol in kitchens and bathrooms, the virus was no longer commonly found in the environment, and when children *were* exposed to it, they had no immunity to it. In other words, while we would *expect* that better hygiene would result in healthier children, the opposite occurred in this case.

In another example, John Wayne was invited to play the role of Matt Dillon in the long-running television Western series *Gunsmoke;* however, he turned the offer down because he didn't want to be typecast as a cowboy. Why is this ironic? Because John Wayne was already a famous cowboy movie star, and he was forever associated with cowboy roles during his long film career.

Recent newspaper articles have examined the thinking of many homeless people. Refusing to endure the degrading environment of shelters, they prefer to fend for themselves on the streets. In addition, they refuse to sign up for welfare programs because they don't want to be caught up in a "dependency mentality" or suffer the degradation of standing in long lines or dealing with rude social workers. Do you sense the incongruity in this thinking? One last example: it is ironic when a firehouse burns down.

IRONY AND ITS SHADES OF MEANING

Armed with these definitions and examples, we can now examine the many forms irony can take. These will be clearer if you imagine a continuum, a horizontal line on which ironic attitudes are plotted. Moving from left to right along the continuum, we move from the most gentle forms of irony to the harshest:

Wit → Irony → Satire → Cynicism → Sarcasm

[1]*Memories*, Spring 1988.

Let us examine each by looking at some examples. Although all of them involve irony, their uses are quite different. Keep in mind that these categories are not fixed and unequivocal; rather they are "slippery," in that one may slide into the next. Do not be overly concerned if at first you have difficulty distinguishing among them. With practice, studying many examples carefully and asking your instructor for clarification if you are unsure, you will begin to see the differences between them.

Wit

Wit, the gentlest kind of irony, relies on mental keenness, or the ability to discern those elements of a situation or condition that are comic and then make a pointed, effective, usually humorous comment on them.

- Samuel Johnson, the 18th-century English man of letters, commenting on a friend's rather hasty remarriage: "A second marriage is the triumph of hope over experience."
- From Ogden Nash, American poet and humorist: "Progress was a good thing once but it went on too long."
- From H. L. Mencken, American critic and newspaper writer: "Criticism is prejudice made plausible."
- Mae West, American actress known for her risqué remarks: "I was as pure as the driven snow—but I drifted."
- From Zsa Zsa Gabor, a Hungarian-American actress known for her many marriages to rich men: "No rich man is ugly," and another, "A man in love is incomplete until he is married. Then he is finished."

Notice that all these examples share a clever turn of phrase or an ingenious play on words.

Irony

Consider again the dictionary definitions of **irony** on page 220. We can now examine the ironic stance with a few short examples.

> It finally happened. The waiting is over. It's here now.
>
> The new off-ramp has opened at San Francisco International Airport.
>
> For years we drove into the airport from the Bayshore Freeway on the old off-ramp. The old off-ramp was a concrete cloverleaf that arched over the freeway and deposited the motorist just past the Airport Hilton Hotel.
>
> Ah, but the new off-ramp! The new off-ramp is a concrete cloverleaf that arches over the freeway and deposits the motorist just past the Airport Hilton Hotel.

Steve Rubenstein, *San Francisco Chronicle*

Rubenstein uses irony to good advantage here. The initial short sentences create an atmosphere of expectation and suspense. Further, he uses identical words to describe the old and new off-ramps. We *expect* something as costly as a new freeway off-ramp to be more efficient, more convenient, perhaps wider and safer than the one it replaced. He does not have to comment on the wastefulness of spending millions of taxpayer dollars for such a project. The ironic stance allows him to criticize the project implicitly and allows us to recognize its ridiculousness.

Like wit, many jokes depend on irony. Consider this anecdote: "When Artur Schnabel, the preeminent Beethoven pianist of his time . . . was teaching a master class at Princeton, Albert Einstein, an ardent but shaky violinist, wormed his way into a quartet. After the great mathematician made several wrong entrances, Schnabel barked, 'For heaven's sake, Albert, can't you *count?*'" (Quoted in Herb Caen, *San Francisco Chronicle,* July 3, 1996.) Why is this ironic?

In this next example, Page Smith, formerly history professor at the University of California, Santa Cruz, uses irony to illustrate memory failure in older people. An old man and his wife are sitting on their front porch:

> Wife: "I certainly would appreciate a vanilla ice cream cone."
>
> Husband: "I'll hobble right down to the drugstore and get you one, dear."
>
> Wife: "Now, remember, I want vanilla. You always get chocolate. Write it down. Vanilla."
>
> Husband: "I can certainly remember vanilla. The store is only two blocks away."
>
> Husband comes back with a hamburger and hands it to his wife. She looks at it disgustedly. "I knew you'd forget the mustard," she says.
>
> Page Smith, "Coming of Age: Jokes about Old Age,"
> *San Francisco Chronicle*

In this last example, Trevor Fishlock explains what he calls "the ambiguity of Alaska, the last frontier."

> In Alaska there is all the ambiguity of the frontier. The Last Frontier slogan is invested with self-consciousness and sadness. It is meant to sound robustly all-American and celebratory, but it has, too, a note of nostalgic longing, regret for vanishing youth. Otherwise, surely, Alaskans would have called their land, in a more forward-looking way, the New Frontier. Men still journey here to be frontiersmen. They grow their whiskers especially for the purpose. They ransack the trading post catalogues for thick wool shirts, thermal underwear, rifles, Bowie knives and books on how to build log cabins and bear-proof larders. They buy devices to get solar electricity

> "free from the midnight sun" and consider whether to invest in "the world's most powerful hand gun, 2000 foot-pounds of raw power! Alaska's answer to bear protection." Thus equipped they thrust their eager bushy faces towards the challenging wilderness—and are dismayed to find parking tickets on their windscreens. Anchorage and Fairbanks have traffic jams, parking congestion and severe carbon monoxide pollution. Even in distant Nome, population 2500, there are irksome regulations. *The Nome Nugget,* Alaska's oldest newspaper (the motto on its masthead states: There's no place like Nome), commented regretfully on the installation of the town's first traffic signal in 1984: "It doesn't make us do anything we weren't already supposed to do. So, no cause for alarm yet. It just makes one wonder who will get the first ticket and how long before the first bullet hole shows up. Big city life is creeping up on us."
>
> Trevor Fishlock, *The State of America*

What does Fishlock find ironic about Alaska and the people who move there?____

Satire

A satire is a piece of writing that seeks to expose folly or wickedness and to hold human behavior up to ridicule. In a tribute to satiric comic Stan Freberg, the irreverent 1950s comedian, John McDonough first writes: ". . . Mr. Freberg is a satirist who views sacred social cows with a presumption of guilt and a fearless willingness to offend." McDonough then defines the satiric intent: "Satire is an outlaw art that loves to live dangerously. It is sustained by skepticism, impertinence and a sense of its own elitism. . . . it feeds on unseen absurdities, especially in times of conformity and reverence."[2]

Here are two examples of satire. The first concerns Newt Gingrich, Speaker of the U.S. House of Representatives, who complained that he had been snubbed on the flight returning from the funeral of Yitzhak Rabin, the assassinated Israeli prime minister, which he had attended with President Clinton. Todd Purdum, writing in *The New York Times,* gives the background:

> **1**Forget, for the moment, the future of Medicare, tax cuts for the middle class, resizing the social safety net or balancing the federal budget in seven, eight, nine or 10 years. Dialogue between Congress and the White House has boiled down to this: Who got to stretch out where, who got to talk turkey with whom and who got equal access to the front door of a Boeing 747.
>
> **2**On Wednesday, House Speaker Newt Gingrich confessed that he had freighted a stopgap spending measure with restrictive conditions that

[2]John McDonough, "Stan Freberg: Curmudgeon of Consequence," *The Wall Street Journal,* August 20, 1996.

> prompted a veto and a government shutdown in part to spite President Clinton for failing to show adequate courtesy to him and Senate majority leader Bob Dole on Air Force One on the way to and from Israel for the funeral of Prime Minister Yitzhak Rabin 11 days ago.
>
> Todd S. Purdum, "Gingrich Takes Flak Over Airplane Gripe," *The New York Times,* November 16, 1995

At the end of the article, Purdum quotes Luis Gutierrez of Illinois, who offers his own satiric "tale of woe": "I had a traumatic experience on an airplane Monday . . . I asked for an aisle seat and they gave me a window. The pilot never came back to say hello. And when we landed, I, a member of Congress, had to walk out with all the rest of the passengers. So I drafted a bill to shut down the government until the airline apologizes to me. Unfortunately, as a Democrat, I was ignored."

Humorist Dave Barry includes a chapter in *Dave Barry's Complete Guide to Guys* titled "Tips for Women: How to Have a Relationship with a Guy." One of Barry's rules is this: "Don't make the guy feel threatened," and he offers this advice:

SITUATION	THREATENING RESPONSE	NONTHREATENING RESPONSE
You meet a guy for the first time.	"Hello."	"I am a nun."
You're on your first date. The guy asks you what your hopes for the future are.	"Well, I'd like to pursue my career for a while, and then get married and maybe have children."	"A vodka Collins."
You have a great time on the date, and the guy asks you if you'd like to go out again.	"Yes."	"Okay, but bear in mind that I have only three months to live."
The clergyperson asks you if you take this man to be your lawful wedded husband, for richer and poorer, in sickness and in health, etc., 'til death do you part.	"I do."	"Well, sure, but not *literally.*"

Dave Barry, *Dave Barry's Complete Guide to Guys*

Cynicism

Cynicism is as difficult to define as irony. You may find these two definitions for the adjective form *cynical* from the *Random House College Dictionary* helpful:

1. Distrusting or disparaging the motives or sincerity of others.
2. Bitterly or sneeringly distrustful, contemptuous, or pessimistic.

The cynical tone is harsher than the ironic and the satirical. It is characterized, as these definitions suggest, by scorn for others' motives and virtues. Politicians are sometimes described as cynical because they underestimate the intelligence of the voting public. But more typically a cynic detects falseness in others and recognizes the impurity in others' motives. The cynical tone is mocking and sneering, often bitter. It may or may not involve irony. Study these examples drawn from real life:

- Mort Sahl, American comedian, during the 1996 presidential campaign: "God bless Bob Dole and Bill Clinton. Long may they waver."
- Voltaire, 18th-century writer and philosopher: "The first clergyman was the first rascal who met the first fool."
- L. Ron Hubbard, founder of Scientology: "The best way to get rich in this country is to start a religion."

Sarcasm

Sarcasm is defined in the usage notes in the *American Heritage Dictionary* as "a form of wit intended to taunt, wound, or subject another to ridicule or contempt." It often involves irony, whereby the writer's or speaker's words are sneering and cutting. (The etymology of the word will help you remember its exact meaning: "flesh-cutting.") A subcategory of irony and sarcasm is the **putdown,** a form of dismissal or rejection, always implying criticism. The degree of offense is hard to determine; some are harmless and clever, but as with any putdown, there seems always to be a nasty edge beneath. Consider these short examples, all coincidentally uttered by Winston Churchill.

- One evening a woman at a dinner party told Churchill that he was drunk. Churchill replied, "And you, madam, are ugly. But tomorrow I shall be sober."
- On Clement Attlee, Churchill's successor as Prime Minister of England, Churchill said, "Attlee is a very modest man. And with reason."
- Joseph Epstein quotes the following exchange in *A Line Out for a Walk:* "George Bernard Shaw once sent Winston Churchill two tickets for the opening night of one of his new plays, noting 'Bring a friend—if you

have one'; to which Churchill wrote back to say that he was otherwise engaged opening night, but would appreciate tickets for the second performance–– 'if there is one.' "

EXERCISES: PART 2—DETERMINING TONE

The directions for this exercise are the same as for the first set of exercises on page 215.

Selection 1

The author, television critic for the *San Francisco Chronicle,* is discussing the birth of WB, the Warner Brothers television network.

> WB has a network symbol, too. CBS has its unblinking eye, NBC its multicolored peacock. The WB symbol is a frog. It shows no early signs of princely aspirations.

John Carman, "New Warner Network Makes Fox Look Highbrow," *San Francisco Chronicle*

Tone ______________________________

Selection 2

These are the opening paragraphs of a review of a movie named "Milk Money," starring Melanie Griffith and Ed Harris, that was released in August 1994:

> [1]If a Martian came to Earth, stayed a day or two and decided to write a heartwarming, family-oriented, romantic comedy, he might come up with something as clueless and distasteful, and as disconnected from anything resembling true human emotion, as "Milk Money," which opens today.
>
> [2]It's hard to figure out for whom this movie was made. Not adults, certainly. Not kids, either. Teenagers would find it too lightweight. I suppose there must be Melanie Griffith fans out there who have to see everything she's in, but no one could call her role here, as an over-the-hill hooker, a flattering showcase. Only the fact that Griffith genuinely seems to invest in this ridiculous movie keeps her from getting demolished by it.
>
> [3]"Milk Money" is another one of those films that have been turning up of late in which little boys, without a hair on them except on their heads, are shown talking about girls in lewd, lustful ways. Has every Hollywood screenwriter forgotten about the "latency period"—you know, that wonderful time of life when you don't need anybody? When bliss is as obtainable as an ice cream cone or a game of whiffle ball?

[4]Michael Patrick Carter plays Frank, a boy who looks to be about 10, who, together with two of his buddies, develops an overwhelming interest in seeing a naked woman—any naked woman. They pool their money, ride their bikes to the nearest city and—in a sequence that is supposed to be absurd, droll, cute or all three—start asking very proper women on the street if they'd be willing to take their clothes off for $100.

[5]Poor kids! Will they *ever* find a good sport out there? But of course. Just as fast as you can say "nadir of her career"—and even faster than you can say "degrading role for a talented actress"—Griffith is on the scene, taking a plastic bag full of loose change from the kids in exchange for dropping her top. (Her back is to the camera, fortunately.)

Mick LaSalle, " 'Milk Money' Comes Up Short," *San Francisco Chronicle*

Tone ____________________

Selection 3 Quotation by Lady Astor, "The only thing I like about rich people is their money."

Tone ____________________

Selection 4 In this excerpt the author is discussing the 1996 Massachusetts Senate race between Republican governor William Weld and the incumbent Democratic senator, John F. Kerry. (Kerry won.) In describing Kerry's background, he writes:

> Kerry's cosmopolitan childhood (his father was a career Foreign Service officer) also hurt him. He was reared in Europe and packed off to boarding school, with weekends spent in places on Boston's North Shore where rich people go and are thin together. Kerry is the least ethnic Massachusetts politician since Michael Dukakis, who discovered he was Greek about an hour before announcing his candidacy for President.

Jack Beatty, "A Race Too Far?" *The Atlantic Monthly*

A bit later in the article Beatty writes: "Then there is Kerry's cool, cerebral manner. Archeologists have searched, but have been unable to discover a single Kerry Joke."

Tone ____________________

Selection 5

Journalist and travel writer Bill Bryson roamed around the United States exploring quirky, out-of-the-way places. He collected these experiences and encounters in *The Lost Continent,* from which this selection comes.

> In the morning I drove on to Wyoming, through scenery that looked like an illustration from some marvelous children's book of Western tales—snowy peaks, pine forests, snug farms, a twisting river, a mountain vale with a cornely name: Swan Valley. That is the one thing that must be said for the men and women who carved out the West. They certainly knew how to name a place. Just on this corner of the map I could see Soda Springs, Massacre Rock, Steamboat Mountain, Wind River, Flaming Gorge, Calamity Falls—places whose very names promised adventure and excitement, even if in reality all they contained were a DX gas station and a Tastee-Freez drive-in.
>
> Most of the early settlers in America were oddly inept at devising place names. They either chose unimaginative, semirecycled names—New York, New Hampshire, New Jersey, New England—or toadying, kiss-ass name; like Virginia, Georgia, Maryland and Jamestown in a generally pitiable attempt to secure favor with some monarch or powdered aristocrate back home. Or else they just accepted the names the Indians told them, not knowing whether Squashaninsect meant "land of the twinkling lakes" or "place where Big Chief Thunderclap paused to pass water."

Bill Bryson, *The Lost Continent*

Tone ______________________________

Selection 6

Lines spoken by Orson Welles, supposedly ad-libbed, in the movie *The Third Man:*

> "In Italy for thirty years under the Borgias, they had warfare, terror, murder, bloodshed—but they produced Michelangelo, Leonardo da Vinci, and the Renaissance. In Switzerland, they have brotherly love, five hundred years of democracy and peace, and what did that produce? The cuckoo clock."

Quoted in John McPhee, *La Place de la Concorde Suisse*

Tone ______________________________

Selection 7

> [1]Dear Miss Manners: Because of a combination of a semi-idiot mother who is, to this day, convinced that a show of any intelligence on the part of a woman is a sure sign of homosexuality; and complete-idiot classmates, who felt the same way, my childhood and adolescence were hell.
>
> [2]As a result, I tend to get testy, now that I am a 29-year-old adult woman, when a waiter or bartender "cards" me. I hate being mistaken for a teenager, since I hated being a teenager.

3 I get even testier when said waiter or bartender patronizingly chastises me for being upset. Evidently, at my advanced age, I should be happy that people mistake me for a teenager.

4 How should I respond to these dim bulbs? Clearly, my life story is none of their damned business, but I would like to know of some reasonably polite churlish response to shut them up, and I am fresh out of ideas.

5 Gentle Reader: You are slightly mistaken in your belief that Miss Manners is in the business of adding to the churlishness in the world. Not only does it seem to her that there is quite enough of that in ready supply, but it strikes her that you have more than your share.

6 The proper response when you are carded is to show proof of your age. If you can manage to do so without churlishness, there will appear to be one fewer of those idiots for whom you have such disdain.

Miss Manners (Judith Martin), "Avoid Being Identified with Churlish Idiots"

Tone ____

Selection 8

In 1995 Calvin Klein's advertising campaign for jeans came under attack because the models were young teenagers wearing very few clothes and posed in provocative, and according to some critics, almost pornographic ways. Klein responded to the attack, saying that American young people show strength of character and independence. In this article that appeared on editorial pages, Maureen Dowd analyzes some of Klein's remarks and follows each with his subtext, the underlying or implicit meaning:

1 Statement from Calvin Klein, Inc. (*With subtext by Calvin*)

2 The message of the CK Calvin Klein Jeans current advertising campaign is that young people today, the most media savvy generation yet, have a real strength of character and independence.

3 (*The message of my jeans campaign is that young people today* should have *sex, lots of sex, straight-up sex, twisted sex, denim sex, multicultural sex. That's the same message I've always had. Wet shots sell dry goods. Why show clothes when you can show a body? I look at the body as being something beautiful. Anyway, these pictures are supposed to make people stop. Stop and shop. But everyone is so blasted media-savvy, it gets harder and harder to push back the edge of the envelope. How do I stay on the border of bad taste when my rivals are doing magazine ads of rape fantasies and black and white men handcuffed together? In the old*

days, it was easy. You got Brooke Shields to vamp in tight jeans . . . You got Marky Mark to clutch himself in boxer briefs. But the edge keeps slipping away. So . . . I was thrilled when Steven Meisel came up with a campaign that had a bunch of hot, half-naked boys and girls being questioned by an old creep in a rec room. So what if it looks like a low-budget porn flick? The idea was so Calvin.)

4They have very strongly defined lines of what they will and will not do—and have a great ability to know who they are who they want to be.

5(*We know exactly what kids will and will not do. Infantile sexuality is older than Cheryl Tiegs. So if Steven can give me that 8-millimeter chickenhawk feel, big deal. Girls exposing their breasts and flashing white cotton panties. Shock, horror! OK, so the boy with bulging briefs, dirty hair, shark tattoo and black nail polish isn't Beaver Cleaver. But this is the '90s. . . . The off-camera creep has this great leering Winstons-and-Wild-Turkey voice. When he asks this stacked Ginalolita, "Do you like to take direction?" and she answers with a Mediterranean accent, "Yes, it's my preferred," I mean, that's truth in advertising. My favorite is when the guy tells the River Phoenix look-alike, "Ya think you can rip that shirt off ya? That's a nice body. You work out? Yeah, I can tell."*)

6We also are conveying the idea that glamour is an inner quality that can be found in regular people in the most ordinary setting; it is not something exclusive to models and movie stars.

7(*Some of the kids and their parents did get upset during the shoots for the TV ads. I kept telling the kids that glamour is an inner quality, so they should go ahead and take their clothes off. Anyway, I hate regular people. We called the agencies and got the coolest models we could find. . . .*)

8However, some people are taking away a different perception of the ads. We have been taken aback by that perception, in part because it differs sharply from our intended message.

9(*I'd have more of a problem if no one cared.*)

10Because of the role the fashion industry plays in shaping the culture in which they grow and form impressions, we have a responsibility to young people—in fact, we share the concerns some have raised about the challenges children face growing up today.

11(*OK, I get it. This year, family values moves the goods. Doesn't anyone in my operation know which way the wind is blowing? I want to exploit, not mis-exploit. And I don't want my picture flashed on the news with the phrase "Kiddie Porn." . . .*)
12We continue to believe in the positive message of these ads.

> [13]*(Controversy is good for business. Kids will want whatever outrages their parents.)*
>
> [14]But since the ads' message about the spirit, independence and inner worth of today's young people has been misunderstood by some, and because we take our responsibility to those young people so seriously, we will cease running the remainder of this campaign as soon as possible.
>
> [15]*(That inner worth line is so hot. My shrink's trainer thought of it. What's next? Steven thinks that, with the outtakes, we've got a video. OK, we'll put a warning label on it.)*
>
> Maureen Dowd, "What Calvin Really Thought . . . ,"
> *The New York Times*

Tone ______________________________

SPECIAL EFFECTS

In this final section of the chapter, we will briefly look at some **special effects** that contribute to tone—understatement, hyperbole, and sentence structure.

Understatement

Actually a form of irony, **understatement** involves deliberate restraint, underplaying a situation to heighten its significance. In this example, Bill McKibben is discussing the way television "levels out" information. He cites the case of the Kogi, an isolated Colombian Indian tribe, who noticed evidence of global warming—what scientists have been warning us about for years. The snow pack that produced their water had diminished. Primitive though they are, they invited the BBC (British Broadcasting Corporation) to come to Colombia and to get across their message: that they "have seen the changes start that mark the end of life; the world is beginning to die." McKibben continues:

> So the film crew came, with helicopters and lights and cameras; the documentary was made, and it was shown in Britain and America and around the world; and quite a few people watched, and many of them must have found it sobering, for here was a long-lived culture speaking out of nowhere at the same time and with the same message as our leading scientists. It was uncanny. But then it was over, and something else came on, and the warning passed unheeded.
>
> Bill McKibben, "Reflections: Television," *The New Yorker*

Locate the phrase where McKibben effectively employs understatement to show irony and to make a dramatic impact.

Hyperbole

Hyperbole (pronounced hī pûr′ bə lē) is a figure of speech using deliberate exaggeration for effect. Jerry Carroll, who writes for the *San Francisco Chronicle,* used hyperbole to good effect in describing the Berkeley, California, living environment of a film writer named Barry Gifford who co-wrote the movie script *Lost Highway* with David Lynch: "He [Gifford] shares the space with artists who leave a colorful mess. An explosion would not be noticed right away." (Quoted in Jerry Carroll, "Gifford's Long Road to 'Highway,' " *San Francisco Chronicle,* March 1, 1997.)

Hyperbole is often used to great advantage in advertising. One notable illustration will suffice: David Brower, president of the Sierra Club during the 1970s, spent enormous energy fighting the Bureau of Reclamation engineers, who were determined to build dams on some of America's most scenic wild rivers. According to Brower, "The Bureau of Reclamation engineers are like beavers . . . They can't stand the sight of running water." One of the Bureau's plans was to build a dam in Marble Gorge, part of the Grand Canyon. Brower went into action, and apparently, these fights were the "bitterest of all."

John McPhee recounts Brower's unorthodox and hyperbolic campaign tactics:

> The Bureau felt that Brower capitalized on literary hyperbole and the mystic name of the canyon. He implied, they said, that the dams were going to fill the Grand Canyon like an enormous bathtub, and that the view from the north rim to the south rim would soon consist of a flat expanse of water. Brower's famous advertising campaigns reached their most notable moment at this time. He placed full-page ads in *The New York Times* and the *San Francisco Chronicle,* among other places, under the huge headline "SHOULD WE ALSO FLOOD THE SISTINE CHAPEL SO TOURISTS CAN GET NEARER THE CEILING?"
>
> John McPhee, *Encounters with the Archdruid*

Though clearly unfair (since the Bureau claimed that its plan was to flood only a fraction of what Brower was claiming), the ads were enormously effective at influencing public opinion. Brower won, the Bureau backed off, and the dam was never built.

Sentence Structure

Writers not only choose words carefully, but they also endeavor to create sentences that reinforce both the content and the mood of the piece. Here are three examples of distinctive sentence structure. In the first, television critic John Carman describes the acting debut of Vanna White, better known as the letter-turner on the television game show

Wheel of Fortune, who appeared in a made-for-television movie, *Goddess of Love.* Carman pokes fun at the movie by writing in overly simple sentences. (For full effect, read this excerpt aloud and exaggerate the simplistic style.)

> [1]This is Vanna White. Vanna is the star of her own movie Sunday night on NBC. Vanna's movie is called "Goddess of Love."
>
> [2]Vanna plays Venus in her movie. Venus is a goddess. Venus comes back to life after 3,000 years. General Electric owns NBC. General Electric brings good things to life.
>
> [3]When General Electric brings Venus to life, Venus falls in love with a hair stylist.
>
> [4]Acting is new for Vanna. Vanna says that "It was very hard. It's very hard to sit there for my first major role on television and say, 'Where dost thou slumber?' "
>
> [5]NBC did not let critics see "Goddess of Love." NBC is very smart. The critics are very sad. They wanted very much to see Vanna act and say, "Where dost thou slumber?"
>
> [6]But NBC says it has not seen the movie either. The man who is in charge of NBC movies has not seen "Goddess of Love," even though it will be on TV Sunday (Channel 4, 9 P.M.). Where can it be?
>
> John Carman, " 'G-dd-ss -f L-v' Must Be Vanna,"
> *San Francisco Chronicle*

Short sentences have a quite different effect in this paragraph in which the author describes the preparations of Harry Houdini, the famous magician, for a bridge jump while manacled.

> Picture the scene as Houdini performs one of his bridge jumps, so often described with such unvarying excitement. The excited crowd, several thousand strong, jostles around. Houdini and his team arrive. A silence falls. Houdini strips to his bathing suit and climbs onto the parapet. The attention of all these thousands of people is focused upon him—a small man, slightly bow-legged, very muscular. The local chief of police comes forward carrying handcuffs, often two sets; leg-irons. Houdini allows himself to be manacled. He stands there, waiting until he "hears the voice." Then he jumps. The crowd surges forward. It is waiting for—what? What it sees, in a minute or so, is Houdini, swimming strongly for the bank or the boat, brandishing the irons in one hand. It is slightly disappointed, but also satisfied. Death has been defeated once more.
>
> Ruth Brandon, *The Life and Many Deaths of Harry Houdini*

Underline the short sentences to see how they heighten suspense and contribute to the dramatic effect.

This final example, by Sherman Alexie, a Coeur d'Alene Indian from Washington state, is the opening paragraph of his 1996 novel *Indian Killer.* In it he describes an Indian Health Service hospital. Composed of sentence fragments, taken together, they create a series of impressions, almost as if he were sketching the hospital scene with words rather than with charcoal. What dominant impression of the hospital does the reader come away with?

> The sheets are dirty. An Indian Health Service hospital in the early sixties. On this reservation or that reservation. Any reservation, a particular reservation. Antiseptic, cinnamon and danker odors. Anonymous cries up and down the hallways. Linoleum floors swabbed with gray water. Mop smelling like old sex. Walls painted white a decade earlier. Now yellowed and peeling. Old Indian woman in a wheelchair singing traditional songs to herself, tapping a rhythm on her armrest, right index finger tapping; tapping. Pause. Tap, tap. A phone ringing loudly from behind a thin door marked PRIVATE. Twenty beds available, twenty beds occupied. Waiting room where a young Indian man sits on a couch and holds his head in his hands. Nurses' lounge, two doctors' offices and a scorched coffee pot. Old Indian man, his hair bright white and unbraided, pushing his IV bottle down the hallway. He is barefoot and confused, searching for a pair of moccasins he lost when he was twelve years old. Donated newspapers and magazines stacked in bundles, months and years out of date, missing pages. In one of the exam rooms, an Indian family of four, mother, father, son, daughter, all coughing blood quietly into handkerchiefs. The phone still ringing behind the PRIVATE door. A cinder-block building, thick windows that distort the view, pine trees, flagpole. A 1957 Chevy parked haphazardly, back door flung open, engine still running, back seat damp. Empty now.
>
> Sherman Alexie, *Indian Killer*

Repetition for Effect

Repeating key words, phrases, or clauses can both bring about a pleasing balance and call attention to important ideas. Such is the effect of Elie Wiesel's repeating the key word "never" in this moving passage. (Wiesel is a survivor of the Holocaust, and this passage, incidentally, is displayed on a large plaque at the U.S. Holocaust Museum in Washington, D.C.)

> [1]Never shall I forget that night, the first night in camp, which has turned my life into one long night, seven times cursed and seven times sealed. Never shall I forget that smoke. Never shall I forget the little faces of the children, whose bodies I saw turned into wreaths of smoke beneath a silent blue sky.

[2]Never shall I forget those flames which consumed my faith forever.

[3]Never shall I forget that nocturnal silence which deprived me, for all eternity, of the desire to live. Never shall I forget those moments which murdered my God and my soul and turned my dreams to dust. Never shall I forget these things, even if I am condemned to live as long as God Himself. Never.

Elie Wiesel, *The Night Trilogy*

EXERCISES: PART 3

Selection 1

[1]One of the greatest and most intrepid travelers of all time, Marco Polo, journeyed to the Far East from the Mediterranean in the thirteenth century and spent twenty years in the court of Kublai Khan in China. [2]On his return to Venice he set down in his book entitled *Description of the World* his impressions of the peoples and places and customs he had seen. [3]There are at least two extraordinary omissions in his account. [4]He says nothing about the art of printing unknown as yet in Europe but in full flower in China. [5]He either did not notice it at all or if he did, failed to see what use Europe could possibly have for it. [6]Whatever reason, Europe had to wait another hundred years for Gutenberg. [7]But even more spectacular was Marco Polo's omission of any reference to the Great Wall of China, nearly 4000 miles long and already more than 1000 years old at the time of his visit. [8]Again, he may not have seen it; but the Great Wall of China is the only structure built by man which is visible from the moon!* [9]Indeed, travelers can be blind.

Chinua Achebe, *Hopes and Impediments*

*About the omission of the Great Wall of China, I am indebted to *The Journey of Marco Polo* as re-created by artist Michael Foreman, published by *Pegasus* magazine, 1974.

A. *Vocabulary*

For each italicized word from the selection, choose the best definition according to the context in which it appears.

1. *intrepid* [sentence 1]: (a) knowledgeable; (b) famous; (c) untiring; (d) fearless.
2. *omissions* [3 and 7]: Things (a) overlooked; (b) misinterpreted; (c) not observed; (d) left out.

B. *Content and Structure*

Complete the following questions.

1. The main idea of this paragraph is expressed in sentence __________.
2. The method of development is (a) comparison; (b) contrast; (c) analysis; (d) example; (e) analogy.
3. The pattern of organization is (a) deductive; (b) inductive; (c) spatial; (d) chronological.
4. If Marco Polo did actually observe that the Chinese knew the art of printing and failed to mention it because he did not see how it could be useful in Europe, such an omission would be an example of (a) a simple oversight; (b) a symbol; (c) cynicism; (d) ignorance; (e) irony.
5. We can infer from sentence 6 that (a) the Chinese gave the idea of the printing press to Gutenberg; (b) Gutenberg traveled to China; (c) Gutenberg invented his printing press independently of the Chinese; (d) Gutenberg's printing process was identical to that of the Chinese.
6. Why does Achebe mention that the Great Wall of China is the only manmade structure visible from the moon, and how does this fact relate to Marco Polo's failure to observe it? ____________________

   ____
7. According to the context in which Achebe uses them, the adjectives *extraordinary* (sentence 3) and *spectacular* (sentence 7) are examples of (a) allusions; (b) denotative words; (c) connotative words with positive overtones; (d) connotative words with negative overtones; (e) euphemisms; (f) sneer words.
8. Which of the following best describes Achebe's tone? (a) surprised; (b) skeptical; (c) objective; (d) sympathetic; (e) confused.
9. As Achebe points out, it is possible that Marco Polo never observed either the art of printing or the Great Wall, yet what piece of evidence in the paragraph makes this seem unlikely or improbable?

   ____

   ____
10. In a sentence of your own, explain Achebe's observation in the last sentence: "Indeed, travelers can be blind." ____________________

   ____

Selection 2

Albert Camus included the following passage in *Between Hell and Reason: Essays from the Resistance Newspaper* Combat, *(1944–1947). Combat,* for which Camus served as editor-in-chief, was published by the French Resistance movement and printed reports of Nazi atrocities and messages from Charles de Gaulle, leader of the French government-in-exile. The dateline of the statement was August 8, 1945, two days after the bombing of Hiroshima; it was subtitled "Thoughts on the Defining Moment of the 20th Century."

1The world is what it is, which is to say, nothing much. That is what everyone learned yesterday, thanks to the formidable concert of opinion coming from radios, newspapers, and information agencies. Indeed we are told, in the midst of hundreds of enthusiastic commentaries, that any average city can be wiped out by a bomb the size of a football. American, English, and French newspapers are filled with eloquent essays on the future, the past, the inventors, the cost, the peaceful incentives, the military advantages, and even the life-of-its-own character of the atom bomb.

2We can sum it up in one sentence: Our technical civilization has just reached its greatest level of savagery. We will have to choose, in the more or less near future, between collective suicide and the intelligent use of our scientific conquests.

3Meanwhile we think there is something indecent in celebrating a discovery whose use has caused the most formidable rage of destruction ever known to man. What will it bring to a world already given over to all the convulsions of violence, incapable of any control, indifferent to justice and the simple happiness of men—a world where science devotes itself to organized murder? No one but the most unrelenting idealists would dare to wonder.

4These discoveries must be reported and given appropriate commentary; they must be announced to the world so that man has an accurate picture of his destiny. But couching these terrible revelations in picturesque or humorous writing is intolerable.

5Even before the bomb, one did not breathe too easily in this tortured world. Now we are given a new source of anguish; it has all the promise of being our greatest anguish ever. There can be no doubt that humanity is being offered its last chance. Perhaps this is an occasion for the newspapers to print a special edition. More likely, it should be cause for a certain amount of reflection and a great deal of silence.

6Let us be understood. If the Japanese surrender after the destruction of Hiroshima, having been intimidated, we will rejoice. But we refuse to see anything in such grave news other than the need to argue more energetically in favor of a true international society, in which the great powers will not have superior rights over small and middle-sized nations, where such an ultimate weapon will be controlled by human intelligence rather than by the appetites and doctrines of various states.

[7]Before the terrifying prospects now available to humanity, we see even more clearly that peace is the only goal worth struggling for. This is no longer a prayer but a demand to be made by all peoples to their governments—a demand to choose definitively between hell and reason.

Albert Camus, *Between Hell and Reason*

A. *Vocabulary*

For each italicized word from the selection, choose the best definition according to the context in which it appears.

1. *formidable* [paragraphs 1 and 3]: (a) unsettling; (b) arousing passions; (c) causing fear, apprehension; (d) causing great admiration.
2. *eloquent* [1]: Written in language that is (a) unintelligible; (b) fluent, forceful; (c) concise, brief; (d) sympathetic.
3. *unrelenting* [3]: (a) inflexible; (b) patriotic; (c) unresponsive; (d) unreasonable.
4. *couching* [4]: (a) disguising; (b) resembling; (c) comparing; (d) expressing in words.
5. *picturesque* [4]: (a) charming, quaint; (b) strikingly vivid; (c) shocking; (d) celebratory.

B. *Content and Structure*

Complete the following questions.

1. The mode of discourse in this passage is (a) narration; (b) description; (c) exposition; (d) persuasion.
2. In which paragraph does Camus express his main idea?

   Paragraph ______.
3. According to the first paragraph, what was the media's opinion about the bombing of Hiroshima? ______________________________

   ____
4. Explain the relationship between paragraphs 1, 2, and 3. ____________
5. In paragraph 3, the phrase "the most formidable rage of destruction" is an example of (a) denotative language; (b) connotative language with negative overtones; (c) connotative language with positive overtones; (d) irony; (e) an allusion.
6. In paragraph 5 Camus writes, "There can be no doubt that humanity is being offered its last chance." This statement is an example of (a) irony; (b) an allusion; (c) understatement; (d) hyperbole.

7. Explain Camus's concern in paragraph 6. ______________________

____

8. In your own words, describe Camus's tone in this passage and point to words and phrases that clearly reveal it. (Note: the tone of this passage is complex and probably cannot be reduced to a single emotional quality.)______________________

____

Selection 3

The chimpanzee who is the subject of this passage, Cholmondeley—or Chumley as he was known to his friends—was being donated to the London Zoo. The author had promised the owner to take the chimp back to England on his way home from Africa.

[1]He arrived in the back of a small van, seated sedately in a huge crate. [2]When the doors of his crate were opened and Chumley stepped out with all the ease and self-confidence of a film star, I was considerably shaken; standing on his bow legs in a normal slouching chimp position, he came up to my waist, and if he had straightened up his head would have been on a level with my chest. [3]He had huge arms and must have measured at least twice my size round his hairy chest. [4]Owing to bad tooth growth, both sides of his face were swollen out of all proportion, and this gave him a weird pugilistic look. [5]His eyes were small, deep-set, and intelligent; the top of his head was nearly bald, owing, I discovered later, to his habit of sitting and rubbing the palms of his hands backward across his head, an exercise which seemed to afford him much pleasure and which he persisted in until the top of his skull was quite devoid of hair. [6]This was no young chimp such as I had expected, but a veteran about eight or nine years old, fully mature, strong as a powerful man, and, to judge by his expression, with considerable experience of life. [7]Although he was not exactly a nice chimp to look at (I had seen handsomer), he certainly had a terrific personality; it hit you as soon as you set eyes on him. [8]His little eyes looked at you with great intelligence, and there seemed to be a glitter of ironic laughter in their depths that made one feel uncomfortable.

[9]He stood on the ground and surveyed his surroundings with a shrewd glance, and then he turned to me and held out one of his soft, pink-palmed hands to be shaken, with exactly that bored expression that one sees on the faces of professional hand-shakers. [10]Round his neck was a thick chain, and its length drooped over the tailboard of the lorry and disappeared into the depths of his crate. [11]With an animal of less personality than Chumley, this would have been a sign of his subjugation, of his captivity. [12]But Chumley wore the chain with the superb air of a Lord Mayor; after shaking my hand so professionally, he turned and proceeded to pull the chain, which measured some fifteen feet, out

of his crate. [13]He gathered it up carefully into loops, hung it over one hand, and proceeded to walk into the hut as if he owned it. [14]Thus, in the first few minutes of arrival, Chumley had made us feel inferior; he had moved in, not, we felt, because we wanted him to, but because he did. [15]I almost felt I ought to apologize for the mess on the table.

Gerald Durrell, "The Life and Death of Cholmondeley"

A. *Vocabulary*

For each italicized word from the selection, choose the best definition according to the context in which it appears.

1. *sedately* [sentence 1]: (a) calmly, in a dignified manner; (b) nervously, apprehensively; (c) arrogantly, haughtily; (d) uncomfortably, awkwardly.
2. *pugilistic* [4]: Having the appearance of (a) a military officer; (b) a movie star; (c) a fighter; (d) a vicious animal.
3. *ironic* [8]: Here, (a) cynical, mistrustful; (b) satirical, ridiculing; (c) sarcastic, suggesting a superior attitude; (d) nasty, cruel.
4. *shrewd* [9]: (a) bored; (b) impartial; (c) deliberately deceptive; (d) keenly perceptive.
5. *subjugation* [11]: (a) boredom, indifference; (b) defeat, enslavement; (c) cooperative spirit; (d) subjectivity, introspective nature.

B. *Content and Structure*

Complete the following questions.

1. Which two modes of discourse are evident in this passage?

   _______________ and _______________
2. The dominant impression of Chumley that Durrell wants to convey is his (a) weird appearance; (b) large size; (c) maturity; (d) superior attitude.
3. With respect to the end of paragraph 1, paragraph 2 serves as (a) an explanation; (b) a contrasting example; (c) an illustration; (d) a conclusion.
4. The relationship between sentences 11 and 12 is (a) cause and effect; (b) general statement and illustration; (c) contrast; (d) steps in a process.
5. The passage contains three figures of speech that describe Chumley's behavior. Identify each in the space provided.

______________________________ in sentence _____

______________________________ in sentence _____

______________________________ in sentence _____

6. Study the figures of speech you wrote for question 5 and, in your own words, state the image of Chumley they are meant to convey.

____

____

7. Which of the following can you accurately infer? (a) Durrell had never seen a chimp before; (b) Chumley was embarrassed by the chains used to tether him to his crate; (c) Chumley insisted on having his surroundings be clean and orderly; (d) Chumley was accustomed to being the center of attention.
8. The tone of the passage can best be described as (a) ironic, wry, and amused; (b) sarcastic, ridiculing; (c) serious, earnest; (d) pensive, thoughtful.

PRACTICE ESSAY

History in Black and White

Michael Wilbon

In April 1997 two significant events in sports history took place: the country's celebration of the fiftieth anniversary of Jackie Robinson's entrance into the previously all-white sport of baseball and Tiger Woods's phenomenal win at The Masters golf tournament in Augusta, Georgia. Tiger Woods is of mixed ancestry. (He calls himself "Cablinasian," a term he invented to describe his mix, which is one-eighth Caucasian, one-fourth black, one-eighth American Indian, one-fourth Thai, and one-fourth Chinese.) After three years of study at Stanford University, Woods left the academic environment to become a professional golfer; within a few months, he had achieved the first of many astonishing victories. Michael Wilbon is a sports columnist at The Washington Post, *where "History in Black and White" was first published. In it, Wilbon finds more significance in these two players' accomplishments than mere baseball and golf statistics.*

1 The image that I cannot shake, even days later, doesn't include Tiger Woods. He wasn't in the frame that's going to stay with me forever. He and his father Earl, not long past bypass surgery, had just concluded a long and loving embrace, which, given the state of fatherhood

in black America, was emotional enough. Tiger had walked in one direction, toward Butler Cabin, to be awarded his green jacket for winning The Masters. But the camera for some reason stayed on Earl Woods, who walked off in another direction.

2 And in the picture, pretty much all you could see was Earl Woods being royally escorted off Augusta National by a legion of what appeared to be Georgia state troopers. At that point, nothing else mattered. A brown-skinned father of a brown-skinned golfer was being guarded by Southern state troopers at a country club where some members only 10 years ago would rather have died and gone to hell than see that man even walk the course, much less play it.

3 Words cannot adequately describe the emotions felt at that moment by millions of people in the country, most of them people of color. The Southern state trooper, second only to the Klan, is the real face of the violent white South, of club-swinging, water-spraying days of the 1960s. Part of me wanted to sit there dispassionately and watch life as it ought to be and should have been. Part of me wanted to go to church and shout.

4 I was fortunate enough to be watching the final moments of The Masters on television with a passionate golfer, my father-in-law-to-be, an accomplished professional black man in his sixties and a Southerner who undoubtedly felt emotions that someone 30 years younger can't feel. After six people in the room had fallen totally silent, he said, "Can you believe all of this?"

5 It is a bit much to take in all at once. Tiger Woods winning The Masters on a Sunday and, 48 hours later, the 50th anniversary of Jackie Robinson breaking baseball's color line being celebrated at Shea Stadium.

6 Nothing like this just happens willy-nilly, this bridge from Robinson to Woods, from Brooklyn to Augusta, Ga., from one ballplayer who endured unspeakable hatred in the name of progress to this young golfer who now has to negotiate unimaginable adulation. It certainly seems the baton has been passed once again, from Jesse Owens to Joe Louis to Jackie Robinson to Muhammad Ali to Arthur Ashe and now to Tiger Woods.

7 Those of us looking for a sign that young Tiger can handle this, that he indeed understands his burden and is willing to carry it, got a clear one even before he received his green jacket. Talking to CBS's Jim Nantz, who asked him about being the first African American and Asian American to win golf's most prestigious tournament, Woods demonstrated a sense of history, of indebtedness and common sense beyond his years when he said, "I may be the first, but I'm not a pioneer." And then he went on to thank, by name, Charlie Sifford, Lee Elder and Ted Rhodes, black golfers—all pioneers—who had not a prayer until recently of walking through the front door at Augusta National.

8 Sifford, Elder and Rhodes are to Woods as Cool Papa Bell, Satchel Paige and Josh Gibson were to Jackie Robinson, the men who took all the earliest hits, who had doors slammed in their faces and roads blocked. It is only through Woods's light that people now will begin to learn more of Sifford, Elder and Rhodes. It's not difficult to find the similarities between them. Both became educated men, Robinson at UCLA and Woods at Stanford. I'm not talking about college degrees, I mean educated, learned, scholarly.

9 It was easy to see in both a great deal of dignity and humility. And it was easy to see in both a sincere sense of family, Woods with his parents and Robinson with his beautiful and tough-minded wife Rachel, who was with him in the trenches and responsible for her husband's endurance in ways most of us will never know. Just as Robinson once did, Woods speaks the King's English, not some mush-mouthed, excuse-making quasi-language that can't do our people any good outside of our own environs, but clear and to the point without hemming and hawing and certainly without struggle. My mother and mother-in-law-to-be, two former schoolteachers, were happier with the way Woods spoke and carried himself than they were with any drive he hit off the tee.

10 I should say at this point that I am not a golfer. I've had two lessons and have only recently started watching televised golf, but it seems clear that Woods and the golf explosion will in short time dramatically change the order of sports in America. This isn't just about sports, however; the venue is sports, and, as is often the case, sports is the earliest setting for significant social change. Jesse Owens and Hitler had their silent confrontation in Berlin three years before the start of World War II. Robinson, remember, came along eight years before Rosa Parks, and before *Brown v. Board of Education.* Title IX preceded by years and years certain mainstream battles for gender equity.

11 This isn't about more black youngsters playing golf, though that will happen automatically and happily. It's about people, particularly people who have been stereotyped and pigeonholed and systematically eliminated from some pursuit or another, to feel free to explore whatever passions are stirring within. It's about letting people explore those passions without restrictions, without having to face bigotry and ignorance.

12 That, not his baseball exploits, is why I think we should honor Jackie Robinson now and forever. Those too young or too far removed to identify with Robinson's struggle can now see the identifiable bridge that has been built across the past 50 years, one that has carried us to a time when a kid of African and Asian descent can be mobbed adoringly by a predominantly white audience in Georgia on land that used to be a slave plantation, and when the uniformed sons of the Confederacy are offering a handshake instead of a billy club.

13 Shut your eyes real tight and imagine Jackie Robinson on one side of that bridge, young Tiger Woods on the other, and all the goodwill in between that can be so wonderful to explore.

A. Comprehension

Choose the answer that best completes each statement. Do not refer to the selection while doing this exercise.

1. For the author, the central image from The Masters tournament is that of (a) Tiger Woods's final victory stroke; (b) the clapping and cheering crowd; (c) the white Georgia state troopers' respectful treatment of Tiger Woods's father, Earl; (d) the lavish attention given to Tiger Woods by the television networks.
2. The winner of The Masters tournament receives (a) red roses; (b) a green jacket; (c) a country club membership; (d) an official golf hat.
3. Wilbon suggests that Tiger Woods's victory in Augusta was emotionally most affecting for (a) young African Americans; (b) current civil rights activists; (c) the Ku Klux Klan; (d) older African Americans who remember the struggles of the 1960s.
4. The affection shown Tiger Woods is as much the result of changed Southern attitudes regarding race as they are of (a) the accomplishments of earlier black athletes who fought for acceptance; (b) the influence of television networks; (c) increased opportunities for blacks to attend college; (d) federal civil rights legislation.
5. According to Wilbon, the venue for "significant social change" in race relations is (a) sports in general; (b) the sport of golf; (c) the sport of tennis; (d) the Olympics.
6. Woods's victory represents a chance for African Americans to (a) identify with Woods as a true cultural hero; (b) explore their interests without confronting bigotry and ignorance; (c) join previously white country clubs; (d) remember and honor Jackie Robinson's accomplishments.

B. Inferences

On the basis of the evidence in the paragraph, mark these statements as follows: PA for inferences that are probably accurate and PI for inferences that are probably inaccurate. You may refer to the selection to answer the questions in this section, and all the remaining sections.

1. ______ Earl Woods, Tiger Woods's father, is also a professional golfer.
2. ______ The author worries that Tiger Woods will be unable to carry the burden that accompanies his Masters victory.
3. ______ Charlie Sifford, Lee Elder, and Ted Rhodes—former black golfers—were not permitted to play in previous Masters tournaments.
4. ______ Jackie Robinson was the greatest baseball player in the history of the sport.

C. *Structure*

1. The mode of discourse in the article is (a) narration; (b) description; (c) exposition; (d) persuasion.
2. Explain in your own words the central metaphor that runs through this article. ____

____
3. Read the last three sentences of paragraph 8 again and explain Wilbon's comment about college degrees. ______________________
4. What quality of Woods is revealed in his quotation (in paragraph 7), "I may be the first, but I'm not a pioneer"? ______________________

____
5. The author's tone can be best described as (a) objective, impartial, neutral; (b) informative, instructive, didactic; (c) sincere, candid, forthright; (d) joyful, exuberant, optimistic.

D. *Vocabulary*

For each italicized word from the selection, choose the best definition according to the context in which it appears.

1. to sit there *dispassionately* [paragraph 3]: (a) pathetically; (b) disparagingly; (c) calmly; (d) cheerfully.
2. Nothing like this happens *willy-nilly* [6]: (a) in an unplanned manner; (b) for better or for worse; (c) traditionally; (d) for no reason.
3. to negotiate *adulation* [6]: (a) complicated contracts; (b) economic barriers; (c) excessive admiration; (d) racially-motivated hostility.
4. excuse-making, *quasi*-language [9]: A prefix meaning (a) false; (b) genuine; (c) incomplete; (d) resembling.

E. *Questions for Analysis and Discussion*

1. In paragraph 10 Wilbon alludes to Rosa Parks and *Brown v. Board of Education.* What do these refer to, and what contributions did each make to the civil rights movement?
2. Consider paragraph 9 again. What are the implications of Wilbon's remarks about language? And what characteristic or quality does it reveal about the author and his identification with race?
3. What are some reasons that athletes—of whatever race—represent role models for so many young people rather than, say, scientists, engineers, business leaders, or teachers?

III

Reading Critically

8

Primary Elements of Critical Reading

From Parts I and II, you learned that analytical reading requires careful attention to many elements: the writer's ideas, both main and supporting; the structure; the choice of words and their connotations, to name a few. With practice, a good reader can follow an author's stream of words almost effortlessly, and at this point in the course, you should be quite proficient at finding the main idea, following the direction of the writer's ideas, discerning modes of discourse, methods of development, tone, and so on.

More than this, however, a good reader must also develop a critical sense, a means of judging an article's worth—its accuracy, fairness, relevance, and significance. The skills taken up in this chapter will help you develop your ability to analyze what you read, in particular argumentative prose that expresses a writer's subjective opinion, whether it is published in a newspaper, magazine editorial, or letter to the editor, in a political speech, in a position paper, or on the World Wide Web. Here are the primary skills you will learn in this chapter:

- Becoming a responsible reader.
- Developing a world view.
- Identifying arguments.
- Detecting unstated assumptions in arguments.

- Evaluating the various kinds of evidence supporting arguments.
- Distinguishing between types of reasoning.

CRITICAL READING DEFINED

The term **critical reading** does not mean "critical" in the sense of tearing down or finding fault. Rather it means evaluating carefully, making sound judgments, and applying our reasoning powers. This requires keeping an open mind, not accepting unquestioningly what you read just because it is in print—but also not rejecting ideas simply because they are different from your beliefs. A middle ground might be called a healthy skepticism. Both to protect our wallets and, more important, to safeguard our ability to think for ourselves and to make up our own minds about the day's important issues, the ability to read material critically, from whatever source—traditional or electronic—becomes ever more necessary.

CRITICAL READING AND THE INFORMATION REVOLUTION

The mass of words that bombards us everyday—from newspapers, magazines, textbooks, the Internet, advertising of all stripes, junk mail, political slogans, and speeches—makes it vital for us to develop a keen critical stance. The increasing popularity and influence of the World Wide Web—a truly revolutionary means of disseminating information—has compounded the problem of information overload. And many people now turn to the Web first, rather than to traditional research tools in the library, as a source of information. (A friend who lives in a rural area 30 miles south of San Francisco wanted to learn how to make wine from his bumper crop of wild blackberries; he found the information in a couple of minutes using the search engine Yahoo!, thereby saving himself a trip to a San Francisco or San Jose library.)

Despite this extraordinary convenience, simple lack of editorial scrutiny is the crucial difference between traditional printed material and material published on the Web. The typical magazine article, for example, is pored over by editors and copy editors before it ever gets into your mailbox or onto the magazine stand. But the Web is completely egalitarian in its origins: Anyone can create a Web site; indeed, thousands of new sites are added each week. If you are experienced in navigating Web sites, you are probably aware that *anyone* with an opinion or interest—no matter how crackpot, no matter how trustworthy—can create a site, resulting in an overabundance of terrifically useful material—

and an overabundance of junk.[1] In essence the Web is an anarchic system, with no rules or strictures as to what can be published—at once its greatest virtue (no censorship) and its greatest handicap (no external objective analysis for fairness, bias, evidence, and the like).

Trying to sort out the fair from the unfair, the true from the false takes time, skill, and, a healthy skepticism, making the critical-reading process ever more difficult. Unbiased information can be found on sites maintained by nonprofit public interest groups (for example, the League of Women Voters), and most organizations involved in political and social issues now maintain Web sites. The important point is this: The same critical reading skills that pertain to conventional reading material must apply, if anything, even more so to Web material. The dangers of the Web are also what make it so exciting—its seductive lure, the enticingly flashy graphics and eye-catching designs, the novelty of finding information with lightning speed by a simple click of the mouse. However, we should not suspend our good judgment and our ability to think critically because we are dazzled by the glitz.

THE STRUCTURE OF ARGUMENTS

According to rules established by rhetoricians in ancient Greece, a sound argument had to conform to a rigid format. Through the centuries, these rules have been relaxed so that the argumentative form today is as varied as any other kind of nonfiction writing. We do, however, distinguish between two kinds of reasoning that underlie arguments: **deductive,** when the writer begins with a proposition and musters evidence in support, and **inductive,** when the writer derives the argument from the evidence. In the next chapter, you will examine deductive and inductive arguments in more detail. Although an argument need not follow the order in this diagram, the conventional argument includes these elements:

Argument (often called the thesis or proposition)

- Evidence
- Evidence
- Evidence (and so forth)
- Refutation (often called the concession)

Conclusion

[1]Mark Willes, chairman of the Times Mirror Company and the publisher of the *Los Angeles Times,* has said that "the Internet is the epitome of an unedited information glut."

THE TEST OF A GOOD ARGUMENT

The preceding diagram refers to the argument's *structure.* But our concern when we read argumentative prose is more apt to be with the quality of the ideas, the content. Some of what is published is very good, some is mediocre, and some is awful. How do you learn to tell the difference? What criteria should you use to determine whether a persuasive or argumentative piece of writing is "good" or "bad," whether the argument is sound or unsound? Here are some simple standards for judging what you read.

The main idea or thesis in persuasive or argumentative prose (usually called the **argument** or sometimes the **proposition**) should be clearly stated. The writer should define key words, especially abstract words open to subjective interpretation or used in a personal way (like *honor, responsibility, evil*). The language should be clear and unambiguous; words should be used consistently to mean the same thing. The evidence in support of the argument should be logically arranged, and it should be relevant to the main idea. Moreover, the evidence should appeal to our intelligence and to our reason, not solely to our emotions. In addition, there should be sufficient evidence to support the point.

Another important element of an argument is the **refutation,** in a short editorial usually just a paragraph or two in which the writer refutes the opposition, meaning that he or she examines opposing arguments and deals with them. With any issue, no single position is either all right or all wrong, and the writer who ignores or disregards the other side or opposing arguments runs the risk of having the reader ask, understandably enough, "Yes, but what about . . . ?" Therefore, in an editorial or opinion piece, a careful writer should include one or two of the opposition's strongest arguments and offer a rebuttal to them. A refutation can take several forms: The writer might concede that the opposition's argument has merit but that his or her own position is more vital or more significant in the long run; he or she might prove the opposing side in error by offering statistics disproving its claims; he or she can dispel myths associated with the opposing side, and so forth. As you work through the editorials at the end of this and the next chapter, it is a good idea to practice separating out these elements.

THE READER'S RESPONSIBILITY

Perhaps we should begin our discussion of specific skills with the reader's responsibility. If the writer's task is to muster convincing and fair evidence in support of an argument and to play by the rules of logic, what should the reader be doing? Why do we all sometimes misinterpret what we read? One cause is laziness. We may not take the trouble to comprehend accurately, being content to graze over the contents with no more concentration than if we were checking out the TV guide. Also, we may not feel like looking up the definitions of important words. Consider, for example, this sentence:

> The defense attorney used a meretricious argument to ensure his client's acquittal.

A reader might encounter this sentence and think, "*Meretricious* sounds sort of like *merit,* and I remember from high-school French that *mère* is the French word for *mother,* so *meretricious* probably means something good." Unhappily, this is way off the mark. Not only does the word have nothing to do with *merit* or *motherhood,* but it really means "attracting attention in a vulgar manner." (Applied to a person, incidentally, *meretricious* can mean "resembling or pertaining to a prostitute"!) So the reader, too lazy to look up the word, concludes from the sentence that the lawyer did something noteworthy, when the writer meant something very different.

Another evasion of our responsibility occurs when we glance through an article and put it aside because we already agree with the author's point of view. Perhaps the author's position is flimsy, supported by equally flimsy evidence. Perhaps the position is not really worth holding or does not stand up to scrutiny. Haphazard reading can never reveal or remedy this problem. Or even worse, we may glance at an article and not read it because we know in advance that we *don't* agree with the author, thus missing an important part of the intellectual experience—examining those opinions we do not share.

Still another obstacle to good reading is prejudice or bias, letting narrow personal experience or parochial values interfere with a clear-headed appraisal of what we read. Naturally, lower-division college students cannot expect to have the same wealth of experience older people do. Yet sensitivity to connotation and a willingness to see events from another perspective are essential components of critical reading (and of the intellectual experience); and they are best developed during the college years when students have the opportunity to be exposed to a wide assortment of political, social, and philosophical ideas. In the years following college, students can refine their thinking and call upon these skills in every aspect of their lives.

An incident that occurred in my advanced reading class illustrates how bias or prejudice can interfere with accurate reading. It involved a recent Polish immigrant in his mid-twenties. The class was discussing a newspaper article about Fidel Castro's playing host to Rajiv Gandhi, the prime minister of India. Wanting to give Gandhi a big send-off at the conclusion to his visit, Castro assembled thousands of Cubans, who lined the streets of Havana, cheering and clapping. Here are the pertinent sentences from the article:

> Rounding up a half-million people on short notice is no small task. But it took only a snap of Castro's fingers. By dawn, Havana was abuzz with activity in preparation for Gandhi's midmorning departure. Mass organizations were alerted and buses normally used to take commuters to their jobs were mobilized. Half a million cheering Cubans saw the Indian leader off that day in 1985.
>
> George Gedda, *San Francisco Examiner*

After reading this passage, the student inferred that Castro had "forced" the population to stop their daily activities and to attend the parade in Gandhi's honor, even though the writer's factual statement implied no coercion. (One could also infer inaccurately that the people gladly dropped what they were doing simply to get out of work.) Nor does the writer's tone convey anything sinister; the phrase, Havana was "abuzz with activity," if anything, indicates more of a positive connotation. In this case, the student's experience of growing up in a Communist country colored his perception, and he read into the writer's words an inference that the writer never implied.

Critical readers try—insofar as it is humanly possible—to maintain an objectivity so that their biases and personal prejudices do not interfere with their understanding.

DEVELOPING A WORLD VIEW

The etymology of the word *educate* means "a leading out," (from the Latin *e,* meaning "from" plus *ducare* meaning "leading"). And although it is impossible for human beings to be completely free of bias and prejudice, we should at least strive to identify the source of our beliefs and to look at ideas from other points of view. This requires us to be aware of or even shed our ethnocentric ideas that everyone else in the world looks at issues and problems the same way North Americans do. **Ethnocentrism** means a belief in the superiority of one's own ethnic group, or—stated more literally—the belief that one's group is at the center of the universe and that any other way of perceiving events is somehow wrong or flawed.

A college education will expose you to a wide range of opinion and thought, and often sorting it all out is difficult. As you grow intellectually and reflect on what you have read, learned, and experienced firsthand, you will develop a **world view**—your perspective on the world, a way of regarding events and issues that reflects your personal point of view. Too often we are content to hang on to our opinions because it is too much trouble to seek other points of view, and then, too, these opinions are so comfortable. They provide a ready-made set of beliefs for us, which may be sufficient for day-to-day life experiences, but which may fall short when we are confronted with serious social, economic, or political issues and complex problems to sort out.

Where does your world view come from? Obviously, from the many influences that you have come into contact with during your formative years: your parents, siblings, teachers, friends, acquaintances, members of the clergy, co-workers, to name a few. But your world view is also formed by intangibles: the value system you were raised with, your family's economic status, their level of education, race or ethnic group, their expectations for themselves and for you, your religious and moral background. All of these intangibles come together to form the person you are—and, for purposes of this discussion—the way you perceive what goes on around you and what you read.

Our world view constantly undergoes change, part of the "leading out" process we experience as students in college and as adults coming into contact with the real world. To characterize your world view, begin by questioning why you think the way you do by reflecting on your upbringing and on those people who have influenced you most. To what extent does your thinking conform to the way you were brought up? to the way you were educated? Becoming an independent adult—and along the way, a good thinker and reader—involves developing one's *own* world view, not someone else's views adopted uncritically.

A personal anecdote will illustrate how one's world view can be at dramatic odds with another person's, and more importantly, how being aware of another's differing world view can be an eye-opening experience. As I am writing this, the long Fourth of July weekend has just concluded. Before the holiday, I called a friend, an African-American woman of two years' acquaintance, and invited her to join us to watch the evening's fireworks display from our deck. Her reply astonished me. She thanked me, but politely declined the invitation, saying that her family had never observed the Fourth of July holiday. She added, "My ancestors didn't come to this country on the Mayflower, and they didn't come through Ellis Island." It had never occurred to me that an African American might not share my white view of the Fourth as a day for parades, barbecues, and fireworks.

Although our world views are different, neither of us is "wrong"; we simply come from different ethnic and geographic backgrounds, and I understand her unwillingness to participate as I know she understands my point of view. World views are personal and unique, and they should be respected, provided that they come from careful thought and conviction, rather than from an automatic conditioned response.

What does all this have to do with reading? Once we are sure we understand a piece of writing, we can then consider whether or not it accords with our world view. And after careful thought, we might discover that our reading has influenced or even altered our world view. It need not, but it might. To illustrate this process, in this section you will read some pieces about bullfighting, a popular spectacle in Mexico, Latin America, and, of course, Spain. (Bullfights also take place in the south of France and in Portugal, but in those countries the bull is not killed.)

The first article is by political writer Christopher Matthews, who describes a bullfight he saw in Barcelona. Before you begin, answer these questions on paper. Doing so will force you to clarify your thinking.

- What do you know/think about bullfighting?
- Do you consider bullfighting to be a sport or an art form?
- What is your opinion based on? For example, have you seen a bullfight on TV? In the movies?
- Have you ever attended a bullfight? If so, what were your reactions? Would you attend another?
- If you answered no to the question above, would you ever attend a bullfight? Why or why not?
- Do you believe bullfighting is cruel?
- Should bullfighting be banned?
- Is a bull an intelligent, sensitive animal in the same way, that, say, a dog is?

Selection 1

1The tragic goring of an American in Pamplona this summer brought to mind images from old Hemingway: the running of the bulls, the taste of wine on a hot afternoon, civil-war Spain. But with it arrives a personal memory that is not as Papa advertised.

2In "Death in the Afternoon," the great writer urged us all to judge the Spanish bullfight not by the squeamish hearsay of old women but from what we see and feel ourselves. With this injunction, I went one Barcelona Sunday to the Placa de Toros Monumental.

3Expecting a classic, if tragic, struggle of courage between man and bull, I saw what we in the press call a "gangland-style execution" of a half-dozen dazed animals. What I felt was the urgent impulse to bolt from my ring seat high above the arena for the exit gates below, mouthing my opinion of this Spanish "sport" the entire route.

4Six bulls were killed, as I said, that Sunday in the Placa de Toros Monumental. On that score at least, our best-known American aficionado got it right. But none of the bulls, I can say with the authority of the eyewitness, met his end "swaying on his legs before going up on his back with four legs in the air." No, it was different.

5The first bull to enter the ring died fastest. Taking the full length of the matador's sword in his back, the huge animal wandered dismally around the edge of the ring before collapsing in the dust.

6It would be wrong to judge an ancient ritual by a newcomer's snapshot, to pass eternal judgment on a spectacle that has diverted tourists for generations and local passions for centuries on the evidence of a single killing. Fortunately, a combination of ticket price, inertia and social pressure kept me in the Placa de Toros Monumental to watch the five other bulls die even more grotesquely than the first. The second to take the matador's blade roamed the full circumference of the arena all the while spewing blood through its mouth like water from a fire hose.

7The deaths of the other four were more complicated, a fact I credit to the clumsiness of the matadors. Not one of them accomplished his work with a single thrust or even a single blade. Each of our heroes was forced by desperation to drive one sword after another into his unimpressed animal.

8Nor did the beast perform according to Hemingway's storyboard. Instead of meeting a quick, exquisite end, it behaved instead like the doomed movie cartoon character who runs off a cliff but fails to fall only because he has not looked down.

9What is a grown man of common sensibility to make of such a thing? Hemingway urged his readers to "go open-mindedly and only feel those things they actually feel and not the things they think they should feel." Fair enough. You know nothing of your true reaction to a bullfight until you have watched one of these once-ferocious animals, a first or second or third sword run clear through him, fighting on against his predators. You know nothing of your reaction to the bullfighters themselves until you have watched the matador and his coterie of banderilleros pursuing and harassing these dying bulls until the wounded beast can run no more.

10But the killing itself is only a part of the grotesquerie. To measure the full moral depravity of the bullfight, one must weigh the entire ritual from beginning to end: the bull charging into the ring, the teasing by the banderilleros, the lancing by the mounted picador, the cape and sword work of the matador.

11At none of these stages did the courage on display in the Placa de Toros Monumental match that depicted by the marvelous old liar who wrote "The Sun Also Rises." From the time the bull entered the ring, he was hectored and confused without mercy by the banderilleros, who spent more time behind the wooden barrera than in the arena. Even when the matador entered the ring, these drugstore cowboys worked relentlessly to keep his rival distracted. Whenever he turned too abruptly or failed to follow his cue, the claque of banderilleros emerged from the barrera and teased the bull away and their hero to safety. Even after several swords had been plunged full length into the beast, the matador's street-corner sidekicks kept at it, torturing the bull even as his blood drained into the dust.

12This confusion and humiliation of the animal plays a critical part in the death ritual ludicrously called a "bullfight." It is much easier to see a beast butchered for sport once he has been made to look stupid.

13But if the bull is so stupid and the matador so cunning, how do we explain the omnipresent banderilleros bent on keeping him confused from the contest's beginning to end? If he is so lacking in basic intelligence, why is the young bull kept from the sight of a dismounted man until he enters the ring to be killed? And if the bull requires so much effort to be confused and subdued, why is he the worthy object of our torture?

14Is there a better word for it? None of the bulls I saw killed in Barcelona died either quickly or with precision. None did the one-point landing in the loving choreography of Hemingway's memory, "swaying on his legs" at the matador's exquisiteness. Bulls do not expire like characters in a Sam Peckinpah movie. Even when they have taken many thrusts of the sword, even when the clock says the match is through, they refuse to play their elegant part. To deal with the embarrassing survivor, a banderillero takes out a pen knife, stabs the wounded bull between the eyes, then sticks the blade deep into the animal's ear, gouging him to death in the manner of a small boy cutting the core from an apple.

15Only then is it time for the band to whip up the distinctive bullfight music, for the dead bull to be chained and dragged through the gates, as the crew of workers sweeps the arena floor much as major league ball park attendants do, leaving in their trail those large smears of red that mark each kill.

Christopher Matthews, "Gored,"
The New York Times Magazine, September 24, 1995

Selection 2

Here is a sampling of letters published in *The New York Times* in response to Matthews' article three weeks after it appeared. I have numbered them for easy reference.

1What Christopher Matthews saw in the corrida in Barcelona was the height of mediocrity (About Men: "Gored," Sept. 24). What I saw in Barcelona in May 1968 was the height of drama, spectacle and artistry. I saw three great matadors: Hernandez, Gomez and Cordobas—that's what Hemingway described. Bullfighting has lasted hundreds of years. Would you stop seeing theater for all the bad plays or movies?

Allan Rich
Los Angeles

[2]Hemingway was not a liar, but people are usually not fortunate enough to see brilliance and art in the bullring the first time. There are many factors that determine the outcome, including the stock of the bulls and the skill of the torero. The truth is that poetry and precision in these fatal dances between man and beast is infrequent.

Marissa Guijarro
Garnerville, N.Y.

[3]As an anthropologist who has spent much time living and working in Barcelona, I know that it is primarily tourism that sustains bullfighting in Catalonia's capital. "Local passions" for the sport run at such a low ebb that the bullring is more often used for political rallies, concerts and other large public events. On weekends, crowds of German, English, French, Japanese and American tourists pay to have their worst prejudices about the Spanish character confirmed. Matthews is no different.

Susan M. DiGiacomo
Amherst, Mass.

[4]In May 1994, I attended a bullfight in Madrid. Aided by the patient explanations of a local señorita, I witnessed a superb display of athleticism and courage. Four Spanish and two Portuguese bullfighters dazzled us with their acrobatic flourishes—one rider, galloping south, going so far as to touch his elbow to the head of a bull charging east.

The women in attendance responded to the bullfighters' flirtations with the bulls with what can politely be described as sexually charged shrieks of delight.

Matthews missed the beauty and the pageantry—a dangerous and exciting ritualization of man's struggle with, and mastery of, the wild beast in the arena and within himself. I encourage Matthews to revisit the bullring.

Paul L. Pusateri
Chicago

[5]I suspect that Matthews's description of the banderillero stabbing the bull between the eyes with a penknife and sticking "the blade deep in the animal's ear, gouging him to death," was blurred by his feelings. For the sake of accuracy, dispatching a mortally wounded bull is not done with a penknife, but with a puntilla, a 12-inch weapon that has a wooden handle and a steel shaft with a lancelike end. A strong thrust at the base of the skull severs the spinal cord and causes instant death.

Most people don't think about how bulls and steers meet their ends. We get involved only in that moment of truth when we must decide on well done, medium or rare.

Marc Simont
West Cornwall, Conn.

6Long ago, I, too, spent a Sunday afternoon at a bullfight in Spain. I left after the first kill, horrified and shaken. I am still haunted by those thousands of faces that seemed brought to orgasmic exhilaration by the suffering of that innocent beast slowly succumbing to a humiliating death. I wonder what disturbs me most—the senseless slaughter or how much everyone seemed to enjoy it?

Barbara Jarmon
Oceanport, N.J.

Letters to *The New York Times Magazine,*
October, 15, 1995

Selection 3

In this last reading, linguist Robert Lado examines the cultural misperceptions of bullfighting.

1A very interesting kind of trouble spot is seen when any element of the form of a complex pattern has different classification or meaning across cultures. The foreign observer gives to the entire pattern the meaning of that different classification of one element.

2*Example.* Bullfighting has always been in my observation a source of cross-cultural misinformation. It is a particularly difficult pattern of behavior to explain convincingly to an unsophisticated United States observer. I therefore choose it as a test case.

3*Form.* A bullfight has a very precise, complex form. A man, armed with a sword and a red cape, challenges and kills a fighting bull. The form is prescribed in great detail. There are specific vocabulary terms for seemingly minute variations. The bullfighter, the bull, the picadors, the music, the dress, etc., are part of the form.

4*Meaning.* The bullfight has a complex of meaning in Spanish culture. It is a sport. It symbolizes the triumph of art over the brute force of a bull. It is entertainment. It is a display of bravery.

5*Distribution.* The bullfight shows a complex distribution pattern. There is a season for bullfights on a yearly cycle, there are favored days on a weekly cycle, and there is a favored time on a daily cycle. The bullfight occurs at a specific place, the bull ring, known to the least person in the culture.

6*Form, meaning, and distribution to an alien observer.* An American observer seated next to a Spanish or Mexican spectator will see a good deal of the form, though not all of it. He will see a man in a special dress, armed with a sword and cape, challenging and killing the bull. He will see the bull charging at the man and will notice that the man deceives the bull with his cape. He will notice the music, the color, etc.

[7]The meaning of the spectacle is quite different to him, however. It is the slaughter of a "defenseless" animal by an armed man. It is unfair because the bull always gets killed. It is unsportsmanlike—to the bull. It is cruel to animals. The fighter is therefore cruel. The public is cruel.

[8]The distribution constitutes no particular problem to the American observer, since he has the experience of football, baseball, and other spectacles.

[9]*Misinformation.* Is there an element of misinformation here, and if so, wherein is it? I believe there is misinformation. The secondary meaning "cruel" is found in Spanish culture, but it does not attach to the bullfight. The American observer ascribing the meaning cruel to the spectator and fighter is getting information that is not there. Why?

[10]Since the cruelty is interpreted by the American observer as being perpetrated by the man on the bull, we can test to see if those parts of the complex form—the bull and the man—are the same in the two cultures.

[11]*Linguistic evidence.* We find evidence in the language that seems interesting. A number of vocabulary items that are applicable both to animals and to humans in English have separate words for animals and for humans in Spanish. In English both animals and persons have *legs.* In Spanish, animals have *patas,* "animal legs," and humans have *piernas,* "human legs." Similarly, in English, animals and humans have *backs* and *necks,* while in Spanish, animals have *lomo* and *pescuezo,* "animal back" and "animal neck," and humans have *espalda* and *cuello,* "human back" and "human neck." Furthermore, in English, both animals and humans *get nervous,* have *hospitals,* and have *cemeteries,* named by means of various metaphors. In Spanish, animals do not get nervous, or have hospitals or cemeteries. The linguistic evidence, though only suggestive, points to a difference in the classification of *animal* in the two cultures. In Hispanic culture the distinction between man and animal seems very great, certainly greater than that in American culture.

[12]By further observation of what people say and do one finds additional features of difference. In Spanish culture, man is not physically strong but is skillful and intelligent. A bull is strong but not skillful and not intelligent. In American culture a man is physically strong, and so is a bull. A bull is intelligent. A bull has feelings of pain, sorrow, pity, tenderness—at least in animal stories such as that of *Ferdinand the Bull.* A bull deserves an even chance in a fight; he has that sportsman's right even against a man.

[13]We can, then, hypothesize that the part of the complex form represented by the bull has a different classification, a different meaning, in American culture, and that herein lies the source of the misinformation.

[14]We should test this hypothesis by minimal contrast if possible. We find something akin to a minimal contrast in American culture in tarpon fishing. In tarpon fishing we have a form: a fight to the exhaustion and death of the tarpon at the

hands of a man with a line and camouflaged hooks. Much of the form is prescribed in detail. There is no large visible audience, but newspaper stories in a sense represent audience contact. In the complex of meaning, it is a sport, and it represents a triumph of skill over the brute fighting strength of the fish. The distribution seems somewhat different from that of a bullfight, but the difference does not seem relevant as an explanation of the difference we have hypothesized.

15We now observe that the very same American who interpreted the bullfight as cruel, and applied that meaning to the spectator and the bullfighter, will sit next to the same spectator on a fishing boat and never think of the fishing game as cruel. I conclude that the part of the complex form represented by the fish is quite distinct from "human being" in both American and Spanish cultures, while the part identified as the bull is much more like "human being" in American culture than in Spanish culture.

16Marginal supporting evidence is the fact that in American culture there is a Society for the Prevention of Cruelty to Animals which concerns itself with the feelings of dogs, cats, horses, and other domestic animals. Recently there was a front-page story in the local papers reporting that the Humane Society of New York City had sent a Santa Claus to distribute gifts among the dogs in the New York City pounds. We would not conceive of a society for the prevention of cruelty to fish.

Robert Lado, "How to Compare Two Cultures,"
Linguistics Across Cultures:
Applied Linguistics for Language Teachers

Clearly, these comments represent a wide spectrum. Which, if any, most corresponds to your point of view? Did any of them persuade you to alter your previously held opinion? No matter what your opinion about bullfighting (sport vs. art), nothing we read obliges us to change our opinion or even to attend a bullfight. But we *can* recognize that there are legitimate cultural differences operating here. Developing cross-cultural awareness means that we have been exposed to different world views from ours.

Two final comments: First, it is wholly acceptable to withhold judgment on any serious issue until you have more information. What other information would help you decide—ultimately—your beliefs? Second, you can discover a lot about your world view by completing an exercise like this. For example, if you are opposed to bullfighting on moral grounds, does your opposition connect in any way to your convictions about animals in other ways? For instance, do you eat meat, or are you a vegetarian? Do you avoid buying products, for example, shampoos and cosmetics, whose manufacturers test them on animals, or do you think it's better to test products on animals before humans use them?

IDENTIFYING ARGUMENTS

Because learning to take arguments apart is a complicated process, we will take it one step at a time—first locating the argument, then identifying any unstated assumptions, and finally evaluating the evidence used in support of the argument.

Before you can evaluate persuasive or argumentative prose, you must first determine what the writer's argument actually is. An **argument,** as defined earlier, is a specific proposition, the main idea, whether stated explicitly or implied, that the writer wants us to accept. Unlike expository or informative writing, the content of which is usually straightforward, the subject matter of persuasive writing involves controversy, it is subject to speculation, and it is capable of eliciting a wide variety of opinion.

To determine whether you truly are encountering an argument or merely a factual statement or innocuous suggestion, first consider the topic and its capacity to generate controversy. Many topics are inherently noncontroversial. No one is going to get worked up about a new program to prevent litter or a proposal to get the municipal bus system running on time. After all, who finds litter attractive or believes that bus service should be erratic? But many topics do inspire concern, great passion, and sometimes even violence. Here are some recent examples of debatable, often controversial, even volatile issues: the right of women to seek an abortion without interference; welfare reform; gay marriage; sending American troops to strife-torn areas like Bosnia; sexual harassment in the workplace; affirmative action programs for college admissions; cloning; and countless others.

Besides the idea itself, a writer's language may suggest a subjective point of view. For example, the words "should," "need," "must," and "ought" as a rule indicate a position that the author wants the reader to accept. Here are some arguments selected from recent issues in the news. Each has been revised to argue for the opposite side.

- The countries of the world should unite to ban human cloning. (*Contrary argument:* Because the cloning of humans might have substantial positive benefits in finding cures for diseases, a universal ban on cloning should not be enacted.)
- Juveniles who commit violent crimes should be tried as adults. (*Contrary argument:* Juveniles who commit violent crimes should not be held to the same legal standard as adults.)
- Introducing different sexual orientations besides heterosexuality to young school children is wrong. (*Contrary argument:* Elementary school children should be taught in school that other sexual orientations exist besides heterosexuality.)

- Distributing free condoms to high school students only encourages sexual experimentation and condones teenage sex. (*Contrary argument:* We as parents must act responsibly and allow high schools to distribute free condoms to any student who requests one.)
- College admissions officers should consider only an applicant's economic class rather than his or her racial or ethnic background. (*Contrary argument:* Decades of discrimination by the nation's colleges can be remedied only by race-based admissions.)
- The world's nations must take strong measures to prevent further global warming. (It is difficult to devise a contrary argument for this example, because the world's scientific community agrees that global warming and the depletion of the ozone layer are truly serious problems. In this case, the contrarian might argue that each nation be allowed to devise its own plan or that corporations and citizens alike must radically change their behavior if global warming is to be brought under control.)

These are all explicit arguments; however, some writers may just imply what "should" be done or what "needs" to be done. Consider these examples:

- English 100 really improved my writing skills. My teacher was helpful and encouraging, and I received an A for all my efforts. The course can help you, too. (*Implied argument:* You should take English 100.)
- Deciding to buy a computer was the best decision I ever made. My son's attitude toward school has turned completely around, and his grades have improved, too. (*Implied argument:* Buying a computer will improve a child's learning.)
- Charging that they were subjected to secondhand smoke that made them sick, in 1997, 60,000 nonsmoking flight attendants sued the tobacco industry for $5 billion in damages. (Although this sounds like a factual statement, the statement also contains these *implied arguments:* Breathing secondhand smoke is hazardous to one's health. The airlines should have protected flight attendants from a known health hazard. The airlines knew that breathing secondhand smoke constituted a health hazard yet denied that one existed.)
- The United States' new "get-tough" policy on legal immigrants who have been convicted of crimes is stripping them of their "due-process" rights and may result in their being returned to countries with repressive political regimes. (*Implied arguments:* America's new "get-tough" policy is unfair. Immigrants should enjoy the same right to due process as citizens. American immigration policy should not punish people by returning them to repressive countries.)

EXERCISE IN IDENTIFYING ARGUMENTS

Practice with these easier examples first. If the argument, or proposition, is stated explicitly, write it in the space provided, using your own words as much as possible. If it is implied, state it in your own words.

1. Timothy McVeigh should receive the ultimate penalty for committing the most infamous act of terrorist murder to ever take place on American soil. His coldly premeditated crime, setting off a huge bomb at a federal building in Oklahoma City, killed 168 men, women and children. ("For McVeigh, a Penalty as Severe as His Crime," *Los Angeles Times,* June 12, 1997.) Note: A few days after this editorial was published, a Denver federal jury sentenced Timothy McVeigh to death for his role in the Oklahoma bombing.

   Argument ____

2. In July 1997, a settlement was announced in which the tobacco industry would pay the states $350 billion to cover health care costs associated with smoking in exchange for immunity from future prosecution. Most cigarette advertising would also be prohibited; this prompted R. J. Reynolds to announce the demise of Joe Camel and Philip Morris to kill off its longtime advertising icon, the Marlboro Man. This excerpt is the opening paragraph of an editorial concerning the settlement.

> America has already had one disastrous experiment in prohibition. The tobacco settlement announced last week puts us on the verge of another. Like the first prohibition in this century, this new one promises an explosive increase in black markets, smuggling, criminality, and general cynicism. What's more, every indication is that the measures proposed by the settlement will serve not to diminish but to *increase* smoking. The settlement calls for spending hundreds of millions of dollars on efforts to discourage and deglamorize tobacco use. But emphasizing that tobacco is dangerous and disapproved will enhance the glamour, prestige and attractiveness—particularly among the young.
>
> Richard Klein, "Prohibition II . . . ,"
> *The Wall Street Journal,* June 26, 1997

   Argument ____

3. The author was the editor of the *Daily Nebraskan,* the University of Nebraska's campus newspaper. This editorial was published in *The Los Angeles Times* after Nebraska won the 1995 Rose Bowl.

> [1]Winning a national football championship brings glory and, with it, the most important force in college athletics—money. Even in sports deemed "amateur," money is the root of all competition.

[2]Since the University of Nebraska won the national football championship on Jan. 1, the Cornhusker state has gotten much richer. The ringing of cash registers can be heard everywhere.

[3]Sports Illustrated sold 300,000 copies of its national championship collector's edition in Nebraska alone. In the first week after Nebraska's success, the largest souvenir retailer in the state sold more than $1 million worth of shirts, hats, doormats and posters. Meanwhile, university coffers grow fatter and fatter.

[4]Yet, none of this newfound wealth will go to the football players. Members of the championship team who played in all 13 games and dedicated four years to the program walked away with only a championship T-shirt, an Orange Bowl watch and a national-championship ring.

[5]It would be silly to get angry at retailers or clever entrepreneurs for this financial "insult" to athletes. Instead, the blame rests with the system.

[6]A myriad of NCAA regulations prohibits compensating athletes. Never mind the billions of dollars these twentysomethings bring to the schools. Never mind that intercollegiate rules prohibit athletes from taking part-time jobs.

[7]This policy should be abandoned.

Jeff Zeleny, "Reward College Athletes by Paying Them for Play," *Los Angeles Times,* February 26, 1995

Argument ______________________________

4. [1]Rarely do we read a newspaper or magazine today without a reference to the information superhighway and its promise of wonders: 500 television channels, access to every movie ever made, 24-hour shopping and the availability of just about any kind of information we might want, all provided in the comfort of our home.

[2]As an avid user of Internet, the vast network of institutional and personal computers linked worldwide, I find the technology inherent in the information highway fascinating and the possibilities intriguing.

[3]As a psychologist, however, certain aspects of it make me very uneasy.

[4]A major cause of violence in our society is the growing economic gap between the urban poor and the suburban upwardly mobile.

[5]If, as U.S. News & World Report recently predicted, the information superhighway will create "a two-tier humanity: those on the net and those who are not," the gap will only widen. The urban poor will not have access to the

equipment, let alone the information, and the resulting frustration will escalate the already rampant violence in our nation.

James M. Jarvis, "Superhighway's Side Effects," *San Francisco Chronicle,* March 12, 1994

Argument ______________________________

Now try these harder ones.

5. Marriage and procreation are at the heart of a serious and flourishing human life, if not for everyone at least for the majority. Most of us know from our own experience that life becomes truly serious when we become responsible for the lives of others for whose being in the world we have said, "We do." It is fatherhood and motherhood that teach most of us what it took to bring us into our own adulthood. And it is the desire to give not only life but a *good way of life* to our children that opens us toward a serious concern for the true, the good, and even the holy. Parental love of children leads once wayward sheep back into the fold of church and synagogue. In the best case, it can even be the beginning of the sanctification of life—yes, even in modern times.

   Leon Kass, "The End of Courtship," *Public Interest,* Winter 1997

   Argument ______________________________

6. This excerpt is from an article discussing recent attempts in Congress to make English the official language of the United States. Also, Arizona adopted an English-only law requiring public employees to conduct all government business in English, which the Supreme Court has promised to review.

Many issues intersect in the controversy over Official English: immigration (above all), the rights of minorities (Spanish-speaking minorities in particular), the pros and cons of bilingual education, tolerance, how best to educate the children of immigrants, and the place of cultural diversity in school curricula and in American society in general. The question that lies at the root of most of this uneasiness is this: Is America threatened by the preservation of languages other than English? Will America, if it continues on its traditional path of benign linguistic neglect, go the way of Belgium, Canada, and Sri Lanka—three countries among many whose unity is gravely imperiled by language and ethnic conflicts? . . .

We like to believe that to pass a law is to change behavior; but passing laws about language, in a free society, almost never changes attitudes or behavior. Gaelic (Irish) is living out a slow, inexorable decline in Ireland despite enormous government support of every possible kind since Ireland gained its independence from Britain. The Welsh language, in contrast, is alive today in Wales in spite of heavy discrimination during its history. Three out of four people in the northern and western counties of Gwynedd and Dyfed speak Welsh.

I said earlier that language is a convenient surrogate for other national problems. Official English obviously has a lot to do with concern about immigration, perhaps especially Hispanic immigration. America may be threatened by immigration; I don't know. But America is not threatened by language.

Robert D. King, "Should English Be the Law?,
The Atlantic Monthly, April 1997

Argument ______________________

7. **1**On a recent segment of the *Late Show* David Letterman and his crew traveled to a New Jersey suburb looking for people willing to make fools of themselves on the air. Most of the people demurred, but a few daring souls belted out songs off-key or launched into embarrassing stunts. One guy even invited Dave into his house to play Twister on the living room floor.

2This was classic Letterman—the "anti-celebrity" hobnobbing with the common folk, while heaping ridicule on them at the same time. It's funny stuff, all right; but what it says about our culture is nothing to laugh at.

3Letterman's shtick,[2] explains Mark Edmundson in *Civilization* (Dec./Jan. 1997), is vintage "insider" humor: cynical, world-weary, and smug—and the dominant form of comedy today. Jay Leno, Jerry Seinfeld, and other comedians also are good at insider humor, but Letterman is the ultimate practitioner. "Letterman is knowingness incarnate," writes Edmundson. "Nothing surprises him. He presides over his show as though he were watching and commenting on a rerun rather than experiencing it in the present tense. Whatever comes along, he's seen it before."

4Considering the level of social confusion and cynicism that exists these days, it's not surprising that Letterman and his kind are so popular. Americans feel out of control, Edmundson argues, and insider humor provides comfort by assuring them that there are plenty of other people worse off than they are. "In a time of widespread social anxiety, when every value seems . . . to be up for grabs," he writes, "it's not surprising that we gravitate to Leno's and Letterman's assurances—not surprising, but not gratifying, either."

5Indeed, insider humor has cheapened our culture and deflated our spirits. What America really needs is a good dose of "outsider" humor, the sort of comedy made famous by the Marx Brothers in the 1930s. "In their best films, the Marx Brothers find themselves in a place where they emphatically don't belong—college classroom, society bash, front office," writes Edmundson.

[2]Yiddish for a show-business routine used to get laughs.

"They're the characters who have no business on the scene, the new people, the ultimate outsiders. But rather than wilting, they take the joint over. They grab a listless world by its expensive lapels and shake it up."

Craig Cox, "Shticks and Stones,"
Utne Reader, March–April 1997

Argument ______________________________

8. Cynthia Tucker is editor of the *Atlanta Journal and Constitution's* editorial pages.

1If you think nothing about race in America has changed in 30 years, take another look at Oprah Winfrey.

2As Winfrey put it in an interview with ABC's Diane Sawyer, the heart of the Texas cattlemen's failed lawsuit against her was that she was powerful enough to drive down beef prices with a casual comment about hamburgers. Thirty years ago, no black woman would have been accused of having such influence.

3If you think nothing about race in America has changed in 30 years, take another look at Vernon Jordan. He has been hauled before a federal grand jury because of his close relationship to the president of the United States. A powerful Washington attorney, Jordan is widely regarded as Bill Clinton's "best buddy" and close confidant. Thirty years ago, the black American closest to the president would have been his valet.

4Despite signs everywhere of progress, there remains a stubborn cottage industry of pessimists and naysayers whose stock-in-trade is bad news about race relations in America—even though their conclusions don't add up. Such is the case with a recent report released by a group founded as the successor to the Kerner Commission, which famously predicted 30 years ago this month that American society was moving toward "two societies, one black, one white—separate and unequal."

5The report by the Milton S. Eisenhower Foundation—founded in 1981 by several members and assistants to the Kerner Commission and other 1960s-era presidential panels—declares that "the Kerner Commission's prophecy has come to pass." while grudgingly acknowledging the growth of the black middle class, the report spends page after page attempting to prove the dubious theory that "progress stopped and reversed."

6Nonsense. I know too many black doctors, lawyers, architects, engineers and entrepreneurs to buy that bleak portrayal. I know too many black homeowners whose expansive suburban lawns and swimming pools are tended by hired hands. I know too many black parents whose children attend trendy private schools and take exchange courses in Europe.

7It is not news to point out—as the Eisenhower report does—that a disproportionate number of black Americans are mired in poverty, stuck in inferior inner-city schools or shunted off to prison for nonviolent drug offenses. Nor is it news to point out that growing income inequality is a troubling trend in this country (a trend affecting black, white and brown, by the way).

8Perhaps Harvard intellectual Henry Louis Gates best summed up the paradox of black achievement coexisting with abject poverty: "There are two Americas, both black." At the same time the black middle class has made substantial gains, too many black Americans have been isolated in neighborhoods growing more destitute, more crime-ridden, more miserable. But it does black Americans left behind no good to pretend that they are there only because of racism.

9The Eisenhower report is not entirely useless. It offers a few time-honored solutions for families stuck in poverty, including fully funding Head Start and increasing parental involvement in public schools. But the authors have failed to make an important distinction in American social life: Class is now more important than race.

10If you don't think so, look again at Oprah Winfrey and Vernon Jordan.

Cynthia Tucker, "Blacks of Consequence
Prove Racial Progress,"
Atlanta Journal and Constitution, March 8, 1998.

Argument ____

THE IMPORTANCE OF DEFINITIONS IN ARGUMENTS

Earlier in the chapter, you learned that one characteristic of good argumentative prose is that the author takes care to define key words, especially an abstract word open to subjective interpretation or one used in a personal or idiosyncratic way. For example, consider this argument:

> Abortion should be prohibited because it means taking the life of a human being.

The crucial phrase here is "life of a human being." Before we can decide on the worth of this argument (along with the many other problems and questions associated with abortion), we need to be sure of what we mean by "life." Roman Catholics believe that life begins at the moment of conception, when the egg and sperm unite. At the other extreme, some believe that a fetus is not truly a human being until it is viable, meaning that it is capable of surviving outside the mother's womb. Your acceptance or rejection of the previously stated abortion argument may, to some degree, depend on whether or not you accept the writer's implicit definition of "human life." Malcolm Potts is a physician who also has a Ph.D. in embryology; he is the Bixby Professor of Population and Family Planning at the University of California at Berkeley. Here is his perspective about the abortion debate and the beginning of life:

> When life begins in the continuum that stretches from setting aside the germ cells in the embryo to the birth of a baby is a judgment where sincere people will always disagree. While the facts of embryology are not in dispute, they can no more answer the question of when life begins than astronomers can determine if heaven exists by looking through a telescope for the Pearly Gates. The assertion that life begins at fertilization is relatively recent. In the Bible (Exodus 21:22) abortion is treated as a crime, but not as murder by giving a life for a life.
>
> "Tolerance in the Abortion Debate,"
> *San Francisco Chronicle,* June 24, 1996

UNSTATED ASSUMPTIONS

The second element in analyzing arguments is to uncover any **unstated assumptions.** All arguments rest on these assumptions or premises—the seemingly self-evident beliefs that underlie our thinking. We accept them, usually without even being aware of them, yet ironically, they are sometimes hard to detect. A simple illustration: If you tell your friend that you will meet him at Gino's Pizza at 6:00 P.M. right after your final exam, your statement implies several assumptions that are so obvious that there is no need to list them:

- You will both be alive tomorrow.
- The bus you rely on to get you to Gino's Pizza by 6:00 P.M. will arrive on time.
- Your final exam will end in enough time for you to get to Gino's by 6:00 P.M.
- Gino's will be open for business.

Here is another example:

> Because my sister is getting married next month in our backyard, we need to hire a caterer to prepare the food and a gardening crew to work on the yard.

Underlying this argument are these assumptions:

- We want the backyard to look nice for the wedding.
- The backyard doesn't look good enough for an event as special as a wedding.
- Hiring a caterer will be less hassle for us than if we prepare the food ourselves.
- We have enough money to pay for a caterer and a gardening crew.

Unlike these two real-life situations where we can safely take the unstated assumptions for granted, the nature of argumentative writing demands that we sort out the external statement and the assumptions that govern the writer's position. This does not mean that unstated assumptions are bad or somehow deliberately manipulative. It does mean that our accepting an argument may depend on our accepting the assumptions propping it up, as you saw in the "human life" example earlier. For example, consider this statement:

> School districts should not spend precious funds on expensive computer equipment at the expense of programs like art, music, and physical education programs.

Can you accept this argument? Can you identify the underlying assumptions, and if so, accept them? I see the two primary ones as being (a) that money allotted to school districts is limited and (b) that developing an appreciation for art and music and participation in sports are more important than developing computer skills. You should recognize that there is no "right" or "wrong" answer here, but rejecting the purchase of computers can at least be questioned, if not refuted. One solution to this either-or situation (i.e., either computers or enrichment programs), obviously, would be to properly fund school districts to permit both kinds of programs to flourish. (In Chapter 9, you will learn another way to analyze this argument, since it represents a fallacy called "false dilemma.")

EXERCISE IN IDENTIFYING UNSTATED ASSUMPTIONS

Let's start with some easy examples. After you consider each argument, write one unstated assumption in the space provided.

1. Colleges should reduce the number of part-time faculty they hire.

   Unstated assumption ______________________________

2. Grades are essential for motivating students to study. Grades let students know where they stand in the class.

   Unstated assumption ______________________________

3. Admitting minority students under affirmative action programs to our nation's colleges and universities will result in a freshman class with lower test scores.

   Unstated assumption ______________________________

4. Eliminating racial preferences in college admissions, particularly for law and medical schools, will result in fewer doctors and lawyers serving minority communities.

   Unstated assumption ______________________________

Now move on to these more difficult ones.

5. Many parents prefer to educate their children at home so that they can enter college at a younger age than their peers who attend traditional schools.

   Unstated assumption ______________________________

6. A college English teacher assigned her students to select a nonfiction book and to write a critique of it. One student chose Truman Capote's *In Cold Blood,* but the instructor rejected her choice, saying that a made-for-TV movie based on the book was going to be aired in the next few days. The teacher thought that the student would simply watch the movie and not read the book.

   Unstated assumption: ______________________________

7. In 1997 the military endured a series of sex scandals, among them charges of sexual harassment in the Army. Democratic Senator Robert C. Byrd of West Virginia questioned whether having men and women in basic training together is a good idea, saying, "I think the scandals which we are seeing . . . must be taken as a danger sign that sexual integration complicates an army's fighting capabilities. . . ." (Quoted in the *San Francisco Chronicle,* May 21, 1997.)

   Unstated assumption: ______________________________

8. From a letter to T. Berry Brazelton, pediatrician and authority on children's health issues and author of the syndicated column "Families Today": A single woman in her mid-30s wrote to Dr. Brazelton saying that she wanted to adopt a baby from another country (which she did not identify). Her question was whether or not raising a child without a father would be unfair to the child. Here is part of Dr. Brazelton's response: "Providing a baby from another country with a caring home is like giving him or her a major gift. You will profit from it as much as the baby." ("Single Woman Wants to Adopt a Baby," *San Francisco Chronicle,* March 18, 1996.)

   Unstated assumption ______________________________

EVALUATING EVIDENCE

The final step in evaluating arguments is looking at the evidence. The term **evidence** refers to the information or support used to prove or support an argument. Without generalizing, it seems fair to say that most good argumentative prose is supported by one or a combination of these types:

- Facts and/or statistics, including survey or poll results.
- Examples and illustrations, whether from the outside world or from the writer's personal experience.
- Good reasons.
- Historical analysis.
- Analogy.

Finally, evidence should meet these criteria: it must be fair, accurate, sufficient, and relevant.

In this excerpt, Andrew Hacker's purpose is to destroy the myth that American black culture is inhospitable to entrepreneurship. He begins by summarizing the arguments used to explain the supposedly small number of black-owned businesses. His evidence is in the form of facts, statistics, and good reasons, all of which refute the myth that blacks are denied business opportunities. By citing figures for all ethnic groups, Hacker convincingly shows that, even in comparison with white-owned businesses, blacks do fairly well. The argument is strengthened by the fact that over 90 percent of whites are on someone else's payroll.

1The so-called "small business" sector can also be a route to wealth and social status. The Census Bureau keeps count of the number of firms owned by black men and women. Its most recent survey found 425,000 such enterprises, numbering about 2.4 percent of the country's corporations, partnerships, and sole proprietorships. By and large, the black businesses are local concerns, with annual receipts averaging around $50,000, and they deal largely in products or services oriented to black clienteles. Indeed, only 70,000 of the 425,000 have any paid employees. In other words, almost 85 percent are one-person enterprises or family-run firms.

2Many arguments have been given for the paucity of black-owned enterprises. There is the difficulty of getting start-up loans and capital from banks and investors stemming from biased attitudes about blacks' business abilities. Nor is it easy for blacks to get experience in corporate management as a prelude to branching out on their own. Some blacks have done

Proportion of Men Who Are Self-Employed in 13 Ethnic Groups	
Korean	16.5%
Japanese	11.1%
Chinese	9.0%
Cuban	8.3%
White	7.4%
Asian Indian	6.6%
Mexican	4.4%
Hawaiian	3.9%
Eskimo	3.7%
Filipino	3.6%
Black	3.0%
Puerto Rican	2.9%
Vietnamese	2.1%

Source: Andrew Hacker, *Two Nations: Black and White, Separate, Hostile, Unequal*

well providing products and services to their own community. Still, the real challenge is to build a wider clientele. In fact, some firms have been successful in this sphere. Most whites who have bought Park's Sausages and McCall's Patterns do not know that those companies are owned and managed by blacks.

[3]It has occasionally been suggested that black Americans do not have a "culture" that encourages entrepreneurship. But it is best to be wary of such sweeping explanations, since they imply that the roots run very deep. There may be some validity to the view that youngsters who grow up in areas with few locally owned enterprises lack models for business careers. But even this need not be an obstacle, since the decision to start up on your own usualiy comes later in life. As it happens, in the generation following emancipation, many blacks set up businesses in Southern cities, just as others prospered in farming. Haitian and West Indian immigrants have brought entrepreneurial ambitions with them; and it will be interesting to see what beocmes of the West African sidewalk vendors who have beocme a New York fixture.

[4]Considering the advantages and opportunities open to white Americans, it is noteworthy that less than 8 percent of them operate enterprises of their own. The table above provides some census

tabulations that suggest that other ethnic groups are well ahead of whites in embarking on entrepreneurship. For this reason, little will be gained by asking whether blacks have a "culture" that inhibits them from establishing their own businesses. Even if that answer is in the affirmative, it also applies to white Americans, 92.6 percent of whom spend their working hours on someone else's payroll.

EXERCISE IN EVALUATING EVIDENCE

Here are some articles or excerpts that contain arguments. As you work through each passage, remember that you do not need to agree with the argument. As you saw above, you may need more information before you can make an intelligent and final judgment. For each, first identify the argument and look for any unstated assumptions. Decide what kind of evidence is used and evaluate it according to the criteria listed above. Again, writing down your evaluations will force you to clarify your thinking.

1. [1]If history really is repeating itself, the schools are in serious trouble. In *Teachers and Machines: The Classroom Use of Technology Since 1920* (1986), Larry Cuban, a professor of education at Stanford University and a former school superintendent, observed that as successive rounds of new technology failed their promoters' expectations, a pattern emerged. The cycle began with big promises backed by the technology developers' research. In the classroom, however, teachers never really embraced the new tools, and no significant academic improvement occurred. This provoked consistent responses: the problem was money, spokespeople argued, or teacher resistance, or the paralyzing school bureaucracy. Meanwhile, few people questioned the technology advocates' claims. As results continued to lag, the blame was finally laid on the machines. Soon schools were sold on the next generation of technology, and the lucrative cycle started all over again.

   [2]Today's technology evangels argue that we've learned our lesson from past mistakes. As in each previous round, they say that when our new hot technology—the computer—is compared with yesterday's, today's is better. "It can do the same things, plus," Richard Riley, the U.S. Secretary of Education, told me this spring.

   [3]How much better is it, really?

   Todd Oppenheimer, "The Computer Delusion,"
   The Atlantic Monthly, July 1997

Argument ___

Unstated assumptions ___

Evidence ___

Evaluation of evidence ___

2. The author is senior minister of the Hamilton Square Baptist Church in San Francisco.

> [1]Government has a fundamental, compelling interest in the reproduction of society, the adequate socialization of the individuals who constitute society and in seeing that its children are induced toward healthy and productive lifestyles. The state very legitimately promotes these fundamental, social objectives—none of which is furthered by homosexual marriage.
>
> [2]Marriage was never intended to be a means for making official an economic partnership or legal or social contract. Nor is it the appropriate means to bring about equality and fairness to a segment of society. Marriage is the social, legal and spiritual uniting of two people (one man and one woman with the capacity to procreate) into "one flesh" in a spiritual act that God makes a reality. As for those who seek to lovingly and compassionately care for the basic needs of others, numerous and very adequate statutory provisions already exist to accommodate hospital visitation, common title to property, inheritance, health care, power of attorney and many other legal necessities.
>
> [3]God has brains! He has very wisely ordered His creation for everyone's good. Violating this created order will only produce chaos and ultimately, destruction. Those who foolishly and arrogantly flaunt or seek to change God's laws will find that they are engaging in the exercise of self-destruction. For those who are willing to face reality there is a much better option—the life-transforming power of Jesus Christ which can utterly change and completely fulfill our lives. This is the message of love, acceptance and hope that we believe and teach.

David C. Innes, from "A Christian View on Gay Marriages," *San Francisco Chronicle,* April 8, 1996

Argument ___

Unstated assumptions ___

Evidence ___

Evaluation of evidence ___

3. [1]The image of teenage girls having babies to receive welfare checks is an emotion-laden but fraudulent cliché. If the availability of welfare benefits causes teen pregnancy, why is it that other industrial countries, with far more generous support policies for women and children, have far lower rates of teen pregnancy?

[2]Welfare benefits do seem to increase the likelihood of unmarried teen mothers moving away from their parents' households, hence increasing the *visibility* of these mothers, but they bear little or no relation to actual birth rates for unmarried women. Harvard economists David Ellwood and Mary Jo Bane compared unmarried women who would be eligible for welfare if they had an illegitimate child with unmarried women who would not be eligible: Even by confining their analysis to states that gave the most generous welfare benefits to single mothers, they found no difference in the rates of illegitimacy between the groups. Mississippi, with the lowest welfare and food stamp benefits for AFDC mothers in the entire country (only 46 percent of the federal poverty guidelines), has the second-highest percentage of out-of-wedlock births in the country; states with higher AFDC benefits than the national average tend to have *lower* rates of illegitimacy than the national average.

[3]Sociologist Mark Rank finds that "welfare recipients have a relatively low fertility rate" and that the longer a woman remains on welfare, whatever her age, the less likely she is to keep having babies. Mothers on AFDC have only one-fourth the number of births while they are on welfare as do mothers who are not on welfare.

Stephanie Coontz, *The Way We Never Were*

Argument ______________________________

Unstated assumptions ______________________________

Evidence ______________________________

Evaluation of evidence ______________________________

4. The author is an obstetrician and gynecologist who practices at the Fayetteville Women's Clinic in Arkansas.

[1]Most of us in medicine now accept that tobacco is associated with major health consequences and constitutes the No. 1 health problem in this country.

[2]What smokers have not yet come to terms with is that if they continue smoking, the probability of developing one or more of the major complications of smoking is 100%. It absolutely will happen. They will develop chronic bronchitis, laryngitis, pharyngitis, sinusitis and some degree of emphysema. It is also highly probable that they will develop serious disease in the arteries of all vital organs, including the brain and heart, markedly increasing their risk of

heart attack and stroke. If they continue, they increase the probability of developing cancer of the lips, gums, tongue, pharynx, larynx, trachea, bronchi and lungs, of the bladder, cervix, gallbladder and other organs. Smoking contributes to rapid aging of the skin and connective tissues—women and men who smoke usually have the skin age of a person 10 to 20 years older than one who doesn't smoke, given the same degree of exposure to the sun.

3About 415,000 people die prematurely each year in the U.S. as a result of smoking—the equivalent of 18 747s crashing every week with no survivors. Many of these victims die after long and excruciating illnesses, burdens to themselves, their families and society. The cost of this misery is incalculable, but we do know that the tobacco industry grosses about $50 billion a year from the agonies it inflicts.

4How does all this damage come about?

5In normal lungs, the trachea and bronchi—the large and small tubes leading to the alveoli (the tiny sacs that do the actual work of the lungs)—are lined with a film of tissue that is one cell layer thick. The surface of these cells is covered with tiny, finger-like structures called cilia. These cilia beat constantly in a waving motion, which moves small particles and toxic substances out of the lung and into the back of the throat where they are swallowed. In a smoker or someone like a coal miner, who constantly breathes in large amounts of toxic substances, many of the cilia soon disappear. If exposure continues, some ciliated cells die and are replaced by squamous cells, the same type that form the skin. Without the cleansing function of the ciliated cells, toxic materials and particles are breathed further into the lungs, staying longer in contact with all the tissue. Each group of ciliated cells killed and replaced by squamous cells decreases by a certain fraction the lungs' ability to cleanse themselves. As this occurs, the amount of damage done by each cigarette increases to a greater and greater degree. By the time one has been a pack-a-day smoker for 10 years or so, extensive damage has already been done. By 20 years, much of the damage is irreversible and progresses more rapidly. After 10 years of smoking, each cigarette may do as much damage to the body as three or more packs did when a smoker first started.

6The longer one smokes, the harder it gets to quit. Smoking is one of the most addictive of human habits, perhaps as addicting as crack cocaine or heroin. One has to quit every day, and there are no magic pills or crutches that make stopping easy. It is tough to do. Only those who keep trying ever quit. And even those who have smoked for only a short time or few cigarettes a day will probably find it difficult to stop. But the sooner a smoker makes this self-commitment, the more probable it is that he or she will quit before having done major damage to the body.

William F. Harrison, "Why Stop Smoking?
Let's Get Clinical," *Los Angeles Times*, July 7, 1996

Argument ______________________________

Unstated assumptions ______________________________

Evidence ______________________________

Evaluation of evidence ______________________________

5. [1]The great American melting pot is becoming more like a stew, and an increasingly exotic and complicated one at that. In its latest report on population trends, the Census Bureau says that nearly one in 10 people in the United States is foreign-born, the highest rate in more than 50 years.

[2]At 24.5 million, the number of foreign-born inhabitants stands at the highest level in U.S. history and is about 2 million more than reported in the previous such survey in 1994. In proportional terms, the foreign-born accounted for 9.3 percent of the total U.S. population—well below the high mark this century of 14.7 percent in 1910 but nearly double the rate since the low point in 1970 and continuing an upward trend since then.

[3]The Census Bureau report—based on a March 1996 survey that included legal and illegal immigrants, naturalized citizens, students and temporary workers—appears to provide ammunition for both camps in the ideological debate over immigration. The bureau reports that the foreign-born, especially the more recent arrivals, are more likely than natives to live in poverty, to be unemployed, to use welfare and to have less than a high school education.

[4]On the other hand, the report says, the longer the immigrants stay here, the better they fare. Those who have lived in the United States for more than six years "seem to have recovered from their initial economic hardship," it says, and those who arrived during the 1970s generally are now earning as much as natives.

[5]Given the economic conditions immigrants must overcome, on the whole, "it's a pretty dark picture," says Mark Krikorian, who heads the Center for Immigration Studies and favors reducing immigration. "The problems that we have with immigration are only becoming sharper," reducing the ability of the United States to unify "the various strands of our people." In any case, he says, this "melting pot" tradition "is no longer considered politically correct."

William Branigan, "The Great American Melting Stew," *The Washington Post,* April 14, 1997

Argument ______________________________

Unstated assumptions ______________________________

Evidence ______________________________

Evaluation of evidence ______________________________

KINDS OF REASONING

In Chapter 5 you learned the difference between deductive and inductive paragraph order. As noted in the preceding chapter, however, in terms of logic the two kinds of reasoning—**induction** and **deduction**—mean something different, referring to two different ways of constructing an argument. In this section you will learn, first, the difference between these two systems of reasoning and then how to identify arguments according to whether they are valid or invalid, sound or unsound.

Inductive Reasoning

Since the conclusion of an inductive argument can become a major premise in a deductive argument, we will start with induction. An **inductive argument** is built upon a set of factual statements serving as evidence. The statements may come from observation or experience, whether personal or scientific. From these statements one comes to a conclusion—either in the form of a *generalization,* a statement asserting that something is true of all members of a class, or a *hypothesis,* a statement of conjecture of what will *probably* occur. In short, inductive arguments move from the specific to the general, as you will recall from Chapter 5. Inductive arguments are also sometimes called **probability arguments** because the conclusion may not necessarily follow from the evidence. Consider this example:

Evidence: English 100 requires five essays.
Evidence: English 220 requires eight essays.
Evidence: English 350 requires ten essays.
Conclusion: All English classes require a lot of writing.

In the above argument, the conclusion represents a **generalization** (by virtue of the word "all") based on three pieces of evidence. The conclusion is probable, but not necessarily true because other conclusions are possible. In this instance, some college English classes, such as survey courses in literature or grammar review may require very little writing. The writing requirement would depend on the individual instructor and the department's standards. But it is equally obvious that the more instances of English courses with demanding writing requirements one provides, the stronger the conclusion derived from them.

Let us now look at an inductive argument with the other sort of conclusion—a hypothesis.

Evidence: Last week I saw my boss and his secretary having dinner together at an intimate little French restaurant.
Evidence: Yesterday I saw my boss and his secretary having lunch at the Mexican restaurant close to the office.

Evidence: This weekend my boss and his secretary are going away together on a business trip.

Conclusion: My boss and his secretary are having an affair.

Is this conclusion reasonable or probable based on the evidence? Although the writer cites three instances of her boss and his secretary's meeting, the conclusion represents only a **hypothesis**—a theory or conjecture—about the reason for their being together. Perhaps they are preparing for the upcoming meeting; perhaps they are just friends who enjoy each other's company; perhaps they *are* having an affair. In the absence of more compelling evidence that would suggest a romantic liaison, this conclusion is possible or somewhat probable, but not necessarily true.

Deductive Reasoning

In Sir Arthur Conan Doyle's first novel, *A Study in Scarlet,* Sherlock Holmes, who has just met Dr. Watson, explains to Watson the usefulness of making deductions in solving mysteries. Watson, apparently, has been skeptical of Holmes's abilities. Holmes says:

> You see I have a lot of special knowledge which I apply to the problem, and which facilitates matters wonderfully. Those rules of deduction laid down in that article which aroused your scorn are invaluable to me in practical work. Observation with me is second nature. You appeared surprised when I told you, on our first meeting, that you had come from Afghanistan.

Watson replies, "You were told, no doubt." And then Holmes demonstrates his deductive powers:

> "Nothing of the sort. I *knew* you came from Afghanistan. From long habit the train of thoughts ran so swiftly through my mind that I arrived at the conclusion without being conscious of intermediate steps. There were such steps, however. The train of reasoning ran: 'Here is a gentleman of a medical type, but with the air of a military man. Clearly an army doctor then. He has just come from the tropics, for his face is dark, and that is not the natural tint of his skin, for his wrists are fair. He has undergone hardship and sickness, as his haggard face says clearly. His left arm has been injured. He holds it in a stiff and unnatural manner. Where in the tropics could an English army doctor have seen much hardship and got his arm wounded? Clearly in Afghanistan.' The whole train of thought did not occupy a second. I then remarked that you came from Afghanistan, and you were astonished."
>
> Sir Arthur Conan Doyle, *A Study in Scarlet*

As he explains it, Holmes has moved from a set of premises regarding Watson's appearance, dress, and behavior to his conclusion. Since they were consistent with Holmes's observations of other Englishmen who served as doctors in the military in Afghanistan, then he could validly conclude that Watson had performed such service.

Unlike inductive arguments, a **deductive argument** moves from reason to conclusion or to specific application with logical necessity. To illustrate, if you know that your textbook is in your backpack and you know that your backpack is in your car, then you can logically deduce that your textbook is in your car. This conclusion is a logical inference that *must* necessarily proceed from the two pieces of evidence, which are called **premises.** Taken together, the two premises and the conclusion derived from them constitute a **syllogism** constructed like this:

Major premise:	My textbook is in my backpack.
Minor premise:	My backpack is in my car.
Conclusion:	Therefore, my textbook is in my car.

As long as the argument follows the prescribed form of the syllogism, it is considered to be *logically valid;* further, if the premises are true, then the argument is considered to be *sound,* in other words, reliable.

To repeat, deduction is the opposite of induction because the conclusion can be logically derived from the major and minor premises, whereas in an inductive argument, the conclusion is a matter of probability or hypothesis. In an inductive argument, the reasons *suggest* that the conclusion is true; as more evidence accumulates, the conclusion becomes stronger. Yet an inductive argument always involves a "leap" from the evidence to the conclusion, again the matter of *probability.* But in a deductive argument, there is no leap or question of probability. Another way to remember the difference between inductive and deductive reasoning is this: Induction is more of an argument of *content,* whereas deduction is an argument of *form,* by virtue of the syllogism.

Here is another example of a deductive argument.

Major premise:	All men are mortal.
Minor premise:	John is a man.
Conclusion:	John is mortal.

This syllogism is valid because (a) the premises are true and (b) the premises already contain or imply the conclusion. By accepting the premises, we must also accept the conclusion, and it is therefore valid.

The following example presents a different syllogism form:

Major premise:	If welfare benefits are cut, former recipients will rise to the occasion, get job training, and enter the workforce.
Minor premise:	Welfare benefits were cut.
Conclusion:	Former recipients rose to the occasion, got job training, and entered the workforce.

This syllogism can be diagramed as follows:

Major premise:	If X, Y (in other words, if X happens, Y will happen).
Minor premise:	X (X happened).
Conclusion:	Y (Therefore, Y happened).

EXERCISE IN IDENTIFYING INDUCTIVE AND DEDUCTIVE ARGUMENTS

For this exercise, decide whether the argument is inductive or deductive.

1. François must be a good lover. He's French, you know.
2. Just look at that gold Lexus! The owner must be really rich.
3. Seven out of ten dentists recommend Trident gum for their patients who chew gum.
4. Our instructor for Film History 10 announced that if students completed all the assignments for the course, they would receive an A. I did all the assignments, and I was thrilled with my final grade!
5. Charlotte, Lindsay, and Gabrielle all got good jobs because they know several computer programs. It's likely that Luisa, who's a whiz on the Macintosh, will get a good job, too.
6. Twenty-five thousand Americans, representing every age group, geographical region, ethnic group, and income and educational level, were surveyed recently about their television viewing habits. Their four favorite television programs were *ER, NYPD Blue, Friends,* and *Seinfeld.* The major networks will undoubtedly air more urban dramas and witty comedies next season.
7. Javier has done a lot of writing in all of his English courses, so he knows he'll have to write a lot when he takes Joan Wilson's critical reading course this year.
8. Since I need something to read on my plane ride, I'm going to buy this novel. I saw it on *The New York Times* bestseller list, so it must be really good.

9. The Catholic Church should follow the example of the Episcopalians and the Presbyterians and allow women to become priests.
10. If dieters follow the rules in the Thin Again Diet Plan, they will safely lose 25 pounds in three months. Kathleen lost 25 pounds between January and April. She must have followed the plan faithfully.

BALANCE

Beyond mustering evidence that meet the criteria discussed above, newspaper and magazine news and feature journalists have a further responsibility to present controversial issues fairly. This is called **balance,** wherein all sides of an issue are presented in approximately equal proportions, leaving the reader free to make up his or her own mind. Unlike editorial writers, whose works typically appear in magazine editorials or in newspapers' op-ed (opinion-editorial) pages and who write from a subjective point of view, reputable news writers also strive—as far as is humanly possible—to maintain objectivity in presenting both sides of a controversial issue.

Let us examine a recent newspaper article for balance. The subject is the controversy over theme parks' performing whales. After you read the article, take a sheet of paper and draw a vertical line down the middle. Label one column "arguments for" capturing and training whales to perform and the other "arguments against."

> **1**At first glance, Yaka and Vigga—the star cetaceans at Marine World in Vallejo—hardly appear likely candidates for national controversy, as they splash and chatter like carefree children on a beach holiday.
>
> **2**Yet animal welfare advocates argue that the pair of whales and the country's 14 other captive orcas are a disgrace. They charge that the seagoing mammals are ripped from their family groups in the wild and worked to premature death in the arenas of an entertainment industry that insists it is acting to preserve the species and to educate the public.
>
> **3**Now, through demonstrations, lawsuits and pressure on regulatory agencies, animal welfare groups are provoking the industry into a high-stakes standoff.
>
> **4**"We see an animal that has intricate social behaviors, and basically they're forced to spend their lives in something that's just a swimming pool," said John Grandy, vice president of wildlife habitat protection for the Humane Society of the United States. "When a wild orca is taken and put into that, we would view that as a tragedy."
>
> **5**Piegen Barrett, executive director of the Marine Mammal Center at Fort Cronkhite, disputes that view. She says Marine World is an exceptionally humane caretaker and deserves credit for its commitment to rescuing stranded cetaceans, adding that it is wrong to associate the facility with others that have lower standards.

6"I do know we're not abusing these animals," Marine World founder and manager Michael Demetrios said in an interview. "The handful we have are ambassadors for their species."

7It has taken a generation of experience with captive marine mammals to prompt a debate over the quality of their care and the ethics of displaying them. In the 1960s, families piled into their gas guzzlers and packed the nation's new aquariums, delighted at the spectacle of dolphins leaping through fiery hoops and cavorting in grass skirts and giant sunglasses.

8Like Flipper, those days are gone.

9"The public is changing its views," Grandy said. ". . . What you're seeing is an evolution of human thought and, perhaps, corporate responsibility."

10Since 1989, protesters encouraged by a more skeptical public have claimed credit for restricting a U.S. Navy dolphin program in Puget Sound and blocking the transfer of a dolphin from a private aquarium to the Navy.

11Last August, in the first such move since it began monitoring theme parks in 1979, the U.S. Agriculture Department charged a Florida exhibitor with low standards of animal care. And just last month, Great America amusement park in Santa Clara announced that it was dropping its live dolphin show, citing public perceptions and the high costs of the exhibit.

12Groups such as In Defense of Animals based in Marin County, are appealing to the emotions of the 15 million Americans who pay money to watch whale shows every year. Hoping to put amusement operators on the defensive and to tweak the consciences of entertainment consumers, they are urging that Yaka and Corky, a killer whale housed at Sea World in San Diego, be returned to their families in Puget Sound.

13At the same time, the groups are massing their legal clout for a battle over the Marine Mammal Protection Act, the 1972 law that gives exhibitors the right to capture, import, move and display whales and dolphins in the name of public education. Advocates believe that if enough members of Congress can be swayed to their side by the time the law is up for review in 1993, the industry could wind up saddled with crippling restrictions.

14Demetrios, who hopes to expand Marine World and acquire a male killer whale so he can try to breed the animals, said the critics "at some point could become a direct threat." He said Marine World is struggling to break even financially.

15Critics not only argue the ethics of capturing marine mammals, they maintain that it is impossible to build adequate facilities for them because so little is known about what they need in order to thrive for many decades.

16Pointing to industry disclosures, they say that more than two killer whales have died in captivity for every one now performing in the United

States. Stress leaves them vulnerable to disease and injury, Susan Rich of the Earth Island Institute told a National Marine Fisheries Service hearing in Washington, D.C. last month.

17Industry executives say the advocates are misleading the public by wrapping self-serving interpretations of mammal longevity in foolish sentimentalism. Further, they say they are the victims of a "protest industry" that deals in warm and fuzzy mammal images for fund-raising. The New England Aquarium was so upset that it fired back at critics with a defamation suit.

18"These people protesting are a very small minority of the public," said John Kirtland, spokesman for the International Marine Mammal Trainers Association. "The sad thing is, in an age of oil spills, pollution, and habitat destruction, their focus is on a small group of animals rather than on the critical issues of conservation of species and preservation of habitat."

19Jim Mullen, assistant director of marine mammal training for Marine World, and Dr. Laurie Gage, the facility's veterinarian, said protest groups have never bothered to see the whales and dolphins for themselves. If they did, Gage said, they would agree that the creatures are thriving in their performing careers.

20Industry supporters acknowledge that plenty of captives died young when parks were in their infancy in the 1960s and 1970s, but they maintain that the average life span of performing whales and dolphins now matches or exceeds that of those in the wild.

21In the case of killer whales, the two sides are divided largely because they disagree on how long an animal should be expected to live in the wild. Protest groups argue that orcas can live to 90. But David Bain, a consultant for the federal fisheries service who has worked with Marine World's two killer whales since 1979, said his research shows that the average life span is about 20 years, although some individuals may last into their 80s.

22Yaka is 25 and has been in captivity since 1969.[3] Vigga, 15 years old, was taken in Iceland in 1981.

23In any cast, industry experts say, it is absurd to suggest that a long-captive animal turned loose again would benefit from the experience. They cite the case of Reno, a harbor seal so named because a Nevada couple picked it up off a San Francisco beach in the early 1970s and fattened it on clams in their bathtub.

24Experts at Steinhart Aquarium slimmed down the animal and tried to put it back in the ocean. But Reno just jumped back into the boat.

[3]Yaka died in October 1997 after performing at Marine World for 27 years. She had been ill for several months.

[25]Still, the concerns over animal welfare are getting through to the public. [26]Adele Gerz illustrates the new awareness. A contributor to the nonprofit Marine World Foundation since 1985, the 29-year-old Vallejo woman visited the park dozens of times and never questioned its educational mission.

[27]That changed a year ago, when she asked a park guide where Yaka came from and was stunned to learn the five-ton female had been abducted from the sea. Yaka and Vigga are the only killer whales in captivity in Northern California.

[28]"The only conclusion I could draw was that they wanted to open a theme park and have this whale as an attraction," said Gerz, who does not belong to any animal welfare group. "It made me feel kind of sick."

Rick DelVecchio, "Performing Whales Drawing Protests," *San Francisco Chronicle*

Now examine your lists. What is DelVecchio's purpose in writing? How well does he maintain his objectivity? Are both sides of the issue presented in roughly the same proportion? Are both sides of the issue presented fairly, in noninflammatory language?

EXERCISE IN ANALYZING EDITORIALS

The last set of exercises consists of four examples of persuasive writing to give you practice in implementing your critical reading skills. These passages represent editorials on current controversial issues from the op-ed pages of major newspapers. For each selection that your instructor assigns (or that you read on your own), consider these questions:

- What is the writer's main argument or proposition? Be sure that you can state it in your own words.
- List two or three assumptions that the argument rests on (assuming that the author has not provided them).
- What kind of evidence does the writer provide in support of the argument?
- Is the argument deductive or inductive?
- Does the evidence meet the criteria discussed in this chapter? Is it fair, accurate, sufficient, and relevant?
- What is the author's tone? (You might want to review the introductory discussion of tone in Chapter 7.) Is the writer straightforward, hostile, sympathetic, outraged, concerned, cynical, sarcastic—to name a few?
- Is the argument, as the author presents it, convincing or at least worth considering?
- Do you accept the argument? Why or why not? If you need more information, what would you need to know?

Selection 1

Arthur Levine is chairman of the Institute for Educational Management at Harvard University.

[1]The merits of reducing the college degree to three years from four are being broadly discussed in academic circles. The debate was started by Fred Starr, the president of Oberlin, and is being fueled by a Stanford University curriculum re-examination that considers whether the time it takes to earn a baccalaureate degree should be reduced to three years.

[2]The idea is appealing on the surface. At a time when college tuitions are soaring, cutting a year from undergraduate study would appear to reduce costs 25%. But like many other academic exercises, it is out of touch with reality.

[3]The idea is not new. Harvard had a three-year degree in the 1640s. Its second president got into a battle royal with his board of trustees when he turned it into a four-year degree. Periodically in the years since, both the debate and "new" three-year degree have reappeared. Most recently, in the early 1970s, the Carnegie Corporation supported the creation of three-year programs at colleges and universities across the country. Nearly all of those programs are now gone. There was too little student interest to justify their continuation.

[4]If anything, three-year degree programs probably would be even less successful now than they were then. There are several reasons:

[5]First, student academic skills have declined since the late 1960s. More than a third of undergraduates report that they are in need of remedial courses. In short, students appear to need more education today, not less.

[6]Second, the average time required to earn a college degree is actually increasing. A growing proportion of students are taking five years of classes, particularly at large public universities, which the majority of students now attend.

[7]Third, a majority of college students work today while attending college. Most work 20 hours or more a week to be able to pay their tuition. The promise of not paying a fourth year of tuition would not eliminate their need to work. As a consequence, the notion of extending the college year or even the college day is impractical.

[8]Fourth, eliminating the final year of college would be a financial disaster for most institutions, which are heavily dependent on tuition or enrollments to fund their operations. Schools would lose a quarter of their student bodies. Outside the West and the South, the demographics of the nation are such that the loss of students simply could not be made up. Colleges might have to raise tuition substantially to compensate.

[9]However, there is a much larger problem for the three-year degree than any mentioned so far: It does not make educational sense. The four-year degree is entirely arbitrary. And so is the three-year degree. Degree time measures how long students sit in class. It is not a measure of how much they learn.

[10]Imagine taking your clothes to a laundry and having the proprietor ask, "How long do you want me to wash them: three hours or four?" The question would be absurd. We don't care how long the clothes are washed. We want them clean. We want the launderer to focus on the outcome of his washing, not the process.

[11]Education should operate similarly. Colleges and universities should define the skills and knowledge a student needs to possess in order to earn a baccalaureate degree, rather than the number of hours of lectures and classes a student should attend to earn a degree.

[12]Students enrolled in college now are more heterogeneous than ever before. More than half of all high-school graduates are going on to some form of post-secondary education, and the fastest-growing group attending college is older adults. As a result there is a greater range of knowledge, skills and experience among college students than in the past. Many will require more than four years of instruction to earn a degree. Others will come to college with such rich backgrounds that they will be able to complete a degree in less than four years and perhaps less than three. For these reasons, it is a mistake for colleges to tie in their degrees to time served.

Arthur Levine, "College—More Than Serving Time,"
The Wall Street Journal, December 21, 1993

Selection 2

[1]Is speech on the Internet like speech in a public square, or is it more like speech in a privately owned mall, where leafleters and demonstrators need permission? And what about universities, where students using university accounts for e-mail and other messages may find themselves subjected to disciplinary rules? The latter problem occurred most recently at Virginia Tech, which has come under challenge for disciplining a student who sent a letter described as abusive to another student.

[2]The difficulty of framing such questions or even of defining the terms they're made up of (Is cyberspace really a "space," or just the ability of a lot of machines to talk to one another?) should be ample illustration of why millions of Internet users are still sloshing around in a state of legal ambiguity. And that ambiguity, though congenial to the anarchically inclined folks who have been in cyberspace since its not-very-remote beginnings, can't be sustained much longer as millions of users pile into cyberspace through commercial, university-owned and workplace hookups.

[3]The providers of these hookups all have an interest in what their users "say" to other users once they're on line, but the interests vary. Some providers are afraid—with cause—that they may be liable for pirated, libelous or other law-breaking material posted on their accounts, or (depending on the outcome of assorted legislation) for transmitting pornographic or indecent material to minors.

[4]Universities have another set of motivations that go beyond fear of legal vulnerability and that have led many—including Virginia Tech—to institute student conduct policies that can be used to curb even non-cyberspace speech.

[5]Virginia Tech authorities say the existing student life policy prohibits "words or acts" that constitute "abusive conduct" that "demeans, intimidates, threatens or otherwise interferes with another person's rightful actions or comfort," whether on line or off. As with the notorious "hate speech" regulations at many campuses, this is a dangerously broad category, though the lines between interfering with someone's comfort and actually threatening him are probably drawable by a court.

[6]Technologically oriented civil liberties groups such as the Electronic Frontier Foundation have been arguing for some time that if First Amendment rights in cyberspace aren't codified and nailed down early, tendencies toward restraint will multiply to cover more and more of the new "sectors," and this will greatly reduce the potential of electronic communication both socially and commercially.

[7]An even more cold-eyed pragmatic argument is that speech restrictions, notoriously hard to enforce in the real world, are even more so in the virtual one: In one formulation much repeated by programmers, the Internet "interprets censorship as a malfunction and detours around it." Add this to the practical impossibility of commercial owners monitoring every message sent via cyberspace, and you have enforcement nightmares.

[8]There are better and broader arguments, though, for being skeptical of any efforts to restrict the content of cyberspace speech in ways that go beyond existing and permitted controls on real-world speech, whether on child pornography, stalking, libel or the rest.

[9]Universities have some wiggle room here, but for the same reason university "hate speech" codes or restrictions on what professors may say in class are a terrible idea, it's bad practice to restrict student speech on-line. Free speech is good for the Internet for the same reasons it's good for the real world.

"Freedom of Net Speech,"
The Washington Post, November 12, 1996

Selection 3

The author of this article is an editorial writer for *The Washington Post.*

[1]There is bad news in the report just issued by the National Commission on Teaching and America's Future. And then there is worse news. Taken together, they show why reform of the education system is a priority for this country as we enter a new century.

[2]The bad news, widely publicized in news stories, is that the current standards for training and hiring teachers are well below the needs of the information-age society and a growing, diverse student body.

[3]The worse news is that more than a quarter of those hired to teach each year lack even those minimal qualifications. They either are unlicensed or given provisional papers just to staff the classrooms.

[4]"In recent years," the report says, "more than 50,000 people who lack the training required for their jobs have entered teaching annually on emergency or substandard licenses. Nearly one-fourth of all secondary teachers do not have even a college minor in their main teaching field."

[5]This is not the first time this point has been made. As this report notes, a similar manifesto, called "A Nation at Risk," issued in 1983, warned that our schools were drowning in "a rising tide of mediocrity."

[6]What is one to make of this? It is instructive to ask what the reaction would be if we were talking not about schools but about the nation's airlines, where the business and professional elite of this country spends so much of its time.

[7]Suppose a report had been issued saying that thousands of unqualified pilots and air controllers were being placed in cockpits and control towers each year. How long would it take the government to stop that practice?

[8]Well, you say, lives would be at stake. Believe me, the lives of these children are at stake. If they are not helped to get the survival skills for this modern economy by competent, motivated teachers, their lives are going to be a misery.

[9]As always, race and class are deeply embedded in this problem. Schools with a high level of nonwhite and/or poverty-impaired students have far higher percentages of unqualified teachers than schools with white, middle-class or affluent constituencies.

[10]"In the nation's poorest schools," the report says, "where hiring is most lax and teacher turnover is constant, the results are disastrous. Thousands of children are taught throughout their school careers by a parade of teachers without preparation in the fields they teach, inexperienced beginners with little training and no mentoring, and short-term substitutes trying to cope with constant staff disruptions. It is more surprising that some of these children manage to learn than that so many fail to do so."

[11]The commission offers a five-step program that would, it says, deal with this problem by 2006. We have heard about such timetables before. Indeed, the commission chairman, Gov. James B. Hunt Jr. of North Carolina, was one of the governors who seven years ago set Goals 2000, the six world-class standards they said it was vital for the nation to meet by the dawn of the new century. Don't hold your breath.

[12]But also don't throw up your hands. As the Hunt commission notes, "This situation is not necessary or inevitable." The practice of hiring unqualified teachers "was almost eliminated in the 1970s" through a combination of financial help to college students preparing to teach, the Urban Teacher Corps and a real drive to raise teacher salaries. But in the past few years, we have slid measurably backward.

13One key is to do what often has been recommended: Require prospective teachers to take a four-year undergraduate major in their subject matter specialty, then add a fifth year of graduate education in teaching techniques and a period of practice-teaching with skilled mentors. The report contains a heartening description of just such a program at the University of Cincinnati.

14But we also need to overhaul the schools, which today are top-heavy with supervisors and administrators. We need to empower qualified teachers to use their skills—and reward them for doing so. That is what the charter school movement, endorsed not just by President Clinton but by such Republican governors as Minnesota's Arne Carlson and Texas's George W. Bush, is all about. It encourages innovative educators to create their own break-the-mold schools.

15But most of all, we have to make a decision to pay for this, to say that the people who teach our children are as important to us as the people who fly our planes and need to be as well qualified.

David S. Broder, "Empower Qualified Teachers,"
The Washington Post National Weekly Edition,
September 23, 1996

9

Evaluating Arguments

Building on the primary skills from Chapter 8, the second chapter of Part III will examine more complex elements of argumentation. Specifically, we will focus on the ways that writers of argumentative prose—whether intentionally or unintentionally—go wrong. Learning to recognize unsound inductive arguments and invalid deductive arguments, generalizations, false appeals, logical fallacies, and other deceptive and manipulative techniques associated with advertising slogans, polls, and statistics will serve you well throughout your life. As before, the chapter ends with some editorials to help you sharpen your critical reading skills. Here are the specific skills addressed in Chapter 9:

- Understanding problems in inductive and deductive arguments.
- Distinguishing between valid and invalid, sound and unsound arguments.
- Detecting false appeals in arguments.
- Identifying common logical fallacies.
- Recognizing bias, the misuse of authority and other manipulative techniques.

PROBLEMS WITH INDUCTIVE REASONING

Sweeping Generalization

The most common error in inductive arguments is the **sweeping generalization,** as you see in this argument.

> You shouldn't buy a Shetland collie. They're all too nervous and high-strung. My sister has a miniature collie, and that dog yaps at every little sound, even when the phone rings, and he jumps all over people, too.

This argument is different from the example in Chapter 8 about the number of papers required in English courses. The number of writing assignments is verifiable. One simply counts the papers assigned, whereas "nervousness" is relative and calls for a subjective judgment. (What some people might call "nervous" and "high-strung," others might call "spirited" or "playful.") This argument rests on a generalization derived from only one example; it is called a sweeping generalization because it "sweeps" all members of a group into a group. The word *all* reveals the flaw in this argument. Temperaments among any members of a breed of dog vary so widely that this conclusion cannot be safely made, and producing even one serene Shetland collie would negate it.

Hasty Generalization

Related to the sweeping generalization, the **hasty generalization,** another kind of false inductive reasoning, results from a generalization drawn too quickly, using insufficient evidence.

> The Hmong (Vietnamese mountain people) have certainly adjusted well to American life. The store owned by a Hmong refugee family in my Minneapolis neighborhood is well-run and profitable, and it's remarkable how easily the family has assimilated into American life.

Notice that in this example the conclusion precedes the evidence; nonetheless, the argument is still inductive because the conclusion represents a generalization that follows incomplete evidence. To make this argument sound, one would have to examine the economic and social situation of hundreds of Hmong families in various regions of the country.

Incorrect Sampling

Inductive arguments often include a **sampling,** and they can be flawed if the sampling is not done carefully. For example:

> Forty percent of the student body at Lincoln State College thinks that the children of illegal immigrants should be denied access to public schools and other government benefits.

From this statistic, the reader might infer that 40 percent of the population as a whole also shares this concern. The method of sampling is crucial: The number of people interviewed should be large; and they should be *representative,* drawn from a cross section of the general population in terms of geographic area, income, ethnicity, religion, and educational level. National polling firms like Gallup, Roper, Harris, the CBS/New York Times poll, and so on have made a science of sampling techniques to such an extent that the chances of statistical error are usually no more than plus or minus one point. Reliable pollsters also disclose information about the number of people surveyed and often include charts showing the breakdown between age groups, gender, race, income levels, and the like. But not all sampling is so reliable.

Here are two real examples of faulty inductive reasoning. The first, described in a sociological study of black men in a South Side Chicago neighborhood, criticizes the sampling techniques used in collecting data for a 1987 *Newsweek* article.

> In 1987, the magazine sent a team of its black reporters to a Chicago housing project, collecting the stories of men who were known to one of the reporters, who had himself grown up in the projects before attending an elite boarding school in the east. In a preface to the special issue, published under the title "Brothers," the magazine's editor-in-chief wrote, "While no single story can sum up an entire community, we believe this special report goes far beyond all the stereotypes and the statistics to tell in important detail what it's like to grow up black and poor in America." The ten men who were selected for coverage in the story were (1) a killer, drug dealer, and heroin user; (2) a former heroin user and high school dropout who now worked at a blue-collar job; (3) a former wife beater who kept a step ahead of the bill collectors; (4) a failed professional basketball player who became a drug dealer; (5) a high school dropout, formerly addicted to heroin, cocaine, and diet pills, now a Jehovah's witness; (6) a high school dropout and former gang member; (7) a former heroin user who spent a year in federal prison; (8) a dropout from Northwestern University who "had a chance but didn't take it," lived off women and abused drugs, and hadn't worked in seven years; (9) a middle-class beneficiary of affirmative action; and (10) a black nationalist yuppie. Many readers undoubtedly concluded that *Newsweek's* choices reflected empirical reality; that those who grow up in the projects are either unstable blacks or middle-class examples of affirmative action. Not a single man among the twelve who grew up in the projects was a stable working-class or working-poor man. Certainly, if the magazine could trace down those who were now living in middle-class neighborhoods, it is not inconceivable that some of those stable working men who had migrated to neighboring working-class districts or who still lived in the projects could also be included. The report, which received widespread attention and acclaim, ironically misled the American public in

> representing itself as going "far beyond all the stereotypes" while actually reinforcing the most common stereotypes of black men.
>
> Mitchell Duneir, *Slim's Table: Race, Respectability, and Masculinity*

The second example concerns a report from a recent *Journal of the American Pharmaceutical Association* outlining the dangers of hair dye. The research team leader, Howard Mielke, an environmental toxicologist at Xavier University College of Pharmacology in New Orleans, reported that some popular hair dyes for covering gray hair contain so much lead that they should be pulled from the market. Mielke and his colleagues targeted three brands in particular: RD Hair Coloring and Groomer; Creme Formula for Men, produced by LT Laboratories; and three Grecian Formula products for men and women. The research team found that although little of the lead penetrates the scalp, significant residue remained on the users' hands, faucets, combs, and other surfaces. The study concluded that these products should be removed from drugstore shelves.

As one would expect, the hair coloring manufacturers named in the study responded swiftly. A representative of Combe, Inc., maker of the various Grecian Formula products, said, "Lead acetate is a safe ingredient in hair dyes." The company cited a six-month clinical study of 53 men and women that "revealed no increase in lead in the blood or urine, nor in the users' enzyme levels. If there were any danger of hand-to-mouth transfer of the material . . . the study would have demonstrated it."[1] The spokesman's argument can be summarized as follows:

> Our hair coloring products are safe because we found no increase in levels of lead in the 53 subjects studied over a six-month period.

In the space provided, write two reasons that the company representative's response represents a faulty inductive argument. ______________

____

As you can see, drawing conclusions in inductive arguments can be risky. One last example: A recent national survey of American college students showed that those students who consumed six or more alcoholic beverages a week consistently had lower grade point averages than those students who drank less or not at all. Even assuming the sampling was done correctly, is this conclusion valid? Looked at another way, which is the cause and which is the effect? Do students'

[1]Quoted in Charles Petit, "Lead Hazard Found in Some Hair Dyes," *San Francisco Chronicle,* February 4, 1997.

grades suffer because going to bars and parties takes time away from their studies, or do they drink to ease the pain and lowered self-esteem that are the results of receiving low grades?

PROBLEMS WITH DEDUCTIVE REASONING

A flawed deductive argument is termed *unsound* if one of the premises is untrue or if it is a generalization. But interestingly, the argument can still be *valid* as long as the syllogism is properly constructed and follows the prescribed form. The following is a valid but unsound syllogism:

Major premise:	All Italians are good singers.
Minor premise:	Luigi is Italian.
Conclusion:	Luigi is a good singer.

Because Luigi has been placed in a class in which all the members are said to share the same characteristic, the statement is valid. Therefore, we can deduce (arrive at the conclusion) that Luigi also shares that characteristic. Yet the argument is *unsound* because the major premise—that all Italians are good singers—is obviously untrue, representing a generalization that could be easily invalidated by only one off-key Italian singer. Note that the major premise above—all Italians are good singers—is the *conclusion* of an unreliable inductive argument:

Evidence:	Frederico is Italian and is an excellent singer.
Evidence:	Antonio is Italian, and he also sings well.
Evidence:	Mario is Italian and is an excellent singer.
Conclusion:	Therefore, all Italians are good singers.

These points are important enough to bear repeating: A deductive argument is *sound* if the premises are true and if it follows the correct form. If the premises are untrue but they follow the correct form, the argument is valid but unsound.

This distinction between validity and truth leads to the question, what in logic does *true* mean? D. L. McDonald defines truth like this: "It is only when terms are defined and mutually accepted that one can begin marshaling evidence to prove the truth of a statement." McDonald goes on to explain the statement that truth is statistically derived:

> A man can insist that fire engines are red because he is expressing a general opinion. Though a "Napoleon" might call them a mass hallucination, he is sure that fire engines exist. Though the color-blind might cavil, he knows they are colored red. And though foreigners or semanticists might do otherwise, he uses the word "red." The reason he speaks the truth and the dissenters do not

> is that he is in the majority. If the majority did not perceive the engines, or saw them as green, or described them as "rouge," he would be locked up as a babbling, color-blind visionary. "Truth" is what people agree to call true.
>
> D. L. McDonald, *The Language of Argument*

Here are some other examples of deductive arguments that are invalid because they violate the prescribed syllogistic form:

Major premise: All students who did not write the term paper in English 100 failed the class.
Minor premise: Dave failed the class.
Conclusion: Dave must not have written the term paper.

This conclusion does not follow logically from the premises because Dave has not been placed in the group of students who did not write the paper. His failing the class could have been for other reasons—failure to write other papers, poor attendance, or low test grades. Because the conclusion cannot be deduced from the premises, the argument is invalid.

Here is another kind of invalid syllogism:

Major premise: If Bill doesn't stop smoking, his wife will leave him.
Minor premise: Bill plans to stop smoking.
Conclusion: Bill's wife won't leave him.

In this syllogism, the conclusion can be valid only if Bill *doesn't* stop smoking, and the minor premise changes the term (from "smoking" to "stopping smoking"), thereby making the argument invalid. The terms must remain constant within the major and minor premises. Bill's wife may leave him for another reason not contained in the major premise.

Another kind of invalid deductive argument occurs when one changes the meaning of the terms in the premises:

Major premise: All squirrels have tails.
Minor premise: This airplane has a tail.
Conclusion: This airplane is a squirrel.

In this example, the major premise is about squirrels' tails, not airplanes' tails; a premise about squirrels cannot lead to a conclusion about airplanes.

In the real world, deductive arguments do not present themselves as neat syllogisms with premises and conclusions outlined. Usually the argument is abbreviated, omitting one of the premises or even the conclusion. For example, consider this argument:

- People shouldn't be allowed to vote if they don't speak English.

  Recast as a valid, though unsound, syllogism, the argument would be written like this:

Major premise:	Only English speakers should be allowed to vote.
Minor premise:	These people cannot speak English.
Conclusion:	These people should not be allowed to vote.

  In this example, the major premise is an unstated assumption.

  Here are some examples of everyday deductive arguments, along with their missing or implied parts:

- If you don't vote, then you can hardly criticize the government.

  Missing major premise: Only voters can criticize the government. This argument is invalid because the major premise is an unfounded generalization.

- To be hired by Acme Publishing Company, you have to be able to type 50 words a minute. Sarah can type only 35 words per minute.

  Missing conclusion: Sarah won't be hired by Acme Publishing, a valid conclusion.

- They say that blondes have more fun, so it's easy to see why Kitsy Snow has so many dates.

  Missing minor premise: Kitsy Snow has blonde hair. This is a valid but unsound argument because the major premise—blondes have more fun—is an untrue generalization.

EXERCISE IN EVALUATING INDUCTIVE AND DEDUCTIVE ARGUMENTS

Consider the following arguments using these steps:

- Determine if the argument is deductive or inductive.
- If the argument is inductive, check its reliability (i.e., look for sweeping generalizations, hasty generalizations, and problems with sampling).
- If the argument is deductive, examine the premises for untrue statements or generalizations.
- Decide if the argument is valid or invalid, sound or unsound.

1. The city of Seattle surveyed a thousand residents who regularly commute by bicycle to work. Nearly 75 percent of the bicyclists felt that the city should build no new freeways.
2. Sign on Interstate 5 in California's San Joaquin Valley:
   No water, no farming
   No farming, no food
3. Seven out of ten dentists recommend Trident gum for their patients who chew gum.
4. The ballot proposition to build a new high school gym will undoubtedly fail. Last week *The Desert Post* announced the results of a new poll, and a majority of the residents of Sunny Dunes Nursing Home were firmly opposed to the measure.
5. Sue Jensen is against abortion. She must be a member of the National Pro-Life Coalition.
6. Last semester I took three sociology classes, and they didn't require very much reading. I guess I'm going to have an easy time this spring if I take Sociology 400.
7. The Department of Agriculture ought to tighten up its eligibility requirements for food stamps. Today I was behind a woman in line at the IGA, and she paid for four T-bone steaks and a pound of shrimp with food stamps!
8. I always take my Volkswagen Jetta to Heinrich Werner for repairs. Germans make the best car mechanics.
9. I don't know what the big deal is about needle exchange programs. Admittedly, the Netherlands has a more liberal drug policy than most other developed nations, but in Amsterdam, police stations offer sterile needles in exchange for used ones, with no names asked. This program has played a major role in stopping the spread of the HIV virus among the city's hard drug users. American cities should follow Amsterdam's example and establish a similar exchange program. If it works there, it can work here.
10. It's no wonder Linda Ng scored so high on the math part of the SAT. Everyone knows that Asians are good in math.
11. Mayor Ruddy has been in office for a month already, and there are more homeless people on the street than before he was elected. He's just like every politician who makes promises during the campaign and then doesn't keep them once elected. I say we should start a recall petition!
12. All roses are red. This flower is red. This flower must be a rose.
13. Naturally, Eduardo Chavez is a poor driver. What do you expect from someone 80 years old?
14. All lemons are yellow. My car is yellow. It must be a lemon.

15. Responsible instructors don't give tests when students aren't prepared for class. I guess we can assume that Ms. Wolf will be nice and not give us a test in English 19 today.
16. University of Maryland professor Lee Bladgett conducted a survey that sought to dispel the myth of a "gay elite," the idea that homosexuals earn more money than heterosexuals. Bladgett collected data from 1989 to 1991, comparing the usual categories of age, education, race, sex, occupation, marital status, and so on. The full survey included 4,426 people, of whom she selected 1680 full-time employees. Roughly 5 percent of these employees were homosexuals—47 gay men and 34 lesbians. The study found that homosexual men make 11 to 27 percent less than heterosexual men in similar jobs, while lesbians earn 5 to 14 percent less than heterosexual women.[2]

OMITTING RELEVANT EVIDENCE

It seems safe to say that the more solid evidence a writer musters in support of the argument, the more convincing and reliable it will be, whether the evidence takes the form of facts and statistics, survey results, examples, good reasons, historical precedent, or analogy. But a reader can reject, or at least question, an argument if relevant information is not supplied that might conceivably change the reader's mind. Whether the omission is deliberate or intentional is nearly impossible to discern. Here are two real examples of arguments that would have been considerably strengthened had certain evidence been included.

The first concerns a 1993 California Supreme Court ruling that manufacturers of nonprescription drugs do not have to print warning labels in foreign languages.[3] The mother of a Modesto, California boy, Jorge Ramirez, brought suit against Schering-Plough HealthCare Products, based in Memphis, because St. Joseph's Aspirin for Children did not provide a warning label in Spanish instructing parents not to administer aspirin to a child with a viral illness. (Aspirin given to a child with fever is associated with Reye's syndrome; after his mother gave him aspirin, Jorge developed the illness and eventually became blind, mentally impaired, and quadriplegic.)

The three points of view concerning this case are as follows:

[2]"A Disputed Study on Salaries of Gays," *San Francisco Chronicle,* August 18, 1994.
[3]Jenifer Warren, "Warnings in Only English OK, Justices Say," *Los Angeles Times,* December 10, 1993.

- The mother's attorneys argued that Schering-Plough had a duty to warn users about Reye's syndrome in her native language, since the bottles carry a warning label in English.
- The company's attorneys argued that requiring foreign-language warning labels would "subject manufacturers to an unreasonable burden, forcing them to translate packaging labels into the 140 languages spoken in the United States."
- Justice Joyce L. Kennard, writing the court's opinion, argued this: "We recognize that if a Spanish-language warning had accompanied [the] product, and if [Jorge's] mother had read and heeded the warning, the tragic blighting of a young and innocent life . . . might not have occurred." However, the Court then said that "the lengths to which manufacturers must go to warn consumers is a task that belongs with the state Legislature, which has proven itself 'able and willing' to make such requirements in other contexts."

Based on this information, what is your position on this issue? Write your remarks in the space provided. ______________________________

____

The first news article I read about this case contained only the preceding information. A subsequent *Los Angeles Times* article, however, included another piece of evidence, which casts a slightly different light on the suit: Schering-Plough widely advertises St. Joseph's Aspirin for Children in Spanish-language media, because, apparently, Spanish-speaking communities have a special fondness for St. Joseph's products. (Though this line of thinking does somewhat strengthen the mother's position, the Court was nonetheless not sufficiently persuaded by it. Indeed, the court agreed with the company's assertion that such a requirement would mean that a warning would have to be printed in the 140 languages spoken in the U.S.) Nonetheless, the information seems of sufficient merit that it should have been included in the first article. Can you suggest a remedy that Schering-Plough could have used to correct this situation and avoid future lawsuits?

____

The second example concerns the 1996 suicide of Naval Admiral Michael Boorda. Following a series of military scandals (cheating and drug busts at the U.S. Naval Academy, the Tailhook sexual harassment incident, among others), *Newsweek* was reportedly ready to publish an article accusing Boorda of wearing Vietnam War combat medals that he had not been awarded and therefore was not entitled to wear. After Boorda's death, *The Wall Street Journal* published an editorial written by John Lehman asserting that the admiral's suicide was the end-product of a decade-long "editorial crusade of the 1980s" by *Newsweek* against the Navy. Proclaiming the accusation "vicious nonsense," John Barry, National Security Correspondent for *Newsweek,* responded in this letter:

Newsweek: We Did Not Attack the Navy

[1]I respect John Lehman's grief and anger at the death of Adm. Mike Boorda. But his assertion (editorial page, May 21) that the admiral's suicide was the end-product of a decade-long "editorial crusade of the 1980s" by Newsweek against the Navy is vicious nonsense.

[2]Mr. Lehman claims that Newsweek "throughout those years" ran "one phony expose after another—alleging that Tomahawk missiles wouldn't work; that Aegis cruisers would tip over; that aircraft carriers couldn't survive; anything and everything to disgrace the Navy."

[3]I have been defense and national security correspondent of Newsweek since the spring of 1985. I have written no such "exposes."

[4]Our library has checked through Newsweek for the first half of the 1980s. There, too, we find nothing supporting Mr. Lehman's charges. Instead, we find the following:

[5]• June 8, 1981: an article on the proposed INF deployments in Europe mentioned, in its last two paragraphs, possible slippage in the Tomahawk test program, but then quoted a Reagan official as saying: "I think we're in pretty good shape."

[6]• Sept. 6, 1982: after the admiral running the cruise missile development program was abruptly fired, Newsweek ran a two-column story on the reasons why. The article said that the missile's development problems were "mostly minor" and "not totally out of line for a new weapon." In its penultimate paragraph, the article also mentioned a congressional report questioning whether the new Aegis cruiser would be "too slow in righting itself in high seas," but in the next paragraph cited Navy experts dismissing this.

[7]• May 17, 1982: the week after HMS Sheffield was sunk by an Exocet missile off the Falklands, Newsweek did run a cover story entitled: "The Falklands Fallout: Are Big Ships Doomed?" It was a careful rehearsal of the debates in Washington about small vs. big carriers, and about the Navy's new "maritime strategy" against the Soviet Navy. It quoted a small fleet of naval officers (serving and retired), senators and Pentagon officials on both sides of the debate, including then-Navy Secretary John Lehman.

[8]To claim, as Mr. Lehman now does, that this sort of reporting showed Newsweek to be "ever a willing conduit for . . . bogus studies and mean-spirited attacks" is preposterous. To go further and regard three articles from 1981 and 1982 as evidence of an "editorial crusade" throughout the 1980s allying Newsweek to "powerful interest groups that wish to pull the Navy down" is, bluntly, paranoid. And to cap this by asserting that, thwarted in their supposed crusade, "Newsweek's editors [now] seem bent

on impugning the character of the Navy's leaders" elevates falsehood into deliberate smear.

[9]In sum, Mr. Lehman's bilious outburst tells us nothing about Newsweek. It does, however, tell us a good deal about the very mind-set that Adm. Boorda was battling to turn around.

John Barry
National Security Correspondent
Newsweek
Washington

The Wall Street Journal, June 5, 1996

Study this letter carefully, and then explain the relevant information omitted from the claim that *Newsweek* did not engage in an "editorial crusade of the 1980s."

____

____

APPEALS IN ARGUMENTS

Now that you can distinguish between induction and deduction and between valid, invalid, sound, and unsound arguments, we can turn our attention to other techniques used in persuasive writing and in advertising. The careful persuasive writer uses sound, accurate, appropriate, and convincing evidence, thereby appealing to our intellect. We can accept the argument because the evidence—no matter what kind it is—persuades us to accept it, or at least to give it some consideration.

Persuasive writers and advertisers—whose aim, after all, is to persuade us to part with our money—often cleverly manipulate our thinking by adopting various **appeals** to our emotions, to our sense of patriotism, to our prejudices, and so forth. To perceive the truth and to make an informed decision, you must strip away the "fluff" from the argument, ignore the appeal, and examine the claim *for itself,* unobscured by emotion or sentiment. Look at a piece of writing or promotional piece and ask yourself: How good is this argument or product *without* the appeal? Is there any evidence underneath the appeal? Let us examine the false appeals.

Appeals to the Emotions

Maintaining objectivity in light of controversial issues is difficult, for writer and reader alike. But to be a good critical reader (and thinker), it is essential to recognize when a writer is deliberately firing your emotions and when you are responding more from emotion than from reason. To paraphrase an old adage: The more emotional the appeal, the weaker the argument. For example:

- "Lower your taxes. Vote No on Proposition 21!"
- "Stop the land grab! Don't let greedy corporations take your most cherished possession away from you!"
- "Don't let the homeless invade Montclair! Vote no on the city's proposal to build a homeless shelter in our neighborhood!"
- "A vote for the school bond issue to build a new gym is a vote for our children."

We respond to emotional appeals on a visceral level because they sound good. After all, who wants higher taxes, a homeless shelter next door, or a school with no gym? Yet, in the absence of reasoned discourse, arguments resting on emotional appeals are unsound and sneaky—because they rest on oversimplification. And they need not be accepted, no matter how stirring the claim. Here, briefly, are five common emotional appeals:

Transfer

Transfer is the appeal most commonly associated with advertising. By using transfer, the writer (or advertising designer or copywriter) deliberately plants the idea that favorable impressions about one thing will transfer or carry over to something else. Ironically, the *association* of the image is almost more important than the product itself. Advertisers identify this phenomenon with this rule: "Sell the sizzle, not the steak." It is for this reason, for example, that Britain has adopted strict prohibitions against showing *anything* attractive in cigarette ads. Cigarette advertisements in Britain cannot show attractive people smoking or even beautiful scenery because of the understandable tendency for readers to transfer the pleasant aspects of the image to the concept of smoking. A glance through *Cosmopolitan, GQ, Esquire, Self,* and other similar glossy magazines will yield many examples of transfer.

Sometimes attempts to use transfer are so clumsy or transparently deceptive that they backfire. One such case occurred in 1995 when Governor Pete Wilson of California announced that he would run in the Republican presidential primaries. Wilson gave his announcement speech in the shadow of the Statue of Liberty, the American symbol of welcome for immigrants. By choosing the site, Wilson hoped that the tolerance and generosity associated with Lady Liberty would somehow be transferred to himself for the assembled crowd (and, of course, that evening's television viewers). But political commentators saw through the ruse and reported the hypocrisy: Wilson had angered immigration supporters by advocating that children of illegal immigrants born on American soil be deprived of citizenship and by strongly supporting California's Proposition 187, which attempted to restrict public services for illegal immigrants.

Flattery

A writer who uses **flattery** tries to put us into a group of people that we might hope to identify with, whether we share their convictions or not. For example, if a writer says, "Every well-educated person knows that James Joyce was one of the most important writers of the twentieth century," we are meant to associate ourselves with "well-educated people." Or this: "Women with good taste shop at Talbot's." We like to think of ourselves as having good taste, so by subtle flattery, we are enticed to become part of the group.

Just Plain Folks

This appeal lies in the writer's desire to have himself or herself perceived as just an "ordinary citizen" or **just plain folks.** It is the opposite of snob appeal. A politician might give a speech to small-town people and use the "plain folks" appeal by stating that he, too, came from a similar little town, went to a school very much like the one there, or came from a family much like theirs. A few years ago, Bartles & Jaymes, the makers of wine coolers, ran some very popular television ads showing two old men dressed in overalls and sitting on a dilapidated front porch of a small house discussing the merits of their beverages. Other examples are restaurants claiming that their food is "just like Mom's" or brand names like "Mrs. Smith's Pies." By means of transfer, we are supposed to picture "Mom" or "Mrs. Smith" cooking up their old favorites just for us.

When Republican Bob Dole was preparing to announce his candidacy for president in 1987, his media consultants scoured suitable locations in Russell, Kansas, Dole's hometown, for "the perfect backdrop." They chose Ol' Dawson's drugstore, where Dole had worked as a soda jerk during his youth. Journalists recognized that the drugstore backdrop was highly symbolic. As Sidney Blumenthal wrote in *The Washington Post,* Dole's home town was "the key to his personality, his politics, his vision." In addition, it was "an irresistible symbol of the small-town virtues that helped Dole overcome a debilitating war injury and climb the ladder of electoral success." (Quoted in Howard Kurtz, "Inside the Media Spin Machine," *The Washington Post National Weekly Edition,* August 11–17, 1995.) Although using the drugstore backdrop is also an example of transfer, the emotional appeal discussed earlier, it also helped solidify Dole's image in voters' minds as an ordinary person with his roots in small-town America.

Testimonial

Television advertisements abound with appeals using **testimonial** as an appeal, using the testimony or endorsements of famous people—movie or television stars, athletes, or other celebrities who are paid large sums of money to plug products. One could probably argue that Chicago Bulls' superstar Michael Jordan is an authoritative representative for Nike athletic shoes, but we can surely question the opinion of an athlete who endorses a certain brand of automobile or a movie star who is paid to speak the praises of a rental car company or a brand of peanut butter.

In recent advertisements, the former Duchess of York, Sarah Ferguson, has been advertising Weight Watchers and Ocean Spray Cranberry Juice; actress Jamie Lee Curtis pitches L'Eggs pantyhose on TV; and in magazines basketball player Anfernee "Penny" Hardaway touts Hillshire Farms Lit'l Links ("The taste that keeps you dunkin'!"). Even defeated Republican presidential candidate Bob Dole has turned up in an ad for American Express. Incidentally, endorsement fees, especially those paid to famous athletes, are so lucrative that they can far exceed the athletes' salaries. For example, the December 1996 issue of *Forbes* published a list of the 20 highest paid athletes in 1996, among them Michael Jordan ($12.6 million in salary, $40 million in endorsements); Shaquille O'Neal ($7.4 million in salary, $17 million in endorsements); and André Agassi ($2.2 million in salary, $13 million in endorsements).

Bandwagon Appeal

The **bandwagon appeal** asks readers to accept an idea by appealing to their desire to "get on the bandwagon" whether we share their convictions or not. For example, "Don't vote for Proposition P. The polls show it is losing 65 to 35." Or "Everyone knows that pornography is the main cause of rape." Beware of arguments that begin, "Everyone knows" or "Everyone agrees." Look for evidence, not appeals to join the crowd. The crowd can be wrong.

Besides emotional appeals, clever writers and advertisers have other appeals in their arsenal of manipulative tricks.

Appeal to Authority

This appeal asks us to accept an argument because some authoritative figure backs it.

- My English teacher says that you should never start a sentence with "and" or "but." He has been teaching for 25 years, so he ought to know what's right.

- A recent medical journal article said that there is no correlation between a high fat diet and certain kinds of cancer. That means I can go ahead and eat all the butter and sour cream I want without worrying about their long-term effects.

Also, do not be deceived by weasely phrases like these that often precede weak arguments: "*Let's face it*—the Constitution is little more than a historical artifact," or "*The fact of the matter is* that gays just don't belong in the military," or "*The truth as I see it is* that we have too many corrupt judges in our courts."

Appeal to Fear

This appeal is obvious: the writer hopes to arouse our fear of what will happen if we adopt a certain course. As with most other appeals, the appeal to fear replaces evidence in the form of good reasons or facts.

- Why would anyone voluntarily move to California? That's earthquake country. And there's no question that the "Big One" will hit sometime in the next 25 years.
- During a strike by the pilots of a national airline in 1985, the newspapers were full of letters to the editor on both sides of the issue. Here is a representative one written by a striking pilot: "I am proud to be a member of the striking pilot's association, and I just hope that all those people who have written attacking us for our stand are not caught on some dark and stormy night, strapped in the seat of an aircraft piloted by a scab hired at the last minute who probably hasn't had adequate training."

Appeal to Patriotism

The **appeal to patriotism** is a deceptive tactic to make us think that we are disloyal to our country if we don't accept an argument. During the Vietnam War, anti-war groups who supported the administration's policy of committing ground troops and ordering napalm strikes against the Viet Cong often used the slogan, "My country, right or wrong!" More recently, Ross Perot warned the public against the North American Free Trade Agreement (NAFTA) on a 1993 TV "infomercial" called "Keeping Your Job in the USA," saying, "If the United States accepts this agreement, so many U.S. companies will flow south that you will hear a giant sucking sound coming from the U.S.-Mexican border."

Appeal to Prejudice

Like the appeal to fear, **appeal to prejudice** works by inflaming negative feelings, beliefs, or stereotypes about racial, ethnic, or religious groups, or gender or sexual orientation. Once again, emotion replaces reasoned discourse.

- Letting so many immigrants into this country is a mistake. They take jobs away from Americans who are out of work, and they don't share our traditional values.
- Why would a man ever want to become a nurse? After all, women are traditionally the caregivers in our culture.

Appeal to Sympathy

By arousing our sympathy, writers and advertisers gain a real advantage over us. We have all seen the advertisements for pet foods using glossy photos of cute kittens and puppies. Consider this example:

- A recent television commercial for StainStick—a pre-wash product manufactured by DowBrands—showed a mother preparing the wash with her little girl, who clearly has Down's syndrome. The mother says, as the daughter applies StainStick to the spots, "We use StainStick because the last place we need a challenge is in the laundry room."

Critics charged that DowBrands was exploiting the child and preying on the viewing public's sympathy to buy the product. In fact, other television ad campaigns are making greater use of the handicapped, showing people in wheelchairs and the like. But the criticism seems justified, since the purpose of the advertisement was to sell StainStick, not to remind us to treat the handicapped fairly.

Here is another example:

- Clearly, the nation's new "get-tough" welfare laws are going to wreak havoc on recipients. Forcing people who aren't equipped to deal with the real world and who have a limited education and no job experience by cutting off their benefits after two years will just increase the number of homeless on the streets.

Welfare is a complex and difficult issue, but these arguments play *solely* on our sympathy, in this case trying to persuade us by generalizing that welfare recipients are helpless victims being pushed around by insensitive lawmakers. The arguments also omit relevant evidence: job-training programs and good counseling have proved to help many unskilled workers get back on their feet and become productive workers.

Appeal to Tradition

The **appeal to tradition** asks us to accept a practice because it has always been done that way.

- The Roman Catholic Church has forbidden women to become priests for nearly 2,000 years. Why should the Church abandon such a long-standing practice?

- My club shouldn't be required to admit women or minorities. Men should have the right to associate with whomever they want without being hassled or threatened with lawsuits.

CLAIMS IN ADVERTISING

Advertisements try to manipulate—or at least to influence—the buying public with any one or a combination of these claims, but some advertising techniques rely on clever slogans and jingles rather than focus on the product's qualities or worth. If you start looking closely at ads—even the cleverest ones—you will quickly see that often they rely on vague, meaningless, or even nonsensical slogans (claims) that, when scrutinized, reveal almost nothing. For example, here is an example of a radio pitch: "More people get their news from KCBS than from any other station." Although this claim could probably be verified with audience surveys, as an *argument* it is certainly questionable. The claim implies a conclusion: you, too, should get your news from KCBS. But since the slogan mentions nothing about the *merits* of KCBS news, it can be dismissed as irrelevant.

Here are some other examples of recent advertisements:

- A television ad: "Bayer Aspirin. Powerful Pain Relief and So Much More."
- A newspaper ad: "Don't Miss Macy's Big Memorial Day Sale. The more you spend, the more you save."
- Ad on the side of a Miller Beer truck: "Miller Beer: Made the American Way."
- Ad in *Sports Illustrated* for Gravity, a men's fragrance, showing an attractive young man and woman seemingly suspended while jumping in mid-air and a picture of the product. The slogan: "Gravity. The Force That Pulls You Closer."
- And this improbable advertising slogan on a Batesville Casket Company truck: "Batesville Caskets—Committed to the Dignity of Life."

EXERCISE IN IDENTIFYING APPEALS

Using the information in the preceding two sections, study these examples and identify the appeal or appeals each contains.

1. By the year 2030, if we continue to admit immigrants at the same level we are today, whites will constitute only 51 percent of the U.S. population. That will be the death of American culture as we know it.

2. When Oliver North and John Poindexter admitted that they were committing illegal acts when they plotted to sell arms to Iran and divert money to the Contras during the Irangate scandal, they claimed they acted out of love for their country.
3. If colleges and universities continue to admit large numbers of minorities under affirmative action programs, soon there won't be any room for whites.
4. Teenage moms really have a tough time. After their boyfriends get them pregnant and abandon them, they have to care for their babies and juggle their schoolwork at the same time. That's why Garfield High School needs an on-campus day care center.
5. Try Auntie Em's frozen pies in five delicious flavors. Low-fat, low-cholesterol, and microwaveable, too. Just like Grandma used to make!
6. Thanks to Megan's Law [a federal law that allows people to view a CD at police stations containing the names and addresses of registered sex offenders], we found out that a scumbag offender has been paroled and is living just two streets away from the park. So what if he's paid his debt to society? We parents won't stand for any sex offenders lurking near our children!
7. Paint store clerk to author: "Why did you choose Benjamin Moore paint to use on your bookcases?"

   Author: "I heard it's the best paint on the market."

   Clerk: "You made the right decision. Benjamin Moore paint is definitely the best paint available. You can't go wrong choosing it."
8. Letter to the editor (paraphrased):

   Those so-called "homeless" people who hold up signs at intersections saying "will work for food" are just a bunch of scam artists. What they really mean is "please give me a dollar." Work is the last thing on these people's minds.
9. The US should not abandon its policy on immigration. This country has always been the refuge for people from all over the world seeking new opportunities.
10. Ad for KitchenAid appliances in *Gourmet:* "Mom Had a KitchenAid Dishwasher. I have a KitchenAid *Kitchen.*"
11. If God wanted homosexuals to marry, he would have created Adam and Steve instead of Adam and Eve.
12. Wal-Mart's proposal to build a superstore in Fredericksburg, Virginia, elicited this letter to the editor in *The Wall Street Journal* (March 15, 1996):

The Wal-Marts Are Coming!

1Wal-Mart's David D. Glass, reported to be banking on construction of 100 new "Supercenters" to reverse recent embarrassing financial results ("Humbled

Wal-Mart Plans More Stores," Marketplace, Feb. 23), is risking a major corporate black eye by plopping one of the three-acre buildings down on George Washington's boyhood farm in Fredericksburg, Va.

[2]Ferry Farm is the only home of our first president left unprotected and unavailable to the public. There are many parcels of nearby land suitable for a Wal-Mart superstore, but there is only one spot where the father of our country spent his formative years. We owe our children's children and their children the chance to stand where young George stood and feel what he felt. The grotesque shadow of a store the size of several football fields encircled by acres of asphalt would rob them of that chance.

Bill Beck
President
Historic Fredericksburg
Foundation
Fredericksburg, Va.

13. *New Yorker* ad for De Beers diamonds: "It's fiery. Feels cool against your finger. Captures light and turns it to brilliance. Sneaking a look at it once in a while, you vow to keep up the manicures. Your diamond, extraordinary and rare. Why wait?"
14. Ad in *Food and Wine* for American Express, showing comedian Jerry Seinfeld with a number of presumably new purchases—an armchair, a globe, a laptop computer, a mountain bike, and so forth: "A Cardmember Goes Shopping. The American Express® Card is welcome at all kinds of places. Just ask Jerry, who uses his Card for everyday items, as well as for the things that make him, well, Jerry. In fact, it's so widely accepted, Jerry uses it wherever he goes. No kidding."
15. Ad in *Mademoiselle* for Camel Light cigarettes showing a woman sitting at a bar sipping from what looks like a martini glass. On the bar is a water ring left by the glass in the shape of Joe Camel. Next to the glass is a tiny picture of a pack of Camel Lights and the slogan "What you're looking for."
16. In December 1996, Hawaii Circuit Court Judge Kevin Chang ruled that same-sex marriages are legal. The ruling goes against an earlier federal ban on such unions. (As of this writing, however, Hawaii has yet to implement Judge Chang's ruling.) In response, Reverend Lou Sheldon of the Traditional Values Coalition in Anaheim, California, said: "Losing this battle doesn't mean that we've lost the war. It means that the very foundation of Western civilization is being given another wake-up call that the homosexuals want to change the culture and want to change the rules in the seventh inning." (Quoted in *San Francisco Chronicle,* December 4, 1996.)

17. Excerpt from a letter received by my husband:

    Dear David: I have exciting news for you and all Spears! Extensive work has been done throughout the world on a project relating to the distinguished Spears name. Now a new book, *The World Book of Spears,* is about to be published and it includes individual Spears who immigrated to the New World between the 16th and early 20th centuries.

    The first Spears we found came to Philadelphia, Pennsylvania in 1820. His name was Henry. Like thousands of others, he sought a better life for himself in this land of opportunity. . . .

    This unique publication also covers how family names originated and what the distinguished Spears name means, the development of family crests with ancient symbols, as well as an artist's drawing of an early Spears Coat of arms dating back centuries, that is translated into everyday language. You'll even find exciting details about how you can trace your heritage in the United States and even back to your homeland and learn even more about your heritage. . . .

LOGICAL FALLACIES: PART 1

Besides the deceptive appeals you saw in the preceding section, an argument may contain **logical fallacies,** errors in reasoning that can make the argument invalid or false. Because many of these fallacies are both challenging and tricky, I have divided them into two groups arranged alphabetically, with an exercise following each group. It should be noted that, unlike appeals to emotion and slanted language, not all fallacies are purposely or consciously intended to dupe the unwary reader. Many writers lapse into them from ignorance or as a result of sloppy thinking.

Ad Hominem Argument

From Latin, *ad hominem* means "to the man." The **ad hominem** fallacy can take two forms: either attacking the character of the person rather than the principles he or she stands for or attacking the character and reputation of a position's supporters. In either case, the argument ignores the person's deeds or character. During the Vietnam War, Vice President Spiro Agnew characterized students and intellectuals (who were generally opposed to President Nixon's war policies) with this famous alliterative phrase—"nattering nabobs of negativism"— thereby attacking their collective character rather than the principles they stood for. Here is another example:

- I'm certainly not going to vote for Proposition 16 in the next election. I just looked at the election pamphlet and discovered that the big oil companies are in favor of it. There must be something in it for them.

Begging the Question

When a writer **begs the question,** he or she presents a proposition and assumes that it has been proved when it has not. A simpler way of understanding the begging-the-question fallacy is this: The writer essentially is arguing in a circle, assuming that a point is true without proof and drawing a conclusion based on it. Stated still another way, the writer assumes to be true that which he or she is supposed to prove. For example: Who is the best person to censor controversial articles in the campus newspaper? In phrasing the question like this, the writer begs the question, assuming without proof that censorship of the campus newspaper is necessary in the first place.

Here is another: During a murder trial, if a prosecuting attorney asks the jury, "Does it make sense to release this murderer so he can commit the same atrocities again and again?" she begs the question, since the very purpose of a trial is to prove whether the defendant actually committed the murder. Study these three examples:

- Detergent ad: "If you want miraculously white clothes, use Soapy detergent. It's a washday miracle!"
- If you can't trust your doctor, whom can you trust?
- Teenagers should be prevented from having abortions. After all, a girl wouldn't get pregnant in the first place if she wasn't allowed to terminate her mistake.

In the last instance, the writer replaces one debatable assumption with another equally debatable one: The option of having an abortion leads to unwanted pregnancies. Therefore, the writer assumes but does not address the idea that removing abortion as an option will solve the teenage pregnancy problem.

Cause-and-Effect Fallacies: False Cause, Questionable Cause, and Post Hoc, Ergo Propter Hoc

You might want to review cause and effect as a method of paragraph development in Chapter 4 before reading this section. There are three common fallacies resting on presumed cause-effect connections. The easiest of the three to identify is the **false cause fallacy,** which results when the cause cited is either irrelevant to the effect or is so *remote,* so far back in time, that its link with the present is only tenuous at best. During the 1992 election, President George Bush took credit for playing a decisive role in the breakup of the Soviet Union. His opponent, Bill

Clinton, responded, "Mr. Bush's taking credit for the breakup of the Soviet Union is like the rooster's taking credit for the dawn." Another example: American essayist Calvin Trillin observed facetiously that the Gulf War finally ended when President Bush learned to pronounce Iraqi president Saddam Hussein's name correctly.

Here are two more examples:

- I knew I should have canceled my tennis match today. My astrological forecast warned me not to engage in anything competitive. No wonder I lost.
- It is obvious that Sam Anderson would grow up to be an ax murderer. According to an interview I read, he was subjected to a rigid toilet-training regime when he was a toddler.

Another problem with cause and effect reasoning is that a writer may identify a single reason to explain a complex situation—whether good or bad—when, in fact, other reasons may be accountable. We call this the **questionable cause fallacy.** For example, many studies have found that college students who attend class regularly receive better grades than those who attend sporadically. One explanation is that regular attendance ensures that students are exposed to ideas in the classroom, but this may not wholly account for higher grades. They may result from better study habits and discipline; further, it is likely that better-disciplined students are also likely to be disciplined enough to get up in time to make their classes. Thus, the statement that exposure to ideas causes higher grades can be termed a *questionable* cause because other factors may affect one's academic achievement, at least as measured by his or her GPA.

For another illustration, social scientists have often pointed to a correlation between the high number of liquor stores per square mile in the nation's inner cities and the high crime rates in these areas. But is this cause-effect relationship justified? Obviously, easy accessibility to liquor could lead to increased drinking, which, in turn, could lead to violent altercations and the like. But this cause is questionable because it is not clear which is the cause and which is the effect. One might argue from a different point of view: that inner-city residents drink more (and also use drugs) to provide solace for the desperate lives they lead, stemming from factors like poverty, lack of decent educational and employment opportunities, and racism, not merely because a greater percentage of liquor stores are located in the neighborhood.

Finally, a perceived cause-and-effect relationship may be purely coincidental. For example, if you break out in hives after eating jalapeño peppers for the first time, you might logically connect the two events. But the hives may have been caused by something quite different—an allergic reaction to something else you ate or to something in the environment, contact with a plant, even stress. To form a good inductive argument, you would have to eat jalapeño peppers perhaps two or three more times and break out in hives each time before you could conclusively connect the two.

The last cause-and-effect fallacy is called **post hoc, ergo propter hoc,** which in Latin means "after this, therefore because of this." It suggests that, because event B occurred after event A, event A caused event B. The post hoc fallacy is similar to the false cause and questionable cause fallacies, but with one important difference: With false cause, there is a "leap" from a remote situation to a present one, and with questionable cause a single cause is credited with producing a complex effect. With the post hoc fallacy, however, the cause-and-effect relationship is based on coincidence—as in the earlier hives-jalapeño pepper example—whereby one event is assumed to have caused a second one.

The post hoc fallacy accounts for many silly superstitions. If you walk under a ladder and are hit by a bus 10 minutes later, it would be fallacious to argue that the accident occurred because you were foolish enough to defy the superstition of walking under a ladder. A broken mirror does not mean that seven years of bad luck will ensue, nor will stepping on cracks in the sidewalk break your mother's back.

Here is a more momentous example. From our study of American history, most of us have grown up believing that Japan surrendered in 1945 as a result of the atomic bombs that the Americans dropped on Hiroshima and Nagasaki. Indeed, not long after the war ended, in February 1947, Secretary of War Henry L. Stimson published an article in *Harper's* titled "The Decision to Use the Atomic Bomb," in which he asserted that the American military agreed to use the bomb from the beginning. However, a recent *New Yorker* article (July 31, 1995) written on the occasion of the 50th anniversary of Hiroshima casts doubt on this assertion. In "Letter from Hiroshima: Did the Bomb End the War?" Murray Sayle explains that this belief is the result of a post hoc, ergo propter hoc fallacy:

> [1]Stimson's defense of the atomic bombs comes down to a familiar pair of propositions: (1) the atomic bombs caused the Japanese surrender, and (2) the surrender saved a large number of American lives.
>
> [2]His version of what happened to end the war has long since hardened into dogma: "We believed that our [nuclear] attacks had struck cities which must certainly be important to the Japanese military leaders, both Army and Navy, and we waited for a result. We waited one day." Aside from his implications that the Japanese Army and Navy had somehow been intimidated by attacks on minor installations, his argument rests on the fallacy post hoc, ergo propter hoc—after, therefore because. But at the time Stimson wrote it was already known that the atomic bombs, in fact, had little

effect on Japan's physical ability to continue the war. The target committee, in drawing up its list, did not consider the military importance of any of them. Above all, Stimson's article pretended that the issue of whether to drop the bomb was seriously studied; we know that it was not.

[3]However, the sequence of events—Hiroshima, Nagasaki, surrender offer—is striking. Could it be that pure coincidence has clouded our understanding of the surrender for half a century? Indeed it could. By themselves, the dates prove nothing. In his article Stimson went further, not simply saying that the atomic bombs were intended to shorten the war, and thus save lives, which was no doubt true (and could be said of any action in any war), but arguing that they actually *did* end the war. This is the only defense he offers for their use—and the only defense seriously put forward by anyone since. This argument needs at least some supporting evidence; there is none.

To end this section, read this portion of a column which parodies false cause-and-effect reasoning, specifically poking fun at the notion that a variety of social changes can be attributed to a single cause. Tom and Ray Magliozzi are auto repair experts whose syndicated question-and-answer column, "Click & Clack Talk Cars," appears in many newspapers.

[1]Dear Tom and Ray: Can you tell me why the auto industry puts computers in cars? It used to be that any mechanically minded person with experience could repair a car. Now, of course, it is necessary to take the car to the dealer or to a factory-authorized repair shop which has factory-trained mechanics. Was this the reason computers were introduced?—Margaret

[2]Ray: No one specifically set out to make cars more complicated. But they certainly have gotten that way. The main reasons for computers are emissions controls and improved fuel economy.

[3]Tom: Computers have allowed cars to have sophisticated fuel injection and engine management systems that would never have been possible with carburetors. Through the use of various sensors, the computer can tell how dense the air is, how cold the engine is, how hard you're stepping on the accelerator, and can calculate from all this data the precise amount of fuel to send into the cylinders. That means minimal waste of fuel and a lot less pollution. Not to mention better performance and greater reliability.

[4]Ray: But it has come at a cost. In my opinion, a social cost more than an economic one. Tinkering with cars used to be a great American pastime. Guys would spend Saturdays out in the driveway taking things apart and then trying to put them back together before it got dark. That's no longer possible.

[5]Tom: And I don't think we realize the widespread ramifications of this change. For example, what do those guys who used to work on their cars do now? They sit around, watching TV, feeling useless and picking fights with their wives. So the increase in the divorce rate is directly attributable to the introduction of computers in cars.

[6]Ray: Tinkering with cars also used to present an opportunity for father-child bonding. That's gone too. And when parents aren't directly involved in their kids' lives, we all know the crime and drug-abuse rates go way up.

[7]Tom: Laundry detergents used to be sold on their ability to remove grease. Where did that grease come from? From engines on Saturday afternoon! And the clothes that couldn't be "Fabbed" and "Duzzed" and "Wisked" fueled the entire Goodwill industry. Gone now, due to computers in cars.

[8]Ray: Plus, being out in the driveway gave neighbors an opportunity to meet and get to know each other. This would often lead to socializing, the building of "communities" and invitations to barbecues.

[9]Tom: That's right. So the decrease in the sales of red meat can also be laid at the feet of computers in cars.

[10]Ray: There's the hope for the future! As soon as the American Beef Association figures this out, they're going to see a major lobbying effort to bring back the carburetor—probably with a series of TV ads starring Robert Mitchum. I think your worries are over, Margaret.

Tom and Ray Magliozzi, "Click & Clack Talk Cars"

Either-Or Fallacy

Sometimes called *false dilemma,* the **either-or fallacy** occurs when the writer reduces a complicated issue to only two choices, thereby ignoring other possibilities or alternatives. In May 1996, it was revealed that a clothing line using Kathie Lee Gifford's name was being manufactured by women in Central American sweatshops toiling in appalling conditions and for very little pay (at least by North American standards). Gifford pledged to pressure companies to take their business away from manufacturers who exploit third-world workers. One often-heard argument against Gifford's position went like this: The impact of Kathie Lee's crusade will drive businesses from Central America, eliminating jobs and making living conditions for the poor even more miserable. Sweatshops are better than no shops at all.

This either-or argument ignores a conspicuous third alternative: Manufacturers could pay workers a decent wage and improve working conditions.

Here are two more arguments using the either-or fallacy.

- Police officers are either brutal or corrupt.

- A married woman should stay home and devote herself to raising her children. If she wants a career, she should forget about having children. (Dr. Laura Schlessinger, call-in radio advice giver, often uses this argument, although to be fair, she does suggest that a husband could work part time to take over the child care duties if his wife wants to work a few hours a week.)

Evasion

Evasion is a fallacy that occurs when a speaker or writer evades or ignores the question altogether by talking about something else. For example, when asked how he plans to solve the community's homeless problem, a mayor would be guilty of evading the question if he talked at length about the importance of finding a solution to homelessness without ever proposing how to go about doing it.

For a more bizarre illustration, consider these remarks made by James Morgan, president of Philip Morris Co., in a deposition given in preparation for airline flight attendants' $5-billion class-action lawsuit. The deposition was videotaped, and excerpts were shown on CBS's *60 Minutes.* When the flight attendants' attorney, Stanley Rosenblatt, asked Morgan if he believes that cigarettes are addictive, Morgan replied: "Pharmacologically, my answer is no. If they are behaviorally addictive or habit forming, they are much more like caffeine, or in my case, Gummi Bears. I love Gummi Bears, . . . and I want Gummi Bears, and I like Gummi Bears, and I eat Gummi Bears, and I don't like it when I don't eat my Gummi Bears, but I'm certainly not addicted to them." (Quoted in "Candy Is as Habit-Forming, Tobacco Executive Says," *San Francisco Chronicle,* May 3, 1997.)

Why is this statement an evasion? ______________________________

For a final example: In August 1997 the Democratic National Committee was under investigation for questionable fund-raising practices. When asked for his reaction to recent revelations about the alleged laundering of foreign money into the DNC coffers, President Clinton responded, "I was sick at heart" and "disappointed," both of which ignored the fact that, according to *The New York Times,* the campaign had been orchestrated from the White House itself and that Harold Ickes, one of Clinton's highest aides, had sent Clinton memos about the matter. (Quoted in "White House Excuses," *The New York Times,* August 8, 1997.)

EXERCISE IN IDENTIFYING LOGICAL FALLACIES—PART 1

Study the following arguments carefully and decide which of the fallacies discussed in this section each represents.

1. Bumper sticker seen in Wyoming: "Wolves, not cows!"
2. It's a good thing that Gary Hart dropped out of the 1988 presidential race. He's the one who, while still married, was caught with a young woman off the coast in a boat appropriately named "Monkey Business."
3. Yesterday I forgot to take my vitamins, and this morning I woke up with a cold. I know for certain that taking vitamins prevent colds.
4. One critic of the Clinton administration wrote in an editorial highly critical of Clinton's first two years in office, "That Mr. Clinton's reign as a national leader was to be a disastrous one was, after all, clear very early—well before he took office." (Dorothy Rabinowitz, "Requiem for the Clinton Presidency," *The Wall Street Journal,* February 6, 1995.)
5. From an essay by Susan Faludi titled "Blame It on Feminism" in her book, *Backlash:* "Law enforcement officials and judges, too, have pointed a damning finger at feminism, claiming that they can chart a path from rising female independence to rising female pathology. As a California sheriff explained it to the press, 'Women are enjoying a lot more freedom now, and as a result, they are committing more crimes.' "
6. Rather than being allowed to receive Credit/No Credit grades in composition courses, college students should be required to receive letter grades for their work. Educators all agree that students work harder when they know they will be graded.
7. Tom remarks to Harry: "I heard that the Asian flu will be worse than usual in the Bay Area this year." Harry replies: "That's because San Francisco has such a large Asian population."
8. In 1996, Pat Buchanan, conservative Republican presidential candidate, campaigned at the Citadel, a formerly all-male military academy in Charleston, South Carolina. The Citadel had tried for years to block women from attending, although it had admitted Shannon Faulkner, who left after less than a week. The Justice Department was threatening the academy with loss of federal funds if it continued to block women from being admitted.

   Expressing sympathy for the Citadel's stance, Buchanan said that if he were elected president, he would tell the Justice Department lawyers: "You are either on the side of the Citadel or you're going back to Berkeley," a reference to UC Berkeley's reputedly liberal atmosphere. (Quoted in a Reuters news release, February 2, 1996.) Note: The Citadel eventually relented, admitting four women students in the fall of 1996 and 20 in the fall of 1997.
9. Sweden is a socialist country, and it has one of the highest suicide rates in the world. Socialism must cause suicide.

10. Because children surely need a mother more than they need a father, women with children should not be allowed to engage in military combat.
11. The President of XYZ Company stated, "The recent settlement between management and the labor union was a huge mistake: Giving in to the union's demands for a wage increase has resulted in low production figures."
12. Why single out welfare recipients and cut off their measly benefits when the rich get tax breaks that allow them to shelter huge chunks of their income from the IRS?
13. Bill Clinton's proposal to curb cigarette advertising is a bad idea. Whether to smoke or not is a a personal decision, one the government shouldn't interfere in. Besides, Clinton's record—from his failure at reforming health insurance to his appointment for Surgeon General—has been poor. He shouldn't make any more pronouncements in this area.
14. Advertisement written by Tony Hueston promoting Nature Cure Bee Caps (printed on a placemat in a Lake Havasu City, Arizona, restaurant):

    In 1986 my mother, Pauline "Grandma" Hueston, was hospitalized in critical condition, suffering from eight separate very serious medical problems. Six years prior she underwent bypass surgery which seemed minor compared to her present condition. We thought we were going to lose her. After extensive hospitalization she was released but was unable to walk or care for herself.

    Shortly thereafter, a friend visiting from Europe brought mom four bottles of the bee products—Royal Jelly, Propolis, Bee Pollen, and Raw Honey. My mother attempted to take them, but her hands were so debilitated that she couldn't remove the bottle caps. One of the major problems remained: she was not eating and could not regain her strength. My hope was that by taking the four bee products she would have an easy way to get nutrition into her system. Using some simple ingenuity, we ground together the contents from the four bottles using a mortar and pestle. Then taking the mixture and placing it into empty capsules, my mother could easily take her bee products. She continued to follow doctors' instructions, took her prescriptions and kept taking the bee capsules. From an initial discharge prognosis of only 2–3 months to live, my mother began to regain her strength, energy and stamina. Miraculously, with the services of an excellent doctor, her medication, good nutrition and trust in God, my mother regained her health. Today at almost 90 years old, she is enjoying herself and loves spending time with her great grandchildren. . . .

15. When Bill Clinton was interviewed during the 1992 presidential campaign about his reported marijuana use in the 1960s during college and law school, he admitted that he had used it. Then he went on to say, "But I didn't inhale."

LOGICAL FALLACIES: PART 2

False Analogy

Although it does not carry the same force as factual evidence or good reasons, arguing by analogy can be effective and persuasive in supporting an argument. As you will recall from Chapter 4 in Part I, an analogy discusses one subject in terms of another, completely different subject. But a logical fallacy called **false analogy** results if there are fewer similarities than differences, if the resemblance is remote or ambiguous, or if there is no resemblance between the two at all.

For example, consider this argument:

- Every red-blooded American serviceman knows that gays should be banned from the military. In the military we're like one big family living in close quarters, and a homosexual just wouldn't fit in.

This argument rests on the dubious idea that people living in military quarters are comparable to a family. To see why the analogy is false, we have to see where it breaks down and if there are more dissimilarities than similarities. First, one chooses to enter the military, but one cannot choose which family to be born into. The analogy also implies that military personnel have no privacy whereas family members do. Further, the writer argues that gays should be excluded from the military because other members wouldn't be "comfortable" being around them, implying—contradictorily—that gays can't "fit in" with a family, either. In sum, when you examine these differences, the only real connection between the military and a family is that both are social institutions.

The tobacco industry has taken many hits in these critical reading chapters for fallacious thinking. Here is yet another example: In 1996 then-governor of Massachusetts William Weld signed a bill that, among other provisions, would force tobacco companies to reveal the additives in each cigarette brand, in particular "ammonia-based compounds that tobacco critics say boost nicotine delivery and make cigarettes more potent." Peggy Carter, a spokeswoman for RJR Nabisco, the parent corporation of its subsidiary, R.J. Reynolds Tobacco Co., responded, arguing: "They wouldn't ask Coke, Pepsi or the Colonel to divulge their soft-drink or chicken recipe, so why should we be deprived of trade-secret privileges? (Quoted in Barbara Carton, "State Demands List of Contents for Cigarettes," *The Wall Street Journal,* August 2, 1996.) Why is this a false analogy? Where does it break down? ______________________________

____

It is important to note that not all analogies used in persuasive writing are false, and in fact, as noted earlier, analogies can be both effective and cogent—as long as the similarities between the two things being compared are greater than the differences. To illustrate, in 1987 a group of parents from Minneapolis (a city with one of the highest Native-American populations in the country), called the Concerned American Indian Parents, designed a poster distributed to local high schools. They were protesting the practice in some high schools of calling their athletic teams the "Indians." The poster depicted the banner of the real Cleveland Indians baseball team, along with three other hypothetical banners for the Pittsburgh Negroes, the Kansas City Jews, and the San Diego Caucasians. The slogan at the bottom of the poster read, "Maybe now you know how Native Americans feel." One of the schools that received the poster, Southwest Secondary School in Minneapolis, announced that it had changed the name of one of its teams from the Indians to the Lakers, demonstrating the compelling power of a good analogy.

Finally, consider this argument supported by an analogy. Education professor Richard Clark was quoted on *The CBS Evening News* as warning schools that trying to teach "by hooking students up to machines and technology" is like "trying to improve the nutrition of a neighborhood by bringing in more trucks to deliver groceries without having the money to buy groceries." Based on what you have learned about analogies, is it false or not? What is being compared to what?

____

Oversimplification

The fallacy of **oversimplification** can involve either reducing a complicated issue to overly simple terms or suppressing information that would strengthen the argument.

- The way to stop drug abuse in this country is to increase dramatically the number of drug enforcement agents and to punish severely anyone caught possessing illegal drugs.

This was the argument used by proponents of the Bush and Reagan Administrations' War on Drugs. Some critics of the War on Drugs program, however, charged that this approach was too simplistic and, in fact, hadn't worked despite the billions of dollars poured into the program. They argued that the only effective approach to fighting drug abuse was in attacking the *causes* of drug abuse, rather than simply putting more money into law enforcement.

Moreover, if the people arguing in favor of the War on Drugs failed to disclose damaging data strongly suggesting that police crackdowns and drug busts have not put a dent in the illegal drug market, they would be deliberately suppressing damaging evidence in order to strengthen their case. A good argument presents the facts and does not conveniently omit relevant, though damaging, evidence. (See the sections on omitting evidence and on refutation to review this important point.)

Non Sequitur

A **non sequitur,** taken from the Latin for "it does not follow," is a conclusion that does not logically follow from the premises or the evidence. Here is an example: In 1994 a disk jockey at Dallas's country radio station KYNG-FM announced that he had hidden five- and ten-dollar bills in books in the fiction section of the Fort Worth public library. Predictably, hundreds of people stampeded through the library, pulling books off the shelves and dumping them on the floor in their frenzy to find the money. A spokesman for the station claimed that the disk jockey who thought up the stunt did so because he wanted to boost public interest in the library.

Rationalization

A **rationalization** is a self-serving but incorrect reason to account for one's actions. For example, the student who gets a D in chemistry and then claims that he didn't do well in the course because he didn't like the instructor is rationalizing. The next example has to do with the nearly-universal practice of senators and congressional representatives receiving honorariums or honoraria (in other words, fees) for speaking engagements.

Here is Senator Robert Byrd of West Virginia's explanation for accepting such fees: "I accept honoraria. I do not like to do it. . . . We do have grandchildren to educate. . . . If it were not for their grandparents, one of these grandsons would not be graduating as a physics major this year. Another grandchild would not be entering as a freshman to college this year. It is important that this country graduate physics majors, majors in mathematics, chemistry, and various other disciplines in order to keep this country ahead in technology, science, and physics." ("The Stupidest Things People Say Calendar," November 6, 1996.)

During the White House sex scandal in early 1998, President Clinton had been accused of having an affair with a 21-year-old White House intern and then persuading her to lie about her involvement. During the investigation conducted by special prosecutor Kenneth Starr, the Treasury Department was notified that Secret Service agents (whose job it is to protect the president) would be subpoenaed to testify about any improper activity they might have observed. According to *The New York Times,* the Treasury Department responded that it would fight any subpoenas seeking testimony from its agents, arguing that "the agents' ability to stay close to the president would be imperiled if they could be forced to disclose what they see and hear." (*The New York Times,* January 29, 1998.)

A final example of rationalization:

- A university fundraiser routinely sent her personal mail, including bills and gifts, using the university's postage, arguing that, because her salary was low, this practice would help compensate her since she believed she deserved higher pay.

Slippery Slope

The metaphoric name of the **slippery slope fallacy** will help you remember it. It suggests that one step in the wrong direction will lead to more and more dire and undesirable occurrences. The image invoked is one of a person being unable to halt his or her descent down a muddy or icy incline once that first tentative step is taken.

In this example, the speaker even admits that his argument is a slippery slope, though he does not suggest that his reasoning is fallacious.

At Baylor University in Waco, Texas, the college's new president, Robert B. Sloan, Jr., overturned the 151-year-old ban on dancing, although he promised that the dancing would be closely supervised and the music carefully chosen. The decision was made in 1995 after years of discussion.

However, Miles Seaborn, president of the Southern Baptists in Texas and a Fort Worth pastor, was unhappy with the decision. "Who's going to be the gyration inspector?" he asked. "Are they going to have a committee, or is the president going to do it?" Seaborn observed what happened at schools "with their roots in divinity, pointing to Harvard and Yale" that allowed dancing. "Baylor has been on the slippery slope for some time, and this is just one more slip. Wherever modern dancing is, there is alcohol and promiscuousness." (Quoted in Allen R. Myerson, "Baylor to Allow Dancing on Campus—But No Gyrations," *The New York Times,* January 30, 1996.) A last example:

- Legalizing marijuana is a terrible idea. Once marijuana is legalized, users will graduate to progressively more dangerous and addictive drugs, like heroin and crack. Eventually, we'll all be a nation of freaked-out zombies!

Two Wrongs Make a Right

The **two wrongs make a right** fallacy is commonly used to make wrongdoing legitimate because others engage in the same practice, as you can see in this example: During the campaign fundraising investigations of 1997, President Clinton admitted that the Democratic National Committee had been guilty of certain abuses (money-laundering, illegal contributions by foreigners, and so forth), but that the Republican National Committee had done exactly the same thing. In fact, the Republicans were in a sticky position concerning the Senate hearings and risked making themselves look ridiculous if they came down too hard on the Democrats for practices that both parties had been guilty of using for years.

Another illustration, commonly cited by speeding drivers after receiving a ticket:

- Policeman to driver: "Sir, did you know you were going 75 in a 65-mile-per-hour zone?"
  Driver: "I don't see why you pulled me over. Didn't you see that guy in the red Acura? He must have been doing 85!"

EXERCISE IN IDENTIFYING LOGICAL FALLACIES: PART 2

Study the following arguments carefully and decide which of the fallacies discussed in the second section each represents.

1. Bumper sticker spotted in Oregon: "Hungry and out of work? Eat an environmentalist."
2. The government's proposal to ban cigarette advertising altogether is a bad idea. When the government begins to tell us what to do, we lose our freedoms. States are already forcing people to wear seatbelts. Pretty soon government officials will be peeking in our bedrooms and dictating how we can make love!
3. I don't see anything wrong with using the office copy machine to make copies of my personal income tax forms. Just yesterday I saw Mike Hulbert making a copy on the office Xerox machine of that mystery novel he's been writing on the side.
4. The traditional football game between archrivals USC and Notre Dame has been lopsided in recent years. USC hasn't won since 1982, losing 11 years in a row before finally tying in 1995. In response to a reporter's comment about the losing streak, Trojan coach John Robinson blamed the string of losses on Southern California's long drought in the 1970s and 1980s.
5. Concerning the question of whether the Miss America Pageant should retain the swimsuit segment of the annual competition, one swimsuit-enthusiast posted a message on the pageant's Internet bulletin board saying that the swimsuit competition should be retained because it allows judges to determine if a contestant is healthy.

6. A dog breeder refused to reimburse me after I purchased a pedigreed German shepherd that later was found to have a serious defect requiring corrective surgery. The breeder refused to pay even half of the surgery's cost, arguing: "You wouldn't expect your doctor to reimburse you if your child needed surgery, would you?"
7. During the Watergate crisis in 1973 that eventually led to President Nixon's resignation, the President's supporters contended that Nixon had not done anything different from any other president. He had just gotten caught.
8. It was revealed that contestants on 1950s quiz shows like *Twenty-One* and the *$64,000 Question* had been fed answers before the programs were aired. The resulting quiz show scandals prompted a national debate over truth and honesty in broadcasting. (This deception was nicely depicted in Robert Redford's film *Quiz Show.*) One quiz show producer was quoted as saying, in defense of the rigged answers, "If we rig the contest and supply [the contestants] with answers, we'll make intellectualism and learning look glamorous."
9. Springfield should round up all the homeless sleeping on the streets and make them live in shelters; otherwise, the city will just be a magnet for all destitute people who will end up sleeping in our public parks and in our doorways.
10. It would be bad for my health if I stopped smoking. I would gain a lot of weight, and that would cause a strain on my heart. Anyway, they'll find a cure for cancer soon.
11. In 1993 the U.S. Government agreed to pay $20,000 and to make an apology to each Japanese-American who had been sent to internment camps during World War II. Some people criticized the government's offer as too little, too late. Others, however, had a different view, like this person: "I'm sick and tired of all these people complaining about the internment camps and about the way Japanese-Americans were treated during the war. What caused all this, anyway? The Japanese attacked the U.S. at Pearl Harbor, and our leaders knew that the Japanese constituted a threat to our national security and our military's policies."
12. The right-to-die initiative should be defeated by the voters in the next election. Although the proposition involves people only with terminal conditions, eventually cooperative doctors will stretch the definition to include chronic conditions, like Alzheimer's or multiple sclerosis. Pretty soon we won't have any control over who lives or who dies. It will be just like ancient Sparta, where babies who did not have the potential to be great warriors were left outside to die.
13. This argument is in response to the 1994 announcement that Lockheed had adopted a policy refusing to hire smokers in an effort to reduce its health care costs: If Lockheed goes ahead and refuses to

hire smokers, I can predict that the results will be disastrous. Eventually, we'll have food police poking through our garbage looking for sour cream containers, steak bones, and Ho-Ho wrappers. Since supermarkets can now link your name, address, and credit card information to their checkout scanners, it's just a matter of time before our health insurance companies will pay to learn about our eating habits and then deny us insurance because we have unhealthy diets!

14. Do corporate executives deserve extra medical insurance? According to a recent article, labor unions and rank-and-file workers say no, but some businesses are promoting "executive health plans" that provide such perks as freedom from making copayments for doctors' visits, from deductibles, and from limits on the choice of a physician, features that are nearly universal in ordinary workers' health insurance policies.

    Defending these perks, Tom Gathers, vice president for human resources at Uno Restaurant Corporation, which operates a chain of pizza restaurants throughout the United States, argued: "Our executives are very busy people. . . . They've tended to ignore their own health. Obviously, for continuity and for good business, you want people to be healthy." (Quoted in "Employee Health Benefits May Be Fine, But Look at What Some Executives Get," *The Wall Street Journal,* October 25, 1994.)

15. We ought to be apprehensive about mandatory seat belt laws. State Highway Patrol officers have vowed to enforce this law vigorously. It wasn't too long ago that citizens in Germany could be stopped at random with the command, "Show me your papers."

16. In 1991 the *Forth Worth Star-Telegram* fired Katie Sherrod, a liberal columnist, for plagiarism. The paper cited many features, including exact wording, that Sherrod had lifted from a 1990 article by William Booth of *The Washington Post.* In response to her firing, Sherrod said that the plagiarism charge was "a pretext designed to cover up the fact that I have been discharged in retaliation for opposing sexually discriminatory practices at the Star-Telegram." Sherrod further contended that she had been "reprimanded" by management when she wrote a column criticizing the paper for naming the woman in the William Kennedy Smith rape case. (Quoted in "Paper Fires Columnist for Plagiarism," *The Washington Post,* July 30, 1991.)

17. In Half Moon Bay, a semirural town near San Francisco, California, each year the local chapter of Future Farmers of America (FFA) sponsors an event at the local high school called Donkey Basketball. Apparently, this involves a basketball game played by players riding on donkeys. Each year this event elicits many angry letters and anonymous messages to the local newspaper's open-line column. (The organizers contend that the donkeys are switched frequently and that they are not harmed by the activity because they are used to it.)

The following anonymous message is typical: "I'm writing in response to those people who are against our FFA Donkey Basketball. . . . Next time you walk, look down at your shoes and see what you're wearing. Maybe there's a piece of leather there. I wonder where that came from?" (*Half Moon Bay Review,* May 3, 1995.)

18. In the debate over high salaries, a recent newspaper article disclosed that the average yearly compensation was $633,000 in 1990 (including benefits and incentives) for chief executives in American corporations. Critics charge that such salaries are immoral, especially when the executives are rewarded for laying off thousands of lower-paid workers by having their own salaries raised still higher.

    In response, Kevin Murphy, a compensation expert and professor at Harvard Business School, replies that this is exactly the situation when a CEO (chief executive officer) *should* be rewarded: "We have too much capacity and the right thing for shareholders and society is no longer to grow the firm, but to close plants, to take the painful steps of laying off people and becoming a more efficient operation. Society is just not very well informed if people are angered by a CEO's pay climbing while he's laying off thousands of people."

    Murphy concluded his remarks by saying that limiting executive pay "would be crazy, a disaster" because it would take away an executive's incentive to do an outstanding job. (Quoted in John Eckhouse, "Boards Taking Closer Look at Pay," *San Francisco Chronicle,* May 18, 1992.)

19. In 1997 the Justice Department filed suit against Microsoft Corporation for violating antitrust laws. The corporation was accused of forcing makers of personal computers to install its web browser, Internet Explorer, on all of its new products, hence creating a monopoly since consumers would not have a choice of which browser to use. Microsoft claimed that its browser was an integral part of Windows 95, the operating system, and if the browser were removed, Windows 95 would not function properly. (Opponents showed that, in fact, Explorer could be easily removed in a couple of minutes and that the browser is also sold as a separate package.) However, defenders of Microsoft's policy countered that Windows 95 is like an automobile and that the Explorer is like a radio. Most car manufacturers provide a radio with a car. And no one objects to GM or Ford or Chrysler selling automobiles equipped with radios.

20. Marion Hammer, president of the National Rifle Association: "I'm being denied the right to own a semiautomatic firearm simply because someone doesn't like the way it looks. . . . If you look at all the different automobiles out there, the majority of them travel on regular roads. So how do you explain the dune buggies or off-road vehicles? They're different, but you don't hear anybody saying, 'Why

> does anyone need to have a dune buggy or an off-road vehicle? What's wrong with your regular run-of-the-mill traditional automobile?' It's all a matter of personal preference." (Quoted in *George,* April 1996.)

OTHER MANIPULATIVE TECHNIQUES

In this last part of Chapter 9, we will briefly look at some other problems and deceptive techniques used in argumentative writing, in politics, and in advertising.

Authority

You will recall that the testimonial appeal uses spokespeople, most often celebrities like movie stars, rock stars, or athletes, to endorse products. However much we admire their talents, we should be skeptical about accepting them as reliable authorities. As noted earlier, they are paid—often enormous sums of money—for their kind words. Second, they may not be knowledgeable about the field as an expert would be. A dietitian would be a more trustworthy authority to speak on the nutritional merits or demerits of a product like Jello Pudding-Pops than Bill Cosby.

An **authority** is defined in the dictionary as "an accepted source of expert information or advice." Certainly an authority should be knowledgeable about the particular field about which he or she is giving information and should comment on matters appropriate to his or her specific field. In May 1997, FBI Director Louis Freeh was criticized by TWA and FAA and National Transportation Safety Board officials when he proclaimed that "catastrophic mechanical failure" was the cause of the TWA crash off Long Island a year earlier. (Quoted on *Meet the Press* and in the Web site maintained by Airwise News for the week ending May 16, 1997.)

Freeh's conclusion was the result of faulty inductive reasoning:

- The TWA crash was not the result of a terrorist attack.
- The TWA crash was not the result of the plane being hit by a missile.
- Therefore, the crash was the result of catastrophic mechanical failure.

To be sure, TWA had a vested interest in the cause being other than mechanical failure; yet Freeh's critics had a point. Freeh was speaking as director of the FBI, but it is questionable if the nation's top FBI authority is also an authority on the causes of airplane crashes. Certainly he is free to speak his mind, but lending his authoritative weight to pronouncements outside his field of expertise is suspect, nor does his opinion have any more authoritative weight than that of ordinary citizens who followed the investigation in the media and on the World Wide Web.

In Chapter 8, you read a selection titled "Why Stop Smoking? Let's Get Clinical" by William F. Harrison of the Fayetteville Women's Clinic in Arkansas. Although Harrison's specialty is obstetrics and gynecology, not pulmonary medicine or cardiology, the fact that he is a physician is sufficient qualification for him to explain the damage smoking does to the human body.

A definite misuse of authority occurs when the high-sounding names of "research organizations" are used to hoodwink the unwary reader or consumer. A particularly blatant instance of this occurred in 1992, when *The New York Times* published an article reporting that chocolate contains cavity-fighting properties. This startling announcement made headlines. A few days later, however, it was revealed that the information had come from a newsletter published by the Princeton Dental Resource Center and distributed to dentists' offices. (The name of this organization, of course, is meant to sound as if it is affiliated with Princeton University; it is not.) As it turns out, the Princeton Dental Resource Center is actually a front for the M&M/Mars Candy Company.

Bias

Bias occurs when a writer favors one side over the other, writing from a subjective viewpoint colored by—and possibly distorted by—his or her political, economic, social, ethnic or racial, or religious views. Knowing the background of a writer—not merely his or her qualifications for serving as an authority—can alert the reader to subtle or not-so-subtle attempts to manipulate our thinking. Although total objectivity is not humanly possible, in a factual news article, we should expect that a writer will attempt to be fair and to exercise careful judgment about what material to select and what material to omit.

In persuasive writing—our concern in this chapter—we should grant a writer somewhat more leeway. Since the writer's purpose is to convince the reader of a particular subjective point of view, we cannot reasonably expect objectivity (which is more closely associated with exposition), nor is a refutation mandatory as would be required in more traditional argumentative forms. To some extent, then, bias is a necessary outgrowth of persuasive writing. The very nature of presenting an argument plainly requires as its starting position a bias—defined in another way as an inclination or an outlook. The critical reader must not assume that evidence of bias assumes a sinister motive. What is important is to distinguish between *acceptable* and *unacceptable* bias. Unacceptable bias is based on racial, ethnic, religious, or political insensitivity or prejudice; on one's own economic self-interest; or on the desire to hide or distort the truth.

Further, to determine acceptable bias, we must consider whether or not the writer is *credible* or believable. Does the writer have any expertise in the subject? What is the basis of the writer's ideas? Has the writer revealed any personal experience that would lend credibility? Assuming that the writer does a decent job of presenting evidence (as discussed in the previous chapter), then one can accept or at least appreciate the argument. In contrast, unfair bias may be accompanied by other manipulative techniques, like slanted language (euphemisms or sneer words), specious arguments, logical fallacies, and so forth.

Let us illustrate with two simple examples: Suppose your English teacher tells you in a conference that your last essay received a D because it was weak. She recommends more specific development in the form of examples, analysis, or explanation. This would be an example of *fair* bias, because your instructor is presumably credible and has expertise (by virtue of his or her academic background and teaching experience). Your teacher's preference for clear, well-developed, and adequately supported prose is consistent with the criteria endorsed by other teachers. However, if your instructor gives your essay a D because you wrote about professional football, which she knows nothing about or finds distasteful, that would be an example of *unfair* bias, based on personal prejudice (a like or dislike that is purely subjective and not necessarily shared by other members of the teaching profession).

In some rare instances, a writer may actually announce his or her subjective point of view, in which case you have at least been alerted up front and know what to expect. Consider these paragraphs by British writer James Fenton in the opening of his essay, "The Fall of Saigon." Fenton, upon being given a chance to go to Vietnam in 1973, states his motivation for going there and the anti-American sentiments that he and his comrades shared:

> [1]I was glad to be going off on a journey. I had been awarded a bursary for the purpose of travelling and writing poetry; I intended to stay out of England a long time. Looking at what the world had to offer, I thought either Africa or Indochina would be the place to go. I chose Indochina partly on a whim, and partly because, after the Paris Peace Agreement in February of that same year, it looked as if it was in for some very big changes. The essence of the agreement was that it removed American military personnel from Indochina and stopped the B-52 bombing raids. The question was how long could the American-backed regime last without that accustomed support. I wanted to see Vietnam for myself. I wanted to see a war, and I wanted to see a communist victory, which I presumed to be inevitable. I wanted to see the fall of a city.
>
> [2]I wanted to see a communist victory because, in common with many people, I believed that the Americans had not the slightest justification for

their interference in Indochina. I admired the Vietcong and, by extension, the Khmer Rouge, but I subscribed to a philosophy that prided itself on taking a cool, critical look at the liberation movements of the Third World. I, and many others like me, supported these movements against the ambitions of American foreign policy. We supported them as nationalist movements. We did not support their political character, which we perceived as Stalinist in the case of the Vietnamese, and in the case of the Cambodians . . . I don't know. The theory was, and is, that when a genuine movement of national liberation was fighting against imperialism it received our unconditional support. When such a movement had won, then it might well take its place among the governments we execrated—those who ruled by sophisticated tyranny in the name of socialism.

[3]There was also an argument that Stalinism was not a simple equivalent of Fascism, that it contained what was called a partial negation of capitalism. Further, under certain conditions it might even lay down the foundations of a socialist organization of society. In the Third World, Stalinism might do the job which the bourgeois revolutions had done in Europe. Even Stalinism had its progressive features.

[4]Our attitudes may have looked cynical in the extreme. In fact they were the formulation of a dilemma. After all, we had not invented the Indochina War, and it was not for us to conjure out of thin air a movement that would match up to our own aspirations for Britain. To remain neutral over Vietnam was to support the Americans. To argue for an end to all US involvement, and leave the matter at that, was to ignore the consequences of one's own argument. If there was a conflict on which one had to choose sides, then it was only right to choose sides honestly, and say: 'Stalinists they may be, but we support them.' The slogans of the Vietnam movement were crude stuff indeed—'One side right, one side wrong, victory to . . . Vi-et-cong!'—but the justice of the cause was deeply felt.

[5]This feeling was shared by many people who were not socialists or communists by any stretch of the imagination, and who did not have any other political axe to grind. Such people had merely to look at what was being done to Vietnam in the name of the Free World to know that the Free World was in the wrong. The broadest support for the anti-war movement was engendered by a disgust at what the Americans were doing.

James Fenton, "The Fall of Saigon,"
The Best of Granta Reportage

Few writers, however, reveal their biases as directly as Fenton does at the outset. And discovering a writer's "hidden agenda," a secondary motive that might not be readily apparent, is probably the most difficult task in critical reading. One solution is to read widely. When you become familiar with the underlying beliefs and agendas of editorial writers by reading their columns over a period of time, after a while, you will have a pretty good grasp of their politics. Still another suggestion is to pay attention to biographical headnotes, for they can contain valuable information about a writer's background and beliefs. Finally, when you read persuasive prose, you should ask yourself this question: What does the writer stand to gain or lose by my accepting (or rejecting) this argument?

If you look over the preceding exercise, "Exercise in Identifying Appeals," you will see that many of these arguments suggest an ulterior economic incentive. Auntie Em's pies may be very good indeed, but it seems hard to believe that anyone would confuse a frozen, microwaveable pie with a homemade one. And if you fall for the "just-like-Grandma-used-to-make," "just-plain-folks" appeal and buy one of the company's pies, you've enriched the pie producer's corporate coffers, not given Auntie Em herself a little extra spending money.

One also has to be alert to the source of information—beyond people who represent themselves as authorities, for example, public-relations and lobby groups that disseminate information to the media. Following an outbreak of E. coli bacteria in Odwalla's unpasteurized apple juice, this letter to the editor was published comparing animal and commercial fertilizers.

Commercial Fertilizer vs. Animal Manure

1Your Nov. 4 article on E. coli bacteria in apple juice ("Odwalla's Woes are a Lesson for Natural-Food Industry") obscures an important difference between commercial fertilizers and animal manure used as fertilizer. Commercially produced fertilizers are not the cause of microbial contamination of food. In fact, they are a key part of safer farming both from environmental and human health standpoints. Commercially produced fertilizer is better for the environment because it contains a specified amount of plant nutrients and can be placed in precise spots at precise times to maximize crop use.

2Because of its efficiency, commercial fertilizer is largely responsible for the productivity of America's farmers. Animal manure, on the other hand, is a far less reliable source of plant nutrients and presents other handling and application challenges such as the presence of harmful bacteria.

Kathleen O'Hara Mathers
Director, Public Affairs
The Fertilizer Institute
Washington

Letter to the editor, *The Wall Street Journal,*
November 22, 1996

A call to The Fertilizer Institute in Washington, D.C., confirmed that the organization is a trade association or lobby, funded by fertilizer companies and established to publicize the industry's products. This connection does not mean that the author is wrong in her statements about the relative merits of commercial fertilizers over the natural variety, but it does mean that her comparison is not impartial.

Since it is virtually impossible for the ordinary citizen, who has precious little time, limited energy, and financial resources, to uncover the truth, one has little choice but to rely on the national media and electronic information sources like World Wide Web sites, to expose discrepancies, tainted findings, and other instances of corruption. To illustrate how bias can tarnish even supposedly impartial research studies and how the media can alert us to such deception, consider this example: A Canadian researcher, Dr. Alexander Logan of the University of Toronto, published an article in the *Journal of the American Medical Association* challenging the conventional belief that lowering one's salt intake would help prevent hypertension (high blood pressure). His study was based on "a re-analysis of 56 earlier trials," which showed that "reducing salt did not lower blood pressure in people who were already healthy and had only minor effects in those with high blood pressure." Logan also stated that avoiding salt could actually be harmful, especially in people who get a lot of exercise. He concluded, "We can no longer accept on blind faith that restricting salt intake is harmless."

But Logan's research was quickly attacked by experts who challenged both the way he had conducted his experiments and his motivation for doing so. As explained in a later *Los Angeles Times* article, experts cited problems with Logan's tests and his conclusions, namely that several trials he used were characterized as "poorly designed"; that he ignored other studies that he should have cited, including a major one published by the *British Medical Journal;* and most damaging, that his research had been paid for in part by the Campbell Soup Company. (Quoted in Thomas H. Maugh, "Disputing Benefits of Low Salt," *Los Angeles Times,* May 22, 1996.)

To put the results of his study and Campbell's interests into perspective, the label on a can of Campbell's tomato soup in my kitchen cupboard indicates that *one* serving contains 730 milligrams of salt, or 30 percent of the recommended daily amount. Maugh cites the amount the American Heart Association recommends—no more than 3 grams (3000 mg) of salt per day for the average American. (Assuming the label is accurate, then, 730 mg from a single serving of tomato soup would be about 25 percent of the AHA figures.) Maugh cites another relevant statistic: The average American consumes between 15 to 20 grams of salt each day, "much of it in processed foods." Since physicians warn their hypertensive patients to restrict the amount of salt they use, Logan's findings, if true, could have helped Campbell's sales.

Following are two newspaper opinion pieces. Read each carefully and then assess each writer's tone, his or her bias, how that bias is conveyed, whether or not the bias is fair or unfair, and the writer's credibility. The first article is by Steven Lubet, a law professor at Northwestern University in Evanston, Illinois, who also identifies himself as a relative of Wisconsin deer hunters.

> [1]In Wisconsin, there is only one time a year when nobody thinks about cheese. For nine consecutive days each fall, they drop their curds and whey and head off to hunt deer. Rising well before dawn, they dress up in day-glow orange bibs, grab their trusty shotguns or rifles, and traipse into the woods to lie in wait at their favorite salt licks, all the better to ambush some innocent, sleepy, unsuspecting ungulate.
>
> [2]Need a haircut? Too bad. The barber's out hunting. Want to buy an airplane ticket? Sorry. The travel agent is breaking in a new 12-gauge. Searching for spiritual redemption? I'm afraid you'll have to find the way yourself. The minister and priest are crouching behind a deer blind, hoping to bag a ten-point buck. A bris?[4] Forget it. The rabbi and mohel have made it an ecumenical foursome. How can you tell a Wisconsin church from a synagogue? Simple. At the churches they just mount the antlers; at the synagogues they turn 'em into menorahs.
>
> [3]Almost everyone is stalking in the woods. Sure, the butcher stays home sharpening knives and preparing to turn dead deer into freezer-ready venison. But the hunters include plenty of bakers, doctors, lawyers, and thieves. And if there were any candlestick makers left, you can bet they'd close up shop and sally forth, dressed like so many thinsulate versions of Elmer Fudd, hot and heavy for the week-long shoot-'em up. The deer hunting mania has become so pervasive that even vegetarians are now taking target practice at scale model moose, constructed entirely out of tofu and root vegetables.
>
> [4]So, given the way that the annual hunt dominates Wisconsin life, you can be sure that scheduling the season has evolved into a high art form. Imagine the way it must be at the Fish and Game Commission—an entire governmental department that does nothing all year but calculate the perfect day for the official deer carnage to begin.
>
> [5]Close your eyes and envision them taking complicated readings that include the annual precipitation in Oconomowoc, the average water temperature in Lake Michigan, the density of the moss on the north side of the

[4]In the Jewish religion, a bris is the circumcision ceremony, performed by a specially trained person called a *mohel.*

tallest birch in the deepest forest. Then they measure the antler-buds on representative specimens of mule deer, white tails, and an occasional stray elk. Next they check the testosterone levels of the stags and the estrus cycles of the rutting does—sure that's dangerous and delicate work, but they probably get special "Badger" points for initiative and ingenuity. And let's not forget the geomancers imported from Hong Kong, who apply the ancient art of feng shui to the alignment of the rock outcroppings along the glacial moraine. Or the Torah sages and Imams who make their fine calibrations according to the lunar calendar.

6Never have you seen a single announcement so eagerly anticipated. Think of the super-lotto results, think of counting electoral votes on election night, think of the white smoke at St. Peter's Basilica. Then double the anticipation—no, triple it—as the hunters wait in rapture (not to mention Gore-Tex) to learn the day when the north woods can at last be transformed into one vast shooting gallery.

7And then, once the astrological, meteorological, climatological, geological, biological, and epistemological results are in—they always end up holding the season during Thanksgiving vacation. So that the hunters won't have to miss too much work (and the workers will be able to get in plenty of hunting). Consider it a subsidy for taxidermists, who have the kind of clout in Wisconsin that defense industry lobbyists can only dream about in Washington, D.C.

8In most parts of the country "fawn" is a color, or maybe an obsequious verb. But in Wisconsin, it's an orphan.

Steven Lubet, "The Deer Hunter,"
The Philadelphia Inquirer, November 30, 1996

What is the writer's tone? ____________________

What is the author's bias? ____________________

How is the bias conveyed? ____________________

Is the bias fair or unfair? ____________________

Is the writer credible? ____________________

The second article is by Kathy Snow Guillermo, the author of *Monkey Business: The Disturbing Case That Launched the Animal Rights Movement,* and a writer for PETA, People for the Ethical Treatment of Animals, a well-known animal rights organization.

1A recent article ("Circus Performs Well on Animal Care," Open Forum, March 12) took People for the Ethical Treatment of Animals (PETA) to task for claiming that circuses abuse elephants. In his account of life with the Carson & Barnes Circus, Mike Echols sounds as ingenuous and naive as

Disney circus tyke Toby Tyler. He waxes lyrical about the enormous Big Top and the convoys that carry animals and people on an annual tour of 18,000 miles. He praises Carson & Barnes for building exercise yards for the elephants at their winter quarters.

[2]But Echols' article raises more questions than it answers. Why, for instance, did Carson & Barnes wait more than 50 years to build a fence around a field so that the elephants could stretch their legs for a few weeks each winter? What about the months of endless travel these animals endure, chained in the backs of tractor-trailers, unable to escape their own waste?

[3]Through freezing desert nights and broiling days, the elephants toil. They must "perform" acts unnatural to them before screaming crowds—always under threat of a jab with a sharp bull hook. The rest of the time they stand, chained at the ankles, waiting for the next assignment. What else can this be called but abuse? Even more troubling, the U.S. Department of Agriculture, which oversees the treatment of animals in circuses, has cited Carson & Barnes with numerous violations of the Animal Welfare Act. In 1994 and 1995, the most recent years for which inspection reports are available, the USDA found at least 20 violations, including elephant trucks with inadequate ventilation; sharp, jagged edges that could injure elephants inside the trucks; and inadequate exercise for one elephant, Paula.

[4]In the summer of 1995, the same year Echols began traveling with Carson & Barnes, I visited the circus at one of its stops in Northern California. I arrived just after sunrise, video camera in hand, to document a typical day. I saw elephants lined up like a 1930s chain gang, legs shackled, unable to step more than a foot or two in any direction. After years of such boredom, elephants begin to act like human inmates in mental hospitals, rocking from side to side in an endless rhythmic motion. This is called stereotypic behavior, and whether exhibited by people or animals, it's a sign of mental disturbance. Every one of the Carson & Barnes elephants swayed back and forth, swinging their trunks, their eyes glazed.

[5]Who wouldn't be driven mad by such deprivation? The people who run this circus may be fond of their elephants, but these magnificent beings, with the largest brains of any land animal, are deprived of nearly everything that makes their lives worth living. Every year brings more stories of circus elephants driven to rebellion. They wield their enormous strength to crush their "trainers" or run crazily through the streets. Such incidents have prompted some cities, such as Vancouver, to ban circuses with animal acts.

[6]Though it's unlikely that any circus trainer can persuade an elephant to stand on a tiny platform or spin in a circle without some form of coercion, a decent life means more than not being beaten. It's difficult to imagine that an elephant would rather live shackled to a truck than roam with her family in her own environment.

> [7]Like elephants, other species suffer under the Big Top. For this reason, PETA believes circuses should retire all animal acts, place the animals in sanctuaries and follow the example of the wildly popular, human-only Cirque du Soleil. And yes, as a mother of three young children, I understand that children love to see animals. But they are too young to understand that the animals are exploited. When we expose kids to twirling elephants, tigers jumping through hoops, and bears on bicycles, we teach them nothing about the natural magnificence of these creatures. We owe our children—and the animals—much better.
>
> Kathy Snow Guillermo, "Circuses—Cruel Shows Can't Go On," *San Francisco Chronicle,* April 11, 1997

What is the writer's tone? ______________________

What is the author's particular bias? ______________________

How is the bias conveyed? ______________________

Is the bias fair or unfair? ______________________

Is the writer credible? ______________________

Though the techniques and emotional tone are quite different, each writer argues forcefully and effectively. Lubet succeeds by using irony, sarcasm, hyperbole, and humor, while Guillermo relies on impassioned yet reasoned discourse. Read this last example and then determine the author's point of view. It is by Dorothy Rabinowitz, a *Wall Street Journal* editorial page writer, who frequently writes about child molestation cases. Would you characterize her discussion as biased or impartial?

> [1]On Labor Day 1984, 60-year-old Violet Amirault—proprietor of the thriving Fells Acres Day School in Malden, Mass.—received a call about a child abuse accusation against her son. Two days later the police arrested 31-year-old Gerald (who worked at Fells Acres) on charges of raping a five-year-old boy, a new pupil.
>
> [2]In short order, the hideous crimes supposedly committed by Gerald began to multiply—as did the number of the accused. Soon, Violet Amirault herself and her newly married 26-year-old daughter, Cheryl, were also charged with having perpetrated monstrous sexual crimes against children ages three to five. Police asked the Amiraults no questions. Instead, they summoned parents of Fells Acres children to a meeting at the station house—where they were instructed to look for symptoms of sex abuse.
>
> [3]Within three years, Gerald Amirault was convicted of assault and rape of nine children. In a second trial his mother and sister were convicted of roughly the same crimes against four children. Gerald, sentenced to 30 to

40 years, has now been in prison since 1986. His mother, now 71, and sister Cheryl, now 37, were given eight to 20 years. Both have been imprisoned, at the Massachusetts Correctional Institute at Framingham, for nearly eight years.

4At the time of their sentencing, prosecutor Lawrence Hardoon complained that the punishment was too light for such crimes: and indeed, the prosecution had brought forth some remarkable accusations against the Amiraults.

A 'Magic Room'

5Children had supposedly been raped with knives—which miraculously failed to leave any signs of wounding or other injury—and sticks, and been assaulted by a clown (allegedly Gerald) in a "magic room." Some children told—after interrogations by investigators—of being forced to drink urine, of watching the Amiraults slaughter blue birds, of meeting robots with flashing lights. Violet Amirault was accused of shoving a stick into the rectum of a child while he was standing up, and of raping him with "a magic wand." Mrs. Amirault was convicted of these charges. The child also testified he was tied naked to a tree in the schoolyard, in front of all the teachers and children, while "Miss Cheryl" cut the leg off a squirrel.

6Who would have credited such witnesses, such testimony? The Amirault family was charged in the midst of the great wave of high-profile child abuse cases sweeping the country in the 1980s—all of them magnets for ambitious prosecutors. Among them was that of day-care worker Kelly Michaels, reported on these pages. But the prime child abuse extravaganza—and the one the Amirault prosecutors clearly took for their model—was the now notorious McMartin Preschool case in California, involving alleged abusers Ray Buckey and his mother, sixtyish administrator Peggy McMartin Buckey.

7True, there was a certain inimitable grandeur to the McMartin epic, involving as it did claims of abuse in underground tunnels, of molestation in hot air balloons, and similar marvels. As recently as three years ago die-hard believers among the plaintiff parents were still to be found at the school site, faithfully conducting their searches for the underground tunnels.

8That the wave of spectacular child-abuse trials emerged in the '80s was no accident. The passage in 1979 of the Mondale Act ensured a huge increase in funds for child protection agencies and abuse investigators. With the outpouring of government money came a huge increase in agencies and staffs, which in turn begat investigations and accusations of child sex abuse on a grand scale. An industry had been born.

9Nowhere was the fervor of the search for abuse more evident than in the case constructed against the Amiraults. Her husband gone from the household, an impoverished Violet Amirault had built her highly successful day care center—in operation for 20 years—alone, and from nothing. Over the years the school became her life, next to her children. It was clear, when the sensational prosecutions began, that of the thousands of children previously graduated from Fells Acres, none had any stories of abuse to tell.

10So the world was left with the state's contention: that Mrs. Amirault, at the age of 60, had suddenly taken to raping small children and terrorizing them into silence. When her daughter, Cheryl, was married in 1983, all the pupils and their parents were invited to the church—an event that occasioned a front page picture of the "kindergarten teacher with a hundred children" in the Boston Herald. Among those children happily giving their teacher kisses were those who some months later would be served up to tell of terrors inflicted by Miss Cheryl, her mother and brother.

11As soon as the accusations surfaced, the school's teachers were grilled—but none could be found who saw anything wrong going on at the school. One or two of them disliked Violet, an exacting school head, but still they could come up with nothing, frightened though they were by unsubtle threats from the police, who repeatedly accused them of lying.

12Still, the police investigators' effort to find abuse testimony pales beside the surreal interrogations conducted by such as pediatric nurse Susan Kelley, who developed most of the children's allegations of abuse. Over and over, the interviews show, the children say nothing happened, nobody took their clothes off, they know nothing about a magic room or a bad clown. But the interviewer persists. In the world of these examiners, children are to be believed only when they say abuse took place. Otherwise, they are described as "not ready to disclose."

13The Fells Acres children were bribed with gifts, assured that their little friends had already told about the bad things and "helped so much." At one point the interviewer tells a child that her friend Sara had said "the clown had you girls take your clothes off in the magic room."

Child: "No, she's lying."

Nurse: "She's lying? Why would she lie about something like that . . . ?"

Child: "We didn't do that."

Next the interviewer tells the child, "I really believed her [Sara] because she told me all about it, and she even told me what the clown said."

Child: "What was it?"

14No sane person reading the transcripts of these interrogations can doubt the wholesale fabrications of evidence on which this case was built. Nor could any reasonable person who looked at the trial transcript doubt that three innocent citizens were sent to prison on the basis of some of the most fantastic claims ever presented to an American jury.

15Forced to come up with motives, the prosecutors hit on child pornography. With no evidence whatsoever that the Amiraults had engaged in such crimes, the Commonwealth brought forth a postal inspector Dunn to regale the jury with detailed descriptions of child pornography. When the Amirault women's appeal was refused, Justice Paul Liacos said, in an eloquent dissent, "the court today condones the admission in evidence of highly inflammatory and prejudicial evidence." Clearly, the justice charged, the Commonwealth wanted the jury to infer that because pornographers having no connection with the defendants took pictures of children, so had the defendants.

16The accused in the McMartin case are now free. Kelly Michaels, too, now has her freedom—but for the Amiraults, a far grimmer story from the outset, prospects remain bleak. The thought of the whole family in prison, Cheryl says, "is too much for any one of us to endure. I can't look into my mother's eyes."

17When the Amirault women were sentenced, Prosecutor Hardoon announced that it was "impudent of them" to continue maintaining their innocence. Nevertheless, after eight years in prison they continue to do so—as does Gerald, in Plymouth Correctional Facility. One parole board member told Cheryl that until she confessed she'd be going nowhere. None of the Amiraults are about to confess to what they have not done.

18After the first time the women were refused parole, the judge who presided over their trial decided they had served enough time and issued an order to revise and revoke their sentence. Agitated prosecutors succeeded in getting the courts to overturn the revise-and-revoke order—a ruling unprecedented in Massachusetts history. As in some crude melodrama, the women, unaware and thankful to be going home again, were stopped just before they got to the exit. Back they went deeper into the system—to be refused parole again and again.

Silence Reigns

19Scott Harshbarger, the district attorney whose office prosecuted the Amiraults—and who ran for re-election advertising that fact—is now attorney general of Massachusetts. Some months after the Amiraults were all convicted and in prison, Mr. Harshbarger presided over a celebratory convocation of the Fells Acres case, billed as "a model multidisciplinary response." Prosecutor Hardoon is now in private practice—in a firm specializing in civil awards for sex abuse.

20In Massachusetts armies of journalists from the Boston Herald, the Boston Globe, and local TV followed this prosecution and its preposterous evidence. Today only silence reigns on the Amiraults and the great abuse trials that occasioned so much fevered reporting. Not long ago a Boston Globe editor dismissed a would-be contributor on the subject, saying "I sent two reporters to cover the story at the time and they said the Amiraults were weirdos."

> [21]Can such a miscarriage of justice—if one can use so bland a term for so horrific a tragedy—be sustained by the will of state prosecutors? As was true of the witch trials of an earlier Massachusetts, this prosecution will, in time, be the source of amazement and horror. In the meantime Violet Amirault lies locked in prison along with her son and her daughter, while the days and years of life slip past.
>
> Dorothy Rabinowitz, "A Darkness in Massachusetts," *The Wall Street Journal,* January 30, 1995

Does Rabinowitz seem biased or impartial? Explain your thinking. ____

____

____

Slanting

You will recall from the discussion of denotation and connotation in Chapter 6 that a writer's carefully chosen words have enormous power to influence our perceptions. **Slanting** is essentially misrepresentation. It is perhaps subtler than bias, which is more typically based on prejudice. Slanting is done with suggestion and innuendo, or as you will see below, with a carefully chosen picture to accompany a piece of writing mirroring the author's subjective stance. Study these next four examples:

School choice has been a matter of much debate in recent years. In 1992 Former Education Secretary, Lamar Alexander, announced a plan to give $1,000 scholarships to one million low- and moderate-income parents, which would allow them to send their children to a public or private school of their own choosing. Alexander labeled his proposal a "G.I. Bill for Kids," adapting the name of the G.I. Bill, which granted educational opportunities to returning war veterans after the Second World War. A favorable editorial in *The Wall Street Journal* explained Alexander's position and then derided the teachers' opposition:

> The administration program is further evidence that empowering parents with choice is an idea whose time has come. Support for choice cuts across income, political and racial lines. Its major opponent is the entrenched education bureaucracy that benefits from the status quo.

Here, the unnamed writer has engaged in slanting by employing two disparaging words: "bureaucracy" and "entrenched."

The editorial goes on to cite a proposed ballot initiative, which the teachers' unions opposed: "Educrats did everything they could to block the initiative, from trying to intimidate potential petition signers to using a Los Angeles cable-TV channel to propagandize." (Quoted in "The Education Revolution," *The Wall Street Journal,* June 25, 1992.)

Aside from the loaded word, "propagandize," the word "educrat" is a sneer word. You won't find it in the dictionary, however, because the writer made it up by combining the first syllables of "educator" with "crat" (as in "bureaucrat"), meaning an "advocate" or "one who is a member of a ruling group." What is the effect of these innuendoes? Not only does the language undermine any serious discussion of an important issue, but it also misrepresents teachers and their unions' concerns, depicting both groups as being more concerned with serving their narrow self-interests than with supporting a quality education for all children.

Published four years later in *The Wall Street Journal,* this article—also on school choice—takes a completely different approach. Although its author, Jeanne Allen, president of the Center for Educational Reform, is clearly pro-school-choice, her purpose is to expose how people who devise surveys and polls use slanted language either to skew the results or to ensure a predetermined desirable result. Her discussion is sufficiently complex to warrant reprinting the article in its entirety. This accompanying chart graphically summarizes the results of one of the survey questions, which asked, "How much do you support providing the option of sending children to the school of their choice rather than to the school to which they are assigned?"

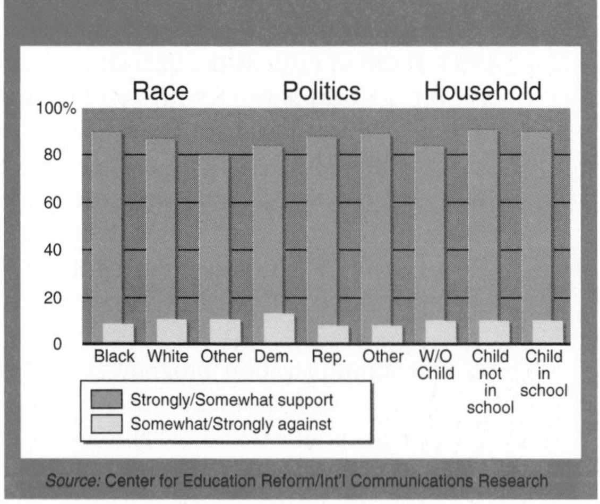

[1]Two recent education polls have made national news, both claiming wide support for public education as we know it and overwhelming opposition to choice programs that would allow parents to send their children to private schools. But both polls were deeply flawed, probably by design. In fact, it may not be an exaggeration to say that the polls lied, in an attempt to ward off popular ideas that threaten the livelihoods of a failing system's defenders.

2"The Public Still Believes in Public Schools," declares a press release from Phi Delta Kappa, a professional educators' association that since 1968 has commissioned an annual Gallup poll on attitudes toward public schools. Each year the survey gives high marks to local schools and finds strong opposition to school choice—although support for choice has risen from 24% in 1993 to 36% this year. (It's also worth mentioning that Phi Delta Kappa changed the wording of its question in 1993. Before then, a more explanatory and objective question annually yielded about 45% in favor of a "voucher system.")

3The other survey, conducted by GOP pollster Linda DiVall for the National Education Association (the nation's largest teachers' union) came up with similar findings. According to the NEA poll, school choice is opposed even by 69% of *Republicans,* allowing the union to claim its views have the overwhelming support of both parties.

4These results seemed suspicious to us. They conflicted with a bevy of state-based polls (in Arizona, Connecticut, Minnesota, Wisconsin and elsewhere) that have found overwhelming support for school choice. Wondering whether Phi Delta Kappa and the NEA were simply asking biased questions, we decided to conduct our own poll.

5We hired a reputable independent polling firm, International Communications Research, to ask nine questions about school choice and the public's perceptions of public schools. We crafted our questions to ensure that they were unbiased and informative enough to make clear what we were asking.

6Our findings differed sharply from those of the union and its allies. Of those surveyed in the Center for Education Reform/ICR poll, 86% said they favor permitting parents to send their children to the public, private or parochial school of their choice. Seventy-two percent believe that state legislators should assist children in failing schools to opt out of that school and attend a school—public, private or parochial—of the parents' choosing. And 73% favor allowing poor children government-funded scholarships to attend any school. On this last question, support was stronger among blacks (90%) than whites (71%), and among Democrats (77%) than Republicans (67%).

7Why were our results so different from those of Phi Delta Kappa and the NEA? Because they designed questions likely to elicit negative responses, using such loaded phrasing as "at public expense" or "with public tax dollars." The NEA even went so far as to ask if school choice is preferable to helping public schools—as if the two were mutually exclusive.

8Now, one can easily object that our group is biased too, since we favor school choice. You decide. Here are questions from the three polls:

[9]**Phi Delta Kappa/Gallup:** Do you favor or oppose allowing students and parents to choose a private school to attend at public expense?

[10]**NEA:** Do you think that tax dollars should be used to assist parents who send their children to private, parochial or religious schools, or should tax dollars be spent to improve public schools?

[11]**Center for Education Reform/ICR:** How much do you support providing parents with the option of sending their children to the school of their choice—either public, private or parochial—rather than only to the school to which they are assigned?

[12]As dishonest as the tendentious polls is the NEA's claim that voters have defeated school choice 21 times at the ballot box. In truth, school-choice ballot initiatives have only been defeated three times—and for reasons having more to do with politics and money than with genuine public opposition to the principle of choice. Women's suffrage took far more attempts than that before it finally won over the public. As for the other initiatives the NEA cites, they were efforts to subsidize private or religious schooling directly—something few choice proponents believe in.

[13]The NEA's claim that school choice means less money for public schools may fool the public for a while. For just as much as we all want things to change, we also want to protect America's long-established tradition of public schooling. The good news is that school choice doesn't threaten public education. On the contrary, the challenge of competition may be just the spur to improvement the educational Establishment needs.

[14]Public education was never intended to be an institution owned and controlled by government alone. Local control has historically been the hallmark of educational excellence. Americans know it, and they want the freedom to educate their children in whatever manner they see fit.

[15]Furthermore, contrary to Gallup's results, both our poll and the more comprehensive Public Agenda survey released earlier this year found widespread dissatisfaction with the quality of public education. With that reality in mind, it's no wonder the unions and their special-interest allies have to skew their polls. If they dared to ask honest questions, they'd be forced to admit they've long outlived their usefulness.

Jeanne Allen, "What Americans Really Think of School Choice," *The Wall Street Journal,* September 17,1996

The next example concerns Proposition 197 on the 1996 California ballot, which proposed amending the California Wildlife Protection Act of 1990 "to remove special protections for mountain lions." (Translation: Mountain lions were moving into previously uninhabited regions, and two or three people had been attacked in recent months, one fatally. The proposition, which lost, would have made the hunting of mountain lions legal again.) Its major sponsor was a group called "Californians for Balanced Wildlife Management," whose name, as Ben Sherwood points out, "sounds good." (Sponsoring groups write the arguments in favor of propositions and rebuttals to the opposition in voting pamphlets.)

Sherwood continues:

> [1]The alternative—Californians for Unbalanced Wildlife Mismanagement—evokes scary images of animals on a rampage.
>
> [2]So who are the Balanced Wildlife Management folks? Among others: the National Rifle Assn.; the Safari Club; the Cattlemen's Assn.; the Turkey Federation; and the Wool Growers. Read between the lines: Mountain lions are eating a lot of cows, turkeys, sheep and other animals. They threaten humans, too. But a more accurate name for this group would have been: Californians Who Want to Hunt and Kill Mountain Lions.

Ben Sherwood, "The Hidden Powers Behind High-Sounding Campaign Names," *Los Angeles Times,* March 31, 1996

Besides innuendo and cleverly misleading names, a picture, cartoon, or drawing accompanying a text may be another form of slanting. A *London Observer* article about Bill Gates, founder of Microsoft, the Redmond, Washington, software company, demonstrates the technique of using a picture to predispose the reader and to mirror the author's point of view. Across the bottom of the article is a large picture showing a crocodile walking along a street, its formidable claws clearly visible on all four feet. But the crocodile's head has been replaced with that of Bill Gates, complete with large scales covering his head and forehead. The article begins like this:

> [1]Appeasement, said Winston Churchill, consists of being nice to a crocodile in the hope that he will eat you last. At the moment, the biggest crocodile in the world is Microsoft, and everybody is busy sucking up to it.
>
> [2]The rewards to be derived from riding the Microsoft bandwagon can be substantial, but are likely to be short-lived because Churchill's Law of Crocodiles still applies. In the end, someone will have to face up to the beast.
>
> [3]But for now, everyone wants to be Bill Gates' friend. Microsoft attracts acres of sycophantic media coverage. His company is held up as the ideal of the thoroughly modern corporation. "Doing things the Microsoft way" has become the goal of many a desperate manager.
>
> [4]Those seeking a more rounded picture of the Microsoft way might therefore appreciate an article by Paul Loeb in the on-line magazine Salon

> (www.salon1999.com/). Loeb describes a company in which outsourcing has been developed to a fine art. The myth that Microsoft is stuffed with happy employees nursing their share options is just so much guff. Most of them have as much stake in the company as the janitor of a privatized British utility.
>
> 5The quest for a place in the Microsoft sun can drive even big corporations crazy. In the last year, hardly a week has gone by without an announcement that Gates has entered into a "strategic partnership" with a television network, a cable company, a Hollywood studio, a bank or two. The list seems endless. The latest one is an alliance with American Express to launch a travel agency on the Net. In each case the blushing corporate suitor cannot wait to tell the world about the megadeal it has struck with the crocodile.
>
> 6What none of them appears to realize is that their deals are death warrants. Gates does not plan to share the on-line banking business—or any other business—with anyone.
>
> 7These "strategic partnerships" are means to a single end: to enable Microsoft to learn enough about particular businesses eventually to dominate them . . .

Naughton concludes: "It was said of the Chicago meat-packing companies that they used every part of the hog except the grunt. By Microsoft standards, they were rank amateurs."

John Naughton, "Courting the Crocodile,"
San Francisco Examiner, July 6, 1997.
Originally published in the *London Observer.*

Distortion

Like slanting, **distortion** involves twisting facts or misrepresenting one's position. Here are two brief examples: The first is a paraphrased version of a letter by a pro-life activist:

> Editor—I have just read your article about women in China aborting their female fetuses after their sonogram reveals the sex of their unborn child. What's the big deal? I wish someone who is in favor of abortion would tell me why selectively aborting female babies is wrong. Isn't it simply the mother's choosing not to have a female child? And isn't this what the pro-abortion movement is all about?

Some women in China do indeed abort their female fetuses (and commit infanticide), a result of China's stringent one-child-per-family policy. In connecting abortion as it is practiced in this country with abortion as it is practiced in China, this writer unfairly distorts the position of pro-abortion supporters.

A second example: According to a generally critical *New Yorker* article, Michael Kelly accuses Bill Clinton of distorting his record in crime and welfare reform. We will look at one instance of this. In 1994, Clinton gave a speech in New Orleans touting his record in crime prevention. He alluded to a provision in his crime bill "to put one hundred thousand police officers on the street." However, the White House was finally forced to admit that this figure was inaccurate. Attorney General Janet Reno said that, in reality, funding had been arranged for only 43,000 positions and only 17,000 officers had actually been hired and put on the street.

Despite Reno's admission that the figure was inaccurate, Clinton continued to use the "hundred thousand figure" in other speeches. How did he get away with this deception? Kelly's explanation is that Clinton is a talented orator who "hide[s] within language of great sweep and promise statements of fact that serve as mitigating clauses." In the New Orleans speech, for example, Clinton said that he had "worked so hard to pass the crime bill, to put one hundred thousand police officers on the streets." According to Kelly, the human ear tends to "hear" that Clinton actually put one hundred thousand police officers on the street, when, in fact, the sentence says only that Clinton "worked hard" to do so. Kelly concludes the explanation by saying, "This sentence is really an escape hatch, a concealed admission that Clinton has, in fact, *not* put a hundred thousand police officers in uniform. He is simply 'committed to keeping on' until he achieves his goal.[5]" In other words both reader and listener must be vigilant and wary when dealing with political speeches.

Demonizing and Scapegoating

We end Part III with **demonizing** and **scapegoating,** two particularly pernicious manipulative techniques. In recent years, as political campaigns have grown more acrimonious, demonizing has been used with increasing frequency as a political tactic. A natural extension of negative campaigning, demonizing goes beyond mere ad hominem attacks. In a recent article[6], Robert Gunnison explains the origins of demonizing and the way it works, citing the opinions of several political theorists and providing examples, as summarized below. Gunnison writes: "Demonizing is a natural extension of negative campaigning and take-no-prisoners partisan politics. But it goes even further: It transforms its

[5]Quoted in Michael Kelly's, "This Year's Model," The New Yorker, June 17, 1996.
[6]" 'Demons' All the Rage in Politics," *San Francisco Chronicle,* February 19, 1996.

subjects into monsters who pose exaggerated threats and raises the prejudice and fear of the targeted audience."

The author quotes Michael Rogin, professor of political science at UC Berkeley, who notes: "You can't say openly racist things any more. You have to find other ways. That is the advantage of this form of demonology." Rogin, author of *Ronald Reagan the Movie, and Other Episodes in Political Demonology,* writes that American politicians create demons "by the stigmatization and dehumanization of political foes." Democrats demonize Republicans as heartless and insensitive for proposing Medicare cuts. Conservative presidential candidate Pat Buchanan and California governor Pete Wilson, and countless other politicians, have demonized welfare recipients and illegal immigrants as undermining the American way and leading the country down a ruinous path.

California Assemblyman Phil Isenberg explains more specifically how demonizing works: "All you have to do is create an enemy. The villains appear clear and obvious and anonymous. And there is no way for them to respond." Elaine Pagels, professor of religion at Princeton University, adds that demonology was embedded in early Christian theology as the struggle between good and evil, between God and Satan. Centuries later, political debate makes use of the same struggle. She goes on to explain: "This apocalyptic vision, in which victory is assured to those who stand on the side of Christ, has taught even secular-minded people to interpret the history of Western culture as a moral history in which the forces of good contend against the forces of evil in the world."

The author offers other examples of groups that have been demonized in American history: "Indians, slaves, Catholics, masons, immigrants, Communists and rum" (the origin of the phrase 'demon rum').

The concept of a scapegoat derives from the Old Testament book, Leviticus, xvi, 10, which describes how Aaron, Moses' older brother, arbitrarily chose a live goat over whose head he confessed all the sins of the children of Israel. The goat was then sent to wander in the wilderness, where it symbolically carried the Israelites' sins until the Day of Atonement. (This day is celebrated as Yom Kippur, the holiest day in Judaism.) **Scapegoating,** closely related to demonizing, refers to the practice of choosing a person to receive the punishment for an entire group, though as you will see in the following editorial, entire groups themselves can become scapegoats—those that take the blame for society's ills. This final selection is written by Jon Carroll, an iconoclastic writer who writes about everyday events and more profound social problems with equal candor, wit, and a healthy sense of skepticism. In it, he examines the way scapegoating is currently practiced and warns us of its dangers.

[1]Very well, it's time to take a little quiz, courtesy of writer Priscilla Labovitz in an Op-Ed page article in the New York Times. Get a pencil and scrawl the answers on the margins of the column—don't think, just write down what seems to you to be an accurate ballpark number. Ready?

[2]What percentage of the United States population is Hispanic? What percentage is Asian? What percentage is African American? What percentage is non-Hispanic Caucasian, what we generally call "white"?

[3]In a moment, the real answers to those questions. But first, consider this: If it is your fate to be murdered, it is overwhelmingly likely that you will be previously acquainted with the person who murders you. Locking your car door when a black teenager crosses the street in front of your automobile might seem like a prudent thing to do, but actually, figuring out which of your lovers or friends is likely to kill you is, statistically speaking, far less paranoid.

[4]In fact, if one name suddenly popped up when you read that previous paragraph, you might want to share that suspicion with someone else.
Mail a letter to your lawyer; leave an "in event of my death" envelope in your top drawer. Didn't help Nicole Brown Simpson; might help you.

[5]These two matters—percentage of nonwhite Americans and statistically probable murderers—may seem unrelated, but I don't think they are. I think that there is a lot of scapegoating going on, scapegoating that is turned into cynical demagoguery by almost anyone running for public office.

[6]So we fret and fuss about violent criminals out on parole stalking innocent victims, about children abused by lowlifes passing through town, when in fact the name of the abuser is most likely to be "Dad" and the name of the murderer is most likely to be "sweetie."

[7]We tell ourselves stories in order to die.

[8]The statistics in Labovitz's article came complete with another set of numbers—the percentage in each of these categories as guessed by white Americans. It makes instructive reading:

[9]Percentage of the United States population that white Americans think is Hispanic: 14.9. Percentage that is Hispanic: 9.5. Percentage that white Americans think is Asian: 10.8. Percentage that is Asian: 3.1. Percentage that white Americans think is black: 23.8. Percentage that is black: 11.8. Percentage that white Americans think is white: 49.9. Percentage that is white: 74.

[10]There is a perception of a flood, but there is no actual flood. There has been a change, yes, and all change is unsettling, but a change is not the

same as a flood. We are not being inundated by immigrants; we are not a nation in which nonwhites are gaining power by sheer force of numbers.

11We're a nation of white people with some other people mixed in, just like we always were. White people are firmly in control. That is the nature of reality; that is (if you will) the nature of the problem. All else is fear-mongering. Been a lot of that around, hasn't there?

12Look at it another way: Corporate downsizing and immigration have nothing to do with each other. If you are fearful for your job, building a fence along the Mexican border or putting guard dogs at all the Asian ports of entry won't help. Two different issues.

13You are being taught to hate in case your hate does the voting.

14We are a more diverse society than we used to be. We attract immigrants. We attract immigrants because we do not actually have a functioning secret police, because we do pay at least lip service and mostly real service to the notion of equality for all, because we are for all our sins a beacon of hope to people whose governments have gone mad.

15So the thing we must guard against is our own government going mad. The thing we must be wary of is big lies that identify some fearsome Other and blame it for our ills. Democracy is in many ways a cumbersome and dreadful system; its one great strength is that we get to tell the truth to each other.

16Let's keep doing that.

Jon Carroll, "Who Are These Foreign People?"
San Francisco Chronicle, March 27, 1996

EXERCISE IN ANALYZING EDITORIALS

As in Chapter 8, the last exercise consists of four examples of persuasive writing to give you practice in implementing your critical reading skills. These passages represent editorials on current controversial issues from the op-ed pages of major newspapers. Note that Selection 1 consists of paired items that should be read together. For each selection that your instructor assigns (or that you read on your own), consider these questions:

- What is the writer's main argument or proposition? Be sure that you can state it in your own words.
- What kind of evidence does the writer provide in support of the argument?
- Does the evidence meet the criteria discussed in Chapter 8? Is it fair, accurate, sufficient, and relevant?

- Does the piece contain any false appeals, logical fallacies, or other manipulative techniques discussed in this chapter?
- Do you accept the argument? Why or why not? If you need more information, what would you need to know?

Selection 1

The author of this editorial, Jesse Shapiro, was the 1997 valedictorian at Stuyvesant High School in New York.

1Welcome to Stuyvesant High School, the Ivy League admissions capital of New York City. Each year Harvard accepts more applicants from Stuyvesant than from any other high school in America. Our school is, in sort, a very special place, populated by similarly unique students.

2To be a student here means passing an SAT-like multiple-choice entrance exam. Sitting for the exam is free—any legal resident of New York City may take it. But only about 800 of the almost 15,000 students who take the exam meet the increasingly steep cutoff.

3Recently, this type of exam-based admissions policy has come under attack by New York City Schools Chancellor Rudy Crew. Mr. Crew has said that tests of this sort, which are employed by many such gifted programs throughout the city, are unfair to "children of color" and "children whose first language is not English." He has advocated replacing intelligence tests with measures of unspecified other talents and abilities. This is part of a growing national revolt among educators against the use of intelligence tests.

4Such a change would do more than just complicate school admissions. It would radically and permanently damage the foundations of these schools and of our city.

5Mr. Crew argues that current admission standards are unfair to those who are talented in nonacademic areas like art, drama and leadership. This almost implies that my classmates and I are automatons, academically skilled but devoid of all other abilities. In fact, Stuyvesant has a wide variety of programs in theater, dance, art, music and comedy. As far as leadership goes, the students do, in many ways, run the school. There are monthly School-Based Planning Committee meetings in which the students discuss school policy with administrators, teachers and parents. At weekly meetings we decide how to spend student activity funds.

6So it's obvious that diversity of talent is not a problem. What about diversity of background? Many of my closest friends are "children of color" and "children whose first language is not English." It is a tribute to their abilities that they were accepted to Stuyvesant and excel here.

7Under a less objective admissions system, criteria would become flimsy and ill-defined. Deserving applicants would be rejected and less-deserving ones accepted. We tried this once before, but then it was on the college level. The City University of New York system, several of whose campuses were once nationally ranked, established a program of "open admissions" in the name of being "inclusive" and "fair." It wasn't long before CUNY had become subpar.

8Nothing could be fairer than a simple multiple-choice exam. It leaves no room for political patronage, racial bias or other discrimination. Unless New York wants talent-blind admissions, it should keep on testing.

Jesse Shapiro, "Talent-Blind Admissions?"
The Wall Street Journal, March 28, 1997

The following letter was published some weeks later in response.

1As a recent graduate and valedictorian of Hunter College, I feel compelled to protest the March 28 editorial-page commentary "Talent-Blind Admissions?" by Jesse Shapiro, valedictorian of Stuyvesant High School. Mr. Shapiro argues that SAT-like entrance exams are the only "objective" way to identify academic talent, and proceeds to denigrate the "open admissions" alternative of the City University of New York system, of which Hunter is a part.

2As a valedictorian from such a good school, Mr. Shapiro should have learned that comparing two wildly dissimilar institutions is illogical. There is not much in common between his high school, which accepts only 800 students a year, and the City University of New York system, which provides two- and four-year degrees, Masters and Ph.D.s as well as professional degrees to more than 200,000 students. Furthermore, "open admissions" does not and never did apply to the four-year CUNY colleges; to use that term is not only a misnomer, but also panders to an already misinformed public. However, Hunter and CUNY do apply a more flexible admissions policy than one based only on written tests.

3For many people, one exam cannot fairly sum up a lifetime of learning or even predict academic ability or future success. But how easily Mr. Shapiro dismisses the more than 14,000 students who do not gain admission to his high school! On the college level, CUNY will often give these students another chance to excel—that is exactly what Hunter College did for me.

4I was a high-school dropout working on an assembly line in a factory. My parents were both illiterate and also did unskilled work in factories in France, where we had immigrated from Portugal. After a few years, I realized that only education would improve my future. I signed up for correspondence courses to prepare for the French equivalent of the GED. When I passed that exam, I moved to New York and took a three-month English course in order to prepare for college. I was a bit older (24), my high-school record was not stellar and English was my third language, but Hunter gave me a chance anyway. Hunter trusted me before I could prove myself, and I did everything I could to deserve that trust. I started with some remedial courses in English and four and a half years later (last June), I graduated summa cum laude (4.0 average) with three majors, one minor, membership in Phi Beta Kappa, valedictorian and other distinctions.

5I am a typical product of Hunter's atypical body of students. My classmates were from Russia or Wyoming; they spoke Spanish or Farsi; they were adults going for a second degree or senior citizens going for a first. They were single, working parents, full-time, part-time students and, oh, yes, high-school graduates, mainly from the public system.

6SAT-like testing would indeed be perfectly objective if the school system were perfect. There are schools in Harlem that, until recently, used social studies books in which the last president mentioned was Jimmy Carter; they, like so many others, are the products of a substandard education. Because the system has failed to educate them does not justify abandoning them.

7I agree that we should not tamper with the proven success of such elite institutions as Stuyvesant High School. Yet Mr. Shapiro simplistically believes that tests are the only way to identify talent. The truth is that finding talent through standardized tests is easy; finding talent where it is not so obvious and fostering it is the far greater challenge, one that ultimately benefits not only fortunate individuals like myself, but all of society.

Osvaldo Da Silva
New York

"From Factory Worker to Valedictorian,"
The Wall Street Journal, April 25, 1997

Selection 2

Ellen Goodman is a syndicated columnist for the *Boston Globe.* Her column appears in many of the nation's daily newspapers.

1AMSTERDAM—Halfway through our conversation, Gerrit van der Wal gets up to consult his dictionary. Surely, he says, there must be an English equivalent for the Dutch word *gedogen.*

2The medical school professor, who conducted the most recent research on doctor-assisted death in the Netherlands, flips through the pages until he comes to the right place. *"Gedogen,"* he reads slowly, "tolerance." Then he shakes his head and says, "No, that isn't quite right."

3If the word is not easily translated, perhaps it is because the concept is so Dutch, so not-American. *Gedogen* describes a formal condition somewhere between forbidden and permitted. It is part of the Dutch dance of principle and pragmatism.

4Here, drugs are *gedogen.* They remain illegal, but soft drugs like marijuana and hash are available in duly licensed coffee shops that dot this city.

5And here, too, euthanasia is *gedogen.* The ending of a life by a doctor remains illegal, but doctors who follow careful guidelines may grant their patients' death wishes.

6I am here in this northern country awash with tulips and controversy because our own Supreme Court has been asked to decide the question of doctor-assisted suicide. Holland has grappled longer and more publicly with the end-of-life issues that we are only now beginning to confront seriously.

7As Ad Kerkhof, a puckish psychologist at the Free University, says, "Holland has become a Rorschach test for euthanasia." Indeed, opponents look to Holland and describe this flat country as a land of slippery slopes.

8In a week of interviewing, people bristled at the notion that Americans think the Dutch are ridding themselves of the old and handicapped. In fact "euthanasia" is defined here as the termination of life by a doctor at the express wish of a patient. Under the guidelines, the patient's suffering must be unbearable and without the possibility of improvement. The requests must be persistent and confirmed by a second physician.

9Dr. Van der Wal, warily leading me through his most recent survey of doctors, points out that only 2.4 percent of deaths in Holland happen with a physician's assistance. Nine out of 10 requests are turned away. Most of those who had assisted suicide were not nursing home patients, but cancer patients in their 60s or 70s. They died in the last days or weeks of their illness, at home, treated by a family doctor they knew for an average of seven years.

10The Dutch system is not fail-safe or without its own ethical dilemmas. Most euthanasia deaths are still (and illegally) not reported to the government. The most troubling discovery is that between 900 and 1,000 patients a year die from what they call "nonvoluntary euthanasia."

11As doctors here note, a bit defensively, this is not the result of Holland's euthanasia policies. It exists unseen and unreported in countries, even our own where doctors deliver lethal painkilling doses of medicine without consent.

12In practice, half of those who were no longer physically able to give consent had expressed the wish for euthanasia earlier. Most were in the last stages of disease. But van der Wal agrees, "It's a weak point in your system if you don't know what the patient really wants. There is always the danger that you are ending life against the will of the patient."

13It's a weak point as well that the Dutch laws don't make a distinction between mental and physical suffering. Not long ago, a psychiatrist performed euthanasia on a physically healthy woman who had lost her children and was in deep despair. He was acquitted in a case that left public confidence rattled.

14The policy of *gedogen* doesn't help the Dutch decide what to think of those who value independence so much they want to control their own death. Nor does it help a doctor who carries the burden and power of deciding when someone has suffered "enough."

15What is notable is that 71 percent of the Dutch remain firm in their support of euthanasia policies. There is a palpable pride in doing things "the Dutch way." Pride in a system in which the law evolves with public consensus.

16Yet time and again, even the strongest supporters of euthanasia told me, as did a retired family doctor, Herbert Cohen: "Euthanasia is not for export." The difference between Holland and America, they say, is universal health care. No one here chooses to die to protect their family finances.

17 Perhaps what is exportable, though, is the Dutch tolerance for ambiguity. For living in the ethical gray zone, grappling with complexity instead of denying it, keeping open to change.

18If there is an American parallel to the Dutch way, it might be a state-by-state experiment, a testing of different rules and experiences with assisted suicide. The truth is that we, too, want to find a way of dying that is both merciful and careful.

19Yet today, in the countryside of canals and *gedogen,* it's not always easy to find the right words in an American dictionary.

Ellen Goodman, "There's No Word in English for It,"
The Sunday Oregonian, April 20, 1997

Selection 3

The writer is on the editorial staff of *The Washington Post.*

1One of our freedoms is the ability to do or say things that are unpopular, as long as they don't harm others. The smoking controversy is about this freedom as well as health, but that has been lost in the hysteria to ostracize smokers and punish tobacco companies. The hysteria—embodied in suits against tobacco companies and strident anti-industry rhetoric by politicians—is so intense that the biggest companies are now in talks to settle. By press reports, Philip Morris and RJR might have the industry pay $225 billion to $300 billion over 25 years and submit to more regulation. In return, it would be spared further liability.

2Massive reparations will strike many people as a fit retribution for merchants of death. The reaction is completely wrong. The cost of a settlement would largely be passed along to smokers. The industry would create a compensation fund for "victims" and then raise prices to pay for it. That would represent a disguised increase in cigarette taxes, which now average 57 cents a pack (24 cents in federal tax, with various state rates). Suppose the price of a pack rose by 50 cents, a 27 percent jump from the current $1.85. The proper questions are who would pay the extra tax and who would receive the benefits.

3Well, we know who would pay: the 25 percent of Americans who smoke. They consist heavily of the poor and lower middle class. About 70 percent have no more than a high school degree. We don't know exactly who would benefit, but the candidates are clear: (a) smokers—or more likely their heirs—if they can show they should be "compensated" for "damages"; (b) trial lawyers, who would represent "victims" in compensation claims or receive a guaranteed payout from the fund; and (c) states that would be paid to offset their allegedly excessive health costs from smoking.

4In short, a compensation fund would be an intricate shell game, with the tobacco companies mainly as middlemen. All smokers would be taxed to pay "damages" to some smokers or their families. In the process, we'd create a welfare program for trial lawyers. Finally, states would receive a hefty slice. Of course, states that feel undercompensated for smoking's costs could raise their cigarette taxes and receive 100 percent of the gain. But a tax increase would, presumably, be unpopular. So 23 state attorneys general have filed suit against the industry, trying to use the courts to enact hidden nationwide tax increases. For this the attorneys general project themselves as heroes.

5Now, I am not defending the tobacco industry's public dishonesty. Nor am I mimicking its posture that cigarettes are no riskier than toothpaste. Smoking is unhealthy. The Centers for Disease Control estimates that it causes about 400,000 Americans to die prematurely each year, with an average loss of life of about seven years. I don't smoke and, as a parent, will fight my children if they start. But otherwise, I don't think I have the right to impose my views. People have a right to choose. Punishing them for their choice denies their freedom. Rewarding them for the ill effects of their choice denies their responsibility.

6Neither can be justified unless smokers lack choice or impose costs on others. Naturally, the anti-smoking ideology presumes (wrongly) that both conditions are true. Smokers are supposedly seduced by the industry's advertising, and once they start puffing, they can't stop, because cigarettes are addictive. Come on. Since the government's first anti-smoking report in 1964, almost everyone has known that cigarettes are dangerous. That knowledge is the main reason the proportion of smokers has dropped from 42 percent in 1965 to the present 25 percent. And everyone has always known that "kicking the habit" is hard, whether smoking is addictive or not. Still, millions have done it.

7Indeed, the main reason there are fewer smokers today is not that fewer Americans start smoking but that more give it up. Consider: In 1994, about 77 percent of Americans over 26 had once smoked. But two-thirds had stopped. In 1974, only 65 percent of this group had ever smoked, but nearly two-thirds still smoked. The trends among the under-26 population are similar.

8Nor do smokers—and the tobacco industry—impose huge economic costs on the rest of society. Just the opposite: Smokers more than pay their own way. They already pay steep cigarette taxes and, by dying early, create future savings in health costs, nursing home care, Social Security and pensions. Even without the taxes, the savings smokers create by early death may exceed the costs they impose by 40 percent, estimates Harvard economist W. Kip Viscusi. Just because this argument is freakish and awkward is no reason to ignore it. If smokers' shorter life expectancy magically vanished tomorrow, government costs would rise.

9Finally, smokers don't pose a major workplace health hazard through "passive" smoke: what's inhaled by nonsmokers. Secondary smoke may be highly irritating, but it's not a major cause of either lung cancer or heart disease. The scientific studies here are weak. Some find that passive smoke causes a small amount of cancer; other studies find no effect. The studies examined nonsmoking wives of smoking husbands. On this meager evidence, a wider danger can be inferred only by assuming (dubiously) that workers face an exposure similar to that of wives of smokers.

10It is smokers themselves who experience the pleasures and horrors of smoking. And that's how it should be. As a society, we ought to clarify that principle, and in this sense, a truce between the industry and its critics—enacted into law by Congress—is desirable. Such a truce would have the industry voluntarily surrender most (or all) of its right to advertise. It might also finance a modest education program for teenagers on the dangers of smoking. In return, it would receive immunity from legal liability. The compact would dispose of the argument that industry ads prey on the ill-informed young, while also denying smokers any reward for their poor health choices.

11Given today's hysteria, I doubt anything so evenhanded is possible. The anti-smoking zealots essentially want to shut the industry. Trial lawyers see the tobacco companies as a huge pot of gold. Politicians see them as fabulous punching bags. The press portrays the story as a struggle of good and evil, barely questioning anti-smoking rhetoric. Hardly any one in this informal coalition of intolerance even senses that freedom is an issue.

Robert J. Samuelson, "A Question of Freedom,"
The Washington Post, April 28, 1997

PART

IV

Reading Essays and Articles

WHY READ ESSAYS IN THE FIRST PLACE?

The essay is the staple of reading assignments in composition and reading courses and, in fact, essays are often assigned in any college course where the textbook is an anthology. The essay form has several advantages. Its relatively short length allows it to be read in one sitting, and it can be discussed thoroughly in one or two class meetings. For the purposes of this book, analytical questions concerning a selection a few pages long are less taxing and overwhelming than they would be if they concerned a book-length work.

In my experience teaching both reading and composition, many college students are unsure of what their instructors specifically expect them to do with essay assignments. Part IV will give you ample practice in the various skills associated with reading essays. A paramount consideration is that you will learn a great deal from your reading assignments if you give sufficient time and attention to understanding an essay's component parts. The truism that practice makes perfect surely applies here. The more experience you get reading your assignments attentively, the more competent you will become and the more you will enjoy preparing your assignments. There is no advantage in *not* reading. Students who seldom read on their own, who speed through assignments, or who sit in the back of the classroom or look down, pretending to be engrossed in the text, hoping to avoid being called on, are missing a significant part of the college experience.

The Characteristics of an Essay

Before we look at the questions you should ask yourself as you read, let us examine an essay's characteristics. If the paragraph is an essay in miniature—as it has often been described—then the essay must exemplify the techniques and characteristics that you studied in Chapters 1–4 in Part I. The essay derives from a form of writing established by the 17th-century French writer Michel de Montaigne. His short pieces were an *attempt* to explain human behavior and the customs he had observed. (In French, the verb *essayer* means "to attempt," and an essay—*un essai*—is the work itself.) Today the term **essay** refers to a sustained piece of nonfiction prose in which the author sets down important ideas, recalls a memory, describes experience, conveys information, analyzes issues, or sets forth a proposition.

Like the paragraph, an essay generally contains a main idea, called a **thesis;** it has a direction; and it has adequate development, unity, and coherence. Unlike the paragraph, whose short length limits its scope, the essay is more flexible and therefore more varied in length, organization, language, and methods of development.

An essay has no fixed length. Though typically, essays published by professional writers run between 500 and 5,000 words, length is not important in defining the form. If you think back to the practice essays you read in Parts I and II, you can easily see that the essay form is a remarkably diverse instrument for communicating ideas.

Finally, the essay has numerous forms. It may be a personal narrative, a description of a scene or an emotion, a presentation of scientific information, a personal confession, an emotional plea to resolve a controversy, a satire on a practice or custom that the writer wants to mock, an explanation of a social or political issue, or an examination of a problem and its repercussions. In short, the essay is infinitely adaptable. It may represent any of the four modes of discourse—narration, description, exposition, persuasion—whether singly or in combination, although usually one mode predominates.

That said, however, let us consider the remarks of two professional writers about the essay form. Richard Marius, director of Harvard College's Expository Writing Program, writes: "The essay inevitably has about it the scent of argument,"[1] by which he means that even in narrative and descriptive essays, the underlying intent is persuasive. Joseph Epstein, the man behind the pseudonym "Aristides" and author of the last essay in Part IV, "Student Evaluations," writes this:

[1] *A Writer's Companion,* 3rd ed., p. 39.

> . . . I think the essay is at its characteristic best when it is not too strongly bullied into being by current events and the intellectual trends of the day. I especially delight in the essay when it allows for a considerable distance from the news and even, for that matter, from the new. I prefer the essay when it is ruminative yet playful, commonsensical yet idiosyncratic, raising lots of questions yet under no strong obligation to provide many answers. I prefer it when the essay takes a small, very particular subject and, through the force of the essayist's artistically controlled maunderings, touches on unpredictably large general matters, makes hitherto unexpected connections, tells me things I hadn't hitherto known, or reminds me of other things I have always known but never thought to formulate so well as has the essayist I am reading at the moment.
>
> Joseph Epstein, Introduction to *Best American Essays 1993*

The Parts of an Essay

Like the paragraph, the essay usually can be divided into three parts: the beginning (the introduction); the middle (the body or supporting paragraphs); and the end (the conclusion). The main idea—comparable to a paragraph's topic sentence—is expressed in a **thesis statement,** the writer's central idea or proposition.

Finding the Thesis

The most important skill in reading any piece of prose is finding the main idea. Given its diverse nature and length, the essay poses greater problems for students than single paragraphs. Where should you look? Some writers announce the main idea in the first sentence, although most good writers avoid this overly obvious placement because the reader has no inducement to continue on. Other writers save the thesis for the end (using inductive order), so that the supporting paragraphs lead to it. Still other writers do not state the thesis at all, preferring to let the supporting paragraphs reveal it. This method is called the **implied thesis.**

So formulating a general rule to help you locate the thesis is impossible. However, many essays do include a thesis somewhere near the beginning of the essay, often following this classic pattern: the opening paragraphs (perhaps two or three) introduce the general subject and orient us to the topic. These paragraphs may include an anecdote or two or a short narrative, they may provide historical background, or they may introduce us to an issue or problem. Following this prefatory section, the writer states the thesis. Some textbooks call this approach the "funnel pattern." But don't expect a bell to sound when you reach the thesis. Few writers announce that a particular sentence is meant to represent the main idea.

Consider the first two paragraphs of a newspaper article from *The Wall Street Journal,* in which the author introduces the topic of cigarette advertising in Britain:

> [1]What does a giant cheese grater have to do with smoking cigarettes? Not much, but never mind. In Britain, where cigarette advertising is heavily restricted, ad writers came up with the image of a cheese grater shredding purple silk to evoke Silk Cut, a cigarette brand from American Brands Inc.'s Gallagher Tobacco. The Ancient Stonehenge ruins covered with blue dots to look like a set of dominos advertise Benson & Hedges Lights. And a current magazine ad simply includes a foldout map of the U.S., above a tobacco health warning, to advertise Marlboro Country.
>
> [2]As U.S. regulators debate the merits of proposed restrictions for tobacco ads aimed at youth, British cigarette ads could provide an important lesson: Restrictions, which include bans on attractive models and cheerful scenes, have triggered a burst of creativity that has produced a new genre of subtle, sophisticated ads.
>
> Tara Parker-Pope, "Tough Tobacco-Ad Rules Light Creative Fires," *The Wall Street Journal,* October 9, 1996

It should be immediately apparent that paragraph 1 "hooks" the reader with some strange examples of British cigarette ads and that paragraph 2 ends with the thesis, which is composed of two parts, just as you learned in Chapter 1. The topic is "restrictions," and the controlling idea is "have triggered a burst of creativity that has produced a new genre of subtle, sophisticated ads."

Separating the Essay's Parts

Once you have found the thesis—assuming that there is one—you can then separate the essay into its component parts: determining where the introduction ends and the body begins, and where the body gives way to the conclusion. It cannot be emphasized too strongly how important this skill is. Rather than drowning in a flood of words, your ability to see the logical progression of ideas will help you distinguish the main points from the support. Often, making a brief outline of an essay's component parts helps you see the overall structure more clearly, just as an aerial view of a city reveals its layout more clearly than a ground-level view does.

The body portion of the essay develops and supports the thesis by whatever methods of development the writer considers appropriate. The body paragraphs explore the implications of the controlling idea. (As you will remember from Part III, in argumentative prose the structure is a little different because careful editorial writers usually include opposing arguments—the refutation section—as well.)

Because of its length, it is even more essential that an essay embody the same principles of unity and coherence that you studied in Parts I and II. To keep you "on track," as each paragraph moves the ideas forward, writers may use devices to ensure coherence: *transitions,* both within as well as between paragraphs; *parallel phrases, clauses, or sentences;* and *repetition of key words or phrases.* The careful writer also organizes the body paragraphs logically, typically arranging them in a least-important to most-important order.

An essay's conclusion is usually quite short—perhaps only a paragraph or two. To find the conclusion, look for a summary, a restatement of the main idea, a logical deduction to be drawn from the evidence, a solution or recommendation, a warning for the future, or a challenge. Again, the form of the conclusion depends on the writer's purpose, subject, and audience.

How to Read an Essay

Armed with this overview of the essay's characteristics and form, you can now turn to the subject of how to tackle assigned readings. The following suggestions constitute what your English teachers ideally hope their students will do to prepare for class discussion. For each assignment, set aside a minimum of an hour preparing, perhaps two hours if the essay is long or difficult. First, read the essay through without stopping. Use a pencil to mark any sentences or paragraphs that will require more attention or to underline any words that are not part of your active reading vocabulary.

Then read the piece again, more slowly the second time, to put the pieces together. Of course, during this reading you should also look up any troublesome words. While you are reading, keep the questions in the next section in mind. When you are done, review the questions to see if you can answer them in your own words. If something eludes your understanding, make a note of it so that you can raise the point in class discussion. Following these steps ensures that you are taking responsibility for your own learning, which will serve you well both in your current English class and all your other academic courses.

QUESTIONS TO CONSIDER WHILE READING

Although your other English texts may provide discussion or "thought" questions after each selection, the following questions are sufficiently extensive and versatile that they can be used with any reading, constituting the sorts of things your instructors want you to look for when you read. Eventually, the process will become automatic so that you will not have to refer to them before each assignment.

1. Who is the author? In most anthologies, as in this text, the writer is identified by a brief biographical source note or headnote. This information is useful for determining the writer's mastery of the subject (his or her authority), audience, purpose in writing, and point of view (or possible bias).
2. This question follows from the first. Whom is the writer writing for? Is the audience the general reading public, or does the vocabulary suggest that the writer is appealing to a narrower group with specialized knowledge? What clues does the author provide that let you know who the audience is?
3. What is the writer's *purpose?* Here, a quick review of the *modes of discourse* in Part I, Chapter 1, might help. Besides the main purpose, does the writer have a secondary purpose in mind, as well? If so, what?
4. What is the *thesis?* Where is it located? Is its placement appropriate for the writer's purpose and subject? If its placement is unusual, is there a reason? Once you have located it, can you paraphrase it—that is, restate it in your own words?
5. What are the main parts of the essay? At what point does the writer stop introducing and begin the support? Where does the body end and the conclusion begin? Can you briefly outline the essay's main parts to see how they fit together?
6. Since we read to learn new information, what are we meant to learn? What are the essay's main ideas? What are the major supporting points for the thesis?
7. What *inferences* are you meant to draw? What conclusions? What has the essay done to educate you about the world? How do the essay's ideas accord with what you already know? What further information do you need?
8. Aside from unfamiliar words—which you should add to your vocabulary notebook as suggested in Part I—are there any instances of words used in unusual ways? Any metaphors or similes? Any strongly connotative words? Is the writer's word choice appropriate for the purpose, audience, and content?

You may find it useful to examine a classic essay in light of these remarks about the essay form and the eight questions you have just examined. "The Spider and the Wasp" by Alexander Petrunkevitch is a widely reprinted essay that presents a fascinating look at one little part of the insect world: the deadly confrontation between the tarantula and its arch-enemy, the digger wasp. After you finish reading it, we will return to the eight questions posed above and attempt to arrive at some answers.

SAMPLE ESSAY

The Spider and the Wasp

Alexander Petrunkevitch

Alexander Petrunkevitch was born in Russia in 1875, and was educated in Moscow and later at the University of Freiberg, Germany. An authority on American spiders, he taught at Harvard, Yale, and Indiana universities, in addition to working as a translator and author on Russian subjects. This essay was originally published in Scientific American.

1 In the feeding and safeguarding of their progeny the insects and spiders exhibit some interesting analogies to reasoning and some crass examples of blind instinct. The case I propose to describe here is that of the tarantula spiders and their arch-enemy, the digger wasps of the genus Pepsis. It is a classic example of what looks like intelligence pitted against instinct—a strange situation in which the victim, though fully able to defend itself, submits unwittingly to its destruction.

2 Most tarantulas live in the tropics, but several species occur in the temperate zone and a few are common in the southern U.S. Some varieties are large and have powerful fangs with which they can inflict a deep wound. These formidable looking spiders do not, however, attack man; you can hold one in your hand, if you are gentle, without being bitten. Their bite is dangerous only to insects and small mammals such as mice; for a man it is no worse than a hornet's sting.

3 Tarantulas customarily live in deep cylindrical burrows, from which they emerge at dusk and into which they retire at dawn. Mature males wander about after dark in search of females and occasionally stray into houses. After mating, the male dies in a few weeks, but a female lives much longer and can mate several years in succession. In a Paris museum is a tropical specimen which is said to have been living in captivity for 25 years.

4 A fertilized female tarantula lays from 200 to 400 eggs at a time; thus it is possible for a single tarantula to produce several thousand young. She takes no care of them beyond weaving a cocoon of silk to enclose the eggs. After they hatch, the young walk away, find convenient places in which to dig their burrows and spend the rest of their lives in solitude. Tarantulas feed mostly on insects and millipedes. Once their appetite is appeased, they digest the food for several days before eating again. Their sight is poor, being limited to sensing a change in the intensity of light and to the perception of moving objects. They apparently have little or no sense of hearing, for a hungry tarantula will pay no attention to a loudly chirping cricket placed in its cage unless the insect happens to touch one of its legs.

5 But all spiders, and especially hairy ones, have an extremely delicate sense of touch. Laboratory experiments prove that tarantulas can distinguish three types of touch: pressure against the body wall, stroking of the body hair and riffling of certain very fine hairs on the legs called trichobothria. Pressure against the body, by a finger or the end of a pencil, causes the tarantula to move off slowly for a short distance. The touch excites no defensive response unless the approach is from above where the spider can see the motion, in which case it rises on its hind legs, lifts its front legs, opens its fangs and holds this threatening posture as long as the object continues to move. When the motion stops, the spider drops back to the ground, remains quiet for a few seconds and then moves slowly away.

6 The entire body of a tarantula, especially its legs, is thickly clothed with hair. Some of it is short and woolly, some long and stiff. Touching this body hair produces one of two distinct reactions. When the spider is hungry, it responds with an immediate and swift attack. At the touch of a cricket's antennae the tarantula seizes the insect so swiftly that a motion picture taken at the rate of 64 frames per second shows only the result and not the process of capture. But when the spider is not hungry, the stimulation of its hairs merely causes it to shake the touched limb. An insect can walk under its hairy belly unharmed.

7 The trichobothria, very fine hairs growing from disklike membranes on the legs, were once thought to be the spider's hearing organs, but we now know that they have nothing to do with sound. They are sensitive only to air movement. A light breeze makes them vibrate slowly without disturbing the common hair. When one blows gently on the trichobothria, the tarantula reacts with a quick jerk of its four front legs. If the front and hind legs are stimulated at the same time, the spider makes a sudden jump. This reaction is quite independent of the state of its appetite.

8 These three tactile responses—to pressure on the body wall, to moving of the common hair and to flexing of the trichobothria—are so different from one another that there is no possibility of confusing them. They serve the tarantula adequately for most of its needs and enable it to avoid most annoyances and dangers. But they fail the spider completely when it meets its deadly enemy, the digger wasp Pepsis.

9 These solitary wasps are beautiful and formidable creatures. Most species are either a deep shiny blue all over, or deep blue with rusty wings. The largest have a wing span of about four inches. They live on nectar. When excited, they give off a pungent odor—a warning that they are ready to attack. The sting is much worse than that of a bee or common wasp, and the pain and swelling last longer. In the adult stage the wasp lives only a few months. The female produces but a few eggs, one at a time at intervals of two or three days. For each egg the mother

must provide one adult tarantula, alive but paralyzed. The tarantula must be of the correct species to nourish the larva. The mother wasp attaches the egg to the paralyzed spider's abdomen. Upon hatching from the egg, the larva is many hundreds of times smaller than its living but helpless victim. It eats no other food and drinks no water. By the time it has finished its single gargantuan meal and become ready for wasphood, nothing remains of the tarantula but its indigestible chitinous skeleton.

10 The mother wasp goes tarantula-hunting when the egg in her ovary is almost ready to be laid. Flying low over the ground late on a sunny afternoon, the wasp looks for its victim or for the mouth of a tarantula burrow, a round hole edged by a bit of silk. The sex of the spider makes no difference, but the mother is highly discriminating as to species. Each species of Pepsis requires a certain species of tarantula, and the wasp will not attack the wrong species. In a cage with a tarantula which is not its normal prey the wasp avoids the spider, and is usually killed by it in the night.

11 Yet when a wasp finds the correct species, it is the other way about. To identify the species the wasp apparently must explore the spider with her antennae. The tarantula shows an amazing tolerance to this exploration. The wasp crawls under it and walks over it without evoking any hostile response. The molestation is so great and so persistent that the tarantula often rises on all eight legs, as if it were on stilts. It may stand this way for several minutes. Meanwhile the wasp, having satisfied itself that the victim is of the right species, moves off a few inches to dig the spider's grave. Working vigorously with legs and jaws, it excavates a hole 8 to 10 inches deep with a diameter slightly larger than the spider's girth. Now and again the wasp pops out of the hole to make sure that the spider is still there.

12 When the grave is finished, the wasp returns to the tarantula to complete her ghastly enterprise. First she feels it all over once more with her antennae. Then her behavior becomes more aggressive. She bends her abdomen, protruding her sting, and searches for the soft membrane at the point where the spider's leg joins its body—the only spot where she can penetrate the horny skeleton. From time to time, as the exasperated spider slowly shifts ground, the wasp turns on her back and slides along with the aid of her wings, trying to get under the tarantula for a shot at the vital spot. During all this maneuvering, which can last for several minutes, the tarantula makes no move to save itself. Finally the wasp corners it against some obstruction and grasps one of its legs in her powerful jaws. Now at last the harassed spider tries a desperate but vain defense. The two contestants roll over and over on the ground. It is a terrifying sight and the outcome is always the same. The wasp finally manages to thrust her sting into the soft spot and

holds it there for a few seconds while she pumps in the poison. Almost immediately the tarantula falls paralyzed on its back. Its legs stop twitching; its heart stops beating. Yet it is not dead, as is shown by the fact that if taken from the wasp it can be restored to some sensitivity by being kept in a moist chamber for several months.

13 After paralyzing the tarantula, the wasp cleans herself by dragging her body along the ground and rubbing her feet, sucks the drop of blood oozing from the wound in the spider's abdomen, then grabs a leg of the flabby, helpless animal in her jaws and drags it down to the bottom of the grave. She stays there for many minutes, sometimes for several hours, and what she does all that time in the dark we do not know. Eventually she lays her egg and attaches it to the side of the spider's abdomen with a sticky secretion. Then she emerges, fills the grave with soil carried bit by bit in her jaws, and finally tramples the ground all around to hide any trace of the grave from prowlers. Then she flies away, leaving her descendant safely started in life.

14 In all this the behavior of the wasp evidently is qualitatively different from that of the spider. The wasp acts like an intelligent animal. This is not to say that instinct plays no part or that she reasons as man does. But her actions are to the point; they are not automatic and can be modified to fit the situation. We do not know for certain how she identifies the tarantula—probably it is by some olfactory or chemo-tactile sense—but she does it purposefully and does not blindly tackle a wrong species.

15 On the other hand, the tarantula's behavior shows only confusion. Evidently the wasp's pawing gives it no pleasure, for it tries to move away. That the wasp is not simulating sexual stimulation is certain, because male and female tarantulas react in the same way to its advances. That the spider is not anesthetized by some odorless secretion is easily shown by blowing lightly at the tarantula and making it jump suddenly. What, then, makes the tarantula behave as stupidly as it does?

16 No clear, simple answer is available. Possibly the stimulation by the wasp's antennae is masked by a heavier pressure on the spider's body, so that it reacts as when prodded by a pencil. But the explanation may be much more complex. Initiative in attack is not in the nature of tarantulas; most species fight only when cornered so that escape is impossible. Their inherited patterns of behavior apparently prompt them to avoid problems rather than attack them. For example, spiders always weave their webs in three dimensions, and when a spider finds that there is insufficient space to attach certain threads in the third dimension, it leaves the place and seeks another, instead of finishing the web in a single plane. This urge to escape seems to arise under all circumstances, in all phases of life and to take the place of reasoning. For a spider to change the pattern of its web is as impossible as for an inexperienced man to build a bridge across a chasm obstructing his way.

17 In a way the instinctive urge to escape is not only easier but often more efficient than reasoning. The tarantula does exactly what is most efficient in all cases except in an encounter with a ruthless and determined attacker dependent for the existence of her own species on killing as many tarantulas as she can lay eggs. Perhaps in this case the spider follows its usual pattern of trying to escape, instead of seizing and killing the wasp, because it not aware of its danger. In any case, the survival of the tarantula species as a whole is protected by the fact that the spider is much more fertile than the wasp.

Here are some suggested responses to the eight questions on page 368.

1. **Who is the author?** The headnote identifies Petrunkevitch as an expert on spiders (an arachnologist). Although he is a scientist, his style is sufficiently clear that even the technical terms are understandable. We can also infer that his report will be a scientific account—objective and impartial in presenting the ideas.
2. **Who is the audience?** His audience is the general reader, *not* other scientists. The information about the tarantula and digger wasp is described specifically, but the language is not formidable. For example, in paragraph 7 Petrunkevitch uses the technical term, tricobothria, to describe the hairs on the tarantula's legs, yet he also defines the term immediately ("very fine hairs growing from disklike membranes on the legs"). Fellow spider experts would recognize this term, so including the contextual definition suggests that he is writing for a wider audience.
3. ***What is the author's purpose?*** Petrunkevitch has two purposes. The primary one is to show that the behavior of these two species presents a classic confrontation between reasoning and instinct. The secondary purpose is to explain these species' reproductive habits. The primary mode of discourse is expository, but there are also strong descriptive elements, especially in paragraphs 6 and 7.
4. **What is the thesis?** Paragraph 1 is a good example of the "funnel pattern" mentioned earlier. Look again at the progression of these three sentences: Sentence 1 orients us to the general subject: the contrast between intelligence and instinct among insects. Petrunkevitch also includes the specific activities that will demonstrate this conflict: the feeding and safeguarding of their progeny. Sentence 2 introduces the two species he will present as his "case," and sentence 3 states his point of view that the confrontation is "strange." Sentence 3 also restates the conflict between reasoning and instinct.

Since the thesis is embodied in bits and pieces in all three sentences, we can suggest this as a paraphrase: *The strange confrontation between the tarantula and its enemy, the digger wasp, is a classic example of the conflict between intelligence and blind instinct.*

5. **What are the main parts of the essay?** Here is a schematic outline of the essay's three-part division:

   Introduction [paragraph 1]
   Body [paragraphs 2–15]
   Conclusion [paragraphs 16–17]

   The middle portion—the support—can be further subdivided, as follows:

   Explanation and description of tarantulas [paragraphs 2–8].
   Explanation and description of digger wasps [paragraphs 9–10].
   Further explanation of the capturing process [paragraphs 11–13].
   Analysis of the significance of these insects' behavior [paragraphs 14–15].

   During our first reading, we might think that the details about the spider's sense of touch, its body hair, and the three tactile responses are irrelevant. But the explanation of the process by which the digger wasp nourishes her larva depends on this information. The main point is that the tarantula behaves uncharacteristically ("stupidly," Petrunkevitch says), doing nothing to defend itself against the wasp's molestation. Once we consider the essay's parts as a whole, we can easily see the importance of details that at first glance appeared trivial.

6. **What do we learn from the essay?** This is obviously an individual matter, but the key points in the essay are these: The digger wasp's search for the correct species of tarantula is the case that serves as the essay's focal point. Despite the tarantula's defense mechanisms, it does nothing to defend itself against the wasp's gruesome pawing. We also learn that the breeding habits and numbers of offspring are vastly different for these two species. The large number of eggs produced by the tarantula contrasts with the wasp's solitary egg, suggesting that the tarantula is a suitable victim and food source. Finally, the wasp's predation keeps the tarantula population in check.

   Most important, Petrunkevitch's explanation of the tarantula's behavior suggests an implicit definition of intelligence. The wasp acts "intelligently" because her actions are purposeful, and she can modify them. The tarantula behaves "stupidly" because it is not in the nature of spiders to attack and because it operates solely from instinct, as evidenced by its inability to change the pattern of its web. (The first of these observations can be confirmed from personal experience if you have ever tried to remove a spider from your living quarters.) Therefore, it can't adapt its behavior to suit the circumstances. Petrunkevitch's working definition for intelligence or reasoning is the ability to adapt to new situations and to resist attacks.

7. **What inferences and conclusions can we draw?** Nature has provided a mechanism for keeping the tarantula population stable. The essay also challenges the conventional wisdom about the severity of tarantula bites and their supposed aggressiveness.
8. **Is the language unusual?** Most unusual here is the use of *anthropomorphic* words, meaning that Petrunkevitch ascribes human characteristics and motivations to a nonhuman. (Another way to look at this is to say that Petrunkevitch imposes his own subjective interpretation of motives and feelings on the insects' behavior.) However you characterize the language, its effect is to make the essay more readable but less "scientific," since true scientific writing is meant to be impersonal and objective, with few authorial intrusions or judgments.

   Consider these sentences:

- [paragraph 11]: "The tarantula shows an amazing tolerance to this exploration. . . . The molestation is so great and so persistent that the tarantula often rises on all eight legs, as if it were on stilts."
- [paragraph 11]: "Meanwhile the wasp, having satisfied itself that the victim is of the right species, moves off a few inches to dig the spider's grave. . . . Now and again the wasp pops out of the hole to make sure that the spider is still there."
- [paragraph 12]: "When the grave is finished, the wasp returns to the tarantula to complete her ghastly enterprise. First she feels all over once more with her antennae. Then her behavior becomes more aggressive. . . . From time to time, as the exasperated spider slowly shifts ground, the wasp turns on her back and slides along with the aid of her wings, trying to get under the tarantula for a shot at the vital spot. . . ."
- [paragraph 12]: "Now at last the harassed spider tries a desperate but vain defense."

Are such intrusions and anthropomorphic language justified? Yes, if you recall that Petrunkevitch is writing for the lay person, not for spider experts. The language is clear, precise, and evocative. The result is a powerful description of the spider's struggle against its enemy.

WRITING SUMMARIES

Why Write Summaries?

A summary is a condensed version of an essay, article, or book that presents only the essential information of the original. Writing summaries is both an excellent intellectual exercise and and a good way to measure your reading and writing skills. Writing a summary requires not only that you understand a piece accurately; it also requires you to weigh the relative worth of ideas, deciding what is essential and what is nonessential, what to retain and what to omit. Further, writing a summary forces you to discern the pattern the writer imposes on the ideas, and it requires you to restate these ideas concisely, accurately, and fairly, without intruding your own opinion or judgment or distorting the thinking. In sum, a true indicator of how well you understand something you read is your ability to restate its main points in your own words.

How long should a summary be? If your instructor does not require you to conform to an arbitrary length, then you can use this formula as a guide: A summary of an essay or article should be between 10 and 25 percent of the original.

How to Write a Summary

At the end of this section is a sample essay and a summary of it. But before you read these materials, here are some general suggestions to consider.

- Read through the passage at least twice so that you have a good understanding of the content. Look up any unfamiliar words.
- Underline important words, phrases, and sentences. You may also make marginal notations, noting main ideas and key supporting statements. (In the sample essay reprinted later, both techniques are illustrated for you.)
- Copy the underlined or annotated material onto a sheet of paper, using double- or triple-spacing to leave yourself plenty of room for changes or additions.
- Study this material. You may have to add information from the original or delete what you don't have room for or what you later decide is not important enough to include.
- Next, rewrite this material by paraphrasing it, using *your own words* as much as possible.
- Insert transitional words or phrases as necessary to show the relationship between ideas.
- Prepare a final draft by rewriting your sentences. Check to see that your summary is accurate and free of your own ideas and opinions. (Note, however, that often instructors assign a summary-response

paper, in which they ask the student both to summarize an essay and then to evaluate it by explaining their objections, criticisms, or points of agreement. In this case, your instructor wants you to offer your point of view.)

- Do a rough word count, making sure that your summary is between 10 and 25 per cent of the original length. For example, the summary of a 2,500 word essay should be between one and two typewritten pages long (250–500 words) to meet the length requirement.

SAMPLE ESSAY

On the Need for Asylums

Lewis Thomas

The physician Lewis Thomas, who died in 1993, specialized in pathology (the study of the nature of diseases). During his long professional career, he was affiliated with such institutions as the Rockefeller Institute, Tulane University, the University of Minnesota, New York University and Bellevue Hospital, the Yale University School of Medicine, and Memorial Sloan-Kettering Cancer Center in New York. Thomas was also a prolific writer. Among the numerous collections of his writings are The Medusa and the Snail, The Lives of a Cell *(which won the National Book Award), and* Late Night Thoughts on Listening to Mahler's Ninth Symphony, *from which this selection comes.*

Structure | *Ideas*

"Medical miracles" have triumphed over many diseases.

Paras. 1–3 orient reader to general subject—funnel pattern.

1 From time to time, medical science has achieved an indisputable triumph that is pure benefit for all levels of society and deserving of such terms as "breakthrough" and "medical miracle." It is not a long list, but the items are solid bits of encouragement for the future. The conquests of tuberculosis, smallpox, and syphilis of the central nervous system should be at the top of anyone's list. Rheumatic fever, the most common cause of heart disease forty years ago, has become a rare, almost exotic disorder, thanks to the introduction of antibiotics for treating streptococcal sore throat. Some forms of cancer—notably childhood leukemias, Hodgkin's disease, and certain sarcomas affecting young

Structure | *Ideas*

people—have become curable in a high proportion of patients. Poliomyelitis is no longer with us.

Many serious diseases still exist.

2 But there is still a formidable agenda of diseases for which there are no cures, needing much more research before their underlying mechanisms can be brought to light. Among these diseases are some for which we have only halfway technologies to offer, measures that turn out to be much more costly than we had guessed and only partly, sometimes marginally, effective. The transplantation of major organs has become successful, but only for a relatively small number of patients with damaged kidneys and hearts, and at a financial cost much too high for applying the technologies on a wide scale. Very large numbers of patients with these fatal illnesses have no access to such treatments. Renal dialysis makes it possible to live for many months, even a few years, with failed kidneys, but it is a hard life.

Focus narrows—a warning.

We may overestimate medical advances—they may lead to unforeseen problems.

3 The overestimation of the value of and advance in medicine can lead to more trouble than anyone can foresee, and a lot of careful thought and analysis ought to be invested before any technology is turned loose on the marketplace. It begins to look as if coronary bypass surgery, for example, is an indispensable operation for a limited number of people, but it was probably not necessary for the large number in whom the expensive procedure has already been employed.

We need to analyze medical advances carefully

Thesis—sentence 2 in para. 4.

Thorazine, used to treat schizophrenia, is an example of such premature acceptance.

4 There are other examples of this sort of premature, sweeping adoption of new measures in medicine. Probably none has resulted in more untoward social damage than the unpredicted, indirect but calamitous effects of the widespread introduction twenty or so years ago of Thorazine and its chemical relatives for the treatment of schizophrenia. For a while, when it was first used in state hospitals for the insane, the new line of drugs seemed miraculous indeed. Patients whose hallucinations and delusions impelled them

Structure	Ideas
Cause-effect chain: ↓ Thorazine ↓ Control of schizophrenia ↓	Positive results: wild behavior was controlled; mental patients could be released; hospitalization no longer necessary.
Closing of asylums ↓	Political side-effects were disastrous.
Opening of community centers	New social policies: to open community mental health centers and return patients to community.

to wild, uncontrollable behavior were discovered to be so calmed by the treatment as to make possible the closing down of many of the locked wards in asylums. Patients with milder forms of schizophrenia could return, at least temporarily, to life outside the institutions. It was the first real advance in the treatment of severe mental disease, and the whole world of psychiatry seemed to have been transformed. Psychopharmacology became, overnight, a bright new discipline in medicine.

5 Then came the side effect. Not a medical side effect (although there were some of these) but a political one, and a disaster. On the assumption that the new drugs made hospitalization unnecessary, two social policies were launched with the enthusiastic agreement of both the professional psychiatric community and the governmental agencies responsible for the care of the mentally ill. Brand-new institutions, ambitiously designated "community mental health centers," were deployed across the country. These centers were to be the source of the new technology for treating schizophrenia, along with all other sorts of mental illness: in theory, patients would come to the clinics and be given the needed drugs, and, when necessary, psychotherapy. And at the same time orders came down that most of the patients living in the state hospitals be discharged forthwith to their homes or, lacking homes, to other quarters in the community.

6 For a while it looked like the best of worlds, on paper, anyway. Brochures with handsome charts were issued by state and federal agencies displaying the plummeting curves of state hospital occupancy, with the lines coinciding marvelously with the introduction of the new drugs. No one noted that the occupancy of private mental hospitals rose at the same time—though it could not rise very high, with the annual cost of

Structure	Ideas
Explanation of political disaster.	Mentally ill wander the streets.
	Patients dependent on public facilities were released—out on the street now, lost and abandoned. New centers provided no custodial care or shelter.

such hospitalization running around $40,000 per bed. The term "breakthrough" was used over and over again, but after a little while it came to be something more like a breakout. The mentally ill were out of the hospital, but in many cases they were simply out on the streets, less agitated but lost, still disabled but now uncared for. The community mental health centers were not designed to take on the task of custodial care. They could serve as shelters only during the hours of appointment, not at night.

Structure	Ideas
	Patients have no refuge.
	Many commit suicide.

7 All this is still going on, and it is not working. To be sure, the drugs do work—but only to the extent of allaying some of the most distressing manifestations of schizophrenia. They do not turn the disease off. The evidences of the mind's unhinging are still there, coming and going in cycles of remission and exacerbation just as they have always done since schizophrenia was first described. Some patients recover spontaneously and for good, as some have always done. The chronically and permanently disabled are better off because they are in lesser degrees of mental torment when they have their medication; but they are at the same time much worse off because they can no longer find refuge when they are in need of it. They are, instead, out on the streets, or down in the subways, or wandering in the parks, or confined in shabby rooms in the shabbiest hotels, alone. Or perhaps they are living at home, but not many of them living happily; nor are many of their families happy to have them at home. One of the high risks of severe mental disease is suicide, and many of these abandoned patients choose this way out, with no one to stop them. It is an appalling situation.

Structure	Ideas
Concession—old hospitals were bad.	"Warehouses for the insane"—a downward course of dependency.

8 It is claimed that the old state hospitals were even more appalling. They were called warehouses for the insane, incapable of curing anything, more likely to make it worse by

Structure	Ideas

the process known in psychiatric circles as "institutionalization," a steady downhill course toward total dependency on the very bleakness of the institution itself. The places were badly managed, always understaffed, repellent to doctors, nurses, and all the other people needed for the care of those with sick minds. Better off without them it was said. Cheaper too, although this wasn't said so openly.

Refutation—what could be done. | *State hospitals could be decent places.*

9 What never seems to have been thought of, or at least never discussed publicly, was changing the state hospitals from bad to good institutions, given the opportunity for vastly improved care that came along with the drugs. It was partly the history of such places that got in the way. For centuries the madhouses, as they were called, served no purpose beyond keeping deranged people out of the public view. Despite efforts at reform in the late nineteenth and early twentieth centuries, they remained essentially lockups.

At least old hospitals provided refuge.

10 But now it is becoming plain that life in the state hospitals, bad as it was, was better than life in the subways or in the doorways of downtown streets, late on cold nights with nothing in the shopping bag to keep a body warm, and no protection at all against molestation by predators or the sudden urge for self-destruction. What now?

Proposal. | *Restore state asylums—spend enough to do it right.* | *Mentally ill should live in decency.*

11 We should restore the state hospital system, improve it, expand it if necessary; and spend enough money to ensure that the patients who must live in these institutions will be able to come in off the streets and live in decency and warmth, under the care of adequately paid, competent professionals and compassionate surrogate friends.

Specifics of proposal, continued.

12 If there is not enough money, there are ways to save. There was a time when many doctors were glad to volunteer their services on a part-time basis, indeed competed to do so, unpaid by state or federal funds and unreimbursed by insurance companies, in order

Structure	*Ideas*	
		to look after people unable to care for themselves. We should be looking around again for such doctors, not necessarily specialists in psychiatric medicine, but well-trained physicians possessing affection for people in trouble—a quality on which recruitment to the profession of medicine has always, we hope, been based. <u>We cannot leave the situation of insane human beings where it is today.</u>
Conclusion: an ethical and moral challenge.	*Judging by the way we treat our mentally ill, our society has failed. We must change.*	13 <u>A society can be judged by the way it treats its most disadvantaged, its least beloved, its mad. As things now stand, we must be judged a poor lot, and it is time to mend our ways.</u>

(Length: approximately 1,550 words)

SAMPLE SUMMARY

Although medical science has conquered many diseases previously thought incurable, some advances have been enthusiastically embraced and implemented before their potential consequences have been clearly thought out. One example is the use of drugs like Thorazine to treat schizophrenics. Even though they could not cure the disease, these drugs calmed patients and controlled their bizarre behavior.

Operating under the assumption that hospitalization for mild schizophrenics was no longer necessary, government agencies and the psychiatric community endorsed closing state-owned mental asylums and replacing them with "community mental health centers." The justification was that schizophrenics and other mentally ill patients, on medication, could be released and returned to the community. However good this idea sounded, the political effect was disastrous. These centers offered no custodial care, and many mentally ill people were left to wander the streets uncared for; some become so desperate that they committed suicide. The plight of these released patients is appalling.

Most agree that the old asylums were little better than hellholes, "warehouses for the insane," where patients weren't cured but nonetheless became dependent on the institutions, bleak as they were. But Thomas suggests that state institutions could be made to work. He proposes reopening and expanding state hospitals and staffing them with a caring, compassionate staff. In answer to the perennial question about adequate funding, Thomas suggests that physicians could volunteer their services on a part-time basis.

If one can judge a culture by the way it treats its mentally ill, then the United States has done a poor job, and it is time we change.

(Length: 258 words or approximately 17 percent)

COMMENT

Both sets of marginal annotations form the basis of this summary. Those on the far left annotate the essay's structure; those on the right pull out and restate the main points in key paragraphs. Remember that this sample summary is only one person's condensed version of the original ideas; other writers might choose to include other information. For example, one problem I had in preparing this summary was how much weight to give the information in paragraphs 1, 2, and 3, which, at first glance, seemed important. In the original version, I included some of Thomas's examples, like medical breakthroughs to combat tuberculosis, smallpox, various cancers, polio, organ transplants, and coronary bypass surgery.

Soon, however, I realized that paragraphs 1–3 form a classic "funnel pattern." Their function is to introduce us to the larger subject of medical advances before the author focuses on his real concern—the use of Thorazine to treat schizophrenics and the side effects of this supposed miracle drug. When examined in light of the whole essay, then, I realized that the information in paragraphs 1 and 3 could be dispensed with in a single sentence.

The remainder of Part IV consists of fifteen essays and articles on a variety of subjects. They are divided into three groups, according to their relative levels of difficulty. It is recommended that you read them all, even if your instructor does not assign the entire lot. Any practice you get in addition to your regular assignments will serve you well in improving your comprehension and analytical skills.

ESSAYS: GROUP 1

Selection 1

A Slave Witness of a Slave Auction

Solomon Northrup

Slave narratives were common before the Civil War, and abolitionists frequently used them in their campaign against slavery. Although many of these narratives were sensational, Northrup's account is fairly objective. It was published in 1853 in a book entitled Twelve Years a Slave: Narrative of Solomon Northrup, a Citizen of New York, Kidnapped in Washington City in 1841, and Rescued in 1853, from a Cotton Plantation near the Red River in Louisiana. *Northrup was finally given his freedom when he was able to get a letter sent to friends in New York. The governor arranged for his release, enabling him to return to his family in Glens Falls, New York.*

1 The very amiable, pious-hearted Mr. Theophilus Freeman, partner or consignee of James H. Burch, and keeper of the slave pen in New-Orleans, was out among his animals early in the morning. With an occasional kick of the older men and women, and many a sharp crack of the whip about the ears of the younger slaves, it was not long before they were all astir, and wide awake. Mr. Theophilus Freeman bustled about in a very industrious manner, getting his property ready for the salesroom, intending, no doubt, to do that day a rousing business.

2 In the first place we were required to wash thoroughly, and those with beards, to shave. We were then furnished with a new suit each, cheap, but clean. The men had hat, coat, shirt, pants and shoes; the women frocks of calico, and handkerchiefs to bind about their heads. We were now conducted into a large room in the front part of the building to which the yard was attached, in order to be properly trained, before the admission of customers. The men were arranged on one side of the room, the women on the other. The tallest was placed at the head of the row, then the next tallest, and so on in the order of their respective heights. Emily was at the foot of the line of women. Freeman charged us to remember our places; exhorted us to appear smart and lively,—sometimes threatening, and again holding out various inducements. During the day he exercised us in the art of "looking smart," and of moving to our places with exact precision.

3 After being fed, in the afternoon, we were again paraded and made to dance. Bob, a colored boy, who had some time belonged to Freeman, played on the violin. Standing near him, I made bold to inquire if he could play the "Virginia Reel." He answered he could not, and asked me

if I could play. Replying in the affirmative, he handed me the violin. I struck up a tune, and finished it. Freeman ordered me to continue playing, and seemed well pleased, telling Bob that I far excelled him—a remark that seemed to grieve my musical companion very much.

4 Next day many customers called to examine Freeman's "new lot." The latter gentleman was very loquacious, dwelling at much length upon our several good points and qualities. He would make us hold up our heads, walk briskly back and forth, while customers would feel of our hands and arms and bodies, turn us about, ask us what we could do, make us open our mouths and show our teeth, precisely as a jockey examines a horse which he is about to barter for or purchase. Sometimes a man or woman was taken back to the small house in the yard, stripped, and inspected more minutely. Scars upon a slave's back were considered evidence of a rebellious or unruly spirit, and hurt his sale.

5 One old gentleman, who said he wanted a coachman, appeared to take a fancy to me. From his conversation with Freeman, I learned he was a resident of the city. I very much desired that he would buy me, because I conceived it would not be difficult to make my escape from New-Orleans on some northern vessel. Freeman asked him fifteen hundred dollars for me. The old gentleman insisted it was too much, as times were very hard. Freeman, however, declared that I was sound and healthy, of a good constitution, and intelligent. He made it a point to enlarge upon my musical attainments. The old gentleman argued quite adroitly that there was nothing extraordinary about the nigger[1], and finally, to my regret, went out, saying he would call again. During the day, however, a number of sales were made. David and Caroline were purchased together by a Natchez planter. They left us, grinning broadly, and in the most happy state of mind, caused by the fact of their not being separated. Lethe was sold to a planter of Baton Rouge, her eyes flashing with anger as she was led away.

6 The same man also purchased Randall. The little fellow was made to jump, and run across the floor, and perform many other feats, exhibiting his activity and condition. All the time the trade was going on. Eliza was crying aloud, and wringing her hands. She besought the man not to buy him, unless he also bought herself and Emily. She promised, in that case, to be the most faithful slave that ever lived. The man answered that he could not afford it, and then Eliza burst into a paroxysm of grief, weeping plaintively. Freeman turned round to her, savagely, with his whip in his uplifted hand, ordering her to stop her noise, or he would flog her. He would not have such work—such snivelling; and unless she ceased that minute, he would take her to the yard and give her a hundred lashes. Yes, he would take the nonsense out of her pretty

[1] This word, now an offensive racial epithet, in the 19th century was a nonjudgmental word referring simply to a dark-skinned person.

quick—if he didn't, might he be d—d. Eliza shrunk before him, and tried to wipe away her tears, but it was all in vain. She wanted to be with her children, she said, the little time she had to live. All the frowns and threats of Freeman, could not wholly silence the afflicted mother. She kept on begging and beseeching them, most piteously, not to separate the three. Over and over again she told them how she loved her boy. A great many times she repeated her former promises—how very faithful and obedient she would be; how hard she would labor day and night, to the last moment of her life, if he would only buy them all together. But it was of no avail; the man could not afford it. The bargain was agreed upon, and Randall must go alone. Then Eliza ran to him; embraced him passionately, kissed him again and again; told him to remember her—all the while her tears falling in the boy's face like rain.

7 Freeman damned her, calling her a blubbering, bawling wench, and ordered her to go to her place, and behave herself, and be somebody. He swore he wouldn't stand such stuff but a little longer. He would soon give her something to cry about, if she was not mighty careful, and *that* she might depend upon.

8 The planter from Baton Rouge, with his new purchases, was ready to depart.

9 "Don't cry, mama. I will be a good boy. Don't cry," said Randall, looking back, as they passed out of the door.

10 What has become of the lad, God knows. It was a mournful scene indeed. I would have cried myself if I had dared.

A. *Comprehension*

Choose the answer that best completes each statement. Do not refer to the selection while doing this exercise.

1. Theophilus Freeman was (a) an animal trainer for the city of New Orleans; (b) the keeper of a slave pen in New Orleans; (c) a sympathetic observer at a slave auction; (d) a slave who was going to be sold to a new owner.
2. The slaves were exercised so that (a) they would be in good physical condition for their future labors; (b) they would be kept busy before the auction began; (c) they would be able to compete in athletic contests; (d) they would look sharp for the customers.
3. Scars on a slave's back, evidence of a rebellious or unruly spirit, meant that (a) the slave would cost more money; (b) the slave would cost less to purchase; (c) the sale would be hurt; (d) the slave would be set free.
4. According to Northrup's narrative, these slaves' primary concern was (a) not being separated from their family; (b) being purchased by a kind owner; (c) living in a place from which escape would be easy; (d) living near their relatives.

5. The man who purchased Randall claimed that he could not purchase Eliza and Emily, too, because (a) he needed only one slave; (b) he needed only a male slave; (c) he had room for only one slave; (d) times were hard.
6. The scene when Randall is sold, as Northrup describes it, is (a) embarrassing; (b) unrealistic; (c) pitiful; (d) maudlin.

B. *Inferences*

On the basis of the evidence in the paragraph, mark these statements as follows: PA for inferences that are probably accurate and PI for inferences that are probably inaccurate. You may refer to the selection to answer the questions in this section, and in all of the remaining sections.

1. ______ Theophilus Freeman was a successful slave broker.
2. ______ Purchasers preferred docile slaves to those who had been beaten for having a rebellious or unruly nature.
3. ______ The customers were not allowed to learn much information about the slaves' condition before they purchased them.
4. ______ Northrup had no intention of trying to escape after his purchase.
5. ______ Eliza was eventually reunited with her children, Randall and Emily.

C. *Structure*

1. The mode of discourse in this selection is (a) narration; (b) description; (c) exposition; (d) persuasion.
2. Northrup's specific purpose is (a) to show the reader how slave auctions were conducted; (b) to explain the criteria slaveowners used to purchase slaves; (c) to make us aware of the terrible hardships the auctions imposed on the slaves; (d) to argue for the abolition of slavery as an institution.
3. In paragraph 1, when Northrup describes Theophilus Freeman, keeper of the slave pen, as "amiable" and "pious-hearted," he is being (a) honest; (b) sarcastic; (c) complimentary; (d) overly sympathetic.
4. The method of development used in paragraph 2 is (a) analogy; (b) classification; (c) definition; (d) example; (e) process.
5. Throughout the essay, Northrup implies that Freeman treated the slaves like (a) family members; (b) objects; (c) luxuries; (d) animals.
6. Northrup dwells on the scene with Eliza and her son to emphasize (a) the inhumanity of slavery as an institution; (b) Northrup's own unselfish attempts to intercede on Eliza's behalf; (c) how hard times were, since the planter could not afford to buy the whole family; (d) the long-term emotional effects on slave families.

D. *Vocabulary*

For each italicized word from the selection, choose the best definition according to the context in which it appears.

1. the very *amiable* Mr. Theophilus Freeman [paragraph 1]: (a) proper; (b) good-natured; (c) honest; (d) religious.
2. the *pious*-hearted Mr. Theophilus Freeman [1]: (a) simple; (b) generous; (c) devoutly religious; (d) superstitious.
3. *exhorted* us to appear [2]: (a) gently encouraged; (b) demanded; (c) urged; (d) threatened.
4. holding out various *inducements* [2]: (a) incentives; (b) threats; (c) bribes; (d) legal pronouncements.
5. the gentleman was very *loquacious* [4]: (a) kindly; (b) talkative; (c) generous; (d) trustworthy.
6. I was of a good *constitution* [5]: (a) state of health; (b) moral character; (c) physical agility; (d) conscience.
7. the old gentleman argued quite *adroitly* [5]: (a) cleverly; (b) impassionedly; (c) skillfully; (d) convincingly.
8. a *paroxysm* of grief [6]: (a) sudden outburst; (b) emotional crisis; (c) example; (d) loud wailing.
9. weeping *plaintively* [6]: (a) quietly; (b) intensely; (c) mournfully; (d) bitterly.
10. She kept on begging and *beseeching* them [6]: (a) imploring; (b) clutching at; (c) annoying; (d) pursuing.

E. *Questions for Analysis and Discussion*

1. Northrup's attitude toward Mr. Freeman shifts during the narrative. What are the purpose and advantage of this seemingly inconsistent point of view?
2. What is Freeman's attitude toward the slaves? How does Freeman reveal it?
3. In paragraph 3, what qualities does Northrup reveal about himself when he talks about his accomplishments as a violinist?
4. In what way does Northrup's account of Eliza's grief over being separated from her son contrast with his earlier method of reporting?

Selection 2

Surviving Deer Season: A Lesson in Ambiguity

Castle Freeman, Jr.

Castle Freeman, Jr., a resident of Newfane, Vermont, is an essayist and short story writer. He is the author of The Bride of Ambrose and Other Stories *(1987),* Spring Snow: The Seasons of New England from The Old Farmer's Almanac *(1995), and* Judgment Hill, A Novel *(1997). This article was published in* The Atlantic Monthly.

1 The foothills of southeastern Vermont were once dairy country, although by the time I arrived, twenty years ago, dairying was mostly finished. One farm in the neighborhood still kept a few milkers, though, and it was there that I became acquainted with a particular local custom that is, I find, rarely celebrated in articles on endearing rural ways through the seasons. Their authors will tell you how to tap a maple in March, mow hay in June, and make cider in October, but by failing to touch on the subject I refer to, they neglect a passage in the turning year that is as venerable as these but darker and more pointed.

2 One morning in November, looking into my neighbor's pasture, I observed an uncanny thing: on the nearest of his animals the word COW had been painted with whitewash in letters two feet high. A further look revealed that the entire herd had been painted the same way. What was this? Was the herd's owner perhaps expecting a visit from city people in need of rural education? Was his tractor painted TRACTOR, his barn BARN? I asked him.

3 "Well, you know what tomorrow is," my neighbor said.

4 "Saturday?" I said.

5 "You're new around here," he said. "You'll see."

6 I saw, all right. More precisely, I heard. The next morning Vermont's two-week deer-hunting season began. Just before dawn the slumbering woods erupted with the fell echo of small arms. Single gunshots, doubles, volleys of three or four, came from all points of the compass, some far off, others seemingly in the living room. By eleven the fire had mounted to a fusillade worthy of Antietam. Across the road, however, my neighbor's cows survived. They hugged the earth

fearfully, like Tommies at the Somme, but they were alive. After all, no deer hunter who could read would shoot a cow.

7 Since then I have become a close student of the lengths to which people go each year on the eve of deer season to provide a margin of safety for themselves, their loved ones, their livestock, their pets. This is the season when dogs wear brightly colored bandannas around their necks, like John Wayne and Montgomery Clift in *Red River.* Cats and smaller dogs, as far as I can tell, have to take their chances along with the deer, although I don't know why the kind of elegant dog vest to be seen on the Pekingeses of Park Avenue shouldn't be produced in hunter orange for the greater safety of their country cousins.

8 That same hunter orange, a hideous toxic color, suddenly appears everywhere in mid-November, like the untimely bloom of an evil flower. Hunters themselves, of course, wear hunter orange to make it less likely that they'll be shot by their peers. But civilians, too, turn up in hunter-orange caps, vests, sweaters, and jackets, as they go about their business outdoors during this uneasy fortnight in the year.

9 Uneasy indeed. Are you a hiker, a birder, an idle tramper through the woods? In deer season you think twice before setting out—think twice and then stay home. If you're a nonhunter, it's painful to avoid the woods and fields as though they were a deserted street in the South Bronx. There is also the trouble of preparing for deer season. It's not as though you don't have enough to do to get the place ready for winter without having to find time to paint the cow, flag the dog, pray for the cat, and plan two weeks' worth of useful projects to do in the cellar.

10 The heaviest demands that deer season makes on the nonhunter, however, it makes not on his time but on his mind. You have to reflect. You have to collect your thoughts. You don't want to move into deer season without having examined your responses, your beliefs.

11 I don't object to deer hunting: let everyone have his sport, I say. I don't for a moment doubt the value, importance, and dignity of hunting for those who do it. Deer hunting teaches skill, discipline, and patience. More than that, it teaches the moral lesson of seriousness—that certain things must be entered into advisedly, done with care, and done right. That hunting provides an education I am very willing to believe. And yet deer season is for me a sad couple of weeks. Because with all its profound advantages for the hunter, the fact remains that deer season is a little tough on the deer.

12 Suddenly deer turn up in strange places: thrown down in the backs of pickup trucks; roped on top of cars; hanging in front of barns; flopped in blood across platform scales in front of country stores and gas stations. It's hard to recognize in those abject, inert cadavers the agile creatures you surprise along the roads at night or see sometimes in the woods picking their way on slender legs and then bounding off, the most graceful animals in North America. It's hard to see them so defeated, so dead.

13 It's particularly hard for children, those instinctive animal lovers, to see deer season's bloody harvest hauled out of the woods. It's especially hard to explain to them why it isn't wrong to kill deer—or, if it is wrong, why nobody can stop it, and how it is that the hunters themselves, who are also your friends and neighbors, are otherwise such familiar, decent, innocent people. It's a lesson in ambiguity, I guess—a lesson in tolerance.

14 I had a number of conversations along these lines with my children when they were young, inconclusive conversations with on their side conviction and passion, and on my own . . . nothing satisfactory. What do you tolerate, why, and how? How do you separate the act from the friend, and condemn the one but not the other? Not an easy matter at any age, in any season.

15 We don't have those talks anymore. The children are older now. They know that with some things all you can do is figure out how you will conduct your own life and let others do the same. Perhaps they have learned this in part from deer season. If so, I'm content. Let the gunners fire at will—and as for the nonhunters, good luck to them, too. It's not only hunters who can learn from hunting.

A. *Comprehension*

Choose the answer that best completes each statement. Do not refer to the selection while doing this exercise.

1. One farmer protected his cows at the beginning of deer season by (a) moving them into barns; (b) moving them into pastures away from woods; (c) painting COW on each animal; (d) putting brightly colored bandannas around their necks.
2. During deer season, to prevent them from accidentally being shot, people wear clothing in (a) hunter green; (b) neon green; (c) neon yellow; (d) hunter orange.
3. For the author, deer season requires him to (a) examine his beliefs carefully; (b) join his friends in hunting; (c) write letters protesting the hunting season; (d) join anti-hunting organizations.
4. The author finds that deer hunting, both for himself and for his children, represents (a) the saddest season of the year; (b) a lesson in ambiguity and tolerance; (c) a chance to learn new skills; (d) the loss of one's innocence.
5. Freeman is very much concerned with how to separate (a) the hunter's professed reason for killing deer and the actual reason; (b) the pros and cons of hunting as a sport; (c) the activity of hunting from the affection he feels for a friend who hunts; (d) the activity of hunting from the hostility he feels for a friend who hunts.

B. *Inferences*

Complete the following questions. You may refer to the selection to answer the questions in this section, and in all the remaining sections.

1. At the end of paragraph 1 Freeman writes that Vermont residents describe all sorts of annual rituals associated with rural living but that they neglect to write about the advent of hunting season. What inference can you make about the reason for this neglect? (a) There is no need to write articles about hunting because the practice is so ingrained and accepted in the community; (b) Vermonters are embarrassed that they enjoy hunting as a sport; (c) Vermonters do not want to call attention to the sport for fear of angering the anti-hunting lobby; (d) The author does not suggest any reason for this neglect.
2. We can infer that the author (a) eventually took up hunting; (b) rejected all of his friends who hunted; (c) had a difficult time resolving his feelings about hunter-friends and their enjoyment of hunting; (d) became a staunch supporter of anti-hunting legislation.
3. We can infer from nonhunters' behavior during deer season as described in paragraphs 7–9 that (a) innocent animals and people have been shot by accident; (b) nonhunters are too intimidated to speak out against hunting; (c) hunters are very careful about who or what they shoot; (d) nonhunters are so accustomed to the sport that they take no special precautions.
4. We can also infer that the author probably (a) dislikes hunting more than he likes it; (b) likes hunting more than he dislikes it; (c) sees both sides of the hunting question objectively; (d) has mixed feelings about hunting.
5. The subtitle of this essay is "A Lesson in Ambiguity." Another good subtitle would be (a) "Vermont Customs"; (b) "Deer Season—Pro and Con"; (c) "A Lesson in Tolerance"; (d) "How to Avoid Danger during Hunting Season."

C. *Structure*

Complete the following questions.

1. The author's purpose is (a) to criticize hunting as a sport; (b) to analyze the advantages and disadvantages of hunting as a sport; (c) to examine the ambiguities hunting as a sport presents to a nonhunter; (d) to explain the positive benefits one can gain from hunting.
2. Find two allusions in paragraph 6 and explain why they are effective.

 ____

____

3. In paragraph 8 Freeman uses a striking simile. Find the simile and then explain what is being compared to what? ______________________

____

Next, explain how the simile shows his point of view toward hunting.

____

4. Look again at this sentence from paragraph 9: "It's not as though you don't have enough to do to get the place ready for winter without having to find time to paint the cow, flag the dog, pray for the cat, and plan two weeks' worth of useful projects to do in the cellar." This is an example of (a) understatement; (b) hyperbole; (c) irony; (d) thematic unity.
5. With respect to the essay as a whole, what is the purpose of paragraph 11? ____
6. The tone of the essay can best be described as (a) contemplative, regretful, and sad; (b) humorous, amused; (c) accepting, condoning; (d) unsure, hesitant, and indecisive.

D. *Vocabulary*

1. a passage as *venerable* [paragraph 1]: (a) awe-inspiring; (b) honest; (c) inspired by tradition; (d) worthy of respect.
2. an *uncanny* thing [2]: (a) uncomfortably strange; (b) magical; (c) bewildering; (d) pragmatic.
3. a hideous *toxic* color [8]: Here, associated with (a) safety; (b) death; (c) garishness; (d) ammunition.
4. those *abject,* inert cadavers [12]: (a) graceful; (b) nimble; (c) deserving pity; (d) miserable.
5. those abject, *inert* cadavers [12]: (a) unmoving; (b) barely alive; (c) terrified; (d) harmless.
6. a lesson in *ambiguity* [13]: (a) patience, forbearance; (b) uncertainty with regard to interpretation; (c) the process of seeing all sides of a question; (d) a steadfast, adamant position.

E. *Questions for Analysis and Discussion*

1. Compare this essay to Steven Lubet's essay on deer hunting in Wisconsin. (See Chapter 9, page 338.)
2. It can be argued that in earlier stages of American history hunting was a necessity if homesteaders and pioneers wanted to eat. But the practice seems less defensible today. Freeman writes of the skill and patience hunting requires. Does the sport have any other virtues?
3. Freeman writes this essay as much to show the importance of tolerance as he does to show his concerns about the sport of hunting.

What is another practice that, fundamentally, you do not accept but that you have developed tolerance for? How did you achieve this tolerance?

Selection 3

Faux Chicken & Phony Furniture: Notes of an Alien Son

Andrei Codrescu

Andrei Codrescu is a Romanian-born poet and nonfiction writer, but he is probably best known as a commentator on National Public Radio's "All Things Considered." First published in The Nation, *this article explores some of the paradoxes associated with the immigrant experience, using his mother's initial infatuation with American products as his starting point. (The word "Faux"—see title—means "fake." Codrescu is referring to supermarket chickens, which are shot full of hormones and raised in cages and which have less flavor than the "free-range" chickens his mother bought in Romania.)*

1 My mother, ever a practical woman, started investing in furniture when she came to America from Romania. Not just any furniture. Sears furniture. Furniture that she kept the plastic on for 15 years before she had to conclude, sadly, that Sears wasn't such a great investment. In Romania, she would have been the richest woman on the block.

2 Which brings us to at least one paradox of immigration. Most people come here because they are sick of being poor. They want to eat and they want something to show for their industry. But soon enough it becomes evident to them that these things aren't enough. They have eaten and they are full, but they have eaten alone and there was no one with whom to make toasts and sing songs. They have new furniture with plastic on it, but the neighbors aren't coming over to ooh and aah. If American neighbors or less recent immigrants do come over, they smile condescendingly at the poor taste and the pathetic greed. And so the greenhorns find themselves poor once more: This time they are lacking something more elusive than salami and furniture. They are bereft of a social and cultural milieu.

3 My mother, who was middle class by Romanian standards, found herself immensely impoverished after her first flush of material well-being. It wasn't just the disappearance of her milieu—that was obvious—but the feeling that she had, somehow, been had. The American supermarket tomatoes didn't taste at all like the rare genuine item back in Romania. American chicken was tasteless. Mass-produced furniture was built to fall apart. Her car, the crowning glory of her achievements in the eyes of folks back home, was only three years old and already beginning

to wheeze and groan. It began to dawn on my mother that she had perhaps made a bad deal: She had traded in her friends and relatives for ersatz tomatoes, fake chicken, phony furniture.

4 Leaving behind your kin, your friends, your language, your smells, your childhood, is traumatic. It is a kind of death. You're dead for the home folk and they are dead to you. When you first arrive on these shores you are in mourning. The only consolations are these products, which were imbued with religious significance back at home. But when these things turn out not to be the real things, you begin to experience a second death, brought about by betrayal. You begin to suspect that the religious significance you attached to them was only possible back home, where these things did not exist. Here, where they are plentiful, they have no significance whatsoever. They are inanimate fetishes, somebody else's fetishes, no help to you at all. When this realization dawned on my mother, she began to rage against her new country. She deplored its rudeness, its insensitivity, its outright meanness, its indifference, the chase after the almighty buck, the social isolation of most Americans, their inability to partake of warm, genuine fellowship, and, above all, their deplorable lack of awe before what they had made.

5 This was the second stage of grief for her old self. The first, leaving her country, was sharp and immediate, almost tonic in its violence. The second was more prolonged, more damaging, because no hope was attached to it. Certainly not the hope of return.

6 And here, thinking of return, she began to reflect that perhaps there had been more to this deal than she'd first thought. True, she had left behind a lot that was good, but she had also left behind a vast range of daily humiliations. If she was ordered to move out of town she had to comply. If a party member took a dislike to her she had to go to extraordinary lengths to placate him because she was considered petit bourgeois and could easily have lost her small photo shop. She lived in fear of being denounced for something she had said. And worst of all, she was a Jew, which meant that she was structurally incapable of obtaining any justice in her native land. She had lived by the grace of an immensely complicated web of human relations, which was kept in place by a thousand small concessions, betrayals, indignities, bribes, little and big lies.

7 At this point, the ersatz tomatoes and the faux chicken did not appear all that important. An imponderable had made its appearance, a bracing, heady feeling of liberty. If she took that ersatz tomato and flung it at the head of the agriculture secretary of the United States, she would be making a statement about the disastrous effects of pesticides and mechanized farming. Flinging that faux chicken at Barbara Mandrell would be equally dramatic and perhaps even media-worthy. And she'd probably serve only a suspended sentence. What's more, she didn't have to eat those things, because she could buy organic tomatoes and free-range chicken. Of course, it would cost more, but that was one

of the paradoxes of America: To eat as well as people in a Third World country eat (when they eat) costs more.

8 My mother was beginning to learn two things: one, that she had gotten a good deal after all, because in addition to food and furniture they had thrown in freedom; and two, America is a place of paradoxes—one proceeds from paradox to paradox like a chicken from the pot into the fire.

A. *Comprehension*

Choose the answer that best completes each statement. Do not refer to the selection while doing this exercise.

1. According to Codrescu, most immigrants come to the United States to escape (a) political persecution; (b) religious persecution; (c) poverty and lack of opportunity; (d) the dislocation that results from years of civil wars.
2. Because immigrating is so traumatic, recent immigrants often seek consolation in (a) acquiring American products; (b) making plans to return home; (c) preserving their language and culture; (d) becoming politically active in their adopted homeland.
3. Codrescu's mother felt betrayed by (a) her American friends; (b) the shoddiness of mass-produced American products; (b) her inability to adapt to American culture; (d) her family members, for turning away from their cultural traditions.
4. Codrescu compares the immigrant experience of leaving their homelands to (a) a release; (b) a second chance at life; (c) an intermediate stage; (d) a kind of death.
5. Eventually, Codrescu's mother realized that in this country she could escape religious and political persecution and savor (a) her family's economic success; (b) acceptance by her neighbors; (c) better quality food; (d) her liberty.

B. *Inferences*

On the basis of the evidence in the paragraph, mark these statements as follows: PA for inferences that are probably accurate and PI for inferences that are probably inaccurate. You may refer to the selection to answer the questions in this section, and in all the remaining sections.

1. ______ For Codrescu's mother, being able to purchase furniture from Sears Roebuck represented the pinnacle of success.
2. ______ Native-born Americans do not experience the same paradoxes as do the immigrants that the author describes.

3. ______ The author's mother was apparently seduced by the lure of plentiful and affordable mass-produced products.
4. ______ Codrescu's mother eventually realized that life in Romania was more stable and more enjoyable than life in the United States.

C. *Structure*

Complete the following questions.

1. The author's purpose is (a) to trace the paradox of immigration and to examine the emotional stages immigrants experience; (b) to criticize Americans for not being more welcoming to new immigrants; (c) to explain his mother's decision to emigrate from Romania; (d) to explain how recent arrivals can avoid making their immigration experience traumatic.
2. Look again at paragraph 2. Although Codrescu is seemingly interested in his mother's Sears Roebuck furniture, what more significant underlying concept does this furniture represent? ______________

____

3. At the end of paragraph 2 Codrescu writes, "And so the greenhorns find themselves poor once more." What does he mean by "poor"?

____

____

4. The two methods of development in paragraph 3 are (a) process; (b) classification; (c) example; (d) comparison; (e) contrast; (f) analogy.
5. Look again at paragraph 7, where Codrescu describes the possibility of throwing ersatz tomatoes at the agriculture secretary or a chicken at Barbara Mandrell. What is he referring to? Are we to take him literally or metaphorically? ______________

____

6. The tone of this article can be best described as (a) arrogant, snobbish; (b) unsympathetic, callous; (c) sympathetic, compassionate; (d) impartial, objective.

D. *Vocabulary*

For each italicized word from the selection, choose the best definition according to the context in which it appears.

1. one *paradox* of immigration [paragraphs 2, 7, 8]: (a) result; (b) a seeming contradiction; (c) fault; (d) an unexplained event.
2. they smile *condescendingly* [2]: Describing an attitude that is (a) guilt-producing; (b) greedy and selfish; (c) patronizingly superior; (d) punishing, reproachful.
3. lacking something more *elusive* [2]: (a) difficult to describe; (b) harmful; (c) corrupting; (d) tangible.
4. they are *bereft* [2]: (a) bewildered by; (b) in mourning for; (c) enslaved by; (d) lacking something necessary.
5. a social and cultural *milieu* [pronounced mĭl yŏo′; 2 and 3]: (a) environment, setting; (b) set of rules; (c) means of advancement; (d) means of assimilation.
6. *ersatz* tomatoes [pronounced er′ zäts; 3]: Describing (a) something lacking nutritional value; (b) an inferior imitation; (c) something juicy, succulent; (d) something of excellent quality.
7. they are inanimate *fetishes* [4]: Describing (a) objects of attention or reverence; (b) examples of industrial output; (c) objects of inferior quality; (d) possessions owned by the rich.
8. go to lengths to *placate* him [6]: (a) allay someone's anger by making concessions; (b) flatter, cajole; (c) do a small favor for; (d) treat with great respect.
9. she was considered *petit bourgeois* [6]: A member of (a) the ruling class; (b) the proletariat or working class; (c) the lower middle class, including tradespeople and shop owners; (d) the professional class, including physicians and lawyers.
10. An *imponderable* made its appearance [7]: Describing something that cannot be (a) seen without special equipment; (b) appreciated without extensive background; (c) seen in advance; (d) precisely evaluated.

E. *Questions for Discussion and Analysis*

1. If possible, interview a recent immigrant to see if that person's experience confirms or refutes that of Codrescu's mother.
2. Explain in your own words the stages that immigrants experience, focusing in particular on the paradoxes his mother encountered with American culture.
3. Based on the information the author includes in paragraph 4, was Codrescu's mother justified or not in her rage against Americans? Explain.

Selection 4

Making the Grade

Kurt Wiesenfeld

Each week Newsweek *publishes a column titled "My Turn," in which people in various professions express personal viewpoints. "Making the Grade" is one such article. This particular column written by Kurt Wiesenfeld, a physicist who teaches at Georgia Institute of Technology in Atlanta, caused much discussion among college students and teachers after its publication in the June 17, 1996, issue.*

1 It was a rookie error. After 10 years I should have known better, but I went to my office the day after final grades were posted. There was a tentative knock on the door. "Professor Wiesenfeld? I took your Physics 2121 class? I flunked it? I wonder if there's anything I can do to improve my grade?" I thought: "Why are you asking me? Isn't it too late to worry about it? Do you dislike making declarative statements?"

2 After the student gave his tale of woe and left, the phone rang. "I got a D in your class. Is there any way you can change it to 'Incomplete'?" Then the e-mail assault began: "I'm shy about coming in to talk to you, but I'm not shy about asking for a better grade. Anyway, it's worth a try." The next day I had three phone messages from students asking *me* to call *them*. I didn't.

3 Time was, when you received a grade, that was it. You might groan and moan, but you accepted it as the outcome of your efforts or lack thereof (and, yes, sometimes a tough grader). In the last few years, however, some students have developed a disgruntled-consumer approach. If they don't like their grade, they go to the "return" counter to trade it in for something better.

4 What alarms me is their indifference toward grades as an indication of personal effort and performance. Many, when pressed about why they think they deserve a better grade, admit they don't deserve one but would like one anyway. Having been raised on gold stars for effort and smiley faces for self-esteem, they've learned that they can get by without hard work and real talent if they can talk the professor into giving them a break. This attitude is beyond cynicism. There's a weird innocence to the assumption that one expects (even deserves) a better grade simply by begging for it. With that outlook, I guess I shouldn't be as flabbergasted as I was that 12 students asked me to change their grades *after* final grades were posted.

5 That's 10 percent of my class who let three months of midterms, quizzes and lab reports slide until long past remedy. My graduate student calls it hyperrational thinking: if effort and intelligence don't matter, why should deadlines? What matters is getting a better grade through an unearned bonus, the academic equivalent of a freebie T-shirt or toaster giveaway. Rewards are disconnected from the quality of one's work. An act and its consequences are unrelated, random events.

6 Their arguments for wheedling better grades often ignore academic performance. Perhaps they feel it's not relevant. "If my grade isn't raised to a D I'll lose my scholarship." "If you don't give me a C, I'll flunk out." One sincerely overwrought student pleaded, "If I don't pass, my life is over." This is tough stuff to deal with. Apparently, I'm responsible for someone's losing a scholarship, flunking out or deciding whether life has meaning. Perhaps these students see me as a commodities broker with something they want—a grade. Though intrinsically worthless, grades, if properly manipulated, can be traded for what has value: a degree, which means a job, which means money. The one thing college actually offers—a chance to learn—is considered irrelevant, even less than worthless, because of the long hours and hard work required.

7 In a society saturated with surface values, love of knowledge for its own sake does sound eccentric. The benefits of fame and wealth are more obvious. So is it right to blame students for reflecting the superficial values saturating our society?

8 Yes, of course it's right. These guys had better take themselves seriously now, because our country will be forced to take them seriously later, when the stakes are much higher. They must recognize that their attitude is not only self-destructive, but socially destructive. The erosion of quality control—giving appropriate grades for actual accomplishments—is a major concern in my department. One colleague noted that a physics major could obtain a degree without ever answering a written exam question completely. How? By pulling in enough partial credit and extra credit. And by getting breaks on grades.

9 But what happens once she or he graduates and gets a job? That's when the misfortunes of eroding academic standards multiply. We lament that school children get "kicked upstairs" until they graduate from high school despite being illiterate and mathematically inept, but we seem unconcerned with college graduates whose less blatant deficiencies are far more harmful if their accreditation exceeds their qualifications.

10 Most of my students are science and engineering majors. If they're good at getting partial credit but not at getting the answer right, then the new bridge breaks or the new drug doesn't work. One finds examples here in Atlanta. Last year a light tower in the Olympic Stadium collapsed, killing a worker. It collapsed because an engineer miscalculated how much weight it could hold. A new 12-story dormitory could develop

dangerous cracks due to a foundation that's uneven by more than six inches. The error resulted from incorrect data being fed into a computer. I drive past that dorm daily on my way to work, wondering if a foundation crushed under kilotons of weight is repairable or if this structure will have to be demolished. Two 10,000-pound steel beams at the new natatorium collapsed in March, crashing into the student athletic complex. (Should we give partial credit since no one was hurt?) Those are real-world consequences of errors and lack of expertise.

11 But the lesson is lost on the grade-grousing 10 percent. Say that you won't (not can't, but won't) change the grade they deserve to what they want, and they're frequently bewildered or angry. They don't think it's fair that they're judged according to their performance, not their desires or "potential." They don't think it's fair that they should jeopardize their scholarships or be in danger of flunking out simply because they could not or did not do their work. But it's more than fair; it's necessary to help preserve a minimum standard of quality that our society needs to maintain safety and integrity. I don't know if the 13th-hour students will learn that lesson, but I've learned mine. From now on, after final grades are posted, I'll lie low until the next quarter starts.

A. *Comprehension*

Choose the answer that best completes each statement. Do not refer to the selection while doing this exercise.

1. According to Wiesenfeld, some college students do not consider grades as a measure of their (a) mastery of the subject; (b) personal performance and effort; (c) ability to organize their time wisely; (d) performance in relation to other students' performance in the class.
2. Some students try to get high grades by (a) cheating; (b) cramming at the last minute; (c) begging and pleading; (d) threatening the instructor.
3. The students described in the article have difficulty with grades because (a) they attend class sporadically; (b) they are unprepared academically for the course work; (c) their long work hours interfere with their studies; (d) they let an entire semester's work slide without doing anything.
4. The idea that students deserve high grades without working for them reflects (a) parental pressure for them to succeed; (b) the larger society's superficial values; (c) the importance of getting into a good graduate school; (d) grade inflation.
5. One particularly serious consequence of undeserved grades in science and engineering courses is that (a) educational standards in other

disciplines are also weakened; (b) unsafely designed buildings and structures can result in loss of lives; (c) graduates expect similar undeserved rewards when they enter the working world; (d) professors feel as if they are under siege.

B. *Inferences*

On the basis of the evidence in the paragraph, mark these statements as follows: PA for inferences that are probably accurate and PI for inferences that are probably inaccurate. You may refer to the selection to answer the questions in this section, and in all of the remaining sections.

1. ______ Many students equate good grades with high salaries rather than with knowledge acquired.
2. ______ It is not only science and engineering students who plead for higher grades; liberal arts students do as well.
3. ______ Parental pressure and the large financial investment college entails may account for some students begging for grades they do not deserve.
4. ______ The designers of the faulty bridge and the Olympic Stadium light tower received higher grades than they should have in their college courses.
5. ______ Professors in engineering courses should give partial or extra credit on examinations or projects.

C. *Structure*

Complete the following questions.

1. The mode of discourse represented in this article is (a) narration; (b) description; (c) exposition; (d) persuasion.
2. From the information in paragraph 1, explain the "rookie error" that Wiesenfeld made. ______________________________
3. The method of development in paragraph 3 is (a) example; (b) classification; (c) process; (d) cause and effect; (e) contrast.
4. The author's tone in paragraphs 1 and 2 is one of (a) despair; (b) confusion; (c) exasperation; (d) nastiness.

5. The purpose of paragraphs 7–10 is (a) to warn the reader about the serious long-term consequences of students' requesting undeserved grades; (b) to explain the origins of this practice; (c) to prove how widespread this practice is; (d) to present the students' point of view.

D. *Vocabulary*

For each italicized word from the selection, choose the best definition according to the context in which it appears.

1. the e-mail *assault* [paragraph 2]: (a) unlawful threat; (b) verbal attack; (c) connection; (d) a series of pleas.
2. a *disgruntled*-consumer approach [3]: (a) disgusted; (b) distrustful; (c) disillusioned; (d) discontented.
3. *hyperrational* thinking [5]: The prefix *hyper-* means (a) lack of; (b) phony; (c) excessive; (d) basic.
4. *wheedling* better grades [6]: (a) using flattery or cajolery; (b) using threats; (c) demanding; (d) offering bribes.
5. sincerely *overwrought* student [6]: (a) tearful; (b) desperate; (c) highly agitated; (d) highly irritating.
6. *intrinsically* worthless [6]: (a) essentially; (b) unusually; (c) fortunately; (d) morally.
7. illiterate and mathematically *inept* [9]: (a) unequal; (b) incompetent; (c) unmotivated; (d) unchallenged.
8. less *blatant* deficiencies [9]: (a) offensively conspicuous; (b) solvable; (c) understandable; (d) predictable.
9. *eroding* academic standards [9]: (a) rising; (b) inconsistent; (c) unreasonable; (d) deteriorating.
10. maintain safety and *integrity* [11]: (a) adherence to old traditions; (b) state of being complete and sound; (c) social cohesion; (d) economic opportunity.

E. *Questions for Analysis and Discussion*

1. Do you see any contradiction in Wiesenfeld's explanation of what grades mean to many students today and what they should mean? (See paragraphs 3 and 4.)

2. Is Wiesenfeld accurate in his criticism of today's students and their attitude about grades? Do you detect any bias? Does he avoid generalizing about his students, and if so, how? From your experience and observation, comment on his most significant points.

Selection 5

This Boy's Life

Tobias Wolff

Tobias Wolff, a professor in Stanford University's creative writing program, is one of America's most respected short story writers. Wolff endured a difficult childhood in Concrete, a gritty working- class town in eastern Washington State. His early life is well documented in This Boy's Life,[1] *the absorbing but dark memoir from which this selection comes. Wolff later served during the Vietnam War, an account of which he published as* In Pharaoh's Army: Memories of the Lost War *(1994). His most recent collection of stories is* The Night in Question *(1996).*

1 Concrete was a company town, home of the Lone Star Cement Company. The streets and houses and cars were gray with cement dust from the plant. On still days a pall of dust hung in the air, so thick they sometimes had to cancel football practice. Concrete High overlooked the town from a hill whose slopes had been covered with cement to keep them from washing away. By the time I started there, not long after the school was built, its cement banks had begun to crack and slide, revealing the chicken wire over which they had been poured.

2 The school took students from up and down the valley. They were the children of farmers, waitresses, loggers, construction workers, truck drivers, itinerant laborers. Most of the boys already had jobs themselves. They worked not to save money but to spend it on their cars and girlfriends. Many of them got married while they were still in school, then dropped out to work full-time. Others joined the army or the marines—never the navy. A few became petty criminals. The boys of Concrete High tended not to see themselves as college material.

3 The school had some good teachers, mostly older women who didn't care if they were laughed at for reciting poetry, or for letting a tear fall while they described the Battle of Verdun. There were not many of them.

4 Mr. Mitchell taught civics. He also acted as unofficial recruiter for the army. He had served during World War II in "the European Theater,"

[1]A watchable film version, also titled *This Boy's Life,* was released in 1993, starring Leonardo DiCaprio as Tobias, Ellen Barkin as his mother, and Robert DeNiro as his vindictively cruel stepfather, Dwight.

as he liked to say, and had actually killed men. He sometimes brought in different items he had taken from their bodies, not only medals and bayonets, which you could buy in any pawnshop, but also letters in German and wallets with pictures of families inside. Whenever we wanted to distract Mr. Mitchell from collecting essays we hadn't written, we would ask about the circumstances of his kills. Mr. Mitchell would crouch behind his desk, peer over the top, then roll into the middle of the room and spring to his feet yelling *da-da-da-da-da*. But he praised the courage and discipline of the Germans, and said that in his opinion we had fought on the wrong side. We should have gone into Moscow, not Berlin. As far as the concentration camps were concerned, we had to remember that nearly all the Jewish scientists had perished there. If they had lived, they would have helped Hitler develop his atomic bomb before we developed ours, and we would all be speaking German today.

5 Mr. Mitchell relied heavily on audiovisual aids in teaching his classes. We saw the same movies many times, combat documentaries and FBI-produced cautionary tales about high-school kids tricked into joining communist cells in Anytown, U.S.A. On our final examination Mr. Mitchell asked, "What is your favorite amendment?" We were ready for this question, and all of us gave the correct answer—"The Right to Bear Arms"—except for a girl who answered "Freedom of Speech." For this impertinence she failed not only the question but the whole test. When she argued that she could not logically be marked wrong on this question, Mr. Mitchell blew up and ordered her out of the classroom. She complained to the principal but nothing came of it. Most of the kids in the class thought she was being a smarty-pants, and so did I.

6 Mr. Mitchell also taught PE. He had introduced boxing to the school, and every year he organized a smoker where hundreds of people paid good money to watch us boys beat the bejesus out of each other.

7 Miss Houlihan taught speech. She had adopted some years back a theory of elocution that had to do with "reaching down" for words rather than merely saying them, as if they were already perfectly formed in our stomachs and waiting to be brought up like trout from a stock pond. Instead of using our lips we were supposed to simply let the words "escape." This was hard to get the hang of. Miss Houlihan believed in getting the first thing right before moving on to the next, so we spent most of the year grunting "Hiawatha" in a choral arrangement she herself had devised. She liked it so much that in the spring she took us to a speech tournament in Mount Vernon. The competition was held outside, and it started to rain while we sat declaiming in The Great Circle. We wore Indian costumes made from burlap sacks that had once held onions. When the burlap got wet it started to stink. We were not the only ones to notice. Miss Houlihan wouldn't let us quit. She walked

around behind the circle, whispering, "Reach down, reach down." In the end we were disqualified for keeping time on a tom-tom.

8 Horseface Greeley taught shop. At the introductory class for each group of freshmen it was his custom to drop a fifty-pound block of iron on his foot. He did this as an attention-getter and to show off his Tuff-Top shoes, which had reinforced steel uppers. He thought we should all wear Tuff-Tops. We couldn't buy them in the stores but we could order them through him. When I was in my second year at Concrete an impetuous freshman tried to catch the block of iron as it fell toward Horseface's foot, and got his fingers crushed.

9 I brought home good grades at first. They were a fraud—I copied other kids' homework on the bus down from Chinook and studied for tests in the hallways as I walked from class to class. After the first marking period I didn't bother to do that much. I stopped studying altogether. Then I was given C's instead of A's, yet no one at home ever knew that my grades had fallen. The report cards were made out, incredibly enough, in pencil, and I owned some pencils myself.

10 All I had to do was go to class, and sometimes even that seemed too much. I had fallen in with some notorious older boys from Concrete who took me on as a curiosity when they discovered that I'd never been drunk and still had my cherry. I was grateful for their interest. I wanted distinction, and the respectable forms of it seemed to be eluding me. If I couldn't have it as a citizen I would have it as an outlaw.

11 We smoked cigarettes every morning in a shallow gully behind the school, and we often stayed there when the bell rang for class, then cut downhill through a field of ferns—ferns so tall we seemed to be swimming through them—to the side road where Chuck Bolger kept his car.

12 Chuck's father owned a big auto parts store near Van Horn and was also the minister of a Pentecostal church. Chuck himself talked dark religion when he was drinking. He was haunted and wild, but his manner was gentle; even, at least with me, brotherly. For that reason I felt easier with him than with the others. I believed that there were at least some things he would not do. I did not have that feeling about the rest. One of them had already spent time in jail, first for stealing a chain saw and then for kidnapping a cat. He was big and stupid and peculiar. Everyone called him Psycho and he had accepted the name like a vocation.

13 Chuck was with Psycho when he snatched the cat. The cat walked up to them while they were standing outside the Concrete drugstore and began to rub against their legs. Psycho picked the cat up to do it some injury, but when he saw the name on its collar he got an idea. The cat belonged to a widow whose husband had owned a car dealership in town. Psycho figured she must be loaded, and decided to put the arm on her. He called the widow from a pay phone and told her he had the cat and would sell it back to her for twenty dollars. Otherwise he would kill it. To show he meant business he held the cat up to the

received and pulled its tail, but it wouldn't make any noise. Finally Psycho moved the receiver back to his own mouth and said, "Meow, meow." Then he told the widow to get the money and meet him at a certain place at a certain time. When Chuck tried to talk him out of going, Psycho called him a pussy. The widow wasn't there. Some other people were.

14 Then there was Jerry Huff. Huff was handsome in a pouty, heavy-lidded way. Girls liked him, which was bad luck for them. He was short but enormously strong and vain. His vanity crested above his head in a stupendous gleaming pompadour. He was a bully. He loitered in the bathrooms and made fun of the boys' dicks and stepped on their white buck shoes and held them over toilet bowls by their ankles. Bullies are supposed to be cowards but Huff confounded this wisdom. He would try to bully anyone, even guys who had already beaten him up.

15 Arch Cook also ran with us. Arch was an amiable simpleton who talked to himself and sometimes shouted or laughed for no reason. His head was long and thin and flat on the sides. Chuck told me that a car had driven over him when he was a baby. This was probably true. Huff used to tell him, "Arch, you might've been okay if that guy hadn't backed up to see what he hit." Arch was Huff's cousin.

16 There were five of us. We piled into Chuck's '53 Chevy and drove around looking for a car we could siphon gas out of. If we found one we emptied a few gallons from its tank into Chuck's and spent the morning tearing up the fire roads into the mountains. Around lunchtime we usually drove back down to Concrete and dropped in on Arch's sister Veronica. She'd been in Norma's class at Concrete. She still had the pert nose and wide blue eyes of the lesser Homecoming royalty she'd once been, but her face was going splotchy and loose from drink. Veronica was married to a sawyer who worked at a mill near Everett and came home only on the weekends. She had two fat little girls who wandered the wreckage of the house in their underpants, whining for their mother's attention and eating potato chips from economy packs almost as big as they were. Veronica was crazy about Chuck. If he wasn't in the mood, she would try to get him in the mood by walking around in short-shorts and high heels, or by sitting in his lap and sticking her tongue in his ear.

17 We hung around the house all afternoon, playing cards and reading Veronica's detective magazines. Now and then I tried to play games with the little girls, but they were too morose to pretend or imagine anything. At three o'clock I walked back up to Concrete High to catch my bus home.

18 Chuck and the others knew a lot of women like Veronica, and girls on their way to being like Veronica. When they found a new one they shared her. They tried to fix me up with some of them, but I always backed out. I didn't know what these girls expected; I did know I was

sure to disappoint them. Their availability unmanned me. And I didn't want it to be like that, squalid and public, with a stranger. I wanted it to be with the girl I loved.

19 This was not going to happen, because the girl I loved never knew I loved her. I kept my feelings secret because I believed she would find them laughable, even insulting. Her name was Rhea Clark. Rhea moved to Concrete from North Carolina halfway through her junior year, when I was a freshman. She had flaxen hair that hung to her waist, calm brown eyes, golden skin that glowed like a jar of honey. Her mouth was full, almost loose. She wore tight skirts that showed the flex and roll of her hips as she walked, clinging pastel sweaters whose sleeves she pushed up to her elbows, revealing a heartbreaking slice of creamy inner arm.

20 Just after Rhea came to Concrete I asked her to dance with me during a mixer in the gym. She nodded and followed me out onto the floor. It was a slow dance. When I turned to face her she moved into my arms as no other girl had ever done, frankly and fully. She melted against me and stayed against me, pliant to my least motion, her legs against mine, her cheek against mine, her fingers brushing the back of my neck. I understood that she didn't know who I was, that all of this was a new girl's mistake. But I felt justified in taking advantage of it. I thought we were meeting rightly, true self to true self, free of the accidents of age.

21 After a while she said, "Y'all don't know how to party."

22 Her voice was throaty and deep. I could feel it in my chest.

23 "Them old boys back in Norville could flat party," she said, "and that's no lie."

24 I couldn't speak. I just held her and moved her and breathed in her hair. I had her for three minutes and then I lost her forever. Older boys, boys I didn't have the courage to cut in on, danced with her the rest of the night. A week or so later she took up with Lloyd Sly, a basketball player with a hot car. When we passed in the hall she didn't even recognize me.

25 I wrote her long, grandiloquent letters which I then destroyed. I thought of the different ways that fate might put her in my power, so I could show her who I really was and make her love me. Most of these possibilities involved death or severe maiming for Lloyd Sly.

26 And when, as sometimes happened, a girl my own age showed some interest in me, I treated her swinishly. I walked her home from a dance or a game, made out with her on her front steps, then cut her dead the next day. I only ever wanted what I couldn't have.

27 Chuck and the others had better luck getting me drunk. Though liquor disagreed with me they were patient, and willing to experiment, and time was on their side. They finally broke through during a basketball game, the last game of the season. It had rained earlier and the air

was steamy. The windows of the school were open, and from our gully outside we could hear the cheerleaders warming up the people in the stands while the players did their lay-up drills.

Who's the team they hate to meet?
Con-crete! Con-crete!
Who's the team they just can't beat?
Con-crete! Con-crete!

28 Huff was passing around a can of Hawaiian Punch cut with vodka. Gorilla blood, he called it. I thought it would probably make me sick but I took a swig anyway. It stayed down. In fact I liked it, it tasted exactly like Hawaiian Punch. I took another swig.

29 I was up on the school roof with Chuck. He was looking at me and nodding meditatively. "Wolff," he said. "Jack Wolff."

30 "Yo."

31 "Wolff, your teeth are too big."

32 "I know they are. I know they are."

33 "Wolf-man."

34 "Yo, Chuckles."

35 He held up his hands. They were bleeding. "Don't hit trees, Jack. Okay?"

36 I said I wouldn't.

37 "Don't hit trees."

38 I was lying on my back with Huff kneeling on me, slapping my cheeks. He said, "Speak to me, dicklick," and I said, "Hi, Huff." Everybody laughed. Huff's pompadour had come unstuck and was hanging in long strands over his face. I smiled and said, "Hi, Huff."

39 I was walking along a branch. I was way out on it, over the far lip of the gully where the cement bank began. They were all looking up at me and yelling. They were fools, my balance was perfect. I bounced on the branch and flapped my arms. The I put my hands in my pockets and strolled out along the branch until it broke.

40 I didn't feel myself land, but I heard the wind leave me in a rush. I was rolling sideways down the hillside with my hands still in my pockets, rolling around and around like a log, faster and faster, picking up speed on the steep cement. The cement ended in a drop where the earth below had washed away. I flew off the edge and went spinning through the air and landed hard and rolled downhill through the ferns, bouncing over rocks and deadfall, the ferns rustling around me, and then I hit something hard and stopped cold.

41 I was on my back. I could not move, I could not breathe. I was too empty to take the first breath, and my body would not respond to the bulletins I sent. Blackness came up from the bottom of my eyes. I was drowning, and then I drowned.

42 When I opened my eyes I was still on my back. I heard voices calling my name but I did not answer. I lay amidst a profusion of ferns, their fronds glittering with raindrops. The fronds made a lattice above me. The voices came closer and still I did not answer. I was happy where I was. There was movement in the bushes all around me, and again and again I heard my name. I bit the inside of my cheek so I wouldn't laugh and give myself away, and finally they left.

43 I spent the night there. In the morning I walked down to the main road and thumbed a ride home. My clothes were wet and torn, but except for a certain tenderness down the length of my back I was unhurt, just creaky from my night on the ground.

44 Dwight[2] was at the kitchen table when I came in. He looked me over and said—quietly, he knew he had me this time—"Where were you last night?"

45 I said, "I got drunk and fell off a cliff."

46 He grinned in spite of himself, just as I knew he would. He let me off with a lecture and some advice about hangovers while my mother stood by the sink in her bathrobe, listening without expression. After Dwight dismissed me she followed me down the hall. She stopped in my doorway, arms crossed, and waited for me to look at her. Finally she said, "You're not helping anymore."

47 No, but I was happy that night, listening to them search for me, listening to them call my name. I knew they wouldn't find me. After they went away I lay there smiling in my perfect place. Through the ferns above me I saw the nimbus of the moon in the dense, dark sky. Cool beads of water rolled down the ferns onto my face. I could just make out the sounds of the game going on up the hill, the cheers, the drumming of feet in the stands. I listened with godly condescension. I was all alone where no one could find me, only the faint excitements of a game and some voices crying Concrete, Concrete, Concrete.

A. *Comprehension*

Choose the answer that best completes each statement. Do not refer to the selection while doing this exercise.

1. According to Wolff, the boys who lived in the town of Concrete (a) were constantly in trouble with the law; (b) dropped out of school early to work or to join the military; (c) faced a life of drudgery working at the cement plant; (d) worked diligently to qualify for college scholarships.
2. The favorite amendment of Mr. Mitchell, the high school civics teacher, was (a) freedom of religion; (b) freedom of assembly; (c) freedom of speech; (d) the right to bear arms.

[2]Dwight was Tobias Wolff's stepfather.

3. Wolff's older friends took him on as a special project because he had never been drunk and had not (a) stolen anything; (b) kissed a girl; (c) lost his virginity; (d) stolen a car.
4. Wolff confesses that the only girls he liked were (a) married; (b) older than he; (c) the ones he couldn't have; (d) his friends' girlfriends.
5. After Wolff got drunk and fell from the cliff, (a) he was knocked unconscious; (b) he was too ashamed and afraid to go home; (c) he was afraid that he would never be found; (d) he deliberately hid from his friends and enjoyed not being found.

B. *Inferences*

On the basis of the evidence in the paragraph, mark these statements as follows: PA for inferences that are probably accurate and PI for inferences that are probably inaccurate. You may refer to the selection to answer the questions in this section, and in all of the remaining sections.

1. ______ Concrete offered limited educational opportunities for young people.
2. ______ The three high school teachers that Wolff describes were conventional, strict, highly predictable, and mediocre.
3. ______ Wolff probably faked his good grades.
4. ______ The police were waiting for Psycho when he tried to collect the ransom for the widow's kidnapped cat.
5. ______ Wolff walked out on the branch, not so much because he was drunk, as because he wanted to prove himself to his friends.

C. *Structure*

Complete the following questions.

1. The mode of discourse in the selection is (a) narration; (b) description; (c) exposition; (d) persuasion.
2. What two main topics does Wolff take up in the body of this essay?

   ______________________________ and ______________________________
3. Look again at the end of paragraph 4, where Mr. Mitchell explains why Americans fought on the wrong side during World War II. His reasoning is an example of a logical fallacy, specifically, (a) false analogy; (b) post hoc, ergo propter hoc; (c) slippery slope; (d) two wrongs make a right; (e) begging the question.
4. In paragraph 5, locate the word "impertinence." After you are certain of its meaning, explain why it is used ironically. ____________________

____

____

5. Throughout the selection, Wolff appears motivated by (a) arrogance and a feeling of superiority to his classmates; (b) a desire to be accepted and yet not to compromise his own values; (c) a desire to be accepted even though it would mean doing illegal or dangerous things; (d) a desire to escape the dreariness of Concrete.
6. Getting drunk on vodka-laced Hawaiian Punch and falling off a cliff represented a rite of passage and proved that Wolff (a) was not cowardly or wimpy; (b) could drink as much as his friends could; (c) was recklessly foolish; (d) was trying to make a reputation for himself as an outlaw and a bid for acceptance by his friends.

D. *Vocabulary*

For each italicized word from the selection, choose the best definition according to the context in which it appears.

1. *itinerant* laborers [paragraph 2]: (a) common, manual; (b) moving from place to place; (c) agricultural; (d) low-paid.
2. for this *impertinence* [5]: (a) imposition; (b) irrelevancy; (c) bit of trivia; (d) improper boldness.
3. we sat *declaiming* [7]: (a) reciting loudly; (b) debating, arguing; (c) fumbling lines; (d) quietly conversing.
4. an *impetuous* freshman [8]: (a) unsophisticated; (b) violent; (c) helpful; (d) impulsive.
5. Huff *confounded* this wisdom [14]: In this context, (a) conformed to; (b) proved true; (c) defeated, proved untrue; (d) learned from.
6. they were too *morose* [17]: (a) stupid; (b) unimaginative; (c) impatient; (d) melancholy.
7. *squalid* and public [18]: (a) embarrassing; (b) inappropriate; (c) dirty; (d) open to ridicule.
8. long, *grandiloquent* letters [25]: (a) heartfelt; (b) emotional; (c) high-minded; (d) pompous.
9. I treated her *swinishly* [26]: (a) politely; (b) brutishly; (c) doltishly; (d) arrogantly.
10. with godly *condescension* [47]: (a) patronizing superiority; (b) contempt; (c) exaggerated politeness; (d) persistence.

E. *Questions for Analysis and Discussion*

1. In the last scene, where Wolff describes lying among the ferns, not wanting to be found by his friends, what emotions does he experience? Why does he hide from his friends?

2. Based on the incidents Wolff describes in this excerpt and on his reactions to the world around him, how would you assess his character? What kind of person is he? How does he look at the world?
3. In what ways does this excerpt represent a boy's rite of passage?

ESSAYS: GROUP 2

Selection 6

The Insufficiency of Honesty

Stephen L. Carter

Stephen L. Carter is the William Nelson Cromwell Professor of Law at Yale University. He is also the author of three books: Reflections of an Affirmative Action Baby *(1991);* The Culture of Disbelief: How American Law and Politics Trivialize Religious Devotion *(1994); and* Integrity *(1996), from which "The Insufficiency of Honesty" is adapted. This version first appeared in the February 1996 issue of* The Atlantic Monthly.

1 A couple of years ago I began a university commencement address by telling the audience that I was going to talk about integrity. The crowd broke into applause. Applause! Just because they had heard the word "integrity": that's how starved for it they were. They had no idea how I was using the word, or what I was going to say about integrity, or, indeed, whether I was for it or against it. But they knew they liked the idea of talking about it.

2 Very well, let us consider this word "integrity." Integrity is like the weather: everybody talks about it but nobody knows what to do about it. Integrity is that stuff that we always want more of. Some say that we need to return to the good old days when we had a lot more of it. Others say that we as a nation have never really had enough of it. Hardly anybody stops to explain exactly what we mean by it, or how we know it is a good thing, or why everybody needs to have the same amount of it. Indeed, the only trouble with integrity is that everybody who uses the word seems to mean something slightly different.

3 For instance, when I refer to integrity, do I mean simply "honesty?" The answer is no; although honesty is a virtue of importance, it is a different virtue from integrity. Let us, for simplicity, think of honesty as not lying; and let us further accept Sissela Bok's definition of a lie: "any intentionally deceptive message which is *stated.*" Plainly, one cannot have integrity without being honest (although, as we shall see, the matter gets complicated), but one can certainly be honest and yet have little integrity.

4 When I refer to integrity, I have something very specific in mind. Integrity, as I will use the term, requires three steps: discerning what is right and what is wrong; acting on what you have discerned, even at personal cost; and saying openly that you are acting on your understanding of right and wrong. The first criterion captures the idea that integrity requires a degree of moral reflectiveness. The second brings in the ideal of a person of integrity as steadfast, a quality that includes keeping one's commitments. The third reminds us that a person of integrity can be trusted.

5 The first point to understand about the difference between honesty and integrity is that a person may be entirely honest without ever engaging in the hard work of discernment that integrity requires: she may tell us quite truthfully what she believes without ever taking the time to figure out whether what she believes is good and right and true. The problem may be as simple as someone's foolishly saying something that hurts a friend's feelings; a few moments of thought would have revealed the likelihood of the hurt and the lack of necessity for the comment. Or the problem may be more complex, as when a man who was raised from birth in a society that preaches racism states his belief in one race's inferiority as a fact, without ever really considering that perhaps this deeply held view is wrong. Certainly the racist is being honest—he is telling us what he actually thinks—but his honesty does not add up to integrity.

Telling Everything You Know

6 A wonderful epigram sometimes attributed to the filmmaker Sam Goldwyn goes like this: "The most important thing in acting is honesty; once you learn to fake that, you're in." The point is that honesty can be something one *seems* to have. Without integrity, what passes for honesty often is nothing of the kind; it is fake honesty—or it is honest but irrelevant and perhaps even immoral.

7 Consider an example. A man who has been married for fifty years confesses to his wife on his deathbed that he was unfaithful thirty-five years earlier. The dishonesty was killing his spirit, he says. Now he has cleared his conscience and is able to die in peace.

8 The husband has been honest—sort of. He has certainly unburdened himself. And he has probably made his wife (soon to be his widow) quite miserable in the process, because even if she forgives him, she will not be able to remember him with quite the vivid image of love and loyalty that she had hoped for. Arranging his own emotional affairs to ease his transition to death, he has shifted to his wife the burden of confusion and pain, perhaps for the rest of her life. Moreover, he has attempted his honesty at the one time in his life when it carries no risk;

acting in accordance with what you think is right and risking no loss in the process is a rather thin and unadmirable form of honesty.

9 Besides, even though the husband has been honest in a sense, he has now twice been unfaithful to his wife: once thirty-five years ago, when he had his affair, and again when, nearing death, he decided that his own peace of mind was more important than hers. In trying to be honest he has violated his marriage vow by acting toward his wife not with love but with naked and perhaps even cruel self-interest.

10 As my mother used to say, you don't have to tell people everything you know. Lying and nondisclosure, as the law often recognizes, are not the same thing. Sometimes it is actually illegal to tell what you know, as, for example, in the disclosure of certain financial information by market insiders. Or it may be unethical, as when a lawyer reveals a confidence entrusted to her by a client. It may be simple bad manners, as in the case of a gratuitous comment to a colleague on his or her attire. And it may be subject to religious punishment, as when a Roman Catholic priest breaks the seal of the confessional—an offense that carries automatic excommunication.

11 In all the cases just mentioned, the problem with telling everything you know is that somebody else is harmed. Harm may not be the intention, but it is certainly the effect. Honesty is most laudable when we risk harm to ourselves; it becomes a good deal less so if we instead risk harm to others when there is no gain to anyone other than ourselves. Integrity may counsel keeping our secrets in order to spare the feelings of others. Sometimes, as in the example of the wayward husband, the reason we want to tell what we know is precisely to shift our pain onto somebody else—a course of action dictated less by integrity than by self-interest. Fortunately, integrity and self-interest often coincide, as when a politician of integrity is rewarded with our votes. But often they do not, and it is at those moments that our integrity is truly tested.

Error

12 Another reason that honesty alone is no substitute for integrity is that if forthrightness is not preceded by discernment, it may result in the expression of an incorrect moral judgment. In other words, I may be honest about what I believe, but if I have never tested my beliefs, I may be wrong. And here I mean "wrong" in a particular sense: the proposition in question is wrong if I would change my mind about it after hard moral reflection.

13 Consider this example. Having been taught all his life that women are not as smart as men, a manager gives the women on his staff less-challenging assignments than he gives the men. He does this, he believes, for their own benefit: he does not want them to fail, and he believes that they will if he gives them tougher assignments. Moreover,

when one of the women on his staff does poor work, he does not berate her as harshly as he would a man, because he expects nothing more. And he claims to be acting with integrity because he is acting according to his own deepest beliefs.

14 The manager fails the most basic test of integrity. The question is not whether his actions are consistent with what he most deeply believes but whether he has done the hard work of discerning whether what he most deeply believes is right. The manager has not taken this harder step.

15 Moreover, even within the universe that the manager has constructed for himself, he is not acting with integrity. Although he is obviously wrong to think that the women on his staff are not as good as the men, even were he right, that would not justify applying different standards to their work. By so doing he betrays both his obligation to the institution that employs him and his duty as a manager to evaluate his employees.

16 The problem that the manager faces is an enormous one in our practical politics, where having the dialogue that makes democracy work can seem impossible because of our tendency to cling to our views even when we have not examined them. As Jean Bethke Elshtain has said, borrowing from John Courtney Murray, our politics are so fractured and contentious that we often cannot even reach *disagreement*. Our refusal to look closely at our own most cherished principles is surely a large part of the reason. Socrates thought the unexamined life not worth living. But the unhappy truth is that few of us actually have the time for constant reflection on our views—on public or private morality. Examine them we must, however, or we will never know whether we might be wrong.

17 None of this should be taken to mean that integrity as I have described it presupposes a single correct truth. If, for example, your integrity-guided search tells you that affirmative action is wrong, and my integrity-guided search tells me that affirmative action is right, we need not conclude that one of us lacks integrity. As it happens, I believe—both as a Christian and as a secular citizen who struggles toward moral understanding—that we *can* find true and sound answers to our moral questions. But I do not pretend to have found very many of them, nor is an exposition of them my purpose here.

18 It is the case not that there aren't any right answers but that, given human fallibility, we need to be careful in assuming that we have found them. However, today's political talk about how it is wrong for the government to impose one person's morality on somebody else is just mindless chatter. *Every* law imposes one person's morality on somebody else, because law has only two functions: to tell people to do what they would rather not or to forbid them to do what they would.

19 And if the surveys can be believed, there is far more moral agreement in America than we sometimes allow ourselves to think. One of

the reasons that character education for young people makes so much sense to so many people is precisely that there seems to be a core set of moral understandings—we might call them the American Core—that most of us accept. Some of the virtues in this American Core are, one hopes, relatively noncontroversial. About 500 American communities have signed on to Michael Josephson's program to emphasize the "six pillars" of good character: trustworthiness, respect, responsibility, caring, fairness, and citizenship. These virtues might lead to a similarly noncontroversial set of political values: having an honest regard for ourselves and others, protecting freedom of thought and religious belief, and refusing to steal or murder.

Honesty and Competing Responsibilities

20 A further problem with too great an exaltation of honesty is that it may allow us to escape responsibilities that morality bids us bear. If honesty is substituted for integrity, one might think that if I say I am not planning to fulfill a duty, I need not fulfill it. But it would be a peculiar morality indeed that granted us the right to avoid our moral responsibilities simply by stating our intention to ignore them. Integrity does not permit such an easy escape.

21 Consider an example. Before engaging in sex with a woman, her lover tells her that if she gets pregnant, it is her problem, not his. She says that she understands. In due course she does wind up pregnant. If we believe, as I hope we do, that the man would ordinarily have a moral responsibility toward both the child he will have helped to bring into the world and the child's mother, then his honest statement of what he intends does not spare him that responsibility.

22 This vision of responsibility assumes that not all moral obligations stem from consent or from a stated intention. The linking of obligations to promises is a rather modern and perhaps uniquely Western way of looking at life, and perhaps a luxury that only the well-to-do can afford. As Fred and Shulamit Korn (a philosopher and an anthropologist) have pointed out, "If one looks at ethnographic accounts of other societies, one finds that, while obligations everywhere play a crucial role in social life, promising is not preeminent among the sources of obligation and is not even mentioned by most anthropologists." The Korns have made a study of Tonga, where promises are virtually unknown but the social order is remarkably stable. If life without any promises seems extreme, we Americans sometimes go too far the other way, parsing not only our contracts but even our marriage vows in order to discover the absolute minimum obligation that we have to others as a result of our promises.

23 That some societies in the world have worked out evidently functional structures of obligation without the need for promise or consent

does not tell us what *we* should do. But it serves as a reminder of the basic proposition that our existence in civil society creates a set of mutual responsibilities that philosophers used to capture in the fiction of the social contract. Nowadays, here in America, people seem to spend their time thinking of even cleverer ways to avoid their obligations, instead of doing what integrity commands and fulfilling them. And all too often honesty is their excuse.

A. *Comprehension*

Choose the answer that best completes each statement. Do not refer to the selection while doing this exercise.

1. Which of the following statements best explains the relationship between honesty and integrity, as the author explains it? (a) Honesty is part of integrity, but integrity requires discernment, while honesty does not; (b) honesty and integrity are so similar in meaning that it is pointless to try to distinguish between them; (c) honesty can be taught, but integrity must be learned; (d) honesty is not as easy to identify in a person's behavior as integrity is.
2. Carter writes that integrity requires three steps. Which of the following was *not* included among them? (a) Distinguishing between what is right and what is wrong; (b) acting upon this distinction, even if it costs you personally; (c) always saying what is right and what is wrong even if it hurts another; (d) stating openly that you are acting upon your distinction between what is right and what is wrong.
3. According to Carter, honesty is the right course of action only when (a) we save our own reputations despite the harm it may do to others; (b) it serves our self-interest; (c) it causes harm to ourselves and spares others from being harmed; (d) we are forced to disclose everything we know, for example, in a court of law.
4. The manager who gives women easier tasks because he is certain they will fail if he gives them harder ones lacks integrity because (a) he has not examined carefully enough whether his beliefs were right in the first place; (b) he has been dishonest with his employees; (c) he has remained true to his own beliefs, even if others do not agree with him; (d) he has made a generalization based on insufficient evidence.
5. A society functions best when its citizens believe in the importance of (a) making contracts to govern every aspect of human relationships; (b) being honest, even if it means abdicating one's responsibilities; (c) keeping promises; (d) recognizing the importance of responsibility rather than mere promises.

B. *Inferences*

Complete the following questions. You may refer to the selection to answer the questions in this section, and in all the remaining sections.

1. Carter suggests that, in any discussion of honesty and integrity, what is most important is (a) to avoid unnecessarily harming another person; (b) to recognize that not everyone knows what these terms mean; (c) to be true to one's beliefs no matter what the consequences; (d) not to disclose everything unless one is absolutely forced to.
2. Look again at the end of paragraph 5. We can infer that (a) racists usually act honestly based on their beliefs; (b) racists have not examined the validity of their beliefs, no matter how honest they think they are being; (c) racists are born, not made; (d) everyone is racist to some degree or other.
3. The hypothetical story of the dying man who confesses his past infidelity to his wife illustrates that (a) his honesty derives from self-interest, not from integrity; (b) it is important to die having confessed to wrongdoings; (c) deathbed confessions are seldom a good idea; (d) he was probably punishing his wife for a miserable marriage.
4. A man who tells a woman that any resulting pregnancy from their relationship is her problem, not his, (a) is not absolved of responsibility just because he has been honest about his feelings; (b) is not responsible morally either for her or for the child; (c) has shown integrity by being up-front from the beginning; (d) is guilty of the worst sort of sexual exploitation.

C. *Structure*

Complete the following questions.

1. The mode of discourse in this essay is (a) narration; (b) description; (c) exposition; (d) persuasion.
2. The *primary* method of development Carter employs throughout the essay, and particularly in paragraphs 4 and 12, is (a) comparison and contrast; (b) cause and effect; (c) classification; (d) definition; (e) explanation.
3. The method of development in paragraphs 7, 8, 13, and 14 is (a) explanation; (b) definition; (c) example and illustration; (d) steps in a process; (e) cause and effect.

4. Why does Carter include paragraphs 17 and 18? What does it add to his discussion? ______
5. The tone of this essay can be best described as (a) reflective, thoughtful; (b) impartial, objective; (c) scholarly, pedantic; (d) uncertain, ambivalent.

D. *Vocabulary*

For each italicized word from the selection, choose the best definition according to the context in which it appears.

1. *discerning* what is right and what is wrong [paragraph 4]: (a) defining; (b) telling the difference between; (c) defending; (d) exhibiting.
2. the first *criterion* [4]: (a) justification; (b) rule; (c) behavior pattern; (d) standard for judging.
3. a person of integrity as *steadfast* [4]: (a) always morally right; (b) hypocritical, phony; (c) firmly resolute; (d) stubborn, unyielding.
4. a *gratuitous* comment [10]: (a) complimentary; (b) unnecessary; (c) tactless; (d) freely stated.
5. honesty is most *laudable* [11]: (a) praiseworthy; (b) jeopardizing; (c) acceptable; (d) damaging.
6. he does not *berate* her [13]: (a) warn; (b) threaten; (c) clash with; (d) rebuke.
7. our politics are so *contentious* [16]: (a) controversial, quarrelsome; (b) difficult to comprehend; (c) resistant to solution; (d) puzzling, confusing.
8. given human *fallibility* [18]: The capability of (a) being perfect; (b) having a misconception; (c) making an error; (d) being an illusion.
9. an *exaltation* of honesty [20]: (a) an example; (b) a raise in status; (c) reliance on; (d) explanation.
10. *parsing* our contracts [22]: (a) breaking down into separate parts and explaining each; (b) revising again and again until each party agrees on terms; (c) defending, upholding; (d) confirming, declaring as true.

E. *Questions for Analysis and Discussion*

1. What is your personal definition of integrity?
2. Is Carter condoning lying? Concerning the hypothetical husband who confesses to an adulterous affair on his deathbed, what would have been the right course of action if she had asked him if he had ever been unfaithful to her?
3. Examine an incident in your life when your behavior showed honesty but not integrity.

Selection 7

Beautiful Girls

Susan Orlean

On December 26, 1996, six-year-old JonBenet Ramsey, was found brutally murdered in the basement of her Boulder, Colorado, home. The case quickly became sensationalized by the media, particularly by tabloid newspapers, for a variety of reasons: Her parents, John and Patsy Ramsey (herself Miss West Virginia in 1977), were wealthy; second, they immediately invited suspicion on themselves because they refused the police's and the FBI's requests to interview them separately. But most of all, JonBenet had been a veteran child beauty pageant contestant, and for months after her death, television viewers saw the same clips of the little girl, heavily made up and provocatively dressed, performing what looked very much like a burlesque show. As of April 1998, the child's murder has not been solved.

Unlike most of the largely negative media publicity about pageants resulting from JonBenet Ramsey's death, in this article, Susan Orlean set out to observe and record the activities behind the scenes at one particular well-known Southern pageant. As Orlean writes near the title in the original magazine article: "The small-town world of children's beauty pageants is as American as mom and apple pie."

Susan Orlean has been a staff writer for The New Yorker *since 1992, where she currently writes a series of columns on American popular culture. Before joining* The New Yorker, *she wrote for the* Boston Globe Sunday Magazine, *the* New York Times Magazine, Spy, *and* Esquire. *She is the author of two books* Red Socks and Blue Fish *and* Saturday Night, *a journal of essays recounting her experiences spending Saturday nights in several American communities.*

1 The Holiday Inn in Prattville, Alabama, is on a grassy rise beside a wide gray highway across from a Waffle House and a McDonald's and several different places to buy gas. One Sunday this spring, the hotel lobby was especially crowded. Some of the people had come straight from church for Sunday lunch: mild-faced women in pastel dresses and men in gray suits and dull-blue ties; boys in white shirts and oxfords and girls in Sunday-school dresses and black Mary Janes. The rest of the people had come for the Universal/Southern Charm children's beauty pageant being held at the hotel. They were wearing stonewashed jeans or leisure outfits, and they were carrying babies or pushing strollers or rushing around leading little girls by the hand, and with a spare finger some of them were balancing hangers that held tiny dresses with ballooning skirts covered by dry cleaners' plastic bags. A few of the littlest babies were fussing. Mothers hurried through the lobby and bumped

their strollers into other mothers' strollers. A miniature dress of green chiffon slid off its hanger and settled onto the carpet with a sigh, and as soon as the woman holding the empty hanger noticed it she yelled, "Nobody move! *Don't step on that dress!*" Then a few three-year-olds started horsing around and squealing, and a cosmetic case slipped out of someone's hand, and, when it landed, out shot a dozen cylinder-shaped things—hair curlers, hairbrushes, lipstick tubes, eyeliner brushes—which rolled in every direction across the floor. A few fathers were sent back to the parking lot to retrieve the shoes or hat or Wet Ones or entry forms that had been left in the car by accident. One mother had spread her baby out on the lobby sofa and was changing her into a lavender Western outfit. In the ladies' room, small dresses and hats were hanging from every ledge they could hang from, and white anklet socks and white shoes and pairs of children's size-2 rhinestone-studded cowboy boots were scattered on the floor, and there was the tangy metallic smell of hot curling irons in the air. In the middle of the room, four women were adjusting the bows in their daughters' hair and smoothing blusher on their cheeks. Across from them, three other women were lined up elbow to elbow. Each one held a Great Lash mascara wand poised like a conductor's baton, and each was facing a lovely little girl in a glittering pageant dress sitting quietly in a sink.

2 I had never been to a beauty pageant before I went to Prattville. For the longest time, the world of children's beauty pageants was invisible to millions of people like me, who don't read *Pageant Life* and *Pageant World,* and don't plan their vacations around the big state finals, and don't have a little girl who has dozens of trophies and crowns and pageant banners in her room. Probably all of that would have remained invisible if someone hadn't murdered JonBenet Ramsey. Once the footage of her in pageant clothes and wearing makeup appeared on the TV news, the world of children's beauty pageants came into sight, and a horrible association was made—not just that a beauty-pageant girl was murdered but that the pageants themselves were depraved and had maybe even contributed to the murder in some way. It was as if you'd never heard of the game of football until the O. J. Simpson trial, and then you'd never been able to separate the crime from the game.

3 But pageants have been taking place all over the country for decades, and in the South, especially, they are as common as barbecue. Pageants are held nearly every Sunday—Sunburst Pageants and Moonbeam Pageants and Miss American Starlet and Glamour Dolls USA Pageants—in meeting rooms at Holiday Inns and Comfort Inns and Best Westerns in places like Florence, Alabama, and Jackson, Mississippi, and Jackson, Tennessee. Every Sunday, pageants have been making winners and losers, inspiring and dashing hopes, wasting some people's money and making some little girls rich. As I left for Alabama, I guessed that I would see some overcompetitive parents and some parents who would

insist on winning even if their kids didn't want to be in a pageant—the same bad things you sometimes see at junior tennis matches and gymnastics meets. I knew that I wasn't going to enjoy seeing three-year-olds wearing eyeliner and crying when they weren't named Supreme Queen. But in spite of what most of the stories that followed JonBenet's murder led me to expect, what I saw in Prattville were not people like the Ramseys, with lots of money and mobility. They were ordinary people: they were dazzled by glamour, and they believed truly and uncynically in beauty and staked their faith on its power to lift you and carry you away. It may be embarrassing or naïve to believe that being Miss America will lead you somewhere in life—unless it happens to be your life, or your daughter's life, and the working-class life that has been assigned to you and your baby feels small and flat and plain. There are only so many ways to get out of a place like Prattville. The crown you win on Sunday might be the chance for your beautiful baby to get a start on a different life, so that someday she might get ahead and get away.

4 Darlene Burgess, who founded the Universal/Southern Charm International Pageant seventeen years ago, told me that ever since JonBenet, people who don't know anything about pageants are peering into the pageant world and then condemning it because they're shocked by the makeup and the dressy dresses and the sexy sophistication of some of the girls. There have been magazine stories and television shows about children's pageants before, but most of them have been for foreign press and TV, so this has really been the first time that the pageant world has been shoved into view. It's not that anyone has anything to hide; it's just that they feel scrutinized and criticized by people who haven't been to a single pageant—people who can't see how proud mothers are when their daughters win, and don't see how pageant people are practically a family, in which everyone knows each other and watches out for each other.

5 Darlene got into pageants purely by accident. She grew up on a farm in Arkansas in the fifties; her mother drove a grain truck, and Darlene lived on her own in town starting at the age of fifteen. She didn't know a thing about pageants and wouldn't have had the money to compete in them even if she had. When she got married, she and her husband, Jerry, who was a pilot for Oral Roberts University, lived in Tulsa. They started their little girl, Becky, in dancing classes at the age of three. Becky was a natural onstage, and Darlene learned to coax out her best performances by waving a flyswatter at her. After a while, Becky's dance teacher entered her in a competition that turned out to be part of a children's pageant. Becky came home that day with a trophy, and Darlene was hooked.

6 Darlene learned about pageants as she went along. One thing she learned was makeup. The dance teacher used some on the girls in their recitals, and Darlene didn't like it at first, but then she agreed that for

pageants Becky needed it. "She was just so pale," Darlene said to me recently. "I just *had* to cake her. Otherwise, she would have been invisible onstage. If you have a baby who's a true blonde, not a browny-blonde, and you put her under those lights, it'll kill her." Darlene herself is tall and substantial and has fair skin and clay-colored hair. She wears big rimless glasses and warmup suits. She has an Arkansas accent, rolling and drawly, and a light, chiming laugh that can put you in an instant good mood. She is self-possessed and capable in a way that is slightly intimidating. When she needed a dress for Becky, she sewed one; when she saw that there was no good pageant-dress business in the area, she started one; when she discovered that no one manufactured mannequins small enough to use for her clients, she built one; and then, when she decided that the pageants Becky was entering were poorly run, she started her own. "I'd hear talk in dressing rooms," Darlene told me. "Like 'If they know you, you win; if they don't, you don't,' and then I was at a pageant and found out that one of the judges was the grandmother of one of the babies, and I thought, I'm going to do my own pageant and do it right." She picked a date, made up flyers, and rented a room. To break even, she had to attract at least fifty kids. She ended up with a hundred and twenty. After a few years, she was able to expand Southern Charm into North Carolina, Mississippi, New York, and Maryland, and she told me that she might soon be adding Virginia and Florida. In each state, Darlene appoints a director to run preliminary pageants and the state finals, and she herself takes care of the national finals. All beauty pageants are owned privately, and most use state directors, as Darlene does. State directors can make money running a pageant, but unless they own a system they need a full-time job. Recently, Darlene's Tennessee directors, a married couple, had to resign, because the man, a Baptist minister, had just got his own church and wasn't free on Sundays anymore.

7 Stacie Brumit, Southern Charm's Alabama state director, arrived at the hotel around noon, loaded down with boxes and bags. The mothers in the lobby hurried with their daughters into a line that started in front of Stacie's registration table and curled down the hall and out the door. Stacie is round-faced and round-shouldered and has a bleached-blond pageboy. She was already heavily into pageants when she signed on to be Darlene's Alabama director—she had competed herself when she was little, and so far she has entered her two-year-old daughter, Brianna, in thirty, starting when Brianna was five months old. "I see how much being in them is giving Brianna, even at her age," she said. "I think she's going to be a great public speaker because of her pageant experience. She's learning poise. She's going to end up being . . . being like the President! I mean, he's not shaky when he's up there speaking." Before becoming a pageant director, Stacie worked at Wal-Mart. This was when she was expecting Brianna, and she says that even though directing a

pageant is hard work, it's nothing compared with sitting on a stool out in the cold in front of a Wal-Mart greeting shoppers when you're six months pregnant and sick as a dog.

8 The kids in line to be registered ranged from six months old to almost but not quite four, and they were beautiful or cute or plain, and they were wearing white satin dresses covered with matching satin capes trimmed with feathers, and peach dresses with beaded bodices and heart-shaped cutouts in the back, and powder-blue dresses with leg-o'-mutton sleeves. The girls who were old enough to have some hair had it swept up, prom style, or left loose and sprayed into curvy shapes, and the bigger girls wore foundation, blusher, eye-shadow, and mascara, and the babies wore no makeup except maybe a little pink gloss on their lips. Some of the mothers wore attractive clothes and had their hair blown smooth, but many were too fat or too thin or looked tired and frayed next to their dazzling daughters. While the mothers were waiting to register, the fathers dawdled in the parking lot having a smoke. The babies napped, and the bigger girls practiced pageant modelling: eye contact with the judges; a wide smile showing one row of teeth; "pretty hands," which means holding your arms straight and slightly lifted, with your hands bent at the wrist and parallel to the floor; and "pretty feet," the pose for the beauty lineup, right heel pressed to left instep, toes wide and apart.

9 To put on a proper pageant, you need trophies and banners and crowns and plaques, and judges who aren't related to any of your contestants, and a master of ceremonies to run the event, and masking tape to make "X"s on the floor showing the kids where to do their modelling turns. If you're giving prize money, you need your prize money, but otherwise you don't need anything else—except in Tennessee and Arkansas, where directors need to post a ten-thousand-dollar bond. Tennessee instituted this practice about twenty years ago, after a pageant director in Nashville was shot and killed by her husband the night before one of her pageants and none of the contestants ever got their entry fees back. Some pageants are scams. Some issue bad checks to the winners or promise scholarships and never come through, and others say they will give you your prize money only if you come to another pageant, and by the time you do that you've spent more money than you would have ever won. There have been occasions when a pageant went bankrupt before any of the winners could collect their money but not before the pageant director had collected a lot of entry fees. Some pageants start late and are run sloppily, and the kids are kept up until all hours and are expected not to complain. Many pageants, though, like Universal/Southern Charm, have been around a long time and are considered quality pageants. Darlene Burgess is strict, and her rules are exacting:

> Contestants should stand still in lineup, no exaggerated poses. Mothers should have control of their child at all times. Baby through 6 years old should wear short dresses. Dresses do not have to be loaded with rhinestones. After 36 months of age, no waving or blowing kisses. Sportswear: This is a garment of your choice but should be dress sportswear such as a jumpsuit . . . something they would wear when dressing up, but not sports related. Black is a very good fashion color now. It is permissible in all age groups if the color is becoming to the contestant. Braces and Missing Teeth: This is just a part of growing up and as long as the contestant smiles and acts naturally you are not to count off. . . . This same principle applies to scratches and similar childhood mishaps. We expect our judges to conduct themselves in a ladylike (gentlemanly) fashion at all times. Judges, No Drinking at any time while you are at this pageant. No exceptions. You must keep in mind that this is a children's pageant and conduct yourselves accordingly.

10 In a stroller in the lobby was Nina from Montgomery, who had a tiny pink face and tiny gold earrings and a scramble of fine red hair. Her pageant dress was still on its hanger. She was napping in a pink sleep suit and a pair of Tweetie Bird shoes. Her mother, Kris Ragsdale, had a long dark braid and a steady, sobering gaze. While she talked, she moved Nina's stroller back and forth, the way you move a vacuum cleaner. Kris told me that she was eighteen and Nina was eight months old. She'd got into pageants this past winter, when she took Nina to the Jefferson Davis Pageant and the Christmas Angel Pageant in Montgomery at the urging of a friend. Kris had never been in a pageant when she was a kid. She mostly lived in foster homes or on her own since she was little, and she got married when she was sixteen. Her husband, James, was dressed in a loose heavy-metal-band T-shirt and an Orlando Magic hat, and he said he worked in Montgomery as a saw sharpener. "He's got a pretty good job," Kris said, rocking the stroller. "Still, I mean, we can hardly save a penny." Until recently, Kris and James shared an apartment with James's ex-girlfriend, James's little son, David, and James's ex-girlfriend's daughter, to save on rent. It cost thirty-five dollars just to enter today's beauty competition, and there were extra fees to enter the contest for Most Photogenic, Most Beautiful, Best Dress, Dream Girl, and Western Wear. There was also the Supreme Special—fifty dollars for all categories except Dream Girl and Western Wear. The fees for national pageants are higher. It costs a hundred and seventy-five dollars to register for the Southern Charm national, and between fifty and a hundred dollars to enter each special category, like Superstar Baby, Talent, Additional Talent, and Southern Belle. Kris said, she'd bought the Supreme Special for Nina today. "You save the money with the Supreme," she explained. "You don't get the Western Wear, but we don't do Western Wear with her yet anyway. The hats are too big for her." She lifted Nina out of the stroller and started changing her carefully into a stiff royal-blue dress.

"My mom got this for me," Kris said. "It was guess how much. Sixty dollars reduced to forty."

11 A woman nearby who heard us talking came over and said to Kris, "Honey, you have to meet Joni Deal. She rents out all sorts of dresses and Western clothes and everything. She'll rent you something nice for the pageants." The woman was here with her granddaughter Rhiannon, who was named for a Fleetwood Mac song and was three years old and big for her age. Rhiannon had been in dozens of pageants and usually won everything except fashion. "We're doing something about that, though," her grandmother said. "We've got something really nice now for her dress. We're not talking about a Kathie Lee off-the-rack-from-Wal-Mart dress, either. I bought her a plain old dress, and then I went to the bridal section at a fabric store and bought a whole lot of trim and beading, and I got out that glue gun and did it myself." She looked at Kris and then said, "For us, losing is not an option."

12 "If we take Nina to the nationals, we're going to have to get her something that's more elegant," James said. "Something more frilly. The judges kill for frilly." In the meantime, Kris said, they had to save for future entry fees, although James hopes they will be able to find a local business that will sponsor Nina; someone told him that a business could claim beauty-pageant fees as a tax deduction. He mentioned that both Nina and David, his little boy, had been offered modelling contracts. "It sounded good," he said, "but it cost about six hundred and fifty dollars just to sign up, and then you had to buy all the makeup and the modelling kit, too, so we decided not to do it." He brightened for a moment. "Something good is definitely going to happen for Nina and David, I think," he said. "Nina's got the pageants, and my ex-girlfriend's talking to some guy right now at Extra Model Management who says he thinks he might be able to get a sitcom for David. That would really be great, but I think it would mean moving to New York, and I don't know how I feel about moving."

13 "It's hard doing pageants, because of the money, but it's worth it," Kris said. "I mean, everybody likes to show off their daughter, right? It's fun for us, and she really enjoys it. It's mother-daughter time, and I know someday we won't have that as much. We're putting all her pageant pictures and scorecards in a scrapbook, so she can have it, and someday she'll be able to see it and all her trophies and say, 'Gee, I did that!' It gives her something she can be proud of."

14 The pageant was about to start, and Kris stood up and attached a bow to Nina's wisps of hair. Nina didn't have enough hair to hold a regular barrette, so Kris had devised something clever with a piece of a zipper she'd cut from a Zip-loc bag. She said she realized that some people might not like pageants, because the thought children shouldn't be exposed to competition this early in their lives, but she and James thought it would be good for Nina—it would give her a head start, especially if Nina

wanted to try for Miss America someday. Kris said, "I know it's a lot of pressure, but, I mean, you know, you're under some kind of pressure your whole entire life."

15 Darlene likes her pageants to start with the babies, because they're at their best in the morning. "You have to do it that way," she said. "Babies just will not put up with an all-day pageant." The room for the competition looked festive. A blue-and-white Southern Charm banner was hanging on the back wall, and beside it was a table loaded with crowns and trophies of all different sizes. The crowns were as big as birthday cakes and were studded with rhinestones. The biggest ones cost almost two hundred dollars apiece. "When Becky was in pageants, she was always getting these so-so crowns," Darlene had complained to me. "I don't want that reputation, so I spend a fortune on my crowns."

16 The judges were two big-boned women with layered haircuts and soft faces. For a few minutes, they murmured to each other, and then looked at Stacie with solemn expressions and nodded. The mothers brought their babies forward one by one and held them facing out toward the judges, fluffing the babies' skirts into meringues of chiffon that billowed up and over the mothers' arms and the babies' dangling legs. Displayed this way, the babies looked weightless and relaxed and sublime, suspended in midair. The judges studied them and scored them in the individual categories while Stacie read introductions: "This is Cheyenne. Her hobbies are playing and cooing. . . . Her favorite food is pears. . . . Her favorite TV show is 'Barney.' She is sponsored today by her friends and family. . . . This is Kayle. . . . Her favorite food is macaroni and cheese. . . . Her hobby is exploring newfound things. . . . This is Taylor. . . . She loves horseback riding and taking her baby cat, Patches, out for walks." One baby picked her nose during her moment at the judging table. Another flailed her arms at the balloons floating above the judges and started to cry. Kris bounced Nina and clucked at her until she finally cracked a gummy smile, but just at that moment both judges happened to look away. Everyone in the audience was standing and waving and aiming toss-away paper cameras at the babies onstage, and everytime a camera flashed the crowns on the table flashed, too.

17 The older girls were divided into age groups of twelve to twenty-three months, twenty-four to thirty-five months, three- and four-year-olds, and so on. Southern Charm accepts girls up to twenty-one years old, but the oldest girl at the Prattville pageant was probably seven. These older children walked onstage by themselves, and some of them even turned the way they were supposed to when they got to the masking-tape "X"s, and a few remembered to do "pretty hands" and "pretty feet" and the grimacing pageant-girl smile. The two-year-olds tended to wander. A blonde from Eclectic named Kendall stood twirling a piece of her hair around her finger and then roamed off the stage. Her

mother was standing next to me, and she said that this would probably be Kendall's last pageant because she hated wearing dresses and was much happier barrel-racing her pony at home.

18 The Southern Charm rules say, "Remember, if you coach from the audience the child will not have eye contact with the judges and they will deduct points for not having eye contact." In spite of that, nearly all the parents were on their feet during the rest of the pageant, making wild hand signals to their daughters which meant "Smile" and "Blow a kiss at the judge" and "Smile much bigger." They pushed to the front of the room, nearly leaning over the judges' shoulders. It was as if someone had set them on a table and then tipped it forward. Just a few minutes after the pageant started, hardly anyone was left sitting in the back of the room.

19 Darlene has forty thousand people on her mailing list, and they are spread out all over the nation. JonBenet Ramsey was one of those names, although she never particularly stood out. Darlene says that in spite of what the papers have said not that many people in the pageant world had heard of JonBenet until she got killed. Right after the murder, Darlene looked up JonBenet's name on her computer and deleted it, so that the Ramseys wouldn't get any upsetting Southern Charm mail.

20 Darlene and Jerry Burgess live about ten miles from downtown Jackson, in an old farmhouse that has been renovated since the days when their daughter, Becky, was at home. (Becky is married and lives in Nashville, where she is studying to go to medical school, and she has a two-year-old daughter, who is just starting on the pageant circuit.) Now the Burgess house is pure pageant. In the outbuildings is a trophy shop and a silk-screening shop where the banners are made and a photography studio where Jerry shoots portfolios of contestants. In the basement is Glitz & Glamour, Darlene's mail-order pageant-dress business, and in the front room are four computers containing all the mailing lists, and eight video machines for copying Jerry's official tapes of the pageants, and Federal Express labels and boxes for the dozen or so Glitz & Glamour dresses and Southern Charm videos they ship out every day.

21 The phone rings all day without stopping, so it is nearly impossible to have an uninterrupted conversation with Darlene. One of the days I was in Jackson, I asked her why she thought people outside the pageant world objected to it so adamantly. "I don't know why they even have an opinion about it at all," she said. "I look at pageants like I look at any other hobby, like golf. I sure wouldn't hit a little white ball around on a lawn and I don't know why anyone else would want to, but that's their business and not mine. Hold on a minute."

22 "Hello, Glitz. . . . Yes, this is Darlene Burgess. . . . O.K., I can send you an entry form. How'd you find out about us? . . . Well, if you want to go to New York, that's a mini-national. Who's crowning in New

York? Let me think. Oh, fiddle! Jerry, who's crowning in New York? Well, I can't remember. . . . So now give me your name and address."

23 Vicki Whitehead, who works at Glitz & Glamour part-time, came upstairs. "Darlene, I have a lady on the phone who has an eight-month-old she says is really tiny and she needs something very dainty for her to wear. And do we have any ultra-suède in an animal print in pink and black? Because I have a lady who's dying for some."

24 Another call for Darlene: "I see. . . . Do you have videos of her in pageants? O.K., send it and I'd be glad to critique it for you." Darlene covered the mouthpiece and said to me, "I'm offering to do it because this lady's up in Illinois and really needs help. They're not too pageant-wise up in places like Illinois. I really think the kids up North are afraid to compete with the kids down South. I remember once Becky said to me, 'Mom, the New York kids are beautiful, but they don't know how to model and they don't know how to dress.' "

25 When Darlene had a break from the phone, she said that nearly every day since JonBenet's murder she has been called by some reporter. So have most of the best known coaches and the owners of the other big pageant systems. Since JonBenet, Darlene has had mothers tell her they weren't going to come to the pageants if reporters would be there, and some mothers have said they had stopped answering their phones because they were sick of being asked to comment on the murder. She is rankled by how dismissive non-pageant people are of everything that she loves about pageants and of how much they mean to these little girls. Some people in pageants have difficult lives and work hard all the time and lose out on a lot, but on any Sunday at a pageant somewhere they have their chance to win. This seems so obvious that Darlene thinks there must be some other reason that pageants have been so maligned. She has finally decided that people who don't appreciate children's pageants probably just don't have their own pretty little girls.

26 From all appearances, Darlene has been a very successful entrepreneur. It happens that most of her state directors are women, and many other pageant systems and pageant-related businesses, like the dress shops, are owned by women. Some of the best-known coaches are women, too. It seems odd that these are the very same women who are certain that a girl's best path in life is to learn how to look good onstage. It's as if they had never noticed that they've made something of themselves by relying on other talents.

27 The first day I was in Jackson, Darlene and I sat in her living room to watch some tapes of last year's Southern Charm national finals, while Jerry was in the other room labelling FedEx boxes with Glitz dresses inside, bound for Irving, Texas, and Lawrenceville, Georgia, and Leesville, Louisiana. To me, all the kids on the tape looked the same—cute, awkward, stiff in their frothy dresses, a little uncertain when they got to the "X"s on the stage. Most of them stared anxiously at their

mothers for directions. Darlene used to judge pageants, and she still has a judge's eye: as we watched the tape, she pointed out winners and losers and which girls had pushy coaches and which girls were wearing makeup that didn't do justice to their skin tone. "This girl, she's beautiful, but her sportswear doesn't do a thing for her, it's too boxy," Darlene pointed out. "I don't like this one's hair all sprayed up like that. I swear, she looks like a Pentecostal! Oh, here's the Southern Belle category. You have to wear something that's historically accurate. My judges get so picky about it that they'll come up onstage and check your dress and make sure you don't have any zippers. . . . Now, look at this baby with her belt sagging. I don't know why these mothers don't realize that a little Velcro under the belt would hold it up. Babies don't have any hips and they have that little potbelly, and a belt just isn't going to stay up on its own."

28 In her personal philosophy, Darlene doesn't like too much eyeliner, and this year she's going to allow only classic Miss America-style modelling in the Swimwear competition. She blames coaches for teaching sexy poses to the girls. "Ten years ago, it wasn't like this," she said. "Now, with the coaches, things are getting out of control." On her granddaughter, Shelby, she likes to see simple makeup and a gorgeous dress, and, since Shelby is doing well, this appears to be working. But some girls do need help to be really big in pageants, according to Darlene. They need coaching, they need advice on their clothes, and, in a few exceptional circumstances, they might even need surgery, although as a rule she doesn't approve. "There was one girl, about thirteen, and it was a special case," Darlene said. "She was a very pretty girl, except she had a really big old honker and it just killed her in the pageants. Even if she hadn't been a pageant child, she was actually better off with a new nose." She has seen kids who are miserable but have been pushed onstage by their mothers, and mothers who yell at their kids when they don't win, and kids falling asleep on their feet because the pageants went on late into the night. "I don't compete the kids at night, but some pageants do," she said. "I remember once Becky had to do her talent at one in the morning. One in the morning! she was exhausted! But the pageant directors insisted on going late. I think that's child abuse."

29 While we talked, Darlene got up to check the chicken in the oven and the fresh bread rising in her breadmaker for lunch. Before we ate, she wanted to show me the winners' speeches at last year's Southern Charm nationals. On the tape, a knock-kneed girl with tawny curls placed a rhinestone Supreme Queen crown on another girl's head. Then the new Supreme Queen started her speech: "I want to say thanks to the Lord Jesus Christ, and thanks to Jerry and Darlene, the directors of the pageant. . . . I want people to know that pageants are about the whole girl, not about who has the best makeup and hair."

30 By the time the Western Wear competition began in Prattville, it was the end of the afternoon. The room was chaotic: people were coming in and out with snacks from a vending machine outside; a lot of the babies were fretting, and a few were yelling as if it were the end of the world. Stacie cast her eye on one of the loudest babies and said into her microphone, "Sounds like we got someone who's not ready for Western Wear!" I was sitting next to this particular loud baby, who was on her mother's lap, and a man behind us was the loud baby's grandfather. He tapped me on the shoulder. "What do you think of this?" he said. "I mean, they're exploiting these kids! Dressing them up, keeping them up all day!"

31 "Daddy, you're supposed to be supporting me, not criticizing me," the baby's mother said. "Look, it's our first pageant and probably our last, but I think it's good to try things. I don't know how I feel about spending so much money. But I like it. It's fun. It's just—Maybe she's not ready." She glanced at her daughter, who was about a year old and was dressed in a satin cowgirl outfit. The outfit looked scratchy. The baby was squirming and weeping. The man said, "Come on, look at her crying, Jeannie! I think it's crazy. And it's a waste of money besides."

32 Stacie Brumit had told me that she'd seen "a lot of mamas dragging their babies kicking and screaming onto the stage." She doesn't like that sort of thing, but she said that some children need extra encouragement. Even Brianna Brumit, who is a veteran, pulls back a little before she has to go onstage. "Once I get her up there, though, she's totally different," Stacie said. "She's just in another world. And it's special for me. For Brianna to go up and win Queen, that's the best thing in the world to me."

33 Nina Ragsdale didn't win Most Photogenic; when Kris asked the judges later, they told her that Nina's pictures needed to show more personality. Nina didn't win Dream Girl, which is based on pure facial beauty; that went to a baby with a peachy face and dark, sleepy eyes. She didn't win Most Beautiful, which is subtly different from Dream Girl, and she didn't win Best Dress; the judges said that blue didn't work for her and that Kris should get her something in turquoise or white. Then the final categories were announced. Nina didn't win Queen or Supreme Queen, and when there were hardly any prizes left to be given out my heart started sinking, but then Nina was named first runner-up and got a medium-sized trophy, and Kris had a moment in which to display her with the trophy on the stage. The baby who won Supreme Queen got a trophy that was taller than any of the children at the pageant. Someone called out, "Honey, if you live in a trailer you're in trouble! You won't be able to get that into your home!"

34 I went back to Alabama a few weeks later to see Nina in another pageant. This one was also at the Prattville Holiday Inn. The pageant was called Lil' American Beauty, and the trophies and the crowns and

the backdrop were different, but the feeling in the air was the same. I recognized some of the kids from Southern Charm. There were only about a dozen girls, so the judging went fast, and just like at the first pageant, I could hardly bear to watch the crowning, Kris Ragsdale stood up there with Nina, who was asleep, her bow sliding out of her hair. The other mothers were also lined up with their babies, shifting them around in their arms like bags of groceries, and they had a little tightness in their faces as they waited to hear what the judges had to say. Most of the babies had curled up and were lost in the folds of their puffy dresses, and suddenly all I could really see were the mothers, wearing their plain outfits and their plain makeup, their husbands and parents standing a few feet away ready to take the picture they were all waiting for, of their beautiful daughters being crowned.

A. *Comprehension*

Choose the answer that best completes each statement. Do not refer to the selection while doing this exercise.

1. Orlean writes that one consequence of JonBenet Ramsey's death was (a) to reveal the previously little-known world of child beauty pageants to the American public; (b) to expose the very real dangers for child beauty pageant contestants; (c) to alert the public to the financial investment beauty pageants entail; (d) to increase public awareness of the riches to be won at such beauty pageants.
2. According to Orlean, most of the people who enter their children in pageants are (a) themselves veterans of such pageants; (b) ordinary people who believe that their children's beauty offers them a way to escape small-town life; (c) living vicariously, deriving secondhand pleasure from their children's success; (d) motivated by greed and the desire to win at any cost.
3. People like Darlene Burgess, founder of Universal Southern Charm International Pageant, believe that JonBenet Ramsey's murder has caused outsiders (a) to demand regulation of the industry; (b) to themselves become involved in these competitions; (c) to scrutinize and unfairly criticize pageants without firsthand knowledge; (d) to ridicule pageants as scams or mere money-making operations.
4. Two states, Tennessee and Arkansas, require (a) pageant sponsors to post a $10,000 bond to cover unforeseen costs; (b) every contestant who enters a child pageant to win a trophy; (c) the directors of such pageants to be certified; (d) the pageant's sponsors to undergo a criminal background check.
5. Some mothers, like Kris Ragsdale, the mother of eight-month-old Nina, justify entering their daughters in such contests because they

are fun and also because (a) they are the required first step for a modeling career; (b) they can provide the child with money for college; (c) they teach a child how to behave in public; (d) they give the child a head start in dealing with pressure.

B. *Inferences*

Complete the following questions. You may refer to the selection to answer the questions in this section, and in all of the remaining sections.

1. In paragraph 3, Orlean discusses her expectations of children's beauty pageants based on the media coverage. What does she imply about this coverage? ____________________________
2. From the details in paragraph 6, what can you infer about Darlene Burgess's contribution to children's beauty pageants? ______________

   ____
3. Again, in paragraph 6, why was Burgess particularly concerned about the people chosen to judge children's pageants? ______________
4. What does Orlean imply in paragraph 8 about the makeup and hair styles that the little girls wear? ____________________________
5. From the details included in paragraph 18, what does Orlean suggest about the behavior of the contestants' mothers? ______________

C. *Structure*

Complete the following questions.

1. The purpose of paragraph 1 is (a) to present the author's point of view; (b) to show the flurry of activity that goes into preparing for a pageant; (c) to justify parents' reasons for entering their daughters in pageants; (d)) to reveal her reason for choosing child beauty pageants as her subject.
2. Read paragraph 2 again. Then write a sentence stating the main idea of the essay. ____________________________________

   ____
3. Why does Orlean restrict her discussion of child pageants to the South?____

4. In paragraph 10, Orlean lists—without comment—some of the entrance fees for regional and national pageants and for the special categories like Superstar Baby, Additional Talent, Southern Belle, and so forth. What contribution to the essay as a whole does this list provide, and how does it serve her purpose?________________

____

____

5. Explain in your own words the impact of the information and details provided in paragraph 34. ________________________

____

D. *Vocabulary*

For each italicized word from the selection, choose the best definition according to the context in which it appears.

1. pageants themselves were *depraved* [paragraph 2]: (a) responsible; (b) morally corrupt; (c) lacking concern; (d) lacking sufficient means for survival.
2. they feel *scrutinized* [4]: (a) beleaguered; (b) threatened; (c) persecuted; (d) under surveillance.
3. the babies looked relaxed and *sublime* [16]: (a) elegant; (b) uncomfortable; (c) heavenly; (d) sleepy.
4. the *grimacing* pageant-girl smile [17]: A facial expression, or in this case, a smile, that shows (a) joy; (b) fear; (c) insincerity; (d) pain.
5. people objected so *adamantly* [21]: (a) unyieldingly; (b) noisily; (c) discourteously; (d) strenuously.
6. pageants have been so *maligned* [25]: (a) defamed; (b) publicized; (c) vulnerable; (d) well-researched.

E. *Questions for Analysis and Discussion*

1. How would you characterize Orlean's point of view, her attitude toward child beauty pageants? Do you see any evidence of bias, whether for or against? As far as you can tell, does she depict the proceedings in a balanced way, or does she betray her sympathies?
2. With respect to the topic of children's beauty pageants and considering your world view, how did you respond to this essay? (More pointedly, would you enter your baby or little girl in such a contest? Why or why not? Clarify your thinking.)

Selection 8

Joe, Montana

Jonathan Raban

In his nonfiction work Bad Land: An American Romance, *from which this excerpt is taken, Jonathan Raban explores the prairie regions of eastern Montana settled by immigrants, who, at the turn of the century, were lured by the promise of 160 acres of free land. The railroad companies and the federal government distributed pamphlets touting the area's potential for wheat farming and promoting the now-discredited technique of "dry farming." Further encouraged by the banks, settlers from Eastern states migrated to the vast empty prairie and tried to establish farms.*

A blend of past and present, Bad Land *recounts the story of these settlers, of their initial successes and their crushing failure during the Depression, and of their descendants. In this selection, Raban visits the town formerly known as Ismay, Montana, which, because of a rock station's promotional gimmick, changed its name to Joe, Montana, in honor of the famous '49er and Chiefs quarterback. Raban is the author of several other nonfiction books, among them* Arabia: A Journey Through the Labyrinth *and* Old Glory: An American Voyage, *and a novel* Foreign Land. Bad Land *won the National Book Critics Circle Award for nonfiction in 1996. (Mike Worsell, mentioned in the middle of the piece, lived in the town as a child and served as the author's traveling companion and tour guide.)*

1 Our course converged with the drab green rift of the cottonwoods on Fallon Creek. We crossed a wooden bridge over the river, still swollen and turbid from the recent rains, jolted over the one-track line of the old Milwaukee Road, and were in Ismay—or what had been Ismay but was Ismay no longer. The name on the sign had been painted out and replaced with *Joe*. Population 28.

2 When it first came into the world, Ismay had been idly, capriciously named, as if it were a goldfish or a hamster. It had nearly jettisoned its name in 1912, when the *Titanic* went down and Bruce Ismay, the chairman of the shipping line, allegedly elbowed his way ahead of the women and children in the race for the lifeboats. Then the town had voted, narrowly, to remain Ismay and tough out the jokes at its name's expense. It had even made it into the gazetteer of the *Times Atlas of the World,* where Ismay, Montana, is sandwiched between Ismaning, Germany, and Ismetpasa, Turkey. But the glue on the name had lost its sticking power, and Ismay was now Joe, at least on a part-time basis. On local maps it was variously represented as Ismay (Joe) and Joe (Ismay). If this went on much longer, the town would boast a patrician string of names like George (Herbert) (Walker) (Bush).

3 Its new *a.k.a.*[1] was a bid to cash in on a celebrity's celebrity. In 1993, when the Kansas City Chiefs bought the star quarterback, Joe Montana, from the San Francisco 49ers, Montana, at thirty-three, was an old man. His knees were going, his upper torso was a monument to the unceasing labour of the surgeon and the chiropractor. He was in his sunset years, and the Chiefs purchased him more for his name, and the glory of his past, than for his continuing abilities on the field. They played him sparingly, a quarter here, a quarter there, wheeling him out on special occasions, as a Mediterranean village might display its famous reliquary of saint's bones.

4 It was a disc jockey at a rock radio station in Kansas City who came up with the idea of turning Joe Montana, or, rather, Joe, Montana, into a place on the map. What was needed was some ailing townlet in the deep sticks, just big enough to have a US Post Office for the souvenir mail frankings. It could become an object of tourist pilgrimage. It could build a museum of Joe Montana memorabilia. It could make a big killing with Joe, Montana, T-shirts. As the people at the radio station saw it, this was an offer that no ailing townlet could afford to turn down.

5 They began calling around the great length and breadth of Area Code 406. They called the one-stoplight towns, the no-stoplight towns, the wide places in the road—and met with a surprising number of gruff refusals. People are sentimentally attached to the names that served their parents and grandparents, even when the names are of the kind that you would have thought anyone would be glad to be rid of, like Molt, Iron, Straw, Yaak, Stumptown, Twodot, Agency, Crackerville. Zero, Montana, might have been a likely taker, but it had lost its post office in 1957.

6 Finally, they got through to Ismay, the smallest incorporated city in the state, six miles from the nearest blacktop road and largely in ruins. Ismay bought the pitch and changed its name. It had been Joe for nearly a year when we arrived, and already the fame of the football player had rubbed off on what was left of the town and set it ostentatiously apart from its mouldering neighbours.

7 Fame transforms—even fame at second remove, like the dilute solution of the stuff that gets sprayed on the brother of a First Lady or the one-time roommate of a celebrated murderer. Taciturn lummoxes suddenly acquire self-consciousness and start taking their own mumblings seriously. They learn to pose for the camera, sticking out their chins to lose their drinkers' jowls, and make the awful discovery that they are *interesting*. Sprinkle a few droplets of the substance on people who have been mutes for the better part of a lifetime, and they cannot be persuaded to stop talking.

[1]Short for "also known as."

8 So it was with Ismay. The town had grown garrulous with signs and messages. From the railroad tracks, it looked much like its sister, Mildred, sixteen miles down the line: a scattered wood-lot; the fuel supply, apparently, for the two or three houses that were still inhabited. Nearly all of the buildings were deeply stooped, sunk to their knees, or pancaked flat and melting rapidly back into the earth. The difference was that in Ismay (Joe) or Joe (Ismay), every heap of bleached grey timber had acquired a new varnished shingle telling the visitor what the heap had been. *The Cass-Hamilton Store. Grey Gables Hotel. J.E. Prindle, Real Estate. Brackett Hotel. Robert, Livery.* A lump of scabbed concrete in the grass had a shingle saying that it had once supported the safe of the Ismay First National Bank. The bank itself, like the high school and the department store, had long gone, its bricks carted off by the local ranchers to build add-ons to their houses.

9 Where Mildred was a wreck, Ismay was a museum. Its dereliction was curated, and the shingles had turned it, at a stroke, into a tourist-attractive *objet,*[2] a slice of authentic Americana. Ismay reached its semiological climax at the mustard-yellow Catholic church, whose south wall had been covered in graffiti. In letters of varying sizes, some in red, some in white paint, the wall now read:

JOE'S CAREER
—
NOTRE DAME → NATIONAL CHAMPS 1977
1975–78

SAN FRANCISCO 1978–93

4=SUPER BOWLS
JOE = 3 MVP'S

KANSAS CITY CHIEFS

I thought the peculiar symbol at the base of the design was an eye, of the kind that Maltese fishermen paint on the prows of their boats to ward off the evil spirits of the deep. Mike, a dour literalist, thought it was a football. I conceded that though it might have been intended to be a football, it was also an eye; Joe's eye, brooding over his damaged body below.

10 'Superstitious people have sometimes seen it wink.'

11 Mike,[3] searching for his childhood here, was lost. All his remembered landmarks were gone, and the shingles were no help.

12 *Ryan Clothing—Millinery & Maternity.*

[2]French for "object," more precisely an object of some artistic value, here used ironically.
[3]Mike Worsell lived in Ismay as a child and served as the author's traveling companion and tour guide. His grandparents had been early settlers in the area.

13 'I don't recall any Ryans.'

14 'Do you think there might be anyone still here from then?'

15 'No—they're all planted in the marble orchard now.'

16 Aside from the grain elevator, much the biggest thing in town was the cinderblock hangar of the new fire hall and community centre. It straddled two blocks, and was an evident statement of faith in Joe's future. We looked through a window at an unfinished room large enough to seat several hundred people. If everyone who lived at present within a twenty-five mile radius were to assemble here, there would still be rows and rows of empty chairs. It would require some astounding renaissance for this great white elephant to earn its keep.

17 'Maybe my grandmother's house is somewhere under there,' Mike said.

18 Five minutes later, he relocated the house on a patch of empty waste ground a block east of the patch of empty waste ground that had been the First National Bank. He walked slowly, making abrupt right-angled turns, opening invisible doors and going from room to non-existent room. 'I think this is it—'

19 Ten minutes later, he found it. The house was still, just, standing, though its roof was hogged, drooping at both ends like the keel of a rotten ship, and it had lost most of its tiles. Here and there, flakes of white paint still clung to the bare planks of the one-story cottage, and a stubborn wisteria vine lived on, trailing from the eaves of the porch and blotting out the front door in a bushy green cascade.

20 'I missed it first time round because of the porch. That porch is new.'

21 *New?* It appeared to be every bit as old and ruinous as the rest.

22 'Shall we go in?'

23 'No. This is enough. I wouldn't want to trouble the mice.'

24 A dust devil haunted the remains of Ismay. It kept on showing over the balding roofs, a whirling cyclone of blown dirt, whose shifting, angular track kept pace with our own. At a street-end, it revealed its source: a frizzy-haired woman in specs and stretch pants, astride a bright red garden tractor with balloon tyres. The postmaster. She wore her government name tag on her blouse: Loreen Nemitz.

25 Her official title did not do her justice. Mrs Nemitz was the *genius loci*[4] of the town. The Nemitzes, newcomers by local standards (Mrs Nemitz and her husband had arrived in Ismay from the Midwest in the 1970s), ran the place. Her husband ran the trucking business; a son ran the grain elevator and was the mayor; her daughter-in-law was the treasurer of the Joe business.

26 The family HQ was a double-fronted trailer, set in a sort of rusty shrubbery of trucks, cars, loose boxes and assorted machine and auto parts.

[4]A Latin phrase meaning, in this context, the guardian deity of a place.

27 'Nice place you have here,' Mike said warmly. He was evidently missing his boatyard. Mrs Nemitz, scenting sarcasm, put his face on trial for a split second, but found it not guilty.

28 Inside the trailer, the mayor and the city treasurer were eating warm brownies from a baking tray and the next generation of Nemitz children were engaged in clumsy espionage activities from behind partially closed doors. Mike explained about his childhood evacuation to Ismay—how he and his brother and sisters had been sent to stay with their grandmother at the house with the wire fence and the wisteria. The old Amundson place . . .?

29 'We own that.'

30 'So what is it you want to know?'

31 Watching the children play at being spies, I thought that perhaps Mike and I were being mistaken for plain-clothes investigators from some federal agency, like OSHA or the EPA. In my bland, know-nothing English voice I said that I was interested in Ismay's transformation into Joe.

32 'You a reporter? You work for a magazine?' Mrs Nemitz said.

33 'No—' But she had my number. And I was a spy.

34 'They did an article about us in *Sports Illustrated.*'

35 A copy was produced. The smiling Nemitzes were in colour, and centre-stage. The text of the piece, about the little town that changed its name, was predictably larksome.

36 'We've been in the *Wall Street Journal,* the *New York Times* . . .'

37 '*USA Today* . . .'

38 'We've been in all the newspapers.'

39 The town now had an agent—a man in Billings, from whose fax machine regular news flashes about the affairs of Joe, Montana, were issued, coast to coast, from New York to Los Angeles. Not since around 1910 had Ismay been the focus of such publicity.

40 The whole town had been flown to Kansas City, where they had watched the Chiefs play and had an audience with Joe Montana. They'd returned home with a clutch of autographed footballs. A San Francisco TV station had made a film about them. Next month they were going to be on David Letterman.

14 'All twenty-eight of you?'

42 'They're flying us out to New York, all expenses paid.'

43 'The date's not quite fixed yet, but they're talking about June 23rd.'

44 'Dave himself is real eager to have us on the show.'

45 'That's going to be a big boost for Joe Montana Day.'

46 Joe Montana Day was to be on 3 July, with a parade, a rodeo, cowboy poetry, the Ismay school reunion, a fiddlers' jamboree and dance, and a firework display. The first Joe Montana Day, held the previous year, had drawn two thousand visitors, even though it was advertised only locally and—in a reversal of the usual story—had been wrecked by

a violent rainstorm. The proceeds had financed the building of the new fire hall and community centre. They'd sold more T-shirts, sweatshirts, bumper stickers, baseball caps and souvenir mugs than they could count, and done a fine trade in commemorative cards and letters franked *Joe, Montana.*

47 This year, after the Letterman show, the Nemitzes were forecasting something more on the scale of the Gold Rush or the Normandy landings. Retired couples in Winnebago motor homes, roaming the country in search of novelties and 'attractions', were already on their way. The media would be there; and where the media went, the people followed, like rats marching to the pied piper.

48 'Joe Montana is coming—'

49 'Maybe. We hope.'

50 'Our agent is talking to his agent.'

51 'Already they say the motels are booked solid for the weekend. You won't find a room between here and Billings . . .' Billings was 200 miles distant.

52 'Sounds like a nice piece of business for the Porta-Potty man.' This was Mike's contribution to the dialogue, and it earned his face another brief trial, and another not-quite-guilty verdict.

53 'You want to see the film the San Francisco people made about us?'

54 The tape was already lodged in the VCR. Maybe it dwelled there permanently. The mayor aimed the remote at the set; a picture of an empty, buff-yellow landscape bloomed on the screen.

55 The film began in happy comedy. In a rented car, on the deserted ribbon of US Highway 12, the TV crew were trying to find Joe, Montana. That we were way back in the back of beyond here was established when the presenter turned on the car radio and set the Scan button to march up and down the airwaves on the FM band. From 76 MHz to 108 MHz, the radio, empty of voices, held only static, like the sound of wind in dry grass. The car stopped. The crew sought directions from a farmer. He'd never heard of Joe, Montana. The name Ismay rang a faint bell with him, however, and he gestured vaguely northwards, to Saskatchewan. And so it went—with people racking their brains, shaking their heads, and pointing unconfidently in the wrong direction. The blacktop gave way to dirt; the crew—a merry bunch of prairie sailors—sighted *Joe, MT,* painted on a plank nailed to a fencepost, and eventually discovered the Nemitzes, living, as it were, in Ultima Thule.[5]

56 In the Nemitz trailer, the film was going out under Jesus's name. On top of the TV set was a puzzle, made of ivory-coloured plastic

[5]An allusion to a place considered by ancient Greek geographers to be the most northerly habitable world, supposedly an island somewhere north of Britain, but also associated with Iceland and Norway. Given the context—the TV crew's inability to find Joe (or Ismay)—Raban means that the town was remote.

blocks; correctly assembled, it spelled JESUS, and this peculiar object, set over the wide screen like a title, was a troubling distraction for the eye. One kept on trying to forge a connection between the title and the picture. The thing generated a kind of wanton irony that attached itself to whatever was happening on screen.

57 The crew were now riding down Main Street on a horse-drawn wagon while the mayor and the city treasurer pointed out the major buildings in the town.

58 'That one?' said the presenter.

59 'Condemned,' said the mayor.

60 'And that?'

61 'Condemned.'

62 Tax-delinquency had put nearly all of the real-estate in Ismay into the hands of the city. The city was, to all intents and purposes, one family. So if the fortunes of the city boomed . . . But the TV crew were not interested in going down that avenue of speculation: after their long drive from Billings airport, they had found the warm, pulsing heart of the heartland, and they were in a celebratory mood.

63 A rubicund cattleman allowed that his ranch was somewhat larger than the entire city of San Francisco. Another was asked to put a price on land hereabouts. Oh, he said; it varied. Could go for as much as a hundred, hundred and twenty; could be as little as fifty.

64 'Fifty! Dollars! An Acre!' said the presenter to camera in his *hear that, folks? voice.*

65 The wrap-up was an earnest paean to life in this crime-free community, where everybody knew everybody else and everybody pulled on the same oar together under an unpolluted sky. The TV crew would, the presenter said, take back with them to San Francisco something more than mere fond memories of Joe: they would carry with them values learned here that had been long lost in urban America—the elemental values of people who live in daily contact with nature, like neighbourliness, humility, good humour and serenity of mind.

66 The camera, which had been tight on the presenter's face, tracked back to take in the cheerful huddle of farming families behind him, and their enormous country, turning gold in the evening light. Its empty treelessness, once famously daunting, was balm for the eye, and the camera loved it.

67 It was a new slant. First, this landscape had been seen as lawless and violent. Then it became a problem to be solved—hard to get in focus, hard to paint and photograph, hard, but possible, to farm. Now it was being perceived as Arcadia,[6] a blessed land of pastoral simplicity and happiness, and going for a song at fifty bucks an acre.

[6]An allusion to a region in ancient Greece that was isolated from the rest of the civilized world. Its residents lived a simple, pastoral life. Raban uses the allusion ironically.

68 The eighteen-minute film was an updated video remake of the railroad pamphlets—and it was every bit as alluring to the 1990s tourist as the pamphlets had been to the 1909 settler.

69 After the show, Mrs Nemitz mounted her tractor and led the Jeep back to the fire hall so that we could buy souvenirs. Inside, the place was even bigger than it had appeared through the window; a gaunt, incomplete secular cathedral, littered with saw-horses and smelling of sheetrock and gypsum. Thousands of caps and T-shirts were stacked up in anticipation of 3 July; enough to clothe a Third World army or the victims of a historic catastrophe.

70 Mike splashed out on a lurid Joe, Montana, football jacket to scandalize his wife. I bought the cheapest and plainest variety of Joe, Montana, coffee mug.

71 'See you on Letterman—' I said.

72 Driving out of town, past the double-fronted trailer, we were chased by a howling mutt.

74 At the Montana Hotel in Baker, a little over twenty miles from Joe, I asked the owner if there was any chance of my finagling a room for the great weekend. She looked in the book. 'Sure. No problem. What room would you like? Number 1 again?'

Postscript: The second annual Joe Montana Day did not live up to the Nemitzes' expectations. Instead of the anticipated crowd of 4,000–6,000 visitors, Raban estimates that around 800 people showed up for the parade, rodeo, and fireworks. The town was also stuck with a huge number of unsold Joe Montana coffee mugs, T-shirts, and bumper stickers. The festival's organizers blamed the day's low attendance on David Letterman's failure to honor his invitation and Joe Montana's failure to show up.

A. *Comprehension*

Choose the answer that best completes each statement. Do not refer to the selection while doing this exercise.

1. Raban writes that the town of Ismay, Montana, changed its name to Joe, Montana, (a) to lure a new generation of settlers to the town; (b) to cash in on the football player's celebrity status; (c) to provide much-needed cash for its annual summer festival; (d) to ensure that the government would not close the town's post office.
2. Raban describes the town of Ismay (or Joe) as (a) a museum preserving beautifully renovated buildings; (b) a thriving community; (c) an ailing town without even a post office; (d) a ruined town except for new signs commemorating the ramshackle buildings.

3. Concerning the turnout for the second annual Joe Montana Day, the townspeople were (a) apprehensive; (b) overly optimistic; (c) convinced that David Letterman would attend; (d) flattered by the attention from the major television networks.
4. Mrs. Nemitz initially thought that Raban and Mike Worsell were (a) television station representatives; (b) spies or federal plainclothes investigators; (c) postal service officials; (d) real estate speculators.
5. The San Francisco television crew that made the film about the town (a) were uncomplimentary in their coverage; (b) had trouble even finding the town; (c) never showed the film; (d) exposed the residents as greedy and publicity hungry.

B. *Inferences*

On the basis of the evidence in the paragraph, mark these statements as follows: PA for inferences that are probably accurate and PI for inferences that are probably inaccurate. You may refer to the selection to answer the questions in this section, and in all of the remaining sections.

1. ______ The plans for the second annual Joe Montana Day were much more elaborate than those for the first one.
2. ______ Several towns in Montana wanted to adopt "Joe" as their new name.
3. ______ The radio station was responsible for exaggerating the benefits that would accrue to the town of Ismay if it changed its name.
4. ______ The television film coverage of Joe, Montana, realistically captured the the town's spirit, its residents, and their values.

C. *Structure*

Complete the following questions.

1. Which *two* of these phrases from the essay best express the irony that lies at the heart of this essay? (a) "The glue on the name had lost its sticking power"; (b) "Fame transforms"; (c) "Ismay's transformation into Joe"; (d) "Where the media went, the people followed, like rats marching to the pied piper"; (e) "a slice of authentic Americana."
2. In the first sentence of paragraph 9, the relationship between the two clauses is (a) comparison; (b) general idea and a supporting example; (c) contrast; (d) cause and effect.
3. Consider these two examples of Raban's style: In paragraph 47, referring to the Second Annual Joe Montana Day, he writes "This year, after the Letterman show, the Nemitzes were forecasting something

more on the scale of the Gold Rush or the Normandy landings," and in paragraph 69, describing the caps and T-shirts amassed for the second festival, he writes that there were "enough to clothe a Third World army or the victims of a historic catastrophe." Both of these are an example of (a) an oxymoron; (b) hyperbole; (c) personification; (d) metonymy; (e) understatement.

4. What is the purpose of paragraph 67 with respect to the essay as a whole?____________________________
5. We can accurately conclude that Joe's residents, and especially the Nemitzes, are (a) psychologically delusional; (b) unrealistic in their expectations and publicity hungry; (c) cynical and mistrustful; (d) justifiably proud of their town and its history.
6. In paragraph 51 one of the Nemitzes remarks that the second festival would draw so many visitors that hotel rooms would sold out from as far as 200 miles away. In light of this remark, when Raban writes that he had no trouble locating a room in the next town, he is (a) nasty and sarcastic; (b) humorously ironic in a pathetic way; (c) complimentary, laudable; (d) only joking.

D. *Vocabulary*

For each italicized word from the selection, choose the best definition according to the context in which it appears.

1. still swollen and *turbid* [paragraph 1]: (a) turbulent; (b) clear; (c) muddy; (d) deep.
2. Ismay had been *capriciously* named [2]: (a) done impulsively; (b) aptly; (c) inaccurately; (d) unluckily.
3. it had nearly *jettisoned* its name [2]: (a) changed; (b) discarded; (c) publicized; (d) hidden.
4. a *patrician* string of names [2]: Referring to names that (a) are hard to pronounce; (b) are notorious; (c) belong to celebrities; (d) belong to aristocratic families.
5. set it *ostentatiously* apart [6]: (a) ostensibly; (b) pretentiously; (c) carefully; (d) clearly.
6. from its *mouldering* neighbors [American spelling *moldering;* 6]: (a) moss-covered; (b) economically thriving; (c) crumbling to dust; (d) bankrupt.
7. *taciturn lummoxes* [7]: (a) untalkative stupid people; (b) arrogant showoffs; (c) slick self-promoters; (d) star-struck groupies.
8. the town had grown *garrulous* with signs [8]: (a) self-congratulatory; (b) wordy; (c) excessively self-absorbed; (d) filled with civic pride.

9. the text was particularly *larksome* [35]: (a) trivial, irrelevant; (b) superficial; (c) expressing cheerful praise; (d) heavily censored.
10. a kind of *wanton* irony [56]: (a) extravagant; (b) weird; (c) inappropriate; (d) delicate.
11. an earnest *paean* to life [pronounced pē'ən; 65]: (a) an expression of celebration and joy; (b) an advertising slogan; (c) a cliché; (d) an exposure of corruption.
12. once famously *daunting* [66]: (a) spirit-lifting; (b) esthetically pleasing; (c) discouraging; (d) seductive.

E. Questions for Discussion and Analysis

1. Is Raban biased, or does he aim to present a fair portrait of an ailing prairie town and its attempts to remain viable?
2. Would you characterize Raban's sense of humor as ironic? cynical? sarcastic? witty and amusing? Point to examples to support your answer.
3. Raban's book explores in great detail the suffering endured by the early 20th-century settlers who moved to eastern Montana with high hopes of turning prairie into productive wheat farms. In light of this area's shared history, do the town's efforts to stay afloat seem more reasonable, or are the residents simply being foolish and unrealistic?

Selection 9

A Neurologist's Notebook: A Surgeon's Life

Oliver Sacks

Born in London, Oliver Sacks received his education in London, at Oxford, in California, and in New York. He is professor of clinical neurology at Albert Einstein College of Medicine in New York, a consultant at the Bronx State Hospital, and the author of many books about odd neurological conditions. Some of his best known books are The Man Who Mistook His Wife for a Hat *(1985);* Seeing Voices *(1989);* Awakenings *(1991), which was made into a movie starring Robin Williams and Robert DeNiro; and* The Island of the Colorblind *(1996). The book from which this excerpt comes,* An Anthropologist on Mars: Seven Paradoxical Tales *(1995), is described like this on the book jacket: "Neurological patients are travelers to unimaginable lands." In this book Sacks offers portraits of seven such travelers, each of whom exhibits a paradox: However abnormal their afflictions may be to us, they have been able to "develop virtues and beauties of their own." Sacks profiles a Canadian surgeon, called here "Carl Bennett," who has Tourette's Syndrome, a neurological disorder marked by compulsive tics and often inappropriate verbal outbursts. Paradoxically, Bennett is an eminent and skilled surgeon.*

1 Tourette's syndrome is seen in every race, every culture, every stratum of society; it can be recognized at a glance once one is attuned to it; and cases of barking and twitching, of grimacing, of strange gesturing, of involuntary cursing and blaspheming were recorded by Aretaeus of Cappadocia almost two thousand years ago. Yet it was not clinically delineated until 1885, when George Gilles de la Tourette, a young French neurologist—a pupil of Charcot's, and a friend of Freud's—put together these historical accounts with observations of some of his own patients. The syndrome as he described it was characterized, above all, by convulsive tics, by involuntary mimicry or repetition of others' words or actions (echolalia and echopraxia), and by the involuntary or compulsive utterances of curses and obscenities (coprolalia). Some individuals (despite their affliction) showed an odd insouciance or nonchalance; some a tendency to make strange, often witty, occasionally dreamlike associations; some extreme impulsiveness and provocativeness, a constant testing of physical and social boundaries; some a constant, restless reacting to the environment, a lunging at and sniffing of everything, or a sudden flinging of objects; and yet others an extreme stereotypy and obsessiveness—no two patients were ever quite the same.

2 Any disease introduces a doubleness into life—an "it," with its own needs, demands, limitations. With Tourette's, the "it" takes the form of explicit compulsion, of a multitude of explicit compulsions: one is driven to do this, to do that, against one's will. Tourette's may seize control at any time. Being "taken over" or "possessed" can be more than a figure of speech for someone with severe Tourette's, and no doubt in the Middle Ages Tourette's was sometimes seen as "possession." (Tourette himself was fascinated by the phenomenon of "possession," and wrote a play about the epidemic of demonic possession in medieval Loudun.)

3 But the relation of disease and self, "it" and "I," can be particularly complex in Tourette's, especially if it has been present from early childhood, growing up with the self, intertwining itself in every possible way. The Tourette's and the self shape themselves each to the other, come more and more to complement each other, until finally, like a long-married couple, they become a single, compound being. This relation is often destructive, but it can also be constructive, can add speed and spontaneity, and a capacity for unusual and sometimes startling performance. For all its intrusiveness, Tourette's may be used creatively, too.

4 Yet in the years after its first delineation, Tourette's tended to be seen not as an organic but as a "moral" disease—an expression of mischievousness or weakness of the will, to be treated by rectifying the will. From the nineteen-twenties to the nineteen-sixties, it tended to be seen as a psychiatric disease, to be treated by psychoanalysis or psychotherapy; but this, on the whole, proved ineffective, too. Then, with the demonstration, in the early sixties, that the drug haloperidol could dramatically suppress its symptoms, Tourette's was regarded—in a sudden reversal—as a chemical disease, the result of an imbalance of a

neurotransmitter, dopamine, in the brain. But all these views are partial, and reductive, and fail to do justice to the full complexity of Tourette's, which may be almost as complex as human nature itself. Neither a biological nor a psychological nor a moral-social viewpoint is adequate; we must see Tourette's simultaneously from all three perspectives—as a biopsychosocial disorder. And one that is far from uncommon: it affects perhaps one person in a thousand.

5 Many professions, one would think, would be closed to someone with elaborate tics and compulsions, but this does not seem to be the case. We find people with Tourette's—sometimes the most severe Tourette's—in virtually every walk of life. There are Tourettic writers, mathematicians, musicians, actors, disk jockeys, construction workers, mechanics, athletes. Some things, one might think, would be completely out of the question—above all, perhaps, the intricate, precise, and steady work of a surgeon. This would have been my own belief not so long ago. But now, improbably, I know *five* surgeons with Tourette's.

6 I first met Dr. Carl Bennett, as I will call him, at a scientific conference on Tourette's in Boston last year. His appearance was unexceptionable—he was fiftyish, of middle size, with a brownish beard and mustache containing a hint of gray, and was dressed soberly in a dark suit—until he suddenly lunged or reached for the ground or jumped or jerked. I was struck both by his bizarre tics and by his dignity and calm. When I expressed incredulity about his choice of profession, he invited me to visit and stay with him, where he lived and practiced, in a town that I will call Branford, in British Columbia—to do rounds at the hospital with him, to scrub with him, to see him in action. Now, four months later, in early October, I found myself in a small plane approaching Branford, full of curiosity and mixed expectations. Dr. Bennett met me at the airport, greeted me—a strange greeting, half-lunge, half-tic; a gesture of welcome idiosyncratically Tourettized—grabbed my case, and led the way to his car in an odd, rapid skipping walk, with a skip each fifth step and sudden reachings to the ground as if to pick something up.

7 The situation of Branford is almost idyllic, nestled as it is in the shadow of the Rockies, in southeast British Columbia, with Banff and its mountains to the north, and Montana and Idaho to the south; it lies in a region of great gentleness and fertility but ringed with mountains, glaciers, lakes. Bennett himself has a passion for geography and geology; a few years ago he took a year off from his surgical practice to study both at the University of Victoria. As he drove, he pointed out moraines, stratifications, and other formations, so that what had at first seemed to my eyes a mere pastoral landscape became charged with a sense of history and chthonic forces, of immense geological vistas. Such keen, fierce attention to every detail, such constant looking below the surface, such examination and analysis, is characteristic of the restless,

questioning Tourettic mind. It is, so to speak, the other side of its obsessive and perseverative tendencies, its disposition to reiterate, to touch again and again.

8 And, indeed, whenever the stream of attention and interest was interrupted, Bennett's tics and iterations immediately reasserted themselves—in particular, obsessive touchings of his mustache and glasses. His mustache had constantly to be smoothed and checked for symmetry, his glasses had to be "balanced"—up and down, side to side, diagonally, in and out—with sudden, ticcy touchings of the fingers, until these, too, were exactiy "centered." There were also occasional reachings and lungings of his right arm; sudden, compulsive touchings of the windshield with both forefingers ("The touching has to be symmetrical," he commented); sudden repositionings of his knees, or the steering wheel ("I have to have the knees symmetrical in relation to the steering wheel. They have to be *exactly* centered"); and sudden, high-pitched vocalizations, in a voice completely unlike his own, that sounded like "Hi, Patty," "Hi, there," and, on a couple of occasions, "Hideous!" (Patty, I learned later, was a former girlfriend, her name now enshrined in a tic.)

9 There was little hint of this repertoire until we reached town, and got obstructed by traffic lights. The lights did not annoy Bennett—we were in no hurry—but they did break up the driving, the kinetic melody, the swift, smooth stream of action, with its power to integrate mind and brain. The transition was very sudden: one minute, all was smoothness and action; the next, all was broken-upness, pandemonium, riot. When Bennett was driving smoothly, one had the feeling not that the Tourette's was in any way being suppressed but that the brain and the mind were in a quite different mode of action.

10 Another few minutes, and we had arrived at his house, a charming, idiosyncratic house with a wild garden, perched on a hill overlooking the town. Bennett's dogs, rather wolflike, with strange, pale eyes, barked, wagged their tails, bounded up to us as we drove in. As we got out of the car, he said "Hi, puppies!" in the same quick, odd, high, crushed voice he had earlier used for "Hi, Patty!" He patted their heads, a tic-like, convulsive patting, a quick-fire volley of five pats to each, delivered with a meticulous symmetry and synchrony. "They're grand dogs, half-Eskimo, half-malamute," he said. "I felt I should get two of them, so they could companion each other. They play together, sleep together, hunt together—everything." and, I thought, are patted together: did he get two dogs partly because of his own symmetrical, symmetrizing compulsions? Now, hearing the dogs bark, his sons ran out—two handsome teen-age kids. I had a sudden feeling that Bennett might cry "Hi, kiddies!" in his Touretty voice, and pat their heads, too, in synchrony, symmetrically. But he introduced them, Mark and David, indi-

vidually to me. And then, as we entered the house, he introduced me to his wife, Helen, who was preparing a late-afternoon tea for all of us.

11 As we sat at the table, Bennett was repeatedly distracted by tics—a compulsive touching of the glass lampshade above his head. He had to tap the glass gently with the nails of both forefingers, to produce a sharp, half-musical click or, on occasion, a short salvo of clicks. A third of his time was taken up with this ticcing and clicking, which he seemed unable to stop. Did he have to do it? Did he have to sit there?

12 "If it were out of reach, would you still have to click it?" I asked.

13 "No," he said. "It depends entirely on how I'm situated. It's all a question of space. Where I am now, for example, I have no impulse to reach over to that brick wall, but if I were in range I'd have to touch it perhaps a hundred times." I followed his glance to the wall, and saw that it was pockmarked, like the moon, from his touchings and jabbings; and, beyond it, the refrigerator door, dented and battered, as if from the impact of meteorites or projectiles. "Yeah," Bennett said, now following my glance. "I fling things—the iron, the rolling pin, the saucepan, whatever—I fling things at it if I suddenly get enraged." I digested this information in silence. It added a new dimension—a disquieting, violent one—to the picture I was building, and seemed completely at odds with the genial, tranquil man before me.

14 "If the light so disturbs you, why do you sit near it?" I asked.

15 "Sure, it's 'disturbance,'" Bennett answered. "But it's also stimulation. I like the feel and the sound of the 'click.' But, yeah, it can be a great distraction. I can't study here, in the dining room—I have to go to my study, out of reach of the lamp."

16 Another expression of his Tourette's—very different from the sudden impulsive or compulsive touching—is a slow, almost sensuous pressing of the foot to mark out a circle in the ground all around him. "it seems to me almost instinctual," he said when I asked him about it. "Like a dog marking its territory. I feel it in my bones. I think it is something primal, prehuman—maybe something that all of us, without knowing it, have in us. But Tourette's 'releases' these primitive behaviors."

17 Bennett sometimes calls Tourette's "a disease of disinhibition." He says there are thoughts, not unusual in themselves, which anyone might have in passing but which are normally inhibited. With him, such thoughts perseverate in the back of the mind, obsessively, and burst out suddenly, without his consent or intention. Thus, he says, when the weather is nice he may want to be out in the sun getting a tan. This thought will begin the back of his mind while he is seeing his patients in the hospital, and will emerge in sudden, involuntary utterances. "The nurse may say, 'Mr. Jones has abdominal pain.' and I'm looking out of the window saying 'Tanning rays, tanning rays.' It might come out five hundred times in a morning. People in the ward must hear it—they can't *not* hear it—but I guess they ignore it, or feel that it doesn't matter."

18 Sometimes the Tourette's manifests itself in obsessive thoughts and anxieties. "If I'm worried about something," Bennett told me as we sat around the table, "say, I hear a story about a kid being hurt, I have to go up and tap the wall and say, 'I hope it won't happen to mine.'" I witnessed this for myself a couple of days later. There was a news report on TV about a lost child, which distressed and agitated him. He instantly began touching his glasses (top, bottom, left, right, top, bottom, left, right), centering and recentering them in a fury. He made "whoo, whoo" noises, like an owl, and muttered sotto-voce, "David, David—is *he* all right?" Then he dashed from the room to make sure. There was an intense anxiety and overconcern; an immediate alarm at the mention of any lost or hurt child; an immediate identification with himself, with his own children; an immediate, superstitious need to check up.

19 After tea, Bennett and I went out for a walk, past a little orchard heavy with apples, and on up the hill overlooking the town, the friendly malamutes gambolling around us. As we walked, he told me something of his life. He did not know whether anyone in his family had Tourette's—he was an adopted child. His own Tourette's had started when he was seven. "As a kid, growing up in Toronto, I wore glasses, I had bands on my teeth, *and* I twitched," he said. "That was the coup de grâce. I kept my distance. I was a loner; I'd go for long hikes by myself. I never had friends phoning all the time, like Mark—the contrast is very great." But being a loner and taking long hikes by himself toughened him as well, made him resourceful, gave him a sense of independence and self-sufficiency. He was always good with his hands, and loved the structure of natural things—the way rocks formed, the way plants grew, the way animals moved, the way muscles balanced and pulled against each other, the way the body was put together. He decided very early that he wanted to be a surgeon.

20 Anatomy came "naturally" to him, he said, but he found medical school extremely difficult, not merely because of his tics and touchings, which became more elaborate with the years, but because of strange difficulties and obsessions which obstructed the act of reading. "I'd have to read each line many times," he said. "I'd have to line up each paragraph to get all four corners symmetrically in my visual field." Besides this lining up of each paragraph, and sometimes of each line, he was beset by the need to "balance" syllables and words, by the need to "symmetrize" the punctuation in his mind, by the need to check the frequency of a given letter, and by the need to repeat words or phrases or lines to himself. All this made it impossible to read easily and fluently. Those problems are still with him, and make it difficult for him to skim quickly, to get the gist, or to enjoy fine writing or narrative or poetry. But they did force him to read painstakingly, and to learn his medical texts very nearly by heart.

21 When he got out of medical school, he indulged his interest in faraway places, particularly the North: he worked as a general practitioner

in the Northwest Territories and the Yukon, and worked on icebreakers circling the Arctic. He had a gift for intimacy, and grew close to the Eskimos he worked with; and he became something of an expert in polar medicine. And when he married, in 1968—he was twenty-eight—he went with his bride around the world, and gratified a boyhood wish to climb Kilimanjaro.

22 For the past seventeen years, he has practiced in small, isolated communities in western Canada—first, for twelve years, as a general practitioner in a small city. Then, five years ago, when the need to have mountains, wild country, and lakes on his doorstep grew stronger, he moved to Branford. ("And here I will stay. I never want to leave it.") Branford, he told me, has the right "feel." The people are warm but not chummy; they keep a certain distance. There is a natural well-bredness and civility. The schools are of high quality, there is a community college, there are theatres, and bookstores—Helen runs one of them—but there is also a strong feeling for the outdoors, for the wilds. There is much hunting and fishing, but Bennett prefers backpacking and climbing and cross-country skiing.

23 When Bennett first came to Branford, he was regarded, he thought, with a certain suspicion. "A surgeon who twitches! Who needs him? What next?" There were no patients at first, and he did not know if he could make it there, but gradually he won the town's affection and respect. His practice began to expand, and his colleagues, who had at first been startled and incredulous, soon came to trust and accept him, too, and to bring him fully into the medical community. "But enough said," he concluded as we returned to the house. It was almost dark now, and the lights of Branford were twinkling. "Come to the hospital tomorrow—we have a conference at seven-thirty. Then I'll do outpatients, and rounds on my patients. And Friday I operate—you can scrub with me."

24 I slept soundly in the Bennetts' basement room that night, but in the morning I woke early, roused by a strange whirring noise in the room next to mine—the playroom. The playroom door had translucent glass panels. As I peered through them, still half-asleep, I saw what appeared to be a locomotive in motion—a large, whirring wheel going round and round, and giving off puffs of smoke and occasional hoots. Bewildered, I opened the door and peeked in. Bennett, stripped to the waist, was pedalling furiously on an exercise bike while calmly smoking a large pipe. A pathology book was open before him—turned, I observed, to the chapter on neurofibromatosis. This is how he invariably begins each morning—a half hour on his bike, puffing his favorite pipe, with a pathology or surgery book open to the day's work before him. The pipe, the rhythmic exercise calm him. There are no tics, no compulsions—at most, a little hooting. (He seems to imagine at such times that he is a prairie train.) He can read without his usual obsessions and distractions.

25 But as soon as the rhythmic cycling stopped, a flurry of tics and compulsions took over; he kept digging at his belly, which was trim, and muttering, "Fat, fat, fat . . . fat, fat, fat . . . fat, fat, fat," and then, puzzlingly, "Fat and a quarter tit." (sometimes the "tit" was left out.)

26 "What does it mean?" I asked.

27 "I have no idea. Nor do I know where 'Hideous' comes from—it suddenly appeared one day two years ago. It'll disappear one day, and there will be another word instead. When I'm tired, it turns into 'Gideous.' One cannot always find sense in these words; often it is just the sound that attracts me. Any odd sound, any odd name, may start repeating itself, get me going. I get hung up with a word for two or three months. Then, one morning, it's gone, and there's another one in its place." Knowing his appetite for strange words and sounds, Bennett's sons are constantly on the lookout for "odd" names—names that sound odd to an English-speaking ear, many of them foreign. They scan the papers and their books for such words, they listen to the radio and TV, and when they find a "juicy" name they add it to a list they keep. Bennett says of this list, "It's about the most valuable thing in the house." He calls it words "candy for the mind."

28 This list was started six years ago, after the name Oginga Odinga, with its alliterations, got Bennett going—and now it contains over two hundred names. Of these, twenty-two are "current" at the present time—apt to be regurgitated at any moment, and chewed over, repeated, and savored internally. Of the twenty-two, the name of Slavek J. Hurka—an industrial-relations professor at the University of Saskatchewan, where Helen studied—goes the furthest back; it started to echolate itself in 1974, and has been doing so, without significant breaks, for the last seventeen years. Most words last only a few months. Some of the names (Boris Blank, Floyd Flake, Morris Gook, Lubor J. Zink) have a short, percussive quality. Others (Yelberton A. Tittle, Babaloo Mandel) are marked by euphonious polysyllabic alliterations. It is only the sound of the words, their "melody," as Bennett says, which implants them in his mind; their origins and meanings and associations are irrelevant.

29 "It is similar with the number compulsions," he said. "Now I have to do everything by threes or fives, but until a few months ago it was fours and sevens. Then one morning I woke up—*four* and *seven* had gone, but *three* and *five* has appeared instead. It's as if one circuit were turned on upstairs, and another turned off. It doesn't seem to have any thing to do with *me*."

30 At seven-twenty-five, we drove into town. It took barely five minutes to get to the hospital, but our arrival there was more complicated than usual, because Bennett had unwittingly become notorious. He had been interviewed by a magazine a few weeks earlier, and the article had just come out. Everyone was smiling, and ribbing him about it. A little

embarrassed, but also enjoying it, Bennett took the joking in good part. ('I'll never live it down—I'll be a marked man now.") In the doctors' common room, Bennett was clearly very much at ease with his colleagues, and they with him. One sign of this ease, paradoxically, was that he felt free to Tourette with them—to touch or tap them gently with his fingertips, or on two occasions when he was sharing a sofa, to suddenly twist on his side and tap his colleague's shoulder with his toes—a practice I had observed in other Touretters. Bennett is somewhat cautious with his Tourettisms on first acquaintance, and conceals or downplays them until he gets to know people. When he first started working at the hospital, he told me, he would skip in the corridors only after checking to be sure that no one was looking; now when he skips or hops no one gives it a second glance.

31 The conversations in the common room were like those in any hospital—doctors talking among themselves about unusual cases. Bennett himself, lying half-curled on the floor, kicking and thrusting one foot in the air, described an unusual case of neurofibromatosis—a young man whom he had recently operated on. His colleagues listened attentively. The abnormality of the behavior and the complete normality of the discourse formed an extraordinary contrast. There was something bizarre about the whole scene; but it was evidently so common as to be unremarkable, and no longer attracted the slightest notice. But an outsider seeing it would have been stunned.

32 After coffee and muffins, we repaired to the surgical-outpatients department, where half a dozen patients awaited Bennett. The first was a trail guide from Banff, very Western in plaid shirt, tight jeans, and cowboy hat. His horse had fallen and rolled on top of him, and he had developed an immense pseudocyst of the pancreas. Bennett spoke with the man—who said the swelling was diminishing—and gently, smoothly palpated the fluctuant mass in his abdomen. He checked the sonograms with the radiologist—they confirmed the cyst's recession—and then came back and reassured the patient. "It's going down by itself. It's shrinking nicely—you won't be needing surgery after all. You can get back to riding. I'll see you in a month." And the trail guide, delighted, walked off with a jaunty step. Later, I had a word with the radiologist. "Bennett's not only a whiz at diagnosis," he said. "He's the most compassionate surgeon I know."

33 The next patient was a heavy woman with a melanoma on her buttock which needed to be excised at some depth. Bennett scrubbed up, donned sterile gloves. Something about the sterile field, the prohibition, seemed to stir his Tourette's; he made sudden darting motions, or incipient motions, of his sterile, gloved right hand toward the ungloved, unwashed, "dirty" part of his left arm. The patient eyed this without expression. What did she think, I wondered, of this odd darting motion, and the sudden convulsive shakings he also made with his

hand? She could not have been entirely surprised, for her G.P. must have prepared her to some extent, must have said, "You need a small operation. I recommend Dr. Bennett—he's a wonderful surgeon. I have to tell you that he sometimes makes strange movements and sounds—he has a thing called Tourette's syndrome—but don't worry, it doesn't matter. It never affects his surgery."

34 Now, the preliminaries over, Bennett got down to the serious work, swabbing the buttock with an iodine antiseptic and then injecting local anesthetic, with an absolutely steady hand. But as soon as the rhythm of action was broken for a moment—he needed more local, and the nurse held out the vial for him to refill his syringe—there was once again the darting and near-touching. The nurse did not bat an eyelid; she had seen it before, and knew he wouldn't contaminate his gloves. Now, with a firm hand, Bennett made an oval incision an inch to either side of the melanoma, and in forty seconds he had removed it, along with a Brazil-nut-shaped wedge of fat and skin. "It's out!" he said. Then, very rapidly, with great dexterity, he sewed the margins of the wound together, putting five neat knots on each nylon stitch. The patient, twisting her head, watched him as he sewed, and joshed him: "Do you do all the sewing at home?"

35 He laughed. "Yes. All except the socks. But no one darns socks these days."

36 She looked again. "You're making quite a quilt."

37 The whole operation completed in less than three minutes, Bennett cried, "Done! Here's what we took." He held the lump of flesh before her.

38 "Ugh!" she exclaimed, with a shudder. "Don't show me. But thanks anyway."

39 All this looked highly professional from beginning to end, and, apart from the dartings and near-touchings, non-Tourettic. But I couldn't decide about Bennett's showing the excised lump to the patient ("Here!") One may show a gallstone to a patient, but does one show a bleeding, misshapen piece of fat and flesh? Clearly, she didn't want to see it, But Bennett wanted to show it, and I wondered if this urge was part of his Tourettic scrupulosity and exactitude, his need to have everything looked at and understood. I had the same thought later in the morning, when he was seeing an old lady in whose bile duct he had inserted a T-tube. He went to great lengths to draw the tube, to explain all the anatomy, and the old lady said, "I don't want to know it. Just do it!"

40 Was this Bennet the Touretter being obsessive or Professor Bennett the lecturer on anatomy? (He gives weekly anatomy lectures in Calgary.) Was it simply an expression of his meticulousness and concern? An imagining, perhaps, that all patients shared his curiosity and love of detail? Some patients doubtless did, but obviously not these.

41 So it went on through a lengthy outpatient list. Bennett is evidently a very popular surgeon, and he saw or operated on each patient

swiftly and dexterously, with an absolute and single-minded concentration, so that when they saw him they knew they had his whole attention. They forgot that they had waited, or that there were others still waiting, and felt that for him they were the only people in the world.

42 Very pleasant, very real, the surgeon's life, I kept thinking—direct, friendly relationships, especially clear with outpatients like this. An immediacy of relation, of work, of results, of gratification—much greater than with a physician, especially a neurologist (like me). I thought of my mother, how much she enjoyed the surgeon's life, and how I always loved sitting in at her surgical-outpatient rounds. I could not become a surgeon myself, because of an incorrigible clumsiness, but even as a child, I had loved the surgeon's life, and watching surgeons at work. This love, this pleasure, half-forgotten, came back to me with great force as I observed Bennett with his patients; made me want to be more than a spectator; made me want to do something, to hold a retractor, to join in somehow in the surgery.

43 Bennett's last patient was a young mechanic with extensive neurofibromatosis, a bizarre and sometimes cancerous disease that can produce huge brownish swellings and protruding sheets of skin, disfiguring the whole body. This young man had had a huge apron of tissue hanging down from his chest, so large that he could lift it up and cover his head, and so heavy that it bowed him forward with its weight. Bennett had removed this a couple of weeks earlier—a massive procedure—with great expertise, and was now examining another huge apron descending from the shoulders, and great flaps of brownish flesh in the groins and armpits. I was relieved that he did not tic "Hideous!" as he removed the stitches from the surgery, for I feared the impact of such a word being uttered aloud, even if it was nothing but a long-standing verbal tic. But, mercifully, there was no "Hideous," there were no verbal tics at all, until Bennett was examining the dorsal skin flap, and let fly a brief "Hid—," the end of the word omitted by a tactful apocope.[1] This, I learned later, was not a conscious suppression—Bennett had no memory of the tic—and yet it seemed to me there must have been, if not a conscious, then a subconscious solicitude and tact at work. "Fine young man," Bennett said, as we went outside. "Not self-conscious. Nice personality, outgoing. Most people with this would lock themselves in a closet." I could not help feeling that his words could also be applied to himself. There are many people with Tourette's who become agonized and self-conscious, withdraw from the world, and lock themselves in a closet. Not so Bennett: he had struggled against this; he had come through and braved life, braved people, braved the most improbable of professions. All his patients, I think, perceived this, and it was one of the reasons they trusted him so.

[1]Cutting off of the last syllable or sound in a word.

44 The man with the skin flap was the last of the outpatients, but for Bennett, immensely busy, there was only a brief break before an equally long afternoon with his inpatients on the ward. I excused myself from this to take an afternoon off and walk around the town. I wandered through Branford with the oddest sense of déjà vu[2] and jamais vu[3] mixed; I kept feeling that I had seen the town before, but then again that it was new to me. And then, suddenly, I had it—yes, I had seen it, I had been here before, for a night in August, 1960, when it had a population of only a few thousand and consisted of little more than a few dusty streets, motels, bars—a crossroads, little more than a truck stop in the long trek across the West. Now its population was twenty thousand, Main Street a gleaming boulevard filled with shops and cars; there was a town hall, police station, a regional hospital, several schools—it was this which surrounded me, the overwhelming present, yet through it I saw the dusty crossroads, and the bars, the Branford of thirty years before, still strangely vivid, because never updated, in my mind.

45 Friday is operating day for Bennett, and he was scheduled to do a mastectomy. I was eager to join him, to see him in action. Outpatients are one thing—one can always concentrate for a few minutes—but how would he conduct himself in a lengthy and difficult procedure demanding intense, unremitting concentration, not for seconds or minutes but for hours?

46 Bennett preparing for the operating room was a startling sight. "You should scrub next to him," his young assistant said. "It's quite an experience." It was indeed, for what I saw in the outpatient clinic was magnified here: constant sudden dartings and reachings with the hands, almost but never quite touching his unscrubbed, unsterile shoulder, his assistant, the mirror; sudden lungings, and touchings of his colleagues with his feet; and a barrage of vocalizations—"Hooty-hooo! Hooty-hooo!"—suggestive of a huge owl.

47 The scrubbing over, Bennett and his assistant were gloved and gowned, and they moved to the patient, already anesthetized, on the table. They looked briefly at a mammogram on the X-ray box. Then Bennett took the knife, made a bold, clear incision—there was no hint of any ticcing or distraction—and moved straightaway into the rhythm of the operation. Twenty minutes passed, fifty, seventy, a hundred. The operation was often complex—vessels to be tied, nerves to be found—but the action was confident, smooth, moving forward at its own pace, with never the slightest hint of Tourette's. Finally, after two and a half hours of the most complex, taxing surgery, Bennett closed up, thanked

[2]French expression, pronounced dé′zhä-vo͞o′ describing the feeling of having experienced something before.

[3]French expression, pronounced zhă′ mā-vo͞o describing the feeling of never having experienced something before.

everybody, yawned, and stretched. Here, then, was an entire operation without a trace of Tourette's. Not because it had been suppressed, or held in—there was never any sign of control or constraint—but because, simply, there was never any impulse to tic. "Most of the time when I'm operating, it never even crosses my mind that I have Tourette's," Bennett says. His whole identity at such times is that of a surgeon at work, and his entire psychic and neural organization becomes aligned with this, becomes active, focussed, at ease, un-Tourettic. It is only if the operation is broken for a few minutes—to review a special X-ray taken during the surgery, for example—that Bennett, waiting, unoccupied, remembers that he *is* Tourettic, and in that instant he becomes so. As soon as the flow of the operation resumes, the Tourette's, the Tourettic identity, vanishes once again. Bennett's assistants, though they have known him and worked with him for years, are still astounded whenever they see this. "It's like a miracle," one of them says. "The way the Tourette's disappears." And Bennett himself is astonished, too, and quizzes me, as he peels off his gloves, on the neurophysiology of it all.

48 Things were not always so easy, Bennett told me later. Occasionally, if he was bombarded by outside demands during surgery—"You have three patients waiting in the E.R.," "Mrs. X wants to know if she can come in on the tenth," "Your wife wants you to pick up three bags of dog food"—these pressures, these distractions, would break his concentration, break the smooth and rhythmic flow. A couple of years ago, he made it a rule that he must never be disturbed while operating, and must be allowed to concentrate totally on the surgery, and the O.R. has been tic-free ever since.

49 Friday afternoon is open. Bennett often likes to go for long hikes on Fridays, or cycle rides, or drives, with a sense of the trail, the open road, before him. There is a favorite ranch he loves to go to, with a beautiful lake and an airstrip, accessible only via a rugged dirt road. It is a wonderfully situated ranch, a narrow fertile strip perfectly placed between the lake and mountains, and we walked for miles, talking of this and that, with Bennett botanizing or geologizing as we went. Then, briefly, we went to the lake, where I took a swim; when I came out of the water I found that Bennett, rather suddenly, had curled up for a nap. He looked peaceful, tension-free, as he slept; and the suddenness and depth of his sleep made me wonder how much difficulty he encountered in the daytime, how much he concealed beneath his genial surface—how much, inwardly, he had to control and deal with.

50 Later, as we continued our ramble about the ranch, he remarked that I had seen only some of the outward expressions of his Tourette's, and these, bizarre as they occasionally seemed, were by no means the worst problems it caused him. The real problems, the inner problems, were panic and rage—feelings so violent that they threatened to overwhelm

him, and so sudden that he had virtually no warning of their onset. He had only to get a parking ticket or see a police car, sometimes, for scenarios of violence to flash through his mind: mad chases, shootouts, flaming destructions, hideous mutilation and death—scenarios that would become immensely elaborated in seconds, and rush through his mind with manic-Tourettic speed. One part of him, uninvolved, could watch these scenes with detachment, but another part of him was taken over, and felt impelled to action. He could prevent himself from giving way to outbursts in public, but the strain of controlling himself was severe and exhausting. At home, in private, he could let himself go—not at others but at inanimate objects around him. There was the wall I had seen, which he had often struck in his rage, and the refrigerator, at which he had flung virtually everything in the kitchen. In his office, he had kicked a hole in the wall, and had had to put a plant in front to cover it; and in his study at home the cedar walls were covered with knife marks. "It's not gentle," he said to me. "You can see it as whimsical, funny—be tempted to romanticize it—but Tourette's comes from deep down in the nervous system and the unconscious. It taps into the oldest, strongest feelings we have. Tourette's is like an epilepsy in the subcortex; when it takes over, there's just a thin line of control, a thin line of cortex, between you and it, between you and that raging storm, the blind force of the subcortex. One can see the charming things, the funny things, the creative side of Tourette's, but there's also that dark side. You have to fight it all your life."

51 Driving back from the ranch was a stimulating, at times terrifying, experience. Now that Bennett was getting to know me, he felt at liberty to let himself and his Tourette's go. The steering wheel was abandoned for seconds at a time—or so it seemed to me, in my alarm—while he tapped on the windshield (to a litany of "Hooty-hoo!" and "Hi, there!" and "Hideous!"), rearranged his glasses, "centered" them in a hundred different ways, and, with bent forefingers, continually smoothed and evened his mustache while gazing in the rearview mirror rather than at the road. His need to center the steering wheel in relation to his knees also grew almost frenetic at this time: he had constantly to "balance" it, to jerk it to and fro, causing the car to zigzag erratically down the road. "Don't worry," he said when he saw my anxiety. "I know this road. I could see from way back that nothing was coming. I've never had an accident driving."

52 The impulse to look, and to be looked at, is very striking with Bennett, and indeed, as soon as we got back to the house he seized Mark and planted himself in front of him, smoothing his mustache furiously and saying, "Look at me! Look at me!" Mark, arrested, stayed where he was, but his eyes wandered to and fro. Now Bennett seized Mark's head, held it rigidly toward him, hissing, "Look, look at me!" And Mark became totally still, transfixed, as if hypnotized.

53 I found this scene disquieting. Other scenes with the family I had found rather moving: Bennett dabbing at Helen's hair, symmetrically, with outstretched fingers, going "whoo, whoo" softly. She was placid, accepting; it was a touching scene, both tender and absurd. "I love him as he is," Helen said. "I wouldn't want him any other way." Bennett feels the same way: "Funny disease—I don't think of it as a disease but as just me. I say the word 'disease,' but it doesn't seem to be the appropriate word."

54 Though Bennett is quite prepared, even eager, to think of Tourette's in neurochemical or neurophysiological terms—he thinks in terms of chemical abnormalities, of "circuits turning on and off," and of "primitive, normally inhibited behaviors being released"—he also feels it as something that has come to be part of himself. For this reason (among others), he has found that he cannot tolerate haloperidol and similar drugs—they reduce his Tourette's, assuredly, but they reduce *him* as well, so that he no longer feels fully himself. "The side effects of haloperidol were dreadful," he said. "I was intensely restless, I couldn't stand still, my body twisted, I shuffled like a Parkinsonian. It was a huge relief to get off it. On the other hand, Prozac has been a godsend for the obsessions, the rages, though it doesn't touch the tics." Prozac has indeed been a godsend for many Touretters, though some have found it to have no effect, and a few have had paradoxical effects—an intensification of their agitations, obsessions, and rages.

55 Though Bennett has had tics since the age of seven or so, he did not identify what he had as Tourette's syndrome until he was thirty-seven. "When we were first married, he just called it a 'nervous habit,'" Helen told me. "We used to joke about it. I'd say, 'I'll quit smoking, and you quit twitching.' We thought of it as something he *could* quit if he wanted. You'd ask him, 'Why do you do it?' He'd say, 'I don't know why.' He didn't seem to be self-conscious about it. Then, in 1977, when Mark was a baby, Carl heard this program, 'Quirks and Quarks,' on the radio. He got all excited and hollered, 'Helen, come listen! This guy's talking about what I do!' He was excited to hear that other people had it. And it was a relief to me, because I had always sensed that there was something wrong. It was good to put a label on it. He never made a thing of it, he wouldn't raise the subject, but, once we knew, we'd tell people if they asked. It's only in the last few years that he's met other people with it, or gone to meetings of the Tourette Syndrome Association." (Tourette's syndrome, until very recently, was remarkably underdiagnosed and unknown, even to the medical profession, and most people diagnosed themselves, or were diagnosed by friends and family, after seeing or reading something about it in the media. Indeed, I know of another doctor, a surgeon in Louisiana, who was diagnosed by one of his own patients who had seen a Touretter on "Donahue." Much of this media emphasis has been due to the efforts of the T.S.A., which had

only thirty members in the early seventies but now has more than twenty thousand.)

56 Saturday morning, and I have to return to New York. "I'll fly you to Calgary if the weather's fine," Bennett said suddenly last night. "Ever flown with a Touretter before?"

57 I had canoed with one, I said, and driven across country with another, but flying with one . . .

58 "You'll enjoy it," Bennett said. "It'll be a novel experience. I am the world's only flying Touretter-surgeon."

59 When I awake, at dawn, I perceive, with mixed feelings, that the weather, though very cold, is perfect. We drive to the little airport in Branford, a veering, twitching journey that makes me nervous about the flight. "It's much easier in the air, where there's no road to keep to, and you don't have to keep your hands on the controls all the time," Bennett says. At the airport, he parks, opens a hangar, and proudly points out his airplane—a tiny red-and-white single-engine Cessna Cardinal. He pulls it out onto the tarmac and then checks it, rechecks, it, and rerechecks it before warming up the engine. It is near-freezing on the airfield, and a north wind is blowing. I watch all the checks and rechecks with impatience but also with a sense of reassurance. If his Tourette's makes him check everything three or five times, so much the safer. I had a similar feeling of reassurance about his surgery—that his Tourette's, if anything, made him more meticulous, more exact, without in the least damping down his intuitiveness, his freedom.

60 His checking done, Bennett leaps like a trapeze artist into the plane, revs the engine while I climb in, and takes off. As we climb, the sun is rising over the Rockies to the east, and floods the little cabin with a pale, golden light. We head toward nine-thousand-foot crests, and Bennett tics, flutters, reaches, taps, touches his glasses, his mustache, the top of the cockpit. Minor tics, Little League, I think, but what if he has big tics? What if he wants to twirl the plane in midair, to hop and skip with it, to do somersaults, to loop the loop? What if he has an impulse to leap out and touch the propeller? Touretters tend to be fascinated by spinning objects; I have a vision of him lunging forward, half out the window, compulsively lunging at the propeller before us. But his tics and compulsions remain very minor, and when he takes his hands off the controls the plane continues quietly. Mercifully, there is no road to keep to. If we rise or fall or veer fifty feet, what does it matter? We have the whole sky to play with.

61 And Bennett, though superbly skilled, a natural aviator, *is* like a child at play. Part of Tourette's, at least, is no more than this—the release of a playful impulse normally inhibited or lost in the rest of us. The freedom, the spaciousness obviously delight Bennett; he has a carefree, boyish look I rarely saw on the ground. Now, rising, we fly over the first peaks, the advance guard of the Rockies; yellowing larches

stream beneath us. We clear the slopes by a thousand feet or more. I wonder whether Bennett, if he were by himself, might want to clear the peaks by ten feet, by inches—Touretters are sometimes addicted to close shaves. At ten thousand feet, we move in a corridor between peaks, mountains shining in the morning sun to our left, mountains silhouetted against it to our right. At eleven thousand feet, we can see the whole width of the Rockies—they are only fifty-five miles across here—and the vast golden Alberta prairie starting to the east. Every so often, Bennett's right hand flutters in front of me, or his hand taps lightly on the windshield. "Sedimentary rocks, look!" He gestures through the window. "Lifted up from the sea bottom at seventy to eighty degrees." He gazes at the steeply sloping rocks as at a friend; he is intensely at home with these mountains, this land. Snow lies on the sunless slopes of the mountains, none yet on their sunlit faces; and over to the northwest, toward Banff, we can see glaciers on the mountains. Bennett shifts, and shifts, and shifts again, trying to get his knees exactly symmetrical beneath the controls of the plane.

62 In Alberta now—we have been flying for forty minutes—the Highwood River winds beneath us. Flying due north, we start a gentle descent toward Calgary, the last, declining slopes of the Rockies all shimmering with aspen. Now, lower, to vast fields of wheat and alfalfa—farms, ranches, fertile prairie—but still, everywhere, stands of golden aspen. Beyond the checkerboard of fields, the towers of Calgary rise abruptly from the flat plain.

63 Suddenly, the radio crackles alive—a giant Russian air transport is coming in; the main runway, closed for maintenance, must quickly be opened up. And another massive plane, from the Zambian Air Force. The world's planes come to Calgary for special work and maintenance; its facilities, Bennett tells me, are some of the best in North America. In the middle of this important flurry, Bennett radios in our position and statistics (fifteen-foot-long Cardinal, with a Touretter and his neurologist), and is immediately answered, as fully and helpfully as if he were a 747. All planes, all pilots are equal in this world. And it is a world apart, with a freemasonry of its own, its own language, codes, myths, and manners. Bennett, clearly, is part of this world, and is recognized by the traffic controller and greeted cheerfully as he taxis in.

64 He leaps out with a startling, tic-like suddenness and celerity—I follow at a lower, "normal" pace—and starts talking with two giant young men on the tarmac, Kevin and Chuck, brothers, both fourth-generation pilots in the Rockies. They know him well. "He's just one of us," Chuck says to me. "A regular guy. Tourette's—what the hell? He's a good human being. A damn good pilot, too."

65 Bennett yarns with his fellow-pilots, and files his flight plan for the return trip to Branford. He has to return straight away; he is due to speak at eleven to a group of nurses, and his subject, for once, is not

surgery but Tourette's. His little plane is refuelled, and readied for the return flight. We hug, and say goodbye, and as I head for my flight to New York I turn to watch him go. Bennett walks to his plane, taxis onto the main runway, and takes off, fast, with a tail wind following. I watch him for a while, and then he is gone.

A. *Comprehension*

Choose the answer that best completes each statement. Do not refer to the selection while doing this exercise.

1. According to Sacks, Tourette's syndrome is (a) a complex biopsychosocial disorder often characterized by compulsive tics and involuntary repetitions of words or actions; (b) a neurological disorder caused by a chemical imbalance in the brain; (c) a psychiatric disorder characterized by unpredictable mood swings and bizarre fantasies; (d) a hereditary illness characterized by violent outbursts followed by periods of passivity and calm.
2. People with Tourette's syndrome often feel as if they (a) are guilty of a moral weakness; (b) enjoy the attention their behavior gets them; (c) are fighting a losing battle against their symptoms; (d) have been taken over or possessed by their compulsions.
3. Tourette's syndrome has made Dr. Carl Bennett, the surgeon that Sacks is writing about, compulsive about things being (a) organized and in their proper place; (b) symmetrical and centered; (c) immaculately clean and germ-free; (d) at right angles to each other.
4. Bennett says that Tourette's syndrome might be called "a disease of disinhibition" because one's thoughts (a) become twisted and contorted, making no sense; (b) are unnaturally suppressed and unable to be expressed; (c) stick in the mind and later burst forth without consent or intention; (d) are associated with musical notes, colors, or natural objects.
5. During surgery, Sacks observed that Bennett (a) is frantic and anxious about the operations he has to perform; (b) has to scrub repeatedly after contaminating his gloves; (c) maintains his focus and concentration and displays no Tourettic behavior; (d) displays Tourettic behavior throughout surgery.

B. *Inferences*

On the basis of the evidence in the paragraphs indicated, mark these statements as follows: PA for inferences that are probably accurate and PI for inferences that are probably inaccurate. You may refer to the selection to answer the questions in this section, and in all the remaining sections.

1. _____ Tourette's syndrome affects all of its victims in the same way. [paragraph 1]
2. _____ People afflicted with Tourette's syndrome may find that the disease can have positive, even creative effects on their lives. [paragraph 3]
3. _____ Sacks believes that a surgeon with Tourette's syndrome is at first surprising, yet not that uncommon. [paragraph 5]
4. _____ Carl Bennett has managed to prevent the dark side of Tourette's from emerging by letting off steam in a variety of athletic pursuits. [paragraph 50]
5. _____ Medical science has not determined the exact cause of Tourette's syndrome. [paragraphs 54–55]

C. *Structure*

1. This essay has a clear beginning, middle, and end. What paragraphs comprise the introduction? ¶ ____ to ¶ ____. What paragraphs comprise the body? ¶ ____ to ¶ ____. And what paragraphs comprise the conclusion? ¶ ____ to ¶ ____.
2. Which of the following quotations *best* represents the central impression of Carl Bennett's character? (a) "I was struck both by his bizarre tics and by his dignity and calm"; (b) "There was an intense anxiety and overconcern; an immediate alarm at the mention of any lost or hurt child; an immediate identification with himself, with his own children; an immediate, superstitious need to check up"; (c) "But being a loner and taking long hikes by himself toughened him as well, made him resourceful, gave him a sense of independence and self-sufficiency"; (d) "There are many people with Tourette's who become agonized and self-conscious, withdraw from the world, and lock themselves in a closet. Not so Bennett: he had struggled against this; he had come through and braved life, braved people, braved the most improbable of professions."
3. Read paragraph 31 again. What strikes Sacks as particularly bizarre in this scene is (a) an outsider's astonishment at what he saw; (b) the location for a medical conversation; (c) his colleagues' lack of concern over Bennett's strange actions; (d) the symptoms of the patient suffering from neurofibromatosis.
4. From the information we are given in paragraph 47, we can assume that, at least for Bennett, the symptoms of Tourette's become apparent (a) without warning, without control; (b) in stressful situations; (c) when the victim remembers he is Tourettic; (d) when others expect him to display such behavior.
5. Explain the irony in the way Carl Bennett learned the name of his condition (see paragraph 55). ________________________________

6. The tone of the article, specifically, Sacks' attitude toward Carl Bennett, can best described as (a) judgmental, critical; (b) admiring, greatly sympathetic; (c) neutral, showing no personal opinion one way or the other; (d) confused, ambivalent.

D. *Vocabulary*

For each italicized word from the selection, choose the best definition according to the context in which it appears.

1. an odd *insouciance* or *nonchalance* [paragraph 1]: These two words are synonyms, meaning: (a) insolence, hostility; (b) tension, anxiety; (c) lack of concern, casual indifference; (d) passiveness, inactivity.
2. I expressed *incredulity* [6—see also *incredulous* in 23]: (a) caution; (b) concern; (c) disbelief; (d) regret.
3. a mere *pastoral* landscape [7]: (a) ordinary, common (b) lush, green; (c) esthetically beautiful; (d) rural, country.
4. a charming, *idiosyncratic* house [10—see also *idiosyncratically* in 6]: (a) distinctive, individual, characteristic; (b) carefully designed; (c) rustic, primitive; (d) mazelike, labyrinthine.
5. a meticulous symmetry and *synchrony* [10]: (a) sequential order; (b) randomness; (c) widely spaced intervals; (d) simultaneousness.
6. a *disquieting,* violent one [13 and 53]: (a) tragic; (b) troubling; (c) vicious; (d) disabling.
7. such thoughts *perseverate* in the back of the mind [17]: (a) lie dormant; (b) become jumbled and confused; (c) gradually become stronger, more intense; (d) spontaneously and uncontrollably recur.
8. Oginga Odinga, with its *alliterations* [28]: (a) repeated number of syllables; (b) rhyming syllables; (c) repeated initial consonant sounds; (d) similar vowel sounds.
9. marked by *euphonious* polysyllabic alliterations [28]: (a) agreeable to the ear; (b) harsh-sounding; (c) unpronounceable; (d) miscellaneous, varied.
10. Bennett had unwittingly become *notorious* [30]: The word is used here ironically; the literal meaning is (a) widely sought after; (b) famous in a positive way; (c) famous in a negative way; (d) instantly famous, to be quickly forgotten.
11. part of his Tourettic *scrupulosity* and *exactitude* [39]: These words are near synonyms referring to one who shows (a) bizarre, uncontrollable tendencies; (b) careful attention to detail; (c) high moral principles; (d) healthy curiosity.
12. a startling, tic-like *celerity* [64]: (a) abruptness; (b) rudeness; (c) swiftness; (d) cheerfulness.

E. *Questions for Analysis and Discussion*

1. For people like Carl Bennett, does Tourette's syndrome, as Oliver Sacks describes its symptoms, appear to be more of a blessing or a liability?
2. What characteristics does Sacks apparently find most fascinating about Bennett?

Selection 10

Arrington v. The New York Times Company: The Case of the Cover Photo

Ellen Alderman and Caroline Kennedy

Ellen Alderman and Caroline Kennedy are attorneys who met at the Columbia University School of Law and the authors of In Our Defense: The Bill of Rights in Action *(1991) and* The Right to Privacy *(1995), from which this excerpt comes. The book examines the legal issues concerning the right to privacy, in particular the ways in which this right has been seriously threatened as the media and technology have become both more sophisticated and intrusive. Here is some pertinent background that will better help you understand the issues in* Arrington v. The New York Times Company.

In 1890 Samuel D. Warren and Louis D. Brandeis (later a U.S. Supreme Court justice) wrote an article titled "The Right to Privacy," after details of a Warren family wedding were published in gossip columns. Their article created the concept of the right to privacy, defined as "the right to be let alone," and its natural counterpart, the right to sue for "invasion of privacy." As Alderman and Kennedy explain, the courts began to accept Warren's and Brandeis's argument, in particular because the Constitution guarantees citizens the right to privacy, but only from government *action. This right of privacy is called a* **tort,** *"a legal cause of action that is specifically set out in a statute (as opposed to the Constitution), or is part of what is known as the general 'common law'—i.e., law that courts recognize based on legal history and other cases."*

In 1960 Dean William Prosser, a legal scholar, further codified the four torts associated with invasion of privacy: intrusion, public disclosure of private facts, false light, and appropriation. **Appropriation** *is defined as "using another's name or likeness for some advantage without the other's consent. For example, a photograph of a famous actress is used without her consent to advertise a product." The purported misuse of Clarence Harrington's photograph is at the heart of this essay.*

1 In the fall of 1978, the staff of *The New York Times Magazine* was preparing its year-end issue. The *Magazine* is part of the Sunday edition of *The New York Times,* which has a nationwide circulation of more than one and a half million. Edward Klein had been hired the year before as editor in chief, and his mandate was to make the *Magazine* more up-to-date and vital by dealing with relevant, even controversial issues. Klein recalls, "I tried early on to grapple with issues that were not yet paid enough attention to and that would grab people's attention because they were important."

2 He found such an issue in a story submitted by William Brashler detailing something the author identified as a new social trend: the rise of the "black middle class." Blacks who had rushed through the doors opened by the civil rights movement in the 1960s had, throughout the 1970s, created a new, upwardly mobile middle class. The existence of this new class directly contradicted findings in a celebrated 1968 study which had concluded that a black middle class could not offer an "escape hatch" from the ghetto. Brashler interviewed a number of African Americans for the article, focusing on two women in particular.

3 Klein recalls that the article "forced itself upon us as an important enough story to warrant running it on the cover." That raised the question of what would appear on the cover of the *Magazine* to illustrate the story. The individuals included in the article had been photographed going about their daily lives. But a cover photo had to be special. It must, as Edward Klein puts it, "drag people inside the magazine and make them want to read this article."

4 *The New York Times* art department contacted a freelance photographer, Gianfranco Gorgoni, and assigned him to "photograph well-dressed blacks on the street." Gorgoni spent several days in New York and Chicago on the assignment, then submitted over a hundred color transparencies to the *Times*. Out of the take, it was decided that the cover of *The New York Times Magazine* would be one of the photographs depicting a black man, clad in a three-piece suit, striding purposefully across a street in New York City.

5 "In no instance did I request permission to take a subject's photograph," Gorgoni would later say. Nor, apparently did anyone at *The New York Times* request the subject's permission to use the photograph on the cover of a magazine.

6 On Sunday, December 3, 1978, Clarence Arrington was at his home in Mount Vernon, a suburb of New York City, getting ready to go to work. Arrington had received an M.B.A. from Columbia University and was working as a senior financial analyst at General Motors. As such, he was responsible for reviewing compensation and benefit plans, as well as preparing summaries of capital budget plans, profit plans, and other financial documents for the GM board of directors. Year-end was a busy time for Arrington and it was not unusual for him to work seven days a

week. He was just about to leave when the telephone rang. It was a coworker, already at the office.

7 Arrington recalls: "My colleague essentially said, 'I didn't know you were doubling as a model.' And I said, 'Well, actually I'm not. What are you talking about?' And he said that there was a full-length color picture of me on the front cover of *The New York Times Magazine.* And I said, 'No, that's not me. You're mistaking me for somebody else.' "

8 Just as Arrington was hanging up the phone, his brother, Lloyd, who lived in the neighborhood, was knocking at the door. Lloyd had gone to the local newsstand to pick up the Sunday *Times*. Now he was standing at Clarence's door with a huge stack of the papers under his arm and a grin on his face. Lloyd handed his brother *The New York Times Magazine.* The headline read: THE BLACK MIDDLE CLASS: MAKING IT. And filling the front cover was a photograph of Clarence Arrington, hand thrust in his pants pocket, crossing Fifth Avenue.

9 "It was rather strange to see it there," Arrington says in an understatement. He had had no idea that his photograph had been taken, much less that it would wind up on the cover of a magazine. Arrington guessed that the picture had been taken one day when he was returning from lunch. He says that the photo was actually quite flattering and at first he got a kick out of the unexpected public exposure. "It was, more or less, kind of a welcome experience," Arrington says. "But," he continues, "that was, of course, before I read the article."

10 The cover story reported on the rise of the "black middle class," stating that this new phenomenon meant that many of the assumptions about race from the 1960s would have to be rethought. The author documented the new social trend with statistics on education, employment, and salaries, but most of all with a detailed depiction of a new class obsessed with making money and acquiring fancy homes, clothes, and cars. The article often reads like a hip insider's guide to a group of former outsiders now consumed by the need to secure the trappings of the white middle class. One exchange between two members of this new class, a receptionist and a visitor to the office, was reported:

> In midmorning, Rachel looks up and greets a visitor she knows.
>
> "Hey, Alvin," she says. "How are ya?"
>
> "Hey, Rachel. What you up to?" Alvin says. He is here on business, looking business-like in a three-piece suit, close-cut natural, an attaché case held with one finger pointing to the ground.
>
> "Gettin' around," Rachel says, just as creamy as ever. "Livin' up on the North Side."
>
> "Oh, yeah? I been up there for some time now. Eugenie Square," Alvin says.
>
> "Still got the Mercedes?" Rachel asks.
>
> "Got it. Four-fifty *es-el,*" Alvin says. He winks.

> "Then you must know Floyd. Lives in Eugenie. Drives a Mercedes."
> "You sure? You really sure?" Alvin says, and looks concerned. "Don't remember the man and I know ev-ree-body in the Square who drives a Benz. . . ."
> Alvin's appointment shows him in, and he walks by Rachel, a most puzzled, troubled look on his face. He *thought* he knew everybody in his building who drove a Benz. It will bother him for the rest of the day.

11 As for Rachel, the article states, "She would like to ride in Alvin's Mercedes."

12 The article also reported that some of the "haves" in the new black middle class are "keeping up the fight," dedicating themselves to finding jobs for black youths and ridding black neighborhoods of drugs. "But it is a struggle," the article continues, "to counteract the prevalent middle-class black backlash against the black underclass." This new class of blacks was "drifting more and more distant from its less fortunate brothers," even from black culture. "Who needs that jive when he drinks Tanqueray and drives a BMW?" the author wrote.

13 The cover story focused on two central characters: an industrial relations manager in her twenties who had worked her way out of a tough neighborhood in Detroit but who had a brother in jail on drug charges ("a street dude who took a fall when he decided to hold up a drug pad"), and a Chicago receptionist who had successfully left behind a life of prostitution but had a sister who was still a prostitute and two brothers in jail. Others mentioned in the article were primarily from Detroit or Chicago.

14 Clarence Arrington was appalled. He objected to almost everything about the article. First of all, Arrington says, "I didn't feel that there needed to be a singling out of a black middle class [as distinct from] the middle class of America." To the extent that a black middle class could be defined, Arrington did not feel that its members were as materialistic and frivolous as the article portrayed them to be. And he did not even think that the people profiled in the article could accurately be called middle class. "In my opinion, they were upper-lower class, or less," Arrington says. He certainly did not identify with the backgrounds or values of those highlighted in the story. And, as he points out, they were not even from the same city as he. Finally, Arrington says it did not help that the article, which he found to be inaccurate and patronizing, was written by a white author. "I was deeply offended by the whole thing," Arrington says.

15 He was not the only one. There was, as Edward Klein recalls, "a minor storm of controversy." Letters to the editor criticized the article for conveying "stereotypes" and "caricatures" of successful blacks. Rebuttals were published in black periodicals. And the *New York Amsterdam News,* a newspaper with a predominantly black readership, stated

that the cover story "managed to bring to new heights the *Times Magazine* tradition of insulting, disparaging and distorting black life. . . . The article is patronizing in the extreme."

16 Most important to Arrington, he began to hear from almost everyone he knew. "Neighbors, friends, cousins, coworkers—they all called," he says. They wanted to know why Arrington would have agreed to pose for a photograph illustrating such an article. Everyone just assumed that a magazine could not put a private person's photograph on the cover without his consent. Therefore, Arrington must have agreed to be featured with the article. Arrington explained over and over that he had quite enough to do at work without "moonlighting" as a model and that he knew nothing about the photograph or the article prior to its publication. "Well, how can the press just use your photograph like that?" his friends and family wanted to know. Arrington didn't think they could and decided to sue *The New York Times* (as well as the photographer and his agent, who sold the photo).

17 A friend who was an attorney at a prominent New York law firm agreed to take the case for free. Otherwise, Arrington says, he never would have been able to afford a lawsuit against *The New York Times,* let alone one which was destined to go all the way to the highest court in New York State. For, contrary to the general public perception, under New York law it was not at all clear that *The New York Times* had done anything wrong.

18 New York has a statute protecting the right to privacy, but it covers only what is generally viewed as the appropriation branch of the four privacy torts. The statute prohibits the use of a person's "name, portrait, or picture . . . for advertising or trade purposes" without the person's consent. For example, the model Christie Brinkley successfully sued under this law to halt the sale of unauthorized pinup posters with her photograph. The New York Statute is one of the earliest laws specifically protecting the right to privacy, and, in fact, grew out of a case similar to Brinkley's that had occurred nearly a century earlier.

19 In 1902, a company used a young girl's photograph, without her consent, on a poster distributed throughout the country advertising the company's brand of flour. The girl's family sued for invasion of privacy. New York's highest court noted that the state legislature had not passed a law protecting the right to privacy. Then, in a crucial part of the ruling, the court refused to find a right to privacy in the "common law" of New York—that is, deriving from legal history or other cases in the state. The court said it could not just declare that a right to privacy existed based on legal tradition. If such a right was to be protected in New York, the court held, then the legislature would have to pass a law. The girl's family lost the case, causing a public outcry. Within a year, the New York legislature enacted the right to privacy statute prohibiting the unauthorized use of one's name, portrait, or picture for advertising or trade purposes—i.e., appropriation.

20 Of the four privacy torts, appropriation is often characterized as the most justifiable. After all, it seems only fair that another should not profit from your name or likeness without your consent. Most important, appropriation, with its emphasis on the *commercial* use of one's identity, appears to pose less of a threat to the core values of the First Amendment than do intrusion, private facts, and false light.

21 The New York statute became a model for other states as the right to privacy grew. However, many other states also wrote laws protecting the other three branches of the right to privacy, or their state courts recognized such causes of action as part of the common law. But in New York, for nearly a century, there remained only the 1903 statute.

22 Under the statute, Clarence Arrington could not argue that his picture had been used for "trade or advertising purposes" simply because *The New York Times* was in the business of selling newspapers. Early on, New York courts decided that if such an argument were to prevail, publishers could not operate. They would have to obtain prior consent for every photograph in every publication, whether it was the President of the United States making a speech, a defendant walking into the courthouse for trial, or an athlete celebrating a victory on the field. New York courts ruled that as long as an article is on a subject of "legitimate public interest" and the photograph used to illustrate the article is "reasonably related" to the subject matter, then the photo has not been used for advertising or trade purposes under the statute.

23 Thus, Arrington first argued that his photograph was not reasonably related to the *Times* story. He did not agree with the views in the article, did not know any of those featured, and did not even feel he was in the same "class" as those portrayed.

24 The *Times* argued that it was enough that Clarence Arrington was indeed a member of the "black middle class," the subject of the article. The press simply had to be free to illustrate such articles with photographs taken in public. If the law were otherwise, the *Times* argued, "Pictures of Sunday strollers down Fifth Avenue, people sitting on a stoop on a hot summer evening, or the faces of people reacting to news of an assassination, would all be banished from the press."

25 Clarence Arrington countered that he was not trying to prevent the press from using crowd shots or covering public events, only that he should not be singled out and featured as the illustration for a story he knew nothing about.

26 The *Times* knew that Arrington had a case that would arouse public sympathy. The newspaper's attorneys said that when they discussed free press issues and mentioned Arrington's situation, even ardent First Amendment supporters said, "Well now, wait a minute. . . ." Nonetheless, the *Times* maintained that it was their First Amendment right to use Arrington's picture as they did, and that there was no way, consistent with a free press, to make a rule to cover Arrington's case. If his complaint was that he had been singled out from a crowd and made to

look as if he had consented to appear in the cover photo, then presumably the answer would be to use a crowd shot. But then could the entire crowd sue?

27 "Some might say that if we had not had just Clarence Arrington, but, say, *three* African Americans crossing the street, all looking prosperous and middle class, that wouldn't have been as 'bad,'" Edward Klein says. "But suddenly the line gets smudged more and more, because why is it okay to have three black people crossing the street? Most people would say, 'Three people, well, that's okay. Two? Well . . . One? Wait a second.'" As always, the question becomes: Where do you draw the line?

28 The media's position is that such lines are necessarily arbitrary and last only until the next set of facts comes along to challenge them. Therefore, no lines should be drawn at all. The press cannot operate freely, the argument goes, if it is under constant threat of a lawsuit, especially from inevitably ill-defined and changing rules.

29 The *Times* asserted that New York courts had long recognized this basic First Amendment principle. The newspaper pointed to several cases indicating that their use of Clarence Arrington's photo was perfectly acceptable under New York law.

30 The cover of *New York* magazine had recently featured a photograph of a man watching the St. Patrick's Day parade under a headline for the cover story: THE LAST OF THE IRISH IMMIGRANTS. It turned out that although the man was dressed in Irish garb, he was not even Irish and had not consented to the use of his picture. In another case, an article on Hindu mystics who used hypnosis to convince audiences that they were watching "Indian rope tricks" was illustrated by a photo of a Hindu man. However, the man was a musician and had nothing to do with hypnosis or rope tricks and, again, had not known his photo would be used. In still another case, a picture of a man at a construction site eyeing a woman passerby was used to illustrate an article on "psychological rape." Not surprisingly, the man had not consented to his photograph being used in this way.

31 Each of the men sued under the New York statute. And each of them *lost.* The photographs were deemed to be "reasonably related to an article of legitimate public interest."

32 But, as often happens in the area of privacy law, Clarence Arrington could point to other cases that seemed to support *his* claim. A photograph of three boys used to illustrate an article on a neighborhood beating was held to be a violation of the statute when it was discovered that the boys had nothing to do with the assault. Also, a college student won under the statute when her photo was used without her consent on the cover of a book about applying to colleges. Thus, Arrington argued, he should prevail under the New York statute as well.

33 Furthermore, Arrington said these cases were part of a trend. Arrington's attorneys asserted that for several years New York courts had

been stretching older rulings under the appropriation statute to allow recovery against the press. Some of these courts had even opined that New York's highest court, the Court of Appeals, was ready to overrule the earlier cases and declare the other privacy torts to be part of the common law of the state. (Most important for Arrington would be the recognition of false light. Arguing that the *Times* had created a highly offensive false impression of him made for a stronger case than alleging that the paper used his likeness for advertising or trade.)

34 By now, most other states recognized at least some of the other privacy torts and allowed greater room for recovery for invasion of privacy than did New York. Arrington's case, his attorneys argued, presented the perfect opportunity for bringing New York in line with these other jurisdictions. It was time, they said, for New York to recognize a general right to privacy under the common law.

35 On April 7, 1982, the New York Court of Appeals declined to do so. Like many people, the members of the court were sympathetic to Arrington's complaint. They agreed that because his picture had been used to illustrate the cover story, "others quite reasonably took the article's ideas to be ones Arrington shared." They also recognized his "perfectly understandable preference that his photograph not have been employed in this manner." Nonetheless, the court held that under New York law, Arrington had no cause of action and his case should be dismissed. The Court of Appeals found that it was indeed enough that Arrington was simply black and middle class for his photograph to be "reasonably related to an article of legitimate public interest."

36 Most important, the court refused to overrule the earlier cases and find a right to privacy in the common law of New York. The court noted that for nearly a century it had consistently refused to do so, stating that it was up to the legislature to protect privacy by statute. The legislature had just as consistently declined to heed the call, content to let cases like Arrington's be dismissed.

37 Then, in a statement that went to the heart of Arrington's case, indeed to the heart of the entire conflict between privacy and the press, the New York Court of Appeals wrote: "An inability to vindicate a personal predilection for greater privacy may be part of the price every person must be prepared to pay for a society in which information and opinion flow freely."

38 However, in a surprise, the court went on to hold that the *photographer* and his *agent* might be liable under the statute. The court said that the sale of the photograph to *The New York Times* was arguably for "trade purposes." Therefore, Arrington could proceed to trial against the photographer and agent, but not the *Times.*

39 Arrington, of course, thought the court had it backwards. He was harmed, he said, not so much by the taking or sale of the photograph, as by its publication on the cover of a magazine. He tried to pursue the

case against the photographer and agent, but after several years of depositions and court papers, he gave up. "Frankly, by that time I had lost interest," he says.

40 Arrington's case ended up having an impact on New York law after all. The New York legislature *did* heed the call and change the privacy statute as a result of the court's opinion in *Arrington v. The New York Times,* but not in the way Arrington expected. The legislature thought that the court was wrong to allow the case to proceed against the photographer and agent—thus, the New York privacy statute was amended to protect photographers and agents from such lawsuits as well.

A. *Comprehension*

Choose the answer that best completes each statement. Do not refer to the selection while doing this exercise.

1. Clarence Arrington's photograph appeared on the cover of an issue of *The New York Times Magazine* to illustrate an article about (a) the impact of the civil rights movement on African Americans; (b) the emerging black middle class; (c) class distinctions among African Americans; (d) successful professional African Americans living in New York City.
2. Arrington was appalled by several things about the *Times* article. Which of the following was *not* mentioned? (a) the author was white; (b) the author had misquoted Arrington's remarks; (c) Arrington disagreed with the author's views about the class system; (d) its subjects were depicted as obsessed with money and material things; (e) the author was inaccurate and patronizing.
3. Arrington's suit against the *Times* for appropriating his picture was actually weaker than he expected because (a) the newspaper had made a good effort to get his permission; (b) a photograph is considered "decorative" and does not have to relate to the article's content; (c) the New York legislature had never passed a law governing citizens' rights to privacy; (d) a newspaper cannot be expected to get permission for every photograph it publishes.
4. In arguing their right to print Arrington's photograph without permission, the *Times* cited (a) the First Amendment; (b) the Fifth Amendment; (c) the Eighteenth Amendment; (d) the Twenty-first Amendment.
5. Apart from the paper's failure to acquire permission, Arrington believed that the *Times* erred in publishing his photograph because (a) it was an unflattering photograph, and he had to endure jokes at his expense; (b) the *Times* had created a highly offensive false impression of him by linking his photograph with the story he

objected to; (c) General Motors, his employer, was annoyed that he was moonlighting as a model; (d) the story had no legitimate public interest.

B. *Inferences*

Complete the following questions. You may refer to the selection to answer the questions in this section, and in all the remaining sections.

1. From the essay as a whole, what is Alderman's and Kennedy's opinion about unauthorized appropriation of a person's photograph?

   ____

2. From paragraph 15, what can you infer about *The New York Times'* track record with regard to printing stories about African Americans, at least according to the *New York Amsterdam News?*

   ____

3. Look again at paragraphs 18, 20, and 22. Explain in your own words how the *Times* was able to get around the prohibition against using a person's "name, portrait, or picture . . . for advertising or trade purposes" without his or her consent. ______________________________

   ____

4. In paragraphs 30 and 31, the authors cite two precedents of two photographs used without permission; the two men sued and lost. What can you infer about the authors' opinion of their legal defeat?

   ____

5. Whose rights did the New York Court of Appeals believe were more important, Clarence Arrington's or *The New York Times'*?

   ____

   What was its reasoning? ______________________________

6. What incorrect assumption did Arrington and his many sympathizers make? ______________________________

C. *Structure*

Complete the following questions.

1. The mode of discourse in this essay is (a) narration; (b) description; (c) exposition; (d) persuasion.
2. The transitional word *nonetheless* used in paragraphs 26 and 35 indicates (a) a contrast; (b) an example; (c) a conclusion; (d) a cause-and-effect relationship; (e) a comparison.

3. The primary method of development throughout the essay as a whole is (a) comparison; (b) definition; (c) contrast; (d) analogy; (e) analysis.
4. Based on the brief examples provided in paragraphs 30 and 32, what conclusion can you draw about the courts' rulings in the four cases cited? ______________________________

____
5. Paraphrase the New York Court of Appeals' statement at the end of paragraph 37. ______________________________

____
6. Ultimately, did Arrington win or lose? ______________________________

D. *Vocabulary*

For each italicized word from the selection, choose the best definition according to the context in which it appears.

1. his *mandate* [paragraph 1]: (a) authoritative order; (b) ambition; (c) obsessive desire; (d) purpose.
2. Arrington was *appalled* [14]: (a) angry; (b) irritated; (c) threatened; (d) dismayed.
3. as materialistic and *frivolous* [14]: (a) not worthy of serious attention; (b) fun-seeking; (c) shallow, superficial; (d) showy, ostentatious.
4. the article was *patronizing* [14]: (a) poorly written; (b) condescending; (c) supportive; (d) apologetic.
5. *"caricatures"* of successful blacks [15]: (a) silhouettes; (b) shop-worn clichés; (c) accurate representations, (d) grotesque imitations.
6. *disparaging* black life [15]: (a) celebrating; (b) belittling; (c) diminishing; (d) mocking.
7. even *ardent* supporters [26]: (a) lukewarm, half-hearted; (b) vacillating, wavering; (c) enthusiastic, passionate; (d) objective, impartial.
8. such lines are always *arbitrary* [28]: (a) subject to whim or individual judgment ; (b) clearly defined; (c) supportive of the moneyed classes; (d) perplexing.
9. the courts had even *opined* [33]: (a) definitively ruled; (b) stated as an opinion; (c) guessed; (d) refused to rule.
10. a stronger case than *alleging* [33]: (a) proving; (b) gathering evidence for; (c) offering as a compromise; (d) asserting without proof.
11. an inability to *vindicate* [37]: In this context, (a) provide justification for; (b) clear of blame; (c) suffer the consequences of; (d) make a persuasive case for.

12. a personal *predilection* [37]: (a) belief in; (b) predetermination for; (c) preference; (d) deviance.

E. *Questions for Analysis and Discussion*

1. Assuming that you correctly understand the facts and the law in *Arrington v. The New York Times,* whose side would you support if it were your decision?
2. Edward Klein, at that time editor in chief of *The New York Times Magazine,* claimed that the issue would have been clearer and easier to resolve if three African Americans had been depicted on the cover rather than only one. Why would this be the case?
3. Can you offer some reasons that might explain why the New York Court of Appeals refused to uphold transgressions against Clarence Arrington's privacy?

ESSAYS: GROUP 3

Selection 11

Helping and Hating the Homeless

Peter Marin

Peter Marin is a free-lance writer who lives in Santa Barbara, California. He has been a contributing editor to Harper's *since 1982, where this essay was first published in 1987. The essay proved sufficiently enduring that it has been widely reprinted in anthologies; it remains one of the most thorough appraisals of the homeless problem ever published. Peter Marin is also the author of* The Limits of Schooling *(1975) and* The World of the Homeless *(1986).*

1 When I was a child, I had a recurring vision of how I would end as an old man: alone, in a sparsely furnished second-story room I could picture quite precisely, in a walk-up on Fourth Avenue in New York, where the secondhand bookstores then were. It was not a picture which frightened me. I liked it. The idea of anonymity and solitude and marginality must have seemed to me, back then, for reasons I do not care to remember, both inviting and inevitable. Later, out of college, I took to the road, hitchhiking and traveling on freights, doing odd jobs here and there, crisscrossing the country. I liked that too: the anonymity and the absence of constraint and the rough community I sometimes found. I felt at home on the road, perhaps because I felt at home

nowhere else, and periodically, for years, I would return to that world, always with a sense of relief and release.

2 I have been thinking a lot about that these days, now that transience and homelessness have made their way into the national consciousness, and especially since the town I live in, Santa Barbara, has become well known because of the recent successful campaign to do away with the meanest aspects of its "sleeping ordinances"—a set of foolish laws making it illegal for the homeless to sleep at night in public places. During that campaign I got to know many of the homeless men and women in Santa Barbara, who tend to gather, night and day, in a small park at the lower end of town, not far from the tracks and the harbor, under the rooflike, overarching branches of a gigantic fig tree, said to be the oldest on the continent. There one enters much the same world I thought, as a child, I would die in, and the one in which I traveled as a young man: a "marginal" world inhabited by all those unable to find a place in "our" world. Sometimes, standing on the tracks close to the park, you can sense in the wind, or in the smell of tar and ties, the presence and age of that marginal world: the way it stretches backward and inevitably forward in time, parallel to our own world, always present, always close, and yet separated from us—at least in the mind—by a gulf few of us are interested in crossing.

3 Late last summer, at a city council meeting here in Santa Barbara, I saw, close up, the consequences of that strange combination of proximity and distance. The council was meeting to vote on the repeal of the sleeping ordinances, though not out of any sudden sense of compassion or justice. Council members had been pressured into it by the threat of massive demonstrations—"The Selma of the Eighties" was the slogan one heard among the homeless. But this threat that frightened the council enraged the town's citizens. Hundreds of them turned out for the meeting. One by one they filed to the microphone to curse the council and castigate the homeless. Drinking, doping, loitering, panhandling, defecating, urinating, molesting, stealing—the litany went on and on, was repeated over and over, accompanied by fantasies of disaster: the barbarian hordes at the gates, civilization ended.

4 What astonished me about the meeting was not what was said; one could have predicted that. It was the power and depth of the emotion revealed: the mindlessness of the fear, the vengefulness of the fury. Also, almost none of what was said had anything to do with the homeless people I know—not the ones I once traveled with, not the ones in town. They, the actual homeless men and women, might not have existed at all.

5 If I write about Santa Barbara, it is not because I think the attitudes at work here are unique. They are not. You find them everywhere in America. In the last few months I have visited several cities around the country, and in each of them I have found the same thing: more and

more people in the streets, more and more suffering. (There are at least 350,000 homeless people in the country, perhaps as many as 3 million.) And, in talking to the good citizens of these cities, I found, almost always, the same thing: confusion and ignorance, or simple indifference, but anger too, and fear.

6 What follows here is an attempt to explain at least some of that anger and fear, to clear up some of the confusion, to chip away at the indifference. It is not meant to be definitive; how could it be? The point is to try to illuminate some of the darker corners of homelessness, those we ordinarily ignore, and those in which the keys to much that is now going on may be hidden.

7 The trouble begins with the word "homeless." It has become such an abstraction, and is applied to so many different kinds of people, with so many different histories and problems, that it is almost meaningless.

8 Homelessness, in itself, is nothing more than a condition visited upon men and women (and, increasingly, children) as the final stage of a variety of problems about which the word "homelessness" tells us almost nothing. Or, to put it another way, it is a catch basin into which pour all of the people disenfranchised or marginalized or scared off by processes beyond their control, those which lie close to the heart of American life. Here are the groups packed into the single category of "the homeless":

- Veterans, mainly from the war in Vietnam. In many American cities, vets make up close to 50 percent of all homeless males.
- The mentally ill. In some parts of the country, roughly a quarter of the homeless would, a couple of decades ago, have been institutionalized.
- The physically disabled or chronically ill, who do not receive any benefits or whose benefits do not enable them to afford permanent shelter.
- The elderly on fixed incomes whose funds are no longer sufficient for their needs.
- Men, women, and whole families pauperized by the loss of a job.
- Single parents, usually women, without the resources or skills to establish new lives.
- Runaway children, many of whom have been abused.
- Alcoholics and those in trouble with drugs (whose troubles often begin with one of the other conditions listed here).
- Immigrants, both legal and illegal, who often are not counted among the homeless because they constitute a "problem" in their own right.
- Traditional tramps, hobos, and transients, who have taken to the road or the streets for a variety of reasons and who prefer to be there.

9 You can quickly learn two things about the homeless from this list. First, you can learn that many of the homeless, before they were homeless, were people more or less like ourselves: members of the working or middle class. And you can learn that the world of the homeless has its roots in various policies, events, and ways of life for which some of us are responsible and from which some of us actually prosper.

10 We decide, as a people, to go to war, we ask our children to kill and to die, and the result, years later, is grown men homeless on the street.

11 We change, with the best intentions, the laws pertaining to the mentally ill, and then, without intention, neglect to provide them with services; and the result, in our streets, drives some of us crazy with rage.

12 We cut taxes and prune budgets, we modernize industry and shift the balance of trade, and the result of all these actions and errors can be read, sleeping form by sleeping form, on our city streets.

13 The liberals cannot blame the conservatives. The conservatives cannot blame the liberals. Homelessness is the *sum total* of our dreams, policies, intentions, errors, omissions, cruelties, kindnesses, all of it recorded, in flesh, in the life of the streets.

14 You can also learn from this list one of the most important things there is to know about the homeless—that they can be roughly divided into two groups: those who have had homelessness forced upon them and want nothing more than to escape it; and those who have at least in part *chosen* it for themselves, and now accept, or in some cases, embrace it.

15 I understand how dangerous it is to introduce the idea of choice into a discussion of homelessness. It can all too easily be used to justify indifference or brutality toward the homeless, or to argue that they are only getting what they "deserve." And yet it seems to me that it is only by taking choice into account, in all of the intricacies of its various forms and expressions, that one can really understand certain kinds of homelessness.

16 The fact is, many of the homeless are not only hapless victims but voluntary exiles, "domestic refugees," people who have turned not against life itself but against *us,* our life, American life. Look for a moment at the vets. The price of returning to America was to forget what they had seen or learned in Vietnam, to "put it behind them." But some could not do that, and the stress of trying showed up as alcoholism, broken marriages, drug addiction, crime. And it showed up too as life on the street, which was for some vets a desperate choice made in the name of life—the best they could manage. It was a way of avoiding what might have occurred had they stayed where they were: suicide, or violence done to others.

17 We must learn to accept that there may indeed be people, and not only vets, who have seen so much of our world, or seen it so clearly, that to live in it becomes impossible. Here, for example, is the story of

Alice, a homeless middle-aged woman in Los Angeles, where there are, perhaps, 50,000 homeless people. It was set down a few months ago by one of my students at the University of California, Santa Barbara, where I taught for a semester. I had encouraged them to go find the homeless and listen to their stories. And so, one day, when this student saw Alice foraging in a dumpster outside a McDonald's, he stopped and talked to her:

> She told me she had led a pretty normal life as she grew up and eventually went to college. From there she went on to Chicago to teach school. She was single and lived in a small apartment.
>
> One night, after she got off the train after school, a man began to follow her to her apartment building. When she got to her door she saw a knife and the man hovering behind her. She had no choice but to let him in. The man raped her.
>
> After that, things got steadily worse. She had a nervous breakdown. She went to a mental institution for three months, and when she went back to her apartment she found her belongings gone. The landlord had sold them to cover the rent she hadn't paid.
>
> She had no place to go and no job because the school had terminated her employment. She slipped into depression. She lived with friends until she could muster enough money for a ticket to Los Angeles. She said she no longer wanted to burden her friends, and that if she had to live outside, at least Los Angeles was warmer than Chicago.
>
> It is as if she began back then to take on the mentality of a street person. She resolved herself to homelessness. She's been out West since 1980, without a home or job. She seems happy, with her best friend being her cat. But the scars of memories still haunt her, and she is running from them, or should I say *him*.

18 This is, in essence, the same story one hears over and over again on the street. You begin with an ordinary life; then an event occurs—traumatic, catastrophic; smaller events follow, each one deepening the original wound; finally, homelessness becomes inevitable, or begins to *seem* inevitable to the person involved—the only way out of an intolerable situation. You are struck continually, hearing these stories, by something seemingly unique in American life, the absolute isolation involved. In what other culture would there be such an absence or failure of support from familial, social, or institutional sources? Even more disturbing is the fact that it is often our supposed sources of support—family, friends, government organizations—that have caused the problem in the first place.

19 Everything that happened to Alice—the rape, the loss of job and apartment, the breakdown—was part and parcel of a world gone radically wrong, a world, for Alice, no longer to be counted on, no longer worth living in. Her homelessness can be seen as flight, as failure of will

or nerve, even, perhaps, as *disease.* But it can also be seen as a mute, furious refusal, a self-imposed exile far less appealing to the rest of us than ordinary life, but *better,* in Alice's terms.

20 We like to think, in America, that everything is redeemable, that everything broken can be magically made whole again, and that what has been "dirtied" can be cleansed. Recently I saw on television that one of the soaps had introduced the character of a homeless old woman. A woman in her thirties discovers that her long-lost mother has appeared in town, on the streets. After much searching the mother is located and identified and embraced; and then she is scrubbed and dressed in style, restored in a matter of days to her former upper-class habits and role.

21 A triumph—but one more likely to occur on television than in real life. Yes, many of those on the streets could be transformed, rehabilitated. But there are others whose lives have been irrevocably changed, damaged beyond repair, and who no longer want help, who no longer recognize the *need* for help, and whose experience in our world has made them want only to be left alone. How, for instance, would one restore Alice's life, or reshape it in a way that would satisfy *our* notion of what a life should be? What would it take to return her to the fold? How to erase the four years of homelessness, which have become as familiar to her, and as much a home, as her "normal" life once was? Whatever we think of the way in which she has resolved her difficulties, it constitutes a sad peace made with the world. Intruding ourselves upon it in the name of redemption is by no means as simple a task—or as justifiable a task—as one might think.

22 It is important to understand too that however disorderly and dirty and unmanageable the world of homeless men and women like Alice appears to us, it is not without its significance, and its rules and rituals. The homeless in our cities mark out for themselves particular neighborhoods, blocks, buildings, doorways. They impose on themselves often obsessively strict routines. They reduce their world to a small area, and thereby protect themselves from a world that might otherwise be too much to bear.

23 Daily the city eddies around the homeless. The crowds flowing past leave a few feet, a gap. We do not touch the homeless world. Perhaps we cannot touch it. It remains separate even as the city surrounds it.

24 The homeless, simply because they are homeless, are strangers, alien—and therefore a threat. Their presence, in itself, comes to constitute a kind of violence; it deprives us of our sense of safety. Let me use myself as an example. I know, and respect, many of those now homeless on the streets of Santa Barbara. Twenty years ago, some of them would have been my companions and friends. And yet, these days, if I walk through the park near my home and see strangers bedding down for the night, my first reaction, if not fear, is a sense of annoyance and

intrusion, of worry and alarm. I think of my teenage daughter, who often walks through the park, and then of my house, a hundred yards away, and I am tempted—only tempted, but tempted, still—to call the "proper" authorities to have the strangers moved on. Out of sight, out of mind.

25 Notice: I do not bring them food. I do not offer them shelter or a shower in the morning. I do not even stop to talk. Instead, I think: my daughter, my house, my privacy. What moves me is not the threat of *danger*—nothing as animal as that. Instead there pops up inside of me, neatly in a row, a set of anxieties, ones you might arrange in a doll-house living room and label: Family of bourgeois fears. The point is this: Our response to the homeless is fed by a complex set of cultural attitudes, habits of thought, and fantasies and fears so familiar to us, so common, that they have become a *second* nature and might as well be instinctive, for all the control we have over them. And it is by no means easy to untangle this snarl of responses. What does seem clear is that the homeless embody all that bourgeois culture has for centuries tried to eradicate and destroy.

26 If you look to the history of Europe you find that homelessness first appeared (or is first acknowledged) at the very same moment that bourgeois culture begins to appear. The same processes produced them both: the breakup of feudalism, the rise of commerce and cities, the combined triumphs of capitalism, industrialism, and individualism. The historian Fernand Braudel, in *The Wheels of Commerce,* describes, for instance, the armies of impoverished men and women who began to haunt Europe as far back as the eleventh century. And the makeup of these masses? Essentially the same then as it is now: the unfortunates, the throwaways, the misfits, the deviants.

> In the eighteenth century, all sorts and conditions were to be found in this human dross . . . widows, orphans, cripples, . . . journeymen who had broken their contracts, out-of-work labourers, homeless priests with no living, old men, fire victims, . . . war victims, deserters, discharged soldiers, would-be vendors of useless articles, vagrant preachers with or without licenses, "pregnant servant-girls and unmarried mothers driven from home," children sent out "to find bread or to maraud."

27 Then, as now, distinctions were made between the "homeless" and the supposedly "deserving" poor, those who knew their place and willingly sustained, with their labors, the emergent bourgeois world.

> The good paupers were accepted, lined up and registered on the official list; they had a right to public charity and were sometimes allowed to solicit it outside churches in prosperous districts, when the congregation came out, or in market places. . . .

> When it comes to beggars and vagrants, it is a very different story, and different pictures meet the eye: crowds, mobs, processions, sometimes mass emigrations, "along the country highways or the streets of the Towns and Villages," by beggars "whom hunger and nakedness has driven from home." . . . The towns dreaded these alarming visitors and drove them out as soon as they appeared on the horizon.

28 And just as the distinctions made about these masses were the same then as they are now, so too was the way society saw them. They seemed to bourgeois eyes (as they still do) the one segment of society that remained resistant to progress, unassimilable and incorrigible, inimical to all order.

29 It is in the nineteenth century, in the Victorian era, that you can find the beginnings of our modern strategies for dealing with the homeless: the notion that they should be controlled and perhaps eliminated through "help." With the Victorians we begin to see the entangling of self-protection with social obligation, the strategy of masking self-interest and the urge to control as *moral duty.* Michel Foucault has spelled this out in his books on madness and punishment: the zeal with which the overseers of early bourgeois culture tried to purge, improve, and purify all of urban civilization—whether through schools and prisons, or, quite literally, with public baths and massive new water and sewage systems. Order, ordure—this is, in essence, the tension at the heart of bourgeois culture, and it was the singular genius of the Victorians to make it the main component of their medical, aesthetic, *and* moral systems. It was not a sense of justice or even empathy which called for charity or new attitudes toward the poor; it was *hygiene.* The very same attitudes appear in nineteenth-century America. Charles Loring Brace, in an essay on homeless and vagrant children written in 1876, described the treatment of delinquents in this way: "Many of their vices drop from them like the old and verminous clothing they left behind. . . . The entire change of circumstances seems to cleanse them of bad habits." Here you have it all: *vices, verminous clothing, cleansing them of bad habits*—the triple association of poverty with vice with dirt, an equation in which each term comes to stand for all of them.

30 These attitudes are with us still; that is the point. In our own century the person who has written most revealingly about such things is George Orwell, who tried to analyze his own middle-class attitudes toward the poor. In 1933, in *Down and Out in Paris and London,* he wrote about tramps:

> In childhood we are taught that tramps are blackguards, . . . a repulsive, rather dangerous creature, who would rather die than work or wash, and wants nothing but to beg, drink or rob hen-houses. The tramp monster is no truer to life than the sinister Chinaman of the magazines, but he is very hard to get rid of. The very word "tramp" evokes his image.

31 All of this is still true in America, though now it is not the word "tramp" but the word "homeless" that evokes the images we fear. It is the homeless who smell. Here, for instance, is part of a paper a student of mine wrote about her first visit to a Rescue Mission on skid row.

> The sermon began. The room was stuffy and smelly. The mixture of body odors and cooking was nauseating. I remember thinking: How can these people share this facility? They must be repulsed by each other. They had strange habits and dispositions. They were a group of dirty, dishonored, weird people to me.
>
> When it was over I ran to my car, went home, and took a shower. I felt extremely dirty. Through the day I would get flashes of that disgusting smell.

32 To put it as bluntly as I can, for many of us the homeless are *shit*. And our policies toward them, our spontaneous sense of disgust and horror, our wish to be rid of them—all of this has hidden in it, close to its heart, our feelings about excrement. Even Marx, that most bourgeois of revolutionaries, described the deviant *lumpen*[1] in *The Eighteenth Brumaire of Louis Bonaparte* as "scum, offal, refuse of all classes." These days, in puritanical Marxist nations, they are called "parasites"—a word, perhaps not incidentally, one also associates with human waste.

33 What I am getting at here is the *nature* of the desire to help the homeless—what is hidden behind it and why it so often does harm. Every government program, almost every private project, is geared as much to the needs of those giving help as it is to the needs of the homeless. Go to any government agency, or, for that matter, to most private charities, and you will find yourself enmeshed, at once, in a bureaucracy so tangled and oppressive, or confronted with so much moral arrogance and contempt, that you will be driven back out into the streets for relief.

34 Santa Barbara, where I live, is as good an example as any. There are three main shelters in the city—all of them private. Between them they provide fewer than a hundred beds a night for the homeless. Two of the three shelters are religious in nature: the Rescue Mission and the Salvation Army. In the mission, as in most places in the country, there are elaborate and stringent rules. Beds go first to those who have not been there for two months, and you can stay for only two nights in any two-month period. No shelter is given to those who are not sober. Even if you go to the mission only for a meal, you are required to listen to sermons and participate in prayer, and you are regularly proselytized—sometimes overtly, sometimes subtly. There are obligatory, regimented showers. You go to bed precisely at ten: lights out, no reading,

[1]According to Marx, *lumpen,* a shortened form of *lumpenproletariat,* were the lowest level of the proletariat, including useless workers, criminals, and assorted vagrants.

no talking. After the lights go out you will find fifteen men in a room with double-decker bunks. As the night progresses the room grows stuffier and hotter. Men toss, turn, cough, and moan. In the morning you are awakened precisely at five forty-five. Then breakfast. At seven-thirty you are back on the street.

35 The town's newest shelter was opened almost a year ago by a consortium of local churches. Families and those who are employed have first call on the beds—a policy which excludes the congenitally homeless. Alcohol is not simply forbidden *in* the shelter; those with a history of alcoholism must sign a "contract" pledging to remain sober and chemical-free. Finally, in a paroxysm of therapeutic bullying, the shelter has added a new wrinkle: If you stay more than two days you are required to fill out and then discuss with a social worker a complex form listing what you perceive as your personal failings, goals, and strategies—all of this for men and women who simply want a place to lie down out of the rain!

36 It is these attitudes, in various forms and permutations, that you find repeated endlessly in America. We are moved either to "redeem" the homeless or to punish them. Perhaps there is nothing consciously hostile about it. Perhaps it is simply that as the machinery of bureaucracy cranks itself up to deal with these problems, attitudes assert themselves automatically. But whatever the case, the fact remains that almost every one of our strategies for helping the homeless is simply an attempt to rearrange the world *cosmetically,* in terms of how it looks and smells to *us*. Compassion is little more than the passion for control.

37 The central question emerging from all this is, What does a society owe to its members in trouble, and *how* is that debt to be paid? It is a question which must be answered in two parts: first, in relation to the men and women who had been marginalized against their will, and then, in a slightly different way, in relation to those who have chosen (or accept or even prize) their marginality.

38 As for those who have been marginalized against their wills, I think the general answer is obvious: A society owes its members whatever it takes for them to regain their places in the social order. And when it comes to specific remedies, one need only read backward the various processes which have created homelessness and then figure out where help is likely to do the most good. But the real point here is not the specific remedies required—affordable housing, say—but the basis upon which they must be offered, the necessary underlying ethical notion we seem in this nation unable to grasp: that those who are the inevitable casualties of modern industrial capitalism and the free-market system are entitled, *by right,* and by the simple virtue of their participation in that system, to whatever help they need. They are entitled to help to find and hold their places in the society whose social contract they have, in effect, signed and observed.

39 Look at that for just a moment: the notion of a contract. The majority of homeless Americans have kept, insofar as they could, to the terms of that contract. In any shelter these days you can find men and women who have worked ten, twenty, forty years, and whose lives have nonetheless come to nothing. These are people who cannot afford a place in the world they helped create. And in return? Is it life on the street they have earned? Or the cruel charity we so grudgingly grant them?

40 But those marginalized against their will are only half the problem. There remains, still, the question of whether we owe anything to those who are voluntarily marginal. What about them: the street people, the rebels, and the recalcitrants, those who have torn up their social contracts or returned them unsigned?

41 I was in Las Vegas last fall, and I went out to the Rescue Mission at the lower end of town, on the edge of the black ghetto, where I first stayed years ago on my way west. It was twilight, still hot; in the vacant lot next-door to the mission 200 men were lining up for supper. A warm wind blew along the street lined with small houses and salvage yards, and in the distance I could see the desert's edge and the smudge of low hills in the fading light. There were elderly alcoholics in line, and derelicts, but mainly the men were the same sort I had seen here years ago: youngish, out of work, restless and talkative, the drifters and wanderers for whom the word "wanderlust" was invented.

42 At supper—long communal tables, thin gruel, stale sweet rolls, ice water—a huge black man in his twenties, fierce and muscular, sat across from me. "I'm from the Coast, man," he said. "Never been away from home before. Ain't sure I like it. Sure don't like *this* place. But I lost my job back home a couple of weeks ago and figured, why wait around for another. I thought I'd come out here, see me something of the world."

43 After supper, a squat Portuguese man in his mid-thirties, hunkered down against the mission wall, offered me a smoke and told me: "Been sleeping in my car, up the street, for a week. Had my own business back in Omaha. But I got bored, man. Sold everything, got a little dough, came out here. Thought I'd work construction. Let me tell you, this is one tough town."

44 In a world better than ours, I suppose, men (or women) like this might not exist. Conservatives seem to have no trouble imagining a society so well disciplined and moral that deviance of this kind would disappear. And leftists envision a world so just, so generous, that deviance would vanish along with inequity. But I suspect that there will always be something at work in some men and women to make them restless with the systems others devise for them, and to move them outward toward the edges of the world, where life is always riskier, less organized, and easier going.

45 Do we owe anything to these men and women, who reject our company and what we offer and yet nonetheless seem to demand *something* from us?

46 We owe them, I think, at least a place to exist, a way to exist. That may not be a *moral* obligation, in the sense that our obligation to the involuntarily marginal is clearly a moral one, but it is an obligation nevertheless, one you might call an existential obligation.

47 Of course, it may be that I think we owe these men something because I have liked men like them, and because I want their world to be there always, as a place to hide or rest. But there is more to it than that. I think we as a society need men like these. A society needs its margins as much as it needs art and literature. It needs holes and gaps, *breathing spaces,* let us say, into which men and women can escape and live, when necessary, in ways otherwise denied them. Margins guarantee to society a flexibility, an elasticity, and allow it to accommodate itself to the natures and needs of its members. When margins vanish, society becomes too rigid, too oppressive by far, and therefore inimical to life.

48 It is for such reasons that, in cultures like our own, marginal men and women take on a special significance. They are all we have left to remind us of the narrowness of the received truths we take for granted. "Beyond the pale," they somehow redefine the pale, or remind us, at least, that *something* is still out there, beyond the pale. They preserve, perhaps unconsciously, a dream that would otherwise cease to exist, the dream of having a place in the world, and of being *left alone.*

49 Quixotic? Infantile? Perhaps. But remember. . . . [w]hat we are talking about here is *freedom,* and with it, perhaps, an echo of the dream men brought, long ago, to wilderness America. I use the word "freedom" gingerly, in relation to lives like these: skewed, crippled, emptied of everything we associate with a full, or realized, freedom. But perhaps this is the condition into which freedom has fallen among us. Art has been "appreciated" out of existence; literature has become an extension of the university, replete with tenure and pensions; and as for politics, the ideologies which ring us round seem too silly or shrill by far to speak for life. What is left, then, is this mute and intransigent independence, this "waste" of life which refuses even interpretation, and which cannot be assimilated to any ideology, and which therefore can be put to no one's use. In its crippled innocence and the perfection of its superfluity it amounts, almost, to a rebellion against history, and that is no small thing.

50 Let me put it as simply as I can: What we see on the streets of our cities are two dramas, both of which cut to the troubled heart of the culture and demand from us a response we may not be able to make. There is the drama of those struggling to survive by regaining their place in the social order. And there is the drama of those struggling to survive outside of it.

51 The resolution of both struggles depends on a third drama occurring at the heart of the culture: the tension and contention between the magnanimity we owe to life and the darker tendings of the human psyche: our fear of strangeness, our hatred of deviance, our love of order and control. How we mediate by default or design between those contrary forces will determine not only the destinies of the homeless, but also something crucial about the nation, and perhaps—let me say it—about our own souls.

A. *Comprehension*

Choose the answer that best completes each statement. Do not refer to the selection while doing this exercise.

1. Marin writes that the word "homeless" (a) is a negatively charged word; (b) is an abstraction; (c) has several meanings; (d) is a confusing term.
2. Marin divides the homeless into two groups: Those who have had homelessness forced upon them and those who (a) are so mentally disturbed that they have little hope of escape; (b) enjoy the stability of city shelters; (c) refuse to live with their families; (d) have deliberately chosen and accepted their homelessness.
3. The story of Alice—the homeless woman from Los Angeles—illustrates a central fact about homelessness, that (a) most homeless people have been victims of crime; (b) a single traumatic event can begin an inescapable downward spiral; (c) city residents are generally unsympathetic to the homeless; (d) homelessness is inevitable for a certain percentage of the population.
4. Our response to homeless people is complex because they represent (a) the breakdown of civic order; (b) the failure of individual responsibility for one's own upkeep; (c) everything dirty and disgusting that bourgeois culture has tried to destroy; (d) a dangerous element of society that disrupts the social order.
5. Marin concludes that homelessness (a) is a national disgrace, proof of the failure of the American dream; (b) a social necessity that reminds us of the importance of having the freedom to be left alone; (c) will require massive infusions of government assistance if cities are to eradicate this growing problem; (d) represents a natural consequence of a polarized society with sharp divisions between rich and poor.

B. *Inferences*

Complete the following questions. You may refer to the selection to answer the questions in this section, and in all the remaining sections.

1. What can we infer about the status of Santa Barbara's "sleeping ordinances" from paragraphs 2, 3, and 4? (a) Sleeping in public is prohibited; (b) sleeping in public is permitted; (c) the city council postponed its vote; (d) there is no way to tell how the council voted on the ordinances.
2. From paragraphs 9–13, we can accurately infer that (a) the homeless are solely responsible for their own plight; (b) the homeless do not consider their situation as desperate; (c) all of society, and especially the military, the government, and industry, are partially responsible for homelessness; (d) the homeless problem is worse now than at any other time in history.
3. In your own words, explain what Marin means in the last two sentences of paragraph 21. ______________________________

   ____
4. Marin implies in paragraph 29 that the Victorians associated (a) uncleanliness with vice and poverty; (b) poverty with lack of ambition; (c) sewage systems with technological progress; (d) charity with hygiene.
5. From paragraph 36 we can infer that the compassion we feel toward the homeless may be (a) sincere; (b) misguided; (c) phony; (d) worthless.

C. *Structure*

Complete the following questions.

1. The mode of discourse in this essay is (a) narration; (b) description; (c) exposition; (d) persuasion.
2. What is the purpose of paragraph 6? ______________________________
3. The method of development in paragraph 8 is (a) facts and statistics; (b) explanation; (c) definition; (d) classification; (e) analogy.
4. Paragraphs 26–30 (a) explain the origins of contemporary attitudes toward the homeless; (b) trace the history of the homeless in Western Europe; (c) show that the roots of homelessness in America are actually in Europe; (d) distinguish between the homeless and the deserving poor.
5. In paragraph 29 Marin emphasizes that, fundamentally, we dislike the homeless because they (a) remind us of our country's failures; (b) remind us of what we might become if we fail; (c) threaten the public order; (d) are often dirty and smell bad.
6. Marin's argument—that the homeless have an important place in our society—would be weakened if he had included (a) a list of

government programs designed to help homeless people; (b) an explanation of the legendary role of the hobo and the tramp in American culture; (c) a discussion of the many economic and social problems the homeless cause; (d) an explanation of what other developed nations have done about the homeless situation.

D. *Vocabulary*

For each italicized word from the selection, choose the best definition according to the context in which it appears.

1. a *marginal* world [paragraph 2] (See also *marginality* in 1): Describing a life (a) of lost opportunities; (b) on the edges of the larger society; (c) economically insecure; (d) lost.
2. the *vengefulness* of the fury [4]: (a) inflicting of punishment; (b) irrationality; (c) excess; (d) lack of good sense.
3. people *disenfranchised* [8]: (a) disinherited; (b) dishonored; (c) deprived of employment; (d) deprived of rights associated with citizenship.
4. many homeless are *hapless* victims [16]: (a) trapped; (b) irresponsible; (c) unlucky; (d) ordinary.
5. voluntary *exiles* [16]: In this context, (a) former military personnel; (b) those who live outside society; (c) those who flee their native country for political reasons; (d) those who reject attempts to help them.
6. the city *eddies around* the homeless [23]: (a) covers up, makes invisible; (b) traps, suffocates; (c) gives birth to; (d) swirls around in the opposite direction.
7. this human *dross* [26]: (a) worthless element; (b) social class; (c) drudgery; (d) condition.
8. an *incorrigible* segment of society [28]: Unable to be (a) convinced; (b) reformed; (c) employed; (d) absorbed.
9. *inimical* to all order [28]: (a) impartial; (b) unaffected by; (c) unrepentant; (d) hostile.
10. tramps are *blackguards* [pronounced *blăg′ ərdz;* 30]: (a) innocent victims; (b) the deserving poor; (c) scoundrels; (d) demons.
11. you are regularly *proselytized* [34]: (a) insulted, treated shabbily; (b) expected to perform household chores; (c) made to repent of one's sins; (d) preached to to bring about religious conversion.
12. the rebels and the *recalcitrants* [40]: (a) those who defy authority; (b) those who obey authority; (c) those who prey on others for money; (d) panhandlers.

E. *Questions for Analysis and Discussion*

1. Is Marin biased? Look through the essay and find examples of his choice of words and examples that reflect his point of view? In addition, what techniques does he employ to ensure balance and fairness?
2. Read Marin's paragraphs 1 and 2 again. Then read paragraphs 46–51. What connection do you see between the ideas in these two sections?

Selection 12

Shiny Happy People Working at the Rat

Jane Kuenz

Inside the Mouse: Work and Play at Disney World, *described as "an outsider's view of Disney World," is the collaborative effort of four people. Susan Willis, a cultural critic and professor of English at Duke University in North Carolina. The other three participants are Shelton Waltrep, an assistant professor at Georgia State University; Karen Klugman, a photographer from Connecticut; and Jane Kuenz, the author of this particular section. A recent recipient of a Ph.D. in English from Duke, Kuenz, who is currently writing about the Harlem Renaissance, currently teaches English at the University of Southern Maine. In this excerpt she focuses on working conditions at Disney World for the workers who portray Mickey Mouse, Minnie Mouse, Goofy, and other assorted characters in the Disney menagerie. (The little interview at the beginning is conducted by Kuenz, here abbreviated "JK.")*

1 TED: *Let's say you were like Pluto, and you were the person in the costume. See, I would never say that to anybody that would write that in the paper, that there was somebody inside the costume. These kids come up and hug you and you sign the autographs and plus, you know, it's just something you have to experience, because you* are *the cartoon. You become Pluto. You have to experience it to understand.*
JK: *Is the "experience" the becoming Pluto or the interaction with the kids?*
TED: *The interaction with the kids.*
JK: *I see.*
TED: *As Pluto.*

2 At one end of the hole under Disney's Magic Kingdom, under the "Carousel," backstage, lies the "zoo." Here, mice and bears, the whole Disney menagerie, gather between their public appearances to kill time without being seen. They must arrive early for their shift to pick up and put on the heavy costumes they negotiate above ground for $5.60 an hour. Inside the huge heads, the heat of a Florida afternoon builds. Some say it gets as high as 130 degrees. All peripheral vision is cut off.

Some of the heads are so unwieldy or the body of its wearer so small that a metal brace is worn on the shoulders with a post extending down the back and up into the head to keep it aloft. Without this, a child's overzealous hug might throw the characters off balance and send them, like grotesque babies, following the head to the ground. The working conditions are so bad that the characters are supposed to go above ground for only 20 to 25 minutes at a time, though in peak seasons they may stay longer. Even then, it is not unusual for the characters to pass out on stage. If you know what to look for you can see them around the park as they wait for a lead to scurry them back to the "zoo," where they can finally remove the head. Learning against replicas of eighteenth-century lampposts or propped against a float's lit backboard, their inhuman heads flashing a permanent smile, they wait, half conscious, hand raised from the elbow, waving absently to no one in particular.

3 Apparently the costumes alone can make wearers sick or, in conjunction with drugs and the Florida heat, can be so painful that wearers are more susceptible to heat exhaustion. Disney has an elaborate roster of height requirements for each kind of costume character: the costumes are built to the specifications of a particular body height and type, although not—as is the case for some performers in MGM Studios—to specific bodies. The bears, for example, require not just height, but strength because of the brace supporting the head. Problems arise when, in the crunch of the summer season, people (usually women, teenagers, and some younger kids) are put into costumes they are not equipped physically to handle:

> When you put a head on, it's supposed to fit on your shoulders. That's why there are height requirements for each individual costume. I have found kids that were 5′ given costumes that should have been given to someone who was 5′4″. So to hold that costume on, they strap the brace on you to make the shoulders stick out. This is how they're walking around for anywhere from 25–45 minutes. I've seen children being hurt by it. They are tired; they're fatigued; their backs, their necks are hurting. And if you were to say "I can't wear this costume," then you can be sure you won't be working there for very long. Your hours would be cut, or you're just not one of the favorites.
>
> It sounds crazy. The gummy bears costumes do not fit somebody that was 4′10″ and they were putting 4′10″ people in them. It was still too large and too heavy for the shoulders of someone with that frame. I played Sunny Gummy and Scruffy—that's the little mean gummy. The heads dig into your collar bones. When you're dancing or even if you're on the moving float, you are in pain. That's metal. There's no way out of it, and there's no relief when you're in it.

4 It's unclear how many of the Disney characters pass out on a given summer day, though everyone is sure that they do. One man reports that during the summer a goodly part of his job is devoted to driving around retrieving characters where they fall. One day he picked up three at one stop—Donald, Mickey, and Goofy: "All of them had passed out within five minutes of each other. They were just lined up on the sidewalk." This is in EPCOT which, unlike the Magic Kingdom with its system of underground tunnels, has a backstage behind the facades of the park's various attractions to which the characters can escape if they have to. If they are in the Magic Kingdom, however, or on a parade float, they must simply ride it out or wait until they've recovered enough to walk to a tunnel entrance in costume and under their own steam. This can get a bit dicey. Passing out is sometimes prefaced by (and probably directly caused by) throwing up inside the head, which cannot be removed until out of public view:

> You're never to be seen in a costume without your head, *ever.* It was automatic dismissal. It's frightening because you can die on your own regurgitation when you can't keep out of it. I'll never forget Dumbo—it was coming out of the mouth during the parade. You have a little screen over the mouth. It was horrible. And I made $4.55 an hour.
>
> During the parades, I've seen many characters in 90° heat vomit in their costumes and faint on the floats and were never taken off the float. There's so much going on during a parade that people are not going to notice if Dopey is doing this [slumps] and he's not waving. . . . I've never seen them take a character off a float.

In one instance described to me, Chip of Chip 'n Dale fame passed out where he stood at the very top of a float, mounted to it by a post that ran up one leg of the costume and into the head. While this was a precaution to keep him from possibly falling off when the float jerked or hit a bump, the visual effect was crucifixion: Chip held up by a post for public exhibition, head hanging to one side, out cold.

5 The cardinal rule among Disney costume characters is never to be seen out of character and specifically out of the head or, alternately, never to let the costume be seen as a costume. Costumes must be black bagged when the characters travel to do work in town or out of the park: "Everything is black bagged. . . . God forbid if that black bag has a tear in it that you didn't know about, and a nose is sticking out of there. You're in trouble." The characters must follow rules about how to and not to move. They can't back up, for example, for the obvious reason that they can see only whatever is straight in front of them and even then only at eye level. They also cannot feel anything around them because the costumes stick out from their body and distort their

sense of space. Sometimes these conditions provide the occasion for delight, as when Minnie Mouse came undone on stage: "I'm walking by the railroad and my pantaloons were around my ankles. You don't feel it because you have so much on you. People were hysterical. Finally, a lead came out, 'Minnie, Minnie, your panties have fallen.'" The fate of Winnie the Pooh, however, is also instructive:

> One time somebody dressed up as Winnie the Pooh backed up. When she backed up she hit a bush and the head popped off. The head popped off Winnie the Pooh, and all the kids see this girl walking around in a Winnie the Pooh costume. And she's fired on the spot because her job is to be the character. And she didn't follow the rules. She should have turned around and walked out. Instead she backed up.

6 Her job is to be the character, and it is on this injunction to "be" a Disney character that the rule not to lose one's head is grounded. Apparently losing her panties is in character for Minnie; Winnie, however, is fired immediately for losing her head, the same way Dumbo would be fired immediately for taking off the one he had just thrown up in because both actions destroy the park's magic, the illusion that the characters are real. One person I spoke with refused for an hour to acknowledge even that there were actual human people inside the Disney character costumes: "That's one of the things I really can't talk about. Not because I work there, but because it keeps it kind of sacred." "Snow White *is* Snow White," another explains. Thus, when she goes to receive an award at a local hospital, Disney officials will not allow her to publicly accept it out of costume. Instead, she must appear as Snow White so those either assembled for the occasion or made privy to it later will not be disillusioned by her transformation into a regular person. In an attempt to impress upon newly-hired employees the significance of the rule not to break character, one management type recounted in a training session the story of taking his visiting niece into the tunnels to find that same Snow White. When they met her, she turned on them, cigarette and Diet Coke in hand, and told them "Get the hell out of here. I'm on break." The child was crushed, the spell broken, and a future shopper permanently lost. It's not a true story, of course—no one can smoke in the tunnels—but it's used apparently to great effect to confirm for new employees the importance of their work and what's at stake—a child's "dream"—in maintaining the company's high standards: "I was very much an idealist about it, about the job, and the whole Disney magic thing that they try to project to the public. I felt that all that magic and happiness was embodied in the character."

7 The extent to which Disney workers seem actually to become their roles and thus embody magic and happiness—and this includes everyone, not just those in head costumes—is one of the most remarked and

generally praised aspects of the park and is said to be the thing that distinguishes Walt Disney World from its neighbor down the street, Universal Studies: "Why is Disney a happier place? Because it's Disney." For those not in character costumes but nevertheless cast and in costume, the transformation to "Disney" via "embodiment" amounts to a kind of leveling out of difference wherever possible. "They deliberately hire blondes," confides one brunette apparently not concerned with reconciling this contradiction. The perception is that they do hire blondes or recreate them as blondes either with wigs or, in one case, enforcing a rule not to have two-toned hair: one woman wanted to stop coloring her hair and let it go gray, but was prevented from doing so by a rule designed to weed out those tending toward fashion experiments. It was okay to be gray; she just couldn't let it go gray. She was left with no choice but to continue coloring it the same honey blonde she had when she came in. Generally, however, it doesn't matter who or what you are when you come in since, once in, you will become whatever you were cast to be: "They have your personality waiting for you. That's literally true: Check it at the door."

8 It's uncanny, in fact, the way Disney's workers once through that door seem not to stop being their roles. One woman explains how it's hard for her to step out of character when she's in the park on her own time:

> I sometimes find myself smiling at people. They're like, "What are you smiling at me for?" I know they're thinking that, but it's because I still feel like I'm constantly this character. I have to say, "Oh, no one notices me, no one recognizes me. It's okay." It's strange sometimes. I'll smile at people or if a child falls down, I go to pick him up, and people probably don't understand that, but I forgot.

During our interviews, many Disney employees would break in and out of character as they spoke, beginning first in a descriptive or narrative mode and switching at some point to direct address as though I were a park guest they encountered in the course of the day. Moreover, their training at Disney University has left permanent marks on their memory. They and the half of Orlando that has worked in the park at some time or another can spout off Disney fun facts at will. How many spots were used in *101 Dalmatians?* 6,469,154. How do you remember the names of the Seven Dwarfs? Two s's, two d's, and three emotions. What kind of popcorn is used in the park? Orville Redenbacher. There's a Disney library and a Disney trivia line for emergencies, but many still have this stuff down years after leaving their jobs. They are information machines, walking advertisements for the park.

9 Apparently this transformation to Disney product is what many of them want when they apply to the park in the first place. These are

frequently people who have migrated to Orlando specifically to work at Disney, often with exceedingly high, perhaps naive, expectations about the park. While these expectations are sometimes only vague notions that Disney must be "the epitome of the fun place to work," at other times they reflect a high level of personal investment with the park and with its power to raise the innocuous or mundane lives of average people into the fantastical and magical existence of the Disney cast member:

> I came down in the summer. I told my parents I was going to work for Disney World, and they said, "Sure you are." I said, "No, really I am. I'm going to go down and work for Disney." They said, "No you're not." And I said, "Yes, I am." So, me and two friends of mine came down—I was just turning 21—in March or April. As soon as you walk in, you are so excited just to be there. Especially me. I'm from Dalton, Georgia. I was a little guy who'd never known anything or been anywhere, and I just decided to come down and do what I wanted to do.
>
> I had six kids in my family. We didn't have a lot of money. But I saw that the park was the one place I saw my parents be relaxed, be kids again. So the park was basically wonderful. What was amazing for me to see would be my dad. He's a truck driver, but he would wear this Goofy hat when he was there. He wouldn't wear it after he left the park, but he would wear it there. And I would see them smile and relax, unlike their usual lives. I saw the behavior change. That is what said to me, "There's something special here."
>
> I was going through a divorce after seventeen years of marriage. I was a dancer many years ago, and I never got the opportunity to do the craft again because I was raising children. I was out of New York. Never knowing what I was going to do and still in the process of raising children, I decided I was going to go to Disney. Why, I don't know; it was a fluke. When you fail at sixteen, it's okay. When you fail at thirty-six, it's kind of rough. It took me seventeen years to get out of my house and get on I-4 and have the courage to go down and apply for something. Well, I go, still never telling anybody, especially my ex-husband who'd said, "What are you going to do? Who's going to want you with three kids? You never worked a day in your life except in the family business, blah, blah, blah." But I thought to myself, I have to do this at least for something just for me.
>
> I was always kind of sentimental about it. I had never been to the park before I worked there. I had just moved down here to Florida from northwest Indiana, the Chicago area, in August 1988, and I got hired in September. It was a very quick thing. It was my senior year in a new school. I didn't know anybody. There was this great opportunity to do something. I picked the character department because it seemed like a lot of fun—the whole concept of "Hey, I'm Pluto."

This is who they are: a twenty-one-year-old homeboy from small town southern Georgia for whom the park represents escape from his parents—their arguments and negative dismissals—so that he can "do what [he wants] to do"; a young woman from a working-class background led back to the park by memories of her parents living one day that is "unlike their [and her] usual lives"; a woman for whom Disney represents a new life and opportunity and the chance to prove she can make it on her own; a seventeen-year-old who finds a place for himself in a new environment at a difficult point in his life by adopting the identity of Pluto. What these stories have in common is the hope that Disney World will provide people with a clean slate and something to write on it; here they can become part of the magic—a Disney item, familiar and reproducible. The park is the site for this transformation, a place where the past—and particularly past identities—is erased, where all bets are off because here a divorced mother of three can and does audition with sixteen-year-olds decked out in their "matching socks and headbands" and get selected over them because, as her director explains, "when she danced, she danced all over."

10 These narratives should be read alongside the various legends and myths that are told and retold in the park and Orlando about miscellaneous millionaires and former executives said to be ladling lemonade at Aunt Polly's Landing. I encountered many tales of these people—though no one who fit the description—who are supposed to have abandoned their former lives either permanently or on a twice-weekly basis to work at Walt Disney World: a former journalist for the *New York Times,* stock analysts in flight from Wall Street, semiretired doctors of various specialties, including a former emergency room doctor from "a New York hospital" (she "couldn't handle the trauma"), bank presidents, disillusioned heirs, and leisured women who jet in from the islands (which they own) for some quality time with the general public. Some of these are the $1-a-year-salary types: "Nothing for me, please. I'm just doing it for the children." Others are said to have walked out of their earlier lives (read: the money, the status, and their attendant problems) to refashion themselves in this new Disney environment. While some of these stories may be true, the veracity of individual cases is less important than the Disney truth produced by the circulation of them: Walt Disney World is the place where truck drivers' daughters work alongside corporate executives in their common mission of producing magic. Furthermore, it's important to see that both the firsthand accounts and the Disney myths trace the same narrative movement. Whether seen from outside as a rise or fall in status or morality, inside the world of Disney they are all the same story, Disney's story, in which everyone moves not up or down—since these implied inequities don't matter or exist in the park—but toward and within the place where each is remade in such a way that anyone can and would want to say "Hey, I'm Pluto. . . ."

11 If reciting the same scripted spiel every fifteen minutes to a new, yet somehow ever more familiar audience is difficult, it is at least made bearable by Disney's rotation system. Ostensibly—and this is its advertised benefit—rotation exposes each employee to the work of those around him or her; this is, in fact, what it does, but only to the extent that the employee is kept going through the shift. Without rotation, says one, "you'd be just sick to death. They tap into a good thing there by moving you around. It does get monotonous as all get-out even then." At a typical Disney attraction, rotation consists of a series of fifteen-minute or half-hour minishifts in which a worker is bumped from monitoring a line outside, to ushering crowds into a theater ("Walk all the way to the end of the row please"), to spieling itself, and back again to the line. In other words, they're not really learning other aspects of the park or of the company's business, but how the particular machinery of their attraction works and how they can function interchangeably as cogs at various points in it. Guests don't register this, of course. What they sense is functionality in its pure and purely invisible form. . . .

12 Those who literally do "put on a face" by putting on a character head routinely claim that park guests seem by their actions not to realize that there are people inside the costumes; guests seem not to see *them.* I find this frankly incredible, but their stories are consistent. A character lead says that "adults and children really believe what they're seeing. . . . Even adults, they believe that's Mickey. The kids go right on with it. That's Mickey that they see." One result of guests temporarily forgetting that Mickey is filled out by a living person is the threat of immediate physical danger. The little kids "pretty much consider you to be a large stuffed animal and treat you the way they treat their stuffed animals at home."

13 You can imagine the possibilities: either they "spot you from twenty yards away and come rushing toward you saying, 'I love you Donald'" or they "hit you, punch you, kick you, bite you." "They think it's fun," he continues. The kids think, "I've seen it in *Home Alone* where the guy gets kicked in the groin and everyone laughs, so, hey, I'll try it with Goofy." Apparently "adults are pretty much like the kids":

> You get the ones that are happy to see you even though you assume that they know better, that I'm not Goofy, that I'm a man wearing a costume that looks like Goofy. You get some that are just really happy to see you just like the kids. They want to get their picture taken. They want to get your autograph. Then you get the adults that are assholes. It's like "Yeah, you're Goofy. I'm going to mess with you." They punch you. I've gotten punched a few times. Punch punched.

14 Other than picking on Goofy for whatever thrill that provides, the more common response to the Disney characters is simple overexcitement, the kind that encourages guests not to think about the people

inside the costume and what they're doing to them. Overexcitement is a bit of a euphemism; as Susan Willis[1] argues, a top priority of Disney guests is to get the right pictures that will document the success of the trip and thus the coherence and happiness of the family so captured in them. Most of the workers understand and are sympathetic to these feelings:

> When people come to Disney and they leave, they don't say, "Oh yeah, we rode Space Mountain, and there was a really nice guy who helped us in line" [in fact, people do say this]. No, it's "We went to Disney" and before they get to anything else they say, "We saw Mickey. We got our picture taken with Mickey."
>
> Visitors are hyped up by their travel agents, and they show them everything they'll get—Mickey and Minnie. These people forget. I really don't believe that they think there's something under the heads. They've got to take that picture home. They need that touch with the characters.

15 This last was told to me by a young woman who, appearing as Minnie, encountered a crowd that apparently needed her touch so badly that it knocked her down and eventually quite unconscious:

> I was taken down by two gentlemen, pulled off the conga line, knocked down to the ground—those heads are very heavy. I lost my balance. The bodice on the costume is wire, and if somebody were to push on that, it will go directly into me. Well, they bent down to help me up. Now there's a crowd of probably fifty people standing around looking at Minnie laying on the floor on Main Street. I was dragged about ten feet. At this point I don't know what's happening. I just think, get me up, get me out of here. That's a mob scene. It's very very frightening. All I know is that this gentleman must have bent down to help me up and his knee hits the body which hits my ribs. At this point I was locked into his head and could not breathe. I thought I was stabbed because there was pain in my side. It's black. There's no way for me to see if there's something sticking out of me. It is horrendous. They left me on Main Street for about fifteen minutes while they were trying to get security. I had passed out. Never to take off my head on Main Street, they took me underground on a stretcher, costume, head and all, and then took it off. I had contusions in two ribs and was out of work for quite a while.

A. *Comprehension*

Choose the answer that best completes each statement. Do not refer to the selection while doing this exercise.

[1]The primary author of *Inside the Mouse.*

1. Ted, a Disney World worker who portrays Pluto, is quoted at the beginning of the essay as saying, "You are the cartoon. You become Pluto," meaning that (a) the costume makes him look like a cartoon character; (b) the Pluto costume is very realistic; (c) portraying Pluto is like acting in a cartoon; (d) playing a cartoon character means completely repressing one's own identity.
2. Those employees who wear costumes portraying Mickey Mouse, Goofy, Pluto, and so forth (a) often suffer from heat exhaustion and pass out; (b) receive the highest pay of any other park employee; (c) are the least experienced workers; (d) rotate roles and play several different characters on each shift.
3. One cardinal rule at Disney World is that employees (a) must not divulge company secrets to the park's visitors; (b) must never be seen out of the character they play or be seen carrying a costume; (c) must submit to random drug tests; (d) must not tell park visitors their real names.
4. When the woman who portrayed Snow White won an award at a local hospital, she accepted it wearing her costume because (a) Disney World wanted her to entertain the hospital patients; (b) Disney World wanted to preserve the illusion of Snow White; (c) her award had been for portraying Snow White in the first place; (d) she wanted to keep her identity a secret.
5. What attracts people to Orlando to work at Disney World is (a) the park's reputation for being a good employer; (b) the park's generous fringe benefits; (c) their desire to climb Disney's corporate ladder; (d) the hope that Disney World will work its magic on their lives and help them erase their pasts.

B. *Inferences*

Complete the following questions. You may refer to the selection to answer the questions in this section, and in all the remaining sections.

1. From the selection as a whole, what can you infer about the working conditions at Disney World? ______________________________
2. From paragraphs 2 and 3, how meticulous is Disney World about observing time limits and height and weight specifications for those employees who portray Disney characters? ______________________________
3. From paragraph 6, what can you infer about Disney's method of training new employees? ______________________________
4. From the information provided in paragraph 9, what attracts many people to seek work at Disney World in the first place? ______________________________

____

5. Concerning the reference in paragraph 10 to the millionaires and business executives who dropped out and came to Disney World to work, why are these "legends and myths . . . told and retold"?

____

____

6. True or false? Based on the evidence, Disney is so concerned with protecting the illusion that the characters are real that it often compromises its workers' health and safety. ______________

C. *Structure*

Complete the following questions.

1. The main idea of the selection is that (a) working at Disney World fulfills the dreams of many people who migrate to Orlando; (b) working at Disney World is demanding and difficult but quite lucrative; (c) Disney World goes to great, almost extreme lengths to protect the image of the park's magic and the illusion that its characters are real; (d) Disney World is a gigantic monolithic entertainment corporation, which, despite employee dissatisfaction, is the enterprise's most profitable element.
2. The mode of discourse in the essay is (a) narration; (b) description; (c) exposition; (d) persuasion. Explain your answer. ______________

____

3. Write the two key ideas examined in paragraph 7. ______________

______________ and ______________

4. Write a main-idea sentence for paragraph 12. ______________

____

5. Look again at the last paragraph that relates an employee's being knocked unconscious and being wheeled away by security. What main idea from the essay does this anecdote reinforce?

____

6. From the examples the author includes and her observations about the "shiny happy people" at Disneyland, how would you describe the author's tone in this excerpt? ______________

____

D. *Vocabulary*

For each italicized word from the selection, choose the best definition according to the context in which it appears.

1. the costumes they *negotiate* [paragraph 2]: (a) arrange for; (b) move around in; (c) design; (d) promote.
2. some of the heads are *unwieldy* [2]: (a) unencumbered; (b) unsteady; (c) poorly designed; (d) not easily handled.
3. a child's *overzealous* hug [2]: *Zealous* means (a) fervent, enthusiastic; (b) clumsy, awkward; (c) done superstitiously to ensure good luck; (d) timid, reluctant.
4. a backstage behind the *facades* [4]: (a) barricades; (b) storage areas; (c) false fronts; (d) inner areas.
5. on this *injunction* [6]: (a) recommendation; (b) directive; (c) advice; (d) request.
6. made *privy* to it [6]: (a) made aware of something secret; (b) made to swear silence about a wrongdoing; (c) made to account for an action; (d) made to participate in something offensive.
7. magic *embodied* in the character [6]: (a) trapped; (b) represented; (c) enhanced; (d) acted out.
8. to raise the *innocuous* lives [9]: (a) innocent; (b) bland, insipid; (c) directionless; (d) ambitious.
9. the *mundane* lives [9]: (a) commonplace; (b) unmotivated; (c) persistent; (d) unfortunate.
10. the *veracity* of individual cases [10]: (a) personal background; (b) scope, dimension (c) truthfulness; (d) lesson, moral.
11. these implied *inequities* [10]: (a) contradictions; (b) inequalities; (c) differences of opinion; (d) subtle nuances.
12. *ostensibly* rotation exposes [11]: (a) from outward appearances; (b) definitely; (c) fortunately; (d) randomly.

E. *Questions for Discussion and Analysis*

1. Do you find any evidence of the author's bias?
2. What is the fundamental contradiction suggested in this essay? Does the author resolve it, and if so, how?
3. At the end of the essay, Kuenz describes the various attitudes and behaviors park visitors exhibit toward the Disney characters. Comment on these behaviors, especially the tendency of some children to punch Goofy. Does this behavior reveal a collective mean streak, or something else?

Selection 13

The Tipping Point and the Epidemic of Crime

Malcolm Gladwell

When he was a child, Malcolm Gladwell and his family immigrated from the West Indies to Ontario, Canada. He is a 1984 graduate of the University of Toronto. From 1987 to 1996, Gladwell was a staff writer at The Washington Post, *covering business and science before serving, for three years, as the paper's New York Bureau Chief. He has been a staff writer at* The New Yorker *since 1996. In "The Tipping Point," published in June 1996, Gladwell writes a thoughtful examination of urban crime and some possible explanations for its recent dramatic decline.*

1 As you drive east on Atlantic Avenue, through the part of New York City that the Police Department refers to as Brooklyn North, the neighborhoods slowly start to empty out: the genteel brownstones of the western part of Brooklyn give way to sprawling housing projects and vacant lots. Bedford-Stuyvesant is followed by Bushwick, then by Brownsville, and, finally, by East New York, home of the Seventy-fifth Precinct, a 5.6-square-mile tract where some of the poorest people in the city live. East New York is not a place of office buildings or parks and banks, just graffiti-covered bodegas and hair salons and auto shops. It is an economically desperate community destined, by most accounts, to get more desperate in the years ahead—which makes what has happened there over the past two and a half years all the more miraculous. In 1993, there were a hundred and twenty-six homicides in the Seven-Five, as the police call it. Last year, there were forty-four. There is probably no other place in the country where violent crime has declined so far, so fast.

2 Once the symbol of urban violence, New York City is in the midst of a strange and unprecedented transformation. According to the preliminary crime statistics released by the F.B.I. earlier this month, New York has a citywide violent-crime rate that now ranks it a hundred and thirty-sixth among major American cities, on a par with Boise, Idaho. Car thefts have fallen to seventy-one thousand, down from a hundred and fifty thousand as recently as six years ago. Burglaries have fallen from more than two hundred thousand in the early nineteen-eighties to just under seventy-five thousand in 1995. Homicides are now at the level of the early seventies, nearly half of what they were in 1990. Over the past two and a half years, every precinct in the city has recorded double-digit decreases in violent crime. Nowhere, however, have the decreases been sharper than Brooklyn North, in neighborhoods that not

long ago were all but written off to drugs and violence. On the streets of the Seven-Five today, it is possible to see signs of everyday life that would have been unthinkable in the early nineties. There are now ordinary people on the streets at dusk—small children riding their bicycles, old people on benches and stoops, people coming out of the subways alone. "There was a time when it wasn't uncommon to hear rapid fire, like you would hear somewhere in the jungle in Vietnam," Inspector Edward A. Mezzadri, who commands the Seventy-fifth Precinct, told me. "You would hear that in Bed-Stuy and Brownsville and, particularly, East New York all the time. I don't hear the gunfire anymore. I've been at this job one year and twelve days. The other night when I was going to the garage to get my car, I heard my first volley. That was my first time."

3 But what accounts for the drop in crime rates? William J. Bratton—who as the New York City Police Commissioner presided over much of the decline from the fall of 1994 until his resignation, this spring—argues that his new policing strategies made the difference: he cites more coöperation between divisions of the N.Y.P.D., more accountability from precinct commanders, more arrests for gun possession, more sophisticated computer-aided analysis of crime patterns, more aggressive crime prevention. In the Seven-Five, Mezzadri has a team of officers who go around and break up the groups of young men who congregate on street corners, drinking, getting high, and playing dice—and so remove what was once a frequent source of violent confrontations. He says that he has stepped up random "safety checks" on the streets, looking for drunk drivers or stolen cars. And he says that streamlined internal procedures mean that he can now move against drug-selling sites in a matter of days, where it used to take weeks. "It's aggressive policing," he says. "It's a no-nonsense attitude. Persistence is not just a word, it's a way of life."

4 All these changes make good sense. But how does breaking up dice games and streamlining bureaucracy cut murder rates by two-thirds? Many criminologists have taken a broader view, arguing that changes in crime reflect fundamental demographic and social trends—for example, the decline and stabilization of the crack trade, the aging of the population, and longer prison sentences, which have kept hard-core offenders off the streets. Yet these trends are neither particularly new nor unique to New York City; they don't account for why the crime rate has dropped so suddenly here and now. Furthermore, whatever good they have done is surely offset, at least in part, by the economic devastation visited on places like Brownsville and East New York in recent years by successive rounds of federal, state, and city social-spending cuts.

5 It's not that there is any shortage of explanations, then, for what has happened in New York City. It's that there is a puzzling gap between the scale of the demographic and policing changes that are supposed to have affected places like the Seven-Five and, on the other

hand, the scale of the decrease in crime there. The size of that gap suggests that violent crime doesn't behave the way we expect it to behave. It suggests that we need a new way of thinking about crime, which is why it may be time to turn to an idea that has begun to attract serious attention in the social sciences: the idea that social problems behave like infectious agents. It may sound odd to talk about the things people do as analogous to the diseases they catch. And yet the idea has all kinds of fascinating implications. What if homicide, which we often casually refer to as an epidemic, actually *is* an epidemic, and moves through populations the way the flu bug does? Would that explain the rise and sudden decline of homicide in Brooklyn North?

6 When social scientists talk about epidemics, they mean something very specific. Epidemics have their own set of rules. Suppose, for example, that one summer a thousand tourists come to Manhattan from Canada carrying an untreatable strain of twenty-four-hour flu. The virus has a two-percent infection rate, which is to say that one out of every fifty people who come into close contact with someone carrying it catches the bug himself. Let's say that fifty is also exactly the number of people the average Manhattanite—in the course of riding the subways and mingling with colleagues at work—comes into contact with every day. What we have, then, given the recovery rate, is a disease in equilibrium. Every day, each carrier passes on the virus to a new person. And the next day those thousand newly infected people pass on the virus to another thousand people, so that throughout the rest of the summer and the fall the flu chugs along at a steady but unspectacular clip.

7 But then comes the Christmas season. The subways and buses get more crowded with tourists and shoppers, and instead of running into an even fifty people a day, the average Manhattanite now has close contact with, say, fifty-five people a day. That may not sound like much of a difference, but for our flu bug it is critical. All of a sudden, one out of every ten people with the virus will pass it on not just to one new person but to two. The thousand carriers run into fifty-five thousand people now, and at a two-percent infection rate that translates into eleven hundred new cases the following day. Some of those eleven hundred will also pass on the virus to more than one person, so that by Day Three there are twelve hundred and ten Manhattanites with the flu and by Day Four thirteen hundred and thirty-one, and by the end of the week there are nearly two thousand, and so on up, the figure getting higher every day, until Manhattan has a full-blown flu epidemic on its hands by Christmas Day.

8 In the language of epidemiologists, fifty is the "tipping point" in this epidemic, the point at which an ordinary and stable phenomenon—a low-level flu outbreak—can turn into a public-health crisis. Every epidemic has its tipping point, and to fight an epidemic you need to understand what that point is. Take AIDS, for example. Since the late

eighties, the number of people in the United States who die of AIDS every year has been steady at forty thousand, which is exactly the same as the number of people who are estimated to become infected with H.I.V. every year. In other words, AIDS is in the same self-perpetuating phase that our Canadian flu was in, early on; on the average, each person who dies of AIDS infects, in the course of his or her lifetime, one new person.

9 That puts us at a critical juncture. If the number of new infections increases just a bit—if the average H.I.V. carrier passes on the virus to slightly more than one person—then the epidemic can tip upward just as dramatically as our flu did when the number of exposed people went from fifty to fifty-five. On the other hand, even a small decrease in new infections can cause the epidemic to nose-dive. It would be as if the number of people exposed to our flu were cut from fifty to forty-five a day—a change that within a week would push the number of flu victims down to four hundred and seventy-eight.

10 Nobody really knows what the tipping point for reducing AIDS may be. Donald Des Jarlais, an epidemiologist at Beth Israel Hospital, in Manhattan, estimates that halving new infections to twenty thousand a year would be ideal. Even cutting it to thirty thousand, he says, would probably be enough. The point is that it's not some completely unattainable number. "I think people think that to beat AIDS everybody has to either be sexually abstinent or use a clean needle or a condom all the time," Des Jarlais said. "But you don't really need to completely eliminate risk. If over time you can just cut the number of people capable of transmitting the virus, then our present behavior-change programs could potentially eradicate the disease in this country."

11 That's the surprising thing about epidemics. They don't behave the way we think they will behave. Suppose, for example, that the number of new H.I.V. infections each year was a hundred thousand, and by some heroic AIDS-education effort you managed to cut that in half. You would expect the size of the epidemic to also be cut in half, right? This is what scientists call a linear assumption—the expectation that every extra increment of effort will produce a corresponding improvement in result. But epidemics aren't linear. Improvement does not correspond directly to effort. All that matters is the tipping point, and because fifty thousand is still above that point, all these heroics will come to naught. The epidemic would still rise. This is the fundamental lesson of nonlinearity. When it comes to fighting epidemics, small changes—like bringing new infections down to thirty thousand from forty thousand—can have huge effects. And large changes—like reducing new infections to fifty thousand from a hundred thousand—can have small effects. It all depends on when and how the changes are made.

12 The reason this seems surprising is that human beings prefer to think in linear terms. Many expectant mothers, for example, stop drinking entirely, because they've heard that heavy alcohol use carries a

high risk of damaging the fetus. They make the perfectly understandable linear assumption that if high doses of alcohol carry a high risk, then low doses must carry a low—but still unacceptable—risk. The problem is that fetal-alcohol syndrome isn't linear. According to one study, none of the sixteen problems associated with fetal-alcohol syndrome show up until a pregnant woman starts regularly consuming more than three drinks a day. But try telling that to a neurotic nineties couple.

13 I can remember struggling with the same theoretical questions as a child, when I tried to pour ketchup on my dinner. Like all children encountering this problem for the first time, I assumed that the solution was linear: that steadily increasing hits on the base of the bottle would yield steadily increasing amounts of ketchup out the other end. Not so, my father said, and he cited a ditty that, for me, remains the most concise statement of the fundamental nonlinearity of everyday life:

> Tomato ketchup in a bottle—
> None will come and then the lot'll.

14 What does this have to do with the murder rate in Brooklyn? Quite a bit, as it turns out, because in recent years social scientists have started to apply the theory of epidemics to human behavior. The foundational work in this field was done in the early seventies by the economist Thomas Schelling, then at Harvard University, who argued that "white flight" was a tipping-point phenomenon. Since that time, sociologists have actually gone to specific neighborhoods and figured out what the local tipping point is. A racist white neighborhood, for example, might empty out when blacks reach five percent of the population. A liberal white neighborhood, on the other hand, might not tip until blacks make up forty or fifty percent. George Galster, of the Urban Institute, in Washington, argues that the same patterns hold for attempts by governments or developers to turn a bad neighborhood around. "You get nothing until you reach the threshold," he says, "then you get *boom.*"

15 Another researcher, David Rowe, a psychologist at the University of Arizona, uses epidemic theory to explain things like rates of sexual intercourse among teenagers. If you take a group of thirteen-year-old virgins and follow them throughout their teen-age years, Rowe says, the pattern in which they first have sex will look like an epidemic curve. Non-virginity starts out at a low level, and then, at a certain point, it spreads from the precocious to the others as if it were a virus.

16 Some of the most fascinating work, however, comes from Jonathan Crane, a sociologist at the University of Illinois. In a 1991 study in the *American Journal of Sociology,* Crane looked at the effect the number of role models in a community—the professionals, managers, teachers

whom the Census Bureau has defined as "high status"—has on the lives of teenagers in the same neighborhood. His answer was surprising. He found little difference in teen-pregnancy rates or school-dropout rates in neighborhoods with between forty and five percent of high-status workers. But when the number of professionals dropped below five percent, the problems exploded. For black school kids, for example, as the percentage of high-status workers falls just 2.2 percentage points—from 5.6 percent to 3.4 percent—dropout rates more than double. At the same tipping point, the rates of child-bearing for teen-age girls—which barely move at all up to that point—nearly double as well.

17 The point made by both Crane and Rowe is not simply that social problems are contagious—that non-virgins spread sex to virgins and that when neighborhoods decline good kids become infected by the attitudes of dropouts and teen-age mothers. Their point is that teen-age sex and dropping out of school are contagious in the same way that an infectious disease is contagious. Crane's study essentially means that at the five-percent tipping point neighborhoods go from relatively functional to wildly dysfunctional virtually overnight. There is no steady decline: a little change has a huge effect. The neighborhoods below the tipping point look like they've been hit by the Ebola virus.

18 It is possible to read in these case studies a lesson about the fate of modern liberalism. Liberals have been powerless in recent years to counter the argument that their policy prescriptions don't work. A program that spends, say, an extra thousand dollars to educate inner-city kids gets cut by Congress because it doesn't raise reading scores. But if reading problems are nonlinear the failure of the program doesn't mean—as conservatives might argue—that spending extra money on inner-city kids is wasted. It may mean that we need to spend even more money on these kids so that we can hit their tipping point. Hence liberalism's crisis. Can you imagine explaining the link between tipping points and big government to Newt Gingrich? Epidemic theory, George Galster says, "greatly complicates the execution of public policy. . . . You work, and you work, and you work, and if you haven't quite reached the threshold you don't seem to get any payoff. That's a very tough situation to sustain politically."

19 At the same time, tipping points give the lie to conservative policies of benign neglect. In New York City, for example, one round of cuts in, say, subway maintenance is justified with the observation that the previous round of cuts didn't seem to have any adverse consequences. But that's small comfort. With epidemic problems, as with ketchup, nothing comes and then the lot'll.

20 Epidemic theory, in other words, should change the way we think about whether and why social programs work. Now for the critical question: Should it change the way we think about violent crime as well? This is what a few epidemiologists at the Centers for Disease

Control, in Atlanta, suggested thirteen years ago, and at the time no one took them particularly seriously. "There was just a small group of us in an old converted bathroom in the sub-subbasement of Building Three at C.D.C.," Mark L. Rosenberg, who heads the Centers' violence group today, says. "Even within C.D.C., we were viewed as a fringe group. We had seven people and our budget was two hundred thousand dollars. People were very skeptical." But that was before Rosenberg's group began looking at things like suicide and gunshot wounds in ways that had never quite occurred to anyone else. Today, bringing epidemiological techniques to bear on violence is one of the hottest ideas in criminal research. "We've got a hundred and ten people and a budget of twenty-two million dollars," Rosenberg says. "There is interest in this all around the world now."

21 The public-health approach to crime doesn't hold that all crime acts like infectious disease. Clearly, there are neighborhoods where crime is simply endemic—where the appropriate medical analogy for homicide is not something as volatile as AIDS but cancer, a disease that singles out its victims steadily and implacably. There are, however, times and places where the epidemic model seems to make perfect sense. In the United States between the early sixties and the early seventies, the homicide rate doubled. In Stockholm between 1950 and 1970, rape went up three hundred percent, murder and attempted murder went up six hundred percent, and robberies a thousand percent. That's not cancer; that's AIDS.

22 An even better example is the way that gangs spread guns and violence. "Once crime reaches a certain level, a lot of the gang violence we see is reciprocal," Robert Sampson, a sociologist at the University of Chicago, says. "Acts of violence lead to further acts of violence. You get defensive gun ownership. You get retaliation. There is a nonlinear phenomenon. With a gang shooting, you have a particular act, then a counter-response. It's sort of like an arms race. It can blow up very quickly."

23 How quickly? Between 1982 and 1992, the number of gang-related homicides in Los Angeles County handled by the L.A.P.D. and the County Sheriff's Department went from a hundred and fifty-eight to six hundred and eighteen. A more interesting number, however, is the proportion of those murders which resulted from drive-by shootings. Between 1979 and 1986, that number fluctuated, according to no particular pattern, between twenty-two and fifty-one: the phenomenon, an epidemiologist would say, was in equilibrium. Then, in 1987, the death toll from drive-bys climbed to fifty-seven, the next year to seventy-one, and the year after that to a hundred and ten; by 1992, it had reached two hundred and eleven. At somewhere between fifty and seventy homicides, the idea of drive-by shootings in L.A. had become epidemic. It tipped. When these results were published last fall in the *Journal of the American Medical Association,* the paper was entitled "The Epidemic

of Gang-Related Homicides in Los Angeles County from 1979 Through 1994." The choice of the word "epidemic" was not metaphorical. "If this were a disease," H. Range Hutson, the physician who was the leading author on the study, says, "you would see the government rushing down here to assess what infectious organism is causing all these injuries and deaths."

24 Some of the best new ideas in preventing violence borrow heavily from the principles of epidemic theory. Take, for example, the so-called "broken window" hypothesis that has been used around the country as the justification for cracking down on "quality of life" crimes like public urination and drinking. In a famous experiment conducted twenty-seven years ago by the Stanford University psychologist Philip Zimbardo, a car was parked on a street in Palo Alto, where it sat untouched for a week. At the same time, Zimbardo had an identical car parked in a roughly comparable neighborhood in the Bronx, only in this case the license plates were removed and the hood was propped open. Within a day, it was stripped. Then, in a final twist, Zimbardo smashed one of the Palo Alto car's windows with a sledgehammer. Within a few hours, that car, too, was destroyed. Zimbardo's point was that disorder invites even more disorder—that a small deviation from the norm can set into motion a cascade of vandalism and criminality. The broken window was the tipping point.

25 The broken-window hypothesis was the inspiration for the cleanup of the subway system conducted by the New York City Transit Authority in the late eighties and early nineties. Why was the Transit Authority so intent on removing graffiti from every car and cracking down on the people who leaped over turnstiles without paying? Because those two "trivial" problems were thought to be tipping points—broken windows—that invited far more serious crimes. It is worth noting that not only did this strategy seem to work—since 1990, felonies have fallen more than fifty percent—but one of its architects was the then chief of the Transit Police, William Bratton, who was later to take his ideas about preventing crime to the city as a whole when he became head of the New York Police Department.

26 Which brings us to North Brooklyn and the Seventy-fifth Precinct. In the Seven-Five, there are now slightly more officers than before. They stop more cars. They confiscate more guns. They chase away more street-corner loiterers. They shut down more drug markets. They have made a series of what seem, when measured against the extraordinary decline in murders, to be small changes. But it is the nature of nonlinear phenomena that sometimes the most modest of changes can bring about enormous effects. What happened to the murder rate may not be such a mystery in the end. Perhaps what William Bratton and Inspector Mezzadri have done is the equivalent of repairing the broken window or preventing that critical ten or fifteen thousand new H.I.V. infections. Perhaps Brooklyn—and with it New York City—has tipped.

A. *Comprehension*

Choose the answer that best completes each statement. Do not refer to the selection while doing this exercise.

1. The main idea of this essay is that (a) crime statistics are confusing and hard to interpret; (b) an understanding of the way infectious diseases behave in an epidemic may help us understand and control violent crime; (c) increased police strategies and improved crime prevention programs are the best solution for the problem of violent crime; (d) epidemics of all kinds have their own set of rules and behave in identical ways.
2. The term "tipping point" refers to (a) the point where an epidemic begins; (b) the point where those people who are going to be infected actually become infected; (c) the point where a previously controllable and stable phenomenon turns into a public-health crisis; (d) the end of an epidemic when the disease disappears.
3. If the number of new infections in a disease—for example, those people exposed to the flu or to the HIV virus—drops even slightly, (a) a dramatic decline in the number of new infections will result; (b) a slight decline in the number of new infections will result; (c) no noticeable effect will occur; (d) the result will be impossible to predict because of the way epidemics behave.
4. Using techniques for understanding epidemics to understand crime (a) has been largely discredited; (b) applies only to the United States because of its unfortunate high crime rate; (c) is still in the planning stage and in need of more funding; (d) is currently the most interesting and hottest area in criminal research.
5. The "broken window" theory is a new method of preventing violence, used to justify (a) longer prison sentences and treating juvenile criminals as adults; (b) stricter gun control and anti-gang laws; (c) cracking down on "quality-of-life" crimes; (d) cleaning up broken glass immediately after it is reported.

B. *Inferences*

Complete the following questions. You may refer to the selection to answer the questions in this section, and in all the remaining sections.

1. From the information in paragraph 5, why do we need a new way to think about crime? ____________________________
2. In paragraph 8, what does Gladwell imply about the spread of AIDS in the future? ____________________________

3. Read paragraph 11 again. Then explain why epidemics don't behave in a linear fashion. ______
4. In paragraphs 13 and 14, what does Gladwell suggest is the relationship between pouring ketchup from a bottle and Brooklyn's murder rate? ______

______
5. From paragraph 25, what is the reader to infer about the relationship between the "tipping point" and "broken window" phenomena?

______
6. From paragraph 25, why it is important to pay attention to seemingly "trivial" crimes by removing graffiti and stopping people who jump over subway turnstiles to avoid paying fares? ______

______

C. Structure

Complete the following questions.

1. Explain why Gladwell focuses on Brooklyn North, an area near New York City, in this essay. ______
2. Write a main-idea sentence for paragraph 2. ______

______
3. Consider these paragraphs and then decide which method of paragraph development is used in each:

   Paragraph 2 ______

   Paragraphs 3 and 4 ______

   Paragraphs 6 and 7______

   Paragraph 8 ______
4. What is the purpose of paragraph 11 in relation to the essay as a whole?______
5. Gladwell's discussion of the connection between epidemics of disease and epidemics of violence (a) is established scientific fact; (b) needs more study before any real conclusions can be drawn; (c) is still a theory with many interesting possibilities that might explain increases and decreases in crime rates; (d) should help communities deal with violence and its root causes.

6. Look again at the second to the last sentence in the essay, which provides (a) a way to tie the central analogies together; (b) a warning for the future; (c) the author's personal opinion; (d) the essay's thesis.

D. *Vocabulary*

For each italicized word from the selection, choose the best definition according to the context in which it appears.

1. *demographic* and social trends [paragraph 4]: (a) population; (b) psychological; (c) transportation; (d) criminal.
2. the economic *devastation* [4]: (a) deviation; (b) materialism; (c) loss; (d) destruction.
3. as *analogous* to diseases [5]: (a) figurative; (b) representative; (c) similar; (d) not comparable.
4. a disease in *equilibrium* [6]: (a) recovery; (b) balance; (c) imbalance; (d) retreat.
5. the language of *epidemiologists* [8]: Specialists in the study of (a) criminal behavior; (b) bacteria and viruses; (c) public health; (d) the causes and control of diseases.
6. the same self-*perpetuating* phase [8]: (a) governing; (b) defining; (c) controlling; (d) continuing.
7. epidemics aren't *linear* [11]: (a) proceeding along a straight line; (b) describing a maze or labyrinth; (c) subject to analysis; (d) easily controllable.
8. every *increment* of effort [11]: (a) example; (b) exertion; (c) sign; (d) slight amount.
9. the heroics will *come to naught* [11]: (a) amount to nothing; (b) be relatively successful; (c) have a long-term benefit; (d) have uncertain results.
10. crime is simply *endemic* [21]: (a) resistant to control; (b) prevalent in a particular location; (c) subject to strong social forces; (d) permanent, fixed.
11. as *volatile* as AIDS [21]: (a) harmful; (b) explosive; (c) uncontrollable; (d) fleeting.
12. singles out victims *implacably* [21]: (a) without regard for economic status; (b) randomly; (c) without warning; (d) inexorably, ceaselessly.

E. *Questions for Discussion and Analysis*

1. Have you observed a neighborhood that has reached the "tipping point"?

2. How strong a case does Gladwell make for the tipping-point phenomenon as a way of understanding how epidemics of disease work? a social problem like teenage sex? homicide rates in urban areas?
3. Gladwell cites the comments of the New York City Police Department commissioner who cites many reasons for the decline in all kinds of crimes. What might be some other reasons—besides Gladwell's theory—that would explain falling crime rates?

Selection 14

Carrie Buck's Daughter

Stephen Jay Gould

Stephen Jay Gould teaches geology, biology, and the history of science at Harvard University. He writes widely on scientific subjects like genetics, biology, and paleontology for the general reader. His best-known books include The Panda's Thumb, Hen's Teeth *and* Horse's Toes, *and the collection of essays from which this selection comes,* The Flamingo's Smile: Reflections in Natural History. *"Carrie Buck's Daughter" presents the case of a young Virginia woman who was an unwitting victim of eugenics (the branch of science concerned with improving humans' genetic stock) and the compulsory sterilization laws popular during the 1920s.*

1 The Lord really put it on the line in his preface to that prototype of all prescription, the Ten Commandments:

> . . . for I, the Lord thy God, am a jealous God, visiting the iniquity of the fathers upon the children unto the third and fourth generation of them that hate me (Exod. 20:5).

2 The terror of this statement lies in its patent unfairness—its promise to punish guiltless offspring for the misdeeds of their distant forebears.

3 A different form of guilt by genealogical association attempts to remove this stigma of injustice by denying a cherished premise of Western thought—human free will. If offspring are tainted not simply by the deeds of their parents but by a material form of evil transferred directly by biological inheritance, then "the iniquity of the fathers" becomes a signal or warning for probable misbehavior of their sons. Thus Plato, while denying that children should suffer directly for the crimes of their parents, nonetheless defended the banishment of a personally guiltless man whose father, grandfather, and great-grandfather had all been condemned to death.

4 It is, perhaps, merely coincidental that both Jehovah and Plato chose three generations as their criterion for establishing different forms of guilt by association. Yet we maintain a strong folk, or vernacular, tradition for viewing triple occurrences as minimal evidence of regularity. Bad things, we are told, come in threes. Two may represent an accidental association; three is a pattern. Perhaps, then, we should not wonder that our own century's most famous pronouncement of blood guilt employed the same criterion—Oliver Wendell Holmes's defense of compulsory sterilization in Virginia (Supreme Court decision of 1927 in *Buck* v. *Bell*): "three generations of imbeciles are enough."

5 Restrictions upon immigration, with national quotas set to discriminate against those deemed mentally unfit by early versions of IQ testing, marked the greatest triumph of the American eugenics movement—the flawed hereditarian doctrine, so popular earlier in our century and by no means extinct today, that attempted to "improve" our human stock by preventing the propagation of those deemed biologically unfit and encouraging procreation among the supposedly worthy. But the movement to enact and enforce laws for compulsory "eugenic" sterilization had an impact and success scarcely less pronounced. If we could debar the shiftless and the stupid from our shores, we might also prevent the propagation of those similarly afflicted but already here.

6 The movement for compulsory sterilization began in earnest during the 1890s, abetted by two major factors—the rise of eugenics as an influential political movement and the perfection of safe and simple operations (vasectomy for men and salpingectomy, the cutting and tying of Fallopian tubes, for women) to replace castration and other socially unacceptable forms of mutilation. Indiana passed the first sterilization act based on eugenic principles in 1907 (a few states had previously mandated castration as a punitive measure for certain sexual crimes, although such laws were rarely enforced and usually overturned by judicial review). Like so many others to follow, it provided for sterilization of afflicted people residing in the state's "care," either as inmates of mental hospitals and homes for the feebleminded or as inhabitants of prisons. Sterilization could be imposed upon those judged insane, idiotic, imbecilic, or moronic, and upon convicted rapists or criminals when recommended by a board of experts.

7 By the 1930s, more than thirty states had passed similar laws, often with an expanded list of so-called hereditary defects, including alcoholism and drug addition in some states, and even blindness and deafness in others. These laws were continually challenged and rarely enforced in most states; only California and Virginia applied them zealously. By January 1935, some 20,000 forced "eugenic" sterilizations had been performed in the United States, nearly half in California.

8 No organization crusaded more vociferously and successfully for these laws than the Eugenics Record Office, the semiofficial arm and

repository of data for the eugenics movement in America. Harry Laughlin, superintendent of the Eugenics Record Office, dedicated most of his career to a tireless campaign of writing and lobbying for eugenic sterilization. He hoped, thereby, to eliminate in two generations the genes of what he called the "submerged tenth"—"the most worthless one-tenth of our present population." He proposed a "model sterilization law" in 1922, designed

> to prevent the procreation of person socially inadequate from defective inheritance, by authorizing and providing for eugenical sterilization of certain potential parents carrying degenerate hereditary qualities.

9 This model bill became the prototype for most laws passed in America, although few states cast their net as widely as Laughlin advised. (Laughlin's categories encompassed "blind, including those with seriously impaired vision; deaf, including those with seriously impaired hearing; and dependent, including orphans, ne'er-do-wells, the homeless, tramps, and paupers.") Laughlin's suggestions were better heeded in Nazi Germany, where his model act inspired the infamous and stringently enforced *Erbgesundheitsrecht,*[1] leading by the eve of World War II to the sterilization of some 375,000 people, most for "congenital feeblemindedness," but including nearly 4,000 for blindness and deafness.

10 The campaign for forced eugenic sterilization in America reached its climax and height of respectability in 1927, when the Supreme Court, by an 8–1 vote, upheld the Virginia sterilization bill in *Buck* v. *Bell.* Oliver Wendell Holmes, then in his mid-eighties and the most celebrated jurist in America, wrote the majority opinion with his customary verve and power of style. It included the notorious paragraph, with its chilling tag line, cited ever since as the quintessential statement of eugenic principles. Remembering with pride his own distant experiences as an infantryman in the Civil War, Holmes wrote:

> We have seen more than once that the public welfare may call upon the best citizens for their lives. It would be strange if it could not call upon those who already sap the strength of the state for these lesser sacrifices. . . . It is better for all the world, if instead of waiting to execute degenerate offspring for crime, or to let them starve for their imbecility, society can prevent those who are manifestly unfit from continuing their kind. The principle that sustains compulsory vaccination is broad enough to cover cutting the Fallopian tubes. Three generations of imbeciles are enough.

11 Who, then, were the famous "three generations of imbeciles," and why should they still compel our interest?

[1]German term meaning a program promoting inherited good health.

12 When the state of Virginia passed its compulsory sterilization law in 1924, Carrie Buck, an eighteen-year-old white woman, lived as an involuntary resident at the State Colony for Epileptics and Feeble-Minded. As the first person selected for sterilization under the new act, Carrie Buck became the focus for a constitutional challenge launched, in part, by conservative Virginia Christians who held, according to eugenical "modernists," antiquated views about individual preferences and "benevolent" state power. (Simplistic political labels do not apply in this case, and rarely in general for that matter. We usually regard eugenics as a conservative movement and its most vocal critics as members of the left. This alignment has generally held in our own decade. But eugenics, touted in its day as the latest in scientific modernism, attracted many liberals and numbered among its most vociferous critics groups often labeled as reactionary and antiscientific. If any political lesson emerges from these shifting allegiances, we might consider the true inalienability of certain human rights.)

13 But why was Carrie Buck in the State Colony and why was she selected? Oliver Wendell Holmes upheld her choice as judicious in the opening lines of his 1927 opinion:

> Carrie Buck is a feeble-minded white woman who was committed to the State Colony. . . . She is the daughter of a feeble-minded mother in the same institution, and the mother of an illegitimate feeble-minded child.

14 In short, inheritance stood as the crucial issue (indeed as the driving force behind all eugenics). For if measured mental deficiency arose from malnourishment, either of body or mind, and not from tainted genes, then how could sterilization be justified? If decent food, upbringing, medical care, and education might make a worthy citizen of Carrie Buck's daughter, how could the State of Virginia justify the severing of Carrie's Fallopian tubes against her will? (Some forms of mental deficiency are passed by inheritance in family lines, but most are not—a scarcely surprising conclusion when we consider the thousand shocks that beset us all during our lives, from abnormalities in embryonic growth to traumas of birth, malnourishment, rejection, and poverty. In any case, no fair-minded person today would credit Laughlin's social criteria for the identification of hereditary deficiency—ne'er-do-wells, the homeless, tramps, and paupers—although we shall soon see that Carrie Buck was committed on these grounds.)

15 When Carrie Buck's case emerged as the crucial test of Virginia's law, the chief honchos of eugenics understood that the time had come to put up or shut up on the crucial issue of inheritance. Thus, the Eugenics Record Office sent Arthur H. Estabrook, their crack fieldworker, to Virginia for a "scientific" study of the case. Harry Laughlin himself provided a deposition, and his brief for inheritance was presented at the

local trial that affirmed Virginia's law and later worked its way to the Supreme Court as *Buck v. Bell.*

16 Laughlin made two major points to the court. First, that Carrie Buck and her mother, Emma Buck, were feebleminded by the Stanford-Binet test of IQ, then in its own infancy. Carrie scored a mental age of nine years, Emma of seven years and eleven months. (These figures ranked them technically as "imbeciles" by definitions of the day, hence Holmes's later choice of words—though his infamous line is often misquoted as "three generations of idiots." Imbeciles displayed a mental age of six to nine years; idiots performed worse, morons better, to round out the old nomenclature of mental deficiency.) Second, that most feeblemindedness resides ineluctably in the genes, and that Carrie Buck surely belonged with this majority. Laughlin reported:

> Generally feeble-mindedness is caused by the inheritance of degenerate qualities; but sometimes it might be caused by environmental factors which are not hereditary. In the case given, the evidence points strongly toward the feeble-mindedness and moral delinquency of Carrie Buck being due, primarily, to inheritance and not to environment.

17 Carrie Buck's daughter was then, and has always been, the pivotal figure of this painful case. I noted in beginning this essay that we tend (often at our peril) to regard two as potential accident and three as an established pattern. The supposed imbecility of Emma and Carrie might have been an unfortunate coincidence, but the diagnosis of similar deficiency for Vivian Buck (made by a social worker, as we shall see, when Vivian was but six months old) tipped the balance in Laughlin's favor and led Holmes to declare the Buck lineage inherently corrupt by deficient heredity. Vivian sealed the pattern—*three* generations of imbeciles are enough. Besides, had Carrie not given illegitimate birth to Vivian, the issue (in both senses) would never have emerged.

18 Oliver Wendell Holmes viewed his work with pride. The man so renowned for his principle of judicial restraint, who had proclaimed that freedom must not be curtailed without "clear and present danger"—without the equivalent of falsely yelling "fire" in a crowded theater—wrote of his judgment in *Buck* v. *Bell:* "I felt that I was getting near the first principle of real reform."

19 And so *Buck* v. *Bell* remained for fifty years, a footnote to a moment of American history perhaps best forgotten. Then, in 1980, it reemerged to prick our collective conscience, when Dr. K. Ray Nelson, then director of the Lynchburg Hospital where Carrie Buck had been sterilized, researched the records of his institution and discovered that more than 4,000 sterilizations had been performed, the last as late as 1972. He also found Carrie Buck, alive and well near Charlottesville, and her sister Doris, covertly sterilized under the same law (she was told that her

operation was for appendicitis), and now, with fierce dignity, dejected and bitter because she had wanted a child more than anything else in her life and had finally, in her old age, learned why she had never conceived.

20 As scholars and reporters visited Carrie Buck and her sister, what a few experts had known all along became abundantly clear to everyone. Carrie Buck was a woman of obviously normal intelligence. For example, Paul A. Lombardo of the School of Law at the University of Virginia, and a leading scholar of *Buck* v. *Bell,* wrote in a letter to me:

> As for Carrie, when I met her she was reading newspapers daily and joining a more literate friend to assist at regular bouts with the crossword puzzles. She was not a sophisticated woman, and lacked social graces, but mental health professionals who examined her in later life confirmed my impressions that she was neither mentally ill nor retarded.

21 On what evidence, then, was Carrie Buck consigned to the State Colony for Epileptics and Feeble-Minded on January 23, 1924? I have seen the text of her commitment hearing; it is, to say the least, cursory and contradictory. Beyond the bald and undocumented say-so of her foster parents, and her own brief appearance before a commission of two doctors and a justice of the peace, no evidence was presented. Even the crude and early Stanford-Binet test, so fatally flawed as a measure of innate worth (see my book *The Mismeasure of Man,* although the evidence of Carrie's own case suffices) but at least clothed with the aura of quantitative respectability, had not yet been applied.

22 When we understand why Carrie Buck was committed in January 1924, we can finally comprehend the hidden meaning of her case and its message for us today. The silent key, again as from the first, is her daughter Vivian, born on March 28, 1924, and then but an evident bump on her belly. Carrie Buck was one of several illegitimate children borne by her mother, Emma. she grew up with foster parents, J.T. and Alice Dobbs, and continued to live with them as an adult, helping out with chores around the house. She was raped by a relative of her foster parents, then blamed for the resulting pregnancy. Almost surely, she was (as they used to say) committed to hide her shame (and her rapist's identity), not because enlightened science had just discovered her true mental status. In short, she was sent away to have her baby. Her case never was about mental deficiency; Carrie Buck was persecuted for supposed sexual immorality and social deviance. The annals of her trial and hearing reek with the contempt of the well-off and well-bred for poor people of "loose morals." Who really cared whether Vivian was a baby of normal intelligence; she was the illegitimate child of an illegitimate woman. Two generations of bastards are enough. Harry Laughlin began his "family history" of the Bucks by writing: "These people belong to the shiftless, ignorant and worthless class of anti-social whites of the South."

23 We know little of Emma Buck and her life, but we have no more reason to suspect her than her daughter Carrie of true mental deficiency. Their supposed deviance was social and sexual; the charge of imbecility was a cover-up, Mr. Justice Holmes notwithstanding.

24 We come then to the crux of the case, Carrie's daughter, Vivian. What evidence was ever adduced for her mental deficiency? This and only this: At the original trial in late 1924, when Vivian Buck was seven months old, a Miss Wilhelm, social worker for the Red Cross, appeared before the court. She began by stating honestly the true reason for Carrie Buck's commitment:

> Mr. Dobbs, who had charge of the girl, had taken her when a small child, had reported to Miss Duke [the temporary secretary of Public Welfare for Albemarle County] that the girl was pregnant and that he wanted to have her committed somewhere—to have her sent to some institution.

25 Miss Wilhelm then rendered her judgment of Vivian Buck by comparing her with the normal granddaughter of Mrs. Dobbs, born just three days earlier:

> It is difficult to judge probabilities of a child as young as that, but it seems to me not quite a normal baby. In its appearance—I should say that perhaps my knowledge of the mother may prejudice me in that regard, but I saw the child at the same time as Mrs. Dobbs' daughter's baby, which is only three days older than this one, and there is a very decided difference in the development of the babies. That was about two weeks ago. There is a look about it that is not quite normal, but just what it is, I can't tell.

26 This short testimony, and nothing else, formed all the evidence for the crucial third generation of imbeciles. Cross-examination revealed that neither Vivian nor the Dobbs grandchild could walk or talk, and that "Mrs. Dobbs' daughter's baby is a very responsive baby. When you play with it or try to attract its attention—it is a baby that you can play with. The other baby is not. It seems very apathetic and not responsive." Miss Wilhelm then urged Carrie Buck's sterilization: "I think," she said, "It would at least prevent the propagation of her kind." Several years later, Miss Wilhelm denied that she had ever examined Vivian or deemed the child feebleminded.

27 Unfortunately, Vivian died at age eight of "enteric colitis" (as recorded on her death certificate), an ambiguous diagnosis that could mean many things but may well indicate that she fell victim to one of the preventable childhood diseases of poverty (a grim reminder of the real subject in *Buck* v. *Bell*). She is therefore mute as a witness in our reassessment of her famous case.

28 When *Buck* v. *Bell* resurfaced in 1980, it immediately struck me that Vivian's case was crucial and that evidence for the mental status of a

child who died at age eight might best be found in report cards. I have therefore been trying to track down Vivian Buck's school records for the past four years and have finally succeeded. (They were supplied to me by Dr. Paul A. Lombardo, who also sent other documents, including Miss Wilhelm's testimony, and spent several hours answering my questions by mail and Lord knows how much time playing successful detective in researching Vivian's school records. I have never met Dr. Lombardo; he did all this work for kindness, collegiality, and love of the game of knowledge, not for expected reward or even requested acknowledgment. In a profession—academics—so often marred by pettiness and silly squabbling over meaningless priorities, this generosity must be recorded and celebrated as a sign of how things can and should be.)

29 Vivian Buck was adopted by the Dobbs family, who had raised (but later sent away) her mother, Carrie. As Vivian Alice Elaine Dobbs, she attended the Venable Public Elementary School of Charlottesville for four terms, from September 1930 until May 1932, a month before her death. She was a perfectly normal, quite average student, neither particularly outstanding nor much troubled. In those days before grade inflation, when C meant "good, 81–87" (as defined on her report card) rather than barely scraping by, Vivian Dobbs received A's and B's for deportment and C's for all academic subjects but mathematics (which was always difficult for her, and where she scored D) during her first term in Grade 1A, from September 1930 to January 1931. She improved during her second term in 1B, meriting an A in deportment, C in mathematics, and B in all other academic subjects; she was placed on the honor roll in April 1931. Promoted to 2A, she had trouble during the fall term of 1931, failing mathematics and spelling but receiving A in deportment, B in reading, and C in writing and English. She was "retained in 2A" for the next term—or "left back" as we used to say, and scarcely a sign of imbecility as I remember all my buddies who suffered a similar fate. In any case, she again did well in her final term, with B in deportment, reading, and spelling, and C in writing, English, and mathematics during her last month in school. This daughter of "lewd and immoral" women excelled in deportment and performed adequately, although not brilliantly, in her academic subjects.

30 In short, we can only agree with the conclusion that Dr. Lombardo has reached in his research on *Buck* v. *Bell*—there were no imbeciles, not a one, among the three generations of Bucks. I don't know that such correction of cruel but forgotten errors of history counts for much, but I find it both symbolic and satisfying to learn that forced eugenic sterilization, a procedure of such dubious morality, earned its official justification (and won its most quoted line of rhetoric) on a patent falsehood.

31 Carrie Buck died last year. By a quirk of fate, and not by memory or design, she was buried just a few steps from her only daughter's grave.

In the umpteenth and ultimate verse of a favorite old ballad, a rose and a brier—the sweet and the bitter—emerge from the tombs of Barbara Allen and her lover, twining about each other in the union of death. May Carrie and Vivian, victims in different ways and in the flower of youth, rest together in peace.

A. *Comprehension*

Choose the answer that best completes each statement. Do not refer to the selection while doing this exercise.

1. The basic assumption proponents of eugenics and compulsory sterilization hold is that (a) parents should be held legally responsible for their children's crimes; (b) human free will should take precedence over all other considerations; (c) the propensity for evil or for mental deficiency is inherited and can be passed down from generation to generation; (d) the Ten Commandments have established historical precedents for sterilization.
2. Gould writes that the eugenics movement, which he characterizes as flawed, specifically advocated preventing biologically fit people from reproducing and encouraged (a) scientific research in the new field of genetics; (b) people who were biologically fit to reproduce; (c) increased immigration to the U.S. to diversify the gene pool; (d) people with mental deficiencies to submit to voluntary sterilization.
3. The ostensible or *stated* reason that Carrie Buck was selected for involuntary sterilization was that (a) she had inherited criminal tendencies from her mother; (b) she, her mother, and her daughter were all feeble-minded; (c) she suffered from a sexually transmitted disease; (d) she had a mental age of nine years according to the Stanford-Binet IQ test.
4. According to Gould, the *real* reason Carrie Buck was confined to a mental institution and sterilized is that (a) her foster parents wanted to get rid of her; (b) she was homeless and had nowhere else to go; (c) she was widely regarded in Charlottesville as a person of "loose morals"; (d) she was illegitimate herself, and after she was raped, produced an illegitimate offspring.
5. Vivian Buck, Carrie Buck's daughter, was judged mentally defective at the age of six months by a social worker, Miss Wilhelm, who (a) studied the baby intensively for several days; (b) looked at the baby briefly and concluded that she didn't look quite right in comparison with another baby of the same age; (c) compared her with her own granddaughter who was also mentally defective; (d) administered the Stanford-Binet IQ test to her.

B. *Inferences*

Complete the following questions. You may refer to the selection to answer the questions in this section, and all the remaining sections.

1. From the essay as a whole, we can infer that (a) it is morally wrong for science or government to tamper with people's reproductive rights; (b) no one takes eugenics seriously any longer; (c) feeblemindedness is a genetic trait that can be handed down to the next generation; (d) eugenics has some positive tenets, among them weeding out undesirables from the population.
2. From paragraph 6 we know that the law requiring castration for people convicted of sex crimes was not always enforced, and we can infer that (a) the law requiring sterilization of the mentally deficient was similarly not enforced; (b) the mentally ill were routinely sterilized; (c) sterilizing the mentally ill was illegal; (d) sterilizing the mentally ill kept the numbers of mentally deficient children low.
3. Gould implies in paragraphs 8 and 9 that Harry Laughlin (a) believed that blindness, deafness, and poverty were hereditary conditions; (b) was not very effective in his campaign to promote eugenic sterilization; (c) ignored those who criticized his eugenics campaign; (d) had solid scientific evidence behind his campaign to stop the "submerged one-tenth of the population" from procreating.
4. We can infer from paragraphs 16 and 20 that (a) Harry Laughlin knew Carrie Buck well; (b) the Stanford-Binet test administered to Carrie Buck was a reliable measure of her intelligence; (c) the Stanford-Binet test administered to Carrie Buck was not a reliable measure of her intelligence; (d) Harry Laughlin lied in court about Carrie Buck's intelligence.
5. Gould implies in paragraph 18 that, in his handling of *Buck v. Bell,* Oliver Wendell Holmes (a) indeed showed judicial restraint; (b) did not show judicial restraint; (c) was uncertain about Laughlin's eugenic theories; (d) established a significant legal precedent that still exists today.
6. From paragraph 22 and from the essay as a whole, we can infer that Carrie Buck (a) was a victim of repressive sexual mores characteristic of earlier times; (b) spoke out vehemently in her defense but was unsuccessful; (c) lost her civil rights because she had been committed to a state hospital; (d) was committed and later sterilized because she refused to name her rapist.

C. *Structure*

1. The primary mode of discourse in the essay is (a) narration; (b) description; (c) exposition; (d) persuasion. Explain your answer.

____

____

2. Gould's purpose in writing this essay is, specifically, (a) to trace the history of an important Supreme Court decision; (b) to tell the story of Carrie Buck's sad life; (c) to analyze the defects in eugenic theories; (d) to set the record straight about forced eugenic sterilization, using the case of Carrie Buck as the focus.
3. Which of the following statements is crucial to understanding the wrong that was done to Carrie Buck? (a) California and Virginia applied forced sterilization more zealously than other states; (b) three generations of imbeciles are enough; (c) [her] supposed deviance was social and sexual; the charge of imbecility was a coverup; (d) inheritance stood as the crucial issue (indeed as the driving force behind all eugenics).
4. With regard to the essay as a whole, paragraphs 5–10 serve as (a) important explanatory background about the eugenics movement; (b) legal evidence in the case against Carrie Buck; (c) the author's own scientific theories; (d) a discussion of constitutional law.
5. The author includes the opinion of Dr. Paul A. Lombardo, whom Gould praises for his generous assistance in researching this case, because (a) he is an authority on *Buck v. Bell;* (b) he interviewed Carrie Buck and found her of normal intelligence; (c) he is a personal friend of Gould's; (d) he also rejects the theories of eugenics supporters.
6. Why is this essay titled "Carrie Buck's Daughter? (and not, say, "The Case of Carrie Buck")? ____________________

D. *Vocabulary*

For each italicized word from the selection, choose the best definition according to the context in which it appears.

1. that *prototype* of all prescription [paragraphs 1 and 9]: (a) relevant example; (b) original model; (c) written document; (d) set of legal precepts.

2. visiting the *iniquity* of the fathers upon the children [1 and 3]: (a) hereditary influence; (b) personality traits; (c) physical characteristics; (d) sin, wickedness.
3. lies in its *patent* unfairness [2 and 30]: (a) exclusive; (b) unsealed; (c) obvious; (d) protected.
4. the misdeeds of their distant *forebears* [2]: (a) descendants; (b) ancestors; (c) relatives; (d) siblings.
5. to remove this *stigma* of injustice [3]: (a) mark of disgrace; (b) principle; (c) representation; (d) damage.
6. *abetted* by two major factors [6]: (a) encouraged; (b) supported; (c) proved; (d) justified.
7. No organization crusaded more *vociferously* [8] (See also *vociferous* in 12): (a) loudly, vehemently; (b) effectively, productively; (c) openly, aboveboard; (d) obsessively, compulsively.
8. his customary *verve* and power of style [10]: (a) reticence; (b) eloquence; (c) liveliness; (d) rigidity.
9. the *quintessential* statement of eugenic principles [10]: (a) definitive, authoritative; (b) pure, concentrated; (c) lucid, clear; (d) rational, reasonable.
10. the old *nomenclature* of mental deficiency [16]: (a) system of naming; (b) description; (c) hierarchy; (d) analytical model.
11. most feeblemindedness resides *ineluctably* in the genes [16]: (a) invisibly; (b) unavoidably; (c) unobtrusively; (d) indestructibly.
12. the *crux* of the case [24]: (a) basic point; (b) highlight; (c) supporting evidence; (d) main argument.

E. *Questions for Analysis and Discussion*

1. How effective is Gould at presenting information exonerating Carrie Buck and uncovering the real story behind her forced sterilization?
2. As Gould states in paragraph 5, the science of eugenics is not extinct today. With the increased availability of genetic counseling, prospective parents can learn the genetic makeup of their unborn children. Those who study ethics fear that soon parents will be able to choose an offspring that meets a certain genetic model (height, eye color, intelligence level, and the like). Comment on this phenomenon. Does it pose ethical concerns for you?

Selection 15

Student Evaluations

Aristides (Joseph Epstein)

Aristides is the pen name of Joseph Epstein, professor of English at Northwestern University and for many years until 1998, editor of The American Scholar, *a publication of the Phi Beta Kappa Society. (Aristides "the Just" was a fifth century political leader in Athens.) Epstein has published many collections, among them,* Plausible Prejudices *(1985) and* With My Trousers Rolled *(1995). Epstein published "Student Evaluations" first in* The American Scholar *and later included it in a collection of essays,* A Line out for a Walk *(1991) retitled* "Autodidact." *This selection is partly a confessional piece in which Epstein discusses his own failings as a student and partly an examination of teachers' expectations of students, revealed by Epstein's characteristic wit and self-deprecating sense of humor.*

1 Socrates may have had to take the hemlock, but at least he was spared the indignity of that relatively recent addition to the teaching transaction known as "teacher evaluation." On these evaluations, generally made during the last minutes of the final session of the college term, students, in effect, grade their teachers. Hemlock may on occasion seem preferable, for turn-about here can sometimes be cruel play, especially when students, under the veil of anonymity, take the opportunity of evaluation to comment upon their teacher's dress, or idiosyncrasies, or moral character. For the most part I have not fared too badly on these evaluations, though my clothes have been the subject of faint comedy, my habit of jiggling the change in my pockets and my wretched handwriting have been noted, and in one instance I have been accused of showing favoritism (a charge I choose to interpret as my preference, in the classroom, for calling upon the relatively intelligent over the complete obtuse). None of these student comments, as you can plainly see, affects me in the least; such personal criticisms roll right off me, like buckshot off a duck's heart.

2 Unless they have long since been rendered catatonic by boredom, or are people on whom everything is lost, teachers of course make similar observations about their students—certainly this teacher does—and the one subject on which all teachers ought to be connoisseurs is that

of the studentry. The difference is that teachers, unlike contemporary students, must keep these observations to themselves. Yet observe one will, nothing for it, and sometimes, as I am standing before a class, the subject of observation, I am myself observing my observers observing me. In this particular zoo, it is not always clear who is the tourist and who the ape. I do know that I carry the mental equivalent of a camera with me whenever I step into a classroom, and it is always clicking away, the monster of observation in me perpetually at work. To alter Christopher Isherwood slightly, "I am a chimera."[1]

3 "Ah, Miss Fogelson, you nod exuberantly, smiling in broad agreement, as if to say, 'I take your point exactly.' All quarter long you imply that you have taken my points. Your smiling nods are meant to convey that we are in some sort of intellectual complicity and are obviously on the same wave length. But beneath that nodding, invariably agreeable smile, why do I sense that in the high noon of your soul you are tuned to a hard rock AM station?"

4 "Mr. Gold, you scowl, sometimes fully glower, at what I say, which implies passion for and penetration into the subject under discussion, which your contemptuous countenance suggests I am making a terrible hash of. I would more readily believe in your perturbation had I not had the displeasure of having read your midterm examination, which reveals you to have greater control over your facial muscles than over your punctuation."

5 "Mr. Kantor, sitting in the back of the room, what are you whispering to and then laughing with Miss Reilly about? Have I stumbled verbally—committed a lip-o, the aural equivalent of a typo—resulting in my having mistakenly said something lewd? Is there a shred of broccoli from lunch stuck between my front teeth? Can my fly be open? Damn it, kiddo, what is so blasted amusing?"

6 "Miss Simpson, need you look so young and fresh and uncomplicatedly beautiful? Your earnest, not very clever presence in this hall of learning is a distraction to a dry man in a cold month, being without much joy, waiting for brains."

7 Thus does my mental camera click away, ever on the lookout for one or another kind of student performance. Of course, I much prefer the genuine article, bright students truly interested in learning, of whom I have had more than my fair share. But my mind is naturally attracted to falsity in student behavior, for I have in my own time been a nodder and smiler, a scowler and glowerer, a whisperer and laugher. For the better part of my sixteen years of formal schooling, I was a fake, a boy and then a young man who in the classroom aspired no higher

[1]A pun on Christopher Isherwood's book *I Am a Camera,* later made into the Broadway musical and movie, *Cabaret.* A chimera was a mythical fire-breathing she-monster who had the head of a lion, the body of a goat, and a tail like a serpent's.

than to mediocrity and frequently fell well short of the mark. I was precisely the kind of student whom today, as a teacher, I should view as obviously hopeless. Lest this seem false humility of a retrospective kind, an attempt to display a phony set of before and after photographs, let me hasten to add that, were I forced to return to school as a student now, I am reasonably confident that I would still be a bad student; and this for reasons I am not altogether clear about but shall nonetheless attempt to discover.

8 The question of what it is that makes for a good or a bad student never occurred to me quite so vividly as it did five or six years ago, when I served on a committee for student awards at the university where I teach. As a member of this committee, I read the classroom essays of an English major—an English major?, Lionel Trilling joked in his story "Of This Time, Of That Place." In what regiment—who was a shoo-in candidate for the best junior-year student in the department. These essays were, each one of them, impeccable. Cold *A*'s, every one—not a semicolon out of place, flawlessly typed, perfectly shaped paragraphs led off by tidy topic sentences. Here was a boy who knew his job, who could deliver the goods.

9 It was only taken together that I found his classroom papers despicable. For a Marxist professor, this boy produced a correctly down-the-line analysis of *Sister Carrie;* for a survey course, he wrote a tribute to Benjamin Franklin as a hero of the American way of pragmatism and capitalist good sense; for a Freudian-minded teacher of nineteenth-century fiction, he discovered unresolved complexes and sexual tensions in *David Copperfield.* (Had he taken one of my courses, doubtless he would have played for me whatever intellectual music it is I wish to hear.) To each of his teachers he gave what he or she asked for—no less and a little bit more. As I read these essays en bloc, I grew first to feel uncomfortable about, then to dislike, finally actively to despise this young man, whom I thought of as an academic stock boy happily filling orders. He went on the following year to graduate with all possible honors. I hope I may be forgiven when I say that I do not wish him any too well. Like others who have chosen early in life to go with the flow, may he one day before too long be made to taste a little lava.

10 I was not a bad student in the way in which I think of this young man, who combined real intellectual gifts with real sycophancy, as a bad student. I did not give my teachers what they wanted; and I was distinctly not a sycophant, for the sound reason that I hadn't the basic skills to mount anything like a decent campaign to please my teachers. I was a bad student in the fundamental sense of being an inept student. Although I believe I was mildly precocious as a very young child—I could print my name before I went to school and my father gave me columns of numbers that I added up with alacrity and joy—once I hit the classroom my brain all but ceased functioning. I was not a discipline

problem, I had no learning disabilities, but I was absolutely, even profoundly mediocre. Almost all the things one was called upon to do in the early grades, I could not do. I could not draw, and my coloring with crayons always strayed outside the lines; I sang badly off key; and my printing and early handwriting looked like the work of an incipient psychopath. I did not use scissors well, I could not draw a straight line, I made my inkwells look as if they were Oklahoma gushers that had just come in, and with paste I was simply out of control. In later grades I brought something like the same impressive ineptitude to making outlines, diagramming sentences, assembling one or another kind of notebook. I remember especially those notebooks in which a student pasted down and catalogued the various kinds of leaves—you're nondeciduous now, so whaddaya gonna do?—easily marking the nadir of my grade-school productions; it was at least four or five full cuts down from disgraceful.

11 I used to say that I had too happy a childhood ever to bother learning grammar. But it would be more accurate to say that I did not learn anything that I found uninteresting. This might put me in the same category as George Santayana, who, reflecting on his years at the Boston Latin School, remarked that "I have always been recalcitrant about studying what doesn't interest me." One of the many differences between Santayana and me, however, is that almost nothing interested me, with the possible exception of spelling. I was all right at spelling, chiefly, I believe, because it was competitive, or at any rate competitively taught through the exercises known as spelldowns, from which I, for some reason, didn't wish to be too soon eliminated. I hope no one reading this will think that, had my teachers taken more "creative" approaches to learning, I would have been a better student, for I am convinced that I would have been even worse. Thinking back on my own early days of schooling, I realize that I reacted to only two stimuli, fear and competition, and when both were absent, so, mentally, was I.

12 As for competition, in my case it was highly selective. I rarely competed when I didn't have a decent chance of, if not winning, at least finishing respectably. I very early knew that I could not compete with the bright kids in my class who had a special aptitude for science, so by the time I was, say, ten or eleven, all science became uninteresting to me. So it went with other subjects. A few of my classmates had only to show strong aptitudes for me to show a countervailingly strong apathy. This, combined with my ability to take my pleasure in life from being a fair playground athlete and a more than fair general screw-off, left me a perfectly mediocre student—one of those children who merely gets by. If I was in any way in doubt about my own mediocrity as a student, I had it confirmed for me when, before going off to high school, I learned that I was not recommended to take Latin, as even the minimally bright students were.

13 Having myself been such a poor student, I naturally adore stories about geniuses who were judged to have been either poor or indifferent students in their day—in the way, I suppose, that failed writers take special delight in learning about classic works that were sorely neglected in their day. The most famous such story is about Albert Einstein's difficulties with mathematics in secondary school, though there is reason to believe that this may be a myth. But it is not mythical that St. Thomas Aquinas when a student was known as "the dumb ox." In the classroom, Henry James was no great shakes. Theodore Dreiser made a rather poor showing in his single year at Indiana University. The physicist and philosopher Ernst Mach was deemed by his teachers to be utterly without talent, and they suggested that he be apprenticed to a cabinetmaker. (I blithely pass by all those geniuses who were splendid students right out of the starting gate.) Yet my guess is that all these men I have named probably failed to do well in school because they were dreamy, or unorthodox, or ran their trains of thought along different, wider-gauged, more farreaching tracks than conventional teaching could accommodate.

14 Along with distinctly not being a genius, I was not dreamy, or unorthodox, or anything other than prodigiously uninterested. I went to a high school with lots of bright kids, but with no intellectual traditions. Anti-intellectual traditions ran much stronger. What are now called "street smarts" were greatly valued, but if there was wisdom in the world, surely no one in his right mind at my high school expected to find it in the words of teachers or in books. "In my school crowd, insofar as I had one," Mary McCarthy has recently recounted of her high-school days, "nobody read." If anyone in my school crowd read, he kept it a secret. I had read the sports stories of John R. Tunis in grade school. I must have been assigned the dreary little project known as "book reports" in high-school English, but I evidently gave mine from Classic Comics, the comic book versions of great works of literature. Many years later, in New York, I met a free-lance writer down on his luck who had actually written some of the scripts for Classic Comics. Acknowledging his important contribution to my education, I thanked him warmly.

15 Over the course of four years in high school, I have no recollection of doing any homework, with the exception of preparation for geometry. Here, I must report, fear operated. I quickly realized that I could not fake or finagle my way through this subject as I could—in fact, did—through every other. Besides, I happened to like geometry, the intellectual order and clarity of it; I also rather enjoyed manipulating theorems and axioms, and being able to close an argument with one of Euclid's rhythmic punch lines: "The angle of the dangle equals the flip of the zip," or "If the square of the hypotenuse equals the longest side, then the giraffe emits a laugh." The point I would underscore, however, is that, liking geometry and working at it, I nonetheless received for my efforts a *C.*

16 One of the fine shiny sociological clichés of our day is contained in the phrase "peer pressure." It might be mildly comforting to me to think that I did so poorly in school owing to peer pressure. Yet I cannot remember feeling any such pressure; it is far more likely that I was one of those peers who put the pressure on other kids. I recall the rather lighthearted contempt with which my friends and I viewed the category of students we referred to as "science bores." These were students who took an earnest interest in such subjects as math, physics, and chemistry (as opposed to my own circle's interest in gin rummy, blackjack, and poker), and who were usually identified by a uniform that consisted of thickish spectacles, rumpled cotton-flannel shirts, unmanageable curly hair, and a light coat of acne. I used to believe that there were no good teachers at my high school, but then it occurred to me that if a teacher was thought to be good—which meant serious and demanding—I steered clear of him. I remember a teacher of chemistry named Dr. Davidson, one of those gallant pedagogues with a Ph.D. who preferred to teach in the trenches of a city public high school. He was dark, with a receding hairline, a perpetually furrowed brow, and rimless glasses. He taught and walked the corridors in a white lab coat and, with every gesture, radiated an air of high intellectual purpose. I would just as soon have taken Dr. Davidson's chemistry course then as I would enter myself in a backwards naked marathon now.

17 I was able to get through what was then called "the general course" in high school without learning a thing—apart from the instruction available in the air provided by Dr. O.S. Mosis—and yet without ever actually failing a single subject. Lest anyone misread this as a chronicle of misgiving, let me hasten to add that during this time I enjoyed myself hugely, while devoting my days to the extracurricular and my nights to the paracurricular. I was able to achieve this through the application of mother wit and the careful selection of the weakest courses taught by the poorest teachers.

18 My parents had a respect for education but, not having gone to college themselves, they had very little interest in schooling. When I would bring home my invariably dismal report cards—a couple of *C*'s, a *D*, a rare *B*, a more frequent *A* in gym—my father would read it, recite a little homily to me about trying harder to do my best, sign it, and let it go at that. I gather that my parents must have concluded that their eldest son's talents, if he had any at all, lay outside the classroom. I am grateful to them for this, especially today when, as a teacher, I regularly encounter students who work under the extreme pressure of parents who have grandiose educational plans for them and who have not been able to conceal their disappointment that their child did not get admitted to Harvard or Yale, Princeton or Brown. (What, I have long wondered, was Brown's first name? Somehow I have the feeling that it wasn't Irving.) If you are looking for a big tax write-off under medical

expenses (therapy chiefly), my advice is that you get behind your children and push them really hard to get into the very best universities.

19 Far from being pushed, I decided quite on my own to go to college. (After about the age of ten, it occurs to me, I made all the educational decisions in my life.) If I had chosen not to go to college but instead directly to work, no one would have been in the least surprised and no one certainly would have been aggrieved. To give my mediocrity a numeric character, I graduated 152 in a class of 211. Today it would be difficult to find a respectable college for a student who had done so poorly—finishing just above the lowest quarter of his class. But in the middle fifties, if you were a resident of the state, the University of Illinois had to accept you as a student, with the single proviso that students who finished in the bottom quarter of their high-school graduating classes were accepted on probation. This can be a bit tricky to explain to the young, but college then was at once more casual and more serious than it is now. Getting in was not so difficult—I never, for example, had to take the College Board Examinations, as I believe the SAT's were then called—but flunking out was much easier. Nowadays the reverse seems to be the case. A friend who has taught at Harvard in recent years remarked to me that, by and large, students at Harvard did not seem to him all that interested in what goes on in classrooms there. "After all," he said, "what is likely to be the greatest achievement in most of their lives has already taken place—this is that they have been admitted to Harvard."

20 In England, in France, in Germany, a boy who had done as poorly as I in secondary school would have been scrubbed, washed up, finished. In education, however, America is the land of the second chance, a condition of which I, for reasons not entirely impersonal, vastly approve. My own experience has left me a half-hearted elitist—someone who feels that everything possible should be done to single out, encourage, and promote true talent, yet who also knows that talent has a way of sometimes not showing up on schedule. In *Out of Step,* his soon-to-be-published autobiography, the philosopher Sidney Hook reveals himself to have been a rebellious high-school student of the wise-guy type; I recently read, in a collection of his letters, that the widely talented poet and painter Weldon Kees never received other than mediocre grades in school. Doubtless hundreds of other names of talented men and women could be adduced who performed poorly in school, and out of this list a National Dishonor Society could be formed, though where exactly the dishonor ought to fall—on the students for not working very hard, or on their teachers for not contriving to get the best of them—is by no means clear. My own rather jaded view is that no matter how efficient and finely meshed an educational system one devises, many children will slip through it and some among them will be the (secretly) talented. A few may scarcely need any schooling at all. "The only school Beethoven attended, and then only

for a short time," reports J.W.N. Sullivan in his study of the composer's spiritual development, "was a lower grade public school in Bonn called the Tirocinium."

21 I blush to speak of the talented, even the secretly talented, for if I had any talent at eighteen, when I went off to the state university that by law was compelled to accept me, it was certainly a secret to me. I had, however, a very keen sense of the talents that I did *not* possess. Most of the friends with whom I went off to the University of Illinois were majoring in business, a subject that I, too, should no doubt have majored in, if only because, in the context of the rather philistine middle-class culture in which I grew up, business sounded so splendidly purposeful. But to major in business meant one had to take several courses in accounting, and I knew, in the nuclei of the cells of the marrow of my smallest bones, that with my handwriting, my penchant for disorder, my unearned disdain for clerical detail, I could turn enrollment in an introductory accounting course into a Venetian tragedy. Out of fear of accounting, then, I chose to study something called "liberal arts," a phrase I heard for the first time only after I had arrived on the campus of the University of Illinois in Champaign–Urbana.

22 If fear of accounting sent me into the liberal arts, fear of flunking out of college kept me studying them, I will not say with intelligence but with ferocious energy. I was less than handsomely equipped for the task of staying in school: I had an unsure grasp of English grammar, knowledge of no foreign language beyond the level of *el burro es un animal importante,* a mind unclogged with even the rudiments of general science, a storehouse of historical fact learned exclusively at the movies, and no study habits whatsoever. My approach to college study was quite simple—I merely memorized everything set before me. Biological taxonomy, French verbs, seventeenth-century English sonnets—hey, as they say nowadays, no problem, I memorized them all. In a composition course then somewhat grandly entitled Rhetoric, I learned that I had a very small knack for writing, a knack I didn't overstrain by doing anything fancy; and anything fancy included using a semicolon, which looked to me like a combination of a Hebrew vowel and a Chinese ideograph and which I wouldn't have touched with a ten-foot dash. Fear of humiliation goading me on all the way, I was able to achieve something like a *B* average at the close of my first semester.

23 Out of the Crockpot into the Cuisinart, I transferred a year later to the University of Chicago, which must have been rather hard up for undergraduates if it accepted me, though I am very grateful that it did. Graduate students greatly outnumbered undergraduates at the University of Chicago, and the school's graduate students set the tone for the place, which was bohemian, slightly neurotic, and very serious. What made the University of Chicago seem especially impressive, at least to my untrained eyes, were the Europeans on its faculty, refugees from

Hitler's depredations in Europe. The undergraduates I encountered were kilometers ahead of me intellectually; the representative undergraduate struck me then as being someone from New York who had been reading the *New Republic* from the age of eleven and decided against going to an Ivy League school because they were all deemed too lightweight. Some among them possessed what seemed to me startlingly arcane information about history, early music, philosophy, politics. Once, in a poetry class taught by Elder Olson, Olson began chanting, quite beautifully and in French, a poem by Baudelaire. He was presently joined in his chant by the student sitting next to me, whose name was Martha Silverman, who also had the poem by heart and in French. Sensing more vividly than ever before how much over my head I was, I felt a strong wave of utter hopelessness wash over me. Oh, Martha, what has become of you since that brilliant performance on that dark morning in Elder Olson's classroom? Did you, I wonder, peak at that very moment, to fall thenceforth gently into decline?

24 I had become more earnest as a student, but I was clearly in the camp of the drones. Even among drones I was a drone. In three years at the University of Chicago I do not believe I ever said anything in a classroom that advanced the discussion in any useful way. On the rare occasions when I spoke at all, usually after being called upon to do so, no teacher ever capped my comments by saying, "A point well taken," or "That is nicely formulated," or "Good, but can you say a little more?" or even "Interesting." The only time I ever knew an answer that no one else in the room knew was when, in a course on the novel, Morton Dauwen Zabel asked if anyone knew what other famous book besides *Madame Bovary* was then—it was 1957—in its centenary year. I happened to have read somewhere, perhaps in the News Notes of *Poetry,* that 1957 was the centenary of *Les Fleurs du Mal.* I raised my hand, decided not to risk the French, and when called upon said, "Charles Baudelaire's *The Flowers of Evil.*" "Correct," said Zabel. "Thank you." I felt flush, as if I had just won the lottery.

25 On the few occasions when I attempted to slip free of dronedom, it proved a mistake. In a course on satire, a very nice professor put forth his theory of satire, which I thought half-baked, and I criticized it in a term paper in which I put forth a completely raw theory of my own. The result was a charitable *C.* In a course in Greek history, I was asked to do an essay on why Philip of Macedon chose Aristotle for his son Alexander's tutor. Cutting through a good deal of historico-political claptrap, I said it was really quite simple: Philip, being no dope, wanted the best possible teacher for his son, and there was none better than Aristotle in the whole of the Peloponnesus. Another icy *C,* this time accompanied by the gentle remonstrance that I should try to control a tendency toward glibness. The evidence was beginning to weigh in: as a drone, I was a *B* student; as an original thinker, I was a *C.*

26 I should have been delighted if, when I was young, some teacher had taken me aside and said, or in his behavior implied, "There is something special in you, and I want to help you develop it." None ever did. But, then, it occurs to me to add, there wasn't anything special in me. I was a rough without a diamond in it. It would be convenient for me now to say of myself that I was obviously a late developer; that, at any rate, is the conventional category in which my intellectual autobiography would seem to fit. But I do not truly think I am a late developer. (I began publishing in magazines, somewhat precociously, in my early twenties.) I think instead that I am someone who has never been able to profit much from the kind of education that is available in classrooms and lecture halls. I may be, in the strict schoolroom sense of the term, ineducable.

27 Not that I was entirely impervious to my teachers, but such influence as they exerted upon me was, in the main, stylistic. Watching a lecture delivered in the grand European manner, or a social scientist unsentimentally dissecting a serious subject, or an art historian passionately conveying his love for Guido Reni—all this was very exciting to me, yet the problem may have been that I *watched* it so intently that I never quite *heard* what they were saying. Observing my professors seemed so much more interesting than actually listening to them.

28 Had I gone on to graduate school, which I never for a moment contemplated doing, I might have fallen under the sway of some powerful teacher and become, say, a Straussian, or Wintersian, or Leavisite. Yet I rather doubt it. I was plenty ignorant, but I wasn't gullible. I had a strong father at home and wasn't looking for one away from home. I also had a street-learned skepticism, and I believed with Santayana (whom I hadn't yet read) that "skepticism is the chastity of the intellect, and it is shameful to surrender it too soon or to the first comer. . . ." In any case, I think I should have bridled under too firm an intellectual influence. One of the things that college taught me was that I cannot be taught in the conventional manner. Autodidactically, I have to go about things in my own pokey way, obliquely acquiring on my own such intellectual skills as I have, assembling such learning as I possess from my odd, unsystematic reading. Are there many such people as I? The inefficacy of teaching in his own life, if I may say so, is an unusual thing to have to admit on the part of a man who himself spends a good part of his own time teaching others. But there it is—or, rather, there I am.

29 As a former poor student who is now a teacher, I study good students rather as Malinowski did the Trobriand Islanders—as an outsider, someone, that is, who is distinctly not one of them. I am tempted to steal a formulation from Tolstoy and say that all good students are alike while every bad student is bad in his own way, except that I don't quite believe it is so. My quotation in the previous paragraph from Santayana

reminds me that one of Santayana's best students was Walter Lippmann, whom he asked to stay on to be his assistant at Harvard, though that young man had other ideas about his career. Traditionally, good students at Harvard have been thought to have a certain intellectual sophistication and suavity without being very deep, whereas good students at the University of Chicago have been thought to be deep but without much in the way of intellectual sophistication or suavity. Owing perhaps to such go-getter alumni as Henry Luce, William Benton, and Chester Bowles, one tends to think of good students at Yale as training themselves for success in the world, while at Princeton the social question—that is to say, snobbery—still seems uppermost, though this may be a hangover from F. Scott Fitzgerald days (Fitzgerald was himself a very poor student, and so was another famous Princetonian named Adlai Stevenson). Good students at St. John's in Annapolis seem almost too earnest—the good life is all very well, but leading it surely cannot entail talking about it so much, as all "great books" education seems to require of its students. But good students have a way of popping up in odd places; and besides, it is probably more sensible today to refer not to good schools—viewed close up, no contemporary school seems very good—but instead to schools that are difficult to get into.

30 Still, I remain astonished at the sheer proficiency of certain students. When I was myself a student, I was much impressed with the type of good student known as "the quick study." The girl-friend of a friend of mine at the University of Chicago, who did not appear to be more than mildly interested in intellectual things, seemed unable to score poorly on an examination or to write an unsuccessful paper. One felt about Dottie that she could write a *B+* paper on John Stuart Mill while sitting under a tree during a monsoon, or score an *A–* on a mathematics exam administered to her during a car crash. At the school where I teach, I have come across a number of students with the happy knack of knocking out term papers that quite simply cannot be given less than a *A*. These students are like beautifully trained retrievers: "T.S. Eliot and Catholicism"—OK, girl, fetch! "Dostoyevsky's Politics"—C'mon, boy, go get it! And they do: efficiently, tidily, sometimes quite brilliantly. Often behind what I have called "the happy knack"—my old tendency toward glibness is still intact, I see—is a great deal of effort; and careful writing is, after all, the best evidence going for having an orderly and lucid mind. And yet the superior writers among my students are often merely those students who best sense what is wanted of them and, through skills they have developed over the years, are able to deliver it. I am generally delighted, in the locution of the car dealers, "to take delivery." Still, in my intellectual greed, I hope that my best students will be more than merely good at school.

31 Everyone who teaches must at some point ask himself what he wants from his students. If one is teaching a science, or a foreign language, or

the skills required for such vocations as law or journalism, the answer ought to be clear—one wants one's students to master the material in the course. But in the teaching of literature, which is what I teach, I don't believe the materials are quite masterable; I have no notion how one masters Henry James or Joseph Conrad. Far from having mastered the materials I teach, I frequently find that, from semester to semester, I cannot even remember them myself, and so have to reread five- and six-hundred-page novels. It would be foolish to expect one's students to be better at this than one is oneself.

32 In my case the matter is complicated by the fact that, so far as I know, I teach no strict doctrine, no clear method; I have no architectonic ideas, or even any very tonic ones. I try to make sense of literary works, convey my appreciation for their subtlety and power and beauty, and make plain their significance. If my teaching has a central message, it is probably the intellectual equivalent of "Don't accept any wooden nickels." (Usually these intellectual wooden nickels have "isms" attached to them.) All this being so, my ideal student is one who has that intolerance for nonsense otherwise known as skepticism. But his must be skepticism of a certain kind—skepticism reinforced by seriousness. By seriousness I mean the understanding that art and ideas have real consequences—consequences over the long haul as great and sometimes greater than those of politics and technology—that life is at once a gift and a puzzle, and that the attempt to make the most of this life through coming to an understanding of the puzzle is not the only game in town but surely the most important one. Of course, in the young such seriousness is almost always inchoate, but it does from time to time turn up, and when it does it is immensely impressive and makes merely being good at school—you will pardon the expression—academic.

33 As a teacher who was not himself good at school, I have a special sympathy for students who do not perform well in class. I rather prize *C* students—were my younger self to walk into one of my current courses, he would doubtless get a *C*, perhaps a *C+*—for in the current day of grade inflation, to be able to give a student a *C* helps convince a teacher that he still has high standards. When I sense a student's nervousness, my own nervousness as a student comes back to me. In a sense, I still am a poor student, or at least have the psychology of a poor student. When an undergraduate, I would occasionally have what I think of as student nightmares: these usually involved my having to take an exam in some branch of higher mathematics or some language, such as Persian, for which I was wholly unprepared. Now, generally near the beginning of a new term, I can count on a teaching nightmare: these usually involve my having lost my notes before a lecture, or being unable to find the room in which I am to teach, or knowing nothing whatever about the subject in which I am to instruct others. Today, even awake, when giving an examination, I feel a slight shudder of terror pass over me—terror and relief at not having to take another college examination myself.

34 A few years after I began teaching, it occurred to me that being a teacher—not being a student—provides the best education. "To teach is to learn twice," wrote Joubert, in a simple-sounding maxim that could have several different meanings. It could mean that one first learns when getting up the material one is about to teach and then tests and relearns it in the actual teaching. It could mean that being a teacher offers one a fine chance for a second draft on one's inevitably inadequate initial education. It could mean that learning, like certain kinds of love, is better the second time around. It could mean that we are not ready for education, at any rate of the kind that leads on to wisdom, until we are sixty, or seventy, or beyond. I favor this last interpretation, for it accounts for the strange feeling that I have had every year of my adult life, which is that only twelve months ago I was really quite stupid.

A. *Comprehension*

Choose the answer that best completes each statement. Do not refer to the selection while doing this exercise.

1. Epstein writes that he observes his students carefully, identifying the obviously bright ones but also looking out for (a) the glowerers and scowlers; (b) budding but undiscovered geniuses; (c) bad students who need extra encouragement; (d) students who are fakes, the way he was as a student.
2. One kind of bad student that Epstein encountered when he served on a student awards committee was a young man who (a) refused to take responsibility for his own learning; (b) produced flawless papers reflecting exactly what each professor wanted; (c) submitted plagiarized essays; (d) exhibited no real intellectual curiosity.
3. As a student, Epstein reacted to only two stimuli: (a) threats from his parents and warnings from the principal; (b) threats from his teachers and competition; (c) fear of humiliation and competition; (d) the desire to get into a good college and to achieve status among his peers.
4. Epstein characterizes himself as a student as (a) concerned only with his social life; (b) lazy and unmotivated; (c) skeptical of teachers' attempts to find what he was good at; (d) profoundly mediocre.
5. When Epstein wrote papers in college in which he tried to say something original, (a) he received lower grades than when he gave the professors what they wanted; (b) he received higher grades; (c) he was accused of plagiarism; (d) he received approving, highly complimentary, comments.
6. Epstein defines the ideal student as one who (a) takes responsibility for his or her own learning; (b) organizes his or her time efficiently and hands assignments in on time; (c) develops a philosophy based

on reading, observation, and thinking; (d) develops a healthy skepticism tempered by a serious appreciation for the importance of ideas.

B. *Inferences*

On the basis of the evidence in the paragraphs indicated, mark these statements as follows: PA for inferences that are probably accurate and PI for inferences that are probably inaccurate. You may refer to the selection to answer the questions in this section, and in all of the remaining sections.

1. ______ Epstein believes that college students should not have the right to evaluate their teachers. [paragraph 1]
2. ______ Epstein's teachers recognized his innate talents but were unsuccessful in their attempts to motivate him. [11]
3. ______ The author decided to go to the University of Illinois probably because he realized that he had wasted his high school years. [19]
4. ______ Teachers are as much to blame for their students turning in unoriginal work as the students are themselves. [8, 9, and 25]
5. ______ Far from being truly mediocre, as his academic performance suggested, the author simply was not equipped to learn in the conventional classroom and with conventional methods. [26]
6. ______ Because of his own experience during his student days, Epstein is probably more sympathetic to mediocre, unmotivated students than most teachers are. [33]

C. *Structure*

Complete the following questions.

1. Explain in your own words what you consider Epstein's primary purpose in writing this essay. ______________________________

   ____

2. The main idea of the essay is that (a) American teachers do not provide enough academic challenges for their students; (b) the American educational system fosters mediocrity; (c) the author's mediocre academic performance was no indication of his real talents and intellectual skills; (d) students today do not know what being a good student requires.

3. Look again at the last sentence in paragraph 1. Explain the simile and explain why it is funny. ______________________________

____

4. In paragraphs 3–6, Epstein gives us imaginary comments on hypothetical students as his mental camera clicks away. Briefly explain what Epstein is thinking about each student:

   Miss Fogelson [3] ______________________________

   Mr. Gold [4] ______________________________

   Mr. Kantor [5] ______________________________

   Miss Simpson [6] ______________________________

5. In paragraph 13, Epstein mentions the names of geniuses who were supposedly terrible students because (a) he doesn't believe these stories; (b) he includes himself in this group; (c) he would like to think that he is part of the group, even though he knows he isn't; (d) he wants to prove that geniuses are self-made, not taught.
6. How would you characterize the tone in the second half of paragraph 18? (a) sincere, earnest; (b) ironic, mocking; (c) objective, impartial; (d) complaining, aggrieved.
7. Explain the point Epstein is trying to make in paragraphs 24–25.

   ____

   ____

8. The tone of the essay as a whole can best be described as (a) confessional, humorous, yet serious; (b) straightforward and objective; (c) philosophical and reflective; (d) confessional, humorous, and arrogant.

D. *Vocabulary*

For each italicized word from the selection, choose the best definition according to the context in which it appears.

1. comment on their *idiosyncrasies* [paragraph 1]: (a) peculiar characteristics; (b) personal weaknesses; (c) inherited traits; (d) virtues, strengths.
2. the relatively *obtuse* [1]: (a) intellectually gifted; (b) slow to understand; (c) comatose, unresponsive; (d) shy, reticent.
3. some sort of intellectual *complicity* [3]: (a) model for correct behavior; (b) majority opinion; (c) conspiracy or partnership; (d) competition.

4. These essays were *impeccable* [8]: (a) brilliant; (b) boring; (c) flawless; (d) difficult to criticize.
5. I was distinctly not a *sycophant* [10] (See also *sycophancy,* 10): (a) a person with a creative mind; (b) a docile, easily led person; (c) a troublemaker; (d) a servile flatterer.
6. the work of an *incipient* psychopath [10]: (a) dangerous; (b) violent; (c) long-established; (d) beginning.
7. the *nadir* of my grade-school productions [10]: (a) lowest point; (b) highest point; (c) main point; (d) ridiculous joke.
8. I have always been *recalcitrant* about studying [11]: (a) eager, enthusiastic; (b) stubbornly resistant; (c) uncompromising, inflexible; (d) difficult to motivate.
9. *prodigiously* uninterested [14]: (a) enormously; (b) seriously; (c) slightly; (d) obsessively.
10. one of those gallant *pedagogues* [16]: (a) politicians; (b) diplomats; (c) taskmasters; (d) schoolteachers.
11. recite a little *homily* to me [18]: (a) short poem; (b) list of rules; (c) moralizing sermon; (d) humorous anecdote.
12. startlingly *arcane* information [23]: (a) earthshaking; (b) deeply philosophical; (c) understood by only a select few; (d) available to everyone.
13. control a tendency toward *glibness* [25 and 30]: (a) shallowness, superficiality; (b) pretentiousness, arrogance; (c) awkwardness, clumsiness; (d) stupidity, dullness.
14. *Autodidactically,* I have to go about things [28] Describing one who is: (a) slow to learn; (b) self-taught; (c) eager to absorb new knowledge; (d) self-restrained.
15. such seriousness is almost always *inchoate* [32]: (a) fully formed; (b) primitive, undeveloped; (c) in its initial stage; (d) impossible to detect.

E. *Questions for Analysis and Discussion*

1. Comment on Epstein's humor. How would you characterize it?
2. Epstein confesses that he was a bad, or at least a mediocre, student. Do you agree with this assessment? In the long run, does it matter? Was there any particular advantage to his academic mediocrity in high school and college?

PART

V

Reading Short Stories

Literature, Aristotle wrote, serves to delight and to instruct. Modern critics do not consider it fashionable to speak of the *didactic* (instructional) aspects of literature; the term has gotten a bad name from moralistic poetry and fiction that has been popular at various times throughout literary history. Aristotle's phrase does not mean that literature "instructs" us in the moral sense. Rather, it means that we read literature for the enjoyment and for its revelation of human experience and behavior. We learn, through the actions of a story's characters, about our own humanity. We learn about all of human experience, far beyond what we as individuals could possibly experience in a lifetime.

I have included short stories in the text not only to provide you with a different opportunity for sharpening reading skills, but also to round out your reading experiences and to give you pleasure. As Sven Birkerts points out in *The Gutenberg Elegies,* reading, especially reading fiction, can take you to an "elsewhere." This is the reason that you should read the four stories in Part V, even if they are not all assigned to you.

ANALYZING THE SHORT STORY

Students commonly complain when they study literature—particularly in high school and introductory college courses—that analysis kills the pleasure of reading, as if examining the structure of a story (or of a poem or a play) somehow destroys their appreciation of it. And deconstruction, one of the many contemporary ways of approaching literature, focuses on the reader's response to the piece rather than on the author's words. Another contemporary development is the tendency among some professors to impose required "-isms" on the way their students respond to literature, subjecting the piece to analysis, in other words, from a predetermined point of view (feminism, Marxist-Leninism, ageism, deconstructionism, postmodernism, and so on). Aristides, at the end of "Student Evaluations" alludes to this phenomenon and his own efforts at resistance. In this book, the focus is not on any particular ideology but on reading for enjoyment, enlightenment, and vicarious experience.

These stories also serve to show you the fundamental means of analyzing short pieces of fiction. **Analysis**—as you may recall from Chapter 4 and from the introduction to Part IV—means breaking down a subject to see how each part functions in relation to the whole. Students occasionally complain that analysis "ruins" their enjoyment of reading. Surely when students are asked to focus on trivia, to "hunt for symbols," or to write papers on topics like "Brand Names in William Faulkner's Fiction," the complaint that analysis kills enthusiasm seems justified. Rather than destroying your enthusiasm or spontaneous enjoyment, however, meaningful analysis of literature has—or should have—the opposite effect: to increase your understanding. And the more you understand how a story or a poem works, the more likely you will "delight"—as Aristotle wrote—in the experience of reading it. The more you will savor being transported to an "elsewhere".

THE SHORT STORY DEFINED

A **short story** can be broadly defined as a fairly brief piece of narrative prose. It is fictional; that is, the people and events in it are made up, as opposed to nonfiction (or prose writing on real topics) such as the essays you have been reading at the end of each chapter and in Part IV. The length is not particularly important. Roughly speaking, a short story can be anywhere from two or three pages to as many as 30 or 40 pages long. Stories longer than that are usually classified as **novellas** ("little novels").

More important than length is what the story accomplishes. Typically, a *short story* presents a series of actions or events that reveal a single aspect of a character. In contrast, a *novel* reveals many aspects of the life and experiences of a character or of several characters. Whereas a novel may describe a character's entire life, or even the lives of several generations of characters, the action of a short story is tightly compressed, so that we see a character at a particular time in his or her life. "Miss Brill" by Katherine Mansfield illustrates this compression well. We see Miss Brill at one stage of her life, and we infer only a few bare facts about her life. She is old and supports herself by giving English lessons and reading aloud to an invalid. She lives alone somewhere on the French coast; she spends her Sunday afternoons at the public garden listening to the music and observing people. The exposition (or background) is subtly woven into the story's brief content, and the bulk of the action, such as it is, takes place on a single Sunday afternoon.

THE PARTS OF A SHORT STORY

A story's action is divided into two parts: rising action and falling action. During the **rising action,** the author provides the background or exposition, introduces the character(s), establishes the setting (location, environment, and often weather or season), and sets the action in motion. The main character, called the **protagonist,** encounters a **conflict,** a tension between himself or herself and something else—often another character (termed the **antagonist**), a custom or belief at odds with his own nature, an element in the physical or social environment, or perhaps even a component in his own nature.

For example, in Alice Munro's "Hired Girl," conflict for Elsa, the hired girl, comes in the form of the Montjoys' wealth and social status. Stephen King's protagonist, nine-year-old Gary, experiences conflict when he encounters evil, personified by the man in the black suit, and must deal with it. In "Miss Brill" the conflict resides in the tension between illusion and reality. And in Tim O'Brien's "On the Rainy River," the conflict is within his fictional alter ego, between his two warring sides. Should he escape to Canada, or should he abide by his draft notice?

In most stories, the tension or conflict increases as the action proceeds until a **crisis,** or turning point, is reached. After the crisis, the action changes to a **falling action,** in which the character resolves the conflict, or increasingly in modern fiction, is defeated by it, but unquestionably is changed in some significant way by the experience embedded in the conflict. In "Hired Girl," Elsa sees through the superficiality of her rich employers, the Montjoys, and discovers her superiority by virtue of her intelligence and her love of the written word. In each story that you read, try to determine the exact point where the crisis occurs and the extent to which it changes the characters.

Not all stories have "happy endings," where tensions are dispelled and problems are ironed out and we are led to believe that everyone will live a fairy tale life. In this group of four stories, only "Hired Girl" ends on a positive note. Despite the unhappy or ambiguous endings in the other three stories, we have learned something about human experience and human relationships. The essential principle in each case is that the story's action, the conflict or tension, and the crisis reveal to us something new about the character—an aspect or truth that we did not know at the story's beginning.

DIAGRAMING THE PLOT

The **plot**—or sequence of events—of a typical story can be diagramed as follows. (Keep in mind that not every story you read will conform exactly to this model.)

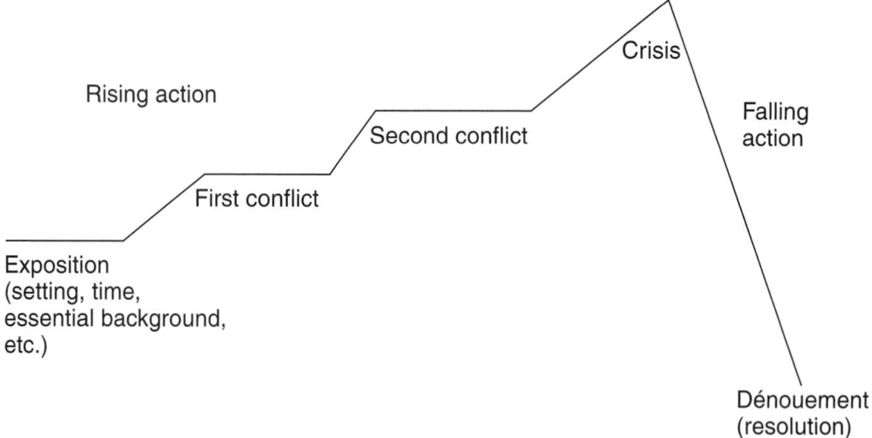

Besides plot, the second primary element in fiction is **character**—the people as they are described and revealed to us, their actions, their responses to events around them, their motivations and behavior. Out of plot and character comes the third basic element in fiction—**theme.** The theme is the underlying idea that the author wishes to get across, the idea that gives rise to plot and character. In other words, the theme is embodied in the story's events and in the way the characters respond to them.

Other considerations are important, too. For example, from whose point of view do we observe the story's events? (Who is the narrator?) What tone do the author's words reveal? Does the weather or the season of the year have a symbolic meaning? In "On the Rainy River," for example, the action takes place during the summer, which, for a recent college graduate, should be a time to rest and to plan ahead for the future. Ironically, however, summer in this story only serves to oppress: O'Brien's job at a meat-packing plant is bad enough, but his draft notice, requiring him to go to Vietnam is grim—throwing his whole future into question—and the oppressive heat of a Minnesota summer reinforces his internal anguish.

In fiction, everything works together, and in a good short story, everything counts. The reader's task is complex, requiring attention not just to structure and events but to small things as well. Little, seemingly insignificant details *are* important. The careful writer embellishes a story with detail to provide texture and reality or perhaps to suggest some strength or foible in the characters. For example, in "Hired Girl," the name of the Canadian island where the Montjoys' summer home is located, Nausicaä, named after a character in Homer's *The Odyssey,* seems to have been chosen deliberately to point up Elsa's superior knowledge: When Mrs. Montjoy brings Elsa to the island, she tells her that the island was named "after some character in Shakespeare." Elsa knows better, though she keeps the information to herself. The first-person narrator comments on this matter: "My superior knowledge gave me a familiar feeling, of satisfaction and misgiving."

Characters' names, too, may be significant. For example, and again in "Hired Girl," the Montjoys' name sounds noble and elegant, befitting their wealth and life of leisure. Perhaps it derives from *mont* (French for *mountain*), combined with *joy,* but given their shallowness, it may have been chosen to convey irony. The hired girl's name, Elsa, sounds countryish and old-fashioned, as does Minnie, the name that one of the Montjoys' guests mistakenly calls her by.

QUESTIONS ABOUT READING FICTION

Each of the four stories in Part V is followed by questions for discussion and analysis. However, they are by no means meant to exhaust the possibilities. Here are some general questions on plot, character, and theme that you can ask yourself after you read each story.

Questions about Plot

1. How are the incidents that make up the plot related to each other? Is there a cause-effect relationship between them?

2. What is the conflict in the story? Who or what is responsible for it?
3. Where in the story does the crisis occur? What provokes it?
4. Is the conflict resolved, and if it is, is it resolved satisfactorily?
5. Is there any evidence of irony in the plot? (In literature, dramatic irony refers to knowledge that the reader has that the characters are unaware of.)
6. Does the plot suggest an additional interpretation, one which perhaps the reader can see but which the characters cannot?

Questions about Character

1. Define each character in terms of his or her "essence," behavior, and motivation.
2. How are the characters revealed to us (through direct comment, through contact with others, through their behavior)?
3. Why do the characters behave as they do? Are their actions consistent with what has been revealed about them?
4. Do any characters change during the course of the story, and if so, how?
5. What is your response to each character? What is the basis for your attitude?
6. Do any of the characters stand for something greater than themselves—that is, are they symbols?

Questions about Theme

1. What is the theme, and how is it embodied in the story?
2. In what ways do plot and character work to convey the theme?
3. Are there minor themes?
4. What do we learn about human existence and human nature from the story?

Short Story 1

On the Rainy River

Tim O'Brien

Tim O'Brien received the National Book Award in fiction for Going After Cacciato. *His collection of stories,* The Things They Carried, *from which this selection comes, is a series of interconnected stories—fusing autobiography and fiction—that detail his experiences serving in Vietnam. O'Brien's most recent novel is* In the Lake of the Woods.

This is one story I've never told before. Not to anyone. Not to my parents, not to my brother or sister, not even to my wife. To go into it, I've always thought, would only cause embarrassment for all of us, a sudden need to be elsewhere, which is the natural response to a confession. Even now, I'll admit, the story makes me squirm. For more than twenty years I've had to live with it, feeling the shame, trying to push it away, and so by this act of remembrance, by putting the facts down on paper, I'm hoping to relieve at least some of the pressure on my dreams. Still, it's a hard story to tell. All of us, I suppose, like to believe that in a moral emergency we will behave like the heroes of our youth, bravely and forthrightly, without thought of personal loss or discredit. Certainly that was my conviction back in the summer of 1968. Tim O'Brien: a secret hero. The Lone Ranger. If the stakes ever became high enough—if the evil were evil enough, if the good were good enough—I would simply tap a secret reservoir of courage that had been accumulating inside me over the years. Courage, I seemed to think, comes to us in finite quantities, like an inheritance, and by being frugal and stashing it away and letting it earn interest, we steadily increase our moral capital in preparation for that day when the account must be drawn down. It was a comforting theory. It dispensed with all those bothersome little acts of daily courage; it offered hope and grace to the repetitive coward; it justified the past while amortizing the future.

In June of 1968, a month after graduating from Macalester College, I was drafted to fight a war I hated. I was twenty-one years old. Young, yes, and politically naive, but even so the American war in Vietnam seemed to me wrong. Certain blood was being shed for uncertain reasons. I saw no unity of purpose, no consensus on matters of philosophy or history or law. The very facts were shrouded in uncertainty: Was it a civil war? A war of national liberation or simple aggression? Who started it, and when, and why? What really happened to the USS *Maddox* on that dark night in the Gulf of Tonkin? Was Ho Chi Minh a Communist stooge, or a nationalist savior, or both, or neither? What about the Geneva Accords? What about SEATO and the Cold War? What about dominoes? America was divided on these and a thousand other issues, and the debate had spilled out across the floor of the United States Senate and into the streets, and smart men in pinstripes could not agree on even the most fundamental matters of public policy. The only certainty that summer was moral confusion. It was my view then, and still is, that you don't make war without knowing why. Knowledge, of course, is always imperfect, but it seemed to me that when a nation goes to war it must have reasonable confidence in the justice and imperative of its cause. You can't fix your mistakes. Once people are dead, you can't make them undead.

In any case those were my convictions, and back in college I had taken a modest stand against the war. Nothing radical, not hothead stuff, just ringing a few doorbells for Gene McCarthy, composing a few tedious, uninspired editorials for the campus newspaper. Oddly, though, it was almost entirely an intellectual activity. I brought some energy to it, of course, but it was the energy that accompanies almost any abstract endeavor; I felt no personal danger; I felt no sense of an impending crisis in my life. Stupidly, with a kind of smug removal that I can't begin to fathom, I assumed that the problems of killing and dying did not fall within my special province.

The draft notice arrived on June 17, 1968. It was a humid afternoon, I remember, cloudy and very quiet, and I'd just come in from a round of golf. My mother and father were having lunch out in the kitchen. I remember opening up the letter scanning the first few lines, feeling the blood go thick behind my eyes. I remember a sound in my head. It wasn't thinking, just a silent howl. A million things all at once—I was too *good* for this war. Too smart, too compassionate, too everything. It couldn't happen. I was above it. I had the world dicked—Phi Beta Kappa and summa cum laude and president of the student body and a full-ride scholarship for grad studies at Harvard. A mistake, maybe—a foul-up in the paperwork. I was no soldier. I hated Boy Scouts. I hated camping out. I hated dirt and tents and mosquitoes. The sight of blood made me queasy, and I couldn't tolerate authority, and I didn't know a rifle from a slingshot. I was a *liberal,* for Christ sake: If they needed fresh bodies, why not draft some back-to-the-stone-age hawk? Or some dumb jingo in his hard hat and Bomb Hanoi button, or one of LBJ's pretty daughters, or Westmoreland's whole handsome family—nephews and nieces and baby grandson. There should be a law, I thought. If you support a war, if you think it's worth the price, that's fine, but you have to put your own precious fluids on the line. You have to head for the front and hook up with an infantry unit and help spill the blood. And you have to bring along your wife, or your kids, or your lover. A *law,* I thought.

I remember the rage in my stomach. Later it burned down to a smoldering self-pity, then to numbness. At dinner that night my father asked what my plans were.

"Nothing," I said. "Wait."

I spent the summer of 1968 working in an Armour meatpacking plant in my hometown of Worthington, Minnesota. The plant specialized in pork products, and for eight hours a day I stood on a quarter-mile assembly line—more properly, a disassembly line—removing blood clots from the necks of dead pigs. My job title, I believe, was Declotter. After slaughter, the hogs were decapitated, split down the length of the belly, pried open, eviscerated, and strung up by the hind hocks on a high conveyer belt. Then gravity took over. By the time a carcass reached my spot on the line, the fluids had mostly drained out, everything except for thick clots of blood in the neck and upper chest cavity. To remove the stuff, I used a kind of water gun. The machine was heavy, maybe eighty pounds, and was suspended from the ceiling by a heavy cord. There was some bounce to it, an elastic up-and-down give, and the trick was to maneuver the gun with your whole body, not lifting with the arms, just letting the rubber cord do the work for you. At one end was a trigger; at the muzzle end was a small nozzle and a steel roller brush. As a carcass passed by, you'd lean forward and swing the gun up against the clots and squeeze the trigger, all in one motion, and the brush would whirl and water would come shooting out and you'd hear a quick splattering sound as the clots dissolved into a fine red mist. It was not pleasant work. Goggles were a necessity, and a rubber apron, but even so it was like standing for eight hours a day under a lukewarm blood-shower. At night I'd go home smelling of pig. It wouldn't go away. Even after a hot bath, scrubbing hard, the stink was always there—like old bacon, or sausage, a dense greasy pig-stink that soaked deep into my skin and hair. Among other things, I remember, it was tough getting dates that summer. I felt isolated; I spent a lot of time alone. And there was also that draft notice tucked away in my wallet.

In the evenings I'd sometimes borrow my father's car and drive aimlessly around town, feeling sorry for myself, thinking about the war and the pig factory and how my life seemed to be collapsing toward slaughter. I felt paralyzed. All around me the options seemed to be harrowing, as if I were hurtling down a huge black funnel, the whole world squeezing in tight. There was no happy way out. The government had ended most graduate school deferments; the waiting lists for the National Guard and Reserves were impossibly long; my health was solid; I didn't qualify for CO status—no religious grounds, no history as a pacifist. Moreover, I could not claim to be opposed to war as a matter of general principle. There were occasions, I believed, when a nation was justified in using military force to achieve its ends, to stop a Hitler or some comparable evil, and I told myself that in such circumstances I would've willingly marched off to the battle. The problem, though, was that a draft board did not let you choose your war.

Beyond all this, or at the very center, was the raw fact of terror. I did not want to die. Not ever. But certainly not then, not there, not in a wrong war. Driving up Main Street, past the courthouse and the Ben Franklin store, I sometimes felt the fear spreading inside me like weeds. I imagined myself dead. I imagined myself doing things I could not do—charging an enemy position, taking aim at another human being.

At some point in mid-July I began thinking seriously about Canada. The border lay a few hundred miles north, an eight-hour drive. Both my conscience and my instincts were telling me to make a break for it, just take off and run like hell and never stop. In the beginning the idea seemed purely abstract, the word Canada printing itself out in my head; but after a time I could see particular shapes and images, the sorry details of my own future—a hotel room in Winnipeg, a battered old suitcase, my father's eyes as I tried to explain myself over the telephone. I could almost hear his voice, and my mother's. Run, I'd think. Then I'd think, Impossible. Then a second later I'd think, *Run.*

It was a kind of schizophrenia. A moral split. I couldn't make up my mind. I feared the war, yes, but I also feared exile. I was afraid of walking away from my own life, my friends and my family, my whole history, everything that mattered to me. I feared losing the respect of my parents. I feared the law. I feared ridicule and censure. My hometown was a conservative little spot on the prairie, a place where tradition counted, and it was easy to imagine people sitting around a table down at the old Gobbler Café on Main Street, coffee cups poised, the conversation slowly zeroing in on the young O'Brien kid, how the damned sissy had taken off for Canada. At night, when I couldn't sleep, I'd sometimes carry on fierce arguments with those people. I'd be screaming at them, telling them how much I detested their blind, thoughtless, automatic acquiescence to it all, their simple-minded patriotism, their prideful ignorance, their love-it-or-leave-it platitudes, how they were sending me off to fight a war they didn't understand and didn't want to understand. I held them responsible. By God, yes, I *did.* All of them—I held them personally and individually responsible—the polyestered Kiwanis boys, the merchants and farmers, the pious churchgoers, the chatty housewives, the PTA and the Lions club and the Veterans of Foreign Wars and the fine upstanding gentry out at the country club. They didn't know Bao Dai from the man in the moon. They didn't know history. They didn't know the first thing about Diem's tyranny, or the nature of Vietnamese nationalism, or the long colonialism of the French—this was all too damned complicated, it required some reading—but no matter, it was a war to stop the Communists, plain and simple, which was how they liked things, and you were a treasonous pussy if you had second thoughts about killing or dying for plain and simple reasons.

I was bitter, sure. But it was so much more than that. The emotions went from outrage to terror to bewilderment to guilt to sorrow and then back again to outrage. I felt a sickness inside me. Real disease.

Most of this I've told before, or at least hinted at, but what I have never told is the full truth. How I cracked. How at work one morning, standing on the pig line, I felt something break open in my chest. I don't know what it was. I'll never know. But it was real, I know that much, it was a physical rupture—a cracking-leaking-popping feeling. I remember dropping my water gun. Quickly, almost without thought, I took off my apron and walked out of the plant and drove home. It was midmorning, I remember, and the house was empty. Down in my chest there was still that leaking sensation, something very warm and precious spilling out, and I was covered with blood and hog-stink, and for a long while I just concentrated on holding myself together. I remember taking a hot shower. I remember packing a suitcase and carrying it out to the kitchen, standing very still for a few minutes, looking carefully at the familiar objects all around me. The old chrome toaster, the telephone, the pink and white Formica on the kitchen counters. The room was full of bright sunshine. Everything sparkled. My house, I thought. My life. I'm not sure how long I stood there, but later I scribbled out a short note to my parents.

What is said, exactly, I don't recall now. Something vague. Taking off, will call, love Tim.

I drove north.

It's a blur now, as it was then, and all I remember is a sense of high velocity and the feel of the steering wheel in my hands. I was riding on adrenaline. A giddy feeling, in a way, except there was the dreamy edge of impossibility to it—like running a dead-end maze—no way out—it couldn't come to a happy conclusion and yet I was doing it anyway because it was all I could think of to do. It was pure flight, fast and mindless. I had no plan. Just hit the border at high speed and crash through and keep on running. Near dusk I passed through Bemidji, then turned northeast toward International Falls. I spent the night in the car behind a closed-down gas station a half mile from the border. In the morning, after gassing up, I headed straight west along the Rainy River, which separates Minnesota from Canada, and which for me separated one life from another. The land was mostly wilderness. Here and there I passed a motel or bait shop, but otherwise the country unfolded in great sweeps of pine and birch and sumac. Though it was still August, the air already had the smell of October, football season, piles of yellow-red leaves, everything crisp and clean. I remember a huge blue sky. Off to my right was the Rainy River, wide as a lake in places, and beyond the Rainy River was Canada.

For a while I just drove, not aiming at anything, then in the late morning I began looking for a place to lie low for a day or two. I was exhausted, and scared sick, and around noon I pulled into an old fishing resort called the Tip Top Lodge. Actually it was not a lodge at all, just eight or nine tiny yellow cabins clustered on a peninsula that jutted northward into the Rainy River. The place was in sorry shape. There was a dangerous wooden dock, an old minnow tank, a flimsy tar paper boathouse along the shore. The main building, which stood in a cluster of pines on high ground, seemed to lean heavily to one side, like a cripple, the roof sagging toward Canada. Briefly, I thought about turning around, just giving up, but then I got out of the car and walked up to the front porch.

The man who opened the door that day is the hero of my life. How do I say this without sounding sappy? Blurt it out—the man saved me. He offered exactly what I needed, without questions, without any words at all. He took me in. He was there at the critical time—a silent, watchful presence. Six days later, when it ended, I was unable to find a proper way to thank him, and I never have, and so, if nothing else, this story represents a small gesture of gratitude twenty years overdue.

Even after two decades I can close my eyes and return to that porch at the Tip Top Lodge. I can see the old guy staring at me. Elroy Berdahl: eighty-one years old, skinny and shrunken and mostly bald. He wore a flannel shirt and brown work pants. In one hand, I remember, he carried a green apple, a small paring knife in the other. His eyes had the bluish gray color of a razor blade, the same polished shine, and as he peered up at me I felt a strange sharpness, almost painful, a cutting sensation, as if his gaze were somehow slicing me open. In part, no doubt, it was my own sense of guilt, but even so I'm absolutely certain that the old man took one look and went right to the heart of things—a kid in trouble. When I asked for a room, Elroy made a little clicking sound with his tongue. He nodded, led me out to one of the cabins, and dropped a key in my hand. I remember smiling at him. I also remember wishing I hadn't. The old man shook his head as if to tell me it wasn't worth the bother.

"Dinner at five-thirty," he said. "You eat fish?"

"Anything," I said.

Elroy grunted and said, "I'll bet."

We spent six days together at the Tip Top Lodge. Just the two of us. Tourist season was over, and there were no boats on the river, and the wilderness seemed to withdraw into a great permanent stillness. Over those six days Elroy Berdahl and I took most of our meals together. In the mornings we sometimes went out on long hikes into the woods, and at night we played Scrabble or listened to records or sat reading in front of his big stone fireplace. At times I felt the awkwardness of an intruder, but Elroy accepted me into his quiet routine without fuss or ceremony. He took my presence for granted, the same way he might've sheltered a stray cat—no wasted sighs or pity—and there was never any talk about it. Just the opposite. What I remember more than anything is the man's willful, almost ferocious silence. In all that time together, all those hours, he never asked the obvious questions: Why was I there? Why alone? Why so preoccupied? If Elroy was curious about any of this, he was careful never to put it into words.

My hunch, though, is that he already knew. At least the basics. After all, it was 1968, and guys were burning draft cards, and Canada was just a boat ride away. Elroy Berdahl was no hick. His bedroom, I remember, was cluttered with books and newspapers. He killed me at the

Scrabble board, barely concentrating, and on those occasions when speech was necessary he had a way of compressing large thoughts into small, cryptic packets of language. One evening, just at sunset, he pointed up at an owl circling over the violet-lighted forest to the west.

"Hey, O'Brien," he said. "There's Jesus."

The man was sharp—he didn't miss much. Those razor eyes. Now and then he'd catch me staring out at the river, at the far shore, and I could almost hear the tumblers clicking in his head. Maybe I'm wrong, but I doubt it.

One thing for certain, he knew I was in desperate trouble. And he knew I couldn't talk about it. The wrong word—or even the right word—and I would've disappeared. I was wired and jittery. My skin felt too tight. After supper one evening I vomited and went back to my cabin and lay down for a few moments and then vomited again; another time, in the middle of the afternoon, I began sweating and couldn't shut it off. I went through whole days feeling dizzy with sorrow. I couldn't sleep; I wouldn't lie still. At night I'd toss around in bed, half awake, half dreaming, imagining how I'd sneak down to the beach and quietly push one of the old man's boats out into the river and start paddling my way toward Canada. There were times when I thought I'd gone off the psychic edge. I couldn't tell up from down, I was just falling, and late in the night I'd lie there watching weird pictures spin through my head. Getting chased by the Border Patrol—helicopters and searchlights and barking dogs—I'd be crashing through the woods, I'd be down on my hands and knees—people shouting out my name—the law closing in on all sides—my hometown draft board and the FBI and the Royal Canadian Mounted Police. It all seemed crazy and impossible. Twenty-one years old, an ordinary kid with all the ordinary dreams and ambitions, and all I wanted was to live the life I was born to—a mainstream life—I loved baseball and hamburgers and cherry Cokes—and now I was off on the margins of exile, leaving my country forever, and it seemed so impossible and terrible and sad.

I'm not sure how I made it through those six days. Most of it I can't remember. On two or three afternoons, to pass some time, I helped Elroy get the place ready for winter, sweeping down the cabins and hauling in the boats, little chores that kept my body moving. The days were cool and bright. The nights were very dark. One morning the old man showed me how to split and stack firewood, and for several hours we just worked in silence out behind his house. At one point, I remember, Elroy put down his maul and looked at me for a long time, his lips drawn as if framing a difficult question, but then he shook his head and went back to work. The man's self-control was amazing. He never pried. He never put me in a position that required lies or denials. To an extent, I suppose, his reticence was typical of that part of Minnesota, where privacy still held value, and even if I'd been walking around with some horrible deformity—four arms and three heads—I'm sure the old man would've talked about everything except those extra arms and heads. Simple politeness was part of it. But even more than that, I think, the man understood that words were insufficient. The problem had gone beyond discussion. During that long summer I'd been over and over the various arguments, all the pros and cons, and it was no longer a question that could be decided by an act of pure reason. Intellect had come up against emotion. My conscience told me to run, but some irrational and powerful force was resisting, like a weight pushing me toward the war. What it came down to, stupidly, was a sense of shame. Hot, stupid shame. I did not want people to think badly of me. Not my parents, not my brother and sister, not even the folks down at the Gobbler Café. I was ashamed to be there at the Tip Top Lodge. I was ashamed of my conscience, ashamed to be doing the right thing.

Some of this Elroy must've understood. Not the details, of course, but the plain fact of crisis.

Although the old man never confronted me about it, there was one occasion when he came close to forcing the whole thing out into the open. It was early evening, and we'd just finished supper, and over coffee and dessert I asked him about my bill, how much I owed so far. For a long while the old man squinted down at the tablecloth.

"Well, the basic rate," he said, "is fifty bucks a night. Not counting meals. This makes four nights, right?"

I nodded. I had three hundred and twelve dollars in my wallet.

Elroy kept his eyes on the tablecloth. "Now that's an on-season price. To be fair, I suppose we should knock it down a peg or two." He leaned back in his chair. "What's a reasonable number, you figure?"

"I don't know," I said. "Forty?"

"Forty's good. Forty a night. Then we tack on food—say another hundred? Two hundred sixty total?"

"I guess."

He raised his eyebrows. "Too much?"

"No, that's fair. It's fine. Tomorrow, though . . . I think I'd better take off tomorrow."

Elroy shrugged and began clearing the table. For a time he fussed with the dishes, whistling to himself as if the subject had been settled. After a second he slapped his hands together.

"You know what we forgot?" he said. "We forgot wages. Those odd jobs you done. What we have to do, we have to figure out what your time's worth. Your last job—how much did you pull in an hour?"

"Not enough," I said.

"A bad one?"

"Yes. Pretty bad."

Slowly then, without intending any long sermon, I told him about my days at the pig plant. It began as a straight recitation of the facts, but before I could stop myself I was talking about the blood clots and the water gun and how the smell had soaked into my skin and how I couldn't wash it away. I went on for a long time. I told him about wild hogs squealing in my dreams, the sounds of butchery, slaughter-house sounds, and how I'd sometimes wake up with that greasy pig-stink in my throat.

When I was finished, Elroy nodded at me.

"Well, to be honest," he said, "When you first showed up here, I wondered about all that. The aroma, I mean. Smelled like you was awful damned fond of pork chops." The old man almost smiled. He made a snuffling sound, then sat down with a pencil and a piece of paper. "So what'd this crud job pay? Ten bucks an hour? Fifteen?"

"Less."

Elroy shook his head. "Let's make it fifteen. You put in twenty-five hours here, easy. That's three hundred seventy-five bucks total wages. We subtract the two hundred sixty for food and lodging, I still owe you a hundred and fifteen."

He took four fifties out of his shirt pocket and laid them on the table.

"Call it even," he said.

"No."

"Pick it up. Get yourself a haircut."

The money lay on the table for the rest of the evening. It was still there when I went back to my cabin. In the morning, though, I found an envelope tacked to my door. Inside were the four fifties and a two-word note that said EMERGENCY FUND.

The man knew.

Looking back after twenty years, I sometimes wonder if the events of that summer didn't happen in some other dimension, a place where your life exists before you've lived it, and where it goes afterward. None of it ever seemed real. During my time at the Tip Top Lodge I had the feeling that I'd slipped out of my own skin, hovering a few feet away while some poor yo-yo with my name and face tried to make his way toward a future he didn't understand and didn't want. Even now I can see myself as I was then. It's like watching an old home movie: I'm young and tan and fit. I've got hair—lots of it. I don't smoke or drink. I'm wearing faded blue jeans and a white polo shirt. I can see myself sitting on Elroy Berdahl's dock near dusk one evening, the sky a bright shimmering pink, and I'm finishing up a letter to my parents that tells what I'm about to do and why I'm doing it and how sorry I am that I'd never found the courage to talk to them about it. I ask them not to be angry. I try to explain some of my feelings, but there aren't enough words, and so I just say that it's a thing that has to be done. At the end of the letter I talk about the vacations we used to take up in this north country, at a place called Whitefish Lake, and how the scenery here reminds me of those good times. I tell them I'm fine. I tell them I'll write again from Winnipeg or Montreal or wherever I end up.

On my last full day, the sixth day, the old man took me out fishing on the Rainy River. The afternoon was sunny and cold. A stiff breeze came in from the north, and I remember how the little fourteen-foot boat made sharp rocking motions as we pushed off from the dock. The current was fast. All around us, I remember, there was a vastness to the world, an unpeopled rawness, just the trees and the sky and the water reaching out toward nowhere. The air had the brittle scent of October.

For ten or fifteen minutes Elroy held a course upstream, the river choppy and silver-gray, then he turned straight north and put the engine on full throttle. I felt the bow lift beneath me. I remember the wind in my ears, the sound of the old outboard Evinrude. For a time I didn't pay attention to anything, just feeling the cold spray against my face, but then it occurred to me that at some point we must've passed into Canadian waters, across that dotted line between two different worlds, and I remember a sudden tightness in my chest as I looked up and watched the far shore come at me. This wasn't a daydream. It was tangible and real. As we came in toward land, Elroy cut the engine, letting the boat fishtail lightly about twenty yards off shore. The old man didn't look at me or speak. Bending down, he opened up his tackle box and busied himself with a bobber and a piece of wire leader, humming to himself, his eyes down.

It struck me then that he must've planned it. I'll never be certain, of course, but I think he meant to bring me up against the realities, to guide me across the river and to take me to the edge and to stand a kind of vigil as I chose a life for myself.

I remember staring at the old man, then at my hands, then at Canada. The shoreline was dense with brush and timber. I could see tiny red berries on the bushes. I could see a squirrel up in one of the birch trees, a big crow looking at me from a boulder along the river. That close—twenty yards—and I could see the delicate latticework of the leaves, the texture of the soil, the browned needles beneath the pines, the configurations of geology and human history. Twenty yards. I could've done it. I could've jumped and started swimming for my life. Inside me, in my chest, I felt a terrible squeezing pressure. Even now, as I write this, I can still feel that tightness. And I want you to feel it—the wind coming off the river, the waves, the silence, the wooded frontier. You're at the bow of a boat on the Rainy River. You're twenty-one years old, you're scared, and there's a hard squeezing pressure in your chest.

What would you do?

Would you jump? Would you feel pity for yourself? Would you think about your family and your childhood and your dreams and all you're leaving behind? Would it hurt? Would it feel like dying? Would you cry, as I did?

I tried to swallow it back. I tried to smile, except I was crying.

Now, perhaps, you can understand why I've never told this story before. It's not just the embarrassment of tears. That's part of it, no doubt, but what embarrasses me much more, and always will, is the paralysis that took my heart. A moral freeze: I couldn't decide, I couldn't act, I couldn't comport myself with even a pretense of modest human dignity.

All I could do was cry. Quietly, not bawling, just the chest-chokes.

At the rear of the boat Elroy Berdahl pretended not to notice. He held a fishing rod in his hands, his head bowed to hide his eyes. He kept humming a soft, monotonous little tune. Everywhere, it seemed, in the trees and water and sky, a great worldwide sadness came pressing down on me, a crushing sorrow, sorrow like I had never known it before. And what was so sad, I realized, was that Canada had become a pitiful fantasy. Silly and hopeless. It was no longer a possibility. Right then, with the shore so close, I understood that I would not do what I should do. I would not swim away from my hometown and my country and my life. I would not be brave. That old image of myself as a hero, as a man of conscience and courage, all that was just a threadbare pipe dream. Bobbing there on the Rainy River, looking back at the Minnesota shore, I felt a sudden swell of helplessness come over me, a drowning sensation, as if I had toppled overboard and was being swept away by the silver waves. Chunks of my own history flashed by. I saw a seven-year-old boy in a white cowboy hat and a Lone Ranger mask and a pair of holstered six-shooters; I saw a twelve-year-old Little League shortstop pivoting to turn a double play; I saw a sixteen-year-old kid decked out for his first prom, looking spiffy in a white tux and a black bow tie, his hair cut short and flat, his shoes freshly polished. My whole life seemed to spill out into the river, swirling away from me, everything I had ever been or ever wanted to be. I couldn't get my breath; I couldn't stay afloat; I couldn't tell which way to swim. A hallucination, I suppose, but it was a real as anything I would ever feel. I saw my parents calling to me from the far shoreline. I saw my brother and sister, all the townsfolk, the mayor and the entire Chamber of Commerce and all my old teachers and girlfriends and high school buddies. Like some weird sporting event: everybody screaming from the sidelines, rooting me on—a loud stadium roar. Hotdogs and popcorn—stadium smells, stadium heat. A squad of cheerleaders did cartwheels along the banks of the Rainy River; they had megaphones and pompoms and smooth brown thighs. The crowd swayed left and right. A marching band played fight songs. All my aunts and uncles were there, and Abraham Lincoln, and Saint George, and a nine-year-old girl named Linda who had died of a brain tumor back in fifth grade, and several members of the United States Senate, and a blind poet scribbling notes, and LBJ, and Huck Finn, and Abbie Hoffman, and all the dead soldiers back from the grave, and the many thousands who were later to die—villagers with terrible burns, little kids without arms or legs—yes, and the Joint Chiefs of Staff were there, and a couple of popes, and a first lieutenant named Jimmy Cross, and the last surviving veteran of the American Civil War, and Jane Fonda dressed up as Barbarella, and an old man sprawled beside a pigpen, and my grandfather, and Gary Cooper, and a kind-faced woman carrying an umbrella and a copy of Plato's *Republic,* and a million ferocious citizens waving flags of all shapes and colors—people in hard hats, people in headbands—they were all whooping and changing and urging me toward one shore or the other. I saw faces from my distant past and distant future. My wife was there. My unborn daughter waved at me, and my two sons hopped up and down, and a drill sergeant named Blyton sneered and shot up a finger and shook his head. There was a choir in bright purple robes. There was a cabbie from the Bronx. There was a slim young man I would one day kill with a hand grenade along a red clay trail outside the village of My Khe.

The little aluminum boat rocked softly beneath me. There was the wind and the sky.

I tried to will myself overboard.

I gripped the edge of the boat and leaned forward and thought, *Now.*

I did try. It just wasn't possible.

All those eyes on me—the town, the whole universe—and I couldn't risk the embarrassment. It was as if there were an audience to my life, that swirl of faces along the river, and in my head I could hear people screaming at me. Traitor! they yelled. Turncoat! Pussy! I felt myself blush. I couldn't tolerate it. I couldn't endure the mockery, or the disgrace, or the patriotic ridicule. Even in my imagination, the shore just twenty yards away, I couldn't make myself be brave. It had nothing to do with morality. Embarrassment, that's all it was.

And right then I submitted.

I would go to the war—I would kill and maybe die—because I was embarrassed not to.

That was the sad thing. And so I sat in the bow of the boat and cried.

It was loud now. Loud, hard crying.

Elroy Berdahl remained quiet. He kept fishing. He worked his line with the tips of his fingers, patiently, squinting out at his red and white bobber on the Rainy River. His eyes were flat and impassive. He didn't speak. He was simply there, like the river and the late-summer sun. And yet by his presence, his mute watchfulness, he made it real. He was the true audience. He was a witness, like God, or like the gods, who look on in absolute silence as we live our lives, as we make our choices or fail to make them.

"Ain't biting," he said.

Then after a time the old man pulled in his line and turned the boat back toward Minnesota.

I don't remember saying goodbye. That last night we had dinner together, and I went to bed early, and in the morning Elroy fixed breakfast for me. When I told him I'd be leaving, the old man nodded as if he already knew. He looked down at the table and smiled.

At some point later in the morning it's possible that we shook hands—I just don't remember—but I do know that by the time I'd finished packing the old man had disappeared. Around noon, when I took my suitcase out to the car, I noticed that his old black pickup truck was no longer parked in front of the house. I went inside and waited for a while, but I felt a bone certainty that he wouldn't be back. In a way, I thought, it was appropriate. I washed up the breakfast dishes, left his two hundred dollars on the kitchen counter, got into the car, and drove south toward home.

That day was cloudy. I passed through towns with familiar names, through the pine forests and down to the prairie, and then to Vietnam, where I was a soldier, and then home again. I survived, but it's not a happy ending. I was a coward. I went to the war.

Questions for Discussion and Analysis

1. To what extent does this story represent a confession?
2. Explain the narrator's attitude toward the war before he is drafted. How has he distanced himself from the war's reality?
3. Why does O'Brien believe himself too good to serve in Vietnam?
4. In relation to the Vietnam war, what is the irony in O'Brien's postgraduation summer job?
5. Explain the moral schizophrenia O'Brien experiences concerning the war and his participation in it. A related question: To what extent are O'Brien's views of the war influenced by the residents of Worthington?
6. In what way is the Rainy River symbolic?
7. When O'Brien writes that Elroy Berdahl saved his life, what specifically does he mean? How did the old man accomplish this?
8. What does O'Brien mean by the phrase "moral freeze"? Explain why O'Brien comes to the decision to stay and not to flee to Canada?
9. Look again at the story's last two sentences? What is their significance? What tone do they convey?

Short Story 2

Miss Brill

Katherine Mansfield

Born in 1888 Wellington, New Zealand, Katherine Mansfield published her first book of stories, In a German Pension, *in 1911. Two more collections followed:* Bliss and Other Stories *(1920) and* The Garden Party *(1922). Like Chekhov, she died of tuberculosis at the peak of her success. She was 34 years old.*

Although it was so brilliantly fine—the blue sky powdered with gold and great spots of light like white wine splashed over the Jardins Publiques—Miss Brill was glad that she had decided on her fur. The air was motionless, but when you opened your mouth there was just a faint chill, like a chill from a glass of iced water before you sip, and now and again a leaf came drifting—from nowhere, from the sky. Miss Brill put up her hand and touched her fur. Dear little thing! It was nice to feel it again. She had taken it out of its box that afternoon, shaken out the moth-powder, given it a good brush, and rubbed the life back into the dim little eyes. "What has been happening to me?" said the sad little eyes. Oh, how sweet it was to see them snap at her again from the red eiderdown! . . . But the nose, which was of some black composition, wasn't at all firm. It must have had a knock, somehow. Never mind—a little dab of black sealing-wax when the time came—when it was absolutely necessary. . . . Little rogue! Yes, she really felt like that about it. Little rogue biting its tail just by her left ear. She could have taken it off and laid it on her lap and stroked it. She felt a tingling in her hands and arms, but that came from walking, she supposed. And when she breathed, something light and sad—no, not sad, exactly—something gentle seemed to move in her bosom.

There were a number of people out this afternoon, far more than last Sunday. And the band sounded louder and gayer. That was because the Season had begun. For although the band played all the year round on Sundays, out of season it was never the same. It was like someone playing with only the family to listen; it didn't care how it played with only the family to listen; it didn't care how it played if there weren't any strangers present. Wasn't the conductor wearing a new coat, too? She was sure it was new. He scraped with his foot and flapped his arms like a rooster about to crow, and the bandsmen sitting in the green rotunda blew out their cheeks and glared at the music. Now there came a little "flutey" bit—very pretty!—a little chain of bright drops. She was sure it would be repeated. It was; she lifted her head and smiled.

Only two people shared her "special" seat: a fine old man in a velvet coat, his hands clasped over a huge carved walking-stick, and a big old woman, sitting upright, with a roll of knitting on her embroidered apron. They did not speak. This was disappointing, for Miss Brill always looked forward to the conversation. She had become really quite expert, she thought, at listening as though she didn't listen, at sitting in other people's lives just for a minute while they talked round her.

She glanced, sideways, at the old couple. Perhaps they would go soon. Last Sunday, too, hadn't been as interesting as usual. An Englishman and his wife, he wearing a dreadful Panama hat and she button boots. And she'd gone on the whole time about how she ought to wear spectacles; she knew she needed them; but that it was no good getting any; they'd be sure to break and they'd never keep on. And he'd been so patient. He'd suggested everything—gold rims, the kind that curved round your ears, little pads inside the bridge. No, nothing would please her. "They'll always be sliding down my nose!" Miss Brill had wanted to shake her.

The old people sat on the bench, still as statues. Never mind, there was always the crowd to watch. To and fro, in front of the flower-beds and the band rotunda, the couples and groups paraded, stopped to talk, to greet, to buy a handful of flowers from the old beggar who had his tray fixed to the railings. Little children ran among them, swooping and laughing; little boys with big white silk bows under their chins, little girls, little French dolls, dressed up in velvet and lace. And sometimes a tiny staggerer came suddenly rocking into the open from under the trees, stopped, stared, and suddenly sat down "flop," until its small high-stepping mother, like a young hen, rushed scolding to its rescue. Other people sat on the benches and green chairs, but they were nearly always the same, Sunday after Sunday, and—Miss Brill had often noticed—there was something funny about nearly all of them. They were odd, silent, nearly all old, and from the way they stared they looked as though they'd just come from dark little rooms or even—even cupboards!

Behind the rotunda the slender trees with yellow leaves down drooping, and through them just a line of sea, and beyond the blue sky with gold-veined clouds.

Tum-tum-tum tiddle-um! tum tiddley-um tum ta! blew the band.

Two young girls in red came by and two young soldiers in blue met them, and they laughed and paired and went off arm-in-arm. Two peasant women with funny straw hats passed, gravely, leading beautiful smoke-coloured donkeys. A cold, pale nun hurried by. A beautiful woman came along and dropped her bunch of violets, and a little boy ran after to hand them to her, and she took them and threw them away as if they'd been poisoned. Dear me! Miss Brill didn't know whether to admire that or not! And now an ermine toque and a gentleman in grey met just in front of her. He was tall, stiff, dignified, and she was wearing that ermine toque she'd bought when her hair was yellow. Now everything, her hair, her face, even her eyes, was the same colour as the shabby ermine, and her hand, in its cleaned glove, lifted to dab her lips, was a tiny yellowish paw. Oh, she was so pleased to see him—delighted! She rather thought they were going to meet that afternoon. She described where she'd been—everywhere, here, there, along by the sea. The day was so charming—didn't he agree? And wouldn't he, perhaps? . . . But he shook his head, lighted a cigarette, slowly breathed a great deep puff into her face, and, even while she was still talking and laughing, flicked the match away and walked on. The ermine toque was alone; she smiled more brightly than ever. But even the band seemed to know what she was feeling and played more softly, played tenderly, and the drum beat, "The Brute! The Brute!" over and over. What would she do? What was going to happen now? But as Miss Brill wondered, the ermine toque turned, raised her hand as though she'd seen someone else, much nicer, just over there, and pattered away. And the band changed again and played more quickly, more gaily than ever, and the old couple on Miss Brill's seat got up and marched away, and such a funny old man with long whiskers hobbled along in time to the music and was nearly knocked over by four girls walking abreast.

Oh, how fascinating it was! How she enjoyed it! How she loved sitting here, watching it all! It was like a play. It was exactly like a play. Who could believe the sky at the back wasn't painted? But it wasn't till a little brown dog trotted on solemn and then slowly trotted off, like a little "theater" dog, a little dog that had been drugged, that Miss Brill discovered what it was that made it so exciting. They were all on the stage. They weren't only the audience, not only looking on; they were acting. Even she had a part and came every Sunday. No doubt somebody would have noticed if she hadn't been there; she was part of the performance after all. How strange she'd never thought of it like that before! And yet it explained why she made such a point of starting from home at just the same time each week—so as not to be late for the performance—and it also explained why she had quite a queer, shy feeling at telling her English pupils how she spent her Sunday afternoons. No wonder! Miss Brill nearly laughed out loud. She was on the stage. She thought of the old invalid gentleman to whom she read the newspaper four afternoons a week while he slept in the garden. She had got quite used to the frail head on the cotton pillow, the hollowed eyes, the open mouth and the high pinched nose. If he'd been dead she mightn't have noticed for weeks; she wouldn't have minded. But suddenly he knew he was having the paper read to him by an actress! "An actress!" The old head lifted; two points of light quivered in the old eyes. "An actress—are ye?" And Miss Brill smoothed the newspaper as though it were the manuscript of her part and said gently: "Yes, I have been an actress for a long time."

The band had been having a rest. Now they started again. And what they played was warm, sunny, yet there was just a faint chill—a something, what was it?—not sadness—no, not sadness—something that made you want to sing. The tune lifted, lifted, the light shone; and it seemed to Miss Brill that in another moment all of them, all the whole company, would begin singing. The young ones, the laughing ones who were moving together, they would begin, and the men's voices, very resolute and brave, would join them. And then she too, she too, and the others on the benches—they would come in with a kind of accompaniment—something low, that scarcely rose or fell,, something so beautiful—moving. . . . And Miss Brill's eyes filled with tears and she looked smiling at all the other members of the company. Yes, we understand, we understand, she thought—though what they understood she didn't know.

Just at that moment a boy and a girl came and sat down where the old couple had been. They were beautifully dressed; they were in love. The hero and heroine, of course, just arrived from his father's yacht. And still soundlessly singing, still with that trembling smile, Miss Brill prepared to listen.

"No, not now," said the girl. "Not here, I can't."

"But why? Because of that stupid old thing at the end there?" asked the boy. "Why does she come here at all—who wants her? Why doesn't she keep her silly old mug at home?"

"It's her fu-fur which is so funny," giggled the girl. "It's exactly like a fried whiting."

"Ah, be off with you!" said the boy in an angry whisper. Then: "Tell me, ma petite chérie—"

No, not here," said the girl. "Not *yet.*"

On her way home she usually bought a slice of honey-cake at the baker's. It was her Sunday treat. Sometimes there was an almond in her slice, sometimes not. It made a great difference. If there was an almond it was like carrying home a tiny present—a surprise—something that might very well not have been there. She hurried on the almond Sundays and struck the match for the kettle in quite a dashing way.

But to-day she passed the baker's by, climbed the stairs, went into the little dark room—her room like a cupboard—and sat down on the red eiderdown. She sat there for a long time. The box that the fur came out of was on the bed. She unclasped the necklet quickly; quickly, without looking, laid it inside. But when she put the lid on she thought she heard something crying.

Questions for Discussion and Analysis

1. Who is Miss Brill? From the details Mansfield provides, what sort of life does she lead?

2. How does Miss Brill perceive herself? How does she perceive those around her? How does she perceive herself as different from the usual occupants of the Jardins Publiques (the public gardens)?
3. Look again at the exchange between the "ermine toque" and the "gentleman in grey"? Who are these people? Whose eyes do we see them through? What has taken place between these two?
4. What is ironic about the description of Miss Brill's reading to the old invalid gentleman?
5. In what way does Miss Brill change during the course of the story? What is the impetus for that change? What is crying when she puts her fur back into its box?
6. Is Miss Brill tragic or merely silly? How are we to see her?

Short Story 3

The Man in the Black Suit

Stephen King

The author of more than 30 books, nearly all of them worldwide bestsellers, Stephen King is most often associated with the genre of horror fiction. "The Man in the Black Suit," first published for the 1994 Halloween issue of The New Yorker, *later won first prize for the 1994 O. Henry Awards, which annually publishes the best in American short fiction. Among King's best known books are* Misery, Salem's Lot, Cujo, Dolores Claiborne, Carrie, Rita Hayworth and the Shawshank Redemption, *and* The Shining. *King lives in Bangor, Maine. The story, according to the O. Henry collection, is "a wonderful reminder of the American roots of the short story as spellbinding tale."*

I am now a very old man and this is something that happened to me when I was very young—only nine years old. It was 1914, the summer after my brother, Dan, died in the west field and not long before America got into the First World War. I've never told anyone about what happened at the fork in the stream that day, and I never will. I've decided to write it down, though, in this book, which I will leave on the table beside my bed. I can't write long, because my hands shake so these days and I have next to no strength, but I don't think it will take long.

Later, someone may find what I have written. That seems likely to me, as it is pretty much human nature to look in a book marked "Diary" after its owner has passed along. So, yes—my words will probably be read. A better question is whether anyone will believe them. Almost certainly not, but that doesn't matter. It's not belief I'm interested in but freedom. Writing can give that, I've found. For twenty years I wrote a column called "Long Ago and Far Away" for the Castle Rock

Call, and I know that sometimes it works that way—what you write down sometimes leaves you forever, like old photographs left in the bright sun, fading to nothing but white.

I pray for that sort of release.

A man in his eighties should be well past the terrors of childhood, but as my infirmities slowly creep up on me, like waves licking closer and closer to some indifferently built castle of sand, that terrible face grows clearer and clearer in my mind's eye. It glows like a dark star in the constellations of my childhood. What I might have done yesterday, who I might have seen here in my room at the nursing home, what I might have said to them or they to me—those things are gone, but the face of the man in the black suit grows ever clearer, ever closer, and I remember every word he said. I don't want to think of him but I can't help it, and sometimes at night my old heart beats so hard and so fast I think it will tear itself right clear of my chest. So I uncap my fountain pen and force my trembling old hand to write this pointless anecdote in the diary one of my great-grandchildren—I can't remember her name for sure, at least not right now, but I know it starts with an "S"—gave to me last Christmas, and which I have never written in until now. Now I will write in it. I will write the story of how I met the man in the black suit on the bank of Castle Stream one afternoon in the summer of 1914.

The town of Motton was a different world in those days—more different than I could ever tell you. That was a world without airplanes droning overhead, a world almost without cars and trucks, a world where the skies were not cut into lanes and slices by overhead power lines. There was not a single paved road in the whole town, and the business district consisted of nothing but Corson's General Store, Thut's Livery & Hardware, the Methodist church at Christ's Corner, the school, the town hall, and half a mile down from there, Harry's Restaurant, which my mother called, with unfailing disdain, "the liquor house."

Mostly, though, the difference was in how people lived—how *apart* they were. I'm not sure people born after the middle of the century could quite credit that, although they might say they could, to be polite to old folks like me. There were no phones in western Maine back then, for one thing. The first one wouldn't be installed for another five years, and by the time there was a phone in our house, I was nineteen and going to college at the University of Maine in Orono.

But that is only the roof of the thing. There was no doctor closer than Casco, and there were no more than a dozen houses in what you would call town. There were no neighborhoods (I'm not even sure we knew the word, although we had a verb—"neighboring"—that described church functions and barn dances), and open fields were the exception rather than the rule. Out of town the houses were farms that stood far apart from each other, and from December until the middle of

March we mostly hunkered down in the little pockets of stove warmth we called families. We hunkered and listened to the wind in the chimney and hoped no one would get sick or break a leg or get a headful of bad ideas, like the farmer over in Castle Rock who had chopped up his wife and kids three winters before and then said in court that the ghosts made him do it. In those days before the Great War, most of Motton was woods and bog—dark long places full of moose and mosquitoes, snakes and secrets. In those days there were ghosts everywhere.

This thing I'm telling about happened on a Saturday. My father gave me a whole list of chores to do, including some that would have been Dan's, if he'd still been alive. He was my only brother, and he'd died of a bee sting. A year had gone by, and still my mother wouldn't hear that. She said it was something else, *had* to have been, that no one ever died of being stung by a bee. When Mama Sweet, the oldest lady in the Methodist Ladies' Aid, tried to tell her—at the church supper the previous winter, this was—that the same thing had happened to her favorite uncle back in '73, my mother clapped her hands over her ears, got up, and walked out of the church basement. She'd never been back since, and nothing my father could say to her would change her mind. She claimed she was done with church, and that if she ever had to see Helen Robichaud again (that was Mama Sweet's real name) she would slap her eyes out. She wouldn't be able to help herself, she said.

That day Dad wanted me to lug wood for the cookstove, weed the beans and the cukes, pitch hay out of the loft, get two jugs of water to put in the cold pantry, and scrape as much old paint off the cellar bulkhead as I could. Then, he said, I could go fishing, if I didn't mind going by myself—he had to go over and see Bill Eversham about some cows. I said I sure didn't mind going by myself, and my dad smiled as if that didn't surprise him so very much. He'd given me a bamboo pole the week before—not because it was my birthday or anything but just because he liked to give me things sometimes—and I was wild to try it in Castle Stream, which was by far the troutiest brook I'd ever fished.

"But don't you go too far in the woods," he told me. "Not beyond where the water splits."

"No, sir."

"Promise me."

"Yessir, I promise."

"Now promise your mother."

We were standing on the back stoop; I had been bound for the springhouse with the water jugs when my dad stopped me. Now he turned me around to face my mother, who was standing at the marble counter in a flood of strong morning sunshine falling through the double windows over the sink. There was a curl of hair lying across the side of her forehead and touching her eyebrow—you see how well I remember it all? The bright light turned that little curl to filaments of gold and made me want to run to her and put my arms around her. In that instant I saw her as a woman, saw her as my father must have seen her. She was wearing a housedress with little red roses all over it, I remember, and she was kneading bread. Candy Bill, our little black Scottie dog, was standing alertly beside her feet, looking up, waiting for anything that might drop. My mother was looking at me.

"I promise," I said.

She smiled, but it was the worried kind of smile she always seemed to make since my father brought Dan back from the west field in his arms. My father had come sobbing and bare-chested. He had taken off his shirt and draped it over Dan's face, which had swelled and turned color. *My boy!* he had been crying. *Oh, look at my boy! Jesus, look at my boy!* I remember that as if it were yesterday. It was the only time I ever heard my dad take the Saviour's name in vain.

"What do you promise, Gary?" she asked.

"Promise not to go no further than where the stream forks, Ma'am."

"Any further."

"Any."

She gave me a patient look, saying nothing as her hands went on working in the dough, which now had a smooth, silky look.

"I promise not to go any further than where the stream forks, Ma'am."

"Thank you, Gary," she said. "And try to remember that grammar is for the world as well as for school."

"Yes, Ma'am."

Candy Bill followed me as I did my chores, and sat between my feet as I bolted my lunch, looking up at me with the same attentiveness he had shown my mother while she was kneading her bread, but when I got my new bamboo pole and my old, splintery creel and started out of the dooryard, he stopped and only stood in the dust by an old roll of snow fence, watching. I called him but he wouldn't come. He yapped a time or two, as if telling me to come back, but that was all.

"Stay, then," I said, trying to sound as if I didn't care. I did, though, at least a little. Candy Bill *always* went fishing with me.

My mother came to the door and looked out at me with her left hand held up to shade her eyes. I can see her that way still, and it's like looking at a photograph of someone who later became unhappy, or died suddenly. "You mind your dad now, Gary!"

"Yes, Ma'am, I will."

She waved, I waved, too. Then I turned my back on her and walked away.

The sun beat down on my neck, hard and hot, for the first quarter-mile or so, but then I entered the woods, where double shadow fell over the road and it was cool and fir-smelling and you could hear the wind hissing through the deep, needled groves. I walked with my pole on my shoulder the way boys did back then, holding my creel in my other hand like a valise or a salesman's sample case. About two miles into the woods along a road that was really nothing but a double rut with a grassy strip growing up the center hump, I began to hear the hurried, eager gossip of Castle Stream. I thought of trout with bright speckled backs and pure-white bellies, and my heart went up in my chest.

The stream flowed under a little wooden bridge, and the banks leading down to the water were steep and brushy. I worked my way down carefully, holding on where I could and digging my heels in. I went down out of summer and back into mid-spring, or so it felt. The cool rose gently off the water, and there was a green smell like moss. When I got to the edge of the water I only stood there for a little while, breathing deep of that mossy smell and watching the dragonflies circle and the skitterbugs skate. Then, further down, I saw a trout leap at a butterfly—a good big brookie, maybe fourteen inches long—and remembered I hadn't come here just to sightsee.

I walked along the bank, following the current, and wet my line for the first time, with the bridge still in sight upstream. Something jerked the tip of my pole down once or twice and ate half my worm, but whatever it was was too sly for my nine-year-old hands—or maybe just not hungry enough to be careless—so I quit that place.

I stopped at two or three other places before I got to the place where Castle Stream forks, going southwest into Castle Rock and southeast into Kashwakamak Township, and at one of them I caught the biggest trout I have ever caught in my life, a beauty that measured nineteen inches from tip to tail on the little ruler I kept in my creel. That was a monster of a brook trout, even for those days.

If I had accepted this as gift enough for one day and gone back, I would not be writing now (and this is going to turn out longer than I thought it would, I see that already), but I didn't. Instead I saw to my catch right then and there as my father had shown me—cleaning it, placing it on dry grass at the bottom of the creel, then laying damp grass on top of it—and went on. I did not, at age nine, think that catching a nineteen-inch brook trout was particularly remarkable, although I do remember being amazed that my line had not broken when I, netless as well as artless, had hauled it out and swung it toward me in a clumsy tail-flapping arc.

Ten minutes later, I came to the place where the stream split in those days (it is long gone now; there is a settlement of duplex homes where Castle Stream once went its course, and a district grammar school as well, and if there is a stream it goes in darkness), dividing around a huge gray rock nearly the size of our outhouse. There was a pleasant flat space here, grassy and soft, overlooking what my dad and I called South Branch. I squatted on my heels, dropped my line into the water, and almost immediately snagged a fine rainbow trout. He wasn't the size of my brookie—only a foot or so—but a good fish, just the same. I had it cleaned out before the gills had stopped flexing, stored it in my creel, and dropped my line back into the water.

This time there was no immediate bite, so I leaned back, looking up at the blue stripe of sky I could see along the stream's course. Clouds floated by, west to east, and I tried to think what they looked like. I saw a unicorn, then a rooster, then a dog that looked like Candy Bill. I was looking for the next one when I drowsed off.

Or maybe slept. I don't know for sure. All I know is that a tug on my line so strong it almost pulled the bamboo pole out of my hand was what brought me back into the afternoon. I sat up, clutched the pole, and suddenly became aware that something was sitting on the tip of my nose. I crossed my eyes and saw a bee. My heart seemed to fall dead in my chest, and for a horrible second I was sure I was going to wet my pants.

The tug on my line came again, stronger this time, but although I maintained my grip on the end of the pole so it wouldn't be pulled into the stream and perhaps carried away (I think I even had the presence of mind to snub the line with my forefinger), I made no effort to pull in my catch. All my horrified attention was fixed on the fat black-and-yellow thing that was using my nose as a rest stop.

I slowly poked out my lower lip and blew upward. The bee ruffled a little but kept its place. I blew again and it ruffled again—but this time it also seemed to shift impatiently, and I didn't dare blow anymore, for fear it would lose its temper completely and give me a shot. It was too close for me to focus on what it was doing, but it was easy to imagine it ramming its stinger into one of my nostrils and shooting its poison up toward my eyes. And my brain.

A terrible idea came to me: that this was the very bee that had killed my brother. I knew it wasn't true, and not only because honeybees probably didn't live longer than a single year (except maybe for the queens; about them I was not so sure). It couldn't be true, because honeybees died when they stung, and even at nine I knew it. Their stingers were barbed, and when they tried to fly away after doing the deed, they tore themselves apart. Still, the idea stayed. This was a special bee, a devil-bee, and it had come back to finish the other of Albion and Loretta's two boys.

And here is something else: I had been stung by bees before, and although the stings had swelled more than is perhaps usual (I can't really say for sure), I had never died of them. That was only for my brother, a terrible trap that had been laid for him in his very making—a trap that I had somehow escaped. But as I crossed my eyes until they hurt, in an effort to focus on the bee, logic did not exist. It was the *bee* that existed, only that—the bee that had killed my brother, killed him so cruelly that my father had slipped down the straps of his overalls so he could take off his shirt and cover Dan's swollen, engorged face. Even in the depths of his grief he had done that, because he didn't want his wife to see what had become of her firstborn. Now the bee had returned, and now it would kill me. I would die in convulsions on the bank, flopping just as a brookie flops after you take the hook out of its mouth.

As I sat there trembling on the edge of panic—ready to bolt to my feet and then bolt anywhere—there came a report from behind me. It was as sharp and preemptory as a pistol shot, but I knew it wasn't a pistol shot, it was someone clapping his hands. One single clap. At that moment, the bee tumbled off my nose and fell into my lap. It lay there on my pants with its legs sticking up and its stinger a threatless black thread against the old scuffed brown of the corduroy. It was dead as a doornail, I saw that at once. At the same moment, the pole gave another tug—the hardest yet—and I almost lost it again.

I grabbed it with both hands and gave it a big stupid yank that would have made my father clutch his head with both hands, if he had been there to see. A rainbow trout, a good bit larger than either of the ones I had already caught, rose out of the water in a wet flash, spraying fine drops of water from its tail—it looked like one of those fishing pictures they used to put on the covers of men's magazines like *True* and *Man's Adventure* back in the forties and fifties. At that moment hauling in a big one was about the last thing on my mind, however, and when the line snapped and the fish fell back into the stream, I barely noticed. I looked over my shoulder to see who had clapped. A man was standing above me, at the edge of the trees. His face was very long and pale. His black hair was combed tight against his skull and parted with rigorous care on the left side of his narrow head. He was very tall. He was wearing a black three-piece suit, and I knew right away that he was not a human being, because his eyes were the orangey red of flames in a woodstove. I don't mean just the irises, because he *had* no irises, and no pupils, and certainly no whites. His eyes were completely orange—an orange that shifted and flickered. And it's really too late not to say exactly what I mean, isn't it? He was on fire inside, and his eyes were like the little isinglass portholes you sometimes see in stove doors.

My bladder let go, and the scuffed brown the dead bee was lying on went a darker brown. I was hardly aware of what had happened, and I couldn't take my eyes off the man standing on top of the bank and looking down at me—the man who had apparently walked out of thirty miles of trackless western Maine woods in a fine black suit and narrow shoes of gleaming leather. I could see the watch chain looped across his vest glittering in the summer sunshine. There was not so much as a single pine needle on him. And he was smiling at me.

"Why, it's a fisherboy!" he cried in a mellow, pleasing voice. "Imagine that! Are we well met, fisherboy?"

"Hello, sir," I said. The voice that came out of me did not tremble, but it didn't sound like my voice, either. It sounded older. Like Dan's voice, maybe. Or my father's, even. And all I could think was that maybe he would let me go if I pretended not to see what he was. If I pretended I didn't see there were flames glowing and dancing where his eyes should have been.

"I've saved you a nasty sting, perhaps," he said, and then, to my horror, he came down the bank to where I sat with a dead bee in my wet lap and a bamboo fishing pole in my nerveless hands. His slick-soled city shoes should have slipped on the low, grassy weeds dressing the steep bank, but they didn't; nor did they leave tracks, I saw. Where his feet had touched—or seemed to touch—there was not a single broken twig, crushed leaf, or trampled shoe-shape.

Even before he reached me, I recognized the aroma baking up from the skin under the suit—the smell of burned matches. The smell of sulfur. The man in the black suit was the Devil. He had walked out of the deep woods between Motton and Kashwakamak, and now he was standing here beside me. From the corner of one eye I could see a hand as pale as the hand of a store-window dummy. The fingers were hideously long.

He hunkered beside me on his hams, his knees popping just as the knees of any normal man might, but when he moved his hands so they dangled between his knees, I saw that each of those long fingers ended in not a fingernail but a long yellow claw.

"You didn't answer my question, fisherboy," he said in his mellow voice. It was, now that I think of it, like the voice of one of those radio announcers on the big-band shows years later, the ones that would sell Geritol and Serutan and Ovaltine and Dr. Grabow pipes. "Are we well met?"

"Please don't hurt me," I whispered, in a voice so low I could barely hear it. I was more afraid than I could ever write down, more afraid than I want to remember. But I do. I do. It never crossed my mind to hope I was having a dream, although it might have, I suppose, if I had been older. But I was nine, and I knew the truth when it squatted down beside me. I knew a hawk from a handsaw, as my father would have said. The man who had come out of the woods on that Saturday afternoon in midsummer was the Devil, and inside the empty holes of his eyes his brains were burning.

"Oh, do I smell something?" he asked, as if he hadn't heard me, although I knew he had. "Do I smell something . . . wet?"

He leaned toward me with his nose stuck out, like someone who means to smell a flower. And I noticed an awful thing; as the shadow of his head travelled over the bank, the grass beneath it turned yellow and died. He lowered his head toward my pants and sniffed. His glaring eyes half closed, as if he had inhaled some sublime aroma and wanted to concentrate on nothing but that.

"Oh, bad!" he cried. "Lovely-bad!" And then he chanted: "Opal! Diamond! Sapphire! Jade! I smell Gary's lemonade!" He threw himself on his back in the little flat place and laughed.

I thought about running, but my legs seemed two counties away from my brain. I wasn't crying, though; I had wet my pants, but I wasn't crying. I was too scared to cry. I suddenly knew that I was going to die, and probably painfully, but the worst of it was that that might not be the worst of it. The worst might come later. *After* I was dead.

He sat up suddenly, the smell of burnt matches fluffing out from his suit and making me feel gaggy in my throat. He looked at me solemnly from his narrow white face and burning eyes, but there was a sense of laughter about him, too. There was always that sense of laughter about him.

"Sad news, fisherboy," he said. "I've come with sad news."

I could only look at him—the black suit, the fine black shoes, the long white fingers that ended not in nails but in talons.

"Your mother is dead."

"No!" I cried. I thought of her making bread, of the curl lying across her forehead and just touching her eyebrow, of her standing there in the strong morning sunlight, and the terror swept over me again, but not for myself this time. Then I thought of how she'd looked when I set off with my fishing pole, standing in the kitchen doorway with her hand shading her eyes, and how she had looked to me in that moment like a photograph of someone you expected to see again but never did. "No, you lie!" I screamed.

He smiled—the sadly patient smile of a man who has often been accused falsely. "I'm afraid not," he said. "It was the same thing that happened to your brother, Gary. It was a bee."

"No, that's not true," I said, and now I *did* begin to cry. "She's old, she's thirty-five—if a bee sting could kill her the way it did Danny she would have died a long time ago, and you're a lying bastard!"

I had called the Devil a lying bastard. I was aware of this, but the entire front of my mind was taken up by the enormity of what he'd said. My mother dead? He might as well have told me that the moon had fallen on Vermont. But I believed him. On some level I believed him completely, as we always believe, on some level, the worst thing our hearts can imagine.

"I understand your grief, little fisherboy, but that particular argument just doesn't hold water, I'm afraid." He spoke in a tone of bogus comfort that was horrible, maddening, without remorse or pity. "A man can go his whole life without seeing a mockingbird, you know, but does that mean mockingbirds don't exist? Your mother—"

A fish jumped below us. The man in the black suit frowned, then pointed a finger at it. The trout convulsed in the air, its body bending so strenuously that for a split second it appeared to be snapping at its own tail, and when it fell back into Castle Stream it was floating lifelessly. It struck the big gray rock where the water divided, spun around twice in the whirlpool eddy that formed there, and then floated away in the direction of Castle Rock. Meanwhile, the terrible stranger turned his burning eyes on me again, his thin lips pulled back from tiny rows of sharp teeth in a cannibal smile.

"Your mother simply went through her entire life without being stung by a bee," he said. "But then—less than an hour ago, actually—one flew in through the kitchen window while she was taking the bread out of the oven and putting it on the counter to cool."

I raised my hands and clapped them over my ears. He pursed his lips as if to whistle and blew at me gently. It was only a little breath, but the stench was foul beyond belief—clogged sewers, outhouses that have never known a single sprinkle of lime, dead chickens after a flood.

My hands fell away from the sides of my face.

"Good," he said. "You need to hear this, Gary; you need to hear this, my little fisherboy. It was your mother who passed that fatal weakness on to your brother. You got some of it, but you also got a protection from your father that poor Dan somehow missed." He pursed his lips again, only this time he made a cruelly comic little *tsk-tsk* sound instead of blowing his nasty breath at me. "So although I don't like to speak ill of the dead, it's almost a case of poetic justice, isn't it? After all, she killed your brother Dan as surely as if she had put a gun to his head and pulled the trigger."

"No," I whispered. "No, it isn't true."

"I assure you it is," he said. "The bee flew in the window and lit on her neck. She slapped at it before she even knew what she was doing—*you* were wiser than that, weren't you, Gary?—and the bee stung her. She felt her throat start to close up at once. That's what happens, you know, to people who can't tolerate bee venom. Their throats close and they drown in the open air. That's why Dan's face was so swollen and purple. That's why your father covered it with his shirt."

I stared at him, now incapable of speech. Tears streamed down my cheeks. I didn't want to believe him, and knew from my church schooling that the Devil is the father of lies, but I *did* believe him just the same.

"She made the most wonderfully awful noises," the man in the black suit said reflectively, "and she scratched her face quite badly, I'm afraid. He eyes bulged out like a frog's eyes. She wept." He paused, then added: "She wept as she died, isn't that sweet? And here's the most beautiful thing of all. After she was dead, after she had been lying on the floor of fifteen minutes or so with no sound but the stove ticking and with that little thread of a bee stinger still poking out of the side of her neck—so small, so small—do you know what Candy Bill did? That little rascal licked away her tears. First on one side, and then on the other."

He looked out at the stream for a moment, his face sad and thoughtful. Then he turned back to me and his expression of bereavement disappeared like a dream. His face was as slack and as avid as the face of a corpse that has died hungry. His eyes blazed. I could see his sharp little teeth between his pale lips.

"I'm starving," he said abruptly. "I'm going to kill you and eat your guts, little fisherboy. What do you think about that?"

No, I tried to say, *please no,* but no sound came out. He meant to do it, I saw. He really meant to do it.

"I'm just so *hungry,*" he said, both petulant and teasing. "And you won't want to live without your precious mommy, anyhow, take my word for it. Because your father's the sort of man who'll have to have some warm hole to stick it in, believe me, and if you're the only one available, you're the one who'll have to serve. I'll save you all that discomfort and unpleasantness. Also, you'll go to Heaven, think of that. Murdered souls *always* go to Heaven. So we'll both be serving God this afternoon, Gary. Isn't that nice?"

He reached for me again with his long, pale hands, and without thinking what I was doing, I flipped open the top of my creel, pawed all the way down to the bottom, and brought out the monster brookie I'd caught earlier—the one I should have been satisfied with. I held it out to him blindly, my fingers in the red slit of its belly, from which I had removed its insides as the man in the black suit had threatened to remove mine. The fish's glazed eye stared dreamily at me, the gold ring around the black center reminding me of my mother's wedding ring. And in that moment I saw her lying in her coffin with the sun shining off the wedding band and knew it was true—she had been stung by a bee, she had drowned in the warm, bread-smelling kitchen air, and Candy Bill had licked her dying tears from her swollen cheeks.

"Big fish!" the man in the black suit cried in a guttural, greedy voice. "Oh, *biiig fiiish!*"

He snatched it away from me and crammed it into a mouth that opened wider than any human mouth ever could. Many years later, when I was sixty-five (I know it was sixty-five, because that was the summer I retired from teaching), I went to the aquarium in Boston and finally saw a shark. The mouth of the man in the black suit was like that shark's mouth when it opened, only his gullet was blazing orange, the same color as his eyes, and I felt heat bake out of it and into my face, the way you feel a sudden wave of heat come pushing out of a fireplace when a dry piece of wood catches alight. And I didn't imagine that heat, either—I know I didn't—because just before he slid the head of my nineteen-inch brook trout between his gaping jaws, I saw the scales along the sides of the fish rise up and begin to curl like bits of paper floating over an open incinerator.

He slid the fish in like a man in a travelling show swallowing a sword. He didn't chew, and his blazing eyes bulged out, as if in effort. The fish went in and went in, his throat bulged as it slid down his gullet, and now he began to cry tears of his own—except his tears were blood, scarlet and thick.

I think it was the sight of those bloody tears that gave me my body back. I don't know why that should have been, but I think it was. I bolted to my feet like a Jack released from its box, turned with my bamboo pole still in one hand, and fled up the bank, bending over and tearing tough bunches of weeds out with my free hand in an effort to get up the slope more quickly.

He made a strangled, furious noise—the sound of any man with his mouth too full—and I looked back just as I got to the top. He was coming after me, the back of his suit coat flapping and his thin gold watch chain flashing and winking in the sun. The tail of the fish was still protruding from his mouth and I could smell the rest of it, roasting in the oven of his throat.

He reached for me, groping with his talons, and I fled along the top of the bank. After a hundred yards of so I found my voice and went to screaming—screaming in fear, of course, but also screaming in grief for my beautiful dead mother.

He was coming after me. I could hear snapping branches and whipping bushes, but I didn't look back again. I lowered my head, slitted my eyes against the bushes and low-hanging branches along the stream's bank, and ran as fast as I could. And at every step I expected to feel his hands descending on my shoulders, pulling me back into a final burning hug.

That didn't happen. Some unknown length of time later—it couldn't have been longer than five or ten minutes, I suppose, but it seemed like forever—I saw the bridge through layerings of leaves and firs. Still screaming, but breathlessly now, sounding like a teakettle that has almost boiled dry, I reached this second, steeper bank and charged up.

Halfway to the top, I slipped to my knees, looked over my shoulder, and saw the man in the black suit almost at my heels, his white face pulled into a convulsion of fury and greed. His cheeks were splattered with his bloody tears and his shark's mouth hung open like a hinge.

"Fisherboy!" he snarled, and started up the bank after me, grasping at my foot with one long hand. I tore free, turned, and threw my fishing pole at him. He batted it down easily, but it tangled his feet up somehow and he went to his knees. I didn't wait to see any more; I turned and bolted to the top of the slope. I almost slipped at the very top, but managed to grab one of the support struts running beneath the bridge and save myself.

"You can't get away, fisherboy!" he cried from behind me. He sounded furious, but he also sounded as if he were laughing. "It takes more than a mouthful of trout to fill *me* up!"

"Leave me alone!" I screamed back at him. I grabbed the bridge's railing and threw myself over it in a clumsy somersault, filling my hands with splinters and bumping my head so hard on the boards when I came down that I saw stars. I rolled over on my belly and began crawling. I lurched to my feet just before I got to the end of the bridge, stumbled once, found my rhythm, and then began to run. I ran as only nine-year-old boys can run, which is like the wind. It felt as if my feet only touched the ground with every third or fourth stride, and, for all I know, that may be true. I ran straight up the right-hand wheel rut in the road, ran until my temples pounded and my eyes pulsed in their sockets, ran until I had a hot stitch in my left side from the bottom of my ribs to my armpit, ran until I could taste blood and something like metal shavings in the back of my throat. When I couldn't run anymore I stumbled to a stop and looked back over my shoulder, puffing and blowing like a wind-broken horse. I was convinced I would see him standing right there behind me in his natty black suit, the watch chain a glittering loop across his vest and not a hair out of place.

But he was gone. The road stretching back toward Castle Stream between the darkly massed pines and spruces was empty. And yet I sensed him somewhere near in those woods, watching me with his grassfire eyes, smelling of burned matches and roasted fish.

I turned and began walking as fast as I could, limping a little—I'd pulled muscles in both legs, and when I got out of bed the next morning I was so sore I could barely walk. I kept looking over my shoulder, needing again and again to verify that the road behind me was still empty. It was each time I looked, but those backward glances seemed to increase my fear rather than lessen it. The firs looked darker, massier, and I kept imagining what lay behind the trees that marched beside the road—long, tangled corridors of forest, leg-breaking deadfalls, ravines where anything might live. Until that Saturday in 1914, I had thought that bears were the worst thing the forest could hold.

A mile or so farther up the road, just beyond the place where it came out of the woods and joined the Geegan Flat Road, I saw my father walking toward me and whistling "The Old Oaken Bucket." He was carrying his own rod, the one with the fancy spinning reel from Monkey Ward. In his other hand he had his creel, the one with the ribbon my mother had woven through the handle back when Dan was still alive. "Dedicated to Jesus" that ribbon said. I had been walking, but when I saw him I started to run again, screaming *Dad! Dad! Dad!* at the top of my lungs and staggering from side to side on my tired, sprung legs like a drunken sailor. The expression of surprise on his face when he recognized me might have been comical under other circumstances. He dropped his rod and creel into the road without so much as a downward glance at them and ran to me. It was the fastest I ever saw my dad run in his life; when we came together it was a wonder the impact didn't knock us both senseless, and I struck my face on his belt buckle hard enough to start a little nosebleed. I didn't notice that until later, though. Right then I only reached out my arms and clutched him as hard as I could. I held on and rubbed my hot face back and forth against his belly, covering his old blue workshirt with blood and tears and snot.

"Gary, what is it? What happened? Are you all right?"

"Ma's dead!" I sobbed. "I met a man in the woods and he told me! Ma's dead! She got stung by a bee and it swelled her all up just like what happened to Dan, and she's dead! She's on the kitchen floor and Candy Bill . . . licked the t-t-tears . . . off her . . . off her . . ."

Face was the last word I had to say, but by then my chest was hitching so bad I couldn't get it out. My own tears were flowing again, and my dad's startled, frightened face had blurred into three overlapping images. I began to howl—not like a little kid who's skinned his knee but like a dog that's seen something bad by moonlight—and my father pressed my head against his hard flat stomach again. I slipped out from under his hand, though, and looked back over my shoulder. I wanted to make sure the man in the black suit wasn't coming. There was no sign of him; the road winding back into the woods was completely empty. I promised myself I would never go back down that road again, not ever, no matter what, and I suppose now that God's greatest blessing to His creatures below is that they can't see the future. It might have broken my mind if I had known I *would* be going back down that road, and not two hours later. For that moment, though, I was only relieved to see we were still alone. Then I thought of my mother—my beautiful dead mother—and laid my face back against my father's stomach and bawled some more.

"Gary, listen to me," he said a moment or two later. I went on bawling. He gave me a little longer to do that, then reached down and lifted my chin so he could look down into my face and I could look up into his. "Your mom's fine," he said.

I could only look at him with tears streaming down my cheeks. I didn't believe him.

"I don't know who told you different, or what kind of dirty dog would want to put a scare like that into a little boy, but I swear to God your mother's fine."

"But . . . but he said . . ."

"I don't care *what* he said. I got back from Eversham's earlier than I expected—he doesn't want to sell any cows, it's all just talk—and decided I had time to catch up with you. I got my pole and my creel and your mother made us a couple of jelly fold-overs. Her new bread. Still warm. So she was fine half an hour ago, Gary, and there's nobody knows any different that's come from this direction, I guarantee you. Not in just half an hour's time." He looked over my shoulder. "Who was this man? And where was he? I'm going to find him and thrash him within an inch of his life."

I thought a thousand things in just two seconds—that's what it seemed like, anyway—but the last thing I thought was the most powerful: if my Dad met up with the man in the black suit, I didn't think my Dad would be the one to do the thrashing. Or the walking away.

I kept remembering those long white fingers, and the talons at the ends of them.

"Gary?"

"I don't know that I remember," I said.

"Were you where the stream splits? The big rock?"

I could never lie to my father when he asked a direct question—not to save his life or mine. "Yes, but don't go down there." I seized his arm with both hands and tugged it hard. "Please don't. He was a scary man." Inspiration struck like an illuminating lightning bolt. "I think he had a gun."

He looked at me thoughtfully. "Maybe there wasn't a man," he said, lifting his voice a little on the last word and turning it into something that was almost but not quite a question. "Maybe you fell asleep while you were fishing, son, and had a bad dream. Like the ones you had about Danny last winter."

I *had* had a lot of bad dreams about Dan last winter, dreams where I would open the door to our closet or to the dark, fruity interior of the cider shed and see him standing there and looking at me out of his purple strangulated face; from many of these dreams I had awakened screaming, and awakened my parents as well. I had fallen asleep on the bank of the stream for a little while, too—dozed off, anyway—but I hadn't dreamed, and I was sure I had awakened just before the man in the black suit clapped the bee dead, sending it tumbling off my nose and into my lap. I hadn't dreamed him the way I had dreamed Dan, I was quite sure of that, although my meeting with him had already attained a dreamlike quality in my mind, as I suppose supernatural occurrences always must. But if my Dad thought that the man had only existed in my own head, that might be better. Better for him.

"It might have been, I guess," I said.

"Well, we ought to go back and find your rod and your creel."

He actually started in that direction, and I had to tug frantically at his arm to stop him again and turn him back toward me.

"Later," I said. "Please, Dad? I want to see Mother. I've got to see her with my own eyes."

He thought that over, then nodded. "Yes, I suppose you do. We'll go home first, and get your rod and creel later."

So we walked back to the farm together, my father with his fish pole propped on his shoulder just like one of my friends, me carrying his creel, both of us eating folded-over slices of my mother's bread smeared with black-current jam.

"Did you catch anything?" he asked as we came in sight of the barn.

"Yes, sir," I said. "A rainbow. Pretty good-sized." *And a brookie that was a lot bigger,* I thought but didn't say.

"That's all? Nothing else?"

"After I caught it I fell asleep." This was not really an answer but not really a lie, either.

"Lucky you didn't lose your pole. You didn't, did you, Gary?"

"No, sir," I said, very reluctantly. Lying about that would do no good even if I'd been able to think up a whopper—not if he was set on going back to get my creel anyway, and I could see by his face that he was.

Up ahead, Candy Bill came racing out of the back door, barking his shrill bark and wagging his whole rear end back and forth the way Scotties do when they're excited. I couldn't wait any longer. I broke away from my father and ran to the house, still lugging his creel and still convinced, in my heart of hearts, that I was going to find my mother dead on the kitchen floor with her face swollen and purple, as Dan's had been when my father carried him in from the west field, crying and calling the name of Jesus.

But she was standing at the counter, just as well and fine as when I had left her, humming a song as she shelled peas into a bowl. She looked around at me, first in surprise and then in fright as she took in my wide eyes and pale cheeks.

"Gary, what is it? What's the matter?"

I didn't answer, only ran to her and covered her with kisses. At some point my father came in and said, "Don't worry, Lo—he's all right. He just had one of his bad dreams, down there by the brook."

"Pray God it's the last of them," she said, and hugged me tighter while Candy Bill danced around our feet, barking his shrill bark.

"You don't have to come with me if you don't want to, Gary," my father said, although he had already made it clear that he thought I should—that I should go back, that I should face my fear, as I suppose folks would say nowadays. That's very well for fearful things that are make-believe, but two hours hadn't done much to change my conviction that the man in the black suit had been real. I wouldn't be able to convince my father of that, though. I don't think there was a nine-year-old who ever lived would have been able to convince his father he'd seen the Devil walking out of the woods in a black suit.

"I'll come," I said. I had come out of the house to join him before he left, mustering all my courage to get my feet moving, and now we were standing by the chopping block in the side yard, not far from the woodpile.

"What you got behind your back?" he asked.

I brought it out slowly. I would go with him, and I would hope the man in the black suit with the arrow-straight part down the left side of his head was gone. But if he wasn't, I wanted to be prepared. As prepared as I could be, anyway. I had the family Bible in the hand I had brought out from behind my back. I'd set out just to bring my New Testament, which I had won for memorizing the most psalms in the Thursday-night Youth Fellowship competition (I managed eight, although most of them except the Twenty-third had floated out of my mind in a week's time), but the little red Testament didn't seem like enough when you were maybe going to face the Devil himself, not even when the words of Jesus were marked out in red ink.

My father looked at the old Bible, swollen with family documents and pictures, and I thought he'd tell me to put it back, but he didn't. A look of mixed grief and sympathy crossed his face, and he nodded. "All right," he said. "Does your mother know you took that?"

"No, sir."

He nodded again. "Then we'll hope she doesn't spot it gone before we get back. Come on. And don't drop it."

Half an hour or so later, the two of us stood on the bank at the place where Castle Stream forked, and at the flat place where I'd had my encounter with the man with the red-orange eyes. I had my bamboo rod in my hand—I'd picked it up below the bridge—and my creel lay down below, on the flat place. Its wicker top was flipped back. We stood looking down, my father and I, for a long time, and neither of us said anything.

Opal! Diamond! Sapphire! Jade! I smell Gary's lemonade! That had been his unpleasant little poem, and once he had recited it, he had thrown himself on his back, laughing like a child who has just discovered he has enough courage to say bathroom words like shit or piss. The flat place down there was as green and lush as any place in Maine that the sun can get to in early July. Except where the stranger had lain. There the grass was dead and yellow in the shape of a man.

I was holding our lumpy old family Bible straight out in front of me with both thumbs pressing so hard on the cover that they were white. It was the way Mama Sweet's husband, Norville, held a willow fork when he was trying to dowse somebody a well.

"Stay here," my father said at last, and skidded sideways down the bank, digging his shoes into the rich soft soil and holding his arms out for balance. I stood where I was, holding the Bible stiffly out at the ends of my arms, my heart thumping. I don't know if I had a sense of being watched that time or not; I was too scared to have a sense of anything, except for a sense of wanting to be far away from that place and those woods.

My dad bent down, sniffed at where the grass was dead, and grimaced. I knew what he was smelling: something like burnt matches. Then he grabbed my creel and came on back up the bank, hurrying. He snagged one fast look over his shoulder to make sure nothing was coming along behind. Nothing was. When he handed me the creel, the lid was still hanging back on its cunning little leather hinges. I looked inside and saw nothing but two handfuls of grass.

"Thought you said you caught a rainbow," my father said, "but maybe you dreamed that, too."

Something in his voice stung me. "No, sir," I said. "I caught one."

"Well, it sure as hell didn't flop out, not if it was gutted and cleaned. And you wouldn't put a catch into your fisherbox without doing that, would you, Gary? I taught you better than that."

"Yes, sir, you did, but—"

"So if you didn't dream catching it and if it was dead in the box, something must have come along and eaten it," my father said, and then he grabbed another quick glance over his shoulder, eyes wide, as if he had heard something move in the woods. I wasn't exactly surprised to see drops of sweat standing out on his forehead like big clear jewels. "Come on," he said. "Let's get the hell out of here."

I was for that, and we went back along the bank to the bridge, walking quick without speaking. When we got there, my dad dropped to one knee and examined the place where we'd found my rod. There was another patch of dead grass there, and the lady's slipper was all brown and curled in on itself, as if a blast of heat had charred it. I looked in my empty creel again. "He must have gone back and eaten my other fish, too," I said.

My father looked up at me. "*Other* fish!"

"Yes, sir. I didn't tell you, but I caught a brookie, too. A big one. He was awful hungry, that fella." I wanted to say more, and the words trembled just behind my lips, but in the end I didn't.

We climbed up to the bridge and helped each other over the railing. My father took my creel, looked into it, then went to the railing and threw it over. I came up beside him in time to see it splash down and float away like a boat, riding lower and lower in the stream as the water poured in between the wicker weavings.

"It smelled bad," my father said, but he didn't look at me when he said it, and his voice sounded oddly defensive. It was the only time I ever heard him speak just that way.

"Yes, sir."

"We'll tell your mother we couldn't find it. If she asks. If she doesn't ask, we won't tell her anything."

"No, sir, we won't."

And she didn't and we didn't, and that's the way it was.

That day in the woods is eighty years gone, and for many of the years in between I have never even thought of it—not awake, at least. Like any other man or woman who ever lived, I can't say about my dreams, not for sure. But now I'm old, and I dream awake, it seems. My infirmities have crept up like waves that will soon take a child's abandoned sand castle, and my memories have also crept up, making me think of some old rhyme that went, in part, "Just leave them alone / And they'll come home / Wagging their tails behind them." I remember meals I ate, games I played, girls I kissed in the school cloakroom when we played post office, boys I chummed with, the first drink I ever took, the first cigarette I ever smoked (cornshuck behind Dicky Hamner's pig shed, and I threw up). Yet of all the memories the one of the man in the black suit is the strangest, and glows with its own spectral, haunted light. He was real, he was the Devil, and that day I was either his errand or his luck. I feel more and more strongly that escaping him was my luck—*just* luck, and not the intercession of the God I have worshipped and sung hymns to all my life.

As I lie here in my nursing-home room, and in the ruined sand castle that is my body, I tell myself that I need not fear the Devil—that I have lived a good, kindly life, and I need not fear the Devil. Sometimes I remind myself that it was I, not my father, who finally coaxed my mother back to church later on that summer. In the dark, however, these thoughts have no power to ease or comfort. In the dark comes a voice that whispers that the nine-year-old fisherboy I was had done nothing for which he might legitimately fear the Devil, either, and yet the Devil came—to him. And in the dark I sometimes hear that voice drop even lower, into ranges that are inhuman. *Big fish!* it whispers in tones of hushed greed, and all the truths of the moral world fall to ruin before its hunger.

Questions for Discussion and Analysis

1. The incident in the story occurred when Gary was nine years old. Why has the narrator waited for so many years to write about it?
2. Is there any significance in Gary's parents not wanting him to go beyond the place where the stream forks?
3. Look up the term "foreshadowing" if you are unsure of its meaning. Where does the narrator use foreshadowing to show that evil is imminent?
4. Examine the narrator's characterization of the man in the black suit. What is the boy's reaction to him? Why does he believe the Devil's report of his mother's death?

5. Of course the devil is evil (impeccably evil, to describe it in an ironic phrase). In what ways does the man reflect the traditional image we have of the Devil? In what ways is he different?
6. Much modern fiction blends dreamlike elements with reality. What details in the story does the narrator provide that suggest that the story is *not* a dream?

Short Story 4

Hired Girl

Alice Munro

Alice Munro, one of Canada's leading writers, grew up in Wingham, Ontario, and attended the University of Western Ontario. She now divides her time between Clinton, Ontario, near Lake Huron, and Comox, British Columbia. Munro's literary forte is the short story, as evidenced by the eight collections of stories bearing her name, among them Something I've Been Meaning to Tell You, Friend of My Youth, *and* Open Secrets, *and most recently,* The Collected Stories of Alice Munro. *"Hired Girl" first appeared in* The New Yorker *in April 1994.*

Mrs. Montjoy was showing me how to put the pots and pans away in her cupboard. I had put some of them in the wrong places.

"Just like our hired girls at home," I said. "The first few days, they were always putting things away where we couldn't find them. We called our maids hired girls, at home."

"Did you?" said Mrs. Montjoy. A moment of silence passed. "And the colander on that hook there."

Nothing about my life could interest or impress her.

Above all things, she said, she hated a higgledy-piggledy cupboard.

A couple of days before this, Mrs. Montjoy had picked me up at the station in Pointe au Baril and brought me to the island. I had got the job through the woman in the Pointe au Baril store, an old friend of my mother's—they had once taught school together. Mrs. Montjoy had asked this woman if she knew of a country girl who would take a summer job, and the woman had thought that I would be about the right age, and trained to do housework.

Mrs. Montjoy wore khaki shorts and a tucked-in shirt. Her short, sun-bleached hair was pushed behind her ears. She had leapt on board the boat like a boy, given a fierce tug to the outboard motor, and we were flung out on the choppy evening waters of Georgian Bay. For thirty or forty minutes we dodged among the rocky wooded islands, with their lone cottages, their boats bobbing beside the dock, and their pine trees jutting out at odd angles, just as they do in paintings.

I held on to the sides of the boat, and shivered in my flimsy new dress.

"Feeling sick?" said Mrs. Montjoy, with the briefest possible smile—it was like a signal for a smile, when the occasion did not warrant the real thing. She had large, white teeth in a long face, and her commonest expression seemed to be one of impatience held decently in check. She probably knew that what I was feeling was fear, not sickness, and she threw out this question so that I—and she—need not be embarrassed. What she did not understand was that fear did not embarrass me.

Here was a difference, already, from the world that I was used to. In that world, fear was commonplace, at least for a female. You could be afraid of snakes, thunderstorms, deep water, heights, rats, and the road through the swamp, and nobody thought any the worse of you. In Mrs. Montjoy's world, however, fear was shameful, always something to be conquered.

The island that was our destination had a name—Nausicaä.[1] It was written on a board at the end of the dock. This name seemed to me a good sign, and I said it aloud as I clambered out of the boat. I was anxious to appear appreciative and at ease.

"Oh, yes," Mrs. Montjoy said. "That was its name when Daddy bought it. It's after some character in Shakespeare."

I opened my mouth to say no, no, not Shakespeare, and to explain all about Nausicaä being the girl on the beach—the princess playing ball with her friends—whom Ulysses surprised when he awoke from his sleep. I was used to giving out information of this sort, without thinking about whether people wanted it. But some briskness in Mrs. Montjoy's tone warned me off, this time. My superior knowledge gave me a familiar feeling, of satisfaction and misgiving.

The dress I was wearing was one I had made myself of pink-and-white striped cotton. The material had been cheap, because it was not really meant for a dress but for a blouse or a nightgown, and the style I had chosen—the full-skirted, tight-waisted style of those days, the early fifties—was a mistake. When I walked, the cloth bunched up between my legs, and I had to yank it free. Today was the first day the dress had been worn, and I still thought that the problem was temporary—with a firm enough yank the skirt could be made to hang properly. But I found when I took off my belt that the day's heat and my sweat on the train had created a worse problem. The belt was wide and elasticized, and it was of a burgundy color, which had run. It had circled my waist with strawberry stains.

[1]From Homer's *Odyssey:* Nausicaä, the daughter of Alcinous, king of the Phaecians, meets Ulysses when he is shipwrecked on her father's seacoast and gives him a kind reception.

I made this discovery in the loft of the boathouse, where I was to sleep. I shared the loft with Mrs. Montjoy's ten-year-old daughter, Mary Anne. Mary Anne was fair-haired and freckled, with a long face, like her mother's. But she didn't have her mother's look of quick judgments waiting, marshalled right at the surface, ready to be tossed out at you. Her expression was benign and serious—she wore her heavy glasses even when she was sitting up in bed. It had taken two operations to get her eyes as straight as they were now. ("Daddy's eyes," she called them.)

"That's too bad about your dress," she said.

I said it was an old dress anyway. "I didn't want to wear anything good on the train."

All night long you could hear the water slapping against the boards of the boathouse. Morning came early here. A hundred miles north of home—could that make a difference? There was a window at each end of the loft. I got up and looked out.

Through one window the silky water, dark underneath but flashing back, from its surface, the light of the sky. The rocky shores of a little cove, the moored sailboats, the open channel beyond, the mound of another island, shores and channels beyond that. I thought that I would never, on my own, be able to find my way back to the mainland.

But maids don't have to find their way anywhere. They stay put, where the work is. It's the other people who come and go.

The other window looked out on a gray rock that was like a slanting wall, with shelves and crevices on it where little pine and cedar trees, and blueberry bushes, had got a foothold. Down at the base of the rock was a path—which I would take later on—through the woods, to Mrs. Montjoy's house. Here everything was damp and almost in darkness still, though the sky was whitening at the top of the rock. The trees here were the strict and fragrant evergreens, with their heavy boughs that don't allow much growth underneath—no riot of saplings and brambles and grapevines such as you find in the hardwood forest. Mostly damp ferns, blueberries. I had noticed this the day before, from the train, and it seemed to me that this was a more authentic forest than the bush lots we had at home—it had eliminated all that lavishness and confusion and seasonal change. And it went on more or less forever.

This morning was the last time that I would feel the shock of this different place on my eyes and skin in this way. What happened after that? It wasn't a matter of things becoming familiar, or housewife's blinkers being put on my eyes—I was not that vigilant, or conscientious. It was just that a barrier went up. A transparent barrier. And perhaps "barrier" is too strong a word—all I mean is that there was something like a heat shimmer in the air, not a warning so much as an indolent reminder. *Not for you.* As if it hardly needed to be said. *Not for you.* And of course I would not admit that such a reminder was there, I would never admit that I was in the least humbled or lonely, or even that I had really become a servant. But I started thinking differently, without admitting it to myself. I stopped thinking about leaving the path, going in among the trees, walking there by myself. I would have had to explain what I was doing, if anybody saw me, and the thought of that made the whole thing too much trouble.

Mary Anne liked to talk when we were lying in our cots at night. She told me that her favorite book was "Kon-Tiki" and that she didn't believe in God or in Heaven.

"My sister is dead," she said. "But I don't believe she is floating around in space in a white nightie. She's just dead, she is nothing."

"My sister was pretty," she said. "Compared to me, anyway. Mother isn't pretty and Daddy is really ugly. Aunt Margaret used to be pretty, but she's fat now, and Nana used to be pretty, but she's old. My friend Helen is pretty but my friend Susan isn't. You are sort of pretty, but it isn't the same thing, because you're a maid. Does it hurt your feelings when I say that?"

I said no. "I'm only a maid when I'm here."

It wasn't that I was the only servant, even on this island. The other servants were Henry and Corrie, and they were not unhappy with their jobs—in fact, they were grateful. Henry and Corrie had come to Canada from Holland a few years before and had gone to work for Mr. and Mrs. Foley, who were Mrs. Montjoy's parents. Mr. and Mrs. Foley spent the summers in a big white house with verandas and awnings, on the highest point of the island. Henry cut the grass and looked after the tennis court and helped Mr. Foley with the boats, the clearing of the paths, and repairs to the dock. Corrie did the housework and cooked the meals and looked after Mrs. Foley. Mrs. Foley spent every sunny morning sitting out on a deck chair on the grass, with her feet stretched out to get the sun and a little awning protecting her head. Corrie came and shifted her around as the sun moved, took her to the bathroom, and brought her cups of tea or glasses of iced coffee. (I often had to go up to the Foleys' house on some errand. I took things there, to put in the freezer, and I got things out. Home freezers were uncommon at that time.)

"You are not going to suck the ice cubes, are you?" I heard Corrie say to Mrs. Foley one afternoon. She stood by and watched, and when Mrs. Foley did begin to suck an ice cube, she said, "Spit it out. Spit it right out in Corrie's hand. You didn't do what I say."

"She could choke to death," Corrie said to me later. "But Mrs. Montjoy, Mr. Foley—they say, 'Give her ice cubes like everybody else.' So I watch her."

I thought it might be interesting if Corrie talked about the war. But all she would say was that everybody had been very hungry and that they had made soup out of potato skins.

"No good," she said. "No good to talk about it."

Corrie never just wiped the counters—she scoured them. Every move she made had the energy and concentration somebody would show when rowing a boat against the current, and every word she said was flung out as if against a high wind. When she wrung out the cleaning rag, she might have been wringing the neck of a chicken.

She and Henry were saving their money to go into business. They meant to start a nursing home. "Lots of them like her," said Corrie, throwing her head back to indicate Mrs. Foley on the lawn. "Soon more and more, because of the doctors; they are not dying soon. Who will be taking care?"

One day, Mrs. Foley called out to me as I crossed the lawn. "Now, where are you going to in this hot sun? You sit down by me and have a little rest."

Her white hair was tucked up under a floppy straw hat, and when she leaned forward the sun came through the holes in the straw, sprinkling her face with pimples of light. Pink and pale-brown spots covered her face, anyway. Her eyes, too, were a pale—an almost extinct—brown, and red around the rims. Her shape was curious—a narrow, flat chest and swollen stomach, under layers of loose, pale clothing. The legs she stuck out into the sun were shiny and discolored and faintly cracked, like old plates.

"I didn't put my stockings on," she said. "I'm afraid I'm having rather a lazy day today. But aren't you the remarkable girl, coming all that way by yourself? Did you get Henry to help you carry the groceries up from the dock?"

Mrs. Montjoy waved to us. She was on her way to the tennis court, behind the Foleys' house. Every morning she gave Mary Anne a tennis lesson, and at lunch they discussed what Mary Anne was doing wrong.

"That's a woman who comes to play tennis," Mrs. Foley said. "She comes every day, so I suppose it's all right. She must be a very dedicated tennis player."

Mrs. Montjoy said to me later, "Did Mrs. Foley ask you to come over and sit on the grass?"

I said yes. "She thought I was somebody who brought the groceries."

"Oh, yes. That was during the war—a girl used to come in a boat. There hasn't been any grocery delivery in years. Mrs. Foley gets her wires crossed occasionally."

"She said you were a woman who came to play tennis."

"Did she really?" Mrs. Montjoy said.

The work that I had to do here was nothing new for me. Like most country girls of my age, I could bake and iron, and clean an oven. This was the reason, in fact, that Mrs. Montjoy had sought out a country girl. In some ways the work was not as hard as it was at home. Nobody tracked barnyard mud into the kitchen, and there were no heavy men's work clothes to wrestle through the wringer and hang on the line. But there was the business of putting every pot and spoon back in its special place and cleaning the burners of the stove after every use, so that it looked as if nothing had ever been cooked there, and polishing the glass door leading to the deck so that the glass disappeared and people were in danger of smashing their faces against it.

The Montjoys' house was modern, built of golden-brown wood, with a flat roof, a deck extending over the edge of the water, and a great many windows, which Mrs. Montjoy would have liked to see as clean as the glass doors.

"But I have to be realistic," she said. "I know if you did that you'd be doing nothing else." She was not by any means a slave driver. Her tone with me was firm and slightly irritable, but that was the way it was with almost everybody. She was always on the lookout for incompetence, which she detested. "Sloppy" was a favorite word of condemnation. Others were "wishy-washy" and "unnecessary." A great many things that people said or did or felt were unnecessary, and some of these unnecessary things were wishy-washy. Other people might have used the word "arty," or "intellectual," or "permissive." Mrs. Montjoy swept all that away. Wishy-washy.

I ate my meals alone, at a table in the kitchen. Mrs. Montjoy and Mary Anne ate their lunch on the deck. I took their salad and sandwiches and drinks out to them, on a tray, and then I did not have to wait on them anymore. I read as I ate. I had found a stack of old magazines—*Life* and *Look* and *Time* and *Collier's*—at the back of the broom closet. I could tell that Mrs. Montjoy did not quite like the idea of my sitting reading these magazines as I ate my lunch. Was it because it was bad manners to read as you ate, or because I hadn't asked permission? More likely she saw my interest in such things as a subtle kind of impudence. Unnecessary.

All she said was "Those old magazines must be dreadfully dusty."

I said that I always wiped them off.

Sometimes a woman friend came over from one of the other islands, to play tennis and have lunch. I heard Mrs. Montjoy saying, ". . . have to keep your girls happy, or they'll be off to the Hotel, off to the Port. They can get jobs so easily, these days."

The other woman said, "That's so true."

"So you make allowances," Mrs. Montjoy said. "You do the best you can."

It took me a little while to understand that they were talking about me, that "girls," meant girls like me. I wondered, then, how was I being kept happy? By being allowed to read those magazines, by being taken along on the occasional alarming boat ride, when Mrs. Montjoy went to get our supplies? By being allowed to wear shorts and a blouse or even a halter, instead of a dark-blue uniform with white collar and cuffs such as Corrie wore?

And what hotel was this? What port?

What are you best at?" Mary Anne said. "What sports?"

"Well—volleyball," I said. We all had to play that, at school.

"Oh, I don't mean team sports," Mary Anne said. "I mean, what are you best at? Such as tennis? Or swimming or riding or what? My really best thing is riding, because that doesn't depend so much on your eyesight. Aunt Margaret's best used to be tennis and so was Nana's, and Granddad's was always sailing, and Daddy's is golf and Uncle Stewart's is sailing and golf, and Mother's is golf and swimming and sailing and tennis and everything, but maybe tennis a little bit the best of all. If my sister Jane hadn't died I'm not sure what hers would have been, but I think swimming, because she could already swim and she was only three."

I had never been on a tennis court. The idea of getting up on a horse or going out in a sailboat terrified me. I could barely swim. Golf was something that silly-looking men did in cartoons. The adults I knew sat down and rested whenever they were not working. That was not often.

"Everybody I know works too hard to do any of those things," I said. "We don't have a tennis court in our town. We don't have a golf course, either." (Actually, we had once had both, but there had been no money to keep them up in the thirties, and they had not been restored since.) "Nobody I know owns a sailboat."

I did not mention the hockey rink or the baseball park.

"Really?" said Mary Anne thoughtfully. "What do they do, then?"

"They work," I said. "And they never have any money. All of their lives."

I told her that most people never saw a flush toilet unless it was in a public building and that old people stayed in bed all winter (these were people too old to work) in order to keep warm. Children walked barefoot until the frost came, in order to save shoe leather, and died of stomach aches and fevers, because there was no money for a doctor. I said that sometimes people had eaten boiled grass for supper.

Not one of these statements—not even the one about boiled grass—was completely a lie. The one about flush toilets came closest to the truth, but it applied to country people—not town people—ten or twelve years earlier. But as I talked to Mary Anne, all the isolated incidents and bizarre circumstances I had heard about spread out in my mind, so that I almost believed that I myself had walked with bare, blue feet on frosty roads—I, who had been given cod-liver oil and inoculations and bundled up for school within an inch of my life, and had gone to bed hungry only because of a refusal to eat beef sausages or junket or bread pudding or liver. And this false impression I was giving seemed quite justifiable because of the real gulf that was there, that could never be made clear. What a difference there was, for instance, between the Montjoys' kitchen and the kitchen at home—but you couldn't explain the difference just by mentioning the worn-out linoleum of one and the perfectly shining surfaces of the other, or the fact that in one of them water was pumped into the sink from a cistern and in the other it came out of a tap. The fact was that one kitchen followed with absolute correctness an idea of what everybody's kitchen ought to be, and the other grew and changed, with improvisations and use, and belonged entirely to one family, to the years and decades of the family's life. And when I thought of that kitchen, with its blackened shelves behind the stove, the historical confusion deep in its cupboards, the smell of the barn clothes hung by the door, it seemed that I had to protect it from contempt—that I had to protect a whole precious and intimate though often unpleasant way of life from contempt, which I supposed to be nourished in the icy hearts of people like the Montjoys.

So I spun out the details of hardship and made no mention of the hired girls I had talked about to Mrs. Montjoy. I eliminated soft, drowsy Olive, whom I would have liked to please, but couldn't, because she lived in a fog of hymns and prophecies and curious prohibitions, also Annie, who marked the cups with lipstick and did her hair up in pin curls at night and kept a list of the boys she went out with, putting strange marks after their names— + ++ ✲ O—and Mavis, who hung the clothes on the line in an eccentric way, by one corner or leg or sleeve. Hired girls had become a thing of the past, anyway, when I got old enough to manage part of the housework. And now my sister was old enough.

"That isn't fair," said Mary Anne. "That's awful." But then she added, "Why don't they go and catch some fish?"

"They haven't got any fishing rods."

"Couldn't they make some?"

"People who don't even need the fish have come and caught them all, anyway. For fun."

I thought that would keep her quiet, but she could not stop mulling over the problem. "Couldn't they go to the Salvation Army?"

"They're too proud," I said.

"Well, I feel sorry for them," Mary Anne said. "I feel sorry for them, but I think that's really stupid. What about the children? They ought to think about their children. Are the children too proud, too?"

"Everybody's proud," I said.

When Mr. Montjoy came to the island on the weekends, there was always a great deal of noise and activity. Some of that was because there were visitors, who came by boat to swim or have drinks and watch sailing races. But a lot of it was generated by Mr. Montjoy himself. He had a loud, blustery voice and a clumsy body. Every weekend he turned red from the sun, and during every week the burned skin peeled away, leaving him splotchy and pink and muddy with freckles, ready to be burned again. When he took off his glasses you could see that one eye was quick and squinty and the other boldly blue but stupid-looking and moving jerkily, as if it had been caught in a trap.

His blustering was often about things that he had misplaced, or dropped, or bumped into. "Where the hell is the—?" he would say, or, "You didn't happen to see the—?," so it seemed that he had also misplaced, or failed to grasp in the first place, even the name of the thing he might grab up a handful of peanuts or pretzels—whatever was nearby—and eat them as if not noticing what he was doing. You felt that he might look at the empty bowl, the minute he had finished eating, and say, "Where the hell are the—?"

One morning I heard him say, "Now where the hell is my—?" when he was crashing around out on the deck.

"Your book?" said Mrs. Montjoy. She was out there having her morning coffee.

"I thought I had it out here," Mr. Montjoy said. "I was reading it."

"That Book-of-the-Month-Club book?" she said. "I think you left it in the living room."

She was right. I was vacuuming the living-room floor, and I had found a book pushed partway under the sofa. Its title was "Seven Gothic Tales." That made me want to see what it was about, so I opened it, and even as I listened to this conversation on the deck I was reading, holding the book open in one hand and guiding the vacuum cleaner with the other: " 'Nay, I speak from my heart,' said Mira. 'I have been trying for a long time to understand God. Now I have made friends with him. To love him truly you must love change, and you must love a joke, these being the true inclinations of his own heart. . . .' "

"There it is," said Mr. Montjoy. "Good girl, you found my book. Now I remember. I was reading it on the sofa last night."

"I just picked it up," I said. "It was on the floor."

He must have seen that I was reading it. "It's a queer kind of book," he said. "But sometimes you want to read a book that isn't like all the others."

"I couldn't make head or tail of it," said Mrs. Montjoy, coming in with the coffee tray. "We'll have to get out of the way here—Elsa has to get on with the vacuuming."

Mr. Montjoy went back to the city that evening. The next day I looked everywhere. I looked under the chairs and behind the curtains, in case he might have left the book behind. But I could not find it.

"I always thought it would be nice to live up here all the year round, the way you people do," said Mrs. Foley. She must have been thinking again that I was the local girl who used to bring the groceries. Some days she said, "Now I know who you are. You're the new girl helping the Dutch woman in the kitchen, but I just can't recall your name," and other days she let me walk by without giving any greeting or showing the least sign of interest.

"We used to come up in the winter," she said. "Sometimes the bay was frozen over and there would be a road across the ice. We used to go snowshoeing. Now, can you tell me, why does nobody go snowshoeing anymore?"

She didn't wait for me to answer. She leaned toward me. "Can you tell me where Jane is?" she said with embarrassment, speaking almost in a whisper.

I said that I didn't know. She reached out a hand, perhaps to touch my face, and I drew back, so that the hand grazed my chest instead. It was a hot day, and I was wearing a halter. I felt her touch on my bare skin just where my breasts divided. Her hand was light and dry as a wood shaving.

"I'm sure it's all right," she said.

After that I didn't want to sit down beside her or speak to her again.

On a Saturday afternoon toward the end of August, the Montjoys gave a cocktail party. The party was given in honor of the friends they had staying with them that weekend—Mr. and Mrs. Hammond.

People arrived in motorboats and sailboats. Some of them went swimming, then sat around on the rocks in their bathing suits or lay on the dock in the sun. Others came up to the house immediately and started drinking and talking in the living room or out on the deck. Some children had come with their parents, and some by themselves, in their own boats. These were not children of Mary Anne's age—Mary Anne had been taken to stay with her friend Susan, on another island—but of mine. Girls and boys fifteen or sixteen years old. They spent most of the afternoon in the water, diving and shouting and having races to the raft.

Mrs. Montjoy and I had been busy since early morning, making all the different things to eat, which we now arranged on platters and offered to these people. This was fiddly and exasperating work—stuffing various mixtures into mushroom caps, sticking one tiny slice of something on top of a tiny slice of toast or bread. All the shapes had to be perfect and of exactly the same size—perfect rounds, perfect squares, perfect triangles, perfect diamonds. Mrs. Hammond came into the kitchen several times and admired what we were doing.

"How gorgeous everything looks," she said. "You notice I'm not even offering to help. It would just be a joke, I'm hopeless."

I like the way she said that. I admired her husky voice, its weary, humorous tone. *I'm hopeless*. I wished I were her, in a sleek, black bathing suit with a tan like dark toast, shoulder-length dark hair, and an exotic orchid lipstick, constantly reapplied. She did not look happy, but her air of complaint and sullenness seemed glamorous to me, her hints of cloudy drama enviable. She and her husband were an altogether different kind of rich people from Mr. and Mrs. Montjoy. They were more like the people I had already met in magazine stories and in books like "The Hucksters"—people who drank a lot, had love affairs, went to psychiatrists. Her name was Carol and her husband's name was Ivan. I already thought of them by their first names—something I had never been tempted to do with the Montjoys.

Mrs. Montjoy had asked me to put on a dress, so I wore the pink-and-white striped cotton, with the smudged material around its waist tucked under the elasticized belt. Nearly everybody else was in shorts or even in bathing suits. I passed among them, offering food. I was not sure how to do this. Sometimes people were talking or laughing so busily that they didn't notice me. I had to say, "Excuse me—would you like one of these?" in a very determined voice, to get their attention. Then they looked startled and amused. "Why, thank you," they said, as if my interruption were a further joke.

"Enough passing for now, Elsa," Mrs. Montjoy said.

She gathered up some glasses and asked me to wash them. "People never keep track of their own—it's easier just to keep giving them fresh ones," she said. "Also it's time to get the meatballs out of the fridge and heat them. Could you watch the oven?"

While I was busy in the kitchen I heard Mrs. Hammond calling, "Ivan! Ivan!" She was roaming through the back rooms of the house. But Mr. Hammond had come in through the kitchen door that led to the woods. He stood there and did not answer her.

He came over to the counter and poured gin into his glass.

"Oh, Ivan, there you are," said Mrs. Hammond, coming in from the hall.

"Here I am," said Mr. Hammond.

"Where else?" she said. "Me, too." She handed him her glass.

Mr. Hammond set her glass down and pushed the gin bottle toward her. He spoke to me. He said, "Are you having any fun, Minnie?"

Mrs. Hammond gave a yelp of laughter. "Minnie. Where did you get the idea her name was Minnie? Her name is Elsa."

"Elsa," said Mr. Hammond. "Are you having fun, Elsa?"

"Oh, yes," I said. I was busy lifting the cookie sheet with the meatballs on it out of the oven and hadn't taken any time with my reply. I immediately wished I had matched his sarcastic tone. I could have said, "Yes, *indeed*."

"I swam around the point," said Mrs. Hammond. "I'm working up to swimming around the entire island."

Mr. Hammond said, "Good."

"Well, then," said Mrs. Hammond. "I'll leave you to it."

I had begun to spear the meatballs with toothpicks and arrange them on a platter. Mr. Hammond said, "Care for some help?" and tried to do the same, but his toothpicks missed and sent the meatballs skittering onto the counter.

"Well, Elsa," he said. Then, as if he could not follow his thought further, he simple repeated himself. "Well, Elsa."

I knew something about him. I knew that the Hammonds were here for a special holiday because Mr. Hammond had lost his job. Mary Anne had told me this. "He's depressed about it," she had said. He did not seem depressed to me. He seemed impatient—chiefly with Mrs. Hammond—but quite pleased with himself. He was tall, he had dark hair combed straight back, and a dark, thin mustache, and I had noticed that when people talked to him he had a way of leaning slightly toward them, as if what they had to say might be very important. The word that described this, in my mind, was "courtly."

"Where do you go swimming, Minnie? Do you go swimming?"

"Down by the boathouse," I said. I thought he must have said "Minnie" for a joke.

"Is that a good place?"

I said yes. It was good for me, because I had never, before this summer, swum in water that was over my head, and I liked being close to the dock.

"Do you ever go in without your bathing suit?"

"No."

"You should try it," he said.

Mrs. Montjoy came through the livingroom doorway, asking if the meatballs were ready.

"This is certainly a hungry crowd," she said. "It's the swimming does it. How are you getting on, Ivan? Carol was just looking for you."

"She was here," said Mr. Hammond.

Mrs. Montjoy dropped parsley here and there among the meatballs. "Now, Elsa," she said. "I think you've done about all you need to here. I think I can manage now. Why don't you make yourself a sandwich and run along down to the boathouse."

I said I wasn't hungry. Mr. Hammond had disappeared into the back part of the house.

"Well, you'd better take something," Mrs. Hammond said. "You might be hungry later."

She meant that I was not to come back.

On my way to the boathouse I met a couple of the guests—girls of my own age, barefoot and in their bathing suits, breathlessly laughing.

They had probably swum partway around the island, climbed out of the water at the boathouse dock, and were sneaking back to surprise somebody. They stepped aside when they saw me but did not quite stop laughing. They made way for my body without looking at me. They were the kind of girls who would have squealed and made a fuss over me if I had been a dog or a cat.

The noise of the party continued for a long time. It was too early, anyway, to go to sleep. I put on my bathing suit and climbed down the ladder into the water and swam around a bit, gradually working up a fantasy about Mr. Hammond. It was not impossible, I thought, that he would come looking for me. And then what? A first touch, I supposed, then kisses, hot pressures, limbs twining in the water, like ribbons of light. The thought of touching a man that old—forty? forty-five?—disturbed me, though I knew I would get pleasure from it. It was like knowing you would get pleasure from touching a crocodile. Mr. Hammond's—Ivan's—skin might be smooth, but his age and his knowledge and his desired corruptness would sit on it like invisible warts and scales.

I let the straps of my bathing suit down, I let my breasts float free. I swam that way, with the water sweetly dividing at my nipples, gliding over my skin. I even dared to lift myself out of the water, though it wasn't dark yet. Holding to the dock with one hand I bobbed up and down and rose into the light like a mermaid, wet and gleaming, with nobody to see.

Then I heard steps—I heard somebody coming. I sank down into the water, by the dock. I held still.

For just a minute I believed that it was Mr. Hammond and that I had actually entered the world of secret signals, lovers' meetings, ruthless desires. I shrank against the dock, horrified and submissive. Then the boathouse light was switched on, and I turned around, noiselessly, carefully, in the water—no longer sure that I would see Mr. Hammond but not sure that I wouldn't see him, either—and there was old Mr. Foley, in his baggy white pants, with his back to me, moving something around on the tool shelf. Earlier that afternoon he had appeared at the party, in his yachtsman's cap and blazer. He had stayed for one drink and explained that Mrs. Foley could not bear the strain of seeing so many people but sent her best to all.

He found what he wanted, or put back what he had taken away earlier, and switched off the light, and left. He never noticed that I was there.

I pulled up my bathing suit and climbed out of the water and went up the stairs. My body seemed such a weight to me that when I got to the top I was short of breath.

The sound of the cocktail party went on. To hold my own against it, I started to write a letter to my friend Eleanor, at home. She was the sort of friend with whom I nearly always talked about sex. I described the party in derogatory terms and spoke of Mr. Hammond as a letch, though I added that he was very good-looking. I said that he had nudged me and fondled me in the kitchen when my hands were occupied with the meatballs, and later he had followed me down to the boathouse and made a determined attack. But I had kicked him and freed myself and he had gone away. *Scurried away* was what I said.

"So hold your breath for the next installment—'The Kitchen Maid's Adventure,' or 'Ravaged on the Rocks of Georgian Bay,'" I wrote. I realized the next day that I should have written "ravished" not "ravaged," but it was all right, Eleanor would not know the difference.

"Mrs. Foley asked me where Jane was," I said to Mrs. Montjoy. We were polishing the silver—I was polishing it and she was standing beside me, inspecting it. All the knives and forks and spoons had to be polished before we left the island. "I didn't know who she meant. Was Jane one of the girls who worked here some other summer?"

"Jane was my other daughter," said Mrs. Montjoy. "She was Mary Anne's sister. She's dead."

"Oh, I didn't know," I said. "Oh, that's too bad."

"Well. It's some time ago now."

"Did she die of polio?" I said cautiously. In those days children still died of polio, every summer.

"No," said Mrs. Montjoy. "She was killed when I moved the corner cupboard in my bedroom. I was looking for my bracelet. I didn't really think it would be there, but I thought I'd look. One of the casters caught on the rug, and the whole thing toppled down on her, and she was killed."

I knew all this, of course. Mary Anne had told me all of it. I knew it the way I knew such things then—the black holes, the horrors that seemed essential in the drama I required of life.

"That's terrible," I said. "I'm terribly sorry." In my guilt, in my queasy triumph, I let a fork slip through my fingers, to the floor.

Mrs. Montjoy picked it up. "Remember to wash this," she said. "It was nothing to do with you, Elsa. It was just one of those things."

At that time I didn't recognize brutality in myself, or boorishness. I thought I had the right—the right to barge in, stir up feelings, demand intimacy, or at least attention. I thought myself blameless, beyond judgment, in my dealings with Mrs. Montjoy. Because I was young and poor and knew about Nausicaä. I didn't have the grace or fortitude to be a servant.

On my last Sunday I was alone in the boathouse, packing up my things in the suitcase that had gone with my mother and father on their wedding trip. When I pulled it out from under my cot and opened it, here, it smelled of home—of the closet at the end of the upstairs hall where it usually sat, close to the mothballed winter coats and the fox-fur scarf and the rubber sheet once used on children's beds. But when you got it out at home it always smelled faintly of train trips and cities where many buildings were still heated by coal—of travel.

I heard steps on the path, a stumbling step into the boathouse, a rapping on the wall. It was Mr. Montjoy.

"Are you up there, Elsa? Are you up there?"

His voice was boisterous, jovial, as it was when he had been drinking. There were friends at the Montjoys' house, toasting the end of summer. I came to the top of the stairs. He put a hand on the wall to steady himself. A boat had gone by out in the channel and sent little waves into the boathouse.

"See here, Elsa," said Mr. Montjoy, looking up at me with his fierce, trapped eye. "See here—I thought I might as well bring this down and give it to you."

It was a book he was handing to me: "Seven Gothic Tales."

"Because I saw you were looking at it that day," he said. "It seemed to me you were interested in it. So I thought, Well, you might as well have it."

"Thank you," I said.

"I thought when I finished it I might as well pass it along to you. It just occurred to me. You might enjoy it."

"Thank you very much."

"That's all right. I just thought you might enjoy it."

"Yes," I said. But very little of the joy I felt got into my voice. I was too surprised at first, then, very quickly, hardly surprised at all. Once I got my hands on the book, I felt as if it had always belonged to me.

"Well, then. I hope you will."

Mary Anne had once said to me, "Daddy used to be poor like you. He grew up in a little place somewhere near Ottawa, and his father was a doctor, but he died. So Daddy had to work his way through university. Nana didn't think Mother should marry him at first but Granddad said he was too smart to stay poor for very long."

I was not sure I was going to give anybody whose father had been a doctor the credit for being poor.

He left the boathouse, and I went back upstairs and pushed the suitcase aside and sat down on the cot. I opened the book just anywhere, and began to read.

"The walls of the room had once been painted crimson, but with time the color had faded into a richness of hues, like a glassful of dying red roses. . . . Some potpourri was being burned on the tall stove, on the sides of which Neptune, with a trident, steered his team of horses through high waves."

Reading this, I felt as if I had just been rescued from my life. Words could become a burning-glass for me in those days, and no shame of my nature or condition could hold out among the flares of pleasure.

Questions for Discussion and Analysis

1. In what ways does Elsa learn about the gulf between her and the Montjoys? How does she accommodate to this awareness?
2. How does the narrator reveal Mrs. Montjoy's coldness?
3. Why does Elsa exaggerate to Mary Anne the poverty that afflicts the people in her hometown?
4. What does Mr. Hammond represent to Elsa—a lecher or a romantic figure who can make the events in bodice-ripping romance novels come true?
5. Why does Elsa deliberately ask Mrs. Montjoy for the details of her little girl's death when she admits later that she knew what had happened?
6. What is Mr. Montjoy's role in the story, especially in the scene in the boathouse?
7. If you are unsure of its meaning, look up the word "epiphany." What is the epiphany in this story?

Permissions Acknowledgments

Abrams, Michael.—From "Life on Lobster Lips" by Michael Abrams, *Discover,* March 1996. © 1996 by Michael Abrams. Reprinted with permission of Discover Magazine.

Achebe, Chinua.—From *Hopes and Impediments* by Chinua Achebe. Copyright © 1988 by Chinua Achebe. Used by permission of Doubleday, a division of Bantam Doubleday Dell Publishing Group, Inc. and Harold Ober Associates Incorporated.

Ackerman, Diane.—From *A Natural History of the Senses* by Diane Ackerman. Copyright © 1990 by Diane Ackerman. Reprinted by permission of Random House, Inc.

Ackerman, Diane.—From "In Praise of Bats" from *The Moon by Whale Light* by Diane Ackerman. Copyright © 1991 by Diane Ackerman. Reprinted by permission of Random House, Inc.

Ackerman, Diane.—From "Sitting on an alligator." from *The Moon by Whale Light* by Diane Ackerman. Copyright © 1991 by Diane Ackerman. Reprinted by permission of Random House, Inc.

Alderman, Ellen and Caroline Kennedy.—"Arrington v. The New York Times Company" from *The Right To Privacy* by Ellen Alderman and Caroline Kennedy. Copyright © 1995 by Ellen Alderman and Caroline Kennedy. Reprinted by permission of Alfred A. Knopf, Inc.

Allen, Jeanne. —"What Americans Really Think of School Choice" by Jeanne Allen, *The Wall Street Journal,* September 17, 1996. Reprinted by permission of The Wall Street Journal, © 1996 Dow Jones & Company, Inc. All Rights Reserved Worldwide.

Anderson, Jervis.—Excerpt from "Black and Blue" by Jervis Anderson. Reprinted by permission; © 1996 Jervis Anderson. Originally published in *The New Yorker.* All rights reserved.

Atwood, Margaret.—From "The View from the Backyard" by Margaret Atwood. Reprinted with permission from the 1986 issue of *The Nation.* © 1986.

Bambara, Toni Cade.—Excerpt from "The Lesson" from *Gorilla, My Love* by Toni Cade Bambara. Copyright © 1972 by Toni Cade Bambara. Reprinted by permission of Random House, Inc.

Barry, John.—"Newsweek: We Did Not Attack the Navy" (letter to the editor) by John Barry as appeared in *The Wall Street Journal,* June 5, 1996. Reprinted with permission by the author.

Beck, Bill.—"The WalMarts Are Coming!" by Bill Beck as appeared in *The Wall Street Journal,* March 15, 1996. Reprinted by permission of the author.

Branigan, William. Excerpt from "The Great American Melting Stew" by William Branigan, *The Washington Post,* April 14, 1997. Copyright © 1997, The Washington Post. Reprinted with permission.

Broder, David S.—"Empower Qualified Teachers" by David S. Broder, *The Washington Post National Weekly Edition,* September 23, 1996. Copyright © 1996 The Washington Post Writers Group. Reprinted with permission.

Buford, Bill.—From *Among the Thugs: The Experience and Seduction of Crowd Violence* by Bill Buford. Copyright © 1991 by William Buford. Reprinted by permission of W.W. Norton & Company, Inc. and Martin Secker & Warburg.

Camus, Albert.—From *Actuelles I* by Albert Camus. © 1950, Gallimard. Reprinted with permission.

Carman, John.—From "'G-dd-ss f- L-v' Must Be Vanna" by John Carman, *San Francisco Chronicle,* November 19, 1988. © San Francisco Chronicle. Reprinted by permission.

Carroll, Jon.—"Who Are These Foreign People?" by Jon Carroll, *San Francisco Chronicle,* March 27, 1996. © The San Francisco Chronicle. Reprinted with permission.

Carter, Stephen L. —From *Integrity* by Stephen L. Carter. Copyright © 1996 by Stephen L. Carter. Published by BasicBooks, A Division of Harper Collins Publishers, Inc. Originally appeared as an article, "The

Insufficiency of Honesty," *The Atlantic Monthly,* February 1996.

Castañeda, Jorge G.—From "Ferocious Differences" by Jorge G. Castañeda, as appeared in *The Atlantic Monthly,* July 1995. Reprinted by permission of the author.

Close, Glenn.—From "Leaving the Role" by Glenn Close as appeared in *The New Yorker,* July 10, 1995. Reprinted by permission.

Codrescu, Andrei.—"Faux Chicken & Phony Furniture" by Andrei Codrescu. Reprinted with permission from the December 12, 1994 issue of *The Nation.* © 1994.

Cox, Craig.—From "Shticks and Stones" by Craig Cox, Utne Reader, March/April 1997. Reprinted with permission from *Utne Reader.*

Da Silva, Osvaldo.—From "Factory Worker to Valedictorian" (letter to the editor) by Osvaldo Da Silva, *The Wall Street Journal,* April 25, 1997. Reprinted by permission of the author.

Del Castillo-Guilbault, Rose.—"Book of Dreams" by Rose Del Castillo-Guilbault, *San Francisco Chronicle,* February 28, 1993. Reprinted by permission of the author.

Del Vecchio, Rick.—"Performing Whales Drawing Protests" by Rick Del Vecchio, *San Francisco Chronicle,* December 18, 1991. © San Francisco Chronicle. Reprinted with permission.

DiGiacomo, Susan.—Letter from Susan DiGiacomo first appeared in *The New York Times Magazine,* October 15, 1995. Reprinted with permission.

Dossey, Larry., M.D.—From "Healing Happens" by Larry Dossey, M.D. as appeared in *Utne Reader,* September/October 1995, p.52. Reprinted by permission of the author.

Dowd, Maureen.—"What Calvin Really Thought . . ." by Maureen Dowd, *The New York Times,* August 31, 1995. Copyright © 1995 by The New York Times Company. Reprinted by permission.

Duane, Daniel.—Excerpt from *Caught Inside: A Surfer's Year on the California Coast* by Daniel Duane. Copyright © 1996 by Daniel Duane. Reprinted by permission of North Point Press, a division of Farrar, Straus & Giroux, Inc.

Duneier, Mitchell.—From *Slim's Table: Race, Respectability and Masculinity* by Mitchell Duneier. Reprinted by permission of the University of Chicago Press as publisher and the author.

Durrell, Gerald.—"The Life and Death of Chomondeley" from *The Overloaded Ark* by Gerald Durrell, Illustrations by Sabine Baur. Copyright 1953, renewed © 1981 by Gerald M. Durrell. Used by permission of Viking Penguin, a division of Penguin Books USA Inc.

Epstein, Joseph.—"Student Evaluations" by Joseph Epstein (Aristides). Reprinted from *The American Scholar,* Volume 56, Number 2, 1987. Copyright © 1987 by the author.

Espen, Hal.—From "American Beauty" by Hal Espen, *The New Yorker,* August 21 & 28, 1995. Reprinted by permission; © 1995 The New Yorker Magazine, Inc. All rights reserved.

Farb, Peter.—"How to Talk About the World" from *Word Play by Peter Farb.* Copyright © 1973 by Peter Farb. Reprinted by permission of Alfred A. Knopf, Inc.

Fenton, James.—From "The Fall of Saigon" by James Fenton from *The Best of Granta Reportage,* 1993. Reprinted by permission of Peters Fraser & Dunlop Group Ltd.

Frazier, Ian.—Excerpt from "Bear News" from *Nobody Better, Better Than Nobody* by Ian Frazier. Copyright © 1987 by Ian Frazier. Reprinted by permission of Farrar, Straus & Giroux, Inc.

Freeman, Castle Jr.—"Surviving Deer Season" by Castle Freeman, Jr. as appeared in *The Atlantic Monthly,* December 1995. Reprinted by permission of the author.

Funk, Charles Earl.—Excerpt from *Thereby Hangs a Tale: Stories Of Curious Word Origins* by Charles Earl Funk. Copyright 1950 by Harper & Row, Publishers, Inc., renewed © 1978 by Beuhal M. Funk. Reprinted by permission of HarperCollins Publishers, Inc.

Garber, Marjorie.—From "Dog Days" by Marjorie Garber, *The New Yorker,* August 8, 1996. Reprinted by permission Sanford J. Greenburger Associates.

Garner, James Finn.—"The Three Little Pigs" by James Finn Garner from *Politically Correct Bedtime Stories.* Reprinted with permission of Macmillan Publishing USA, a Simon & Schuster Macmillan Company, from Politically Correct Bedtime Stories by James Finn Garner. Copyright © 1994 by James Finn Garner.

Gladwell, Malcolm.—"The Tipping Point" by Malcolm Gladwell, as appeared in *The New Yorker,* June 3, 1996. Reprinted by permission of the author.

Gladwell, Malcolm.—From "The Science of Shopping" by Malcolm Gladwell, as appeared in *The New Yorker,* November 4, 1996. Reprinted by permission of the author.

Gladwell, Malcolm.—From "The New Age of Man" by Malcolm Gladwell, as appeared in *The New Yorker,* September 30, 1996. Reprinted by permission of the author.

Goldstein, Warren.—From "Time Out for a Change In College Athletics" by Warren Goldstein as appeared in *The Washington Post National Weekly Edition,* September 23–29, 1996. Reprinted by permission of the author.

Goodman, Ellen.—"There's No Word in English for It" by Ellen Goodman as appeared in *The Sunday Oregonian,* April 20, 1997. Copyright © 1997, The Boston Globe Newspaper Co./Washington Post Writers Group. Reprinted with permission.

Gopnik, Adam.—From "Carry That Weight" by Adam Gopnik. Copyright © 1995 by Adam Gopnik, as printed in the May 1, 1995 issue of *The New Yorker.* Reprinted with the permission of The Wylie Agency, Inc.

Gossage, Howard Luck.—From "25 Years Ago" by Howard Luck Gossage as appeared in *The Atlantic Monthly,* September 1994.

Gould, Stephen Jay.—"Carrie Buck's Daughter" from *The Flamingo's Smile: Reflections in Natural History* by Stephen Jay Gould. Copyright © 1985 by Stephen Jay Gould. Reprinted by permission of W.W. Norton & Company, Inc.

Graham, Lawrence Otis.—Excerpt from *A Member of the Club* by Lawrence Otis Graham. Copyright © 1995 by Lawrence Otis Graham. Reprinted by permission of HarperCollins Publishers, Inc.

Grimsley, Kirsten Downey.—From "Defining the Problem is a Start" by Kirsten Downey Grimsley, *The Washington Post National Weekly Edition,* January 27, 1997. Copyright © 1997 The Washington Post. Reprinted with permission.

Guijarro, Marissa.—Letters from Marissa Guijarro as appeared in *The New York Times Magazine,* October 15, 1995.

Guillermo, Kathy Snow.—"Circuses-Cruel Shows Can't Go On" by Kathy Snow Guillermo as appeared in *San Francisco Chronicle,* April 11, 1997. Reprinted by permission of the author.

Guterson, David.—From "Moneyball!" by David Guterson, *Harper's,* September 1994. Copyright © 1994 by David Guterson. Reprinted by permission of Georges Borchardt, Inc. for the author. Essay originally appeared in *Harper's.*

Hall, Donald.—From "Argument and Persuasion" from *The Ideal Bakery* by Donald Hall. Copyright © 1987 by Donald Hall. Reprinted with permission of Gerard McCauley Agency.

Harrison, Dr. William.—"Why Stop Smoking? Let's Get Clinical" by William F. Harrison, *Los Angeles Times,* July 7, 1996. Reprinted by permission of the author.

Hiss, Tony.—From *The Experience of Place* by Tony Hiss. Copyright © 1990 by Tony Hiss. Reprinted by permission of Alfred A. Knopf, Inc.

Innes, David C.—From "A Christian View on Gay Marriages" by David C. Innes as appeared in *San Francisco Chronicle,* April 8, 1996. Reprinted with permission of author.

Jarmon, Barbara.—Letter from Barbara Jarmon as appeared in *The New York Times Magazine,* October 15, 1995. Reprinted by permission.

Jarvis, James M.—From "Superhighway's Side Effects" by James M. Jarvis as appeared in *San Francisco Chronicle,* March 12, 1994. Reprinted by permission of the author.

Jenkins, Bruce.—From "Dark Day Our Pastime in Ruins" by Bruce Jenkins, *San Francisco Chronicle,* September 15, 1994. © The San Francisco Chronicle. Reprinted with permission.

Jones, Ann.—From "Where Penguins Dare" by Ann Jones, *Lear's,* March 1992. Reprinted by permission.

Jordan, Mary.—From "Fascinated by Guns" by Mary Jordan, *The Washington Post National Weekly Edition,* March 24, 1997. Copyright © 1997, The Washington Post. Reprinted with permission.

Kass, Leon.—From "The End of Courtship" by Leon Kass. Reprinted with permission of the author from *The Public Interest,* No. 126 (Winter 1997), p. 60. © 1997 by National Affairs, Inc.

Kelley, Kevin J.—From "R.I.P. for the CIA?" by Kevin J. Kelley as appeared in *Utne Reader,* July/August 1995. Reprinted by permission of the author.

King, Robert D.—From "Should English Be the Law?" by Robert D. King. © 1997 Robert D. King, as first published in *The Atlantic Monthly,* April 1997. Reprinted by permission.

King, Stephen—"The Man in the Black Suit." Copyright © 1994 by Stephen King. All rights reserved. First published in *The New Yorker,* October 31, 1994. Reprinted by permission of Darhansoff & Verrill Literary Agency.

Kuenz, Jane.—"Shiny Happy People" by Jane Kuenz from *Inside the Mouse: Work and Play at Disney.* Copyright © 1995, Duke University Press. Reprinted with permission.

Lado, Robert.—From "How to Compare Two Cultures" by Robert Lado from Linguistics Across Cultures: Applied *Linguistics for Language Teachers,* University of Michigan Press, 1957. Reprinted by permission of The University of Michigan Press.

Lancaster, Hal.—From "Chaos in a Box: Messy Computer Files Can Strain Your Job" by Hal Lancaster, *The Wall Street Journal,* July 2, 1996. Reprinted by permission of The Wall Street Journal, © 1996 Dow Jones & Company, Inc. All Rights Reserved Worldwide.

LaSalle, Mick.—From "Milk Money Comes Up Short" by Mick LaSalle, *San Francisco Chronicle,* August 31, 1994. © San Francisco Chronicle. Reprinted with permission.

Levine, Arthur.—"College—More Than Serving Time" by Arthur Levine, *The Wall Street Journal,* December 21, 1993. Reprinted by permission of The Wall Street Journal, © 1993 Dow Jones & Company, Inc. All Rights Reserved Worldwide.

Lubet, Professor Steven.—"The Deer Hunter" by Steven Lubet, *The Philadelphia Inquirer,* November 30, 1996 and The Chicago Tribune, November 24, 1996, Reprinted by permission of the author.

Lutz, William.—Excerpt from *The New Doublespeak* by William Lutz. Copyright © 1996 by William Lutz. Reprinted by permission of HarperCollins Publishers, Inc.

Magliozzi, Tom and Ray.—"Click & Clack Talk Cars" by Tom and Ray Magliozzi, *San Francisco Chronicle,* November 24, 1995.

Martin, Judith.—"Avoid Being Identified with Churlish Idiots" by Judith Martin. Reprinted in *The San Francisco Chronicle,* February 26, 1997. Copyright 1997 by Judith Martin. Distributed by United Feature Syndicate, Inc.

Mathers, Kathleen O'Hara.—"Commercial Fertilizer vs. Animal Manure" by Kathleen O'Hara Mathers as appeared in *The Wall Street Journal,* November 22, 1996. Reprinted by permission of the author.

Matthews, Christopher.—"Gored" by Christopher Matthews, *The New York Times Magazine,* September 24, 1995. Reprinted by permission.

Max, D.T.—From "The End of the Book?" by D.T. Max, first appeared in *The Atlantic Monthly,* September 1994. Reprinted by permission of the author.

McKibben, Bill.—From The Age of Missing Information by Bill McKibben. Copyright © 1992 by Bill McKibben. Reprinted by permission of Random House, Inc. Originally published in *The New Yorker.*

Morain, Genelle.—"Kinesis and CrossCultural Understanding" by Genelle Morain, *Language in Education: Theory and Practice,* No. 7, 1978. Washington, DC. Center for Applied Linguistics. ERIC Clearinghouse on Languages and Linguistics. Reprinted by permission.

Morris, Desmond.—Reprinted from *Manwatching: A Field Guide to Human Behavior* by Desmond Morris. Published by Harry N. Abrams, Inc., New York. All rights reserved.

Munro, Alice.—"Hired Girl" by Alice Munro. Originally published in the April 11, 1994 issue of *The New Yorker.* Copyright © 1994 by Alice Munro. Reprinted by permission of the Virginia Barber Literary Agency, Inc. All rights reserved.

Murphy, Cullen.—From "In Praise of Snow" by Cullen Murphy, *The Atlantic Monthly,* January 1995. © 1994 by Cullen Murphy. Reprinted with permission.

Naughhton, John.—From "Courting the Crocodile" by John Naughton, *London Observer,* June or July 1997. Reprinted by permission of The Observer.

Northrup, Solomon.—"A Slave Witness of a Slave Auction," *A Southern Reader,* edited by Willard Thorp. Alfred A. Knopf, 1955. Reprinted by permission of the Willard Thorp Estate.

O'Brien, Tim.—"On the Rainy River" from *The Things They Carried.* Copyright © 1990 by Tim O'Brien. Reprinted by permission of Houghton Mifflin Co./Seymour Lawrence. All rights reserved.

Oppenheimer, Todd.—From "The Computer Delusion" by Todd Oppenheimer, as appeared in *The Atlantic Monthly,* July 1997. © Todd Oppenheimer. Reprinted by permission of the author. The article won a 1998 National Magazine Award.

Orlando Sentinel.—"Chickens of the Sea." Originally published in *Florida,* The Sunday Magazine of the *Orlando Sentinel,* November 24, 1991. Reprinted by permission.

Orlean, Susan.—"Beautiful Girls" by Susan Orlean, *The New Yorker,* August 4, 1997. Reprinted with permission of the author.

ParkerPope, Tara.—From "Tough Tobacco-Ad Rules Light Creative Fires" by Tara ParkerPope, *The Wall Street Journal,* October 9, 1996. Reprinted by permission of The Wall Street Journal, © 1996 Dow Jones & Company, Inc. All Rights Reserved Worldwide.

Petrunkevitch, Alexander.—From "The Spider and the Wasp" by Alexander Petrunkevitch, *Scientific American,* August 1952. Copyright © 1952 by Scientific American, Inc. All rights reserved.

Pusateri, Paul.—Letter from Paul Pusateri first appeared in *The New York Times Magazine,* October 15, 1995. Reprinted by permission of the author.

Raban, Jonathan.—From Bad Land, *An American Romance* by Jonathan Raban. Copyright © 1996 by

Jonathan Raban. Reprinted by permission of Pantheon Books, a division of Random House, Inc.

Rabinowitz, Dorothy.—"A Darkness in Massachusetts" by Dorothy Rabinowitz, *The Wall Street Journal,* January 30, 1995. Reprinted by permission of The Wall Street Journal, © 1995 Dow Jones & Company, Inc. All Rights Reserved Worldwide.

Regan, Tom.—Excerpt from *Matters of Life and Death,* 3E by Tom Regan, 1993. Reprinted by permission of The McGraw-Hill Companies.

Reid, Jeff.—From "The DNA-ing of America" by Jeff Reid, *Utne Reader,* September/October 1995. © 1995 Jeff Reid. Used by permission of the author.

Remnick, David.—From *The Devil Problem and Other Stories* by David Remnick. Copyright © 1996 by David Remnick. Reprinted by permission of Random House, Inc.

Rich, Allan.—Letter from Allan Rich as appeared in *The New York Times Magazine,* October 15, 1995.

Rushdie, Salman.—"On Leavened Bread" by Salman Rushdie. Copyright © 1996 by Salman Rushdie, first printed in the December 23 and 30 issue of *The New Yorker.* Reprinted with the permission of The Wylie Agency, Inc.

Sabato, Ernesto., trans by Helen Lane.—From *On Heroes and Tombs* by Ernesto Sabato, translated by Helen Lane. Reprinted by permission of Helen Lane.

Sacks, Oliver.—"A Neurologist's Notebook: A Surgeon's Life" from *An Anthropologist on Mars* by Oliver Sacks. Copyright © 1995 by Oliver Sacks. Reprinted by permission of Alfred A. Knopf, Inc.

Samuelson, Robert J.—"A Question of Freedom" by Robert J. Samuelson, *The Washington Post,* April 28, 1997. Copyright © 1997, Washington Post Writers Group. Reprinted with permission.

Sayle, Murray.—From "Nerve Gas and The Four Noble Truths" by Murray Sayle. Reprinted by permission; © 1996 Murray Sayle. Originally in *The New Yorker,* April 1, 1996. All rights reserved.

Sayle, Murray.—From "Did The Bomb End The War?" by Murray Sayle. Reprinted by permission; © 1995 Murray Sayle. Originally in *The New Yorker,* July 31, 1995. All rights reserved.

Schapiro, Mark.—From "The Fine Art of Sexual Harassment" by Mark Schapiro, *Harper's.* Copyright © 1994 by *Harper's Magazine.* All rights reserved. Reproduced from the July issue by special permission.

Schapiro, Mark.—From "Muddy Waters" by Mark Schapiro as appeared in *Utne Reader,* November/December 1994. Reprinted by permission of the author.

Schlosser, Eric.—From "Reefer Madness" by Eric Schlosser, *The Atlantic Monthly,* August 1994.

Shapiro, Jesse.—"TalentBlind Admissions?" by Jesse Shapiro, *The Wall Street Journal,* March 28, 1997. Reprinted by permission of The Wall Street Journal, © 1997 Dow Jones & Company, Inc. All Rights Reserved Worldwide.

Simont, Marc.—Letter from Marc Simont to *The New York Times Magazine,* October 15, 1995. Reprinted by permission.

Solomon, Andrew.—From "A Death of One's Own" by Andrew Solomon. Copyright © May 2, 1995 by Andrew Solomon, first printed in *The New Yorker Magazine.* Reprinted with the permission of The Wylie Agency, Inc.

Solomon, Norman.—Excerpts from *The Power of Babble* by Norman Solomon. Reprinted by permission.

Steinhart, Peter.—Excerpt from *The Company of Wolves* by Peter Steinhart. Reprinted by permission of Random House, Inc.

Stevens, Mark.—From "Chief Joseph's Revenge" by Mark Stevens as appeared in *The New Yorker,* August 8, 1994. Reprinted by permission of the author.

Stille, Alexander.—"Who Burned Atlanta?" by Alexander Stille. Copyright © July 29, 1996 by Alexander Stille, first printed in *The New Yorker Magazine.* Reprinted with the permission of the Wylie Agency, Inc.

Svitil, Kathy A.—From "Just Trying to Fit In" by Kathy A. Svitil, *Discover,* July 1996. © 1996 Kathy A. Svitil. Reprinted with permission of Discover Magazine.

Thomas, Lewis.—"On the Need for Asylums," copyright © 1981 by Lewis Thomas, from *Late Night Thoughts on Listening To Mahler's Ninth* by Lewis Thomas. Used by permission of Viking Penguin, a division of Penguin Books USA Inc.

Tisdale, Sallie.—Excerpt from "The Only Harmless Great Thing" by Sallie Tisdale. Reprinted by permission; © 1989 Sallie Tisdale. Originally in *The New Yorker,* January 23, 1989. All rights reserved.

Tisdale, Sallie.—Excerpt from "The Pacific Northwest" from *Stepping Westward: The Long Search for Home in the Pacific Northwest* by Sallie Tisdale. First published in The New Yorker, August 26, 1991. Reprinted by permission of the author.

Walinsky, Adam.—From "The Crisis of Public Order" by Adam Walinsky, *The Atlantic Monthly,* July 1995, p.52. Reprinted with permission or author.

Washington Post Editorial.—"Freedom of Net Speech," *The Washington Post,* November 12, 1996. Copyright © 1996, The Washington Post. Reprinted with permission.

Whitehead, Barbara Dafoe.—From "The Failure of Sex Education" by Barbara Dafoe Whitehead, as first published in *The Atlantic Monthly,* October 1994. © 1994 by Barbara Dafoe Whitehead. Reprinted by permission.

Wiesel, Elie.—Excerpt from *Night* by Elie Wiesel, translated by Stella Rodway. Copyright © 1960 by MacGibbon & Kee. Copyright renewed © 1988 by The Collins Publishing Group. Reprinted by permission of Hill and Wang, a division of Farrar, Straus & Giroux, Inc.

Wiesenfeld, Kurt.—"Making the Grade" by Kurt Wiesenfeld. From *Newsweek,* June 17, 1996. All rights reserved. Reprinted by permission.

Wilbon, Michael.—"History in Black and White" by Michael Wilbon, *The Washington Post National Weekly Edition,* April 21, 1997. Copyright © 1997 The Washington Post. Reprinted with permission.

Wolff, Tobias.—From *This Boy's Life* by Tobias Wolff. Copyright © 1989 by Tobias Wolff. Used by permission of Grove/Atlantic, Inc.

Wright, Lawrence.—From "Orphans of Jonestown" by Lawrence Wright, *The New Yorker.* Reprinted by permission of The Wendy Weil Agency, Inc. Copyright © November 22, 1993 by Lawrence Wright.

Zeleny, Jeff.—From "Reward College Athletes by Paying Them for Play" by Jeff Zeleny, *Daily Nebraskan.* Reprinted with permission from the Daily Nebraskan.

Index

N

O

P

Q

R

S

Y

Z